Keep this book. You will need it and use it throughout your career.

About the American Hotel & Lodging Association (AH&LA)

Founded in 1910, AH&LA is the trade association representing the lodging industry in the United States. AH&LA is a federation of state lodging associations throughout the United States with 11,000 lodging properties worldwide as members. The association offers its members assistance with governmental affairs representation, communications, marketing, hospitality operations, training and education, technology issues, and more. For information, call 202-289-3100.

LODGING, the management magazine of AH&LA, is a "living textbook" for hospitality students that provides timely features, industry news, and vital lodging information.

About the American Hotel & Lodging Educational Institute (EI)

An affiliate of AH&LA, the Educational Institute is the world's largest source of quality training and educational materials for the lodging industry. EI develops textbooks and courses that are used in more than 1,200 colleges and universities worldwide, and also offers courses to individuals through its Distance Learning program. Hotels worldwide rely on EI for training resources that focus on every aspect of lodging operations. Industry-tested videos, CD-ROMs, seminars, and skills guides prepare employees at every skill level. EI also offers professional certification for the industry's top performers. For information about EI's products and services, call 800-349-0299 or 407-999-8100.

About the American Hotel & Lodging Educational Foundation (AH&LEF)

An affiliate of AH&LA, the American Hotel & Lodging Educational Foundation provides financial support that enhances the stability, prosperity, and growth of the lodging industry through educational and research programs. AH&LEF has awarded millions of dollars in scholarship funds for students pursuing higher education in hospitality management. AH&LEF has also funded research projects on topics important to the industry, including occupational safety and health, turnover and diversity, and best practices in the U.S. lodging industry. For more information, go to www.ahlef.org.

MANAGING SERVICE in FOOD and BEVERAGE OPERATIONS

Educational Institute Books

MANAGING SERVICE in FOOD and BEVERAGE OPERATIONS

Fourth Edition

Ronald F. Cichy, Ph.D., CHA
Philip J. Hickey, Jr.

**American
Hotel & Lodging
Educational Institute**

Disclaimer

This publication is designed to provide accurate and authoritative information in regard to the subject matter covered. It is sold with the understanding that the publisher is not engaged in rendering legal, accounting, or other professional service. If legal advice or other expert assistance is required, the services of a competent professional person should be sought.

—*From the Declaration of Principles jointly adopted by the American Bar Association and a Committee of Publishers and Associations*

The authors, Ronald F. Cichy and Philip J. Hickey, Jr., are solely responsible for the contents of this publication. All views expressed herein are solely those of the authors and do not necessarily reflect the views of the American Hotel & Lodging Educational Institute (the Institute) or the American Hotel & Lodging Association (AH&LA).

Nothing contained in this publication shall constitute a standard, an endorsement, or a recommendation of AH&LA or the Institute. AH&LA and the Institute disclaim any liability with respect to the use of any information, procedure, or product, or reliance thereon by any member of the hospitality industry.

Cover photo: The Fairmont Royal Pavilion, Barbados. Courtesy of Fairmont Hotels & Resorts.

Dedication

The Rune of Hospitality*

I saw a stranger yesterday;
    I put food in the eating place,
Drink in the drinking place,
    Music in the listening place,
And in the sacred name of the Triune,
    He blessed myself and my house,
My cattle and my dear ones.

A rune is literally magic or mystery, spirit or soul. Hence, this Celtic message conveys the spirit or magic of hospitality. We dedicate this book to all who practice the spirit of hospitality service, and especially to our hospitality business mentors, who taught us by their examples, coached us when we needed a guide, and saw potential in us when we were young. We thank our mentors very much, and we accept the responsibility for mentoring the future.

*A message posted on the wall of the guesthouse at The Abbey of Gethsemani in Trappist, Kentucky.

Contents

Preface

We present to our readers the fourth edition of *Managing Service in Food and Beverage Operations*. We have discovered through our research that simply focusing on service is not enough to create positive, memorable experiences for today's guests. Instead, great service has to anticipate the needs and wants of guests and deliver service at a level above simply meeting expectations. It is the strength of the experience created that compels guests to return to a food and beverage operation and bring their friends.

Why did we write this book? We have experienced very delightful and very awful service in businesses that advertise the importance of guests. We hope to have a positive effect on those in the hospitality industry—both individuals and operations—who could benefit from our experiences and, in turn, improve the service experiences they provide to their guests.

Secondly, we again invite students of hospitality and other service businesses to practice what we have discovered works when it comes to superior service and wowing guests. We hope that these future leaders of food and beverage operations will go on to delight their guests, and that someday we will have the honor of being in their food and beverage operations to experience what they have created.

We begin at the end: the creation and delivery of a positive experience within a food and beverage operation. An experience that is so caring and restorative that it compels us to come back and bring our friends. A system for the creation and delivery of an experience is part science, but a larger part art, as it is very personal and authentic. Managers are leaders, and leaders involve their teams in the day-to-day drama of the operation, suggesting better ways to serve guests, and delivering to guests their very best.

Service styles, pre-shift meetings, suggestive selling and upselling, anticipatory service, and teamwork are all present in those operations that set out to do what it takes to satisfy guests. From menu planning and purchasing, through receiving, storing, issuing, preparing, cooking, holding, serving, and cleaning and maintenance, the food and beverages must be safe, quality controls in place, and results constantly monitored from the guests' perspectives. Staff members are the most important resource in a food and beverage operation, yet their labor costs must be controlled. In addition, revenue management is receiving increased attention as operators are focused on maximizing the sales captured from each guest in each meal period/day part offered by the operation.

From casual-dining restaurants to fast-casual dining, from full-service to quick-service restaurants, from banquets to catered events, and from in-room dining to on-site managed food and beverage operations, the ultimate goal is to build guest loyalty and enhance the operation's relationship with each guest. This is how repeat business and positive word-of-mouth referrals are built and disseminated into the community so that additional business can be generated.

The creation and delivery within food and beverage operations of positive, memorable experiences is a wonderful calling. To those who are called, we hope our book helps you, in some small way, to understand what it takes to answer that call.

Acknowledgments

A book is never simply the result of efforts by its author or authors. Many people helped us dramatically change the third edition into the fourth edition that you are holding in your hands.

We received and incorporated ideas from two-year and four-year, international and domestic, instructors and students. We thank all of you for taking the time.

We thank Mi Ran Kim and Praneet Randhawa, who volunteered to assist us with the research for this fourth edition.

We thank Lena Loeffler, who prepared and edited the writing initially. We thank the dedicated members of the editorial, production, and sales teams at the American Hotel & Lodging Educational Institute, including Writer/Editor Jim Purvis, for all their kind assistance.

A book is a project that should contain some of the soul of the author. We have attempted to show a new way of managing service.

Ronald F. Cichy   *Philip J. Hickey, Jr.*
Okemos, Michigan   Santa Rosa Beach, Florida

Ronald F. Cichy   Philip J. Hickey, Jr.

Ronald F. Cichy, Ph.D., NCE5, CHA Emeritus, CHE, CFBE, is the director of and a professor in *The* School of Hospitality Business at Michigan State University, positions in which he has served at his *alma mater* since 1988. Dr. Cichy's work on four continents has developed managers and leaders, team builders and trainers, and helped businesses become high-performance organizations.

His most recent books are *Managing Beverage Operations*, Second Edition (co-authored with Lendal Kotschevar), *Your Emerging Leadership Journey* (co-authored with John H. King, Jr.), and *Food Safety: Managing with the HACCP System*, Second Edition. Dr. Cichy is recognized as a pioneer researcher on leadership qualities, keys, secrets, and essentials, and on the emotional intelligence of hospitality leaders, both in the United States and Japan. Along with other researchers he continues to study the private club industry. His research has led to his identification as one of the most influential scholars in hospitality management.

Dr. Cichy serves on the boards of several hospitality industry institutes, foundations, and associations. In 1999, the American Hotel & Lodging Educational Institute honored Dr. Cichy as the Outstanding Hospitality Educator with the Lamp of Knowledge Award. In 2001, he was inducted into *The* School of Hospitality Business Alumni Association's Wall of Fame Class of Contributors. *The* School's Alumni Association honored him as a Distinguished 75th Anniversary Year Alumnus in 2002. The Eli Broad College of Business presented Dr. Cichy with its Distinguished Alumnus Award in 2003. He has been recognized by MSU's President Lou Anna K. Simon and MSU's Provost and Associate Provost for his scholarly publications in 2004, 2005, 2007, 2008, 2009, and 2011. In 2006, Dr. Cichy received the Anthony G. Marshall Award, presented by the American Hotel & Lodging Educational Institute, acknowledging his significant long-term contributions to the hospitality industry in educating future leaders. Dr. Cichy was honored with the prestigious Certified Hotel Administrator (CHA) Emeritus by the American Hotel & Lodging Educational Institute in 2008. He lives in Okemos, Michigan, with his wife Shelley and a Labrador Retriever named Soda.

Philip J. Hickey, Jr., currently serves as chairman of the board of O'Charley's, Inc., a multi-concept public restaurant company based in Nashville, Tennessee. Mr. Hickey served as chairman of the board/chief executive officer of RARE Hospitality International, Inc., until October 2007, at which time RARE Hospitality was acquired by Darden Restaurants, Inc. RARE Hospitality was an Atlanta-based restaurant company whose concepts included LongHorn Steakhouse and the award-winning Capital Grille. RARE operated more than 300 restaurants, employed over 20,000 people, and served more than 55 million guests per year. From 1997 to 2007, Mr. Hickey and his team grew RARE Hospitality's market capitalization from $90 million to $1.3 billion.

As a veteran of more than 35 years in the industry, Mr. Hickey has experienced the restaurant business from many perspectives. In addition to his roles at O'Charley's and RARE, Mr. Hickey has been a single-restaurant owner-operator, has co-founded a restaurant company and taken it public, and grew a concept from 6 to 50 restaurants.

In 2002, Mr. Hickey was named "Restaurateur of the Year" by the Georgia Hospitality and Travel Association, and in 2004 he was inducted into the "Wall of Fame" at *The* School of Hospitality Business at Michigan State University. In 2005 Mr. Hickey received the Golden Chain Award from *Nation's Restaurant News*, as well as the "Chain Leadership Award" from *Chain Leader* Magazine. In 2006, he received the Elliott Motivator of the Year Award, and in addition received the People Report 2008 Legacy Award.

Mr. Hickey earned his bachelor's degree in Hospitality Business from Michigan State University and has served as an adjunct instructor at the Massey Business School at Belmont University. He currently serves on the board of directors as the treasurer of the National Restaurant Association and on the executive board of directors of *The* School of Hospitality Business Alumni Association at Michigan State University, and has served on the board of directors of the Atlanta Convention & Visitors Bureau; Hemisphere, Inc.; the Metro Atlanta Chamber of Commerce; and the Georgia Tourism Foundation.

A frequent guest lecturer at colleges and universities, Mr. Hickey is a founding board member of the YMCA Community Action Project, an active member of the World Presidents' Organization, and recently served as chairman of the Board of Councilors for the Jimmy Carter Center in Atlanta.

Mr. Hickey currently operates a nationwide consulting practice specializing in the hospitality industry. He lives in Santa Rosa Beach, Florida, with his wife Reedy.

Part I

Chapter 1 Outline

Food and Beverage Industry Developments
    and Trends
Leadership: Knowing and Leading
    Knowing Self
    Leading Self
    Knowing Others
    Leading Others
    Leading Change
Creating Positive, Memorable Experiences
    Anticipatory Service
    Making Positive First Impressions
    Managerial Contributions
Economic Considerations
    Aligning Business and Guest Values
Thinking and Acting Like an Owner
    Six Entrepreneurial Practices

Competencies

1. Describe current developments and trends in the food and beverage industry. (pp. 3–5)

2. Identify and discuss the five practices of know-lead leadership. (pp. 5–9)

3. Explain how anticipatory service, positive first impressions, and committed managers can contribute to creating positive, memorable experiences for guests. (pp. 9–12)

4. Discuss how economic considerations impact sales in food and beverage operations, and describe how the alignment of values between a food and beverage operation and its guests can build guest loyalty. (pp. 12–13)

5. Outline the six entrepreneurial practices food and beverage managers and staff can use to think and act like an owner. (pp. 13–15)

Leadership in Food and Beverage Operations

THERE ARE NEARLY one million food and beverage operations in the United States alone. These operations can be independently owned, part of a chain, or located in a hotel or some other lodging operation. They are often categorized by the type of service they offer:

- Quick-service (McDonald's, KFC, Taco Bell, Arby's)

- Fast-casual (Chipotle, Panera Bread, Qdoba, Subway)

- Family-dining (Bob Evans, Cracker Barrel, Sweet Tomatoes)

- Casual-dining (Applebee's, Chili's, LongHorn Steakhouse, Olive Garden, P.F. Chang's)

- Fine-dining (The Capital Grille, Morton's)

In addition, various specialty markets—such as the transportation, recreational, business/industry, educational, health care, corrections, and military markets—have their own food and beverage operations that have unique operating processes and challenges.

In this chapter we will concentrate on food and beverage industry development and trends, leadership, creating positive dining experiences for guests, economic considerations within the industry, and the goal to have everyone in a food and beverage operation thinking and acting like an owner.

Food and Beverage Industry Developments and Trends

Food and beverage industry developments and trends are constantly changing as the needs and expectations of consumers evolve. It is critical for food and beverage managers to study these developments and trends so that operational changes and improvements can be made in a timely way. For example, menus must continually evolve so that they feature menu choices that guests want; the result is that the food and beverage operation becomes more profitable. While some of today's trends (e.g., mobile food trucks) began many years ago, others (e.g., the explosion of social media marketing) are emerging and strengthening right now.

What follows are some developments and trends currently seen in the food and beverage industry:

- What began years ago as coffee and donuts delivered to construction workers has evolved into various types of mobile high-end eateries such as the Kogi trucks in Los Angeles, which feature Korean barbecue to go. Mobile food trucks are everywhere in Seattle and Los Angeles, and more operators are seeing this type of food and beverage operation as a way to beat the high cost of real estate.

- Pressure for both the development and consumption of ethically sourced foods is coming from many areas. PETA (People for the Ethical Treatment of Animals), for example, is one organization that strongly advocates for ethically sourced foods, but many chefs and companies are buying and featuring ethically sourced foods simply because they think "it's the right thing to do."

- Another long-term trend that has picked up steam in recent years is the local food movement—also called the "farm to fork," "farm to table" or "plow to plate" movement—which was spearheaded by chefs Alice Waters and Jeremiah Tower decades ago. Chef-owned restaurants are still leading the charge. *Tāyst*, for example—"the first and only green certified restaurant in Nashville"—lists the names of all the local farms where its products are sourced, but chains such as Chipotle Mexican Grill and Silver Diner are responding to this trend as well.

- The rapidly increasing Hispanic population in the United States means opportunity. Antonio Swad's Pizza Patrón, for example, is a highly successful Hispanic-focused pizza chain that requires all of its staff members to speak English and Spanish.

- The recent explosion of social media marketing is an incredibly effective tool in attracting 20-somethings. Social media marketing takes place on websites such as Facebook, foursquare, twiddish, Twitter, and YouTube.

- There is currently a huge movement away from casual dining toward quick-casual dining concepts. This movement is across all cuisines (e.g., Mexican such as Chipotle Mexican Grill, Italian such as Red Brick Pizza) and will continue.

- There has been impressive growth of many quick-casual concepts such as Five Guys Burgers and Fries, which has expanded to over 625 locations since 2003.

- Focus on reduction of energy consumption is a recent trend. Darden, for example, a company that includes Red Lobster, Olive Garden, and other restaurant chains, intends to reduce energy and water use by 15 percent within five years.

- Baby Boomer behavior is driving change in the food and beverage industry, as these guests want great taste, smaller portions, healthy menu options, lively atmosphere, value, great service, and have a huge amount of disposable income available.

- In the spirit of creating community, more restaurants are offering free Wi-Fi, encouraging people to linger and mingle.

- Cause marketing, i.e., "doing well by doing good," is a current trend driven primarily by socially conscious members of Generation Y.

- Finally, customers across all demographic lines are looking for and expecting value. From Morton's to McDonald's, everyone at every level in the restaurant business is either offering a deal or about to offer one to attract guests. Value is not just about discounting, however. In fine-dining restaurants, value is also a combination of specialty menu items (e.g., dry-aged steaks, live lobsters), renowned chefs, and distinctive décor. In the casual-dining segment, restaurants are promoting value by advertising how they are better than the competition, i.e., special and unique as perceived by their guests. In fast-casual restaurants, guests are offered lower menu prices than can be found in fine-dining or casual-dining restaurants. Fast-casual restaurants also offer value in the form of convenience and speed of service, since guests are becoming more strapped for time in this busy and increasingly demanding world. Quick-service restaurants promote value through still lower menu prices and combination meals.

These food and beverage industry developments and trends are taking place in small and large restaurant chains, independent restaurants, and indeed across the board in all types of food and beverage operations. These developments and trends represent shifts in the ways that food and beverage operations are creating excellent dining experiences for guests.

Leadership: Knowing and Leading

A leader is someone who is trustworthy, is a role model for others, and guides others to becoming the best they can be. A leader also trusts him- or herself to make the right decisions. Some people believe incorrectly that leaders are only born—i.e., an individual's leadership cannot be improved unless he or she was born with leadership skills and qualities. That thinking is nonsense. Virtually anyone can develop leadership skills if they work hard enough. Leadership is not about perfection; it is about practicing, practicing, and practicing again to improve. Leadership should be viewed as a journey of improvement that can be pursued by following the five practices of know-lead leadership:

1. Knowing self
2. Leading self
3. Knowing others
4. Leading others
5. Leading change

These five practices of know-lead leadership are the hallmarks of food and beverage managers and operations that are committed to quality guest service. Through knowing and leading, these operations and the people in them improve each day. They are not stagnant, but are ever-evolving and growing in dynamic ways. Exhibit 1 shows how these five practices build off one another to form a continuous path that ends in leading change.

Exhibit 1   The Five Practices of Know-Lead Leadership

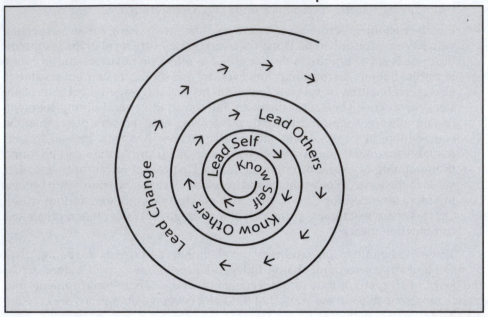

Knowing Self

The first step in acquiring self-knowledge is gaining an understanding of personal values. Values are beliefs or ideas people hold to be important; a person's values generally determine how he or she approaches situations. For example, a person who values hard work will continue to work at a problem, trying different solutions until it is solved; a person who values serving others and takes pride in creating positive memories will gladly take on the challenges associated with a career in a food and beverage operation. Honesty and integrity are values that help define individual ethics as well as how a person acts in both personal and professional situations. A person generally forms values at a young age. Family members, friends, role models (e.g., teachers, youth organization leaders), and even the media can influence a person's values. These values are the foundation upon which a person builds his or her life.

The next step in gaining self-knowledge involves planning for the future. When individuals have strong self-knowledge, it implies that they have some kind of plan for their future. As the future becomes more distant, however, knowing what you want to do may become less clear. For example, it may be easy to envision a career progressing from food and beverage supervisor to food and beverage manager in the next five years; however, it is more difficult to see what a career will look like twenty years down the line.

The third requisite for an individual to achieve self-knowledge is to determine a life mission—what he or she wants to accomplish both personally and professionally. This encompasses recognizing personal strengths and weaknesses, likes and dislikes, hopes and dreams for the future, and overall life purpose.

Once an individual's values, vision for the future, and mission are understood, then he or she can begin searching for an organization that has similar values, a similar vision, and a similar mission. This alignment is crucial for individuals who want to be positive contributors to the organization while at the same time meeting personal goals.

Leading Self

Self-leadership follows self-knowledge. Self-leadership requires practice, self-awareness, and knowing how to act in every situation. The more self-leadership is practiced, the more likely it will become a habit. Others in the organization look to leaders as role models and guides on how to behave in certain situations. People in organizations closely observe the organization's leaders, looking for consistency in words and actions. Consider a food and beverage manager who talks at staff meetings about how guest service is the operation's top priority and then complains during work shifts that it's troublesome to serve guests and that they are unreasonable. In this case, the manager's actions are not consistent with what was said; i.e., the manager does not "walk the talk" and is not leading self consistently.

Knowing Others

To know others in the way that leadership requires takes empathy and awareness. Empathy is the ability to see situations from another person's point of view; awareness includes recognizing that each person is different and respecting those differences. Leaders should not "treat others as you would like to be treated," but rather "treat others as each of them individually would like to be treated."

Getting to know others does not just mean getting to know the organization's guests (external customers). While guests are very important, they are not the operation's only important customers; leaders also need to consider their "internal customers." Internal customers are the operation's managers and staff members—those who create the operation's products and services and deliver them to external customers. Without internal customers, there would be no ability to serve external customers. If a food and beverage operator takes care of and ensures that internal customers are satisfied, the possibility that guests (external customers) will also be satisfied skyrockets.

Additional people that a leader must know include the investors and owners of the food and beverage operation. Sometimes the food and beverage operation is owned by an entrepreneur, other times it will be owned by a corporation that may be owned by an individual or other private group, or the public (as in a corporation with stocks). In all of these cases, the owners have a right to and an expectation of a fair return on their investments. A leader must know what these owners and investors want, need, and expect.

In addition, leaders must know the distributors who provide the products that the food and beverage operation transforms into the menu items and other products desired by guests. Leaders must also know the community. The community expects the food and beverage operation to act ethically, to enhance the value of the community, and to be a good citizen by paying taxes and supporting community causes.

Finally, last but certainly not least, leaders must know and stay closely connected with their own families. In the twentieth century, when one would ask food and beverage leaders about priorities, usually they responded that the business was their most important priority, with family a distant second. Today, food and beverage leaders are seeking a healthier balance between work and family life and between their professional and personal lives.

Leading Others

Leading others requires a blend of management and leadership. While management is focused on planning, organizing, directing, controlling, and evaluating, leadership is centered on values, vision, and mission tied to strategic goals with measurable outcomes. Both qualities are important in a food and beverage operation. Without management, there would be no organization to serve the needs of external and internal customers, owners and investors, and others. Without leadership, there would be no alignment between the individual values, visions, and missions of the food and beverage operation's staff members and those of the operation. Both leadership and management are necessary; both are related.

Leaders who lead others effectively realize that their role is to coach, mentor, and guide, rather than to dictate or command. They get to know their staff, including each person's position and what he or she hopes to contribute. A team focus in a food and beverage operation revolves around the feeling of "we," not "I," and of "us," not "me." When staff members hear a manager constantly referring to "me, me, me, I, I, I, me, me, me," they quickly know that this person is only in it for him- or herself, with staff members, guests, and the operation itself taking a back seat.

Leading a team requires the leader to think positively rather than negatively. People want a leader who sees not only the problems to be solved, but the possibilities to realize or move toward. Positive leaders see the glass as half full rather than half empty. They do not only see the weaknesses in others; they are aware of their strengths as well. Leaders understand that everyone has strengths that can help an organization succeed.

Leading others often requires being a mentor. A mentor is a guide who has experienced situations similar to the ones his or her mentees are experiencing. Mentors should be trustworthy and honest in coaching others through the challenges they face. A mentor understands both the personal and the professional side of a person, as well as that of a situation. Mentors are "go-to" people who can advise and help others avoid unnecessary hazards on their career journey. Mentors light the path for their mentees so that they do not have to learn everything the hard way through making mistakes.

Leading Change

Leading change begins with the practice of continuously improving self. Regular self-analysis leads to self-confidence and self-development. Leaders must adapt to change and be flexible in changing their leadership practices when leading both themselves and others. Leading change in self is driven by continuous learning and improvement.

Leading change also helps the leader improve his or her ability to lead others. In addition, putting new ideas and information into practice encourages others to grow. Finally, by leading change the leader can improve the food and beverage operation and contribute to moving it forward by adding value for its guests, staff members, and owners.

Creating Positive, Memorable Experiences

Memories are our recollections of the past. Memories are often triggered by feelings and emotions. Sometimes memories surface because of smell, sights, or sounds a person might experience. Memories can be simply categorized as positive or negative. In the food and beverage industry, positive memories are formed when people experience service in a food and beverage operation that exceeds their expectations, such as a server who provides a bib for a family with a small child without anyone having to ask. A positive, memorable experience is something that guests seek in a food and beverage operation. When guests have a good experience at a food and beverage operation, they often tell others and return to the operation for more.

Positive, memorable experiences are authentic, not contrived. How can food and beverage operators, managers, supervisors, and staff members create these experiences for guests? Quite simply, by learning the needs, wants, and expectations of each guest and acting to satisfy them.

Anticipatory Service

A positive, memorable experience begins with recognizing the guest's needs, wants, and expectations. Sometimes guests openly state them, saying, for example, "A steak sounds so good right now," or "I'm thirsty for a martini." Other times, they go unsaid, yet the perceptive service professional can sense what they are and create and provide what guests need and want. This is called anticipatory service. Anticipatory service results when a service professional "knows" what guests want and is eager to provide it before being asked. For example, consider a guest carrying a briefcase who arrives at a full-service restaurant alone at lunchtime. The mere fact that the guest chose a full-service restaurant shows that the guest wants to enjoy the experience of being served at lunch; otherwise, the guest would have selected a quick-service or fast-casual restaurant. In addition, since the guest is dining alone, being seated in an area where there is some privacy may be important to the guest. Perhaps the guest needs some privacy so business papers can be reviewed during lunch in preparation for a very important meeting that afternoon. If that is the case, clearly this guest should not be seated in a high-traffic area with all its distractions. The best way for the manager or host to discover this guest's preferences is to simply ask a question: "Would you prefer to be seated at a table in a quieter section of the dining room?" The answer to the question helps identify the guest's needs.

After the guest's wants and needs have been identified, the guest's expectations can be considered. If a server knows what a guest expects, the server can then meet or exceed those expectations. Continuing with our example, perhaps this guest's expectation is to have a quick, light lunch before returning to the office to make final preparations for an important meeting and is looking for efficient, friendly service that does not interrupt the guest's concentration on the work that needs to be done during lunch. If so, this guest likely will scan the menu quickly, make selections, and expect service to proceed promptly, including the presentation of the check. Service that proceeds at a steady pace with no hassles, no delays, and no lengthy conversations with the server would make for a positive, memorable experience for this guest. On the other hand, imagine how guest needs, wants, and expectations would differ if two businesspeople arrived for lunch to sign a contract and celebrate, or if a party of ten guests arrived in one of the restaurant's private dining rooms to honor a colleague who is retiring. In these instances, the service pace should be slower to accommodate guests who are in the mood to relax and celebrate, and the server is freer to make food and beverage suggestions to enhance the event for these guests. As you can see, a "one size fits all" approach to guest service will not produce positive, memorable dining experiences for all of an operation's guests. Rather, service must be customized for each dining experience to suit each individual guest or group of guests.

Making Positive First Impressions

A positive, memorable dining experience begins with making a good first impression. For example, the first impression could be made when a guest phones to make a reservation. The ensuing conversation is where the guest can first be made to feel that a dining experience at the operation will be special. A friendly voice, a quick greeting, use of the guest's name, and a personalized message (e.g., "We're really excited that you will be here to celebrate your birthday" or "So nice to chat with you again, Ms. Rodriquez") all begins the guest's experience with the operation in a positive way.

Contrast this good first impression with the following: a guest arrives at a restaurant with three colleagues without a reservation for lunch and the host greets him in this manner:

GUEST: Hello, can we have a table for four, please?

HOST: Do you have a reservation?

GUEST: No, we don't. We would prefer a table rather than a booth, if possible.

HOST: We have many reservations today. I don't know if it's possible to seat you at a table.

This guest (and the three colleagues) may feel that it is an imposition to seat them for lunch. They may not feel welcome, and if after they are seated the service is just so-so or too slow, the overall experience will be a negative one.

An opportunity for a good first impression could occur before the guest approaches the host or even enters the restaurant, in the form of the restaurant's valet parking service. If the guest is greeted with a smile after the valet opens the guest's car door, the seeds of a positive dining experience are sown. This good first impression is reinforced if the valet greets the guest by name, e.g., "Welcome back to our restaurant, Mr. Pellingham."

After the host has seated a guest, there is a transition from the host to the server. So far, the guest may have encountered a staff member who took the guest's reservation over the telephone, the valet (if provided by the operation), the host, and now the server. While all four people have an opportunity to contribute to a positive, memorable dining experience for the guest, the server is likely to have the greatest influence on the overall experience simply because the server is with the guest for the most time.

Prompt attention from the server after guests are seated is important. If the server is busy taking an order or delivering an order to another table, then some-one else—another server, a manager, a busperson—should acknowledge the newly seated guests sooner rather than later. This is part of making guests feel valued by the operation. Immediate attention to a newly seated table is particularly impor-tant when the guests have arrived during lunch and only have a limited amount of time before they have to return to work, or the guests include small children who are hungry and have little patience for waiting.

When a server approaches guests for the first time, a warm greeting is essen-tial. The server must convey to the guests how appreciated they are for choosing the restaurant and spending their time (and money) there. It is very important for servers to listen to guests as they express their needs and wants, ask questions, and place orders. By doing so, the server will be well on the way to exceeding the expectations of those guests.

Giving continual attention to guests is another hallmark of servers who know how to create and deliver a positive, memorable dining experience. When guests order beverages, they should be delivered as soon as possible. Courses should be served in the correct sequence—i.e., appetizer, soup, salad, main course and sides, dessert. When a server forgets to serve soup before the main course, or serves the soup and then delivers the salad at the same time as the main course, it will likely appear to the guest that the server is rushing the meal or has not been properly trained. This impression will detract from the dining experience. In addition, used tableware and flatware should be removed promptly throughout the meal. This also gives the busperson an opportunity to make a positive impact by quickly removing used utensils and even refilling beverages if the server is busy. Finally, the server should deliver the check soon after dessert is served or, if dessert is not ordered, after the main course.

Once the check is delivered to the table, the server should thank the guests for coming to the food and beverage operation. The server should then continue to pay close attention to the table because, for example, if the guests at the table are engaged in an important conversation they may not attend to the check immedi-ately. If they do quickly attend to the check, the server should promptly process the transaction and deliver the receipt and payment card or change back to the table, remembering to thank the guests again. Sometimes guests like to linger at the table even after a check has been delivered; at other times, they want to dash for the door and be on their way. Observant servers will be in tune with their guests and act accordingly.

Managerial Contributions

Ideally, during a guest's visit to a food and beverage operation featuring table ser-vice, a manager has greeted the guest, either at arrival, during the meal, or upon his or her departure. Managers and supervisors who are committed to providing positive, memorable experiences in their food and beverage operations know that they cannot singlehandedly do so. It takes, using the previous example, the reservationist, the valet, the host, the server, staff in the dining room, the kitchen staff, and the managers all working together to provide the total dining experience.

Once a manager or supervisor understands the need for this team approach, he or she can make a commitment to selecting the very best staff members, ensuring that their skills and attitudes fit with the positions they hold, and train and retrain them at every opportunity. In addition, managers and supervisors should act as role models in terms of providing superior service to guests. This means, for example, that during the food and beverage operation's busiest time periods they are not in an office working on reports but are on the floor or working the host area. In addition, they are supporting and encouraging their staff in providing excellent service. These managers also stop at guests' tables, not because they have been asked to because there is a problem, but because they genuinely care about the guests' experience. By visiting guests' tables, eye contact and a smile can be delivered, and the opportunity to use a regular guest's name will come up; if the guest is not a regular, the manager has the opportunity to meet new guests. Either way, relationships can be built through these personal connections.

Another opportunity for managers to thank guests occurs when the guests are exiting the restaurant. It is not possible to thank a guest too many times. If a guest feels appreciated, that guest is more likely to tell others about his or her positive experience and return in hopes of a similar one. In addition, if the guest is thanked by name and invited to return soon by the manager, staff members who observe this will be more likely to act in the same way toward that guest and others. Managers should constantly model ways to go the extra mile and do what it takes to provide superior service to guests.

Economic Considerations

Money spent by guests in food and beverage operations is usually discretionary money. When the local, regional, or national economy takes a dive, many personal incomes are reduced and many businesses decrease their spending. This means that there is less discretionary money available to spend in food and beverage establishments.

At times when there is less discretionary money to spend, some guests will "trade down" and dine at less expensive places than they would in better economic times. For example, instead of dining at a full-service restaurant they might go to a fast-casual restaurant. Other guests will trade down from fast-casual restaurants to quick-service restaurants where they can stretch their discretionary dining-out dollars even more. Still other guests may choose to eat at home rather than dine out.

There is one certainty in a down economy: guests are going to seek out food and beverage operations that they perceive are offering the greatest value. Guests may have fewer discretionary dollars to spend; however, many will choose to spend them in a food and beverage operation if they feel they are treated hospitably and valued as special guests in that operation.

Aligning Business and Guest Values

Many guests today are looking for food and beverage operations that have values that are consistent with their own personal values. For example, if a guest who likes Indian cuisine values authenticity, that guest may seek out a food and beverage business that prepares and serves authentic Indian cuisine, including menu selections cooked in a tandoor (a traditional Indian clay oven). If another guest values sustainability, that guest may frequent a food and beverage operation that has energy-saving equipment and a water-saving dishwashing machine, uses products from local suppliers, recycles, and is in a building that has LEED (Leadership in Energy and Environmental Design) certification. A third guest may value small cafés and entrepreneurs who own and manage single food and beverage businesses in the community. This individual may be more likely to visit a niche café, such as a bubble tea shop, a cereal bar with all-day breakfast, a chocolate café featuring a selection of chocolate desserts, a coffee roasterie and dessert café, a noodle bar, or a tea lounge with exotic beverages.

These examples illustrate the increasing importance of alignment between guests' individual values and the values of a food and beverage operation. This alignment creates a very strong guest-to-business bond and builds guest loyalty. In order for a food and beverage operation to explain its values to present and potential guests, it must first define and understand those values. In addition, both the operation and the staff must make their actions consistent with the operation's values. For example, if a business values social networking, it should have a high-profile presence on social networking sites, create and consistently update a blog, and offer free Wi-Fi at its location. The business can then advertise this information to current and potential guests, which will attract those guests who also value social networking. Effective marketing is vital to communicating a business's values to its guests.

Thinking and Acting Like an Owner

Most people who work in or have careers in food and beverage operations are not owners of those operations. They are paid by the owner to serve guests and deliver a return on investment for the owner, whether the owner is a solitary entrepreneur or a large corporation that is publicly owned by shareholders.

One of the most difficult actions for an owner to take is to give up control of a business that he or she owns to someone else. In order to do so successfully, the owner has to let go and realize that if managers and staff members understand the operation's overall goals and are given the freedom to act like owners, they can help the operation become even more successful. Mistakes may be made along the way if managers and staff are given this kind of freedom. The best way to handle mistakes is to use them as teachable moments, i.e., learning experiences.

Those who care about the food and beverage operation as much as the owner and act accordingly should be recognized and rewarded for their behaviors. Owners who reward staff members who act in the best interests of the organization will find others eager to contribute. Recognizing staff members in front of their peers allows them to be seen as positive examples for others. Those who are recognized are encouraged to do even more to improve the food and beverage operation.

Six Entrepreneurial Practices

Owners typically are entrepreneurs. Research has found six practices important to successful entrepreneurship in the hospitality and service industries:

1. Intrapersonal communication
2. Interpersonal communication
3. Agility
4. Creative savviness
5. Problem-solving pragmatism
6. Legacy leader

If managers, supervisors, and staff members want to exceed the expectations of their owners (as well as their guests), they will adopt and adapt for their own use these six practices for thinking and acting like an owner.

Intrapersonal Communication. Intrapersonal communication is about communication with one's self. As important as it is to listen to others, it is equally essential to listen to self. Intrapersonal communication includes honesty, listening skills, and patience. Honesty with one's self starts with self-awareness and self-understanding about personal values, vision, and mission; strengths; areas that need improvement; and goals. By listening carefully to his or her inner voice, an individual's needs, wants, expectations, requirements, dreams, and vision can become clearer. Patience is needed to conceive, launch, and build a business, and people who think and act like owners are patient with first themselves, then with others.

Interpersonal Communication. Interpersonal communication involves conversations with others. An owner must effectively communicate to staff what he or she wants to see happen with the food and beverage operation. To do this, the owner must give a detailed description of his or her vision for the operation. This gives staff members an idea of exactly what the owner wants to accomplish so they can help make the vision a reality. Owners also listen to staff input and commentary. Listening is the most important communication skill. It requires empathy, which means considering things from other people's perspectives. Effective interpersonal communication is focused on listening to others' words and being sensitive to the meaning behind the words, which is often indicated in non-verbal ways (facial expressions, body language, and so on).

Agility. Agility, the third of the six entrepreneurial practices, requires skills such as autonomy, independence, and resourcefulness; however, the most important skills it requires are adaptability and decision-making. Agility is the ability to quickly change direction if something new surfaces. Agility is also characterized by adjusting to conditions—those you have some control over and those you have no control over—as they develop. Agility is vital to surviving today's economic challenges. Owners work hard and are determined to do what it takes, even if it means changing course, to achieve their dreams.

Creative Savviness. The creative savviness practice covers creativity, intuition, and inventiveness. All of these qualities are embodied in an entrepreneur who sets out to develop something new and innovative. Creativity is one of the key strategies for staying ahead of the competition; it is embedded in anticipatory service, the type of service that fosters guest loyalty. Savvy owners have a "sixth sense" and are able to anticipate guests' needs and desires before guests express them. Such owners are inventive and look for hidden opportunities others do not see. They capitalize on those opportunities and advance their organizations accordingly. Politically savvy entrepreneurs understand that the food and beverage industry is becoming increasingly regulated and complex, and are able to position their businesses competitively within this environment.

Problem-Solving Pragmatism. An owner who practices problem-solving pragmatism is one who is both objective and knowledgeable about financial matters. Owners who are problem-solving pragmatists have a detailed understanding of balance sheets, budgets, cash flow, profit-and-loss statements, and return on investment. These owners make fact-based decisions. They constantly scan the environment, including market demographics, to determine which market segments have unmet needs and wants for products, services, and experiences, which they then provide. Strong problem-solving capabilities help owners to be great operators. Problem solving can become a strategy to continuously improve all areas of the business. Owners who are good problem solvers learn from their mistakes, from reading, by benchmarking successful businesses, by being curious, by asking questions, and by holding themselves and others accountable for achieving desired outcomes. Pragmatic owners are realistic and practical. They have the ability to balance personal life and work life. They lead the business and do what it takes to make it successful, but they also pay close attention to personal and family requirements.

Legacy Leader. The legacy leader practice, the last of the six entrepreneurial practices, embodies a desire on the part of an owner to leave a significant mark. Owners are focused on their vision for the future, and often, when describing a concept or product/service that is still in the development stages, they will do so as if it already exists. They visualize their legacy and work hard to achieve it. They are gratified when they see their products and services create positive, memorable experiences for guests and financial success for their operations.

These six practices of hospitality and service industry owners can help managers, supervisors, and staff members within food and beverage operations focus on what is important to be successful. Thinking and acting like an owner helps them meet the needs, wants, and expectations of owners who have risked and invested their capital in their food and beverage operations. Staff should keep in mind that the more successful an operation is, the more secure are the jobs of those working within it and the more opportunities for career development and advancement.

? Review Questions

1. What are some current developments and trends within the food and beverage industry?

2. What are the five practices of the know-lead leadership model?

3. How can managers and staff create positive, memorable dining experiences for guests?

4. How does a down economy affect the food and beverage industry?

5. Why is alignment between food and beverage operations' values and guests' values important?

6. How can managers, supervisors, and staff members think and act like an owner?

 Case Studies

Cultivating Culture

Ed Hastings knew he had a challenging assignment. He had just been named president and CEO of Victory Restaurants, Inc., a 600-unit casual-dining restaurant chain, a division of the worldwide conglomerate, Interconstellation Enterprises, Inc. Of the 600 Victory Restaurants, 100 are company-owned and 500 are franchised.

Ed was the senior vice president of marketing for another of the parent company's business units. He enjoyed remarkable success in his previous position. His boss, Greg Benson, felt that Ed was just the right person to inject new life into a restaurant chain that just seemed to be treading water instead of moving forward.

Ed has encountered such turnaround situations before. He knew that he would have to change the culture of Victory Restaurants to get the employees energized. He reminded himself of the slogans, mottos, and mantras of successful organizations that describe their company cultures to the world. For example:

- Ritz-Carlton: "We are ladies and gentlemen serving ladies and gentlemen"

- United Airlines: "Fly the friendly skies of United"

- General Electric: "Progress is our most important product"

- Ford Motor Co. "Quality is job one"

Ed knew that these phrases go to the heart and mind of employees and customers. He began to formulate a plan and jotted his ideas down on paper to help prioritize his agenda. Here is what he has developed so far:

- We will not call our employees "employees." We will call them "teammates."

- We will change the sign on our building that says "World Headquarters" to read "Victory Team Resource Center."

- I will call a meeting of all staff members in the organization and tell them that they are to consider themselves as resources and service providers to the operations personnel and franchisees. We will no longer have a "headquarters knows best" attitude.

- I will call a meeting of all managers of company-owned units and ask for their suggestions as to what improvements and/or changes should be made.

- I will call a meeting of all the franchisees and ask for their input as to improvements and changes that should be made.

- I will personally visit a minimum of one franchisee and one company store per week.

- We will establish a "Top 10" list of all 600 units. Every month, we will acknowledge the top 10 restaurants in the system with respect to increased sales and profits.

- We will give every teammate a "Victory" pin to wear once he or she has been a member of our team for one year. Different color pins will recognize one year, five years, ten years, etc., of service.

- We will have an annual awards banquet recognizing the top 10 units of the year, with engraved plaques presented to each such unit.

- We will provide a $20,000 bonus pool to be shared among all teammates of the unit that shows the greatest growth in profitability.

Discussion Questions

1. How would you assess the approach Ed Hastings is taking to changing the culture at Victory Restaurants, Inc.?

2. What would you delete, add, or alter on his list of things to accomplish?

3. What do you believe is the most important item on his list?

4. Should the $20,000 bonus pool be divided in equal shares (distinguishing between full-time and part-time employees)? Or should management personnel receive a larger share?

This case was taken from William P. Fisher and Robert A. Ashley, *Case Studies in Commercial Food Service Operations* (Lansing, Mich.: American Hotel & Lodging Educational Institute, 2003).

The New Food and Beverage Director

Julie Simmons has just been hired as the food and beverage director of the Parkway Hotel. The property is a 300-room, full-service hotel, with a main dining room seating 220 guests, several banquet/meeting rooms that can accommodate up to 24 guests each for meal service, a 100-seat coffee shop, and a 400-seat banquet hall. The hotel provides room service and does some outside catering on request. It also has a 60-seat cocktail lounge.

Julie has been in food and beverage ever since she graduated from college. She recently transferred to this city, as her husband, a government employee, received a promotion that required relocation. Julie was previously the assistant food and beverage director with an independent hotel. This is the first time she has held the top position in food and beverage.

Julie is poised, knowledgeable, organized, competent, and epitomizes the image of the professional woman.

As she commutes to work on her first day, she begins to organize a list of things she will do and look into. A lot of thoughts race through her mind and she tells herself, "I better categorize my approach to be sure I have all the bases covered, then I can become more detailed in my approach to each area." She thinks, for example, of such matters as: an organization chart and staffing levels, equipment maintenance schedules, health inspection reports and self-inspection checklists, menus and menu analysis, financial measurements, guest satisfaction measurements, and …

"Wow," she exclaims. "I better jot the category headings down and then draft some questions under each so I can delve into what I need to know and do."

Discussion Question

1. What categories should Julie write down, and what questions or points should she list under each so she can be fully immersed in her responsibilities as quickly as possible?

This case was taken from William P. Fisher and Robert A. Ashley, *Case Studies in Commercial Food Service Operations* (Lansing, Mich.: American Hotel & Lodging Educational Institute, 2003).

References

Cichy, Ronald F., Jeffrey A. Beck, and Jeffrey Elsworth. "Six Practices of Hotel Entrepreneurship." *Lodging Hospitality* 65, no. 6 (April 15, 2009).

"Dining Trends and the Equipment That Supports Them." *Chain Leader* 16, no. 12 (February 2009).

King, Jr., John H., and Ronald F. Cichy. *Your Emerging Leadership Journey: How to be Promoted to a Leadership Position in Less than 10 Years*. Bloomington, IN: iUniverse, 2010.

Luebke, Patricia. "Management 101." *Restaurant Startup & Growth* (April 2008).

———. "Management 101…Eight Ways to Maintain a Positive Attitude in Tough Times." *Restaurant Startup & Growth* 6, no. 2 (November 2009).

Lynott, William J. "When the Going Gets Tough." *Restaurant Hospitality* 92, no. 9 (September 2008).

Main, Bill. "Why Service in Restaurants Stinks." *Restaurant Hospitality* 89, no. 5 (May 2005).

Marvin, Bill. "Westward Ho! Becoming a Better Operator by Becoming a Better Leader." *Restaurant Startup & Growth* 5, no. 11 (November 2008).

———. "Who's Minding the Store? How to Groom Managers to Run the Day-to-Day Enterprise Without You." *Restaurant Startup & Growth* (October 2007).

Rowe, Megan. "Secrets to Great Service." *Restaurant Hospitality* 90, no. 3 (March 1, 2006).

Tanyeri, Dana. "What Makes a Great Manager?" *Restaurant Business* (May 2006).

"What's Hot in 2009: Here's What San Francisco-Based Hospitality Consultant Andrew Freeman & Company Sees in the Year Ahead." *Restaurant Hospitality* 93, no. 2 (February 2009).

Internet Sites

For more information, visit the following Internet sites. Remember that Internet addresses can change without notice. If the site is no longer there, you can use a search engine to look for additional sites.

Adventures in Hospitality Careers
www.hospitalityadventures.com

American Hotel & Lodging Association
www.ahla.com

American Hotel & Lodging
 Educational Institute
www.ahlei.org

American Institute of Wine & Food
www.aiwf.org

Commercial Food Equipment Service
 Association
www.cfesa.com

Culinary Cult
www.culinarycult.com

Culinary Institute of America
www.ciachef.edu

eHospitality Institute
www.ehiedu.org

Food Channel
www.foodchannel.com

Food Institute
www.foodinstitute.com

Foodservice Consultants Society
 International
www.fcsi.org

Gallup, Inc.
www.gallup.com

GuestMetrics, Inc.
www.guestmetrics.com

Hcareers.com
www.hcareers.com

International Demographics, Inc.
www.themediaaudit.com

International Food Service Executives
 Association
www.ifsea.com

National Restaurant Association
www.restaurant.org

Nation's Restaurant News
www.nrn.com

New Strategist Publications
www.newstrategist.com

NPD Group, Inc.
www.npd.com

Pizza Today
www.pizzatoday.com

QSR
www.qsrmagazine.com

Restaurant Associates
www.restaurantassociates.com

Restaurant Hospitality
www.restaurant-hospitality.com

Restaurant Report
www.restaurantreport.com

Restaurant Marketing Group
www.rmktgroup.com

Technomic, Inc.
www.technomic.com

RestaurantOwner.com
www.restaurantowner.com

Whole Foods Market
www.wholefoodsmarket.com

Sandelman & Associates
www.sandelman.com

Zagat Survey, LLC
www.zagat.com

Chapter 2 Outline

Food and Beverage Staff
    Managers
    Production Personnel
    Service Personnel
The Team Approach in a Food and Beverage Operation
    Trust in Work Relationships
    Service Teams
Basic Elements of a Food and Beverage Operation
    Telephone Courtesy
    Taking Reservations
    Tipping Policies
    Menus
    Food Production
    Service Styles
    Point-of-Sale Equipment
    Service Trays
Food and Beverage Guests
    Serving Different Generations
    Guest Complaints
    Guest Feedback
    Retaining Guests

Competencies

1. Identify staff members needed in a food and beverage operation. (pp. 23–31)

2. Explain general issues and tasks involved in working in a food and beverage operation, such as trust in work relationships, service teams, telephone courtesy, taking reservations, tipping policies, menus, food production, service styles, point-of-sale equipment, and service trays. (pp. 31–44)

3. Discuss issues involving food and beverage guests, including generational issues, guest complaints, guest feedback, and retaining guests. (pp. 44–50)

2

Food and Beverage
Operations

THE FOOD AND BEVERAGE industry is labor-intensive: a large number of people are required to do the work necessary to successfully create and deliver positive, memorable experiences for guests. The people working in food and beverage operations must be able to work together to successfully deliver these experiences. To do this, many successful food and beverage operations employ the team approach when providing guest service. The team approach helps all staff members who directly serve guests to view guest service as an activity to which everyone must be committed. It involves cross-training each staff member to perform a variety of service functions, which might include taking orders, using suggestive-selling techniques, delivering orders, and resolving guest complaints. This chapter will take a look at typical food and beverage staff positions, service teams and various other service elements, service styles, and food and beverage guests.

In any table-service restaurant, a guest's full enjoyment of the meal depends in large part on the quality and style of service. The menu items may be prepared faultlessly and the décor may be interesting and attractive, but if staff members display no courtesy, personality, or interest in serving guests, the dining experience will be unsatisfactory and the guests probably won't return. Poorly prepared menu items can produce the same result; excellent service can do a great deal to soften the disappointment of a below-standard meal, but the guest will not totally enjoy the experience. All aspects of the meal must be excellent in themselves to add up to a great overall experience for guests.

In hotels, the food and beverage division is an important revenue center. In fact, it is typically second only to the rooms division in the amount of revenue it earns. A good food and beverage operation can help establish the quality of the hotel in the eyes of guests and provide a competitive advantage over other lodging properties. This can justify higher room rates and may help keep occupancy levels high. The primary departments that make up the food and beverage division of most large lodging properties include:

- Restaurant operations—responsible for food and beverage service in all food outlets. Types of food outlets in lodging properties include gourmet and specialty restaurants, casual-dining restaurants, coffee shops and cafes, and lounges or dining rooms where live music or shows are performed.

- Culinary operations—responsible for food production.

- In-room dining—responsible for serving food to guests in their guestrooms.

- Banquet and catering—responsible for providing food, beverages, and service for banquets and other special functions.

- Stewarding—responsible for warewashing and other clean-up duties.

Food and beverage service in hospitality suites and for staff members may be additional food and beverage operations found in lodging properties.

The key to continued success for all types of food and beverage operations is *building guest loyalty.* This loyalty is earned through repeated superb dining experiences delivered by motivated, competent service professionals.

Food and Beverage Staff

The people in food and beverage operations can be grouped into three general categories: managers, production personnel, and service personnel. (Before we start, it should be noted that position titles may vary from operation to operation, and not all of the positions described in this section are found in every food and beverage operation.)

Managers

In general—especially in chains and other large organizations—there are three levels of managers: top managers, middle managers, and supervisors. How top, middle, and supervisory levels are determined, and the typical duties for each level of management, will vary from organization to organization. Whether department heads are considered top or middle managers, for example, depends on the size of the organization they work for; chefs are top managers in some operations, middle managers in others. Exhibits 1 and 2 show, respectively, job descriptions for a restaurant general manager and a beverage manager. These exhibits describe typical responsibilities of these managers and list many of their specific tasks. As the person in charge of operations for the restaurant, the general manager is responsible for all aspects of the operation. Much of this work involves setting objectives, creating plans to reach those objectives, assembling the team to achieve the objectives, and evaluating the extent to which objectives have been attained.

Top managers are concerned with long-term plans and goals. They focus more than other managers on the business environment in general. Top managers watch for environmental opportunities and threats such as changes in strategy by competitors, changes in the national and local economy, and changes in the business climate of the local community.

Middle managers are in the middle of a food and beverage operation's chain of command. They are in key positions through which communication flows up, down, and throughout the organization. They are concerned with shorter-term goals than top managers and are typically less concerned with large, environmental issues. They supervise lower-level middle managers or supervisors.

Supervisors are sometimes referred to as "linking pins." They must represent higher levels of management to staff members and, at the same time, transfer the wishes and concerns of the staff upward. A supervisory position is the first level

Exhibit 1 Job Description—Restaurant Manager

I. Basic Responsibilities

Responsible for meeting all budget goals; for ensuring that quality standards for food and beverage production and service to guests are constantly maintained; for meeting with clients and booking special catered events; for supervising, scheduling, and training the food and beverage controller and assistant manager; for delegating general management tasks to the Assistant Restaurant Manager; for verifying through analysis of source documents that all income due is collected from food and beverage sales; for designing/improving existing cash security and recordkeeping/accounting systems; for supervising department heads in absence of the Assistant Restaurant Manager.

II. Specific Duties

A. Develops, with department head assistance, operating budgets.

B. Monitors budget to control expenses.

C. Serves as restaurant contact for all advertising/marketing activities.

D. Supervises, schedules, and trains Food and Beverage Controller and Assistant Restaurant Manager.

E. Provides required information needed by the controller for payroll, tax, and financial statement purposes.

F. Reviews all operating reports with department heads; conducts regular and ad hoc meetings to correct operating problems.

G. Meets with clients; plans and prices special catered events.

H. Designs and improves restaurant cash security and cash disbursements systems.

I. Conducts cost reduction/minimization studies.

J. Audits source documents to ensure that all monies due have been collected.

K. Delegates miscellaneous administrative tasks to assistant managers.

L. Serves as restaurant's contact with insurance agent, attorney, banker, and accountant.

M. Works on special problems as assigned by owner.

N. Reviews department reports; makes recommendations and follows up to ensure that all problems have been corrected.

O. Is available to provide assistance as needed during busy periods.

III. Reports to

Owners.

IV. Supervises

Assistant Restaurant Manager, Food and Beverage Controller; department heads in absence of the Assistant Restaurant Manager.

(continued)

Exhibit 1 *(continued)*

V. Equipment Used

Must be able to operate all equipment in restaurant.

VI. Working Conditions

Works in all areas of restaurant; long hours, standing, and walking are routine components of the job.

VII. Other

Must know how to operate and do minor maintenance and repair work on all food and beverage production and service equipment, as well as building heating, ventilating, air conditioning, plumbing, and electrical systems. Must be tactful and courteous in dealing with the public.

---

of management. Food and beverage supervisors generally use their technical skills more than higher-level managers, and are concerned with such short-term goals as preparing staff schedules and helping staff members through the rush times that occur in almost every meal period.

Staff members who exhibit superior knowledge and skills and who desire positions with more responsibility often become supervisors. It is a more complex position—certainly not for everyone—but an interesting position to which staff members can aspire. Staff members who move into supervisory positions (this is commonly described as "promotion from within") often use them as stepping stones to successful careers in management and leadership in food and beverage operations.

Production Personnel

Production personnel are concerned primarily with food production and usually have little contact with guests. There are certain basic production tasks that must be assigned to staff members regardless of a food and beverage operation's type or size. Typical production staff positions include:

- Chefs
- Cooks
- Assistant cooks
- Pantry-service assistants
- Stewards
- Storeroom and receiving staff
- Bakers

Chefs. Executive chefs, sometimes given the title Chef de Cuisine, are managers in charge of production personnel in the kitchen. In large operations, an executive chef may perform managerial duties only, while other chefs assume production duties. In smaller operations, the executive or head chef (he or she may be the

Exhibit 2   Job Description—Beverage Manager

OVERVIEW

The Beverage Manager is responsible to the Director/Manager of Restaurants or the Assistant Director/Manager of Food and Beverage for the successful and profitable management of the lounges and bars to maximize the profitability of the restaurants and of the hotel.

SPECIFIC RESPONSIBILITIES

Responsible for:

1. Maintaining warm, hospitable guest relations in all guest contacts.

2. Meeting or exceeding budgeted goals in sales and profits for the lounges and bars.

3. Developing accurate and aggressive long- and short-range financial objectives relating to liquor sales.

4. Operating within budgeted guidelines.

5. Facilitating highest-quality beverage and service related to the operation of the restaurants.

6. Maintaining the property's housekeeping and sanitation standards in lounges and bars.

7. Implementing corporate sales promotion programs and developing and implementing local sales promotions in the lounges and bars.

8. Knowing the competition and keeping current with industry trends and developments.

9. Maintaining effective controls in the Beverage Department.

10. Implementing and supporting company policies and procedures.

11. Maintaining a high level of professional appearance, demeanor, ethics, and image of self and staff members.

12. Sustaining professional development of self and staff members.

13. Communicating effectively between departments and corporate office personnel within area of responsibility.

14. Operating in compliance with all local, state, and federal laws and government regulations.

15. Maintaining fair wage and salary administration in the department in accordance with corporate policy.

16. Assessing and reviewing the job performance of staff members and maintaining personnel records of assigned staff as described in the hotel personnel policy manual.

17. Conducting and attending regular department meetings.

18. Directing and coordinating the activities of all assigned personnel and meeting department responsibilities.

(continued)

Exhibit 2 *(continued)*

19. Hiring, inducting, orienting, and training assigned personnel to meet department responsibilities.

20. Maintaining positive staff relations in a supportive environment.

21. Interfacing department and self with other departments of the food and beverage operation or hotel to ensure a harmonious working relationship.

22. Ensuring good safety practices of staff members and guests throughout the operation and assisting in the maintenance of proper emergency and security procedures.

23. Performing special projects as requested.

only chef) has both managerial and production duties. Executive chefs may plan menus with the restaurant manager, be responsible for recipe standardization and overall food quality, assist in developing food purchase specifications, prepare daily entrées, plan and oversee special events, develop procedures for food production, and perform miscellaneous production responsibilities. Executive chefs may directly supervise a number of different types of chefs, including sous chefs (the principal assistants to the executive chef) and chefs garde-manger (chefs in charge of cold food production).

Cooks. Cooks assist chefs and prepare soups, sauces, and food items to be sautéed, baked, poached, steamed, braised, roasted, grilled, broiled, or fried. They carve and cut meats and prepare cold meat and seafood salad plates, cold sandwiches, hors d'oeuvres, and canapés. Types of cooks include soup cook, sauce cook, fish cook, roast cook, pastry cook, and relief cook.

Assistant Cooks. Assistant cooks help cooks prepare foods for cooking. They trim, peel, clean, grind, shape, mix, or portion foods before cooking and may do simple cooking under the instruction or guidance of cooks or chefs.

Pantry-Service Assistants. Pantry-service assistants supply dining room and banquet pantries with items such as utensils, china, glassware, flatware, and other supplies. These staff members may also prepare beverages and assist in serving food when required.

Stewards. Chief stewards are managers who typically oversee buspersons, dishwashing staff, and related personnel. A chief steward may also be in charge of purchasing at some operations. Chief stewards and their staffs perform cleaning tasks to maintain a high level of cleanliness and food safety. They may also scrape, wash, and store pots, pans, and other cooking utensils and equipment. Additional duties may include performing janitorial and special cleaning tasks in food and beverage areas, and cleaning and storing china, glass, flatware, and related equipment according to acceptable sanitation procedures.

Storeroom and Receiving Staff. Storeroom staff members assist in storing, checking, and dispensing supplies from the storeroom. Receiving clerks help distributors unload food and other supplies and verify that the quality, size, and quantity of incoming products meet the operation's specifications. They also check to make sure the prices of items ordered are correctly recorded on the distributors' invoices.

Bakers. Bakers include senior bakers, bakers, and bakers' assistants. Senior bakers are managers who specialize in all phases of bakery preparation and must be able to prepare a wide variety of bakery products following standard recipes. Bakers prepare less complex bakery products such as bread, rolls, pies, and plain cakes, and may assist senior bakers with other tasks. Bakers' assistants help senior bakers and bakers prepare various bakery products. Compared to the other production positions in restaurants, the baker position is relatively rare and is usually only found in fine-dining restaurants or those featuring bakery products as signature menu items. Most restaurants purchase their bakery products from outside distributors and do not have a bakery staff.

Service Personnel

While the number and variety of food and beverage service positions will depend on the size and complexity of the food and beverage operation, some basic positions include:

- Dining room managers
- Hosts
- Restaurant servers
- Banquet servers
- Buspersons
- Bartenders
- Beverage servers
- Cashiers/checkers

Dining Room Managers. In small food and beverage operations, the dining room manager not only manages the dining room but often performs the duties of host as well. In large organizations, the dining room manager directly supervises an assistant, whose title may be assistant dining room manager, host, or something similar. The dining room manager helps his or her assistant greet guests and supervise other service staff. The dining room manager has many other duties as well; typical duties are listed in Exhibit 3.

Hosts. Hosts, called dining room captains or maitre d's at some operations, directly supervise servers, buspersons, and other service staff. Hosts check all phases of dining room preparation, complete *mise en place*—a French term meaning "to put everything in its place"—and discuss menu specials, expected regular guests, and anticipated total number of guests with servers and other service staff. The host may greet and help seat guests, present menus, and take guests' orders. Other tasks can include serving wines, planning for and providing tableside preparation, helping servers when necessary, and preparing flaming desserts. The host may also offer after-dinner drinks and coffee to guests and present the check.

Exhibit 3   Duties of a Dining Room Manager

- Checking the physical condition of the dining room before it opens

- Checking the place settings on tables and the condition of the china, glassware, and flatware (at full-service operations)

- Making sure the menus are in good condition

- Noting the number of reservations that have been made

- If necessary, rearranging tables to accommodate large guest groups

- Checking the schedule to make sure enough service personnel will be on hand

- Observing and, when necessary, recording the job performances of service staff

- Making sure that guests are satisfied and following up on any guest complaints

- Detecting dishonest servers and guests

- Taking appropriate action in case of an emergency or an accident

- Dealing with intoxicated or hard-to-handle guests in a discreet and appropriate manner

- Providing special services (within reason) to guests who request them

- Maintaining a pleasant atmosphere in the dining room

- Performing closing duties, such as turning off lights and adjusting heat or air conditioning levels

- Providing reports and other data requested by upper management

Restaurant Servers. Restaurant servers take guests' orders and serve food and beverages to guests. The skills that servers require differ, depending on the type of restaurant and the level of service. Typically, restaurant servers are responsible for:

- Preparing for service.
- Inspecting tables for cleanliness and proper setup.
- Greeting guests.
- Taking guest orders.
- Serving guest orders.
- Creating a friendly atmosphere where guests can enjoy themselves.
- Closely monitoring guests' alcohol consumption.
- Completing service.
- Helping co-workers as needed.

Banquet Servers. Banquet servers provide food and beverage service to banquet guests. Banquet servers are responsible for:

- Preparing for service.
- Inspecting tables for cleanliness and proper setup.

- Greeting guests.

- Serving food and beverages.

- Completing service.

- Breaking down function rooms and service areas.

- Keeping a count of the number of guests served.

Banquet servers rely heavily on banquet event orders (BEOs). BEOs tell servers what the banquet is (a wedding banquet, for example) and what needs to be done; they are detailed documents that include all the important details of the event.

Buspersons. The primary responsibilities of a busperson are to set and clear tables and help restaurant servers and guests as much as possible. Buspersons are responsible for:

- Preparing tables for service.

- Prepping **sidestations,** condiments, and silverware.

- Busing soiled dishes, glasses, silverware, and linens (where applicable) from tables.

- Assisting servers and guests to ensure total guest satisfaction.

Buspersons may be the earliest arriving staff members to the restaurant and, along with servers, may be expected to help set up the restaurant dining area for service.

Bartenders. Bartenders prepare mixed drinks and other alcoholic and nonalcoholic beverages and serve them directly to guests or to beverage servers. There are two basic types of bars: public bars and service bars. Bartenders working at public bars serve beverages directly to guests sitting or standing at the bar, or to servers who take the beverages to guests seated in the bar or lounge. Bartenders working at service bars typically do not serve beverages directly to guests; they serve beverages to servers who present them to guests—usually guests in the dining room. Many bars are combination public/service bars. There are age restrictions for serving alcohol that vary by state.

Beverage Servers. Beverage servers serve beverages and food items to guests in bar and lounge areas.

Cashiers/Checkers. Cashiers or checkers total the price of food and beverages on guest checks and collect guest payments. They may also take reservations.

The Team Approach in a Food and Beverage Operation

As previously noted, most food and beverage operations encourage their staff members to use the team approach when delivering service. Before the implementation of this strategy, it is important that everyone in a food and beverage operation understand the significance of trust and teamwork in work relationships, as well as the basics of telephone courtesy, restaurant reservations, tipping policies, menus, food production, service styles, point-of-sale equipment, and service trays.

Trust in Work Relationships

Trust between staff members, supervisors, managers, and owners is the cornerstone for teambuilding, staff attraction, staff retention, and just plain having fun at work. Trust is characterized by honesty, acting ethically, treating all fairly, and bringing people together to collaborate rather than tearing them apart with gossip or constantly pointing out their weaknesses.

In a recent poll conducted by the employee satisfaction research firm Maritz Research, employees across all hospitality industry segments were surveyed to measure the amount of trust these employees placed in their bosses and co-workers. Of the respondents, only a little more than one in ten (11 percent) said they strongly agree that their direct managers are consistent with their words and actions. Actions speak louder than words; staff members watch the actions of their supervisors, managers, and owners to make sure there is complete consistency between what these leaders say and do. Inconsistency leads to a lack of trust.

In the same survey, merely one fifth (20 percent) of those who responded believed that their leader was completely honest and ethical, while only one quarter (25 percent) said they trusted management to make the right decisions in times of uncertainty. Being able to act honestly and ethically as well as make the right decisions are all part of being effective as leaders. When owners, managers, and supervisors are seen as ineffective by staff members, trust diminishes or disappears.

Another discovery was that nearly two thirds (63 percent) who had strong trust in management said they would be happy spending the rest of their careers in their present organization. This feeling of wanting to stay and continuing to contribute is reinforced when leaders point out a task well done, engage with and get to know staff members, and build relationships based on trust. Once that foundation of trust is built, relationships can be deepened, which not only benefits staff members and guests, but also supervisors, managers, and owners.

Service Teams

Teamwork in a food and beverage operation requires management to (1) believe that one of the organization's top priorities is serving internal customers (i.e., staff members), and (2) actively demonstrate that belief. If staff members know that managers desire to serve them, it makes them more willing to give guests (external customers) that extraordinary service that makes the dining experience special. One of the ways that supervisors and managers build teamwork is by working alongside staff members and knowing firsthand what they do. Supervisors and managers can empower staff members by making sure they receive adequate training for their positions—when staff members are properly trained, they feel empowered to act.

Managers who select team members based primarily on attitude generally are more successful than those who place experience at the top of their criteria when hiring. The philosophy behind this method is to select for attitude and personality, then train for specific responsibilities. A good food and beverage service attitude includes the following:

- Understanding and leading of self

- Focusing on others

- Being upbeat with a positive outlook

- Taking action when there is a problem to be solved or an issue to address

- Not complaining to others about others—that is, not complaining to staff members about guests, to staff members about other staff members, etc.

- Using "we" or "us" rather than "me" or "I"

- Disagreeing in an agreeable, nonconfrontational way; for example, by saying, "My opinion is different" rather than "You are wrong"

- Being aware of how nonverbal actions (e.g., crossed arms, no eye contact, lack of attention) can indicate a lack of interest and a closed mind

One of the proven strategies for strengthening a food and beverage team is holding regular meetings focused on discussing how everyone—servers, hosts, buspersons, cooks, kitchen staff—can work together to create a more positive experience for guests. This creates unity of purpose and reminds everyone of what the primary mission of the food and beverage operation is—the creation and delivery of great dining experiences for guests. Team meetings are also opportunities to introduce and taste new menu items and wine selections, and review special promotions. These meetings are a good time to recognize individuals and teams within the larger team. This recognition boosts the sense of accomplishment of those being recognized and calls attention to behaviors that others on the team should emulate.

Teams require a coach, or more accurately, a number of coaches. Coaches are mentors and teachers who train staff members to accept more responsibility and help them develop within their positions. With this increased responsibility and development, staff members will feel more empowered and respected by others. In addition, developing staff members in this way helps to retain them in the food and beverage operation.

Coaches delegate responsibilities based on the staff members' abilities to accept and follow through with assignments. Delegation helps individual staff members develop and shifts responsibilities so both the coach and the staff member can contribute more value to the operation. When a manager delegates, it is important that the staff member understands the desired outcome and has the information necessary to make a good decision. However, the delegating manager sometimes needs to be reminded that one person's methods of reaching an outcome may be different than another person's. The delegating manager must be comfortable with this fact, as well as the concept that sometimes people will make mistakes along the way. As long as mistakes are viewed as learning opportunities for all, they will be seen as occasions for further development rather than punishment.

Coaches focus on the strengths of individuals and recognize how people's strengths contribute to results in the food and beverage operation. It is the strengths of both the service staff and the kitchen staff combined with management's strengths that deliver the full guest experience. Coaches also place people in the organization based upon where their individual talents can best be utilized and further developed. Coaches are great listeners because they know that this is the most important of all communication skills. Listening to members of the food and beverage team to obtain the true meaning of their messages promotes understanding and respect among team members.

Basic Elements of a Food and Beverage Operation

In the following sections we will discuss basic service and production elements of a food and beverage operation.

Telephone Courtesy

Some food and beverage staff members make frequent use of the telephone while performing their duties. A telephone call is often the first point of contact a guest has with a food and beverage operation, so telephone courtesy is a critical skill that all staff members should possess. Guests call to make reservations, ask questions, or order take-out food or in-room dining service. Food and beverage staff members should try to make every caller feel important by being friendly, polite, and professional on the telephone. They should:

- Smile when they talk. A smile helps them sound more relaxed and pleasant.

- Speak clearly into the receiver. They should avoid slang, technical terms, or hospitality words that callers may not understand.

- Use proper grammar and diction. They should avoid "yep," "uh-huh," and "okay." Instead, staff members should use "yes," "certainly," or "absolutely."

- Answer the phone promptly. A phone that rings and rings gives a caller the impression that the operation doesn't want to take the call.

- Refrain from putting a caller on hold for more than one minute. The caller may become irritated by excessive waiting time.

- Always tell the caller their name, the operation's name, and their department (if applicable). Each operation may have a specific way for staff members to answer the phone.

- Give the caller a friendly greeting, such as "good morning" or "good evening," and ask how they can help.

- Give the caller their complete attention. One way to do this is to pretend that the caller is standing right in front of them.

- Talk only to the person on the phone, not to anyone around them.

- Properly hand off the call, if necessary. If the call is for a manager, they should ask the caller if they may put him or her on hold, then get the manager immediately, or take a message if they discover the manager is not available. If the caller is looking for a guest, they should ask a co-worker to help them locate the guest. (If they cannot find the guest within one or two minutes, they should take a message.) If a work-related call is for another staff member, they should ask the caller if they may put him or her on hold and then go find the person.

To take a message, staff members should write down the caller's name, the time and date of the call, the message, and their name as the message-taker in case there are any questions. In some operations, callers may have the option of leaving a voice mail for the person they are trying to reach.

As just mentioned, sometimes staff members must put callers on hold. They should always first ask callers if it is all right to put them on hold. If the caller gives them permission, they should put the caller on hold for no longer than one minute, then thank the caller for waiting when they return to the line.

Each phone call should be ended with a sincere thank you. Staff members should offer to be of assistance in the future, and let the caller hang up first. The end of the call is the last chance to leave a good impression with a potential guest.

Automated Telephone Answering Systems. Due to today's broad array of communication technology, food and beverage operations may not have persons answer telephone calls initially; rather, callers may be greeted with a recorded message that invites them to proceed via button- or voice-activated options. There are many schools of thought on this topic, one being that while providing electronic or digital answering options may be efficient, it might also have the effect of depersonalizing the operation's first point of contact with a guest. Managers should carefully consider how an automated telephone answering system affects the total guest experience.

Taking Reservations

Successful food and beverage operations can be very busy. During these busy times, the host may need help taking reservations. Therefore, it is desirable that other food and beverage staff members be familiar with taking reservations as well. This helps the staff work better as a team and provides faster service to guests. When taking a reservation, food and beverage staff members should:

- Greet the guest warmly. If it is a phone reservation, they should answer the phone promptly and use proper phone etiquette. If someone is making a reservation in person, they should first warmly welcome the guest to the restaurant.
- Find out:
  — The name the reservation will be under
  — Whether the guest wants a booth or table (if both are available)
  — The date and time of the reservation
  — The number in the party
  — Whether there are any special requests
  — The guest's phone number or (for hotel restaurants) guestroom number

- Repeat the information back to the guest to make sure it is correct.

- Thank the guest for making the reservation. The staff member should then initial the reservation in case someone has questions about it later.

In today's web-based communication world, electronic reservations are easy to make and electronic confirmations are easy to send. The electronic notice, in addition to confirming the reservation, should require the person making the reservation to furnish his or her e-mail address. See Exhibit 4 for an example of a confirmation e-mail and follow-up thank-you message.

Tipping Policies

Some types of food and beverage staff members—servers, for example—receive tips for performing their duties. In some food and beverage operations, these tips are shared. Sharing tips with other food and beverage staff is one way to recognize that excellent service is only possible with the efforts of everyone on the service team. All members of the team depend on one another to provide positive, memorable experiences to guests.

Every food and beverage operation has its own tipping policies. Two of the most common ways tips are handled are:

- Servers are allowed to keep all of their individual tips

- Servers share their tips with a few specific co-workers, such as the buspersons they work with

  An operation's tipping policies must follow federal and state regulations.

Tip Pooling. Some operations use a tip pooling strategy. Tip pooling is essentially a sharing of a portion of server tips with a pool of other staff members. Those in the tip pool usually include buspersons, counter staff members (who serve guests), servers, and service bartenders. Those usually excluded from the tip pool include cooks, chefs, dishwashers, supervisors, and managers.

When tips are pooled, each person who contributes cannot be required to give a greater percentage of his or her tips than is customary and reasonable. Food and beverage operators may, for example, decide that 10 percent of a server's tips is a fair amount for each server to contribute to the tip pool.

Managers must weigh the advantages of a tip pool against the disadvantages. If, for example, a server believes that there is no reason to increase efforts to satisfy guests because he or she will be expected to contribute a larger dollar amount to the tip pool, this policy may be counter to enhancing the guest experience. This lower productivity could result in less than acceptable service and higher labor costs.

Menus

A successful food and beverage operation begins with the menu. Much planning and design goes into deciding what foods and beverages an operation will offer to its guests. In fact, the menu is the first and best marketing tool an operation has. It entices guests with its offerings, and can sell guests with its scrumptious

Exhibit 4 Sample Reservation Confirmation and Follow-Up E-Mail

Reservation Confirmation E-Mail:

From: "Barker, Barney" <Barney@sodarestaurant.com>
Date: March 14, 20XX: 1:34 PM EDT
To: Ellie@lab.com
Subject: Reservation Confirmation #WEB1325 for SODARESTAURANT on 4-17-20XX at 6:15 PM

Dear Ellie,

THANK YOU for selecting Soda Restaurant for your dining experience. We are pleased to confirm the following dinner reservation:

Confirmation Number:	WEB1325
Party of:	5
Time of Reservation:	6:15 PM
Day/Date:	Wednesday, April 17, 20XX

Please phone us at 517-555-1234 if you need to cancel your reservation at least 24 hours in advance.

THANK YOU and we look forward to serving you.

Soda Restaurant

Follow-Up Thank-You E-Mail:

From: "Barker, Barney" <Barney@sodarestaurant.com>
Date: April 17, 20XX: 10:24 PM EDT
To: Ellie@lab.com
Subject: THANK YOU from Soda Restaurant

Dear Ellie,

It was our pleasure having you dine with us at Soda Restaurant this evening. Please feel free to contact me if you have suggestions for improving the dining experience, special requests, or future reservations with which I can assist you.

THANK YOU.

Barney Barker
Restaurant Manager
Soda Restaurant
Phone: 517-555-1234

descriptions. The menu dictates what resources are needed and how they must be expended. Typically, the more complex and varied the menu, the more expensive and elaborate the food and beverage operation.

When planning a menu, managers should consider the following factors:

- What are the target markets for the operation—that is, what types of guests will it attempt to appeal to? What are these guests' requirements and preferences?

- What type of food, beverages, and services will be offered?

- Where will the operation be located?

- Who are the operation's competitors?

- What can we do to create a unique and memorable service experience?

  It is also necessary to determine how the menu will affect the following:

- *Labor requirements.* An adequate number of qualified staff members with the appropriate skills are required to produce all menu items.

- *Equipment needs.* Equipment must be available to produce all of the items required by the menu.

- *Space requirements.* The menu in large part determines the space that will be required for equipment and storage, production, serving, and other facilities.

- *The operation's layout and design.* The menu can affect the operation's layout and design.

- *Ingredient (food and beverage products) requirements.* Standard recipes specify the ingredients necessary to prepare each item on the menu. All ingredients should be readily available at costs that support anticipated menu item selling prices.

- *Production and service times.* The types and complexity of the items offered on the menu will affect production and service times.

- *Costs.* Equipment, space, staff, and time concerns can all be translated into costs. The menu will also affect costs for utilities and supplies.

  All servers should read the operation's menu and become familiar with it. It is their responsibility to know all of the items on the menu. Guests will often ask questions about the food on the menu. All servers should be able to answer the following questions about any item offered:

- What are the ingredients?

- How is it prepared? (See Exhibit 5 for basic food preparation terms.)

- How large are the portions?

- What goes with it?

- How does it taste?

- What may guests substitute for this item?

- What cannot be substituted for this item?

- Which beverage products (wines, for example) would best accompany this item?

  Managers should ensure that food and beverage servers are able to sample as many of the menu items as possible. If they try something and like it, it is easier for servers to suggest that item to a guest. Servers should also be able to explain any words on the menu that a guest may not understand.

Exhibit 5   Basic Food Preparation Terms

One of the best ways to describe the food offered in a restaurant is to describe how it is prepared. Successful food and beverage staff members use the following terms accurately when describing menu items:

Baked	Cooked by dry heat in an oven.
Boiled	Cooked in boiling liquid.
Braised	Browned in a small amount of fat, then cooked slowly in a small amount of liquid.
Broiled	Cooked by direct heat from above.
Deep-fried	Cooked in enough fat to cover the food.
Fried	Cooked in fat.
Grilled	Cooked on a grid over direct heat (usually hot coals).
Poached	Cooked in enough simmering liquid to cover the food. A liquid is simmering when it is just below the boiling point.
Roasted	Cooked uncovered without water added, usually in an oven, by dry heat.
Sautéed	Browned or cooked in a small amount of hot fat.
Steamed	Cooked in steam with or without pressure.
Stewed	Simmered slowly, usually for a long period of time, in enough liquid to cover the food.

Menus change regularly in many food and beverage operations. Successful servers stay current regarding any new items or changes in recipes. Guests often are interested in daily or chef specials because they typically offer value and variety. Servers should be able to describe these specials, along with their prices. They should also know which items on the menu are considered house specialties, as guests will often try these if they are described well.

During busy times, a food and beverage operation may run out of a popular menu item. Servers should know what's no longer available (a daily special, for example) before approaching a table to take an order and should be prepared to suggest another item instead.

Food Production

Excellent food is a basic requirement for a successful food and beverage operation. An operation will not continue to operate long-term unless the food served is as good or better than nearby competing operations.

Excellent food requires quality ingredients. To get the best results from the quality ingredients, menu items should be prepared as close as possible to the time of service. Proper cooking methods must be followed as menu items are produced. For instance, if a recipe calls for a stew to be simmered for two hours, it should be simmered, not boiled violently. Once food is prepared, it must be properly cared for until it is served. Food safety requires that hot foods must be held hot and cold foods held cold until they are served, and holding times should be as short as possible before service.

Excellent service depends on correctly timing meals. Guests want meals at the correct temperature, courses brought promptly after a previous one is finished, and all the entrées for the entire party brought at the same time. This requires careful coordination in the food production area.

The Kitchen. A kitchen in a typical large food and beverage operation may consist of a range section (which may include ranges, stock kettles, broilers, grills, steamers, fry kettles, and roasting ovens); a garde-manger (cold food) section; a pantry (salad) area; and a scullery (dish and pot washing) area. Kitchen facilities in hotels may include a staff cafeteria kitchen, a banquet kitchen, and an in-room dining kitchen. Some large hotels may also have a butcher, pastry, and/or bake shop.

Excellent food can be produced only when the food and beverage production staff has the proper tools and equipment with which to work. Therefore, it is important that the kitchen and all its equipment be kept in proper working condition at all times.

Correct Plate Presentations and Garnishes. Guests like to see attractive-looking meals. The way a plate or glass is presented and garnished can make the difference between an average experience and a memorable one. Plate presentation changes from operation to operation, but some common rules of plate presentation are as follows:

- The correct plate is used

- Hot foods are served on hot plates, chilled foods on cold plates

- The food looks fresh and appealing

- There are no drips down the side of the glass or plate

- The entrée portion is placed at the six o'clock position when the food is served to the guest

- An appropriate garnish is used

Garnishes are often used to accent food on a plate. They add color, form, and texture to the presentation. Some common garnishes are parsley, lemon slices or wedges, orange slices or wedges, cherries, tomato wedges or cherry tomatoes, carved or grated carrot, chocolate curls, endive, and fresh (edible) flowers.

Service Styles

There are many variations in the procedures and techniques food and beverage operations use to serve food to guests, but most can be categorized under one of four main styles of service: plate service, cart service, platter service, and family-style service. In addition to table-service styles, buffet service is being used by an increasing number of operations, often in combination with a table-service style. Some operations give guests a choice between a buffet or selecting items from a menu.

Plate Service. Plate service (also called American service) is the most common style of table service in the United States. Plate service follows these basic procedures:

1. Servers take guests' orders in the dining area, then enter the orders into the POS system.

2. Kitchen staff members produce food orders, portion them, and place them on plates in the kitchen.

3. Servers deliver the prepared plates to the guests.

4. Buspersons assist servers and clear tables.

Standards for a table's "guest ready" appearance vary from restaurant to restaurant. For example, staff members in some casual-dining restaurants may set tables with all but the plates required for the entrée, so that bread and butter plates, water and wine glasses, napkins and flatware, and other items are already on the table when guests are first seated. Some restaurants, especially high-check-average and full-service, upscale restaurants, also preset tables with a **show plate** or base plate.

In restaurants using plate service, servers generally serve several tables simultaneously. The actual number depends on how much experience the server has, the distance from his or her sidestation to the food pickup area, the menu itself, the number of servers on duty, and the number of guests that can be seated at each of the tables in the server's assigned section.

Well-designed, well-stocked sidestations for food servers are a must for plate service. The dining area should be designed so that staff members have convenient access to the sidestations. At the same time, these stations should not be a cause of disturbance to guests seated near them—there should be no excessive noise or traffic jams caused by service staff, for example, or unattractive views of service supplies and equipment.

Plate service requires that servers clear each course's emptied plates and used flatware before serving the next course (unless the guest prefers otherwise).

With the plate-service system, food quality is solely controlled by the chef and the production staff. The policy in many restaurants is that the chef has the overall responsibility for food quality during its presentation in dining areas as well as during its production in the kitchen. Plate service easily accommodates this policy, since production staff members prepare and plate food products under the chef's direction. Although the chef has the ultimate responsibility for food quality, it is still the responsibility of each server to visually check the food quality and presentation of each order before delivering it to guests.

Cart Service. Cart service (also called French service) is popular internationally, but used less frequently in the United States. Cart service is an elaborate service style in which menu items are prepared on a cart or *guéridon* beside guest tables by specially trained staff members; menu items are cooked—sometimes flambéed—in front of the guests via the cart's portable heating unit *(réchaud)*. In the United States, the limited number of restaurants that use cart service are generally full-service, upscale, high-check-average operations. Restaurant managers who are considering using this high-priced and labor-intensive service style should undertake detailed feasibility studies to confirm the existence of a guest base sophisticated enough to support it, and be ready to implement an extensive training program so that staff members can deliver it.

In dining rooms that offer cart service, a maître d' who knows the intricacies of cart service is required to seat guests, supervise the dining room, and perform other duties. A sommelier typically helps guests select wines and then serves them. At least two food service staff members are needed in each dining area station for cart service: the *chef du rang* and the *commis du rang*. The *chef du rang* is generally responsible for taking orders, serving drinks, preparing food at the table, and collecting guest payments. He or she must be very experienced and skilled. Normally, production staff members partially prepare the food in the kitchen, then the *chef du rang* finishes preparing it at tableside. The *commis du rang* assists the *chef du rang*. He or she is responsible for taking food orders to the kitchen, placing the orders, picking up food in the kitchen, and bringing it to the tableside carts, often on silver trays. When the *chef du rang* is busy with preparation duties, the *commis du rang* also delivers drink orders and serves food to guests.

Platter Service. Platter service (also called Russian service) requires servers to deliver platters of fully cooked food to the dining room, present the platters to guests for approval, and then serve the food. This type of service is featured in many of the best international restaurants and hotels; some food and beverage operations in the United States, particularly banquet operations, also use it.

With platter service, the food is prepared (and sometimes precut for easier service) by food production staff members in the kitchen. They arrange the food attractively on the service platters for food servers to deliver to the dining room. Generally, servers use a team approach; one server carries the entrée and a second carries the accompaniments. Servers line up in the kitchen and, at the appropriate time, parade into the dining area. After presenting (showing) the food to the guests, they place the platters on tray stands while they position a hot, empty dinner plate in front of each guest. Holding the platter in the left hand, the server transfers the food to guest plates by artfully manipulating a fork and spoon held in the right hand. Service proceeds in this way around the table counterclockwise.

Platter service can be as elegant as cart service, but it is more practical because it is faster and less expensive. Platter service can provide a special touch and still allow managers to control labor and product costs closely. Like cart service, platter service incorporates many traditions that mean elegant and superior service for guests.

Family-Style Service. Family-style service (also called English service) requires food to be placed on large platters or in large bowls that are delivered to the guests' tables by servers. Guests at each table then pass the food around their table and serve themselves. Family-style service is relatively easy to implement, because service staff members do not need to be highly skilled. In fact, with family-style service, servers generally put more effort into clearing tables than into presenting and serving the food.

One possible disadvantage of family-style service is that it is difficult to implement portion-control procedures. The last guests may not receive as much of an item as they would like if the first guests took more than their share. This problem can be reduced if the initial amount of food placed in the bowl or on the platter is generous. The informal atmosphere of family-style service can also be a disadvantage if guests expect a more formal atmosphere or desire a great deal of attention from servers.

Buffet Service. Buffets display food on counters or tables, and guests help themselves to as many and as much of the items as they wish to eat. There are many popular layouts for **buffet service** that can be used in place of the traditional straight-line setup. Buffets can range from a simple offering of several basic food items to elaborate presentations of more sophisticated menu items that appeal to guests with those tastes. Buffet service is sometimes used in combination with (rather than in place of) table service; for example, servers may serve drinks and desserts using plate service while allowing guests to serve themselves at a buffet for the main course.

Typically, the chef plans the buffet menu, since his or her responsibility for the food extends into the dining area. However, concerns such as the placement of the buffet, the flow of guests as they pass through the buffet line, and related service details are generally the responsibility of the dining room manager. As the manager plans the buffet line, he or she should pay a great deal of attention to the presentation of the food. For instance, ice sculptures, fresh flowers, or vegetable or fruit centerpieces can be attractive focal points on the buffet line. Decorative service platters or bowls also can enhance the food presentation. Increasingly popular is the use of shelves and stands to allow food and beverage products to be displayed at various heights.

Foods are usually placed on buffets in the following order: salads and other chilled meal accompaniments; hot vegetables; and meats, poultry, fish, and other hot entrées. Some buffets feature whole beef filets, whole hams, racks of lamb, or turkey breasts that servers or production staff carve as guests request a portion. Such items as crepes and omelets are sometimes cooked to order on a buffet line at so-called "action stations." Sauces, dressings, and relishes should be placed close to the menu items that they accompany.

Some organizations use a **scramble system** for their buffets. The term "scramble system" was first used to describe cafeterias in which guests could go to separate stations to be served, rather than waiting in a single line. For example, hot foods might be at one station, beverages at another, and desserts and salads at still others. Using this plan for buffets simply involves making each station a small buffet. While requiring more setup space than other buffet-service styles, the scramble system lessens bottlenecks because it does not force guests into a single line.

Point-of-Sale Equipment

A food and beverage operation's computerized **point-of-sale (POS) system** is often made up of a number of individual POS units. Some units are pre-check terminals that servers use to create and track guest orders, others are like cash registers in that they can add up guest charges and print a bill. In hotel restaurants, POS units may be linked to the front desk so that a guest's restaurant check can be transferred and automatically added to a guest's folio if the guest so desires; the check will then be paid along with guestroom charges and other charges when the guest checks out.

Most computerized point-of-sale systems require servers to sign onto the system at the beginning of a shift using a password number called a "server number." Then, whenever they open a new guest check, add orders to an open guest check, or total a guest check, they must enter their server number again. At the end of their shift, servers must sign off the system. At that time, the system may automatically print a report summarizing their shift transactions.

Service Trays

Service trays are used to help transport food, dishes, and equipment throughout the restaurant. Servers most commonly use two types of trays:

- A 12- to 14-inch beverage tray, which should be used only for serving beverages or serving food for a single guest.

- A large restaurant service tray, usually 27 inches long and oval in shape, to be used for serving food for a party of more than one and clearing tables.

Service trays are often used when servers are delivering or clearing items. They are usually washed in the kitchen at the end of the meal period and periodically sprayed with sanitizing solution and then wiped throughout service. Servers often help clean the trays, set them up, and stock their sidestations with trays.

Servers and others should follow safe lifting procedures when carrying large trays. When picking up a loaded tray, they should bend at the knees so that their shoulder is below the tray. They can then pull the tray with one hand onto the palm of the other hand. They should balance the tray at shoulder level on their fingertips, not on their forearms (trays carried on a forearm have a greater likelihood of tipping over). They should keep their back straight as they stand up and steady the tray with their free hand. Trays should always be loaded with the heaviest items near the center of the tray.

Food and Beverage Guests

We have discussed food and beverage staff members, the team approach to organizing and running a food and beverage operation, basic elements of a food and beverage operation, and the different service styles possible within a food and beverage facility. Last but certainly not least, we will now discuss food and beverage guests. Obviously, without guests, food and beverage operations would not survive. In the following sections we will cover guest issues ranging from generational age groups and their differing wants and needs as guests, to strategies food and beverage operations use to retain guests.

Serving Different Generations

While a detailed discussion of food and beverage preferences based on generational age groups is beyond the scope of this chapter, this section will highlight some important fundamental information. In general, guests of all age groups seem to be searching for value today. One way this is seen is in the growing preference for dining at fast-casual restaurants rather than at full-service restaurants. A second commonality is that there are more food and beverage operations competing for the same guests. For that reason, it is even more important for a particular food and beverage operation to be seen as the guest's primary choice. A third fact, which is associated with a struggling economy, is that guests of all ages are dining out less frequently. There is less discretionary money to spend, so the choice of dining at a particular food and beverage operation is more deliberate; this means some guests may choose to eat at home more frequently. A fourth factor true for all guests is that many food and beverage operations are reducing portion sizes, along with prices for those portions, in an attempt to attract today's value-conscious consumers.

Guest markets are sometimes looked at in terms of age. The mature market comprises those guests who are 50 years old or older. The Baby Boomers (people born between the mid 1940s and early 1960s) are already in or are about to enter the mature market. In the last century, one might refer to the individuals within this market as "senior citizens." Today, these guests fit anything but the traditional concept of a senior citizen, as they are a multi-generational, active, youth-oriented group. This market has embraced fitness and improved health, focusing on attaining a longer life with a better quality of life. Because Baby Boomers are generally physically active and committed to living longer, they tend to like light and healthy food options when dining out. Baby Boomers still enjoy a burger and fries on occasion, but more often order salads, fish and shellfish, and vegetables that are not fried. They also prefer, more so than other generations, carbonated soda, coffee, and iced tea. Baby Boomers more frequently choose mid-scale food and beverage operations with variety on the menus.

Generation X is made up of those people born between the mid 1960s and the early 1980s. They tend to be more autonomous and self-reliant than earlier generations. They are less interested in loyalty to an organization and more committed to balance between their personal and professional lives. They want what they want when they want it and have been described as somewhat self-centered. Generation X guests choose a food and beverage operation that they consider to be consistent with their personal values. If the Gen-X guest values community support by food and beverage businesses, for example, then that guest will most likely choose an operation that contributes to the local community through cash or in-kind contributions. Most of all, Generation Xers seek value in food and beverage operations as defined not by the operation, but by the guest.

Generation Y consists of those born between the early 1980s and the turn of the century; there are roughly 75 million Generation Y individuals in the United States. This generation consists of many adventurous eaters who enjoy various cuisines, along with intense flavors and healthy menu options. Generation Y will be guests of food and beverage operations for many decades, so it is important for food and beverage operators to understand and get to know this generation's dining preferences.

Guest Complaints

Guest complaints should be interpreted as meaningful feedback, not looked upon as just the same old complaining that servers always hear. Guest complaints are actually reality checks revealing how guests truly perceive a food and beverage operation. As retailer J. C. Penny, a twentieth century innovator in customer service, once said, "If you want to sell what the customer buys, you must see the world through the customer's eyes." Guest complaints help owners, managers, supervisors, and staff members see the operation through the customers' eyes and provide information that can either be ignored or used to help enhance guests' experiences.

Guest complaints help alert staff to areas that need attention and improvement. Rather than viewing a complaint as annoying, disruptive, unwanted, unreasonable, silly, or invalid, operators should take complaints seriously and be alert for any hidden messages that might be behind them. For example, a guest complaining about rolls not being warm, the time it took for a server to visit the table after he or she was seated, and the doneness of a steak may genuinely be upset with these individual items; however, the guest's complaints could also stem from his or her initial discomfort in being seated at a table that is too close to the noisy kitchen. It is the server's responsibility to engage such a guest in conversation to find out the root cause of the complaint, and then do everything possible to handle it.

Not all guests who have a complaint register it. Sometimes they feel sorry for the server and hesitate to voice their displeasure because the reason for the complaint (e.g., wrong degree of a steak's doneness) was the fault of the cook, not the server. Guests generally do not like to be perceived as too pushy or rude. Other guests do not think their complaint will be used to help the operation improve, so they don't bother. Guest are further discouraged from complaining if a server responds to a complaint by making a remark similar to "I've never heard that complaint before!" which implies, first, that "You are the only person petty enough to complain about this" and second "Who cares what you think?"

Some operators view a complaint in terms of who is right or wrong; ultimately, that doesn't matter. What matters is why the complaint was made, what the true source of the complaint is, and how it can be resolved. Obviously, resolving guest complaints is critical if the food and beverage operator wants positive word-of-mouth referrals. Studies have shown that more than 80 percent of people who have a problem with a business never return. These people are not happy, but often they leave without saying a word to the people in the operation. Frustrated, they instead may tell their co-workers, family, friends, and all they meet about their dreadful experience.

In some cases, not satisfying a guest may cause a simple complaint to escalate into a major problem. For instance, the guest could contact the local Better Business Bureau, Chamber of Commerce, or health department; the media; and others to bring additional attention to the unresolved complaint. Therefore, it is always better to resolve a complaint immediately to the guest's satisfaction if at all possible. If a server simply asks the guest what it will take to satisfy his or her complaint, often the guest will volunteer the information.

In some cases, people may try to scam a food and beverage operation with a bogus complaint. Often the scammer will invent a story in an attempt to get a free meal, such as finding an insect or a piece of glass in his or her food. It is important to treat such complaints as legitimate until checked for accuracy.

When a complaint, whether legitimate or made up, is lodged, it is important to take action as soon as possible. The staff member handling the complaint needs to first identify and record the facts surrounding the complaint; second, apologize to the guest; and third, follow up to fix the problem and eliminate the "why" behind the complaint.

In the process of identifying and recording the facts, the guest and any staff members or supervisors who were directly involved with the situation should be interviewed. Guests should be asked to define specifically the nature of the complaint. For example, "I didn't like my main course" does not give as much information as "The flavor in my main course made me believe that one or more of the ingredients was spoiled." Try to find out the guest's real concerns regarding the complaint.

The person handling the complaint should apologize profusely. He or she should listen to the meaning behind the guest's words, apologize, ask the guest what can be done to remedy the situation, and make sure the guest leaves satisfied. Truly listening to the complaint can help get to the source of the problem.

Finally, after doing what it takes to resolve the complaint, the staff member should follow up to determine if there is additional action required. The problem should be resolved as quickly as possible, and the guest should not be made to feel awkward about complaining. The staff member should thank the guest for bringing the problem to his or her attention and clearly state what is being done (or going to be done) to satisfy the guest.

Guest Complaints and the Internet. In the past when a guest complained, it often was to a friend in a later one-on-one conversation or perhaps to a group of friends at a party. No more. Today a guest's complaints might be read by hundreds of friends who are on Facebook or tweeting on Twitter. TripAdvisor is just one example of a website where unfavorable reviews of food and beverage operations may be posted on the Internet for thousands to read.

Food and beverage operations are increasingly concerned about their online reputation, so many of them monitor and respond to online comments. Some operations have retained consultants to develop social media strategies and help in these monitoring efforts. As technology continues to change and social media becomes more popular, some food and beverage operations are asking staff members to be on the lookout for what guests are saying about their dining experiences on various social networking sites. Staff members who discover guest complaints online are urged to write apologies on behalf of the operation and then relay this information to the operation so that staff can find the root cause of the problem and fix it. If the full name of the complainer and the operation is listed on a review, the operation is more likely to see the complaint as legitimate and take action.

Sometimes action can be taken immediately. For example, if a hotel guest who posts a complaint online is still staying at the hotel at the time of the post, the hotel can contact the guest and offer him or her a complimentary dinner (if the guest's dining experience was the problem). It is far better to address the problem before the guest leaves the operation.

Guest Feedback

There are many ways for an operation to seek and obtain guest feedback. One way is to have servers engage their guests in conversation by asking questions such as:

- How did you find out about our food and beverage operation?

- Is this your first visit?

- What did you like about us earlier that brought you back for this visit?

Another way to gather guest feedback is to ask guests to complete an evaluation at the end of their dining experience. The evaluation can ask guests:

- To rate the operation on its ambience, cleanliness, food quality, hospitality, telephone courtesy, and welcome.

- If they have any ideas on how the operation can be improved.

- For contact information such as e-mail addresses, telephone numbers, and home address so the restaurant can contact them if necessary.

Increasingly, food and beverage operations are encouraging guests to utilize e-mail for feedback. For example, some restaurants are sending guests both reservation confirmation and follow-up e-mails to garner feedback. Typically, the restaurant manager sends the guest an e-mail confirmation after he or she makes the reservation (either by e-mail, by phone, or in person), reminding the guest of the reservation time and date. Following the visit, the same manager sends an e-mail to thank guests for their visits and to solicit feedback through a short survey.

Phoning customers is another way to obtain feedback. To be effective, guests have to receive the telephone call very soon after their visits. Questions that might be asked include:

- Was this your first dining experience with us?

- If so, what led to your choice?

- If not, how many times have you been our guest?

- What did you order? If this was not your first time visiting us, have you ordered this item before?

- Of the restaurants that you frequent, how do we match up?

- What could we do better?

- Are you dining out more or less frequently than six months ago?

An advisory council of guests can also help an operation obtain feedback. Similar to a focus group, an advisory council can be utilized for feedback on the operation's food and beverage product quality, service delivery, cleanliness, and potential new menu items. Council members can also share their perceptions of the operation and what they would like to see done differently at the operation. The members on the council should reflect the operation's customer-base demographics in terms of gender, age, geographical area, and other attributes.

Retaining Guests

Keeping a current guest is less expensive than attracting a new guest. In order to retain guests, a food and beverage operation's staff must commit to getting to know individual guests and then doing everything possible to keep them satisfied and coming back.

There are a number of ways to get to know guests while at the same time working to retain them. One way is to simply engage guests in conversation with questions such as:

- What do you like most/least about our food and beverage operation?

- What do you like most/least about our competitors' food and beverage operations?

- What can we do to better satisfy you?

Another way to learn about guests is to administer a survey. These surveys should be made available online or on paper. A paper-based survey may be given to guests before they leave or may be mailed to them. The survey could ask for information about the demographic characteristics of each guest such as age, gender, ethnicity, etc. This information can assist the food and beverage operator in choosing menu items to feature, selecting portion sizes, developing pricing strategies, deciding hours of operation, and many other operational aspects of the food and beverage business. A survey may also help the operator identify buying patterns of guests if it asks guests to provide information such as how often they go out to eat in a specific time period, how much they typically spend when they go out, and so on.

Other questions to consider for a guest survey are those related to why a guest chose that particular food and beverage operation—i.e., for the location, the menu, a special occasion, a business reason, or some other reason. It is also important in a guest survey to find out what guests like and do not like about the operation. Often these questions are framed in terms of products (e.g., menu items, beverages), services (e.g., hospitality, friendliness, courtesy, attention to detail, server appearance and knowledge), ambience (e.g., cleanliness, organization, atmosphere, facility appearance), and other attributes of the operation.

Usually, a guest survey asks what the operator can do to improve the operation. Sometimes a combination of current offerings (e.g., daily menu specials, foods prepared to go) and offerings that the operator may be considering (e.g., off-site catering) are presented in surveys to gauge how well the current offerings are being received and to obtain a "read" from guests prior to the implementation of new offerings.

Guest surveys sometimes include questions about the competition, such as, "When you are not dining in our operation, where else do you dine?" It is important to keep in mind that it is not simply just other food and beverage operations that are considered to be competition. Rather, it is any other dining activity that a guest chooses instead of deciding to dine at the food and beverage operation.

A final topic for a guest survey could be general guest satisfaction. For example, one question might ask about the quality of the food and beverages served, while another could ask about the level of service quality. A third question might inquire about the overall food and beverage experience. These questions would help identify guest satisfaction levels in three general areas—product, service, overall—and could be used to track and compare guest satisfaction over time.

An alternative way to obtain guest information that can help an operation retain guests is to survey them by telephone. Interviewers could be hired for this purpose, or supervisors and managers could be required to phone a predetermined number of guests with questions about their most recent dining experience. This not only provides valuable feedback, it also strengthens the operation's relationship with these guests.

Key Terms

buffet service—A typically large assortment of foods attractively arranged for self-service by guests.

cart service—A table-service style in which specially trained staff members prepare menu items beside the guests' tables using a cart; the food is prepared and plated on the cart, then served to the guests. Also called French service.

family-style service—A table-service style in which servers take food on large platters or in large bowls from the kitchen and deliver it to guest tables; the guests at each table then pass the food around their table, serving themselves. Also called English service.

garnishes—Decorative, edible food items that accent food on a plate. They add color, form, and texture.

guéridon—A cart or rectangular table mounted on wheels with workspace, shelves, and a heating unit *(réchaud);* used for tableside food preparation in cart service.

mise en place—A French term that means "to put everything in its place."

plate service—A table-service style in which fully cooked menu items are individually produced, portioned, plated, and garnished in the kitchen, then carried to each guest directly. Also called American service.

platter service—A table-service style in which servers carry platters of food to the dining room and present them to guests for approval. Servers then set hot plates in front of each guest and place food from the platters onto the plates. Also called Russian service.

point-of-sale (POS) system—A computer network of pre-check terminals and electronic cash registers that keeps track of guest orders through order placement, order production, and guest payment.

réchaud—A portable heating unit used for food preparation on the cart or *guéridon* in cart service.

scramble system—A system used for cafeterias and buffets in which guests go to separate stations for their food rather than wait in a single line. For example, hot foods might be placed at one station, beverages at another, and desserts and salads at still others.

service trays—Platters used by food and beverage personnel to transport food, dishes, and equipment.

show plate—Often ornately designed with the organization's logo or made of fine china, pewter, or another attractive material, this plate enhances the table presentation when guests first arrive. Also called a base plate. The plate holding the entrée and other food items is placed on top of the show plate.

sidestation—A service stand in the dining area that holds equipment (such as a coffee maker) and service supplies (such as tableware and condiments) for easy access by servers and other staff members. Also called a server station, sidestand, or workstation.

Review Questions

1. What are typical responsibilities and concerns of top managers, middle managers, and supervisors?

2. What types of food production positions are commonly found in food and beverage operations?

3. What types of service positions are commonly found in food and beverage operations?

4. How can trust in work relationships be fostered?

5. What are some ways food service staff members can display telephone courtesy to callers?

6. How does a restaurant's menu impact the restaurant?

7. What are some basic food preparation terms?

8. What are the basic characteristics of plate service? cart service? platter service? family-style service? buffet service?

9. What are some of the differences among Baby Boomer, Generation X, and Generation Y guests?

10. What are some examples of questions staff members could use to engage guests in conversation for the purpose of getting feedback?

11. What kinds of questions should be considered when formulating a guest survey?

Case Studies

Moments of Truth: A Very Unhappy Birthday

Martin Hagadorn swore under his breath as he pulled into the parking lot of Xavier's, the upscale restaurant his wife, Francine, had chosen for her birthday dinner.

"What did I tell you, Fran. Every kid in town is here tonight for a fancy dinner before the prom," he grumbled. "Are you sure you want to eat here—and tonight? We could always come back next week when it's not so crowded. Besides, I brought Charlie Rogers here for lunch last week, and it wasn't all that great. I haven't been impressed the last few times I've been here with clients."

"But today's my birthday, not next week," Fran protested. "I'm not asking for much, Martin. This is my favorite restaurant, and I've got my heart set on the Maine lobster. I'm sure you'll find a parking spot around back."

The back parking lot was eerily dark; a light was burned out. Fran stepped out of the car, then gave a yelp of surprise and dismay.

"What's wrong?" Martin demanded, hurrying to her side of the car. Fran was shaking her foot.

"I didn't see this can of pop someone left in the parking lot. Now I've ruined my new suede pumps," she explained.

Martin was still grumbling about the lousy lighting as they entered the restaurant. He strode up to the host's station while Fran dashed to the restroom to clean her shoe. He was still waiting when she returned.

"Is our table ready, dear?" she asked hopefully.

"I wouldn't know. There doesn't seem to be anyone working here tonight," he said, craning his neck to try and spot the host, who was seating a large party of teenagers in formal attire. "See, I told you this was a bad idea."

He finally caught the host's eye, and she hurried over to greet them. "Hagadorn, party of two, eight o'clock," Martin barked.

"Oh, yes, Mr. Hagadorn. I see you're here for pleasure rather than business this time," said Monica, the host. "I'm sorry about the wait. I've got your table all ready in the smoking section."

"No-smoking, you mean," said Martin. "I specifically asked for no-smoking. My wife's very sensitive to smoke."

Monica knew there were no available tables in no-smoking, so she suggested that the Hagadorns go to the bar for a 20-minute wait until a table was ready. Martin looked disgruntled, but Fran tried to make the best of it.

"That's a fine idea. I can start my birthday dinner off with a glass of wine," she said as they sat down in the dusky bar. She ordered her favorite, a white zinfandel. When the bartender brought her drink, though, it was not what she had ordered.

"I'm sorry, ma'am, that's my mistake," said the bartender. "Let me bring you another glass—on the house." He returned with her drink as well as the bill for Martin's Rob Roy. "I'll take that whenever you're ready, sir," he said.

Martin looked at the bartender in surprise—usually the bar transferred his bill to the dinner tab. But he paid nonetheless. Nothing's gone right yet, he thought, except for Fran's free drink. He excused himself to check on the status of their table.

"Is the table ready yet?" he asked Monica. "It's my wife's birthday, and I'd really like the rest of her evening to be special, if that's not too much to ask."

"Certainly, sir, I understand. Your table will be ready in a moment," said Monica. She started to jot down "Hagadorn—birthday" on the log to remind herself to tell their server to present them with a complimentary cake, when the phone rang. I wish the other host hadn't called in sick tonight, she thought as she answered the phone. After she hung up, she noticed that a table was free and went to get the Hagadorns.

When Richard Merrill, the manager, glanced over the log a few minutes later, he saw that there was a couple celebrating an anniversary, and an 18th birthday for one of the prom-goers. I'll have to stop by those tables, he thought. Just then, his attention was diverted by a commotion near the kitchen. Monica was attempting to seat an older couple at a table near the swinging doors, and the gentleman looked near apoplexy as he loudly refused the seats.

"Is there anything I can help you with, Mr. Hagadorn?" Richard asked, sizing up the situation and smiling reassuringly at Monica. He spotted a table near the window that had yet to be bussed. "We can have that table ready in a jiffy, sir," he said, striding over and starting to bus the table himself. If only it wasn't prom night, we'd have more busers on duty to speed things up, he thought.

The Hagadorns stood gamely in the middle of the dining area, abandoned by Monica, who had hurried back to her station to greet more patrons. The manager called a busboy over to help him finish preparing the table, then was called away to deal with a situation in the kitchen. The couple continued to wait, until another busboy, assessing the scene, hurried over to escort them to their table.

"Please let me seat you. I hope you haven't been waiting long," Marco chatted cheerfully. "Here's some water and a basket of bread for you. Andrea will be your server tonight. Can I get you anything else?"

"We're finally getting the attention we expect when we come here," muttered Martin to the busboy as Fran smiled her thanks to him. But Marco forgot one detail—the menus—so the brief bright spot in their evening soon flickered and died as they waited in vain for their server to notice them.

"Andrea, table 26," hissed Marco as he passed her on the way to the kitchen. She sauntered over and smiled pleasantly at Martin and Fran and asked if they were ready to order.

"It's kind of tough to order without any menus, don't you think?" snarled Martin. "Don't bother," he said as she started to fetch some. "We're hungry and we know what we want. Give my wife the Maine lobster special and bring me the veal marsala. French dressing on the salads, and start us off with the stuffed mushrooms."

"Yes, sir," Andrea said. "What a crab," she whispered as she passed Marco on the way to the kitchen, nodding toward the Hagadorn's table. "Wonder what's wrong with them?"

Martin started to cool off as the food began to arrive. The stuffed mushrooms were perfect, and the salads were delicious. He ordered a carafe of wine, and even that was correct—this time. Andrea noticed that "the crab" was smiling as she cleared the salad plates. Well, he seems to have gotten over whatever was bothering him, she thought.

She went to the kitchen to pick up their orders, and saw only the veal marsala. "Where's the Maine lobster for table 26?" she called.

"We've been trying to find you to tell you we're out of lobster," said the chef.

"Someone forgot to mark it on the out-of-stock board," Andrea complained, glancing at the 86 board. But now she saw that someone had hastily scrawled "lobster" on the bottom of the list. She knew it hadn't said that when she had checked it earlier.

"Oh, great," said Andrea. "I'm not dealing with this. Where's Mr. Merrill?"

Richard listened to the server's explanation, then approached the table.

"Excuse me, Mr. and Mrs. Hagadorn. I'm sorry to have to tell you this, but we're all out of the Maine lobster because of our prom crowd. We do have lobster tails, though, and I'd be happy to have the chef prepare our surf and turf special for you—on the house, of course," said Richard.

Fran threw down her napkin. "I can't believe this!" she cried. "All I wanted was a nice lobster dinner and we've had nothing but trouble! I don't know whether I even want to stay here anymore." Seeing the manager's earnest face, she tried to calm down. "Okay, surf and turf. I'd like the filet medium rare."

Richard placed the order, then continued with his other duties, convinced he'd picked up the pieces of what could have been a bad scene. If he'd checked back, he would have learned that the "medium rare" filet came to the table well done. Fran, too hungry to fight about it, ate what she could and left the rest. She was subdued as the meal ended without even a little slice of cake to acknowledge her birthday. Usually her husband made certain the restaurant knew it was a special occasion. Oh well, nothing else had gone right. What did I expect? she thought.

When the server brought the check and asked how everything was, Martin blew his top with a tirade that brought Richard Merrill running from across the restaurant.

"I can't believe you have the audacity to ask that question!" Martin yelled. "I have never had such lousy service in my life, and this has got to be the worst birthday dinner my wife has ever had. This will be the last bill I ever pay in this place, because it's the last time you'll ever see us here! And I'm going to tell my friends and business partners, too. You'll never hear the end of this disaster!"

Richard was astounded. All this because of a bad table and no lobster? What could have gone wrong?

Discussion Questions

1. What went wrong with the Hagadorns' visit to Xavier's? Identify at least 10 (there may be more) service recovery opportunities that were missed by the restaurant's staff. What could have been done at each opportunity to prevent or minimize the problems experienced by the Hagadorns?

2. How should the manager respond on the spot to recover with the Hagadorns?

3. What steps does the manager need to take to develop a strategy for ensuring quality guest service and service recovery?

The following industry experts helped generate and develop this case: Timothy J. Pugh, Regional Manager, Damon's—The Place for Ribs (Steve Montanye Enterprises, East Lansing, Michigan); and Lawrence E. Ross, Assistant Professor, Florida Southern College, and owner of Sago Grill, Lakeland, Florida.

Tips, Tip Pooling, and Service Charges

Fred and his family have just returned from Europe where they enjoyed a two-week vacation. Fred is the owner/manager of Fred's Feast, a 150-seat restaurant in a mid-sized city. He inherited the business from his father and the establishment has been a fixture in the community for 52 years.

While traveling, Fred experienced what he already knew. European restaurateurs add a service charge to the guest check. On the way home, he pondered whether he should add a service charge on all guest checks. (He already adds a 16 percent service charge to parties of eight or more people.) It would certainly simplify reporting for tax purposes, which the servers might appreciate. It would also guarantee a more stable income for servers, which is important when they apply for home mortgages, car loans, etc. Customers might also appreciate it, as it takes the calculation effort away and some customers may just be glad that they don't have to make a tipping decision.

As he was contemplating the service charge issue, he recalled that Monica, one of his new servers, asked him if he ever considered having employees pool their tips into one large treasury from which distributions could be made by a formula for buspersons, servers, etc. Monica said she's worked in other establishments where they had such a system and it really helped the teamwork among the service personnel. Fred wondered whether kitchen personnel should be included in such a tip pooling system.

He casually mentioned tip pooling to Jackie, one of his long-term employees, and she quickly said, "No way! I don't want to subsidize poor performers."

Fred continued to contemplate making changes, but has done nothing at this point.

Discussion Questions

1. What are the advantages and disadvantages of service charges that you would mention to Fred?

2. What are the advantages and disadvantages of tip pooling?

3. What would you recommend that Fred do?

This case was taken from William P. Fisher and Robert A. Ashley, *Case Studies in Commercial Food Service Operations* (Lansing, Mich.: American Hotel & Lodging Educational Institute, 2003).

 References

Barol, Bill. "Just Take the Money!" *Time* 161, no. 23 (2003).

Clark, Kim. "Customer Disservice." *U.S. News & World Report* 135, no. 5 (2003).

Crouch, Michelle. "20 Secrets Your Waiter Won't Tell You." *Reader's Digest* (December 2009).

Durham, Emily. "Survey Says...10 Objectives of a Successful Guest Survey." *Restaurant Startup & Growth* (November 2007).

"Existing Customers Hold Key to Operator Survival." *Nation's Restaurant News* 43, no. 15 (April 27, 2009).

Gillett, Wendy. "It's the Little Things That Count: Small Service Touches that Go a Long Way to Upgrade Your Image." *Restaurant Startup & Growth* (December 2007).

Glazer, Fern. "NPD: Baby Boomers Represent Potential Boon to Industry Traffic." *Nation's Restaurant News* 43, no. 4 (February 2, 2009).

Hollister, Julia. "Quality Restaurant Service is Standard Fare for Skilled Servers." *Job Journal* (September 4, 2005). See www.jobjournal.com/article_full_text. asp?artid=1511

Luebke, Patricia. "Making Lemonade Out of Lemons." *Restaurant Startup & Growth* (March 2007).

———. "New Culinary Trend Report Highlights Booming Specialty Cafés Market." *Restaurant Startup & Growth* (December 2007).

———. "Youth-Oriented 'Mature Market' Wields $1.6 Trillion in Spending Power." *Restaurant Startup & Growth* (August 2007).

Nassauer, Sarah. "'I Hate My Room,' The Traveler Tweeted. KaBoom! An Upgrade!" *The Wall Street Journal* (June 24, 2010).

Ruggless, Ron. "RCA Experts: Gen Y Eaters Demand Flavor, Portability." *Nation's Restaurant News* 43, no. 10 (March 16, 2009).

"The U.S. Mature Market." Packaged Facts." June 1, 2000. See www.packaged-facts.com/Mature-143465. Accessed on September 17, 2010.

Vermillion, Len. "Managing in an Era of Mistrust." *Lodging Magazine*. 35, no. 9 (June 2010).

Internet Sites

For more information, visit the following Internet sites. Remember that Internet addresses can change without notice. If the site is no longer there, you can use a search engine to look for additional sites.

Adventures in Hospitality Careers
www.hospitalityadventures.com

American Culinary Federation
www.acfchefs.org

American Hotel & Lodging
 Association
www.ahla.com

American Hotel & Lodging Educational Institute
www.ahlei.org

American Institute of Wine & Food
www.aiwf.org

Commercial Food Equipment Service
 Association
www.cfesa.com

Culinary Cult
www.culinarycult.com

Culinary Institute of America
www.ciachef.edu

eHospitality Institute
www.ehiedu.org

Food Channel
www.foodchannel.com

Food Institute
www.foodinstitute.com

Foodservice Consultants Society
 International
www.fcsi.org

Gallup, Inc.
www.gallup.com

GuestMetrics, Inc.
www.guestmetrics.com

Hcareers.com
www.hcareers.com

International Demographics, Inc.
www.themediaaudit.com

International Food Services Executives
　Association
www.ifsea.com

National Restaurant Association
www.restaurant.org

Nation's Restaurant News
www.nrn.com

New Strategist Publications
www.newstrategist.com

NPD Group, Inc.
www.npd.com

Organic Trade Association
www.ota.com

Pizza Today
www.pizzatoday.com

QSR
www.qsrmagazine.com

RestaurantOwner.com
www.restaurantowner.com

Restaurant Associates
www.restaurantassociates.com

Restaurant Hospitality
www.restaurant-hospitality.com

Restaurant Marketing Group
www.rmktgroup.com

Restaurant Report
www.restaurantreport.com

Sandelman & Associates
www.sandelman.com

Service Management Group, Inc.
www.servicemanagement.com

Technomic, Inc.
www.technomic.com

Whole Foods Market
www.wholefoodsmarket.com

Zagat Survey, LLC
www.zagat.com

Chapter 3 Outline

Competencies

3

Select Restaurant Food and Beverage Staff

STAFF MEMBERS are the individuals that managers must lead wisely and well if their food and beverage organizations are to be successful. A motivated staff is the key to success in any food and beverage operation.

Staff members are just as valuable as guests, in the sense that, without them, the restaurant fails: if there is no one to perform the work, no work gets done, nothing of value is produced, no guests come, and the restaurant must close its doors. In a strictly economic sense, the value of staff members is reflected in the wages and benefits managers pay them for their work. But in the context of quality service—that is, in the sense of consistently meeting or exceeding guest expectations—their true value is in their ability to keep guests coming back by providing excellent service and delivering positive, memorable experiences.

Hiring and retaining staff members who are able to provide quality service is a key element to a successful restaurant, and that will be the subject of the first section of the chapter. Two of the key staff positions in restaurants—whether the restaurants are free-standing or part of a lodging property—are servers and buspersons. These two positions have the greatest amount of contact with guests, and the performance of these staff members can make or break a restaurant; therefore, we will look at these two positions in detail. Next, the chapter will discuss how restaurants can attract and retain good managers. The chapter closes with a look at staff evaluations.

Attracting and Retaining Restaurant Food and Beverage Staff

The process of attracting and retaining excellent staff members begins with recruitment, followed by selection, orientation, training, and retention. This process is designed to find people who are the very best fit within the culture and philosophy of the restaurant. Selection of staff members should be based, first and foremost, on the service attitude required in the position. That is to say, experience in a position is not the primary consideration; more important is an attitude that serving others is an honorable profession. The needs and expectations of guests must come first. Those who create positive memories for guests are "other focused," which is an essential quality of a successful restaurant staff member.

Recruitment

Recruiting encompasses more than simply hiring. In a restaurant, it often involves staff members as well as managers. Staff members who are currently successful in delivering positive, memorable experiences for guests can help the operator find others who may be able to do the same. Individuals who advocate for the restaurant where they are employed can convince others—friends, staff members at another food and beverage operation, or even current guests—to at least investigate the career opportunities at that restaurant. Other sources for talent recruitment include newsletters; the Internet; social media such as LinkedIn, Twitter, Facebook, etc.; and distributors who sell foods, beverages, and other items to the restaurant. Staff members, however, are generally one of the best sources, particularly those staff members who understand how to exceed guests' expectations. When staff members are treated well, they are more likely to scout out others who would also enjoy working at the restaurant.

Showing excitement and enthusiasm about the restaurant, the opportunities available there, and the people who work there helps encourage potential recruits. Enthusiasm about guests and guest interaction also helps paint the opportunity in a positive light. Interviewers can illustrate these positive points by telling stories about experiences staff members have had with fellow staff members, guests, and others. Above all, having a positive attitude will attract positive people to the organization. Candidates who have a positive attitude are usually preferred to those who have a large amount of work experience, because it is relatively easy to teach the required skills and knowledge for the position, while it is difficult to develop the right attitude.

When recruiting talent for the restaurant, it is important for managers to plan enough time to complete the recruitment process. If, for example, a restaurant in a ski resort is in need of seasonal staff members during its peak ski season (say, December through March), it would be essential to start the recruiting process no later than mid-summer. It is the responsibility of the manager or staff member who is recruiting the candidate to give the recruit some background about the organization, including its values, vision, and mission. The recruiter should also list the advantages of working in the restaurant, such as a location with short commute time from where the candidate lives, training programs, flexible work hours, attractive facilities, great ambience, staff camaraderie, and benefits such as health care. The recruiter can also encourage the candidate to ask other staff members about their job perspectives and experiences. In addition, important information about the local community can be useful to a candidate.

Staff should always be on the watch for people who can contribute to the goals of the restaurant. Spreading the word will help attract the very best talent.

Selection

Once a pool of well-qualified candidates is identified, selection can take place. As just mentioned, selection should be based, first and foremost, on the candidate's positive attitude, not his or her experience. An individual's attitude is evident in how he or she approaches problems. Does the individual view problems as opportunities or does he or she take a more pessimistic view? Indicators of a great attitude include self-confidence, the ability to cooperate with others, and taking pride in being part of a team where each member contributes to a job well done. Often, attitude is revealed by the way people dress, the words they use, and their facial expressions. People with positive attitudes describe a hopeful future. They enjoy being of service to others through both their individual efforts and the efforts of the teams in the organizations they have joined.

Job candidates should be asked to share their personal and professional goals. Once candidates have identified their goals, it is easier to decide whether they would fit in with the organization. Alignment of a candidate's personal vision, values, and mission with those of the organization is beneficial for both parties because it gives them mutual support; the individual has the opportunity to work with others who have similar goals, while the organization reaps the benefits of this collective work.

The selection process should include a background check for prospective staff members before an offer is made. Background checks search an individual's history via criminal records, driving records, or education records, depending on the organization. Companies may also require drug tests. All of these pre-employment screening procedures are designed to protect the organization's guests and staff as well as the organization's assets (e.g., cash, tangible items) and reputation.

The policy of many restaurants is to have a trial employment period for those who are newly selected. If the individual or operator feels that the position is not a good fit for the staff member's talents, either one of them can decide to part ways within this period.

Orientation

Orientation is an investment in the staff member who is selected. An orientation program pays dividends through more productive and satisfied staff members, as well as satisfied guests. Effective orientation can reduce turnover because it gives new staff members the tools they need to become familiar with their new positions and the operation as a whole. New staff members who do not receive orientation, on the other hand, might grow frustrated with the position if they are simply thrown into the job without any type of introduction as to how the restaurant works or the way in which the various positions of the staff function together. Without effective orientation, a restaurant operator runs the risk of high turnover and the subsequent expenditure of time and other resources on continuous recruiting.

A restaurant's standard orientation process should be planned and organized in writing. The orientation plan should include the topics that will be reviewed during orientation, the desired outcomes of these reviews, and the overall results managers and owners are expecting orientation to produce in terms of performance improvement and the retention of staff members. Orientation should include a general introduction to familiarize new staff members with the restaurant, including its mission, policies, values, vision, and specific goals, as well as outline ways in which each department and individual in the restaurant can help the restaurant achieve those goals. The orientation plan also needs to include a specific description for each position in the restaurant. In the case of restaurants that hire seasonal staff, it is important to provide new seasonal staff members with the same orientation that nonseasonal staff receive.

Some restaurants compile all the information they plan to provide to staff members at orientation into an orientation manual that is distributed at the orientation. When orientation materials are organized, it gives new staff members the impression that the restaurant is organized as well. Furthermore, an orientation manual that includes a statement from a restaurant leader, such as the food and beverage manager, general manager, or other leader, demonstrates to new staff members the importance of the information provided in the orientation.

Training

The most effective way to train staff members is via job instruction training. Job instruction training begins by defining in writing the most important training results, outcomes, and strategies. Job instruction training consists of four steps:

1. Preparation
2. Presentation
3. Trial performance
4. Follow-through

Preparation begins with writing training objectives based on desired training results. After this has been accomplished, the training methods (one-on-one or group) must be chosen. Breakdowns of the position's responsibilities are then prepared to be later utilized to help the trainee become more familiar with the position's responsibilities. Trainers must also establish a timetable—that is, a scheduled length for each training session, as well as the overall length of the training period. A training location (preferably where the trainee will work) needs to be chosen and training materials assembled, along with any necessary equipment. The final preparation consideration is to discuss with the trainee what he or she already knows in terms of the position and the restaurant.

In the presentation step, the trainer demonstrates the position procedures alongside the trainee, taking care to explain each action as it is being performed. The model for the training presentation should be the previously prepared position breakdown. It is important for the trainer to take adequate time and have patience with the trainee, and realize that the trainee is most likely seeing the position tasks performed for the first time.

The trial performance step provides an opportunity for the trainee to practice performing the position responsibilities. In this step, the trainer supervises the trainee while he or she performs the job operations that were demonstrated in the presentation step. The trainee should explain each step of whatever operation he or she is performing, including an explanation as to the rationale of the procedure (the "why" behind the procedure). The trainer coaches the trainee, reinforcing positive behaviors while pointing out areas needing improvement.

In the follow-through step, the trainee is allowed to work independently. During this step the trainer provides performance feedback to the trainee and evaluates the training in terms of its effectiveness in achieving the desired results and the effectiveness of the training methods. Training is a continuous process; trainers should continue to check in with newly trained staff members after this step has been completed.

After the training is completed, it is important to assess the knowledge and skills of the trainee in at least the following areas:

- The restaurant's history

- The restaurant's values, mission, and vision

- The restaurant's policies

- The trainee's core job responsibilities

Additionally, staff members are sometimes certified by a third party, as in a food safety certification or Controlling Alcohol Risks Effectively (CARE) certification. Not only do these types of assessments and certifications reinforce and complement what was learned, they also may help lower the operation's liability insurance premiums.

Newly trained staff members should never start on a busy shift (a Saturday night, for example). It is best instead to schedule them to work slower shifts at first. In addition, since the start of any shift is typically busy, new staff members should be brought in after the shift has begun. It is also important to regularly touch base with new staff members throughout their training periods.

Servers. Because servers are so important to a restaurant's success—guests typically perceive servers as the "face" of the restaurant—we will discuss their training specifically in this section. It is essential that newly selected servers receive adequate training. Server training programs must be thoughtfully prepared in advance. Checklists are extremely useful, as there is too much detail for either the trainer or the trainee to try to remember to cover or write down during the training.

Servers must be trained to, among other things:

- Greet guests properly.

- Take beverage and food orders.

- Serve the beverage and food orders.

- Present guest checks.

- Collect payment for the checks.

- Remove soiled tableware at appropriate times.

- Thank guests properly.

Effective server training should also include a review of the restaurant's policies and procedures. These should be presented in writing; oftentimes restaurants incorporate them into a server handbook, which can be used as a ready source of information when questions arise. Such handbooks should also explain the restaurant's expectations of staff members, supervisors, and managers, along with its disciplinary procedures. There should be a section about the menu, with explanations of unique preparation methods, ingredients used, what substitutions are allowed, and which menu items the restaurant prepares and serves best—servers can suggest these items when guests ask for recommendations.

Server training requires a training schedule prepared by a qualified trainer. The training schedule should indicate which topics will be presented in each session; it is better to plan shorter sessions than longer sessions when possible. Persons who are qualified to train servers generally include those who communicate well; use written objectives, goals, and guidelines when training; display patience and understanding with new trainees; possess strong service skills and qualities characteristic of good servers; and enjoy and see value in training others.

Properly trained servers know to greet guests in a hospitable and authentic manner. They smile, use the guest's name when possible, and work to establish a rapport with the guest. Guests do not feel welcome when they are ignored, which means servers should use a team approach. For example, if a server whose station is momentarily slow sees that a fellow server is too busy to immediately stop and greet his or her new guests, that server should take the initiative to greet those guests even though they are not in his or her section. On the other hand, when the restaurant is not experiencing peak demand, servers should make sure they do not become distracted by, for example, side conversations with other staff members when guests are seeking attention; this behavior gives guests the impression that they are not important or valued.

Servers must be trained to appear professional. This means they must wear the uniforms designated by the restaurant in which they work, which can range from a golf shirt and a cap in a sports-themed restaurant to a more formal uniform in an upscale full-service restaurant. In any case, the uniform must be clean; dirty uniforms can cause guests to have qualms about the overall cleanliness of the restaurant. Restaurant managers should also make clear their expectations regarding servers' hygiene practices and appearance issues apart from their uniforms, such as how many pieces of jewelry are acceptable and how servers with long hair should wear it.

To provide excellent service, servers must be good communicators. They should know that, as important as it is to ask questions to identify guests' needs and wants, it is more important to actually listen carefully to their responses. Guests not only communicate with words, but also with actions. Servers need to listen to guests' words and watch for body language. Listening requires reading the meaning behind the spoken words; for example, the phrase "I'm not really interested in *dessert*" might suggest to a server that the guest may want a different item, such as a cup of coffee or tea.

Superb service consists of, first and foremost, a positive attitude, followed by the knowledge and skills needed to create a great dining experience for guests. Server training is focused on knowledge and skills, although the service attitude expected must be clearly communicated during training. Friendliness is one of the most important components of a service attitude. Friendly people make others feel welcome and comfortable. Guests who are served by friendly staff feel as if they have a real relationship with their servers, rather than feeling that they are seen only as potential sources of tips or just numbers to be served. As guests leave the operation they should be thanked, not just by their servers, but by other staff

Quality Service From Restaurant Servers: One Guest's Definition

A restaurant server should strive to provide quality service to guests without going overboard. In this newspaper article, columnist John Schneider outlines some of the behaviors that he as a guest finds obnoxious in restaurant servers (or "waiters," as he refers to them):

A long time ago, I heard an adage that went something like this: "You're not a man until you know how much to tip a waiter."

I've known all along that the saying referred to a calculation: service rendered versus reward provided. But only in recent years have I come to truly appreciate the intricacies of that equation.

Indeed, it takes experience and maturity to understand the sometimes subtle differences between a mediocre waiter and a fine one.

That's not to say it takes a trained eye to spot all those differences. Some are as subtle as a glass of ice water in the lap. Take, for example, the waiter as performance artist. A stand-up comic, maybe, or actress in a one-woman play called, "Ain't I Adorable?"

Here's a generous tip: Bring the food in a timely, civil fashion and leave the theatrics to the professionals.

Fine Dining

It was a local waiter who put me on this soap box. Following my daughter's recent high school graduation ceremony, five of us went out for a celebratory dinner.

We got lucky. From the moment this waiter approached our table, it was clear that he was no run-of-the-mill server. There was something about the way he spoke and carried himself. He was respectful, but reserved; polite, but not presumptuous. Everything that followed—from the wine to the check—reinforced the impression that we were in the hands of a professional.

It was an afternoon of fine dining. And the food was pretty good, too.

What, exactly, did the waiter do? Well, it may be more relevant to report what he *didn't* do:

- He didn't tell us his name, or otherwise call attention to himself.

- He didn't describe the kind of day he was having, his attempts—sporadic or otherwise—at a college education, or the poor treatment he received from previous customers.

- He didn't pretend that he wanted to be our friend.

- He didn't interrupt our conversations.

- He didn't run down the menu items that he personally enjoyed.

- He did not once use the phrase, "Are you still working on that?" It always makes me think of an overstuffed ogre sweating over a haunch of something or other, straining to put away yet another mouthful.

(continued)

(continued)

On the Job

Somehow, while managing to avoid all those things, the waiter kept our water glasses and bread basket filled. He made our main courses appear after our salads were eaten. He neither crowded nor neglected us.

He was, in a phrase, attentive without being obtrusive.

I couldn't help but notice in my recent trips to France and Italy that waiters there routinely strike that crucial balance.

It could be that waiters in Europe are better trained, or better paid. Or it could be that food service is viewed as a legitimate career in those countries, rather than as something short of a real job.

Or maybe waiters play to their audiences. Maybe Europeans prefer cool professionalism from their food servers, while Americans, in general, like chirpy familiarity.

Give me the waiter whose gift is to be inconspicuous. I have all the pals I need.

---

members and managers as well. Guests who are genuinely thanked feel genuinely appreciated.

Servers must be trained to act in ways that enhance both the guest's experience and the reputation of the restaurant. Creating a positive guest experience requires competence in service skills and an understanding of guests. Well-trained servers know how to delight guests, and delighted guests are likely to be repeat guests.

Retention

Staff members in restaurants generally have higher morale if the restaurant pays attention to their needs, wants, and expectations. Higher morale means less staff turnover and helps the restaurant avoid all of the associated costs with recruiting, orienting, training, and trying to retain someone new.

Staff members who have high morale are better service providers than those who have low morale. They are more productive and more satisfied because they work in a place that helps them meet or exceed some of their own personal expectations. In some restaurant chains, top executives travel to individual restaurants to meet staff members and chat with them one-on-one. Others phone each restaurant once a week at a predetermined time to check in and do a quick morale assessment. Some chains are also trying to connect with those who actually supervise and manage/lead the individual operations by bringing them to corporate headquarters to meet peers (e.g., other general managers and supervisors in the system) in hopes that they will network, figure out ways to solve common problems, and continue to stay in contact after the meeting.

If a manager or supervisor is to have a positive effect on morale in the restaurant, he or she must be able to communicate. The most important communication skill is listening. To build morale, managers should listen to staff (staff members should be looked upon by managers as their internal customers) as well as guests (external customers). Managers should ask questions of both internal and external customers, plus the restaurant's suppliers/distributors, owners, and surrounding community, and listen to the words as well as the true meaning behind the words. As morale increases, staff members feel more and more that they are a part of the operation and that their ideas and opinions are valued; when this takes place, staff members are more likely to stay with the restaurant.

Another strategy to retain staff members and build morale is to plan friendly competitions. Competition in the workplace may include not only sales contests but may also involve guest comment scores, food safety goals and inspection results, reports by secret shoppers, and other metrics. Such contests not only raise staff morale but are good for the restaurant as well, since they result in greater sales or in improving the restaurant in some way. Cash incentives, local tickets to theaters, coupons for merchandise at retail stores, and other items can be used as rewards for winners in such competitions.

Other ideas for staff member retention are less typical but can be highly effective. One operator cooks breakfast for the servers once per week and the team eats that breakfast together, while discussion about important restaurant issues takes place. Other restaurants have formed teams to donate blood to the local community, or host an annual picnic or awards dinner where the family members of staff members are invited. Some restaurants reimburse their staff members for educational expenses (usually after the class is taken and successfully completed).

Additional actions to retain staff may include a supervisor or manager meeting with each new team member to assess the progress of the orientation and training since the person joined the team. Some managers insist that staff satisfaction surveys be administered at least one time each year. In these same organizations, staff members have the opportunity to evaluate their supervisors and managers at least one time per year.

On average, one in five people change jobs each year; however, that number is closer to one in two in hospitality businesses. To do a better job of retaining staff members, restaurants must begin by recruiting and selecting the right people. Once the right people have been brought on board, they must be oriented and trained so that they have the knowledge and skills required for their positions. New staff members should be informed of the very important role they play on the restaurant team; the values, goals, mission, and vision of the restaurant; and the challenges the restaurant is facing. Current staff members should be encouraged to coach new ones. This coaching reinforces the restaurant's formal training efforts and builds staff retention.

Restaurant Servers

A restaurant server helps make a guest's dining experience positive and memorable by providing anticipatory food and beverage service. Servers are responsible for:

- Preparing for service.
- Greeting guests.
- Taking the order.
- Serving the order.
- Creating a friendly atmosphere where guests can enjoy themselves.

- Closely monitoring guests' alcohol consumption.
- Completing service and thanking guests.
- Helping co-workers as needed.

Server duties vary based on the type of restaurant. Restaurants can be categorized as full-service, casual-dining, fast-casual, and quick-service. In full-service restaurants, servers may be asked to acquire skills and perform duties—such as prepare fresh salads or specialty desserts for guests at their tables—that servers in casual-dining restaurants would not usually have to know. Exhibit 1 lists many of the tasks that most restaurant servers typically perform.

Working as a Team

Servers are part of a service delivery system. They should give guests *and* co-workers (i.e., internal customers) great service. To be excellent team players, servers and other serving staff can help the restaurant's hosts and hostesses by:

- Greeting and seating guests.
- Answering the telephone.
- Letting them know when there are guests who are ready to leave so that they can plan which guests to seat there next.

They can help buspersons by:

- Immediately removing from tables the items guests do not need anymore.
- Clearing and resetting tables.
- Restocking sidestations so that supplies are always available.

They can help the kitchen staff by:

- Writing orders neatly and completely (in restaurants that use manual systems) or inputting orders accurately (in restaurants that use computer systems).
- Asking guests all the necessary questions when they take orders, such as, "How would you like that prepared?"
- Pointing out special or unique orders to the chef or cook.
- Properly sorting and stacking used glasses, china, silverware, and other tableware.

An additional duty servers may be asked to take on is helping to train other service staff. Many supervisors ask qualified servers to work with new servers or current servers who are having trouble with certain responsibilities.

Superior Performance Standards

The quality of the food, drinks, and service at a restaurant should enhance each guest's overall experience and create positive memories. Providing excellent service, beverages, and meals at a reasonable price is every restaurant's ultimate goal. Well-trained servers:

Exhibit 1   Typical Tasks for Restaurant Servers

Here is a list of typical tasks that restaurant servers might perform, depending on the restaurant. The number and complexity of tasks that a restaurant server is expected to perform depends on the style of the restaurant and other factors. Not all of these tasks will be discussed in the chapter.

1. Set up the restaurant for service
2. Stock and maintain sidestations
3. Fold napkins
4. Prepare breads and bread baskets or trays
5. Prepare service trays
6. Take restaurant reservations
7. Work efficiently
8. Greet and seat guests
9. Approach the table
10. Provide appropriate service for children
11. Lift and carry trays, bus tubs, or dish racks
12. Serve water
13. Check IDs of guests ordering alcohol
14. Take beverage orders
15. Process beverage orders
16. Prepare and serve coffee
17. Prepare and serve hot tea
18. Prepare and serve iced tea
19. Prepare and serve hot chocolate
20. Take food orders
21. Serve bread and butter
22. Prepare ice buckets
23. Serve wine or champagne by the bottle
24. Serve the meal
25. Check back to the table
26. Respond to dissatisfied guests
27. Maintain tables
28. Sell after-dinner items
29. Prepare takeout items
30. Present the guest check
31. Settle guest checks and thank guests
32. Clear and reset tables
33. Handle soiled restaurant linens
34. Inventory, requisition, and restock restaurant supplies
35. Perform closing sidework

- Demonstrate professional behavior within the operation.
- Make sure the dining room is properly lit, has a comfortable temperature, and looks clean and organized.
- Are familiar with all restaurant menus and food and beverage offerings.
- Are familiar with all menu items, including specials and desserts.
- Know whether the kitchen is out of any menu items, and find out what will be offered in place of sold-out items.
- Quickly approach guests and greet them warmly.
- Introduce themselves to guests, and use guests' names whenever possible.
- Accommodate special guest requests when appropriate.
- Use suggestive selling throughout the guest's visit to make his or her experience more memorable.
- Make sure food is served at the correct temperature, attractively presented, and pleasing to the guest.
- Frequently check back to the table to ensure guest satisfaction.
- Stay alert to safety procedures at all times.
- Wash their hands after taking a break.
- Thank guests sincerely.

Restaurant Server Duties

In the following sections we will discuss typical responsibilities of restaurant servers.

Sell. Many restaurants expect their servers to be not merely order-takers but also salespersons who can use various sales techniques to increase the size of a guest's check while at the same time enhancing the guest's dining experience. Restaurant managers should make their sales expectations clear to servers at the onset of their employment. If these expectations change, servers should be informed as soon as possible. Regardless of whether sales expectations remain consistent or are constantly changing, management needs to regularly discuss them with staff. This can be done both at staff meetings and one-on-one with individual servers, and may be especially necessary if a particular server is consistently not making his or her sales numbers. Those who are meeting or exceeding sales expectations should be rewarded. Managers can reward a server during his or her performance review or at other times as appropriate. Those servers who are good at selling should be asked to share their techniques with those who are struggling.

Sales techniques that servers should be trained in include suggestive selling and upselling. **Suggestive selling** is based on making suggestions that add to both a guest's dining experience and his or her final bill. A common suggestive selling example is when a server greets his or her guests and, before taking their orders, suggests a specific appetizer such as grilled spicy chicken wings or potato skins with chipotle sour cream. Suggesting items that are unique to the restaurant is especially beneficial because it reminds guests of why this particular restaurant stands out. Keep in mind that suggestive selling is best done from a point of knowledge—it is much easier to suggest a particular menu item if the server has tasted it and can describe it in an appealing manner.

Upselling is based on making suggestions that upgrade the quality of an item the guest has already ordered. These upgrades are generally more expensive, thus adding to both the guest's satisfaction and his or her bill. Alcoholic beverages are items that are often upsold. A guest, for example, may ask for a dry vodka martini on the rocks with two olives and one cocktail onion. If the server suggests a premium, more expensive vodka such as Ciroc or Belvedere and the guest takes the server up on the suggestion, the restaurant will capture more revenue from that guest than if he or she had just ordered the martini with call or house vodka as originally intended. Another menu category often upsold is the side items; a server might suggest creamed spinach, Lyonnaise potatoes, and onion rings instead of the house vegetable and baked potato that would have otherwise come with the steak dinner. Upselling strategies also include suggesting a salad or soup to start the meal if these items are priced separately (i.e., à la carte), a bottle of wine with the main course, or a dessert at the end of the meal.

The following are some techniques servers use for more effective suggestive selling and upselling:

- Develop a selling attitude.

- Be enthusiastic. It is easier to sell something that you are excited about.

- Make food sound appetizing. Use words like "fresh," "popular," and "unique" when describing menu items.

- Ask questions. For example, find out if guests are really hungry or just want something light; whether they like chicken or beef; or if they feel like having something hot or cold.

- Suggest specific menu items. Do not simply ask, "Would you like soup with your meal?" Instead, suggest something specific: "A cold cup of gazpacho would go nicely with your salad on a hot day like this."

- Suggest personal favorites. Try as many menu items as possible, and tell guests you have tried them: "You will like the Chicken Romano—it's one of my favorites here." But be honest—do not say that something is your favorite when it is not.

- Offer a choice: "Would you like a slice of our famous cheesecake or our home-made cherry pie for dessert?"

- Suggest the unusual. People dine out to get away from the routine fare they have at home. And most people don't know what they want to order when they arrive.

- Suggest foods and beverages that naturally go together—soups and sandwiches, bacon and eggs, steak and Lyonnaise potatoes, coffee and dessert.

- Compliment guests' choices. Make them feel good about their choices, even if they don't order what you suggest.

Finally, professional servers ask for the sale. After they suggest and describe an item, they ask if the guest would like it. A good way to ask for the sale is to describe several items and ask which the guest would prefer.

Servers who are effective sellers are, above all, in tune with guests' needs. They listen closely to guests' comments (e.g., "I'm so hungry," "I just want to relax") and try to accommodate their guests as much as possible (e.g., combining appetizers for guests who cannot decide which one they want more, or offering a flight of several two-ounce soups to a guest who wants to try them all). These servers also strive to make occasions like birthdays and anniversaries special by providing a complimentary dessert (if it adheres to the operation's policies) or making some other celebratory gesture.

Set Up the Restaurant for Service. Servers work with buspersons to set up tables in their area. They should make sure that each table in their section is perfect. This includes checking:

- Silverware.

- Glasses.

- Napkins.

- Salt and pepper shakers or grinders.

- Sugar bowls or caddies.

- Tablecloths.

- Place mats.

- Condiments.

- Chairs and booths.

- Flower arrangements and other centerpieces.

- Table lamps.

- Other tabletop items.

- Floor and carpets.

- Overall table appearance.

- Ice buckets.

For servers, providing anticipatory, superior service often lies in the details. Every detail that they make sure is correct helps guests to have a memorable experience.

Silverware must be clean and free from food and water spots. Most health departments prohibit hand polishing of silverware; wiping sanitized silverware with a cloth can place germs back on the silverware. Regular silverware includes knives, forks, and spoons. Special silverware may include fish forks, small tongs, demitasse spoons, and other flatware required for special menu items. Glassware should come from the dishwasher clean and ready for use. As with silverware, hand polishing glassware is unsanitary.

Most health departments do not allow loose sugar to be served on the table. Instead, food service operations put out sugar caddies filled with sugar packets

Top Restaurant "Ouch Points"

According to a survey by Opinion Research Corporation, the top restaurant "ouch points" for guests are:

- **Rude Servers.** Rude servers are often self-centered and not mindful of others' needs, wants, and expectations. Sometimes a server comes off as rude when trying to be a comedian; trying to be funny rarely works. Rude servers often have lousy work experiences and share their problems with guests. This is not fair to guests, who bring their most precious possession—time—to the restaurant and are paying not only for the food but for the overall experience. If management receives a report of a rude server, management should speak to the server about the behavior. If the behavior problems continue, the server should be retrained, disciplined, or let go, depending on the server, the circumstances, and the operation's policies.

- **Hosts Who Underestimate Waiting Times.** Hosts should try to accurately estimate waiting times and do all they can to enhance the guests' experiences while they wait. They could suggest that guests wait in the lounge, serve complimentary appetizers, or serve samples of drinks featured in the latest drink promotion to those of age. Hosts should keep in mind that if they tell a guest it will be "ten to fifteen minutes," the guest might practice selective hearing and expect to be seated within ten minutes, rather than allowing for the "extra" five minutes.

- **Slow Servers.** Slow service often is the result of a packed house, or what some in the restaurant business call "getting slammed." For example, when all the tables in a server's section are seated at the same time, service will most likely be slower than usual. When a restaurant is in a peak sales situation, it is especially important for the host to help out servers whenever possible by, for example, taking drink orders for a server whose tables have all filled at once.

- **Poorly Prepared Food.** Poorly prepared food may result from a number of mistakes made in the heart of the house. In some cases, food might be left too long under holding lamps in the kitchen. As soon as food is prepared, it must become a priority to deliver the food as soon as possible. If a server has a large table or is busy because he or she is slammed, all available servers should make an effort to help by taking out the food orders when they come up. Sometimes it's not a delivery problem; sometimes the food really is poorly prepared. Therefore, to help prevent this kind of complaint, it is important that those who prepare food receive the proper training, especially in the use of standard recipes and portion control.

- **Cold Food (Intended to Be Hot).** When food is not served at the proper temperature, it not only makes the food taste differently (generally, worse) than it should, but also creates the possibility of a food safety violation. Many times the mistake is in serving lukewarm or cold food that should be hot. To help avoid this problem, hot food should be placed and served on hot plates as soon as the food is ready. Restaurant operators who train servers to make serving hot food hot (and cold food cold) a top goal know that when a guest's order arrives at the correct temperature, his or her perception of the operation's quality and

(continued)

(continued)

attention to detail will be positive. Server paging systems help the person in charge of the kitchen notify a server when one of his or her table's food is ready to serve. Picking up and delivering the food should then become the highest priority for that server, as well as other servers who are able to assist if possible. In other restaurants, the call "Hot food ready!" is used to summon any available server to serve ready food immediately, even if the food is not going to that particular server's table.

- **Being Ushered Out.** Lingering after a meal with family and friends is often something guests like to do. Usually this is not a problem unless there is a long wait for guests to be seated or the restaurant is about to close. When there is a long wait, it is understandable for the operator to want to maximize revenues and reduce the waiting time of waiting guests. It is also understandable that, when the restaurant is closing, sometimes staff members want to send obvious signals to guests in an attempt to get them to leave sooner rather than later (such as vacuuming the floor, turning up the lights, or constantly stopping and interrupting the table conversation by asking if there is anything else the guests need). Just because both cases are understandable, however, does not mean that these actions are excusable. Both operators and servers should do their best to be patient in situations where they want to rush guests out the door, and instead concentrate on doing other activities that might speed up the table turnover or closing process, such as cleaning up other tables or refilling items like salt and pepper shakers.

- **Dirty Menus.** Given that a restaurant's menu presents its product offerings and that just about every guest will see a menu, restaurant staff should take care that all of a restaurant's menus will contribute positively to the operation's image and the guests' memories. This is not possible if the restaurant provides its guests with spotted, stained, or otherwise unclean menus. Guests do not like dirt, period, including dirty floors, dirty light fixtures, dirty restrooms, and dirty kitchens. Therefore, restaurants should not be introducing guests to what they will be eating via dirty menus.

- **Fast Service.** Sometimes fast service is preferred by guests, but at other times it feels too rushed. The dinner period is often a time when guests appreciate a slower service pace. Fast service can be appropriate when guests are facing a deadline, such as when they need to return to work from lunch by a certain time. Fast service during the breakfast meal period is often appropriate, since many guests are on their way to work. Fast service is never appropriate, however, no matter what the time of day, when such service makes guests feel uncomfortably rushed.

and artificial sweetener packets. Most managers direct servers to place packets upright and facing the same way so that guests can read the printing on them.

Operations that use tablecloths do so to communicate a specific image. Many will use two tablecloths—a top cloth over a base cloth. Servers should adjust each tablecloth so that it hangs evenly on all sides with the seams facing down. They should replace any tablecloths that have holes, wrinkles, or stains. Operations that cover their tablecloths with large sheets of paper can often end up irritating guests because the paper can get caught on guests' sleeves; using paper can also make the operation appear as being too cheap to change tablecloths in between guests. "We just change the paper to save money" is not something guests want to hear from servers. Operations that do not use tablecloths may use place mats. Place mats should always be clean and free from holes, tears, or stains; tables should be wiped down with a damp cloth and sanitizing solution and dried before mats are placed on the table. Servers should make sure they are placed neatly and consistently, right-side-up with the printing facing the guests. Each mat should be lined up with the table edge and with the mat on the opposite side of the table. Every time a table is reset, paper place mats should be thrown away and new ones placed on the table.

Condiment containers should be clean and full of fresh condiments. Servers should make sure there are no spots, spills, or fingerprints on any condiment packets or bottles. They should also check the rims of containers or dispenser lids to make sure they are clean; honey and syrup dispensers are especially prone to stickiness and require frequent wiping. Condiments that do not require refrigeration can be preset according to the operation's tabletop guidelines for each meal.

Servers should check chairs and booths to make sure they are free from crumbs, dust, and fingerprints. They should pay special attention to the arms, legs, and spindles of the chairs. When necessary, they should wipe the chairs and booths clean with a damp cloth and sanitizing solution, followed by a dry cloth —the cloths used to clean and dry chairs and booths should be different than those used to clean tabletops. (Linen napkins should not be used for this purpose!) If there are seating cushions that can be pulled out, servers should pull them out and wipe up any crumbs. They should also check under tables and chairs for gum, removing any that they find. Upholstery stains, burns, rips, and tears should be reported to the supervisor. Chairs that are in good order should be placed so that the edge of the seat is even with the table edge. Servers should also make sure that highchairs and booster seats are cleaned between each use. Small children often place their food directly on the highchair tray, so those trays need to be sanitized between each use and then wrapped with a food service film to keep them sanitary. Servers should also check the safety straps on highchairs to make sure they are clean and in working order. Any missing or broken straps should be replaced.

While others are usually responsible for preparing dining room flower arrangements or other centerpieces, servers can help maintain them. They can check vases for cracks, chips, and fingerprints, cleaning or replacing them as needed. They can make sure that live flowers are fresh and neatly arranged, and that artificial arrangements are free from dust. Likewise, servers should make sure that table lamps are clean and free of chips and cracks. If lamps have brass or silver trim, the trim should be free from spots and tarnish. Servers should place new candles in each candle lamp as needed, or refill lamps using liquid fuel.

Finally, servers should check the overall appearance of their tables, making sure that all of them are set the same way. They should make sure there is enough room to pass between the tables without disturbing guests, adjusting tables as necessary to provide enough aisle space for proper traffic flow and service.

Servers also may sign out guest checks, if the restaurant uses a manual guest check system. Guest checks help the operation track sales and control its income.

Every server is accountable for the checks he or she signs for at the beginning of the shift. However, many operations use computerized point-of-sale equipment that produces guest checks from register tape. If this is the case, no guest checks will be issued.

Stock Sidestations. Sidestations are service areas in the dining room where supplies are stored. They are stocked with such items as glasses, silverware, and dishes. These supplies help servers work more efficiently, because they reduce the distance that servers have to go to get the supplies that guests need. Servers should make sure that all items in their sidestations are stocked to par levels. They should also make sure there is a bucket of sanitizing solution and a clean cloth at their station.

Servers should maintain their stations throughout their shifts. A **sidework checklist** lists sidework and the server who is assigned to complete each task. Common sidework tasks include folding napkins and wiping service trays. Sidework tasks are an important part of keeping a restaurant running well. Servers cannot provide anticipatory service if they waste time returning to the kitchen for items that should be in the sidestations.

Work Efficiently. Servers should work smartly to keep up their energy and provide better guest service—especially during busy times. They should rarely move between the kitchen and the dining room with empty hands; they should almost always be carrying something—food, beverages, condiments, coffee, and other supplies each time they move between the two. If they have nothing else to carry, they can always clear used plates, glasses, and other items from tables before entering the kitchen, which means they should carry a tray with them so they are prepared to clear items.

One technique that veteran servers use is to think of their entire section as one big table and look at all guests to see if they need anything each time they are in the dining room. Whenever they have nothing else to do, they start cleanup duties.

Greet and Seat Guests. A host will usually handle seating, but sometimes servers are called on to help out. When they are seating guests, servers should smile and give a warm greeting. They should then ask the guests whether the restaurant is holding a reservation for them, and whether they have any seating preferences. Some guests may have special needs such as braille menus, highchairs, or booster seats, to name a few.

Servers usually use a seating chart to decide where to seat a group of guests who are dining together. Each restaurant will have a different policy for how to balance tables. Overloading one section will make good service difficult. However, if a group requests a certain table and it is available, servers will usually give it to them even if it overloads a section. (The dining room manager can take this into account and adjust the workload among servers.)

Once they have selected a table, servers should pick up enough menus for each guest in the group and ask the group to follow them. They can communicate confidence by:

- Holding the menus high on their arm.

- Standing up straight and giving their full attention to the group they are seating.

- Moving service equipment to one side to clear a path for the guests.

- Describing the restaurant's signature menu items as they move toward the table.

Servers should then help the guests with seating by pulling highchairs away from the table, helping guests with disabilities as appropriate, and pulling out a chair for a guest. Servers should never touch a child or any other guest unless they have permission. They should also let the guests decide who will sit in the chair they have pulled out. Servers can then present the menu with their right hand (the menu should be closed and/or right-side-up) to each guest, from the guest's right side. Before departing, the server should remove any extra place-settings.

Approach the Table. Greeting guests immediately puts guests at ease and assures them that a server has noticed them and will take care of them. The server's greeting is one of the guests' first impressions of the server and the restaurant; thus, a brief "How you guys doin'?" is never acceptable as a professional service greeting. Servers should instead develop a warm and sincere greeting such as "Good afternoon and welcome."

Guests do not like to wait, and they hate to be ignored. Giving guests a brief hello and a sincere apology if a delay in greeting them occurred will usually overcome any negative feelings. A common service standard is that servers should greet guests within thirty seconds after they are seated. Servers should be relaxed, pleasant, and professional during their greeting and introduce themselves by name.

During the initial greeting, servers can encourage guests to tell them whether they have any special needs or requests. They should also try to read their guests right away, being especially alert to guests who may have already been drinking and therefore may become intoxicated quickly. Reading guests helps servers determine the type of service they want.

If the busperson did not serve water as soon as the guests were seated, the server should do so during the greeting, and deliver menus if necessary. (In some operations, the host passes out menus when seating guests.)

Provide Appropriate Service for Children. Servers who give special attention to children will help the children and their parents have an enjoyable restaurant experience. Servers should:

- Ask parents if their children will need highchairs or booster seats.

- Seat guests with children away from the center of the room.

- Remove knives from the place settings of small children.

- Make sure highchairs, trays, bibs, menus, coloring books, and toys are clean.

- Provide the children with menus, coloring books, toys, bibs, crackers, and other appropriate items.

- Serve children their meals first, as quickly as possible.

Highchairs and booster seats should be cleaned and sanitized after each use, and their trays wrapped in food service film to keep them clean.

Serve Beverages. The first beverage typically served is water. In some restaurants, servers or buspersons will bring full water glasses to the table. In other restaurants, guests may choose tap water (no charge) or bottled water. Water may be served only by request or may be delayed until after beverage orders have been taken. Servers should refill water glasses whenever they are less than half-full, usually pouring from a pitcher.

All servers should use the same order-taking system to help remember who ordered which menu items. In some restaurants, servers write beverage orders on the back of the guest check, and the point-of-sale unit prints the order neatly on the front side. In those cases, servers do not have to worry about **standard food and drink abbreviations**. However, most servers do have to find out which food and drink abbreviations are used by the restaurant and use those on the guest check. Servers typically pre-ring drink orders on the restaurant's point-of-sale equipment.

In many restaurants, bartenders set up the drink glasses (and ice, if needed). In other restaurants, servers set up the correct glasses in the order that they will call the drinks and then place the glasses on the kitchen or bartender side of the service bar. When they call orders, they say in a clear voice, "Ordering," and then announce the drink order, including any special instructions. The reason servers follow a specific **calling order** is that some drinks take more time to prepare than others, or they do not hold up as well as other drinks.

Either the server or the bartender will garnish the drinks that require garnishes after they have been prepared. Servers should collect one beverage napkin for each drink and then check the entire order, asking themselves:

- Do I have all of the beverages for the order?
- Are the beverages in the correct glasses?
- Are the garnishes correct?
- Have special instructions (if any) been followed?
- Has anything spilled over the side?

If the order is correct, the server should center the glasses on the tray so that the tray is well-balanced. If possible, heavy or tall glasses should be placed in the center of the tray.

Once they have returned to the table with the guests' beverages, servers should place beverage napkins in front of the guests before putting down the drinks. If there is a logo on the napkin, the logo should be readable to the guest. Once the napkin is placed on the table, the beverage should be placed in the center of the napkin. Servers should always handle glasses away from the rim or lip, and handle stemmed glasses by the stem or base (because their hands will warm the drink if they touch the outside of the glass). Because of sanitation concerns, servers should never put their fingers inside a glass or on surfaces that will come into contact with the guest's mouth.

When guests have finished their drinks and order other drinks, servers should clear the empty glasses and old napkins before bringing the new drinks and fresh napkins.

Take Food Orders. When servers take food orders, they should begin by telling guests about the menu specials. It is their responsibility to always know about the daily specials—the soup of the day, the vegetable of the day, the entrée of the day, and any other special the restaurant is offering. If the chef does not announce the specials, the servers should ask. Many guests get annoyed if they ask about the daily specials and then have to wait for the server to go to the kitchen to find out.

Servers should take orders in a standard clockwise fashion so that they or someone else can serve their guests without having to ask who ordered what. Most operations will create a numbering system for the chairs at each table. Chair #1 at each table is typically the chair closest to the front door or some other easily identifiable landmark in the restaurant. When writing orders on the order pad or guest check, servers should write the order for the guest in chair #1 on the first line of the order form. The chair numbers identify each seat at the table; they do not stand for the order in which servers write things down.

Servers should ask questions about preferred preparation ("How would you like your steak prepared?") and obtain as much information as possible while taking orders so that they do not have to interrupt their guests later to find out this information. They should also work at not sounding mechanical when describing food choices, and attempt to make every item sound good. They should stand up straight and look at each guest as they take orders. If they notice a guest hesitating while making a decision, they can make a suggestion.

Servers can also suggest additional courses such as appetizers, soups, and salads when they take the food order. They should consider what entrée the guest has selected and only suggest items that will go well with it. If guests are celebrating a special occasion such as a birthday or anniversary, they may want to have wine or champagne with their meal. Servers should learn which wines go well with certain foods so that they can suggest appropriate wines while taking orders. By suggesting additional items, servers can enhance the guests' dining experience, increase revenue for the restaurant, and increase their own tips.

Some guests may request an item to be prepared in a way not listed on the menu. Servers should write all special requests on their order pads and tell kitchen staff about the requests when they place the orders. They may need to check with the chef or a supervisor before they promise a guest they can fulfill a special request.

While taking the food order, servers can check on drink levels and suggest another drink if a beverage is one-half to three-fourths empty, and if (when the drinks in question are alcoholic) the guests are not nearing intoxication. As previously mentioned, servers should clear empty glasses before serving new beverages.

Servers then collect the menus (and, in some restaurants, wine lists) and pre-ring the food orders. In restaurants with point-of-sale systems, food checks must be rung into a point-of-sale unit before the kitchen will prepare any food. Servers sometimes have to speak with the chef to explain special orders. In such cases, they should make an effort to always be polite and limit conversations to a mini-mum, particularly when the restaurant is busy.

Serve the Meal. The timing of food preparation is important to a smooth dining experience. All of the guests in a group should get their meals at as close to the same time as possible. Planning and organization help servers to serve all of their guests quickly.

Servers should turn in the order for each course when guests are about three-fourths finished with the previous one. If the kitchen is busy, they should turn the orders in sooner. Unless guests request a different order, most establishments will serve courses in the following order:

- Appetizers
- Soup
- Salads
- Entrées
- Dessert
- After-dinner drinks
- Coffee

Servers and cooks should work together to make sure orders are being prepared in a reasonable amount of time. They try not to make guests wait without an explana-tion from the server or a supervisor. If servers are too busy to pick up their orders as soon as they are ready, they should ask other servers for help.

Part of memorable service is preparing the table for each course before serv-ing it. This involves clearing away empty plates and glasses, bringing out condi-ments and accompaniments, and bringing extra plates if guests are sharing an item. Servers should wait to clear away empty plates until more than one guest is done, so that those who are still eating will not feel rushed. Bringing out the condi-ments before the next course helps ensure that food will not have to wait under a heat lamp while the condiments are being collected.

Before taking a food order out of the kitchen, servers should check it carefully, asking themselves:

- Does the food look fresh and appealing?
- Have all preparation instructions been followed?
- Is the food garnished?
- Have all special requests been met?
- Is the plate clean?
- Is hot food hot on hot plates and cold food cold on cold plates?

Then the servers deliver the food on a tray. Tray service saves steps and lets serv-ers take care of many guests at once. Servers can use their order pad or guest check to help them remember who ordered what; they should not have to ask the guests. Anticipatory service is so smooth that guests are hardly aware of the servers. When servers are able to serve each course without asking questions, guests are not interrupted.

Servers should serve food from the guest's left side with their left hand (whenever possible) and avoid reaching in front of guests. They should place the plate with the first course on top of the base plate, if a base plate is included in the restaurant's table setting. They should place the entrée plate so that the main food item on the plate is closest to the guest. They should then place side dishes to the left of the entrée plate. If a guest asks for something extra, servers should deliver it as quickly as possible so that the meal does not get cold while the guest waits for it. Servers should also ask whether guests would like them to bring or do anything else for them at this time.

Check Back to the Table. Attentive servers make sure that their guests are satisfied with their meals. They approach guests after they have taken a few bites and ask specific questions about the food, such as, "How is your whitefish?" or "Are you enjoying your salad?" They also ask if there is anything else they can bring. Business is built when satisfied guests keep returning and tell their friends about their positive dining experiences, so servers should work at making each guest's experience as positive and as memorable as possible. If a food or beverage item is unsatisfactory, servers should apologize to the guest and take care of the problem immediately.

Respond to Dissatisfied Guests. Guests do the restaurant a favor when they complain—they are giving servers a chance to fix the problem. A guest with a problem who does not complain to the server is probably complaining to other potential guests. Servers can respond to dissatisfied guests by:

- Listening to the guest.

- Apologizing to the guest.

- Taking appropriate action.

- Thanking the guest for speaking up.

Maintain Tables. Servers should maintain their tables throughout the meal to keep the guest experience a pleasant one. An important part of maintaining a table's appearance is to remove items throughout the meal that the guests no longer need. This is called **pre-busing**. Some restaurants clear items as soon as a guest finishes a course; others wait until all guests in the group have completed the course. By the end of the meal, before dessert service, only beverages and items that go with them (cream, sugar, lemons, and so on) should remain on the table. Maintaining tables includes:

- Being aware of guest needs. Professional servers use proper manners and are especially attentive to the needs of children.

- Checking food and beverage levels. Servers should refill water glasses, coffee cups, hot tea pots, iced-tea glasses, and other beverages that are refilled at no charge to the guest whenever they are half-full. They should refill bread baskets as needed.

- Pre-busing the table.

Sell After-Dinner Items. After-dinner items are great sales-builders. Many people will be tempted by a dessert if the server describes it well and as soon as possible after the meal. Once servers have cleared the entire table, they should bring the dessert cart or display tray to the table and describe each dessert using mouth-watering terms, and perhaps suggest their personal favorites. If guests say they are too full to have dessert, the server might point out the lighter dessert items, or suggest that guests share a dessert. Servers should also offer coffee and tea when taking dessert orders. Many guests who have dessert will also order coffee or tea.

Prepare Take-Out Items. Servers may be asked to prepare foods to-go or help box leftovers. Servers should wash their hands thoroughly before putting take-out items in sanitary take-out containers. They should use serving utensils, not their fingers. They should place lids on cups and provide straws for cold beverages. They can then add paper napkins and individual packets of appropriate condiments (such as salt, pepper, mustard, ketchup, and salad dressing) to the take-out order. For leftover food, servers should bring a take-out container to the table. In some restaurants, servers give the container to the guest and the guest puts the leftover food into it; in other restaurants, the server uses serving utensils to neatly transfer the leftover food from the guest's plate to the container. In some full-service restaurants, servers then wrap the container with aluminum foil and fashion the foil into a swan or some other decorative figure for the guest. Other restaurants have take-out bags featuring their logo that servers can give to guests for transporting their leftovers.

Present the Guest Check. Finally, servers should present the guest check to the guests according to their restaurant's policies. In most restaurants, the check will be printed by a point-of-sale unit. Servers should review the check carefully to be sure it is complete and accurate before taking it to the table. At the end of the meal, some guests may become impatient to leave and will become annoyed if they have to wait for the check, so servers should work hard to make sure their guests do not have to wait for them. It is also important that guests do not feel as if they are being rushed out if the check has been presented but they prefer to linger. Servers should place the check with a pen near the center of the table unless a guest specifically asks for the check.

Most restaurants use **guest check folders**. Guest check folders keep checks clean and provide a place for guests to put their money or payment cards. If the restaurant uses comment cards, they are often included in the check folder.

Settle Guest Checks. In most restaurants, guests have many payment options for settling their checks: cash, payment card, personal check, traveler's check, coupon, voucher, or gift certificate. In hotel restaurants, guests might also choose to charge their meal to their room, or charge it to their city account.

When a guest pays with cash, the server should present any change due back to the guest in the guest check folder. Servers should never ask the guest if he or she needs change. If the guest leaves while the server is settling the check, the change is the server's tip.

When a guest settles a check with a payment card, the server must get an approval code and imprint the card on the back of the guest check and/or on a payment card voucher. The server then completes the voucher and presents it with a pen to the guest in a guest check folder. The guest then totals the bill (if adding a tip to the food and beverage charges) and signs the voucher.

It is extremely important that servers get information such as a driver's license number, an address, and a telephone number from guests who are paying for their meals by personal check. This information helps assure that a personal check can be traced if it is returned for non-sufficient funds.

Traveler's checks must be signed in the server's presence. Once servers have verified that the signature is valid by comparing it to the signature already on the check, they should then treat the check like cash.

Servers should be taught their restaurant's policies for each type of coupon, voucher, or gift certificate that the restaurant issues. For example, many restaurants do not give change for gift certificates and coupons; however, guests might receive smaller gift certificates in the place of change. Whether a coupon, voucher, or gift certificate, servers should carefully read the document to make sure it is valid and unexpired. If it is still usable, they should treat it like cash. Today, many restaurants offer gift cards with a specific balance that declines as guests use the cards.

Guests in hotel restaurants who are staying at the property and have approved credit may charge restaurant meals and drinks to their room. This is called a **house account.** (Some hotel staff members, such as salespeople or top-level managers, may also have house accounts.) Servers ask guests who wish to charge their meals to their rooms to print their names and room numbers on the guest checks and sign them.

Some frequent guests of hotel restaurants who live in the local community may have charge accounts at the hotel that allow them to be directly billed each month (i.e., receive a bill in the mail for their hotel food and beverage charges). Such local accounts are called **city accounts**. When settling these accounts, servers should ask guests to print their name (or their company's name or group's name — whatever name the account is under) on the check, along with their city account number. The guest should then be asked to sign the guest check.

Thank the Guests. Finally, servers should always remember to thank guests as they return their change and receipts to them, and invite them to return. A sincere and gracious thank you leaves guests feeling that their business is appreciated and they are valued. A genuine thank you helps build guest loyalty.

Clear and Reset Tables. It is important that tables be cleared and reset promptly. This makes it possible to seat waiting guests quickly, and adds to the neat appearance of the dining room. Servers work with buspersons to clear and reset tables. While it is important to clear and reset tables as quickly as possible, the needs of the servers' other guests always come first. Servers clear and reset tables by:

- Gathering items needed to reset the table.
- Clearing away used dishes, silverware, glasses, and linens.
- Cleaning the table with a sanitizing solution.
- Replacing tablecloths (if applicable).

- Resetting the table.
- Cleaning the chairs.
- Giving the tables a final check.
- Taking soiled items to the dish room.
- Breaking down the tray of soiled items.
- Storing sanitizing solution and the tray stand at the sidestation.

Perform Closing Sidework. Servers typically work from a closing duty checklist at the end of their shift. It usually includes such tasks as:

- Remove soiled linens
- Store condiments
- Store bread and butter
- Restock silverware
- Disassemble and clean the coffee station
- Clean ice buckets
- Clean water pitchers
- Reset all tables
- Straighten, clean, and restock sidestations

Buspersons

A busperson can be defined as someone who sets and clears tables and helps servers. While this definition is technically correct, it leaves out the heart of a busperson's job. A better definition might be: A restaurant staff member who does everything possible, within reason, to make each guest's dining experience exactly what the guest wants it to be, and who exceeds guest expectations whenever possible. Buspersons are responsible for:

- Preparing for service.
- Setting tables.
- Helping servers provide high-quality guest service.
- Maintaining tables.
- Clearing tables.
- Creating a friendly atmosphere where guests can enjoy themselves.

Buspersons can make a positive difference in the guest's service experience.

Working as a Team

One secret of a restaurant's success is that everyone works together—as a team—to give guests a positive, memorable experience. Buspersons are part of a service delivery system. They must give guests *and* internal customers great service for the system to work. To be excellent team players, buspersons can help:

- Hosts and hostesses by:
  - Greeting and seating guests when necessary.
  - Answering the phone.
  - Taking reservations when hosts and hostesses are busy.
- Servers by:
  - Setting tables according to restaurant policy.
  - Providing beverage service for guests when servers are busy.
  - Clearing and resetting tables promptly after guests leave.
  - Checking sidestations periodically to make sure they are stocked.

Superior Performance Standards

The quality of the food, drinks, and service at a restaurant should enhance each guest's overall experience. Providing excellent anticipatory service, beverages, and meals at a price that guests find reasonable is every restaurant's ultimate goal. A restaurant's superior performance standards help everyone achieve that goal. To display superior performance standards, buspersons must:

- Be familiar with all restaurant menus and food and drink offerings.
- Demonstrate professional behavior.
- Quickly approach guests and greet them warmly if servers and hosts or hostesses are busy.
- Be alert to safety procedures.
- Keep tabletop items clean and attractively arranged.
- Keep coffee, tea, water, and other nonalcoholic beverages filled at each table.
- Clear and reset tables promptly after guests leave.
- Keep dining room floors neat and clean.

Busperson Duties

The primary responsibilities of a busperson are to set and clear tables and help servers. In general, buspersons are responsible for preparing tables for service; prepping sidestations, condiments, and silverware; busing soiled linens, dishes, glasses, and silverware from tables; and assisting servers and guests to ensure total guest satisfaction. Buspersons and servers often act together in teams.

Buspersons may be the earliest arriving staff members to the restaurant and, along with servers, may be expected to help set up the restaurant dining area for service. These duties may include:

- Polishing brass.
- Adjusting drapes and blinds.
- Adjusting environmental controls in the restaurant.
- Setting up serving trays.

Exhibit 2 lists the most common tasks that buspersons are expected to be able to perform and perform well.

Inspect and Stock China. When people eat at a restaurant, the **china**—plates, bowls, cups and saucers, and serving pieces—tells them a lot about the type of restaurant they are in. China tells people whether an establishment is casual, fine-dining, trendy, or traditional. Typically, restaurants choose their china carefully to present a certain image to guests. Buspersons can enhance that image by taking care of the following responsibilities:

- Inspect all china carefully to make sure it is spotless and free of cracks or chips. Report any cracked or chipped china to a supervisor. Return spotted china to the dishwasher.

- Stock enough of each type of china in sidestations and other areas so there is always plenty on hand and guests always receive food on the correct china.

Provide Silverware. Forks, knives, spoons, and other silverware items are typically made of stainless steel (true silverware, which is made of silver, is extremely expensive and rarely used). Think of silverware as the tools that guests need to eat their meals comfortably. At home, the basic "tools"—a fork, knife, and teaspoon—may be enough. But there are more than forty additional types of silverware used for various occasions and situations, and guests expect buspersons to provide the right silverware at their tables.

Anticipate Guest Needs. Guests tend to remember positive restaurant experiences in which the server and busperson kept their table exactly the way they wanted it by bringing food and beverages just when they wanted them, and clearing items as soon as they were through with them. These delightful dining experiences make guests feel appreciated and valued. It is this type of service that buspersons should provide for guests. Whenever appropriate, they should take the steps necessary to make sure each guest has a positive experience. As buspersons perform their tasks, they can also help servers by observing guests and determining their needs. For instance, buspersons can:

- Ask guests arriving with young children if they would like child seats or highchairs.

- Refill water glasses as soon as they are half full or less.

- Remove unwanted items from tables promptly.

- Notice when guests are looking around and stop at their table to assist them, or tell them their server will be right with them, then go find the server.

By anticipating guest needs, buspersons can exceed guest expectations and help make each guest's dining experience positive and memorable.

Prepare Tables for Service. As stated previously, no guest likes to wait for a table. That is why one of the most important responsibilities buspersons have is to quickly and correctly set tables to the restaurant's standards.

The guest's first impression of the table is important in setting the tone for the dining experience. Every table in the restaurant should look presentable, whether

Exhibit 2   Typical Tasks for Buspersons

Here is a list of typical tasks that buspersons might perform, depending on the restaurant. The number and complexity of tasks that a busperson is expected to perform depends on the style of the restaurant and other factors. Not all of these tasks will be discussed in the chapter.

1. Set up the restaurant for service
2. Prepare flower arrangements or other centerpieces for the dining room
3. Prepare butter for sidestations
4. Prepare breads and bread baskets or trays
5. Prepare condiments and crackers
6. Prepare sugar bowls or caddies
7. Prepare salt and pepper shakers and grinders
8. Fold napkins
9. Stock silverware
10. Prepare service trays for servers
11. Lift and carry loaded trays, bus tubs, and dish racks
12. Prepare chilled forks and plates
13. Prepare table-side service carts
14. Prepare ice bins in service stations
15. Set up the water station and water pitchers
16. Prepare ice buckets and ice bucket stands
17. Prepare and serve coffee
18. Prepare and serve hot tea
19. Prepare and serve iced tea
20. Prepare and serve hot chocolate
21. Set up, maintain, and take down the salad bar
22. Prepare tables for service
23. Take reservations
24. Greet and seat guests
25. Serve water
26. Serve bread and butter
27. Maintain tables
28. Assist servers to ensure total guest satisfaction
29. Respond to dissatisfied guests
30. Help serve wine or champagne
31. Clear and reset tables
32. Bus soiled dishes to the dish room
33. Handle soiled restaurant linens
34. Maintain sidestations
35. Pick up and restock restaurant supplies
36. Prepare take-out items
37. Perform closing sidework and cleaning duties

it was set before the restaurant opened or just a few minutes ago when the last group of guests left the table. When tables are kept clean and set consistently, it shows guests that the buspersons care about providing a memorable dining experience.

Table setup specifications vary with each restaurant and may change with each meal period. Table setup tasks involve:

- Cleaning tables and chairs.
- Cleaning children's seating.
- Checking floors.
- Placing tablecloths or place mats.
- Positioning tabletop items such as centerpieces, salt and pepper shakers and grinders, sugar bowls/caddies, condiments, and cracker baskets.
- Placing base plates (in fine-dining restaurants).
- Placing silverware.
- Placing bread and butter plates.
- Placing glassware.
- Placing napkins.
- Placing cream, butter, flowers, and other perishable items.
- Checking the overall appearance of the table.

Fold Napkins. Fresh, clean linens and crisply folded napkins are an important part of professional food presentation in full-service restaurants, whether guests are having an entire meal or just having coffee and a snack. One of the many duties buspersons may be responsible for in these restaurants is to fold clean napkins to prepare for each meal period.

Stock Silverware. Silverware used in most restaurants includes knives, forks, and spoons. Special silverware—depending on the food served—may include fish forks, snail tongs, demitasse spoons, and other silverware required for the service of specialty menu items. Buspersons may be responsible for stocking the silverware trays that are usually located in the restaurant's sidestations. Buspersons should never touch the eating surfaces of the silverware. While stocking the silverware, buspersons should check each silverware item to make sure it is clean and without any water spots or food residue. Any soiled silverware should be returned to the kitchen for further washing.

Prepare Chilled Forks and Plates. Some restaurants that serve chilled salads, appetizers, or other similar items provide chilled forks and/or plates to guests who order those items. Buspersons may be responsible for making sure these forks and plates are chilled in advance. Plates and forks may be chilled in a freezer, refrigerator, or a special chiller designed for the purpose. When using a refrigerator, buspersons should line a stainless steel pan with a clean linen napkin and place the forks or plates in the pan. They then should place a second clean linen napkin over the pan, to prevent contamination of the clean forks/plates. Plates should be stacked upside-down. The pans should then be carefully placed in the refrigerator, in an area where food will not be spilled on them. Buspersons should always check that the forks and plates are clean before chilling them.

Prepare Table-Side Service Carts. Table-side cart service turns a routine dining experience into a form of entertainment and a memorable service experience. Table-side carts may include dessert carts, salad carts, and table-side cooking carts. These carts will vary in style and setup based on the menu items. Restaurants featuring higher-priced items on their menus are more likely to have this kind of special service.

Buspersons may be responsible for cleaning and preparing table-side carts for service. A clean, wet cloth, along with soapy water, is used to wash the shelves, pedestals, legs, and wheels of the cart, in that order. The cart should then be wiped down with a new, clean cloth, and finally, polished with yet another new, clean cloth. The necessary condiments, equipment, linens, and silverware are then placed on the cart. If the cart is a cooking cart, the cooking burner will need the appropriate fuel supply. Once the cart is loaded, buspersons should check the overall appearance of the cart and check that the wheels do not squeak.

Prepare Sidestations. The responsibilities of buspersons include setting up and stocking the restaurant's sidestations. Sidestations store extra supplies; buspersons and servers can eliminate some trips to the kitchen by going to sidestations instead. This means quicker, more efficient service for guests.

A restaurant's sidework checklist lists sidework tasks and the buspersons who are assigned to complete them. Some sidework tasks are shared with servers. These tasks are important to the smooth operation of the dining room; professional buspersons review the checklist before their shifts to determine their responsibilities. By following the sidework checklist and fully stocking the sidestations, buspersons can help servers save steps and serve guests more efficiently during rush periods, without running out of supplies.

Buspersons make sure sidestations are kept clean by removing soiled items and washing the stations as needed. They empty used ice buckets and full trash cans. They also keep the sidework station stocked. Sidestations are stocked before the restaurant opens. On busy days there may not be enough time between meal periods to completely restock the sidestations. Buspersons should monitor the supply levels in the sidestations and keep them as full as possible. Servers and buspersons cannot provide high-quality service if they waste time returning to the kitchen for items that should be in the sidestation.

In some restaurants, stocking sidestations involves working with butter and other food items. Before they do any food preparation of any kind, buspersons must thoroughly wash their hands—both sides—with warm water and soap for at least twenty seconds.

Butter. Generally, a supervisor or restaurant manager will tell buspersons how to prepare butter and how much butter to prepare, based on expected business volume. Butter is typically prepared in one of four ways:

- Butter chips
- Curls

- Rosettes

- Molds

As the butter is portioned, it is placed on a butter dish or ramekin, covered with food service film, and placed on a bed of ice.

Condiments. Condiments that most restaurants typically provide include ketchup, hot sauce, mustard, steak sauce, jelly, jam, honey, and syrup. They are usually served in their original containers or in specialty dispensers. Buspersons should make sure that these containers are kept clean. This might include removing the condiment lids, wiping the tops of the containers or dispensers with a paper towel, washing the condiment lids in a sink to remove any food residue, rinsing the lids and spraying them with an approved sanitizing solution, and completely drying them before replacing the lids. Containers or dispensers that are chipped, cracked, or dented should not be used.

Buspersons may also be responsible for refilling and restocking condiments when needed. It is common practice to combine contents of partially full containers or dispensers using a small kitchen funnel. However, it is necessary to check with local health laws to determine whether this is permitted. Generally, small individual-use bottles are not reused or combined; they are simply thrown away when the tables are cleared.

Some restaurants use single-service packets of mustard, ketchup, or specialty sauces. Many restaurants provide individually packaged crackers in baskets on the dining tables. Buspersons may be responsible for ensuring that these baskets stay full and for removing cracker crumbs, broken crackers, or open or empty wrappers from the baskets.

As with condiment containers, buspersons should routinely check sugar bowls (if their use is permitted by local food safety laws) to make sure they are full, clean, and free from chips or cracks. Damaged bowls should be discarded. Buspersons can use a clean, damp cloth to wipe away dust or crumbs from the sugar bowls. Bowls that are excessively dirty should be sent to the kitchen for washing.

At most restaurants, sugar is not served in a bowl; rather, it is served in individual packets that are placed in a caddie on the table. Non-sugar artificial sweeteners are often served in the same manner. Buspersons should place the proper number of sugar packets on one side of the caddie and artificial sweetener packets on the other; a common ratio is two sugar packets to every artificial sweetener packet. Packets are placed upright and facing the same direction so guests can plainly see the printing or logo on them. Packets that were not used during a meal can be reused unless they are stained, damaged, or partially opened. Buspersons also make sure that the sidestations have extra sugar caddies.

Ice bins. A typical restaurant will have ice bins at each sidestation. These bins need to be kept full throughout each shift. Buspersons and servers often share this duty.

Because guests consume ice, it is handled like food. A sanitary container is always used to transfer ice from the ice maker to each ice bin. In addition, each ice bin is kept covered when it is not in use, and an ice scoop is used to dispense the ice. Scoops are always left near each ice bin but never inside the ice bins.

Typically, at the end of each shift or meal period, buspersons empty and clean the ice bins. They wipe down the inside walls of the bins with a clean cloth and an approved detergent. They then rinse and drain the bins completely and allow them to air dry before adding ice.

Restaurants that offer wine, champagne, and bottled water or other chilled, bottled beverages may serve them in an ice bucket on a stand. Buspersons may be responsible for preparing these buckets and stands for service. The buckets must be checked for cleanliness and washed, if necessary, before they are filled one-half to two-thirds full with ice. Crushed ice is preferable to cubed ice because using crushed ice makes it easier to nest bottles in the bucket. Sometimes water is then added, filling the bucket up so that the shoulder of the bottle is covered. Once the bucket is filled, it is placed on the bucket stand, with a clean linen cloth draped over the top. Buspersons then place the stands in the proper location at the sidestations.

Water pitchers. In addition to ice bins, most restaurants also have designated locations for water pitchers, usually at the sidestations. These areas should be cleaned or wiped with a cloth before and after each shift or meal period. Clean water glasses are also stored at the same station as the water pitchers. Because racks of glasses are heavy, buspersons should always use proper lifting techniques when carrying them to and from the sidestations. Buspersons should make sure to check that all glasses and pitchers are clean before they are stocked or filled.

A clean linen cloth is usually placed on the counter at the sidestation to serve as a drip base for the water pitchers. This will prevent the sidestation from becoming messy from moisture or drips.

Buspersons fill the water pitchers by first filling them with ice, using an ice scoop—buspersons should never use the pitcher itself to scoop ice. Pitchers are always filled with more ice than water so that the pitchers stay cold longer. The filled pitchers are then placed back on the drip base.

Coffee. In some restaurants, buspersons make fresh coffee when the pot in the sidestation is nearly empty or if the coffee becomes stale. Having fresh coffee readily available is a mark of good service.

Prepare Salad Bars. In some restaurants, buspersons may be responsible for setting up, maintaining, and taking down the salad bar. When setting up the salad bar, buspersons should always handle the food safely and check to make sure that the food meets the restaurant's standards. The first step in this task is to gather the needed supplies onto a cart. These supplies may include the following:

- Linen skirts for the salad bar, table decorations, a sneeze guard, a soup tureen, and crocks of food and salad dressing

- Salad plates, soup cups, saucers, soup spoons, bread and butter plates, and serving utensils

- Condiments, salt and pepper shakers and grinders, and oil and vinegar cruets

Buspersons should check the salad bar and make sure it is clean. The sneeze guard can be cleaned by using glass cleaner and paper towels before the food is placed on the bar. The edges of the soup tureen can be kept clean with a clean, damp cloth. Linen skirts can be placed on the salad bar by using special "T-pins"; the skirts should then be fluffed if necessary. Before placing these skirts, buspersons should check them to make sure they do not have any rips, tears, or stains. Additional tasks involved with preparing and maintaining the salad bar include:

- Placing table decorations on the salad bar.

- Adding ice to the salad bar.

- Placing crocks of food and salad dressing onto the salad bar.

- Plugging in and turning on the soup tureen.

- Stocking the salad bar with salad plates.

- Routinely checking the salad bar and surrounding floor area for crumbs or food particles.

- Keeping all food and dressing crocks filled.

- Restocking salad plates, as needed.

- Ensuring that food is stored and displayed safely.

  At the end of the meal period, buspersons can disassemble the salad bar by:

- Placing all food containers back onto a cart.

- Storing food that can be reused in the kitchen, adhering to food safety principles.

- Discarding food that cannot be reused.

- Taking salad plates to the kitchen for washing.

- Storing condiments in their proper place.

- Removing the linen skirts and taking them to the laundry bins.

- Draining the melted ice from the salad bar.

- Cleaning the sneeze guard with paper towels and glass cleaner.

- Wiping down the salad bar with a clean, damp cloth and a sanitizing solution.

Clear and Reset Tables. Tables must be cleared and reset promptly and quietly. Most restaurants want tables cleared within five minutes of guest departure. This makes it possible to seat waiting guests quickly, and it adds to the neat appearance of the restaurant. When buspersons keep up with this process, there will only be a few tables to reset as part of the closing duties later.

Buspersons, of course, must wait until after guests leave the table to clear used dishes, silverware, and glasses. Food and debris can be scraped into a **bus tub.** Whenever possible, buspersons should avoid scraping plates in view of guests; in some restaurants, the dishes are simply placed in the tub, to be scraped later in the dish room. Buspersons should work with their backs to nearby guests and place soiled dishes in the bus tub, stacking like items together. If the restaurant uses linen napkins and tablecloths, these should be removed and the busperson should make sure no silverware, small dishes, or glasses get accidentally folded into the linens. Once everything is removed, the table surface can be cleaned, or the table-cloth replaced. Buspersons at full-service operations may be taught how to replace a tablecloth so that guests are never able to see the table surface. Then the table can be reset with glassware, silverware, and dishes. The chairs or bench seats (if the busperson is working in a booth) should be checked and cleaned as needed. Before leaving, buspersons should do a final check to make sure the table looks right, then take the soiled dishes and linens to the dish room or other designated area.

Bus Soiled Dishes. Busing occurs throughout meal service as new courses are served and old courses are cleared, when clearing and resetting tables, or whenever a server requests it. In addition, buspersons bus the sidestations as needed. Once a dining table has been cleared and reset, buspersons take the filled bus tubs back to the kitchen or dish room for washing.

Because the task of carrying soiled dining items back to the kitchen is performed so frequently, buspersons should take care that they are properly loading and lifting the trays, tubs, or racks in order to prevent spills or injury to themselves or others. The weight of the items placed in the tray, tub, or rack should be spread evenly to allow for better balance with lifting. Heavy items should placed in the center; light items around the edges. Professional buspersons know that making two trips is better than overloading a cart, tub, or tray in order to make one trip.

When buspersons lift loaded trays, they should bend at the knees in order to place their shoulder below the tray. They can then pull the tray with one hand onto the palm of the other hand. By balancing the tray at shoulder level on their fingertips instead of their forearm, buspersons can help prevent tipping as they straighten their legs. The long end of a loaded tray or tub should be next to their bodies and kept close to their bodies as they move through the restaurant.

Buspersons should always keep their backs straight when lifting. Other safety-conscious steps that buspersons can take when carrying include looking out for opening doors, watching for wet spots on the floor, avoiding passing others in aisles, and calling out "Behind!" to alert other staff members to their presence.

Once buspersons have carried the soiled items to the kitchen or dish room, they typically sort the items according to a decoy system. Most restaurants have decoy systems that consist of bus tubs and dish racks with one dirty dish, glass, or other item to be washed to show where each item should be placed. Often these tubs are filled with water and a soaking solution. This sorting makes the dishwashing work easier. Buspersons finish by rinsing the empty bus tub and wiping it dry with a clean cloth.

Handle Soiled Restaurant Linens. In restaurants that use linen napkins and table-cloths, buspersons may be required to gather these used linens and take them to the laundry area for cleaning if the operation does not have a laundry service that picks them up. Buspersons use a linen bag or a rack to gather and transport the soiled linens. This may be done periodically throughout a shift as well as at the end of each shift. This helps keep the dining area clean.

Buspersons should check each linen item to make sure it does not contain silverware, plates, glasses, condiment containers, or other non-linen items. Not only are these items costly to replace, but they could also tear the linens once they are in the washer or dryer. They could also potentially cause injury to those doing the laundry.

The tablecloths and linen napkins are always separated from other restaurant laundry when laundry items are sorted; other laundry items may include cleaning towels and aprons. The restaurant may have a specific sorting process. Buspersons should follow this process to make the laundry job easier.

Assist Servers. A very important responsibility that buspersons have is to assist servers in providing service to restaurant guests. One way that buspersons help servers is by providing beverage service to guests when servers are busy. When helping servers by serving beverages, buspersons should follow these basic steps:

1. Have the right glass or cup for the beverage.

2. Make sure the glass or cup is sparkling clean and without cracks, chips, or spots before pouring the beverage. Cracked or chipped glasses or cups should be removed from service immediately and reported to a supervisor. Spotted glasses/cups should be returned to the dishwasher.

3. When pouring at a table, leave the glasses and cups on the table. Never pick up a glass or cup to pour unless there is no other way to pour without spilling.

4. Pour from the right side with the right hand.

5. Never add ice to a hot glass. Always use an ice scoop or tongs—not hands or a glass—to pick up ice.

In general, successful buspersons are always aware of guest needs. If guests request something from buspersons, the buspersons should either help the guests themselves or quickly alert a server. Buspersons should always use good manners when interacting with guests. They should be attentive to children, pick up items on the floor, and provide extra napkins as needed.

When buspersons remove items from dining tables while the guests are still eating, they should first ask the guests if they are done with the item. Items are cleared from the right side of guests with the right hand. Cleared items are placed in the bus tub or tray as are any crumbs, food particles, or soiled linens. Buspersons should leave drinks and condiments on the table until the end of the meal. Full bus tubs or trays can then be taken to the kitchen.

Perform Closing Sidework. Once the dining period is over, or when a shift ends, buspersons can perform their closing sidework and cleaning duties. Typically, buspersons will have a checklist that they use to keep track of their end-of-shift tasks. Tasks that may be required of buspersons at the end of their shifts include:

• Remove soiled linens

• Store condiments

• Store bread and butter

• Restock silverware

• Break down the coffee station

• Break down ice buckets

- Break down water pitchers
- Clean the dining room chairs and tables
- Wipe all furnishings, displays, railings, and other appropriate surfaces
- Vacuum carpeted areas
- Sweep floors
- Reset all tables
- Straighten, clean, and restock all sidestations
- Set music, HVAC, and light system controls, as appropriate

Attracting and Retaining Restaurant Managers

The old saying "select for personality and train for talent" is true, to an extent. A person who is friendly and outgoing will make a much better service professional than one who is abrasive and combative. Experience, however, is another qualification employers generally look for when hiring managers. This is because it takes time to develop the skills, competencies, and capabilities a manager must have. One of the most important skills a manager can have is the ability to train staff members, so they in turn can go on and train others. Promoting staff to supervisor and manager positions from within allows the restaurant to "grow their own" when it comes to management talent. Promoting from within not only ensures that individuals receive managerial training specific to the restaurant, it also allows staff members to see that the restaurant provides for internal advancement.

Management Practices and Responsibilities

Managers who do well in restaurants have several traits in common. They see themselves as people who should focus on improving the restaurant's processes and systems overall, rather than simply as another pair of hands working in the restaurant. They also understand the critical importance of guests and how vital it is to maintain an accurate database of the restaurant's guests and their preferences, frequency of visiting, and so on. These managers keep in touch with their guests via e-mail or social media such as Facebook and Twitter. They track guest responses to various restaurant promotions. They utilize financial statements and selected ratios to track the restaurant's financial performance.

Managers who enjoy interacting with and pleasing people seem to do better in restaurants than those who do not have these interpersonal and social skills. Desirable personality traits for restaurant managers include the following:

- Readily acknowledging mistakes and admitting to being wrong
- Being positive
- Being consistent and fair
- Taking a personal interest in each staff member
- Being open to suggestions (i.e., not being a know-it-all)

- Praising in public and correcting in private
- Smiling and being able to laugh at self
- Working hard and leading by example

One of the biggest responsibilities of managers is increasing the operation's profitability. It may be possible to build revenues and profits by providing catering or promoting the restaurant's gift cards for holidays, anniversaries, or special occasions. Managers are also responsible for the overall experience that each guest receives. They know that this experience is not just about products, or even service. Providing guests with a positive, memorable experience in which an operation's mission and values are brought to life is best accomplished by those managers (and staff members) who authentically enjoy serving and taking care of others.

Management Incentives

Financial payouts are sometimes given to managers, usually once a year, as rewards for good performance. A manager's performance may be measured in terms of sales, net income, profit, guest satisfaction, staff member satisfaction, and other indicators. Managers receive these bonuses in addition to their salaries. Sometimes managers' bonuses are affected by how well they control the restaurant's labor costs. Additional factors that can affect the rewarding of bonuses include controllable expenses (food, beverage), staff turnover, and net operating profits. In order for a bonus program to be successful, it must:

- Be based on reasonable and attainable objectives.
- Have reasonable deadlines for completing various parts of the plan. Usually, annual or quarterly bonus plans are preferred to monthly bonus plans because the fluctuations sometimes seen from month to month can become more level over the course of a year or quarter.
- Assess progress at regular intervals, e.g., monthly, quarterly, annually, to detail achievements, look for areas needing improvement, and set new deadlines for the next time period.
- Mutually benefit the individual and the organization.

Plans for awarding management bonuses should include setting management goals for each of the controllable expense categories—food, beverage, labor—as well as goals for facility maintenance and capital improvements, sales, and marketing. The tracking of guest and staff satisfaction is often factored into a bonus plan. Greater weight may be placed on one item (e.g., guest satisfaction) than on another (e.g., facility maintenance). Continuous improvements in processes (such as inventory control) should also be a metric in bonus plans. Specific steps toward improvement, however, can only be taken after a process is reviewed and input from those involved is sought and received.

Managers should be involved in setting their incentive and other management goals. Like staff members, managers are more likely to align with goals they help develop than goals that are handed down to them from corporate headquarters or higher-level managers.

Evaluating Staff Performance

Performance evaluations are used to measure the progress of individual staff members. They are typically conducted annually, although some operations might provide evaluations for new staff members after their trial hiring period is over. Every staff member should be evaluated, including managers.

An effective method used to evaluate staff members is to simply rate the staff member's performance regarding specific tasks or requirements. This can be done using the following scale:

5 = Excellent—exceptional performance; exceeds expectations

4 = Very good—performance is better than expected

3 = Good—performance meets expectations

2 = Not good—performance is less than expectations; requires improvement

1 = Unsatisfactory—performance is below position requirements; requires substantial improvement

0 = Not applicable (N/A)

If each staff member is rated on this or a similar scale in each area, comparisons can be made over time and improvements tracked. Bar managers, for example, could be rated on the following:

- Training of other bar staff
- Cost control (products, labor)
- Ordering procedures
- Par levels
- Portion control
- Presentation of beverages
- Quality (recipes, service)
- Waste (spills, wrong orders)
- Inventories

Staff members who work in dining service could be evaluated on:

- Training and supervision of other staff members (when applicable).
- Cost control (products, labor).
- Timeliness of greeting guests.
- Sales.
- Accuracy of order-taking.
- Telephone etiquette.
- Secret shopper reports.

- Ability to follow service steps and procedures.
- Completion of side work.
- Appearance.

Areas in which managers or staff members need to improve should be identified, and goals for improvement should be developed. These goals need to be articulated and agreed to by all involved in the evaluation.

Sometimes restaurants utilize secret shoppers to evaluate, among other things, staff member performance. Secret shoppers are individuals who pose as guests and later report back to the restaurant on their experiences. Because secret shoppers experience the operation as an actual guest would, they can help staff members better understand the guest's perspective. Observations by secret shoppers may point to areas in which staff are not doing a good job and may need additional training. Secret shoppers can also help reinforce desirable behavior and boost staff morale by including positive feedback in their reports.

Dealing with Performance Issues

Staff performance issues can range from absenteeism to below standard performance in one or more areas. In any case, it is important for management to deal with those staff members who have performance issues sooner rather than later. To minimize poor performance, service expectations should be made clear during the selection and orientation processes and reinforced during training. They should also be put in writing.

Staff members must understand what the restaurant expects from them and act accordingly. If a staff member's behavior is not aligning with the restaurant's standards and values, the appropriate manager must discuss the situation with the staff member as soon as possible. Additional coaching and training may be necessary; if the problem continues, disciplinary action might be required.

Key Terms

bus tub—A container that is used to carry soiled dishes from the dining room to the dish room.

calling order—The sequence in which servers place drink orders. The specific sequence is necessary because some drinks take more time to prepare than other drinks or do not hold up as well.

china—The plates, bowls, cups, saucers, and serving pieces that a restaurant uses.

city account—The charge account of local hotel customers who are directly billed each month.

condiments—Assorted dressings and spices that are served with a meal. They could include ketchup, mustard, steak sauce, jelly, jam, honey, or syrup. They are usually served in their original containers or in specialty dispensers.

guest check folders—A folder in which guest checks are placed to keep them neat and clean.

house account—The charge account of guests who are staying at a property with approved credit accounts. They can charge restaurant meals and drinks to their room—or the house account.

pre-busing—Removing items throughout the meal from the table that the guest no longer needs.

sidestations—Service areas where supplies are stored. They are stocked with such items as glasses, silverware, and dishes.

sidework checklist—A list of all the sidework that needs to be completed and the staff member who is assigned to complete each task.

standard food and drink abbreviations—Shorthand used by all staff members to indicate specific food and drinks.

suggestive selling—A selling method that encourages guests to buy additional food and beverages.

table-side cart service—A special service where a cart is wheeled up to the table to display desserts, salads, cheese, or tableside cooking.

upselling—A selling method in which staff members suggest more expensive and possibly better quality items to guests.

 ## Review Questions

1. What are some of the ways restaurants attract and retain food and beverage staff?

2. What are some ways that servers can work as a team?

3. What are some of the duties of servers?

4. What are some of the ways that guests can settle checks?

5. How can buspersons work as a team with servers and others to provide great guest service?

6. What are some of the duties of buspersons?

7. What are some desirable personality traits for restaurant managers?

8. How might restaurant managers evaluate staff performance?

 ## Case Studies

Hobson's Choice: Finding the Best Server for the Job

Bill Hobson, general manager of McFitzhugh's, an independent, casual-dining restaurant, was working late on a Thursday night, reviewing the interview notes he had gathered for a server opening he had to fill right away. On Monday, his assistant manager, Gretchen Jensen, conducted the first round of interviews and eliminated seven of the applicants. This morning he personally interviewed the remaining three candidates and this afternoon he asked the staff who had met them for their own impressions. Bill had told each candidate that he would let them know his decision by three o'clock Friday afternoon.

But the decision was not as easy as he had anticipated. Each candidate had arrived for the interviews well-groomed, well-dressed, and on time. They all had either some restaurant experience or hospitality education. Even so, none was an obvious choice for the job; each person came with his or her own strong points and weak points. Bill hoped that by going over his second-interview notes one more time he would at last be able to make a decision.

Because service skills and availability already seemed a given for these three candidates, Bill had focused on a series of questions designed to find out how well each applicant would fit in with the McFitzhugh's team. How well would they hold up under pressure? Were they able to laugh at themselves? Did they have a guest-friendly, team-friendly personality? To find out, he had developed four specific questions:

1. How well do you think you work with people?

    Although most of the McFitzhugh's team is made up of people under the age of 25, they have various education, family, and lifestyle backgrounds. They don't all share the same work ethic. Yet, when they are on the job, everyone has to work smoothly together if they're going to successfully serve their guests. There's no room for lone rangers or prima donnas.

2. What's the funniest thing that has happened to you in the last week?

    Bill knew that some people scoffed at the importance of a sense of humor, but he had found that a positive and constructive sense of humor can be an invaluable asset when problems or stressful situations arise. And guests enjoy a pleasant, smiling server who can laugh along with them.

3. Can you tell me about a time when you weren't treated fairly? What did you do?

    The answer to this question would help Bill know whether the applicant could be cool under pressure—such as when the kitchen makes a mistake on an order, when two servers are out sick on a busy night, or when guests refuse to be pleasant no matter what you do.

4. Has your personality ever helped you out of a tough situation?

    Over the years, Bill had hired more than his share of job applicants who described themselves as "people persons," but were unable to relate well with people who spoke, dressed, or acted differently than they did. When high-tension situations arose, they were flustered—or worse. McFitzhugh's needed servers who could relate well to a wide variety of guests and co-workers and diffuse even difficult situations comfortably.

Now Bill turned to the notes Gretchen had prepared for him after her initial interviews.

Applicant 1, Preston Clark, had impressed Gretchen with his knowledge of the hospitality industry. "This guy knows more of the terminology than I do!" she wrote on a page in the same folder with his application. He was currently a student in the hospitality program of a local community college, and his professors had nothing but glowing comments about his academic proficiency. He had no previous hospitality experience, although he emphasized his position as a "movie theater clerk" on his application.

Applicant 2, Gwen Farrell, had told Gretchen that she had been a stay-at-home mom since she and her husband moved to town from another state and her son was born. But now she was ready to start earning a second family income again. Previously, she had worked for seven-and-a-half years as a server in a well-known casual-dining franchise in Texas. "Shy and nervous at first," Gretchen had noted, "but soon got comfortable and really opened up."

Applicant 3, Charity Lambert, had graduated from college three years ago and worked as a restaurant server ever since. The details weren't immediately clear on Charity's application, but Gretchen had learned that she had worked at three different restaurants in as many years. "Very bubbly and relaxed," Gretchen penciled in the notes section of the application. "Seems extremely guest-service oriented."

After refreshing his memory about Gretchen's perceptions, Bill shifted his attention to his own interviews from this morning. Studying his notes, he replayed the conversations in his mind.

"Tell me, Preston, how do you think you work with people?"

"Oh, I work great with people," the young man responded. "To be honest, I've never met anyone yet who didn't like working with me."

"Okay," Bill said, taking notes. "If I asked what was the funniest thing that has happened to you in the last week, what would you say?"

"That's easy. It would have to be when Professor Mickelson, who's teaching a seminar on the gaming industry—that's what they call gambling now, you know—anyway, he's telling us something about the win percentage for slot machines, and he got the number wrong! Anyway, I'd been doing some extra reading and looking at sites on the Web, so I knew right away that he had blown it. Everybody else was apparently clueless. So I corrected him in front of the whole class. My friends and I are still laughing about that."

Bill nodded, writing. "Tell me about a time when you weren't treated fairly. What did you do?"

"That's another easy one. Once, I was supposed to work the 4:00 to 10:00 shift at the theater on a Saturday afternoon. I left my house on time, but I ended up getting stopped by a train. So I found a phone, called in, and said I'd be late, and they said 'okay,' but when I finally got there, the manager told me the popcorn machine had to be cleaned. I mean, right! Like nobody else could clean that. I think I got the bum job because I was late, but it wasn't fair."

"So what did you do about it?"

"Well, I cleaned it, of course—but since I was only twenty minutes late, I only worked on it for twenty minutes. It's usually a 45- to 50-minute job, but that's only fair, right?"

Bill went on. "Has your personality ever helped you out of a tough situation?"

"Yes, I believe it has. In one of my classes, we had been divided into teams of seven people each. Well, on my team, three of us seemed to be doing all the work for the whole group. The other four weren't contributing much of anything. So the other two people I was working with were getting really frustrated. They talked about just working on their own thing and letting the other four sink. Since I knew the professor wouldn't go for that, I talked to them, got them to voice their concerns to the other four, and eventually work things out so we could finish the assignment."

Bill turned to his notes on Gwen Farrell, Applicant 2. When he asked how well she worked with people, Gwen noted that she had had some problems working with young people in the past.

"Could you explain?"

She answered that some of her young co-workers had been more concerned about talking with their friends than actually doing their jobs. "I'm sure there are lots of good young people out there, but in my experience they don't always have a good understanding of what it means to deliver great service. Sometimes they just want to be entertained, rather than go the extra mile for excellence."

"What's the funniest thing that happened to you during the last week?" Bill asked next.

"I was waiting in the car to pick up our son from preschool when my husband called on the cell phone. Well, the reception wasn't very good, so he suggested I get out of the car. What I forgot was that I had locked the doors while I was wait-ing—and locking the doors arms the car alarm. I pulled hard on the door handle and set the alarm off. So, my husband is hollering through the static on the phone, my son is coming out of school wondering why his mother is calling all this atten-tion to herself, and someone inside the school was already on the phone to the police!"

Bill next asked Gwen about being treated unfairly, and she mentioned that she had once offered to switch shifts with another server at the restaurant where she used to work. So Gwen worked the other woman's shift and the woman thanked her profusely for trading. But when it came time for her to work Gwen's shift, she said her child was sick and she couldn't do it. "You know, her child probably was sick," Gwen said, "but I felt that she should have worked something out so she could be there. I ended up working that shift for her, but I decided right then and there that, if I ever had a child to look after, I would make arrangements to ensure I met my work responsibilities."

Finally, Bill asked, "Has your personality ever helped you out of a difficult situation?"

"Once I carded a guest who was actually 42! His wallet was out in his car, and he was pretty indignant—not only because he was going to have to go get his I.D., but because I'd even asked for it in the first place. When he came back, I had to smile when I saw his birth date. 'Well,' I told him, 'you sure seem young at heart to me.' Apparently, that was exactly what he wanted to hear. He was a great guest after that."

Now to Applicant 3, Bill thought. Charity Lambert had not made the best first impression. As they shook hands, Bill could not help noticing that she was wearing too much makeup and perfume. But that could easily be adjusted, he told himself.

("Believe me, Bill, she didn't dress like that when I interviewed her," Gretchen had assured him that afternoon.) She did have good experience, though, a bright smile, and an outgoing personality that seemed tailor-made for a restaurant server.

"How well do you think you work with people?" Bill had asked, settling into his four important questions.

"Well, I think I work great with people," Charity said. "I love meeting all the different guests and making sure their visit is a memorable one. In fact, you should probably be aware that lots of guests seem to move with me from restaurant to restaurant. I think I'm good for business."

"What's the funniest thing that's happened to you in the last week or so?"

Charity bit her bottom lip. "That's a tough one. Well, this was probably a month ago, but I was working at Kilby's downtown, and I had this huge tray loaded with an order for a table of six and there was this spill right by the coffee station and—whoosh—down I went! Oh, but now that I think about it, that probably wasn't all that funny at the time."

"Tell me about a time when you weren't treated fairly, and what did you do about it?"

"Wow, these are great questions. Oh, I know. I had this one job where I was working with about five other servers all the time, and they got mad at me because they said I was spending too much time at guests' tables. I don't know what they thought I should have been doing. I mean, the whole point of the job is guest service, right?"

"So what was your response?"

"I just tried to ignore them."

"Has your personality ever helped you out of a tough situation?"

"Well, I don't want to brag, but I think it has. I've heard that traffic cops really like to pick on people who drive red cars, and that's true because they're constantly harassing me about speeding or something. Anyway, when they pull me over, I'm usually able to be charming enough so that they just let me off with a warning instead of a ticket."

Bill set aside the interview notes and applications, leaned back in his chair, and took a deep breath. "Well," he said to himself, "I think that settles it." Leaning forward, he made a notation in his planner to call his new server tomorrow morning.

Discussion Question

1. Based on the information provided, which applicant do you think Bill Hobson hired, and why?

   The following industry experts helped generate and develop this case: Christopher Kibit, C.S.C., Academic Team Leader, Hotel/Motel/Food Management & Tourism Programs, Lansing Community College, Lansing, Michigan; and Jack Nye, General Manager, Applebee's of Michigan, Applebee's International, Inc.

The "Seat of the Pants" Training Program

Tom Madison, an experienced director of food and beverage, has just accepted a position with the Arcadia Hotel, a 400-room, full-service property in a Midwestern city. The hotel was once the leading property in the city, but in recent years has lost the luster that once made it the place to stay. It had been family owned and the property grew tired as the ownership grew older and the younger generation of family members chose other careers.

As of last month, the hotel has new owners who have vowed to restore the property to a level of prominence. Tom Madison is part of that turnaround vision.

The hotel has a 200-seat main dining room, which is adjacent to an 80-seat cocktail lounge. There is a 120-seat coffee shop on the corner of the building, which enjoys considerable off-the-street traffic. There are 12 meeting rooms that can also serve as small banquet rooms in addition to a main ballroom that can accommodate up to 1,000 guests.

One of the first things Tom notices is that many of the food and beverage employees have been with the hotel for a number of years. The oldest employee is 80 years old and was recently honored on her 50th anniversary of employment with the hotel. In reviewing the records, Tom estimates the average age of the employees to be 40 to 50 years, and the average time of employment to be 12 years.

The financial records show that profitability of the food and beverage operations has been declining, except for the corner coffee shop. Tom knows that the average occupancy of the hotel has also been steadily declining from an 80-percent level ten years ago to the 60-percent level currently.

Tom calls a meeting of the supervisors that report to him—the executive chef, chief steward, kitchen manager, dining room manager, and head bartender. He asks them to tell him about the training programs that are in use so that new employees can be trained properly and current employees can be updated.

His request is met with silence and no one makes eye contact with him. "Well," he says, "do you want me to repeat the question?"

After five seconds or so, Delores, the dining room manager, says, "We don't really have a training program per se. When we have a new employee, we just have someone show the new person around, where things are, how to do something, and tell the person to ask any of us any questions he or she may have. We are all willing to help." The other meeting attendees all nod in agreement with Delores.

Tom thanks Delores for her input but thinks, "That's totally unacceptable. No wonder this hotel is going downhill. I'd better start formulating a training program for the food and beverage department."

Discussion Questions

1. How does Tom go about establishing a training program? Who should he talk to?

2. Does he need to motivate anyone, and if so how does he do that? Will there be resistance? Will there be a fallout?

3. What are the benefits of establishing a training program?

This case was taken from William P. Fisher and Robert A. Ashley, *Case Studies in Commercial Food Service Operations* (Lansing, Mich.: American Hotel & Lodging Educational Institute, 2003).

Adrift in a Sea of Apathy: Putting Dining Room Service Back on Course

Owen O'Brien, a general manager for CJ's, a casual-dining restaurant chain, had a reputation as a troubleshooter with a knack for turning around underperforming units within the chain. That's why corporate headquarters was sending him to the CJ's in Westmont, Illinois, a Chicago suburb. While other Chicago-area CJ's were thriving, the Westmont restaurant posted merely average operational results, and was below standards in a number of areas, particularly service. Given the restaurant's size and location, the company felt the operation should have been performing better than it was. Owen's assignment was to uncover problem areas and implement solutions that would bring the operation up to speed.

Owen decided to spend his first week at the restaurant simply observing staff members and guests and gathering information about the operation, rather than trying to jump in with quick-fix solutions. What he saw was certainly at odds with the glowing staff member and supervisor performance evaluations he had read in preparation for his move. Where was the teamwork, the attention to detail that CJ's stressed in its training? Everyone seemed to be doing just enough to get by.

The Thursday dinner shift was typical of what Owen had witnessed during his first week in Westmont. It wasn't that service was really bad, but the lackluster attitude of the servers contrasted with the upbeat, friendly image called for in CJ's server training manual. One of the more experienced servers, Laura, started out the evening with what Owen considered the best attitude, but as the night wore on, Laura seemed to lose her sparkle. He saw her arguing with another server over by the kitchen, and when the shift supervisor ignored the altercation, Owen walked over to intervene.

"What seems to be the trouble, ladies?" he asked in a calm voice.

"Well, Erin here delivered entrées to my table, but she mixed up everyone's order," said Laura. "If she can't do her job right, she should leave my tables alone."

"But we're supposed to help each other, aren't we?" asked Erin. "I thought we weren't supposed to let orders sit. I've seen you take orders to other servers' tables. Why are you on my case?"

"The problem," snapped Laura, "is that you didn't get the orders right, and that makes me look bad."

"Wait a minute," Owen cut in. "Don't you use the company's pivot point system for taking and delivering orders?"

Erin looked confused, then explained that Ned, her supervisor, had said something about training the newer servers to use that system, but had never gotten around to it. She had been on the job for three months, and figured that it must not be a big deal since it never came up.

Owen commended Erin for her willingness to pitch in with getting orders to tables in a timely fashion, but suggested that she concentrate on her own tables until she and the other newer servers were more fully trained.

Owen learned that Laura had been delayed in picking up the food order because she was explaining to guests at another table that their meal would take longer than expected. Apparently John, the head cook, had taken an order of chicken fajitas meant for Laura's table and had given it to Grace, who had forgotten to place the order for a guest at one of her tables.

"Then shouldn't Grace have been the one to wait?" asked Owen. This was definitely not standard procedure for CJ's, or any other restaurant he knew of, for that matter.

"Oh, John and Grace are an 'item,' so of course she can do no wrong," grumbled Laura. "You'll see what kind of favoritism goes on after you've been here a few more weeks."

Later that evening, as Owen visited at tables and poured coffee for guests, he caught snatches of conversations about mixed-up orders, servers who didn't know—and didn't care—about the specials, and about the futility of having free refills on soft drinks if the servers never seemed to notice when the glasses became empty.

Owen saw Carl, a veteran server, carrying a soda pitcher past a table of diners who were conspicuously rattling the ice cubes in their empty glasses. Thinking Carl just hadn't noticed them, Owen pointed them out. Carl returned to the table and filled the glasses.

"Thanks, Carl," said Owen. "I know that's not your table, and I appreciate your help. At CJ's, it's everyone's job to see that our guests don't go thirsty."

Carl sighed. "Yeah, I know the routine. But I got tired of being the only one doing it. None of the other servers, except maybe Laura, even knows that 'ever-full' soft drinks are a CJ's tradition. I finally decided that if they're not going to do it, then neither am I."

"I can understand your frustration," said Owen. "But perhaps you can be a role model for the others. We need experienced servers like you to show the newer staff members what it means to be a CJ's server."

Carl smiled at the implied compliment. "You know," he told Owen, "it used to be really fun to work here. That's why I came to CJ's. But now, nobody seems to care. Poor Ned is so busy finding new servers to replace the ones who split after two or three months that he barely has time to train them on the basics, much less on the standards I learned when I started here. Confidentially," he whispered, "I think Ned's getting burned out, especially since he's had to be acting manager, until you showed up."

The next day, Owen learned that Ned was not the only one dropping the ball. It was evident during the line check before the 4 p.m. shift that Jeanette, the kitchen manager, was passing on the same slipshod attitude in the kitchen that Ned was conveying to the dining room staff.

Owen watched as Jeanette checked off items on her list with barely a glance at the coolers. She lifted the lids on the steam table as she passed by, stirred the sauces, but neglected temperature and quality checks, including tasting the sauces.

He followed behind, tasting as he went, and made a horrible face as he tried the sweet-and-sour sauce.

After the line check was completed, Owen motioned Jeanette away from the kitchen and told her in a low voice that the sweet-and-sour sauce tasted like it was made with salt instead of sugar.

"Oh, no, not again. Julie must be working today," said Jeanette. "It looked fine to me."

"That just emphasizes how important it is to taste the sauces," said Owen. "And what do you mean, 'not again'?"

She explained that at least twice before, Julie had mistaken salt for sugar in that sauce. When Owen commented that he hadn't seen any mention of that on Julie's performance evaluation, Jeanette just shrugged.

"It's tough enough keeping cooks who'll work well with John. I find it's easier to overlook minor things like this than risk losing them over a poor evaluation," she said.

"But we risk losing guests if we serve them inedible food," Owen replied. "And it's not fair to Julie to let her think she's doing a good job if she's not. Please have her prepare a new batch of sweet-and-sour sauce—I don't want this going out to guests."

Owen left the kitchen and joined Ned and the servers at their preshift meeting. Ned was reading off the evening's specials and Owen heard him say, "It's that chicken pasta thing corporate's trying to push on us. Try to make a big deal about it, if you want to." Two of the servers were talking throughout Ned's description of the dish, and Owen doubted they'd be able to "make a big deal" about the special to their guests, if they even bothered to try after Ned's less-than-enthusiastic presentation.

As Ned assigned workstations for the night, Owen saw another storm brewing as Erin complained that Ned was once again giving Laura the best section.

"She always gets the best tables, so she always gets the best tips," Erin whined.

Laura retorted, "Did you ever think that maybe it's because I give the best service?"

"Well, that's not my fault," said Erin. "Maybe if I'd had the training you got, I'd be as good as you. I'm doing the best job I know how."

Owen stepped in. "An argument is not the best way to start a shift. Let's all do the best jobs you can at the stations you've been assigned tonight. After the weekend, I'd like to sit down and hear your ideas for how we might do things better. You know I've called an all-staff-member meeting for Monday, and I'd like everyone to bring at least one idea to share, or you can write down your suggestions if you can't make it. I've got some ideas of my own, but I'd like to know what you think needs to be done, too."

Owen asked Ned if he could meet with him privately before the meeting, then returned to the kitchen to remind Jeanette about Monday's brainstorming session.

Discussion Questions

1. What are some of the problem areas at the Westmont CJ's restaurant?

2. What are some possible causes of these problems?

3. What steps can Owen take immediately to start to turn around operations at CJ's?

4. What long-term strategies could be implemented to turn around operations at CJ's?

The following industry experts helped generate and develop this case: Christopher Kibit, C.S.C., Academic Team Leader, Hotel/Motel/Food Management & Tourism Programs, Lansing Community College, Lansing, Michigan; and Jack Nye, General Manager, Applebee's of Michigan, Applebee's International, Inc.

 # References

Berta, Dina. "Efforts Grow to Boost Staff Morale Amid Tight Economy: Perks Like Free Food, Awards Aid HR Goals." *Nation's Restaurant News* 42, no. 37 (September 22, 2008).

Erickson, Joe. "Training for the Front Line: The Fundamentals of an Effective Server Training Program." *Restaurant Startup & Growth* 5, no. 4 (April 2008).

Goldstein, Jay. "8 Simple Points for Making Good Hiring Choices." *Restaurant Startup & Growth* 5, no. 4 (April 2008).

Hauswirth, William F. "Know Your Employees." *Restaurant Hospitality* 91, no. 1 (January 1, 2009).

Laube, Jim. "Dominant Traits: 10 Common Practices and Characteristics of Successful Independent Restaurant Operators." *Restaurant Startup & Growth* 5, no. 1 (February 2008).

Luebke, Patricia. "Handle Your New Employees with Care (or You'll Be Doing a Lot More Hiring)." *Restaurant Startup & Growth* 5, no. 7 (July 2008).

———. "Help! I've Hired the Wrong Person." *Restaurant Startup & Growth* (March 2007).

———. "Management 101." *Restaurant Startup & Growth* 11, no. 5 (November 2008).

———. "Management 101." *Restaurant Startup & Growth* 6, no. 6 (June 2009).

———. "Management 101…Secret Shoppers." *Restaurant Startup & Growth* 7, no. 5 (July 2008).

———. "Managing People." *Restaurant Startup & Growth* 11, no. 5 (November 2008).

———. "No Fly Zone: Make Sure Your Restaurant Buzzes with Business, Not Flies." *Restaurant Startup & Growth* (August 2006).

———. "Recruit, Don't Just Select." *Restaurant Startup & Growth* (March 2007).

———. "Service vs. Sustenance: Polite Waiters Trump Good Cuisine." *Restaurant Startup & Growth* (November 2007).

———."The Three Dumbest Things Your Servers Are Saying." *Restaurant Startup & Growth*. (July 2007).

Mullen, Rosalind. "Time for Training." *Caterer & Hotelkeeper* (January 13, 2005).

Simos, Pam. "How to Create a Sales Culture." *Restaurant Hospitality* 90, no. 6 (June 2006).

Sullivan, Jim. "Recruiting the Right Seasonal Staff is Essential for Successful Sales and Seamless Execution." *Nation's Restaurant News* 43, no. 16 (May 4, 2009).

Tripoli, Chris. "A Real Bonus: Management Incentives That Work." *Restaurant Startup & Growth* 5, no. 11 (November 2008).

Internet Sites

For more information, visit the following Internet sites. Remember that Internet addresses can change without notice. If the site is no longer there, you can use a search engine to look for additional sites.

American Hotel & Lodging Association
www.ahla.com

Restaurant Marketing Group
www.rmktgroup.com

GfK MRI
www.mediamark.com

Waiter Training
www.waiter-training.com

National Restaurant Association
www.restaurant.org

Appendix

Service Techniques	American System					European System			
	Plate	Platter	Cart	Family-Style	Butler	Plate	Platter	French or Butler	Side Table
Service to the left of the guest									
• Platters presented to guest/host		•			•	•		•	
• Plates held with left hand, served with left hand	•								
• Platters carried on left forearm		•			•		•	•	
• Move counterclockwise	•	•	•	•	•	•	•	•	•
• Fingerbowl (placed above dinner fork)	•					•			
• Food served with spoon and fork in right hand of servers		•					•		
• Guest serves self with spoon and fork					•			•	
• Serve bread and butter	•	•	•			•	•	•	
• Serve salad (as side dish)	•	•	•			•	•	•	
• Crumb table	•	•	•	•		•	•	•	
• Clear salad plate	•	•	•	•		•	•	•	
• Clear B & B plate	•	•	•	•		•	•	•	
• Food plated on guerdon			•						
• Soup	•								
Service to the right of the guest									
• Set hot or cold plates (movement clockwise)			•			•		•	•
• Clear plates	•	•	•	•		•	•	•	•
• Change flatware	•	•	•	•		•	•	•	•
• Move clockwise	•	•	•	•		•	•	•	•
• Pour beverages	•	•	•	•		•	•	•	•
• Present wine bottles	•	•	•	•		•	•	•	•
• Soup						•	•	•	•
• Food plates held and served with right hand			•			•			

(continued)

Appendix *(continued)*

Service Techniques *(continued)*	American System					European System			
	Plate	Platter	Cart	Family-Style	Butler	Plate	Platter	French or Butler	Side Table
Service performed near table									
• Food is cooked in kitchen and finished at tableside			•						
• Food is carved/boned for plating			•						•
• Food is finished on rechaud (stove)			•						•
• Food is plated from silver platter			•						•
• Two hands (fork and spoon) used to plate food			•						•
Service performed by guests									
• Side dishes, sauces, and vegetable on table to pass				•				•	
• Meat carved and plated by host and served by butler or passed by guest				•					

Task Breakdowns: Dining Service

The procedures presented in this section are for illustrative purposes only and should not be construed as recommendations or standards. While these procedures are typical, readers should keep in mind that each food and beverage operation has its own procedures, equipment specifications, and safety policies.

RESTAURANT SERVER: *Stock and Maintain Side Stations*

Materials needed: A sidework checklist, glasses, silverware, dishes, napkins, condiments, garnishes, cleaning cloths, a bar towel, sanitizing solution, and gloves.

STEPS	HOW-TO'S
1. Stock the side stations.	❑ The items that need to be stocked vary among properties. Items should be stocked at par levels. A "par" is the number of supplies you will need to get through one workshift.
	❑ If you used items from your side stations when you checked your tables, replace these items so that the side stations are fully stocked for service.
	❑ Side stations should be completely stocked with items such as glasses, silverware, and dishes before a new shift begins.
	❑ Bring clean glasses, silverware, and dishes from the dish room to replace the used ones.
	❑ Fold extra napkins.
	❑ Make sure there is always a fresh supply of condiments at the side stations.
	❑ Make sure there is a bucket of sanitizing solution and a clean cloth at each side station.
2. Maintain the stations throughout your shift.	❑ Check the sidework checklist to see which tasks you are responsible for. A sidework checklist lists sidework and the restaurant server who is assigned to complete each task. Common sidework tasks include folding napkins and wiping service trays.
	❑ Perform your assigned sidework duties throughout your shift. Sidework tasks are a very important part of keeping your restaurant running well.

RESTAURANT SERVER: *Stock and Maintain Side Stations* (continued)

STEPS	HOW-TO'S
	❑ Wipe up spills, bread crumbs, etc., as soon as possible.
	❑ Pick up broken glass with a linen napkin or gloves to prevent cuts. Throw away broken glass in the proper container.
	❑ Throw away wilted or discolored garnishes. Wash and dry the garnish container. Refill the container with fresh garnishes as needed.
	❑ Empty used ice buckets and wipe them out with a bar towel. Store them until they are needed.
	❑ Ask buspersons or stewards to empty full trash cans for you.
	❑ Check the side stations throughout the meal period. Work with the busperson assigned to each station to restock the area as needed.
	❑ Keep side station supplies and equipment orderly.
3. Clean the side stations.	❑ Take soiled items to the dish room. Wipe the shelves and countertop with a clean, damp cloth and a sanitizing solution.
	❑ Keep the cleaning cloth in the sanitizing solution when you are not using it.
	❑ Change the sanitizing solution periodically throughout your shift.
	❑ Throughout service, clean side stations as needed and as your time permits.
	❑ Do not overlook the needs of guests while maintaining the side stations.
	❑ Work as a team with buspersons to complete all tasks.

RESTAURANT SERVER: *Greet and Seat Guests*

Materials needed: Menus, special supplies (such as booster seats, highchairs, braille menus), snacks, and a wine list.

STEPS	HOW-TO'S
1. Approach guests who are waiting to be seated.	❑ Smile and give a warm greeting, such as "Good morning!" or "Welcome to (name of the restaurant)." ❑ Be positive when greeting guests. Your manner will affect guest satisfaction.
2. Direct guests to the coatroom if your restaurant has one.	❑ Do not take responsibility for guests' coats, packages, or other articles.
3. Ask guests if you are holding a reservation for them.	❑ The steps to record in the reservations book, either paper or electronic, that a party has arrived vary among properties. ❑ If guests do not have a reservation, ask them if anyone else will be joining them. Then check available seating to see if you can accommodate them.
4. Accommodate special guest needs.	❑ Ask guest with visual impairments if they would like braille menus, if they are available. ❑ Ask guests with disabilities if they have special seating needs. A guest in a wheelchair may prefer to sit in a chair. ❑ Ask guests with small children if they would like a highchair or a booster seat. ❑ Ask the busperson to rearrange tables or to set up special equipment if necessary. ❑ If necessary, ask the party to wait while you meet their needs.

RESTAURANT SERVER: *Greet and Seat Guests*
(continued)

STEPS	HOW-TO'S
5. Look at the seating chart and decide where you are going to seat the party, according to your restaurant's seating policies.	❏ Overloading one section will make good service difficult. However, if a party requests a certain table and it is available, you should seat them at that table, even if it overloads a section. Then tell the dining room manager so he or she can adjust the server's workload. Also, let the server for that section know about the guests.
6. Direct guests to their table.	❏ Pick up enough menus for each guest, plus one wine list, if appropriate.
	❏ Ask the party to follow you, and lead the way to the table at a reasonable pace.
	❏ Hold the menus high on your arm, not down by your side.
	❏ Stand up straight and give your full attention to the party you are seating. Do not stop along the way to talk to co-workers unless it relates to seating the party you are leading.
	❏ Move service equipment to one side to clear a path for the guests. Make sure the party is following.
	❏ As you walk, describe restaurant highlights, such as a salad bar, buffets, or house specials.
7. Help the guests with seating.	❏ Help children get into booster seats. Pull highchairs away from tables so that guests can place small children into them. Never touch a child—or any other guest—unless you have permission
	❏ Help guests with disabilities as appropriate. If you're not sure how to help, ask guests what you can do for them.

(continued)

RESTAURANT SERVER: *Greet and Seat Guests*
(continued)

STEPS	HOW-TO'S
	❑ Pull out a chair for a guest and adjust the chair as the guest sits. Help others with seating as appropriate. Let the guests decide who will sit in the chair you pull out.
8. Present the menus.	❑ Give a closed menu, right-side-up, to each guest in the following order: • Children (children's menu when available) • Women • Men
	❑ Present the menu from the guest's right side, using your right hand.
	❑ The procedures for when and how to present menus vary among properties.
	❑ Hand the wine list to the host of the party if there is one. If not, place the wine list on the table.
	❑ Introduce yourself and tell guests who their server will be.
	❑ Serve water (if appropriate) and items such as crackers, bread sticks, or other snacks (if appropriate).
9. Remove extra place settings.	

RESTAURANT SERVER: *Take Food Orders*

Materials needed: An order pad or guest checks and a pen.

STEPS	HOW-TO'S
1. Tell guests about specials.	❏ Know the daily specials. If appropriate at your restaurant, try to taste each one. ❏ Always describe specials and chef's choice items, such as the soup of the day, before guests ask. ❏ Describe the ingredients and the preparation of specials in an appealing way. Always give the price of specials.
2. Ask for the food order.	❏ Offer to help guests with menu selections. Answer any questions about the menu. ❏ Ask if they are ready to order.
3. Follow an order-taking system.	❏ Know the numbering system for the chairs at each table. Chair #1 at each table is typically the chair closest to the door or some other landmark in your restaurant. By taking orders in a standard clockwise fashion, you make it possible for someone else to serve your guests without having to ask who ordered what. ❏ When writing orders on your order pad or guest check, write the order for the guest in chair #1 on the first line of the order form. Remember that the chair numbers identify each seat at the table. They don't stand for the order in which you'll write things down. ❏ Take the orders of children first, then women, and then men. Write their orders in the corresponding places on the order pad. For instance, if the guest in chair #2 is the only woman at the table, take her order first and write it on line #2 on the order pad.

(continued)

RESTAURANT SERVER: *Take Food Orders* (continued)

STEPS	HOW-TO'S
	❑ Your supervisor will show you abbreviations and other tips for writing food orders that will be understood by everyone who works at the restaurant.
	❑ Continue to take food orders in a clockwise pattern around the table.
4. Stand in the correct position to take orders.	❑ The place where you stand to take orders may be one of the following: • In different positions around the table so you can speak one-on-one to each guest. • In one position to get the attention of the entire table so that everyone can hear your suggestive selling. • It depends on the table and the guests.
	❑ Always stand up straight as you take orders. Do not rest the order pad on the table or sit down at the table with guests.
	❑ Look at each guest when he or she is ordering. Watch for hesitation in making a decision. This provides you an opening to offer a suggestion.
5. Ask the appropriate questions.	❑ Pay attention to details and know your menu thoroughly. Try not to sound mechanical when describing choices. Make every item sound good.
	❑ Know what questions to ask for each item to determine the guests' choices. For instance, know if a guest must choose soup or salad. If you don't ask the right questions when taking the order, you will have to interrupt your guests to find out necessary preparation and service information. This is embarrassing to you and annoying to your guest.
	❑ Repeat each completed order to the guest, especially if there are special details or requests regarding preparation or service.

RESTAURANT SERVER: *Take Food Orders* (continued)

STEPS	HOW-TO'S
6. Suggest additional courses.	❑ Suggest additional courses such as appetizers, soups, and salads when you take the food order. By suggesting additional items, you can enhance the dining experience, increase revenue for the restaurant, and increase your tips. ❑ Think about what the guest has selected and suggest items that will go well with the entree.
7. Suggest a bottle of wine.	❑ Try to sell a bottle of wine after taking the food order. If guests are celebrating a special occasion such as a birthday, anniversary, or other celebration, they may want to have wine or champagne with their meal. ❑ Know which wines will go well with certain foods. ❑ Always know how much alcohol your guests are drinking. Don't suggest wine or other alcoholic beverages if your guests are intoxicated or are close to becoming intoxicated.
8. Try to meet special requests.	❑ Some guests may request that an item be prepared in a way not listed on the menu. ❑ Write all special requests on your order pad and tell the kitchen staff about the requests when you place the order. ❑ You may need to check with the chef or your supervisor before making a promise to a guest.

(continued)

RESTAURANT SERVER: *Take Food Orders* (continued)

STEPS	HOW-TO'S
9. Ask if guests would like another beverage.	❑ Check on drink levels. Suggest another drink if a beverage is one-half to three-fourths empty and guests are not nearing intoxication. ❑ If guests are drinking alcoholic beverages but do not want another, suggest a nonalcoholic beverage. ❑ Clear empty glasses before serving new beverages.
10. Collect the menus and wine list, if you haven't already done so.	
11. Tidy the table to keep it as fresh as possible.	
12. Pre-ring the food order.	❑ The steps to pre-ring orders vary among restaurants. ❑ Food checks must be rung into the point-of-sale unit before the kitchen will prepare any food.
13. Place food orders with the kitchen.	❑ The steps to place an order with the kitchen vary among restaurants. ❑ Special orders may require speaking with the chef. Always be polite and limit conversations to a minimum when possible.

RESTAURANT SERVER: *Serve the Meal*

Materials needed: An order pad or guest check, a service tray, and condiments.

STEPS	HOW-TO'S
1. Time the preparation of the food.	❑ The timing of food preparation is important to a smooth dining experience. Each guest in a party should be served at the same time.
	❑ Turn in the order for each course when guests are about three-fourths finished with the previous one. If the kitchen is busy, turn in the orders sooner.
	❑ Serve courses in the following order, unless guests request a different order: • Appetizers • Soup • Salads • Entrees • Dessert • Cordials • Coffee
	❑ Check with the cook or your supervisor if you are concerned that an order is not being prepared in a reasonable amount of time. Don't make guests wait without an explanation from you or your supervisor. If there is a problem with a guest's order, do not avoid the table. Guests appreciate knowing what's going on.
	❑ If you are too busy to pick up an order as soon as it is ready, ask another restaurant server for help.
2. Prepare the table for each course before serving it.	❑ Clear any empty plates or glasses from the guest's right with your right hand. Always ask guests if they are finished.
	❑ Wait to clear glasses or plates until more than one guest at a table is finished so guests who are still eating or drinking do not feel rushed.

(continued)

RESTAURANT SERVER: *Serve the Meal* (continued)

STEPS	HOW-TO'S
	❑ Never stack dirty plates in front of guests. Pick them up separately and stack them away from guests.
	❑ Bring all condiments and accompaniments to the table before serving the order. You shouldn't have to set food under a heat lamp or on your tray while you collect condiments.
	❑ Only bring full—not partially full—condiment bottles to guests.
	❑ If you will be serving an item that guests will share, bring a plate for each guest.
3. Pick up the food order.	❑ The steps to pick up food orders may vary among restaurants.
	❑ Planning and organization will make it possible for you to serve all of your guests quickly.
	❑ Check the food before you take it out of the kitchen: • Does the food look fresh and appealing? • Have all preparation instructions been followed? • Is the presentation garnished? • Have all special requests been met? • Is the plate clean? • Is hot food hot and cold food cold?
	❑ Ask the cook to make any corrections necessary to meet the restaurant's food standards.
	❑ Notify your supervisor immediately of any problem in the food preparation so that he or she can speak to the guests and correct the situation.
	❑ If you are having trouble meeting guest needs, ask your supervisor or another server for help until you can catch up.

RESTAURANT SERVER: *Serve the Meal* (continued)	

STEPS	HOW-TO'S
	❑ Don't let the guests suffer because you are busy.
	❑ Thank the kitchen staff for their cooperation.
4. Deliver food.	❑ The way food is delivered may be by:
	• Using a tray draped with a napkin
	• Using a tray without a napkin
	❑ Use your order pad or guest check to help remember who ordered what. You shouldn't have to ask the guests. Good service is so smooth that the guests are hardly aware of you. When you are able to serve each course without asking questions, guests are not interrupted.
	❑ Serve the children first, women next, then men, and the host last.
	❑ Serve food from the guest's left side with your left hand whenever possible. Don't reach in front of guests.
	❑ Place the plate with the first course on top of the base plate, if a base plate is included in your restaurant's table setting.
	❑ Place the entree plate so that the main item is closest to the guest.
	❑ Place side dishes to the left of the entree plate.
	❑ If a guest asks for something extra (e.g., more sauce, extra fresh lemons), deliver it as quickly as possible so that the meal does not get cold.
	❑ Ask if guests would like you to bring or do anything else for them at this time.
	❑ Remove empty beverage glasses.

RESTAURANT SERVER: *Settle Guest Checks and Thank Guests*

Materials needed: A guest check, a guest check folder, a credit card voucher, a credit card imprint machine, and a pen.

STEPS	HOW-TO'S
1. Settle guest checks paid by cash.	❑ The steps to settle guest checks paid by cash vary among restaurants. ❑ Do not ask: "Do you need change?" ❑ Present change in the guest check folder. Do not claim a tip until guests leave. If the guest leaves while you are settling the check, the change is your tip. ❑ Always provide a receipt with the change.
2. Settle guest checks paid by traveler's check.	❑ Ask the guest to sign the traveler's check in your presence. ❑ Ask to see a driver's license if the guest signed the check when you were not present. ❑ If the signatures do not match, calmly report the problem to your supervisor. ❑ The steps to keep a record of traveler's checks vary among restaurants. ❑ Always put the receipt and any change in the guest check folder and give it to the guest.
3. Settle guest checks paid by credit card.	❑ Get an approval code. ❑ If a credit card is declined, politely ask the guest for another card or form of payment. If necessary, ask the guest to step away from his or her group so that he or she will not be embarrassed. ❑ Imprint the card on the back of the guest check and on a credit card voucher. ❑ Underline the account number and the expiration date on the imprint. If the card has expired, return it and ask for another form of payment.

RESTAURANT SERVER: *Settle Guest Checks and Thank Guests* (continued)

STEPS	HOW-TO'S
	❑ Complete the voucher. Enter the date, your name, the guest check number, which credit card is being used, the approval code, and the amount of the purchase.
	❑ Present the voucher and a pen to the guest in a guest check folder. Ask the guest to total and sign the voucher.
	❑ Make sure the voucher is totaled and signed.
	❑ Return the card along with the guest's copy of the credit card voucher.
4. Settle guest checks charged to house accounts (for food and beverage operations in hotels).	❑ Ask guests to print their names and room numbers on the guest checks and to sign them. Guests who are staying at the property with approved credit accounts may charge restaurant meals and drinks to their room. This is called a "house account."
	❑ Ask guests to present their room keys as identification, unless the point-of-sale unit verifies occupancy.
5. Settle guest checks charged to city ledger accounts (for food and beverage operations in hotels).	❑ Ask guests to print the company name or group name on the check. Some local guests may have charge accounts. This allows them to be directly billed each month. Such local accounts are called "city ledger accounts."
	❑ Ask guests to provide the city ledger account number.
	❑ Ask guests to sign the guest check.
	❑ Verify with the front office staff that guests who don't know the account number are authorized. Get the account number from the front office.
	❑ Give guests a receipt showing the charge.

(continued)

RESTAURANT SERVER: *Settle Guest Checks and Thank Guests* (continued)

STEPS	HOW-TO'S
6. Settle guest checks paid by personal check.	
7. Settle checks paid by coupon, voucher, or gift certificate.	❑ Read the document carefully to determine if it is valid and unexpired. Find out what charges are covered. Many restaurants do not give change for gift certificates and coupons. However, guests may receive smaller gift certificates in place of change.
	❑ Make sure your restaurant accepts the coupon or other documents presented. Know your restaurant's policy for each type of coupon, voucher, or gift certificate.
	❑ Treat the document as cash if it is valid. Collect the balance of the account if the document doesn't cover the full amount.
	❑ Always put the receipt and any change or gift certificates in the guest check folder and give it to the guest.
8. Thank the guest when you return the change and receipt, and invite the guest to return.	
9. Inform security and your manager immediately if a guest leaves without settling the bill.	

RESTAURANT SERVER: *Perform Closing Sidework*

Materials needed: *A closing duty checklist, a clean kitchen funnel, cleaning cloths, a condiment requisition, clean silverware, water pitchers, and a bar towel.*

STEPS	HOW-TO'S
1. Consult your closing duty checklist.	
2. Remove soiled linens.	❑ Check side stations and the entire dining room for scattered soiled linens.
3. Store condiments.	❑ Remove condiments from the side stations and return them to the kitchen pantry. Combining condiments reduces costs and improves the appearance of the condiment containers. But only combine condiments if your local health department allows it.
	❑ Use a clean kitchen funnel to combine each type of condiment. Wipe the containers with a damp cleaning cloth before storing them.
	❑ Complete a condiment requisition for the next day. Order enough condiments to bring stock back to par levels.
4. Store bread and butter.	❑ Return unused butter and unserved rolls or bread to the kitchen. The chef will decide if the bread will be saved for future use or thrown away. Unserved bread is sometimes used for making other items, such as croutons or stuffing.
	❑ Follow sanitation rules in judging what to save and what to throw out.
	❑ Place unserved butter in the proper kitchen cooler.
5. Restock silverware.	❑ Take soiled silverware to the dish room. Follow dish room procedures for unloading soiled silverware.
	❑ Pick up clean silverware from the dish room and restock the side station

(continued)

RESTAURANT SERVER: *Perform Closing Sidework*
(continued)

STEPS	HOW-TO'S
6. Break down the coffee station.	❑ Empty all coffeepots into an approved sink. ❑ Throw away coffee grounds. Rinse the grounds holder and return it to the coffee maker. ❑ Take coffeepots to the dish room for washing. ❑ Throw away open cream or cream that has been out of the refrigerator too long. ❑ Return all other cream to the correct kitchen cooler. ❑ Store all unused coffee filter packs. ❑ Wipe the coffee maker and the surrounding area with a clean, damp cloth. ❑ Clean the nozzle head on the grounds holder, and clean the area around the nozzle head.
7. Break down ice buckets.	❑ Remove corks, foil scraps, labels, and other debris from buckets to avoid plugging drains. ❑ Empty ice and water into the appropriate sink. ❑ Return empty wine and champagne bottles to the bar for inventory. ❑ Dry the ice buckets with a bar towel. ❑ Store buckets in the designated side station.
8. Break down water pitchers.	❑ Empty ice and water into an appropriate sink. ❑ Take pitchers to the dish room for washing. Pitchers should be washed and sanitized between meal periods. ❑ Restock the side stations with clean pitchers.

RESTAURANT SERVER: *Perform Closing Sidework*
(continued)

STEPS	HOW-TO'S
9. Reset all tables.	❑ Follow table setup polices for the next meal period.
	❑ In a restaurant with tablecloth dinner service and place mat breakfast service, do not strip and reset tables for breakfast while guests are still seated in the area.
	❑ Clear the table down to the tablecloth and centerpiece, and wait to reset the table until the guests leave.
	❑ Turn glasses upside-down so they will not collect dust.
	❑ Check the appearance of each table to be sure it is complete.
10. Straighten, clean, and restock all side stations.	❑ Restock side stations after the rest of the area has been cleared.
	❑ Remove all soiled equipment and restock with clean dishes, silverware, and glassware. Leave everything in spotless condition at the end of your shift.

BUSPERSON: *Set Up the Restaurant for Service*

Materials needed: *A pen, an opening duty checklist, a vacuum cleaner, caution signs, cleaning cloths, brass polish, and a blinds duster.*

STEPS	HOW-TO'S
1. Pick up and store restaurant linens.	
2. Dust wine displays.	❑ Carefully remove each wine bottle and wipe it with a clean, dry cloth. Do not use a wet cloth. Dusty wine racks and bottles ruin the effect of the wine display. A wet cloth will damage the label. ❑ Return each bottle to its original location.
3. Polish brass.	❑ Use approved brass polish, and a soft cloth. ❑ Apply polish and rub the brass to remove tarnish and spots. Buff with a soft, dry cloth. ❑ Never use steel wool or other abrasive materials on brass.
4. Adjust drapes and blinds.	❑ Check drapes to be sure they are hanging neatly. Adjust them to give the best appearance. ❑ Set blinds based on the angle of the sun to ensure guest comfort. ❑ Use a special blinds duster to clean blinds as needed. This helps maintain the restaurant's image. ❑ Report any food residue or stains on drapes or blinds to the restaurant manager so that cleaning can be scheduled with the housekeeping department.
5. Vacuum carpeted areas.	❑ Place caution signs. ❑ Empty the vacuum cleaner bag if necessary. ❑ Use a damp cloth followed by a dry cloth to remove spills before vacuuming. Do not use a linen napkin to clean up spills. Use only designated cloths or cleaning towels.

BUSPERSON: *Set Up the Restaurant for Service*
(continued)

STEPS	HOW-TO'S
	❑ Report stained or damaged upholstery or carpeting to your supervisor.
	❑ Unwind the cord and plug the vacuum cleaner into an outlet near the door. Make sure the cord is out of the way so that no one trips. To avoid being shocked, do not stand in water when plugging in the vacuum cleaner.
	❑ Begin vacuuming at the far side of the room and work toward the main entrance.
	❑ Move tables and chairs as needed.
	❑ Pay special attention to room corners, carpet edges, high-traffic areas, and areas under booths or banquettes. Careful vacuuming improves the restaurant's appearance and reduces problems with pests and rodents.
	❑ Vacuum booth seats and upholstered chairs if necessary.
	❑ Unplug the vacuum and carefully wind the cord.
	❑ Empty the vacuum cleaner bag if needed.
	❑ Store the vacuum cleaner as soon as you finish vacuuming to prevent accidents.
	❑ Report carpet or equipment problems to your supervisor.
6. Adjust the environmental controls in the room.	❑ Adjust heat, ventilation, air conditioning, lighting, music, and other environmental controls if assigned to do so.
	❑ If controls are automatic, do not adjust them unless instructed to do so by a manager.
7. Check off this task on your opening duty checklist.	

BUSPERSON: *Prepare Tables for Service*

Materials needed: *Tablecloths or place mats, cleaning cloths, sanitizing solution, foodservice film, packets of crackers, a broom, a dustpan, a service tray, a tray jack, a dish dolly or cart, napkins, cream, butter, and flowers.*

STEPS	HOW-TO'S
1. Clean tables and chairs.	❑ Clean all tables and chairs before setting up the side station, even if they were cleaned at the end of the previous meal period.
	❑ Wipe tabletops with a damp cloth and sanitizing solution followed by a dry cloth. Clean tabletops before wiping table legs and chairs.
	❑ Wipe the legs, rungs, and bases of the tables with a different cloth. Rinse the cloth as needed.
	❑ Wipe chair seats, backs, legs, and rungs. Wipe booths, banquettes, and any other seats. If possible, pull out seating cushions and wipe up crumbs.
	❑ Check under tables and chairs for gum, and remove any gum you find.
2. Clean children's seating.	❑ Wipe highchair trays with a damp cloth and sanitizing solution and let them air-dry. Children may eat directly from the tray, and parents will appreciate the cleanliness.
	❑ After trays have dried, place two packets of crackers on each tray and wrap each tray with foodservice film.
	❑ Wipe the seats, backs, and legs of highchairs and all children's booster chairs.
	❑ Check that the safety straps on highchairs are clean and in working order. Replace any missing or broken straps.
3. Check floors.	❑ Check under tables for crumbs, food spills, or stains. Sweep up crumbs.
	❑ Use a damp cloth followed by a dry cloth to wipe up spills.

BUSPERSON: *Prepare Tables for Service* (continued)

STEPS	HOW-TO'S
	❑ Report stubborn stains to your supervisor before setting up the station for service.
4. Place tablecloths or place mats.	❑ Setting and resetting tables is a very important duty of the busperson. The guest's first impression of the table is important in setting the tone for a pleasing dining experience.
	❑ Check each new tablecloth or place mat for: • Correct size • Stains • Tears or holes • Unsightly wrinkles
	❑ If place mats are used, make sure the pattern is right-side-up and facing the guest so words on the place mat can be read.
	❑ Line up place mats with the table edge and with the place mats on the opposite side of the table.
	❑ Place the tablecloths on the tables. Make sure they are right-side-up and centered on the tables.
5. Position tabletop items.	❑ Pick up tabletop items from your side station. Get enough of each of the following items to set all tables: • Centerpieces • Salt and pepper shakers and grinders • Sugar bowls • Condiments and cracker baskets
	❑ Check the condition and appearance of each item. Clean or replace any items if necessary.
	❑ Place the items on a service tray. Do not overload the tray. Make as many trips as necessary to safely carry items.

(continued)

BUSPERSON: *Prepare Tables for Service* (continued)

STEPS	HOW-TO'S
	❑ Carry the tray to the dining room and place it on a tray jack.
	❑ Place each item neatly in the center of the table according to standard table setup specifications.
	❑ If you are setting booths or tables that are against the wall, place the items at the end of the tabletop, near the wall.
	❑ Get a rack of clean plates from your side station or the dish room. In fine-dining restaurants, the base plate enhances the appearance of the table and acts as an underliner for cocktails and starter courses.
6. Place base plates (if called for by the meal).	❑ Carry the rack into the dining room. At some restaurants, you will need to empty items from the rack onto a service tray lined with linen napkins before carrying items into the dining room.
	❑ Place the rack on a tray jack. Most dish racks will fit on a tray jack.
	❑ Only use a dish dolly or cart to transport dishes when the restaurant is closed.
	❑ Check each base plate to be sure it is clean and free of water spots, chips, and cracks.
	❑ Return soiled or spotted plates to the dish room. Give chipped or cracked plates to your supervisor.
	❑ Place a base plate directly in front of each chair about two inches from the table edge.
	❑ If the plate has a logo, place the plate so that the guest can read the logo.
	❑ Return empty dish racks, dollies, or carts to the dish room.

BUSPERSON: *Prepare Tables for Service* (continued)

STEPS	HOW-TO'S
7. Place silverware.	❑ Get a rack of clean silverware from your side station or the dish room.
	❑ Carry the rack to the dining room and set it on a tray jack.
	❑ Check each knife, fork, and spoon for cleanliness.
	❑ Return spotted or soiled silverware to the dish room.
	❑ Use a linen napkin to place silverware on the table. Touch the silverware only by the handle.
	❑ If no base plates are called for by the meal, leave a 12-inch space directly in front of each seat.
	❑ Place forks to the left of the base plate or space.
	❑ Place knives to the right of the base plate or space, with the cutting edge of the knife toward the plate or space.
	❑ Place spoons to the right of the knives.
	❑ Leave small spaces between pieces of silverware.
	❑ Line up all silverware handles about two inches from the table edge.
8. Place bread and butter plates.	❑ Get a rack of clean bread and butter plates from your side station or the dish room.
	❑ Carry the rack to the dining room and place it on a tray jack.
	❑ Check each bread and butter plate to be sure it is clean and free of chips or cracks. Return soiled plates to the dish room. Throw away chipped or cracked plates.
	❑ Place bread and butter plates to the left of or above the forks at each place setting.
	❑ Return the empty rack to the dish room.

(continued)

BUSPERSON: *Prepare Tables for Service* (continued)

STEPS	HOW-TO'S
9. Place glassware.	❑ Get racks of clean glasses from your side station or the dish room. ❑ Carry one rack at a time to the dining room. ❑ Place the glassware rack on a tray jack. ❑ Make sure glasses are clean and free of water spots, lipstick, food residue, chips, or cracks. ❑ Return soiled glasses to the dish room. Throw away chipped or cracked glasses. ❑ Place a water glass one-half inch above the tip of the knife blade at each place setting. ❑ Place wine glasses (if appropriate) to the right of and slightly below the water glass. ❑ Return empty racks to the dish room.
10. Fold and place napkins.	❑ Napkins may be folded earlier as an opening sidework duty. ❑ Place one napkin at each place setting.
11. Place cream, butter, flowers, and other perishable items.	
12. Check the overall appearance of the table.	❑ Place each chair so the edge of the seat is even with the table edge. ❑ Step away from the table and view the results. ❑ Make sure place settings are lined up. ❑ Adjust tables and chairs as needed.

BUSPERSON: *Clear and Reset Tables*

Materials needed: A bus tub, a service tray, a tray jack, clean tablecloths and napkins, clean serviceware, cleaning cloths, sanitizing solution, candles or lamp fuel.

STEPS	HOW-TO'S
1. Gather items needed to reset the table.	❑ Place the correct number of place settings, napkins, and other tableware needed to reset the table on a service tray. Get a clean tablecloth if necessary. ❑ Carry the tray to the table and place it on a nearby tray jack. ❑ Always carry a clean, damp cloth when clearing and resetting tables. ❑ Get an empty bus tub.
2. Clear used dishes, silverware, glasses, and linens after guests leave the table.	❑ Clear tables within five minutes of guest departure. It is important that tables are cleared and reset promptly. This makes it possible to seat waiting guests quickly, and it adds to the neat appearance of the dining room. ❑ You may work with the server to clear and reset tables, but if he or she is busy, you should clear and reset the tables yourself. Teamwork is important to the success of the restaurant. ❑ Scrape food and debris from dishes into a bus tub. ❑ Do not scrape plates in view of guests. Work with your back to nearby guests to shield them from seeing the clearing process. ❑ Place soiled dishes in the bus tub. Carefully stacking dishes will help prevent breakage. ❑ Stack like items together. ❑ Clear tables as quietly as possible. ❑ Sort used linens. Place the soiled linens in the bus tub.

(continued)

BUSPERSON: *Clear and Reset Tables* (continued)	
STEPS	**HOW-TO'S**
	❑ Remove any silverware, small dishes, or glasses from the liners and place them in the bus tubs.
3. Clean the table.	❑ If tables don't have tablecloths, clean and sanitize the tabletops. There should be sanitizing solution at each side station.
	❑ Always use a clean, damp cloth to wipe tabletops and condiment containers.
	❑ Wipe under condiment containers and the centerpiece.
	❑ Wipe the condiment containers that will be left on the table.
4. Replace tablecloths if necessary.	❑ Remove the top cloth from a double-clothed table. Replace only the top cloth if the base cloth is not soiled.
	❑ If there are stains on the base cloth that will show, change both cloths, and clean and sanitize the table.
	❑ To change tablecloths, move flowers, condiments, and so on to the edge of the table away from the side where you are standing.
	❑ On your side of the table, fold the edge of the soiled cloth to the top of the table.
	❑ As you fold the soiled tablecloth up, unfold the new tablecloth on the part of the table you are uncovering. Do not shake out or completely unfold the clean cloth before spreading it onto the table. In a formal dining area, a table should never be stripped in view of guests. Guests should not be able to see the table surface when you change a tablecloth.
	❑ Check to make sure the new tablecloth's seam is facing down.

BUSPERSON: *Clear and Reset Tables* (continued)

STEPS	HOW-TO'S
	❑ Spread the new cloth halfway across the tabletop, moving the dirty cloth out of the way as you spread the new cloth. Arrange the new cloth on your side of the table so it is centered and hangs evenly.
	❑ Move to the opposite side of the table. Move flowers, condiments, and so on to the clean cloth to keep it in place.
	❑ As you pull the new cloth toward you, remove the soiled cloth in the same motion.
	❑ Roll up the soiled cloth so crumbs are caught in the middle of the cloth. Do not dump crumbs onto the chairs or floor.
	❑ Place rolled-up soiled linens on a chair until you have completely reset the table. Do not place soiled linens on the floor.
	❑ Make sure the new cloth is centered and hangs evenly with no wrinkles.
	❑ Wipe the condiment containers and centerpieces with a clean, damp cloth and move them back to the correct spot on the table.
5. Reset the table.	❑ Make sure all glassware, silverware, and dishes are clean, polished (if appropriate), and free from spots, chips, and cracks.
	❑ Place the serviceware on the table. Set all tables the same way to give the restaurant a neat and appealing appearance.
	❑ Handle glassware by the base—never near the lip. Never put your fingers inside glasses.
	❑ Handle plates by the edges. Never place your fingers on the food surface of the plates.
	❑ Handle silverware by the handles.

(continued)

BUSPERSON: *Clear and Reset Tables* (continued)

STEPS	HOW-TO'S
	❑ Relight table lamps that have gone out. Replace candles or fuel as needed.
	❑ Wipe clean and replace promotional table tents as needed.
6. Clean chairs.	❑ Remove soiled linens from the chair and place them in a bus tub.
	❑ Wipe crumbs from chairs into your cleaning cloth.
	❑ Brush crumbs into the bus tub, and not onto the floor.
	❑ Push chairs to the table so the front edge of the seat is even with the edge of the table.
7. Check tables.	❑ Adjust anything that is not lined up properly.
	❑ Check the centerpiece to make sure it is still attractive.
8. Take soiled dishes and linens to the correct area.	❑ Use safe lifting techniques.

BUSPERSON: *Bus Soiled Dishes to the Dish room*

Materials needed: A clean cloth and a bus tub or a service tray.

STEPS	HOW-TO'S
1. Carry soiled dishes to the dish room.	❑ Bussing soiled dishes to the dish room will occur: • Throughout meal service as new courses are served and old courses are cleared • When clearing and resetting tables • When cleaning side stations at the end of the meal period • Whenever requested by a server
2. Unload soiled dishes.	❑ In the dish room, sort the items according to the decoy system set up by the stewards. Scrape dishes (if you haven't already scraped them) and stack them by type. ❑ A decoy system consists of bus tubs and dish racks with one dirty dish, glass, etc., in them to show you where to place dirty items. ❑ Put broken glass in the proper trash can, not in the soiled linen bin. ❑ Place glasses upside-down in the correct washing racks. ❑ Place silverware in the silverware-soaking solution.
3. Rinse the bus tub or tray and wipe it dry with a clean cloth before returning it to its proper place.	

Sources: Adapted from the "Restaurant Server Guide" and "Busperson Guide" in the *Hospitality Skills Training Series* (Lansing, Mich.: American Hotel & Lodging Educational Institute, 1995).

Chapter 4 Outline

Banquet Servers
    Working as a Team
    Superior Performance Standards
    Banquet Server Duties
In-Room Dining Attendants
    Working as a Team
    Superior Performance Standards
    In-Room Dining Attendant Duties
Concierges
    Concierge Duties

Competencies

4

Select Hotel Food and Beverage Staff

FULL-SERVICE HOTELS rely on their food and beverage staffs to help transform the hotel into a home away from home for guests. While few guests choose hotels based on their food and beverage operations, the service they receive from these operations may make the difference in whether they return.

Banquets and catered functions play an important part in hotels because of the revenue they provide. A hotel with excellent banquet facilities and service can increase its room sales by hosting meetings, conventions, and conferences.

While restaurants located in hotels need all the staff members that non-hotel restaurants need, most hotels hire additional service personnel for non-restaurant food and beverage duties. These staff members include banquet servers, in-room dining (room service) attendants, and concierges.

Banquet Servers

Banquet servers provide food and beverage service to banquet guests. Perhaps a better definition, though, would be that banquet servers are food and beverage staff members who do everything possible, within reason, to make each guest's dining and meeting experience exactly what he or she wants it to be, and who exceeds guest expectations whenever possible. Banquet servers are responsible for:

- Preparing for service
- Inspecting tables for cleanliness and proper setup
- Greeting guests
- Serving food and beverages
- Completing service
- Resetting function rooms and service areas
- Keeping a count of the number of guests served
- Helping take inventory

Exhibit 1 lists many of the tasks that banquet servers are expected to perform.

145

Exhibit 1   Typical Tasks for Banquet Servers

Here is a list of typical tasks that banquet servers might perform, depending on the food and beverage operation. The number and complexity of tasks that a banquet server is expected to perform depends on the formality of the food and beverage operation and other factors. Not all of these tasks will be discussed in the chapter.

1. Follow banquet event orders and change orders
2. Receive, store, and ship packages for guests
3. Fold napkins
4. Place tablecloths on tables
5. Skirt and flounce tables
6. Prepare salt and pepper shakers and grinders
7. Prepare sugar bowls or caddies
8. Set tables for banquets
9. Prepare bread
10. Prepare and serve coffee
11. Prepare and serve hot tea
12. Prepare and serve iced tea
13. Prepare and serve hot chocolate
14. Prepare, lift, and carry service trays
15. Serve water
16. Take and serve beverage orders
17. Check IDs
18. Serve bread and butter
19. Prepare ice buckets
20. Serve wine or champagne by the bottle
21. Serve each course at sit-down banquets
22. Maintain tables during service
23. Maintain buffets
24. Set up and maintain hors d'oeuvres for receptions
25. Provide service for cocktail receptions
26. Provide break or continental breakfast service
27. Refresh meeting rooms
28. Provide appropriate service for children
29. Respond to dissatisfied guests
30. Promote restaurants and other property facilities
31. Settle individual guest checks
32. Settle group checks
33. Clear tables
34. Perform end-of-shift duties

Working as a Team

To be excellent team players, banquet servers can:

- Follow dish room procedures when dropping off dirty tableware.

- Report needed equipment repairs to maintenance, using the maintenance request system.

- Take soiled linens to the laundry department to help the laundry manage its production.

- Interact with "internal customers" (kitchen staff, maintenance staff, laundry staff, and other staff members) with the same care and concern that they show guests.

Superior Performance Standards

The quality of the food, beverages, and service at a lodging property should enhance each guest's overall banquet experience. Providing excellent service, beverages, and meals at a reasonable price is every property's ultimate goal. Superior performance standards help banquet servers achieve that goal. Banquet servers must:

- Demonstrate professional behavior within the property.

- Refresh function rooms as needed.

- Greet guests warmly as they enter the room.

- Serve food and beverages according to high-quality service standards appropriate for the type of function.

- Anticipate and quickly respond to guests' needs.

- Be alert to safety procedures at all times.

- Make sure food is served at the correct temperature, attractively presented, and pleasing to the senses.

Banquet Server Duties

In the following sections we will discuss typical banquet server duties and other related issues.

Banquet Event Orders. Banquet servers rely heavily on **banquet event orders (BEOs)**. BEOs (called "function sheets" at some properties) tell servers what the banquet is and what needs to be done. All function preparation begins with the BEO.

The BEO typically states the type of banquet service that will be provided. At a buffet banquet, guests serve themselves some or all of the meal. Banquet servers replace items on the buffet line as needed, serve beverages, and clear tables. At a sit-down banquet, food is plated in the kitchen and servers bring it to the table. A BEO also lists:

- The name of the organization that scheduled the function; the organization's address, phone number, and e-mail address; and the organization's contact person

- The hotel salesperson who booked the function
- The type of function
- The room in which the function will take place
- The number of guests expected and the number guaranteed
- Room setup specifications
- Table setup specifications
- Special equipment needed
- Costs of special equipment, flowers, and other miscellaneous items
- Complete menu for the function, including beverages and all the courses
- Time the food should be plated
- Time each course should be served
- Prices of all food and beverage items
- Any special requests

Promote Restaurants. Banquet servers have many opportunities to promote the other restaurants and services of the hotel. They should be prepared to tell guests the following about each restaurant at the property:

- Hours of service
- Type of food and beverages served and price range
- Signature menu items
- Reservations policy
- Dress code (if any)

Banquet servers can suggest the property's restaurants by mentioning specific items served. For example, they can say, "If you're still here tomorrow, try the cafe. It has an excellent breakfast buffet." They can also suggest the property's other facilities to guests who show an interest in recreation. Features such as pools, spas, and fitness centers contribute to repeat business.

Linens and Napkin Folding. Fresh, clean linens and crisply folded napkins are a necessary and important part of professional food presentation, whether guests are having coffee and a snack or a seven-course banquet.

Banquet servers should always check linens for rips, stains, and wear, and replace linens that do not meet the property's standards. The supervisor will inform the laundry department about problems with the napkins and determine which napkins to rewash and which to throw away.

Banquet servers should always wash their hands thoroughly before folding napkins, as guests will wipe their mouth with napkins. Napkins should get the same sanitary care as food. There are many napkin folds that can be used to enhance the appearance of tables. The way banquet servers fold napkins will vary with the type of function, the season, and the time of day. The combination of silverware wrapped in a linen napkin is often referred to as a **linen roll-up**. Once

Exhibit 2   Common Ratios for Table Items and Table Seating

Amount	Per
1 salt and pepper shaker	Every 10 people or every table of fewer than 10 people
1 sugar bowl or caddy	Every 10 people or every table of fewer than 10 people
8 places	Five-foot round table
10 places	Six-foot round table

folded, napkins should be stored in clean areas of the sidestations, well away from the danger of splatters and spills.

Standard Place-Setting Arrangements. All of the tables in a function room should look the same, even if several different banquet servers set them. When tables are set consistently, with evenly lined-up tableware, attractive centerpieces, and straight, crisp tablecloths, it shows guests that banquet staff members care about providing a quality dining experience.

Place-setting arrangements will change with the type of function and type of service provided. It is important to know the standard place-setting arrangement for each type of function held at a property.

All tables for a function should be set and ready no later than 15 minutes before the banquet's scheduled start time. Depending on the policy of the banquet department, a supervisor or banquet captain may then check all of the tables. Once the table setups have been approved, banquet servers should be in the room, ready to welcome guests.

The banquet event order will direct how tablecloths should be placed and how many place settings are needed for each room. Banquet servers must collect the tableware and other serviceware and make sure that the silverware, china, and glasses are clean and have no spots, cracks, or chips. Servers should be careful to handle all items by the edges and not touch anywhere food or a guest's mouth will touch. Exhibit 2 lists common ratios for table items and table seating.

Banquet servers place silverware before guests arrive, leaving a 12-inch space on the table directly in front of each chair for the dinner plate. The dinner fork is placed to the left of the plate space, the salad fork or second dinner fork is placed to the left of the first fork. The dinner knife is placed on the right of the plate space with the sharp edge toward the plate space. Spoons are placed to the right of the knife. Banquet servers ensure that the handles of the silverware line up evenly from the table edge (two inches from the edge is a common standard). They then preset any specialized silverware that the meal requires, such as fish forks, appetizer forks, steak knives, or dessert spoons.

Water glasses are placed above the tip of the dinner knife (one-half inch above is a typical standard). Wine glasses are then set up according to the banquet department's policy. If more than two wine courses are to be served, banquet servers usually clear and reset glasses rather than preset the table with more than two wine glasses. If an appetizer wine is to be served, banquet servers set a small aperitif glass to the right of and slightly below the other wine glasses. Mugs or cups and saucers are placed to the right of and slightly below the outermost wine glass. Banquet servers typically turn the handle of the cup or mug to the right and at an angle specified by the banquet department.

Finally, banquet servers should carefully check each table to make sure everything looks consistent and meets the department's standards. If there are table lamps or candles on the table, they must be turned on or lit before the arrival of guests.

Prepare Condiment Containers. Before a banquet begins, banquet servers should prepare and clean such items as salt shakers, pepper shakers, pepper grinders, and sugar bowls or caddies.

Salt and pepper shakers and grinders should be cleaned before they are set out. If shakers and grinders are cleaned and refilled regularly and stored in a warm, dry place between meal periods, they work with few problems. If shakers or grinders are not completely dry before being filled, however, the contents will clump together and not come out properly. Salt and pepper shakers typically are filled with a small kitchen funnel up to the threads of the shaker. Servers can place the shakers on a service tray to catch any spills that occur during the filling process.

Pepper grinders are also called pepper mills. Guests often like fresh ground pepper on their salads, pasta, and red meat entrées. To fill grinders, servers must unscrew the retainer nuts from the tops of the grinders and remove the tops. The grinders can then be filled with whole peppercorns. They should be filled only three-quarters full, as overfilling can interfere with the grinding action.

Sugar bowls and caddies should be cleaned with a cleaning cloth to wipe dust and crumbs away. Sugar packets can then be placed neatly in one side of each bowl or caddy, and artificial sweeteners placed in the other side. If a property serves unrefined sugar, the bowls or caddies should be filled with an equal number of packets of unrefined sugar, white sugar, and artificial sweetener. Sugar and sweetener packages from previous meals can be re-used if they are undamaged and free of stains. All packets should be placed upright and facing the same direction so that guests can more easily see the printing and/or logo on them.

Prepare Bread. Banquet servers are often called upon to put bread onto trays or into baskets to serve at each table. Pre-prepared breads may be delivered by storeroom personnel or picked up at the storeroom. Breads prepared in the bakery are picked up in the bakery or delivered by the baker. The amount of bread needed for the banquet will be listed on a food requisition form.

Banquet servers must remove all crumbs and food residue from bread baskets before setting them up for service; bread trays should be cleaned and polished. Generally speaking, servers set up one bread basket or tray per table (for tables of 10 or fewer guests), or one basket/tray for every 10 guests, if banquet tables are placed in such a way that many guests are seated at very long tables. A folded linen napkin should be placed in each basket or on each tray, then the baskets or trays can be stored in the pantry or in sidestations until they are needed. Just before serving time, the bread is placed in the baskets or on the trays.

Sometimes the BEO calls for the bread to be warm when served. Breads should never be heated in a microwave oven; this causes the bread to lose its moisture and quickly become tough and hard. Instead, bread warmers should be used. Many bread warmers have a water tank to keep the bread from drying out. The bread can be placed in the warming units until it is time to serve it. Banquet servers should avoid warming more bread than is needed for each table, as once-warmed bread cannot be warmed again and served at a later time.

Prepare Beverages. Banquet servers may prepare several types of beverages for any given banquet. The most common beverages that require advance preparation are:

- Coffee

- Hot tea

- Iced tea

- Hot chocolate

Other beverages, such as carbonated soft drinks and water, are also commonly served at banquets, of course, but they require little or no advance preparation.

Coffee. Coffee pots should be checked for cleanliness. If a coffee pot was left on the burner too long, it may have coffee residue in the bottom. At the end of the night, pots must be returned to the dish room and washed in the dish machine.

Banquet servers make coffee either by the pot in a drip coffee maker or by the urn. Many lodging properties use filter packs that are premeasured to meet the tastes of most guests. To make coffee by the pot, banquet servers empty these filter packs onto the filter in the grounds holder. The grounds holder is then returned to the coffee maker. A clean pot is then placed under the grounds holder. Water is poured from a measured pitcher or a clean coffee pot into the coffee maker.

Coffee strength **layers** as water passes through the ground coffee. Generally speaking, the first third of the pot is too weak, the second third is too strong, and the final third is too weak. To get the right flavor, banquet servers should let the full pot drip so that the layers have a chance to blend and the coffee in the pot arrives at the desired strength. The full pot of fresh coffee should then be moved to a reserve burner, the used grounds thrown away, and the grounds holder rinsed.

Coffee begins to deteriorate in quality immediately after it is brewed; the oils in the coffee start to break down and a foul odor and taste starts to develop. That is why it is important to serve coffee as soon after it is brewed as possible.

To make coffee in urns, banquet servers should:

1. Check to make sure the urn is clean.

2. Add water to the urn.

3. Heat the water until it boils.

4. Place a cloth or paper filter in the brew basket.

5. Measure the correct amount of ground coffee into the filter and spread it evenly.

6. Place the brew basket in the coffee urn.

7. Put the water arm over the brew basket, replace the lid, and press start.

Some coffee urns have two compartments; one is for heating water and the other for brewing coffee. Other urns have three compartments—one for hot water and two for coffee. In this case, one compartment is typically used for decaffeinated coffee. Just as with coffee made by the pot in coffee makers, coffee brewed in urns should be prepared as close to the time of service as possible. Water should never be run through the grounds twice to reach a desired strength with less coffee.

Hot tea. Hot tea for banquets is commonly served either in two-cup teapots or by the individual cup. If a property uses ceramic teapots, banquet servers should preheat them by filling them with hot water from the drip coffee maker. Items that typically accompany hot tea (sugar, artificial sweeteners, spoons, and honey) should be placed on the service tray along with the tea cups. (Since banquet servers often serve the same items to many people, they will typically use a service tray, not a beverage tray.) Tea bags and lemon wedges can be placed on side dishes or bread-and-butter plates. Finally, hot water from the coffee maker is run into teapots and the teapots are placed on the tray.

Iced tea. To make iced tea in a drip coffee maker, banquet servers place the correct number of tea bags in a clean, empty coffee pot. The pot is placed on a drip-coffee-maker burner and a clean, empty grounds holder is placed in the coffee maker to funnel the water. The tea is then brewed and allowed to steep in the hot water for eight to ten minutes. Banquet servers can then fill clean plastic pitchers with ice and—after removing the tea bags—pour the brewed tea into the pitchers. They then stir the tea with a clean iced-tea spoon to help cool the tea (warm tea will melt the ice in a guest's glass and make the tea too watery). If a property garnishes its iced-tea glasses, banquet servers should garnish the glasses during setup and place them (along with lemon wedges, sugar, spoons, and beverage napkins) on a service tray.

Hot chocolate. Hot chocolate is usually made with a hot chocolate machine. As each machine is different, banquet servers learn on the job how to use it and make hot chocolate.

Serve Beverages. When booking a function, the host selects the beverages that will be served; these choices are listed on the banquet event order. When first arriving at a table, the banquet server should tell guests which beverages are available and ask them what they would like to order. If a guest asks for a beverage not included on the BEO, the banquet server should tell the guest whether there is an extra charge and what that charge is.

Beverage orders should be written on the guest check according to how the guests are seated. Each property will provide banquet servers with a system to write checks, usually using the same reference point in a function room. Banquet servers also should use standard drink abbreviations so that anyone can deliver the beverage orders.

Beverages are carried out to guests on a service tray and the tray is placed on a tray stand in the function room. Banquet servers can show guests that they are service professionals by following these steps when serving beverages:

1. Use the right glass for the beverage.

2. Pour beverages only into sparkling clean glasses without cracks, chips, or spots. Throw away glasses with cracks or chips, and return spotted glasses to the dish room.

3. Leave the glasses on the table when pouring at a table. (Servers should never pick up a glass to pour unless there is no other way to pour without spilling.)

4. Use their right hands to pour from the guest's right side.

5. Never add ice to a hot glass.

6. Always use an ice scoop or tongs—not their hands or a glass—to pick up ice.

Water may be poured a few minutes before the guests arrive or as soon as guests arrive. Water glasses are refilled whenever they are less than half-full unless the guest declines a refill.

Only coffee that is less than 30 minutes old should be served; coffee drinkers instantly know the difference between fresh and stale coffee. Also, old, stale coffee gives off an offensive odor that will spread throughout the room. If coffee is made in an urn, guests will probably serve themselves, in which case the banquet servers only need to make sure there is enough cream, sugar, artificial sweetener, and mugs or cups and saucers.

Coffee cools quickly. Guests expect banquet servers to keep their coffee hot and fresh. Therefore, banquet servers should refill coffee cups or mugs as soon as they are less than half-full or until the guests signal that they have had enough.

Serve Bread and Butter. Bread and butter service varies slightly from function to function. Generally speaking, prepared butter ramekins or dishes are pulled from a service refrigerator and placed on a tray. Butter dishes and knives are placed on small plates. Bread is placed in a napkin-lined basket or on a bread tray. The basket or tray should be placed in the center of the table so guests can serve themselves. Butter dishes are usually placed near the bread basket. Banquet servers should check baskets and trays throughout the meal and bring fresh bread and butter when the original bread is gone.

At a formal, sit-down banquet, bread is served with the first course. If a basket of crackers, bread sticks, or other specialty breads was served with the appetizers, banquet servers should remove this basket from the table before serving breads for the main course.

Serve Each Course. The banquet manager or captain will signal when to serve each course. Courses are typically served in the following order:

- Appetizers
- Soup
- Salads
- Entrées
- Desserts

- Cordials
- Coffee

The table has to be prepared for each course before it is served. Once the meal has begun, this is done by clearing away empty plates or glasses and bringing all necessary condiments and accompaniments to the table before serving the course.

As each order is brought out of the kitchen, banquet servers should check it by asking the following questions of themselves:

- Does the food look fresh and appealing?
- Have all preparation instructions been followed?
- Is the presentation garnished?
- Have all special requests been met?
- Is the plate clean?
- Is hot food hot and cold food cold?

If there is a problem with any of the plates, the banquet servers should ask the cook to fix it—always thanking the kitchen staff for its cooperation.

Typically, courses are delivered on service trays and placed on tray stands in the function rooms. Generally speaking, plates are delivered to guests in this order:

1. Children
2. Women
3. Men
4. Host

Whenever possible, food is served from the guest's left side with the server's left hand. The plate with the first course is placed on top of the base plate (if a base plate is included in the table setting). The entrée plate should be placed so that the main food item is closest to the guest. Side dishes are placed to the left of the entrée plate.

Banquet servers should ask guests whether they would like the server to bring or do anything else for them. If a guest asks for a special condiment or some other item, the server should deliver that item as quickly as possible so that the guest's meal is not delayed.

Clear Tables. All banquet servers should work together as a team to clear tables. It is usually very important to clear tables quickly, as servers should be out of the function room by the time a speaker begins speaking or some other banquet program begins.

Typically, banquet servers clear tables by carrying a service tray to a tray stand near the tables they are going to clear. They then remove dishes, glasses, silverware, and napkins from the table. They may also scrape food and debris from all dishes onto one dish, out of the sight of guests. They stack the same kinds of dishes in small piles and place the dish with the food and debris on the top of the stack. They then place glasses on the tray in several spots so that one area is not heavier than the others. Likewise, silverware, beverage napkins, and linen napkins are all placed in their own area of the tray. Because silverware and other items left in linen napkins can tear linens in the washer or dryer and injure laundry attendants, banquet servers should be careful to remove them.

The filled tray is then carried to the dish room, where the silverware and dishes are unloaded using a decoy system. A typical decoy system consists of dish machine racks with one dirty dish, glass, or some other piece of tableware in each rack to show servers where to place dirty items. Glasses are placed upside-down in the correct racks; silverware goes into a silverware-soaking solution.

Banquet servers can then wipe the tray and return to the room to remove all condiments and centerpieces from their tables. If the function is over and the guests have left, servers can remove the tablecloths by folding the ends into the middle; this prevents crumbs from falling on the floor. The servers can then inspect the chairs and clean those that have crumbs or minor spills on them.

Settle Individual Guest Checks. The banquet captain or food and beverage manager will typically handle the banquet bill. However, if a guest orders an item that was not on the banquet event order, the server will have to process an individual guest check. The bartender will usually prepare a check for beverages. If the guest ordered something from the restaurant, the restaurant's cashier will prepare the check. Many properties use guest check folders, as they keep the checks clean and provide a place for guests to put their money or credit cards. Guests who are staying at the property with approved credit accounts at the front desk may charge their food and beverage items to their room; that is, charge them to their "house account." Guests who live nearby and often entertain clients at the hotel may have approval to charge their meals to their company or to a group account. These are called "city accounts." If a guest is paying by check, it is extremely important to record the guest's address, telephone number, and other information to ensure that the hotel's accounting department will be able to take appropriate action if the check is returned to the hotel for non-sufficient funds.

Perform End-of-Shift Duties. At the end of the shift, banquet servers help return everything to its place. While the exact tasks will vary according to the functions that were worked, some general tasks include:

- Empty and wipe out ice buckets
- Empty water pitchers and take them to the dish room
- Empty and clean the coffee station
- Clean and restock banquet sidestations

Function Rooms. Function rooms are rooms where banquets, meetings, and receptions take place. Banquet servers need to be familiar with their property's function rooms. Each function room may vary in size, style, and the number of people it will hold. Certain rooms may be used only for certain types of functions. Banquet departments will often create diagrams of standard function room setups. These are helpful aids to banquet setup staff members and banquet servers.

Buffets. During a **buffet**, guests serve themselves to the food that banquet servers put on the buffet tables. The job of a server is to keep the food on the buffet tables full, looking attractive, and at the right temperature. Many buffets have items that must be held hot, cold, or at room temperature during the buffet. Hot food can be held hot with **chafing dishes**. Banquet servers should monitor the amount of water in the liners of the hot chafing dishes and make sure that the heating elements stay on. When guests are not in the serving line, servers can put the lids back on the chafing dishes to help keep foods hot. Cold food is held cold by ice on the buffet. Servers should replace ice as needed and remove any ice that gets into food containers.

When a container of food is less than one-quarter full, servers should get a full container from the kitchen and replace the old container. Food from the old container should not be combined with the new container. Instead, the old food should be taken to the kitchen and given to the appropriate person. Entrée plates and other dishes should be restocked when there are fewer than ten in a stack; a stack should never get below five dishes. Each food container needs an appropriate serving utensil, and any utensil that falls on the floor must be replaced with a clean one from the kitchen. Banquet servers also should wipe up any spills on the buffet tables.

Receptions. Receptions can be a function for anything from a small business gathering to a large wedding. Hors d'oeuvres and snack foods are served from buffet tables as finger foods at many receptions. The buffet tables are often decorated with food or flower displays.

Banquet servers are usually asked to bring out the equipment for the hot and cold food. They set up ice beds for cold items and chafing dishes or electric warmers for hot items. If a chafing dish is heated by canned, gel-type fuel, servers should place one can on a bread-and-butter plate under a half-size chafer and two cans under a full-size chafer. Cans of fuel should be lit ten minutes before putting the food in the chafing dishes.

Servers can arrange stacks of beverage napkins on the service table and then place cocktail forks or picks, knives, and small plates on the table. About 10 to 15 minutes before the guests are expected, servers should bring out the food and place it in the beds of ice or chafing dishes.

Continental Breakfast Service. Many lodging properties of all sizes offer continental breakfast to their guests. Banquet servers usually collect food, beverages, and service items and take them to the room or area where the food will be served. Service items may include:

- Small plates
- Linen or paper napkins
- Forks, spoons, and knives
- Glasses
- Mugs or cups and saucers

Ice beds should be set up for cold items (including soft drinks/sodas, juices, and bottled waters). Chafing dishes or electric warmers are set up for hot food. Decaffeinated coffee dispensers are usually clearly labeled and placed next to the regular coffee dispensers.

Meeting Rooms. When guests reserve a function room to hold a meeting, they often order beverage service or snack service. The banquet event order will indicate when guests plan to take breaks in their meeting and what should be served. During the breaks, banquet servers can enter the meeting room to:

- Pick up any trash in the room
- Replace dirty tablecloths
- Refill food and beverages
- Replace dull pencils (if they belong to the property) and restock notepads
- Make sure the tables are fresh and neat

When a room for a function continues beyond one day, the banquet setup staff members will typically refresh the rooms.

In-Room Dining Attendants

In-room dining attendants take guests' food and beverage orders, place orders with the kitchen, deliver orders to guestrooms, and serve guests in their rooms. At some properties, in-room dining order-takers record guests' orders and in-room dining attendants serve the orders. Having food delivered to the guestroom is a luxury many guests at a lodging property want to experience; in-room dining attendants can make guests feel special and pampered by providing this service. In-room dining attendants:

- Help businesspeople stay on schedule by delivering food and beverages that allow them to keep working
- Make a private dinner for two possible
- Help guests host functions for friends, family members, or business associates

  In-room dining attendants are responsible for many tasks, including:

- Selling food and beverages
- Delivering food and beverages
- Presenting food and beverages to guests in guestrooms or hospitality suites
- Removing tableware and other items when guests are done with them
- Helping co-workers as needed

Exhibit 3 lists common tasks that in-room dining attendants are called on to perform.

Working as a Team

To be excellent team players, in-room dining attendants can:

Exhibit 3   Typical Tasks for In-Room Dining Attendants

Here is a list of typical tasks that in-room dining attendants might perform, depending on the hotel. The number and complexity of tasks that an in-room dining attendant is expected to perform depends on the formality of the hotel and other factors. Not all of these tasks will be discussed in the chapter.

1. Perform beginning-of-shift duties
2. Preset in-room dining trays and carts
3. Process express breakfast orders
4. Deliver VIP amenities
5. Use the point-of-sale equipment
6. Take and record in-room dining orders
7. Handle special in-room dining requests
8. Place the in-room dining order
9. Perform pantry prep for in-room dining orders
10. Prepare coffee
11. Prepare hot tea
12. Prepare iced tea
13. Prepare hot chocolate
14. Assemble the beverage order and food condiments
15. Pick up the in-room dining order
16. Deliver the in-room dining order
17. Serve the in-room dining order
18. Serve coffee or hot tea
19. Check IDs
20. Present and settle the guest check
21. Retrieve trays and carts
22. Close out the guest check
23. Follow up with guests
24. Respond to dissatisfied guests
25. Clear and reset trays and carts
26. Handle soiled in-room dining linens
27. Set up portable bars in suites or guestrooms
28. Set up and serve small group dinners and receptions
29. Set up and serve small buffet banquets
30. Set up and serve coffee breaks
31. Maintain in-room dining sidestations
32. Pick up and restock in-room dining supplies
33. Perform closing shift duties
34. Make shift deposit and collect due-backs
35. Use the in-room dining logbook

- Deliver food and beverage orders promptly to the kitchen or bar to prevent last-minute rushing for everyone involved

- Deliver soiled linens to the laundry department throughout their shift to prevent linen shortages and laundry work back-ups

- Keep hallways clear of used in-room dining items so that others will not trip over them

- Conduct supply inventories and restock items as necessary to ensure that other in-room dining attendants will not run out of supplies

- Report guestroom mechanical problems that guests relay to them to the engineering department, and fill out maintenance request forms if necessary

- Bus soiled tableware often, so stewards will not fall behind

Superior Performance Standards

Successful in-room dining attendants strive to meet the following superior performance standards:

- Answer the telephone promptly ("by the third ring" is a common property standard)

- Be familiar with all menu items, including specials and desserts

- Suggest daily specials and signature appetizers, desserts, beverages, and other menu items

- Tell each guest the approximate time of delivery, and deliver food and beverages by that time

- Use portable heaters for all hot food

- Knock, then ask for permission to enter the guestroom when the door is opened

- Set in-room dining tables, remove coverings, and arrange tableware attractively for guests

- Use only full, capped, and clean condiment containers

- Politely ask guests to phone in-room dining when finished so that the dirty dishes can be retrieved

- Remove service trays and dishes promptly, so that no trays or dishes remain in the hall from one meal period to the next

In-Room Dining Attendant Duties

In the following sections we will discuss typical in-room dining attendant duties and other related issues.

Guestroom Safety. As a function of their duties, in-room dining attendants use carts and trays to deliver food and beverages to guestrooms. While restaurant servers are able to make sure their work area (the dining room) is clean, in-room dining attendants can never be sure what the condition of a guestroom will be.

There might be water spilled on the floor, clothes hanging from a chair, or smoldering cigarettes and scattered newspapers on the table. That is why in-room dining attendants should be careful when they enter and work in a guestroom. The following tips can help keep in-room dining attendants, guests, and equipment safe. In-room dining attendants should:

- Watch where they push their cart.

- Look at the floor of the guestroom before they enter.

- Pick up obstructive items off the floor before pushing the cart into the room, or politely ask the guest to move his or her belongings.

- Refrain from confronting guests if they see a weapon, drugs, controlled substances, pets, or damage to the room. Instead, they should deliver the order and then report the problem to their supervisor. If they feel uncomfortable, they can excuse themselves right away and tell their supervisor about the problem.

- Make it their goal to wheel the cart into the guestroom and deliver the food and beverages to the guest. However, if a guest does not want them to enter the room, they should not leave the cart until the guest takes all the items off the cart; with the cart emptied, servers can take the cart with them when they return to their duty station. In-room dining carts left in the hallway can be a safety hazard.

- Take along a doorstop so they can prop open the door while they are wheeling the cart through the doorway and working in the guestroom. Keeping the door open provides extra security.

Elevator Courtesy. Most properties that offer in-room dining also have service elevators that the in-room dining attendants use to transport food and food service carts. However, since there may be times when in-room dining attendants must use the guest elevators, they should be aware of proper elevator courtesy.

Riding an elevator can often be socially uncomfortable. Guests may not be sure who should get off first, whether to make conversation, or who should push the buttons. In-room dining staff members can help guests be more comfortable by being confident and knowing what to do. Riding the elevator with guests gives in-room dining attendants a chance to provide superior service.

In-room dining attendants and other hotel staff should always be the last one on the elevator and the last one off. This allows them to hold the door open for all the guests each way. If they see guests approaching the elevator—even if they are moving slowly—they should hold the elevator for them. When they are on the elevator with guests, in-room dining attendants should make small talk with them. Not only will this get rid of the uncomfortable silence, it gives in-room dining attendants a chance to make guests aware of the property's services. Their friendliness can make a good impression on guests.

If it does not appear that the in-room dining cart will fit comfortably on the elevator with the guests, attendants should wait for the next elevator.

Presetting Trays and Carts. Many lodging establishments have charts that show in-room dining attendants how to set up in-room dining trays and carts. Having standard setups for trays and carts helps attendants save time loading and unloading guests' orders. It also helps them arrange items so they are properly balanced, which allows them to carry items on trays or push items on carts efficiently and safely.

In-room dining attendants typically begin and end each shift by cleaning their service trays and carts. Cork-lined trays can be rubbed with lemon wedges, metal trays washed with hot water and an approved sanitizing solution. Carts should be sanitized and then polished with a clean, dry cloth. Most establishments put tablecloths over in-room dining carts. Attendants then organize and preset the trays and carts before the meal period begins. Some things that they may place on a tray or cart include packets or containers of salt, pepper, ketchup, mustard, mayonnaise, sugar, and artificial sweetener. As they place each item, attendants should check it to ensure it is clean.

In-room dining carts may be equipped with hot boxes, which might be electrically powered or use canned, gel-type fuel. Attendants should check the gel cans and replace them as needed. They should always wash their hands right away after handling these gel cans, because gel-type fuel is poisonous.

Express Breakfast. Express breakfasts are offered at many properties for the convenience of guests. Typically, doorknob menus are provided in the guestroom; guests mark which items they want for breakfast and the time they would like the breakfast delivered, then hang the completed menu on the outside doorknob of the guestroom door. Security staff members or bell attendants may pick these up for the in-room dining department. Menus are typically collected by 3 A.M. so that the breakfast orders can be prepared and delivered on time to guests.

In-room dining attendants arrange the menus according to delivery time, with the earliest delivery times first and the latest ones last. On an express breakfast control sheet, they record the names of guests and the times the breakfasts are to be delivered. The orders are then placed with the chef and the in-room dining attendants begin preparing beverages to accompany the in-room dining orders.

In-Room Dining Orders. In this section we will look at typical tasks in-room dining attendants may perform when taking and delivering in-room dining orders.

Taking the order. The task of taking in-room dining orders may be divided between in-room dining attendants and in-room dining order-takers, depending on the size of the property. Whomever takes the order should pick up the phone promptly and greet the caller warmly, using good telephone etiquette. The in-room dining staff member should ask the guest for his or her name and the guestroom number, even if the computerized telephone system displays the guest's name and room number. Asking for the name and room number allows staff members to confirm that they are speaking with the registered guest.

Most guests simply sign the guest check for in-room dining orders so that the charges, including any tips, will be added to their house account at the hotel. In-room dining attendants should check the cash-only list while taking the order to see whether the guest's name is on that list. If it is, they must politely explain that the guest will have to pay for the order when it is delivered. If the guest's name and room number are not on the cash-only list, attendants should take the order without discussing payment.

While on the phone, in-room dining attendants have the opportunity to use suggestive selling. They can suggest unique appetizers, soups, and salads; menu specials; profitable entrées, desserts, and wine; and other signature items, such as premium-brand alcoholic beverages. Attendants are most effective when they recommend specific items to enhance the guest's meal. For instance, rather than saying, "Would you like an appetizer?" they can say, "Would you like a fresh vegetable assortment or mini–crab cakes to begin your meal?"

Describing the daily menu specials helps guests "see" the items. Guest may be more likely to order items they can picture. In-room dining attendants should vividly describe the items' ingredients and preparation in an appealing way.

In-room dining attendants can help increase the property's beverage sales by being prepared with wine or champagne suggestions. In general, white wines go best with white meats and seafood, red wines go best with red meats and game. Rosé, blush, and sparkling wines go with any type of food. In-room dining attendants should be prepared to answer any questions guests have about wines or champagnes and provide general guidelines, but they should always support the guests' preferences and allow them to make their own decisions. Guests are never wrong in their selection of wines, regardless of the general rules. Nor should any food service staff member ever argue with a guest over the selection of a wine or the pronunciation of a wine's name.

While taking orders, in-room dining attendants should pay close attention to the guests. They should ask questions to find out the guest's choices or preferences for service, such as how he or she would like an item cooked or prepared (e.g., medium rare, or "on the rocks"). They should ask guests for their choices of salad dressings and for any special requests; these should be written down and highlighted on the guest check or input into the computerized order-taking system. Attendants should ask the guest how many people will be dining (if it is not otherwise obvious) so the attendants can be sure to properly set up the trays or carts based on those numbers.

Finally, the in-room dining attendant should politely read the order back to the guest and repeat all details. If the guest confirms that the order is correct, the attendant should tell the guest how long the delivery will take (trying to never underestimate the amount of time needed) and thank the guest for the order. The attendant can then tell the guest what the total charges will be, including tax and service charges. This prevents unpleasant surprises and allows cash-only guests to have the money ready when the order is served.

Placing the order. At some properties, in-room dining attendants hand-carry orders to the kitchen; other properties use point-of-sale equipment that automatically transmits orders to the kitchen. Attendants should let the cook or expediter know about any guest requests, such as the degree of doneness for eggs and steaks, a fat-free preparation, extra sauce, or removing bread or buns.

When food orders are almost ready, in-room dining attendants should place the beverage orders with the bar. The timing of in-room dining drink orders is important. Food must stay at the correct temperature, and the ice in beverages must not melt and water down the drinks.

Pantry prep. Good organization of an in-room dining order helps keep the in-room dining operation running smoothly. In-room dining attendants should set up a service tray or the in-room dining cart ahead of time, to the extent that they can, so that the order can be delivered as soon as the food is ready. The guest check will help determine what items need to be set up. When in-room dining attendants are gathering the china, glasses, and silverware they need for the order, they should check all items to make sure they are clean and free from chips, cracks, water spots, and food residue before arranging them attractively on the tray or cart. Anything that is chipped or cracked should be thrown away; any soiled items should be returned to the dish room.

Next, they perform **pantry prep.** Pantry prep is the process of gathering the uncooked or precooked food needed to complete the order. These might include salads, crackers or bread and butter, and desserts. Butter dishes, salads, and other food items should be covered with foil, food service film, or lids. Condiments (ketchup, mustard, vinegar, syrup, grated cheese, steak sauce, jams and jellies) are important items to remember. Items needed for the beverage order, such as cream, lemon wedges, hot chocolate garnishes, and other beverage accompaniments, should be gathered at this time as well. If the order includes food for children, attendants should include straws and extra napkins.

Attendants should preheat containers that will be used to carry hot beverages to the guestroom; this ensures that a cool container will not cool the hot beverage while it is being delivered. They can do this by filling the containers with hot water from the drip coffee maker and allowing them to stand for three to five minutes.

Cold beverages without ice should be poured into the correct glass when the hot food is nearly ready. In-room dining attendants pour beverages without ice—such as milk, juice, and some soft drinks—first. Then hot drinks (such as coffee, hot tea, and hot chocolate) are poured into the preheated containers. Finally, drinks with ice are poured. If the glasses were previously filled with ice, attendants should drain off any water from the melted ice before adding the beverage. Then all of the beverages should be placed on the service tray or cart. Glasses should be covered with food service film or lids to prevent spills. If the guests ordered bottled beer or wine, the attendant should pick up an ice bucket filled with ice and place the beer or wine in the ice. At some properties, attendants put a clean linen napkin through the ring of the bucket or drape it over the top of the bucket. Dishes filled with items that should be kept cold should rest in a bed of ice to keep the items cold during delivery. This setup is called an **ice compote.**

Picking up the order. While many of the basic, nonalcoholic beverages are prepared by in-room dining attendants, bartenders will prepare alcoholic and other specialty drinks. Attendants pick these orders up from the bar and check that they have been prepared and garnished correctly. They then pick up the food order as soon as it is ready and make sure that it meets property standards. Hot food is usually covered with aluminum foil or plate covers and placed in a hot box.

Delivering the order. Double-checking orders before leaving the kitchen helps save unnecessary return trips to pick up items that were missed. In-room dining carts must be moved carefully. They should be eased over uneven surfaces—such as where carpet meets a tile floor—and pulled into and out of elevators so that the attendant can see where he or she is going.

Most properties set up routes for in-room dining attendants to take through the property. These routes usually take them away from congested areas such as public elevators, lobbies, and restaurant entrances. Quick delivery keeps the food at the proper temperature and prevents drinks from being watered down by melting ice.

After arriving at the guestroom, attendants should knock on the door firmly three times and announce, "In-room dining." If there is no answer, they should knock and announce again. If the guest still does not answer, they should check the room number on the order again. If they have the right room according to the order, the attendant should call the in-room dining department and inform a supervisor of the situation.

When the guest opens the door, attendants should greet the guest by name in the form of a question to verify that they have the right room: "Ms. Lily?" As soon as guests acknowledge that the attendants have the right room, the attendants should follow up with a greeting. They should not enter the room until the guests acknowledge them and invite them in. The guestroom is the guest's "home away from home." Just as they would not enter someone's home uninvited, in-room dining attendants should not enter a guestroom unless they are invited.

Serving the order. Once they have been invited into the guestroom, attendants can enter the room and set up the order. They should offer to place the order on the table, desk, or credenza, whichever the guest prefers. If they are using an in-room dining cart, they should fold out the wings of the table and spread out the tablecloth. They can then place the linen napkins and silverware on the table. The food is served by removing the hot food from the hot box and placing it on the table. Entrée plates are placed so that the main item is closest to the guest. Side dishes are placed to the left of the entrée plate. Attendants should remove the foil or plate covers from the hot food and then place the condiments within the guest's reach, but out of his or her way. Beverages, beverage napkins, glasses, mugs, cups, and saucers should be placed to the right of the entrée plate, and the food service film or lids removed.

At some properties, in-room dining attendants present the check to guests before serving their orders. This gives guests time to review and sign the check while the order is being set up. After the meal is set up, attendants should ask their guests whether they would like anything else. If the guests are satisfied, attendants should ask the guests to phone the in-room dining department for any further service, and collect the signed check (or other form of payment). They should also ask the guests to let the in-room dining department know when they are ready for the tray or cart to be picked up after their meal.

Guest Checks. Most guest checks are presented in a check folder with a pen. The folders keep checks clean and provide a place for guests to put their money or payment cards. Comment cards can also be included in the check folder.

Guest checks for in-room dining will normally be settled as a room charge or by cash. Many properties give in-room dining attendants small amounts of cash so they will not have to make return trips to make change for guests paying with cash. On rare occasions, a guest will pay with a payment card, coupon, gift certificate, or voucher. Personal checks are usually not accepted for in-room dining. If they are, attendants should make sure the check has the guest's name, address, telephone number, and driver's license number on it, so it can be traced if it is returned for non-sufficient funds. Attendants should provide a receipt if guests choose to pay for their order rather than charge it to their room.

Most properties include a mandatory tip on in-room dining checks. If the guest desires, he or she may add an additional gratuity to the check or offer a cash tip, but attendants should not expect it.

Retrieving Trays and Carts. In-room dining attendants pick up trays and carts when guests phone the in-room dining department and request their removal from their guestrooms. Attendants should also retrieve trays and carts whenever they see them in hotel corridors. Trays and carts in guestrooms and corridors are hazards; people can easily trip over them or bump into them. Soiled tableware and equipment left in corridors are unsightly and indicate a poorly run in-room dining department. When a guest phones from a guestroom to retrieve an in-room dining tray or cart, attendants should follow the same procedures to enter a room as they did when delivering the food.

VIP Amenities. A property may give gifts (amenities) to VIPs (very important persons), especially if they are frequent guests of the hotel brand. If the hotel's management orders a VIP amenity, VIP amenity slips will be sent to the in-room dining department listing the amenity, room number, time of delivery, and guest's name.

Fruit and cheese trays are common VIP amenities; they may be assembled in the property kitchen or bought elsewhere. In-room dining attendants often deliver these items before guests check in. Before they deliver them, they should phone the front desk to make sure that the guestrooms listed on the VIP amenity slips are available and have been inspected by housekeeping. They should also double-check each room number before delivering the amenity in case there was a room change, due to a maintenance or other problem.

Even when attendants are sure there is no one in the room, they should still knock before entering, just in case. If the guest does answer the door, they should greet the guest and say that they have a gift to deliver, then present the gift to the guest or take it into the room and place it on a table or credenza. They should avoid placing food in direct sunlight. They should then wish the guest a pleasant stay and leave promptly. If a VIP guest offers a tip, they should politely decline it ("Thank you, but I can't accept your generosity"), since the amenity is a gift from the property. In-room dining attendants should never ask for special favors from VIPs, such as pictures or autographs.

Concierges

Concierges are front desk staff members who are responsible for answering guest questions and meeting special guest needs, but many properties also ask their concierges to assist with some food and beverage functions. These functions often include breakfast buffets and cocktail receptions, especially in VIP lounges or concierge-level floors. Concierges may also work with the in-room dining department, preparing gifts for VIP guests or passing along VIP food or wine preferences stored in guest history files.

Concierge Duties

In the following sections we will discuss the food and beverage duties that some concierges perform at some hotels.

Concierge-Level Kitchens. As just mentioned, some lodging properties have concierge-level or club-level floors set aside for VIPs and others interested in superior guest service. Some of these floors have their own food and beverage facilities for the exclusive use of these guests. These facilities usually have their own distinctive china, silverware, and glasses. Concierges sometimes work with the food and beverage staff members on these floors to ensure that the proper inventory levels for all of these distinctive items are maintained.

Some of these floors feature a food buffet for guests. Before and throughout the buffet, concierges make sure all utensils and service equipment stored in the buffet bar meet par stock requirements. They refill utensils and equipment as needed and wipe the bar with an all-purpose cleaner and a sanitary food service cleaning cloth. When the buffet bar is not in use, they lock its doors.

The kitchen typically also contains a beverage bar which also must be kept fully stocked and cleaned. The refrigerator should be stocked with food and beverage items according to par stock levels established by the property. The concierge may be the staff member assigned to keep track of inventory levels and fill out requisition forms when more items are needed. Often the concierge kitchen will have its own dishwasher. Though not of the industrial size found in commercial kitchens, it is large enough to wash the dishes, glasses, and silverware used during a daily reception or buffet. Other items found in the kitchen or lounge area include microwave ovens, ice makers, and coffee urns.

Breakfast Buffets. Concierges in charge of breakfast buffets on concierge-level or club-level floors typically consult arrivals lists and in-house guest lists to find out what the daily guest count is for the floor; this lets them know how many items they need to set out for the breakfast buffet. They will use these counts to put out an appropriate number of dishes, cups, silverware, napkins, juices, fresh fruits, and pastries. They will then brew coffee and boil water for tea, setting out all the accoutrements for tea and coffee service. Often, they will also set out newspapers and magazines for club-floor guests.

Some concierges will include special touches such as flowers or other decorations as part of the buffet. If there is a television in the lounge, they will usually turn it on to a station that broadcasts the morning news, with the volume turned down to an acceptable level for that hour of the morning.

Concierges work at knowing each VIP guest by name so they can greet each one personally as he or she arrives for breakfast. They then usually stay at the concierge desk or in the room throughout the breakfast buffet so they are available to offer help and refill items as needed. After the breakfast, they take down the breakfast setup and clean the area.

VIP Amenities. Special amenities are often offered to the property's most important guests. Many properties will develop a list of standard amenities that concierges use as a menu when preparing gifts for guests. Typically, a concierge will fill out a VIP supply requisition form, recording the guests' names, arrival and departure dates, food or beverage items needed, and the date and time the items are needed. They then submit the form to the appropriate food and beverage staff member. The items are either delivered by in-room dining attendants or picked up by the concierges when the items are ready.

Cocktail Receptions. Complimentary cocktail receptions are growing in popularity not just for club-level floors, but for all property guests. Concierges are often asked to set up and maintain the cocktail reception. During cocktail service, there is usually a selection of hot hors d'oeuvres and cold hors d'oeuvres. Menu items may include:

- Antipasto salad
- Buffalo wings
- Peel-and-eat shrimp
- Smoked fish
- Chicken and chili quesadillas
- Cheeses
- Vegetables and dip
- Crackers and breads

Concierges can use flowers, props, candles, and other items to make the reception room look more attractive. Cocktail receptions allow concierges to get to know guests better, which can help them provide better service.

While some properties have an honor system where club-floor guests are allowed to pour their own drinks, most control the beverages by having a bartender, a banquet server, or the concierge serve drinks. These staff members are then able to monitor alcohol service and keep beverages well-stocked. During cocktail receptions, alcoholic beverages such as wine, beer, and cocktails may be free to guests for a period of time. Later, cocktails may be available on an honor basis, in which guests keep track of their charges on an honor bar slip. However, as many states restrict the hours of alcohol sales, alcohol must be removed during time periods when sale is prohibited by law.

When the reception is over, the concierge tells any remaining guests that the lounge is closing and wishes them a good evening. After the final guest has departed, the concierge closes and locks the lounge doors and then begins breaking down the cocktail reception. Food is taken to the concierge-level kitchen; dishes and glasses are placed in the dishwashing machine for cleaning. Any tablecloths or taffeta that are soiled are either taken to the laundry or spot cleaned. All surfaces are then washed. If breakfast is being served the next day, preliminary setup will be done before the end of the shift.

Key Terms

banquet event orders (BEOs)—Forms that detail all aspects of a banquet, including menus, number of guests, types of tableware, entertainment, and other details.

banquet servers—Food and beverage staff members who provide food and beverage service to banquet guests.

buffets—Functions where food is placed on a table and the guests serve themselves.

chafing dishes—Special containers in which hot food is held hot either by electricity or gel-can burners.

function rooms—Rooms where banquets, meetings, and receptions take place.

ice compote—A bed of ice that keeps cold in-room dining food and beverage items cold during delivery.

layers—A word describing what coffee does as it is being brewed. The first third of the pot is too weak, the second third is too strong, and the final third is too weak.

linen roll-ups—Silverware wrapped in linen napkins.

pantry prep—The process of gathering the uncooked or precooked food needed for meals.

receptions—Functions where food and drink is typically served for anything from a small business gathering to a large wedding.

 ## Review Questions

1. How do superior performance standards for banquet servers translate into better experiences for guests?

2. What tasks do banquet servers need to perform to prepare for functions?

3. How do the details of correct service procedures enhance a function?

4. What is the difference between buffets, receptions, breakfast service, and meeting room service?

5. What can an in-room dining attendant do to practice safety?

6. What are the steps to taking, preparing, and delivering in-room dining orders?

7. What role does a concierge play in food and beverage service?

8. How is a concierge's work similar to a banquet server's work? an in-room dining attendant's work?

 ## Internet Sites

For more information, visit the following Internet sites. Remember that Internet addresses can change without notice. If the site is no longer there, you can use a search engine to look for additional sites.

Banquet and Catering Software
www.wineasi.com

Chicago Hotel Concierge Association
www.chca.info

Les Clefs d'Or USA
www.lcdusa.org

WebEventPlanner
www.webeventplanner.com

Appendix

Service Techniques	American System					European System			
	Plate	Platter	Cart	Family-Style	Butler	Plate	Platter	French or Butler	Side Table
Service to the left of the guest									
• Platters presented to guest/host		•			•		•	•	
• Plates held with left hand, served with left hand	•								
• Platters carried on left forearm		•			•		•	•	
• Move counterclockwise	•	•	•	•	•	•	•	•	•
• Fingerbowl (placed above dinner fork)	•	•	•	•	•	•	•	•	•
• Food served with spoon and fork in right hand of servers		•					•		
• Guest serves self with spoon and fork					•			•	
• Serve bread and butter	•	•	•		•	•	•	•	•
• Serve salad (as side dish)	•	•	•		•	•	•	•	•
• Crumb table	•	•	•	•	•	•	•	•	•
• Clear salad plate	•	•	•	•	•	•	•	•	•
• Clear B & B plate	•	•	•	•	•	•	•	•	•
• Food plated on guerdon			•						
• Soup	•								
Service to the right of the guest									
• Set hot or cold plates (movement clockwise)			•			•		•	•
• Clear plates	•	•	•	•	•	•	•	•	•
• Change flatware	•	•	•	•	•	•	•	•	•
• Move clockwise	•	•	•	•	•	•	•	•	•
• Pour beverages	•	•	•	•	•	•	•	•	•
• Present wine bottles	•	•	•	•	•	•	•	•	•
• Soup						•	•		
• Food plates held and served with right hand			•			•			

(continued)

Appendix *(continued)*

Service Techniques *(continued)*	American System					European System			
	Plate	Platter	Cart	Family-Style	Butler	Plate	Platter	French or Butler	Side Table
Service performed near table									
• Food is cooked in kitchen and finished at tableside			•						
• Food is carved/boned for plating			•						•
• Food is finished on rechaud (stove)			•						•
• Food is plated from silver platter			•						•
• Two hands (fork and spoon) used to plate food			•						•
Service performed by guests									
• Side dishes, sauces, and vegetable on table to pass				•				•	
• Meat carved and plated by host and served by butler or passed by guest				•					

Chapter 5 Outline

Beverage Server
    Suggestive Selling and Upselling
    Preparing for Service
    Taking Orders
    Serving Drinks
    Maintaining Tables
    Guest Checks
    Clearing Tables
    Last Call and Closing
Bartender
    Key Control
    Standard Drink Recipe Development
    Converting Recipes
    Standard Portable Bar Setup
    Opening Sidework
    Wash Bar Glasses
    Prepare Beverages
    Prepare Orders for In-Room Dining
    Clean Bartop and Lounge During
       Service
    Balance Bank, Make Shift Deposit, and
       Collect Due-Backs
    Clean and Secure the Bar and Lounge
Specific Beverage Service Procedures
    Coffee
    Tea
    Beer
    Wine and Champagne

Competencies

1. Describe the duties of a beverage server. (pp. 173–184)

2. Explain the role that a bartender plays at a beverage operation. (pp. 184–195)

3. Identify the rituals and procedures associated with the service of coffee, tea, beer, wine, and champagne. (pp. 195–204)

5

Select Beverage Service Staff

A CERTAIN MYSTIQUE has grown up around beverage service over the centuries. A plethora of rituals and ceremonies are brought to each beverage sale. Even those who serve the beverages do not escape the expectations of guests. Some guests expect staff members to be chummy confidantes. Other guests look for elegance and refinement from experienced sommeliers.

Given the allure of beverage service, the staff members who provide it hold important roles in a food and beverage operation. The two positions that are most often responsible for serving alcoholic beverages to guests are the beverage server (sometimes called a cocktail server) and the bartender. Both of these positions have a high amount of guest contact, so the people in them must be thoroughly trained in and knowledgeable about the operation's beverages, service styles, standards, and policies.

Beverage Server

A beverage server could be defined as someone who takes and serves guests' beverage orders. While this definition is technically correct, it leaves out the heart of a beverage server's responsibilities. A better definition might be: a food and beverage staff member who does everything possible, within reason, to make each guest's experience at least exactly what he or she wants it to be, and who exceeds guest expectations whenever possible, creating positive, memorable experiences.

Beverage servers are responsible for:

- Preparing for service
- Greeting guests
- Taking the order
- Serving the order
- Creating a friendly atmosphere where guests can enjoy themselves
- Closely monitoring guest alcohol consumption
- Completing service
- Helping other staff members as needed

One secret of success is that everyone works together as a team to give guests great service. Beverage servers are part of a service delivery system. They must give guests and other staff members great service for the system to work.

To be an excellent team player, beverage servers can:

- Help other staff members whenever possible.

- Ask other staff members for help when they need it, so guest service doesn't suffer and all staff members can concentrate on guests' needs.

- Say "hello" to guests and staff members when they see them, and use their names if they know them.

- Say "please" and "thank you" to guests and staff members.

- Share supplies.

- Take pride in their work.

- Always clean up after themselves.

- Immediately remove from tables the items guests do not need anymore.

- Clear and reset tables.

- Restock sidestations so that supplies are always available.

- Write drink orders clearly and completely.

- Ask guests all necessary questions when they place beverage orders, such as, "Do you want that 'up' or 'on-the-rocks'?"

- Turn in drink orders promptly.

- Pick up drinks promptly.

- Properly sort and stack used glasses, china, silverware, and other tableware.

The quality of the food, drinks, and service at a restaurant, club, and lounge should enhance each guest's overall experience. Providing excellent service, beverages, and meals at a reasonable price is each operation's ultimate goal. One way to achieve this goal is to set superior performance standards.

Beverage servers help to meet these superior performance standards. What are some of these standards? They must make sure:

- Alcoholic beverages are served in accordance with state and local laws, ordinances, rules, and regulations.

- The bar and lounge area is clean and attractive.

- Table and bar surfaces are free of spills, spots, chips, cracks, and warping.

- Glasses are clean, sparkling, and free of chips and cracks.

- Each beverage is served with a clean glass and a new beverage coaster or napkin.

- A nonalcoholic beverage menu is available.

- They are familiar with all restaurant menus and food and drink offerings.

- They demonstrate professional behavior.

- Guests are acknowledged within at least two minutes after being seated.

- They quickly approach guests and greet them warmly.

- They introduce themselves to guests, and use guest names whenever possible.

- The initial order is delivered within five minutes or less.

Suggestive Selling and Upselling

Suggestive selling encourages guests to buy additional food and beverages. An example of suggestive selling is suggesting an appetizer to go with beverage orders. **Upselling** means suggesting more expensive and possibly better quality items.

Suggestive selling and upselling require tact and good judgment. If guests know exactly what they want, beverage servers should not try to change their minds. Instead, they could suggest additional items that might improve the guests' experience. One way for servers to increase their success at suggestive selling and upselling is to be familiar with food and beverage trends. (See the chapter appendix for more information about some of today's trends.)

Suggestive selling makes some servers nervous. This is probably because selling reminds them of a pushy salesperson they've known. Using suggestive selling and upselling techniques, however, is not being pushy. These techniques are part of providing good service; guests are merely being offered choices. Done properly, suggestive selling and upselling are not pressure-selling tactics but rather gentle invitations for guests to select what they prefer from options presented to them by the server.

The key to effective selling and upselling is a good knowledge of the menu. Servers have to know all of the products the lounge or restaurant sells. When they are completely familiar with the menu and how each item is prepared, they can suggest dishes confidently and professionally.

Many food and beverage managers encourage servers to suggest the most popular call brands when a guest does not specify a brand. When a guest is not sure what to order, servers can suggest a specialty drink. Other suggestive selling techniques include asking guests whether they would like a glass of wine or a nonalcoholic drink when they decline cocktails. Servers can also always suggest specific alcoholic and nonalcoholic drinks, such as a Bombay Sapphire gin and tonic, a sparkling water, or a mango daiquiri.

Here are some techniques beverage servers can use for more effective suggestive selling and upselling:

1. Develop a selling attitude.

2. Be enthusiastic. It is easier to sell something you are excited about.

3. Make beverages sound appetizing. Use words like "fruity," "icy," and "thirst-quenching" when describing them.

4. Ask questions. Find out if guests are unhurried or only have time for a quick drink; whether they like sweet or tart beverages; if they feel like having something hot or cold.

5. Suggest specific menu items. Don't simply ask: "Would you like soup with your drinks?" Instead, point out: "A cup of gazpacho would go nicely with your martini on a hot day like this."

6. Suggest personal favorites. Try as many beverages as possible, and tell guests that you have tried them: "I think you would like our mint chocolate chip martini, one of our new beverages; it's one of my favorites here." But be honest—don't say that something is your favorite if it isn't.

7. Offer a choice: "Would you like Belvedere or Ketel One in your vodka and tonic?"

8. Suggest the unusual. People go to bars and lounges to get away from their routines, and most guests don't know what they want to order when they arrive.

9. Suggest foods and beverages that naturally go together—beer and pizza, wine and cheese, margaritas and nachos.

10. Compliment guests' choices. Make guests feel good about their choices, even if they don't order what you suggest.

And finally, effective beverage servers ask for the sale. After they suggest and describe a beverage, they ask if the guest would like it. A good way to do this is to describe several items and ask which the guest would prefer.

Beverage servers must always keep responsible beverage service techniques in mind when they sell. A beverage server should never attempt to sell alcoholic beverages to an intoxicated guest or encourage a guest to drink more alcohol than that person wants to have. Rather, beverage servers should focus on selling other nonalcoholic drinks and food when a guest is nearing intoxication or is intoxicated.

Preparing for Service

Beverage servers work with buspersons to set up tables in their area. They should make sure that each table in their section is perfect. This includes checking:

- Silverware
- Glasses
- Napkins
- Salt and pepper shakers or grinders
- Sugar bowls or caddies
- Tablecloths
- The evenness of place mats
- Condiments
- Chairs and booths
- Flower arrangements
- Table lamps
- Floor and carpets
- Overall table appearance
- Ice buckets

Most lounges or restaurants provide beverage servers with an opening-duty checklist that lists all of the tasks they must complete before the lounge opens for service. Some of these tasks may include vacuuming (if housekeeping does not do it), cleaning tables and chairs, checking table lamps, checking flower arrangements, adjusting drapes and blinds, supplying lounge tables with appropriate items, restocking guest checks, and setting up a cash bank.

Sidestations store extra supplies that help eliminate trips to the kitchen for beverage servers. This means more efficient service for guests.

The **sidework checklist** lists sidework tasks and the servers who are assigned to complete each task. These tasks are important to the smooth operation of a bar and lounge. Common sidework tasks include folding napkins and filling salt and pepper shakers.

Taking Orders

Beverage servers are encouraged to greet guests as soon as they are seated. Many properties have a standard greeting time of two minutes or less. Some have only a 60- or 30-second greeting time. Servers who are unable to greet their guests within that time are told to at least stop by the table and let the guests know they'll be back soon. Then they apologize for the wait when they return.

During the greeting, beverage servers tell guests about the specials. They also attempt to read their guests right away. **Reading guests** means determining what type of service they need, want, and expect. Two guests just seated together in a lounge may want privacy to complete a business negotiation; two other guests may be starting an evening devoted to celebrating an anniversary—obviously, these two sets of guests will need, want, and expect two different styles of service, and servers must adjust their service delivery accordingly. Servers must also be alert to newly arrived guests who may have been drinking already and who therefore may become intoxicated quickly.

When guests order alcoholic beverages, beverage servers verify that they are of legal drinking age by checking the identification of anyone who looks under the age of 30. The server should examine the ID and politely ask for another form of identification if it appears the first one has been tampered with or is a false identification.

Most operations use an order-taking system to take orders. Frequently, beverage servers will place a beverage napkin in front of each guest as they take orders to help keep track of who has ordered. They should place the napkin so that any logos are facing the guests. If guests are not ready to order, leaving a beverage napkin at the table will let other servers know that someone has checked with the guests. It is another way to use teamwork to provide excellent guest service.

Beverage servers typically write orders on the guest check or order pad according to how the guests are seated, following a clockwise direction. By using a standard order-taking system, anyone can serve guests without having to annoy them by asking who ordered which items. Servers will usually assign a number to each chair at a table. Chair number one at each table is typically the one closest to the main door or some other landmark in the lounge. All beverage servers use the same reference point as a starting point. Beverage servers then write the order for the guest in chair number one on the first line of the guest check or order pad. They write the order for the guest in chair number two on the second line of the guest check or order pad and continue until all guests have ordered. At some operations, beverage servers write the orders on the back of a guest check and the point-of-sale equipment prints the orders neatly on the front side.

Orders are taken using standard drink and food abbreviations. While taking the orders, beverage servers should listen carefully to each guest's order and repeat the order and details. Any special requests should be noted on the guest check or order pad. Because each guest may have widely different preferences for drinks, servers need to ask what their preferences are for such things as "on-the-rocks" or "straight up."

After taking drink orders, beverage servers often bring complimentary food to guests. Some types of food, such as pasta or pretzels, increase the absorption of alcohol into the bloodstream. Foods high in fat, such as fried cheese, slow the absorption of alcohol into the bloodstream.

If complimentary food is offered on an hors d'oeuvres table, servers should offer to bring items to the guests. If the guests wish to be served, beverage servers should select food items from the hors d'oeuvres table and place them on a small service plate for each guest. They should also bring the appropriate silverware and present it to each guest on a dinner napkin. For serving food in the bar or lounge, silverware may be wrapped in linen napkins in advance. These are typically called **roll-ups.**

If complimentary food is not offered, servers should try to sell appetizers such as seafood cocktails or nachos along with each drink order.

Placing Orders. After taking orders, beverage servers must place the orders with the bartender. This might be done through either point-of-sale systems or by clipping the guest check to a rail.

Many beverage operations ask the beverage servers to set up glasses for drink orders. If so, they should set up the glasses in the order in which they will "call" the drinks. They should place the glasses near the edge of the bartender's side of the service bar. They should also fill glasses with ice (always with a scoop) for drinks that require ice.

One way beverage servers can help bartenders is by being organized when giving drink orders. This means combining drink orders for more than one table and calling the drinks in a specific order to the bartender. To call a drink, servers should use a clear voice and say "Ordering," and then tell the bartender the drink orders, including any special instructions. A calling order is necessary because some drinks take longer to prepare than other drinks or do not hold up as well. Exhibit 1 shows a standard calling order for drinks.

After calling the drinks, the written order is placed where the bartender can refer to it. The beverage server then places one beverage napkin for each glass on the beverage tray and inserts stirrers or straws if needed.

Serving Drinks

Mixing, pouring, garnishing, and serving drinks the same way every time is the mark of a quality operation. To help create this quality, beverage servers should

Exhibit 1   Standard Drink Calling Order

A standard calling order for drinks is:

- Bottled beer
- Frozen drinks
- Highballs
- Cognacs
- Liqueurs or cordials
- Mixed drinks
- Blended drinks
- Cream drinks
- Plain sodas and juices
- Wine by the glass
- Draft beer

check all beverages to make sure they are complete as ordered before serving them. If something is amiss, they must fix it before serving the drink. They can check each beverage by asking themselves:

- Is it the correct beverage?
- Is it in the correct glass?
- Is the garnish correct?
- Have special instructions been followed?
- Has anything spilled over the side?
- Should it have a chaser?

Beverage Trays. Beverage trays are often lined with a linen napkin to improve the look of the tray. Typically, there are two types of trays. A 12- to 14-inch beverage tray is used only for serving beverages or serving food to a single guest. A large restaurant service tray, usually 27 inches long and oval in shape, is used for serving food to a party of more than one and for clearing tables. Many operations use cork-lined trays so glasses won't slip. Beverage servers also often keep an extra pen and extra beverage napkins on the tray. They center glasses on the tray so that it will be balanced. Heavy or tall glasses are put in the center of the tray. Servers must also keep in mind the order in which they will serve the drinks so that the tray will be balanced until the last drink is removed.

Safe work habits should come into play whenever servers carry trays. When filled with beverages, the trays are often heavy and potentially treacherous. Safe lifting and carrying involves bending at the knees and lowering the shoulder below the tray. Servers then pull the tray with one hand onto the palm of the other

Sommeliers deliver outstanding wine experiences for guests.

hand. They balance the tray at shoulder level on their fingertips, not on their forearms. (If the tray is carried on the forearm, it may tip over.) They then keep their back straight as they stand up and steady the tray with their free hand.

Serving Beverages. Traditionally, servers have served women first and the host of the group last. In a no-host situation, they simply serve women first and men last. The first step is to place a beverage napkin on the table in front of the guest, unless they have already placed one. They then move around the table and serve every guest from the guest's right side with the server's right hand when possible. They avoid reaching across guests.

Servers handle glasses away from their rim or lip. Stemmed glasses are handled by the stem or base. Hands warm drinks when they touch the outside of the glass and it is unsanitary to put fingers inside a glass.

A sign of a quality operation is that beverage servers know who ordered which drink and they do not have to ask who ordered what. They also repeat the name of the drink and any special requests as they serve each drink so that they can ensure all is correct.

At some beverage operations, beverage servers pour bottled beer into a glass at the table, while at other operations, guests pour their own beer from the bottle.

Maintaining Tables

The beverage server's job does not end with the delivery of a single round of drinks. Guests will frequently want refills. Also, when empty glasses and other items are quickly cleared away, the entire operation looks neater and guests can have a more relaxing time with a less cluttered table. Maintaining a table typically involves:

- Clearing items such as dirty tableware, linens, and any other items that are not being used.

- Keeping the bar and lounge area neat at all times.

When a guest's glass is half to three-quarters empty, beverage servers should ask guests whether they would like another beverage. They suggest alcoholic drinks only to guests who are not intoxicated or nearing intoxication. This means that servers must count the number of drinks each person has had and what type of drink they've had. The amount of alcohol in a mixed drink with one ounce of alcohol is about equal to one beer or to one glass of wine. Drinks are served only to guests who want them; servers do not simply bring another round for everyone if some guests do not want another drink. Also, as operations allow, servers will provide nuts, buttery popcorn, or other high-fat snacks to slow the absorption of alcohol into the bloodstream.

When writing the second order on the order pad or guest check, servers typically draw a line under the first order and write the new order below the line. They write "repeat" on the order pad or guest check if all guests in a party order the same thing for the next round.

Servers should clear empty glasses and beverage napkins before serving additional beverages and always bring a fresh glass with each fresh bottle of beer.

Guest Checks

Prompt service in processing payment is the guest's last impression of a beverage operation. It is a key service point for all beverage servers. The exact procedures for totaling guest checks and presenting the check to guests will vary among operations and will often be dictated by the point-of-sale system.

If guests get up to leave before beverage servers present the check, servers should ask, "Are you ready to settle your tab?"

Most operations present checks in a check folder. Check folders keep checks clean and provide a place for guests to put their money or payment card. It is also an ideal place for operations to put guest comment cards.

Cash. When guests pay by cash, servers should take the money to the point-of-sale system and then present change in the guest check folder (they should never ask, "Do you need change?"). They should not claim a tip until guests leave. If the guest leaves while the server is settling the check, the change is then taken as a tip. Operations should always provide a receipt with the change.

Traveler's Checks. Traveler's checks must be signed in the presence of the beverage server. If the server was not present, he or she must ask to see a driver's license and compare the signatures on the two documents.

Payment Cards. Beverage servers must always get an approval code when taking payments by payment card. If a payment card is declined, they can discreetly and politely ask the guest for another card or form of payment. If necessary, a beverage server might ask the guest to step away from his or her group to avoid embarrassment.

Typically, servers will imprint the card on the back of the guest check and on a payment card voucher. They may be asked to underline the account number and the expiration date on the imprint. If the card is expired, they should return it and ask for another form of payment. They then complete the voucher by entering the date, their name, the guest check number, which payment card is being used, the approval code, and the amount of the purchase. The voucher is then presented with a pen to the guest. The guest totals and signs the voucher. Guests will often include a tip before signing the voucher. Servers return the card along with the guest's copy of the payment card voucher.

House Accounts. Guests who are staying at a lodging property with approved credit accounts may charge restaurant meals and drinks to their room. This is called a "house account." These guests print their names and room numbers on the guest checks and sign them. Often operations will ask guests to present their room key as identification. In addition to guests, some associates, such as sales staff members or managers, may also have house accounts.

City Ledger Accounts. Some local guests may have charge accounts. This allows them to be directly billed each month. Such local accounts are called "city ledger accounts." When settling guest checks charged to city ledger accounts, servers ask guests to print the company name or group name on the check. They also ask for the city ledger account number and then have the guests sign the guest check. They then provide a receipt showing the charge.

Personal Checks. It is extremely important that beverage servers get as much information as possible from the guest who is settling the bill by using a personal check. This information helps assure that a personal check is good or can be traced if it is returned for non-sufficient funds.

Coupons, Vouchers, or Gift Certificates. Each operation will have its own policy for each type of coupon, voucher, or gift certificate. For example, many operations do not give change for gift certificates and coupons. However, guests may receive smaller gift certificates in place of change. Servers should carefully read any document they are given to determine whether it is valid and unexpired. They also check to see which charges are covered, as some coupons might exclude alcoholic beverages or particular meals. If the document is valid, servers should treat it the same as cash. They collect the balance of the guest check if the document doesn't cover the full amount. They then put the receipt and any change or smaller gift certificates in the guest folder and return it to the guest. Many operations are now issuing debit cards rather than paper gift certificates or vouchers.

Transferring Checks. If an operation has a separate lounge and restaurant, there may be times when a guest transfers his or her bar charges into the restaurant and pays both at the end of the visit. This is possible only if the operation's point-of-sale system allows it; otherwise, servers must settle guest checks before the guests move into the restaurant. However, transferring a bar tab to the restaurant is one way to show guests that an operation's first priority is service.

Also, beverage servers may offer to deliver unfinished drinks to the restaurant after guests are seated. This must be done promptly so that the ice does not melt and ruin the drinks.

Clearing Tables

While most restaurants have server assistants (or buspersons), it is common for beverage servers to clear lounge tables after the guests have left. A sign of quality in an operation is to have the tables cleared within five minutes of guest departure. This helps to seat other guests quickly and keeps the operation looking good.

When clearing tables, servers should place a service tray on a nearby tray jack or bring out a bus tub. They place all dirty tableware on the tray or in the bus tub, being alert to broken glass, personal articles left behind by guests, and missing items that belong to the property. They are also careful to not put their fingers in glasses. Clearing the table also involves removing all used napkins. When possible, servers should avoid stacking plates in front of guests.

After the table is cleared, it must be cleaned and sanitized. Sanitizing solution is kept at each sidestation. Crumbs can be brushed into a beverage napkin. Servers also clean chairs by brushing crumbs off, wiping the seats with a clean, damp cloth (*not* the same one used for the tabletop), and placing the chairs so that the seats are even with the table edge.

Once the tables are cleared, servers should reset them so that the tables are as neat and attractive as they were when the operation first opened. Every newly set table in an operation should look the same, whether it was set before the lounge opened or right after the last group of guests left the table. When tables are set consistently, it shows guests that the staff cares about providing a quality food and beverage experience. Table setup specifications may change with the time of day (no tablecloth at lunch, for example).

Last Call and Closing

Many states and localities require beverage operations to stop alcohol service at a particular time. Where this is the case, an operation will often issue a "last call" at least 20 minutes before closing.

Beverage servers are typically the ones who deliver the last call message. They typically tell guests it is the last call and ask whether they would like another beverage before the bar closes. They do not offer to serve alcoholic beverages to guests who are intoxicated or who are almost intoxicated. They also don't serve double orders during last call.

Exhibit 2   Last Call Alerts

During last call, beverage servers are especially alert to:

- Guests who try to leave without settling an open check.
- Guests who appear intoxicated and should not be allowed to drive.
- Guests who may need assistance to their guestrooms.
- Guests who harass employees to go out with them after closing.
- Guests who try to take alcohol with them in open containers if this is illegal in the establishment's area.

After the last drink is served, beverage servers prepare the lounge for closing by cleaning and storing equipment.

Guests may ask servers to keep the operation open later or to sell items after closing. It is important that no alcohol is sold after the closing time the operation's liquor license specifies. Beverage servers are in charge of the guests in their section. If guests resist closing, servers should be pleasant and simply tell guests that management sets closing time and they must comply. Exhibit 2 lists some of the things that servers should watch for during last call.

Closing duties vary with different operations. Typically an operation will have a closing duty checklist. If the beverage servers have performed cleaning chores throughout the shift, they will have less work to do at closing time. Common closing duties include:

- Cleaning tables and chairs
- Taking soiled tableware to the dish room
- Cleaning out and storing ice buckets
- Cleaning service trays
- Storing food
- Removing flowers from tables
- Cleaning the side station
- Vacuuming carpets
- Turning in guest checks
- Removing all trash and relining trash cans

Bartender

Bartenders prepare and serve drinks to bar and lounge guests and sometimes serve food as well. They prepare beverages for beverage servers, restaurant servers, and in-room dining (room service) attendants to bring to their guests.

On May 11, 1911, H. L. Mencken described bartenders in the *Baltimore Evening Sun:*

> The average bartender, despite the slanders of professional moralists, is a man of self respect and self possession; a man who excels at a difficult art and is well aware of it; a man who shrinks from ruffianism as he does from uncleanliness; in short, a gentleman…the bartender is one of the most dignified, law abiding, and ascetic of men. He is girt about by a rigid code of professional ethics; his work demands a clear head and a steady hand; he must have sound and fluent conversation; he cannot be drunken or dirty; the slightest dubiousness is quick to exile him to the police force, journalism, the oyster boats or some other Siberia of the broken.

Today, bartenders are as likely to be women as men, but many of the traits Mencken describes continue to hold true. Bartenders are responsible for:

- Monitoring guests' alcohol consumption.
- Controlling alcohol risks effectively.
- Ensuring that drinks are prepared consistently and to quality standards every time.
- Knowing how to use bar equipment efficiently and safely.
- Helping control waste and costs.
- Maintaining bar sanitation.
- Preparing drinks promptly.
- Accommodating the taste preferences of individual guests.
- Making drinks look attractive.
- Promoting the operation's facilities.

In addition, experienced bartenders may help train new bartenders and beverage servers, and they may test new drink recipes.

Bartenders contribute to the operation's team by:

- Helping co-workers and guests whenever possible.
- Turning in food orders promptly to the kitchen to prevent last-minute rushing for everyone involved.
- Picking up food from the kitchen when beverage servers are busy.
- Conducting inventories according to the inventory schedule to ensure that other bartenders won't run out of supplies.
- Reporting repairs to engineering using a maintenance request system, and filling out a maintenance request form, if necessary.
- Providing the same excellent service to other staff members that they provide to guests.

Key Control

Bartenders use many different keys. At any given operation, they might control keys to the cash bank, alcohol storerooms, bars, and other limited-access areas. All bartenders should be trained in proper key control to protect these areas.

Key control guidelines for bartenders include:

- Following procedures for signing keys in and out.

- Never leaving keys in a door's lock and never setting them down. They should keep keys with them or secured in a cash drawer at all times.

- Always turning in any keys before leaving the operation for any reason.

- Reporting any lost keys immediately to the manager-on-duty.

Standard Drink Recipe Development

Every standard drink recipe an operation uses has been thoroughly tested. Typical testing procedures include the following:

- A skilled bartender creates a tested recipe or one is selected from a published source.

- Several people prepare and test the drink. Guests participate in the testing. The bartender collects feedback about the drink's flavor, color, and strength.

- Adjustments are made to the recipe based on the feedback, and testing continues until the recipe produces a perfect result.

- Preparation testers consider the difficulty of the recipe, how guests will like it, potential service problems, and how many servings might be sold.

- Final adjustments are made.

Although individual bartenders may find some ingredients or methods odd, they should be instructed to follow the exact recipe so that the drinks are consistent no matter who mixes the drink.

Converting Recipes

When several guests in the same party order the same type of drink, most bartenders will make the drinks in a batch to save time. Making drinks in batches involves converting drink recipes. Bartenders must be well trained in converting drink recipes because, if they convert incorrectly, they end up wasting ingredients or not having enough drinks for their guests.

Most standard drink recipes make one drink. To convert most recipes, bartenders can simply count the number of guests ordering the drink, and multiply the ingredients by the number of guests. For a sample conversion, see Exhibit 3.

When several drinks are made in a batch, bartenders must use equipment large enough to accommodate the amount of their ingredients. Some drinks—such as layered drinks, in which lighter ingredients are floated on top of others—must be made one at a time and cannot be made in a batch.

Exhibit 3   Recipe Conversion

Most standard drink recipes make one drink. To convert a recipe, simply count the number of guests ordering the drink, and multiply the ingredients by the number of guests. For example, if five guests have ordered margaritas, you will multiply all of the ingredients in your recipe by five:

Margarita for 1				Margarita for 5
1 ounce Tequila	×	5	=	5 ounces Tequila
½ ounce Triple Sec	×	5	=	2 ½ ounces Triple Sec
1 ounce lime juice	×	5	=	5 ounces lime juice

When you make several drinks in a batch, always be sure to use equipment large enough to accommodate the amount of your ingredients.

Standard Portable Bar Setup

Bartenders may work in a lounge, restaurant, banquet room, suite, or reception room. In such service areas as banquet or reception rooms, bartenders prepare and serve drinks from a portable bar. Being able to easily find the correct spirits, mixers, glassware, napkins, and other items in a portable bar conveys an image of professionalism and quality service to guests.

Bartenders should stock the bar for the number of people they will be serving, plus an additional percentage. The number of people that will be served is typically available on a banquet event order.

Opening Sidework

Like beverage servers, bartenders have several tasks that fall under opening sidework. These tasks include:

- Picking up, verifying, and setting up a cash bank.
- Setting up the point-of-sale equipment.
- Setting up guest checks.
- Reviewing the bar logbook.
- Reviewing the daily function sheet.
- Picking up and transporting liquor and food issues from storerooms.
- Storing items.
- Preparing the bar area.
- Preparing mixes and garnishes.
- Preparing service areas.

There may be other tasks for bartenders to complete, depending on the opening-duty checklist used at their operation.

Exhibit 4   Receipt of Cash Bank

By signing on the last unsigned line below, I acknowledge receipt of cash in the amount of $_____ to be used as a cash register bank. The total amount is due and payable before checking out at the end of the shift.

Name	Date of Shift	Returned (Signature of Manager on Duty)

Picking Up, Verifying, and Setting Up a Cash Bank. Bartenders must be given a cash bank at the beginning of their shifts. In many operations, a bartender completes a form similar to the one shown in Exhibit 4. In this way, the bartender certifies that the cash bank has been received and that he or she is responsible for the amount of cash in the bank until the bank is returned at the end of the shift.

Setting Up the Point-of-Sale Equipment. Bartenders start their shift by taking preshift readings on the point-of-sale (POS) units and recording those readings on the cashier's report. This reading establishes a starting point for sales during the shift. As POS units become more sophisticated, such sales records are able to be further broken down.

Setting Up Guest Checks. Every staff member at a food and beverage operation is accountable for his or her own checks. They typically pick up and sign for these checks when they pick up the cash bank, unless the point-of-sale unit produces guest checks. If the latter is the case, then the operation will not distribute guest checks. Often, bartenders will be responsible for issuing guest checks to beverage servers. When this is the case, they record the range of check numbers on the checks servers receive. Depending on how busy the operation is, the bartender may bundle servers' checks in batches of 15, 25, or 35 to save issuing time.

Reviewing the Bar Logbook. Bar logbook entries are extremely important—if the operation is ever sued in any matter related to alcohol service, the entries are legal records. The logbook keeps bartenders informed about important events and decisions that happened during previous shifts. Some of the incidents that might be noted in the bar logbook include the following:

*   Service is cut off for an intoxicated guest.

*   A dissatisfied guest is compensated in any way, including complimentary service.

*   A staff member is harassed by a guest.

- Something is spilled on a guest.

- An accident or injury involves guests or staff members.

- A sick guest requires medical help.

- Bar products or money is stolen.

- Bar equipment breaks down.

- A guest demands a service that the operation cannot provide.

- Food and beverages are unavailable.

- A foreign object is found in a food or beverage item.

Reviewing the Daily Function Sheet. The daily function sheet tells bartenders what activities and meetings are taking place at the operation. These are most common in operations that are attached to lodging properties.

Picking Up and Transporting Liquor and Food Issues from Storerooms. Bartenders should pick up the exact type and quantity of items listed on the food requisition and beverage requisition and sign for it. At some operations, storeroom personnel may be responsible for delivering items.

Storing Items. Bartenders should rotate old stock to the front and new stock to the rear. As they rotate the stock, they should check expiration dates and inform their supervisor about any items that have expired or are about to expire.

Preparing the Bar Area. To start the shift, bartenders set up portable equipment such as mixers or blenders. The supplies and portable equipment used at each operation will vary according to menus and service styles. Some common equipment and supplies include: heavy-duty blenders, spindle drink mixers, cocktail shakers, bar spoons, corkscrews, ice buckets, ice scoops, cork-lined beverage trays, bar glassware, coffee cups and saucers, stir sticks, tall straws, beverage straws, round toothpicks, beverage napkins, linen napkins and silverware roll-ups, cutting boards, paring knives, salt shakers, pepper shakers, and others.

When setting up liquor, bartenders should create a speed rail for house brands. Many operations will have a standard speed rail setup for house brands. Otherwise, a common order is:

- Vodka

- Gin

- Rum

- Whiskey

- Scotch

- Bourbon

- Sweet vermouth

- Dry vermouth

- Brandy

- Grenadine
- Lime juice

Next, bartenders should set up display bottles of call brands and assemble and set up draft-beer and soda-dispensing equipment. They should also check pre- and post-mix tanks and beer kegs, changing them as needed. Clean glasses should be set up according to type and in the amounts the operation sets. Bartenders may also set up manual glass-washing equipment for the washing of bar glasses.

Next, bartenders should set up for coffee service and make sure the ice bins are clean and filled with fresh ice. In some operations, the bartenders may also set up food such as popcorn machines or hors d'oeuvres tables. Finally, they should sanitize the bar and counter by spraying an approved sanitizing solution on them and wiping them with a clean, foodservice-safe cloth.

Preparing Mixes and Garnishes. To provide more efficient service, bartenders often prepare some mixes and garnishes ahead of time. If there are leftover mixes or garnishes, they should check them for freshness and appearance, discarding anything doubtful or unusable. Mix and garnish ingredients range from types of juices to fruits and vegetables to sugar and salt.

Preparing Service Areas. Along with the beverage servers, bartenders should check the lounge tables. Table cards and displays are sometimes used to promote food or drink items; displays may be used to promote wines or champagnes. Bartenders should make sure this material is neat and in good shape, replacing whatever is worn. They should also refuel table lamps or replace candles and make sure that table cards, chairs, and stools are clean and arranged properly.

Wash Bar Glasses

Many bars will hand wash some of the bar glasses—especially those glasses in which beer will be served.

To wash glasses, bartenders should fill a washing sink with water that is at least 110 degrees Fahrenheit (43 degrees Celsius). A washing sink is one with brushes mounted in the bottom. A thermometer is typically kept on hand to check water temperature. A detergent is added to the first sink and the center sink is filled with clean, clear rinse water that is at least 120 degrees Fahrenheit (49 degrees Celsius). The third sink is filled with clean, clear water and a sanitizing solution. The proper temperature of the water will depend on the type of sanitizing solution being used and will typically be provided with the manufacturer's guidelines.

When hand washing bar glasses, each glass should be moved up and down 12 to 15 times on the brush mounted on the bottom of the sink, to be sure to clean away all lipstick and residue. Each glass is then thoroughly rinsed in the rinsing and sanitizing sinks.

It is necessary to test and change the sanitizing solution often, because the detergent residue from glasses will break down the sanitizer. Footed glasses are hung on a rack to dry and unfooted glasses are placed on a stainless steel drain board. If the rinse water is hot and changed often, the glasses should drain and air dry without spots. After drying, they can be moved to shelves.

Bar glasses are not hand dried or polished. Drying and polishing violates the health code because it puts germs on the glasses from your hands and the towel. Glasses are stored upside-down to prevent contaminants from falling into them.

Prepare Beverages

Standard recipes keep drinks consistent. Bartenders should make it their goal to memorize the standard recipes used at their operation. Those who have not memorized the recipes should read all recipes twice before preparing drinks.

Once bartenders have read the recipe, they should gather all of the needed ingredients and equipment. Each time they prepare a drink, they should measure all the ingredients. Exhibit 5 gives several standard measurements. Some bartenders think they are doing guests a favor by over pouring; however, a strong drink is not necessarily a quality drink. Many operations have automated liquor guns for pouring well-brand liquor. These guns will pour a standard shot of alcohol whenever used. Certain mixes, such as water or soda, may also be poured from a gun. This speeds service and provides additional cost control for the bar.

Good drink recipes specify the type of glass needed for each drink. The bar glass sizes at each operation are related to the pour size (the standard amount of liquor poured for each drink recipe) and the prices charged for drinks.

Special precautions must be taken when handling ice used for drinks. Guests consume ice, especially after it melts, so sanitary guidelines must be followed. The ice bin should be cleaned each day before ice is added. Bartenders should use a clean ice scoop or tongs to handle ice and should not scoop it with a glass or their hands. Cubed or cracked ice is used for stirred or shaken drinks, crushed ice is used for mists. If glass breaks in the ice bin or anything spills into the ice bin, the bartender must empty all ice, clean the bin, and refill it with fresh, clean ice.

Stirred Drinks. To prepare stirred drinks, bartenders place all ingredients in a mixing glass. If several guests order the same stirred drink, the drinks are prepared in a batch. If the beverage is mixed with fruit juices or aromatics, it is stirred with a spoon and a scoop of ice is added. The drink should be stirred three to four times to mix and chill it. Bartenders must be careful not to over-stir, or the alcohol will be watered down by the melting ice. After stirring, the ingredients are strained from the mixing glass into the correct serving glass. If drinks are being made in a batch, drinks are strained so that each glass is filled to the midpoint. Then the remainder is evenly divided among the glasses.

Shaken or Blended Drinks. Preparing drinks in a shaker is one way many bartenders add artistic flair to their work. Some bartenders hold the mixing glass and shaker over their head and shake vigorously to put on a show for guests. This type of showiness works well in a noisy "action" bar, but would be in poor taste in a quiet, intimate bar and lounge. Good bartenders match their bartending style to their bar.

When bartenders shake or blend drinks, ice is placed in a mixing glass, followed by the nonalcoholic ingredients and then the alcohol. A metal shaker is placed firmly upside down on top of the mixing glass. Holding the two securely together, the bartender shakes hard and fast. After shaking, the drink is strained into the correct glass and garnished according to the recipe.

Exhibit 5   Measurement Cross-Check Chart

Mixologist's Measurement Cross-Check Chart

	Dash	Barspoon	Tsp	Tbsp	oz	Jigger	Wine Glass	Cup
Dash	1	$1/3$	$1/6$	$1/18$	$1/36$	$1/54$	$1/144$	$1/288$
Barspoon	3	1	$1/2$	$1/6$	$1/12$	$1/18$	$1/48$	$1/144$
Teaspoon	6	2	1	$1/3$	$1/6$	$1/9$	$1/24$	$1/48$
Tablespoon	18	6	3	1	$1/2$	$1/3$	$1/8$	$1/16$
Ounce	36	12	6	2	1	$2/3$	$1/4$	$1/8$
Pony	36	12	6	2	1	$2/3$	$1/4$	$1/8$
Jigger	54	18	9	3	$1 1/2$	1	$3/8$	$3/16$
Wine glass	144	48	24	8	4	$2 2/3$	1	$1/2$
Cup	288	96	48	16	8	$5 1/3$	2	1

Measurement Relationships—American Units

8 oz	=	2 gills	=	1 cup	=	½ pint			
16 oz	=	4 gills	=	2 cups	=	1 pint	=	½ quart	
32 oz	=	8 gills	=	4 cups	=	2 pints	=	1 quart	=	¼ gallon
		16 gills	=	8 cups	=	4 pints	=	2 quarts	=	½ gallon
		32 gills	=	16 cups	=	8 pints	=	4 quarts	=	1 gallon

15 3/4 gallons   =   1 keg   =   1/2 barrel   =   1/4 hogshead
31 1/2 gallons   =   2 kegs   =   1 barrel   =   1/2 hogshead
63 gallons   =   4 kegs   =   2 barrels   =   1 hogshead

Metric System Measures for Distilled Spirits

Old Bottle Size	U.S. Measure	New Metric Measure	U.S. Measure	Servings per Bottle (1 ½)
Miniature	1.6 oz	50 ml	1.7 oz	1
Half pint	8 oz	200 ml	6.8 oz	4½
Pint	16 oz	500 ml	16.9 oz	$11 1/4$
Fifth	25.6 oz	750 ml	25.4 oz	17
Quart	32 oz	1 Liter	33.8 oz	22
Half gallon	64 oz	1.76 l	59.2 oz	39½

Wine Bottle Measures

Name	Metric Measure	U.S. Measure	Servings per Bottle (4 ½ oz)
Split	187 ml	6.3 oz	1½
Tenth	375 ml	12.7 oz	3
Fifth	750 ml	25.4 oz	6
Quart	1 Liter	33.8 oz	8
Magnum	1.5 l	50.7 oz	12
Double magnum	3l	101.4 oz	24

Bartenders shake or blend drinks with a mixing glass and shaker.

Frozen Drinks. Frozen drinks include daiquiris and margaritas. Bartenders begin by placing a scoop of ice in a blender cup and adding the other ingredients. The mixture is placed in an electric blender and blended until the ice is crushed and the ingredients are pureed. Bartenders must be careful not to over-blend frozen drinks. They then pour the drink from the blender cup into the correct glass and garnish as the recipe directs.

Building Drinks. Some drinks are prepared using what is called a "build" method. To make drinks in this fashion, bartenders place ice in the correct serving glass, then add the liquor. Next, they add the correct amount of mixer, the garnish, and a swizzle (stir) stick. The drink is served without mixing, stirring, or shaking.

Layered Drinks. Bartenders create a layered drink by pouring each beverage on top of the previous one in layers to form multicolored stripes in the glass. Some layered drinks have only one alcoholic beverage, and sweet cream (whole cream, not whipped) is "floated" on top. Ice is not used for layered drinks. The heavier ingredients are poured first so that the lighter ingredients will float on top of the heavier layers. If a recipe calls for floating an ingredient off the back of a spoon, the ingredient is poured over the rounded part of a spoon into the glass. The spoon method reduces the chance of disturbing the layer below.

Coffee Drinks. Coffee drinks can be a good seller in cold weather, especially as an after-dinner drink. With the increasing growth in popularity of coffee shops, specialty coffee drinks are being ordered more frequently. Most coffee drinks are begun by pouring fresh hot coffee into the correct glass or mug. The other ingredients are added according to the recipe. A bartender gently stirs the ingredients with a bar spoon and adds whipped cream as called for by the recipe.

Prepare Orders for In-Room Dining

Bartenders who work at lodging properties may help prepare drinks for in-room dining. Most small properties will provide beverage service from a main bar rather than from a separate in-room dining bar.

An in-room dining attendant typically picks up prepared drinks. There will usually be some sort of covering for the glass, either plastic wrap or a paper covering.

Many properties use a control procedure called red-lining. This involves bartenders drawing a red line under the last beverage listed on the order. Operations will also have control procedures to account for full-bottle sales. Tight controls are required for all beverage activities. These controls help to properly charge revenue to the appropriate departments.

Clean Bartop and Lounge During Service

Bartenders and beverage servers work together to keep the bar and lounge neat at all times. This involves:

- Removing glasses, napkins, food plates, and silverware that are not being used

- Clearing empty plates from guest tables

- Picking up any popcorn or snacks on the floor

Balance Bank, Make Shift Deposit, and Collect Due-Backs

A **cash bank** is the smallest amount of cash that allows bartenders to do their business. It is individual to each bartender and each individual should be the only one using his or her own cash bank.

Bartenders are responsible for maintaining security over their cash bank at all times. This involves counting their cash bank money at least twice before starting the shift. The count should be in a private place away from the public. Most operations will ask bartenders to sign a cash-bank contract assuming responsibility for the bank when it is issued. The cash bank is locked in a safe-deposit box between shifts and the bartender must maintain key control over the safe-deposit key.

At the end of each shift, bartenders prepare a deposit and cashier's report. They begin by counting any vouchers for tips paid out as cash, since that amount will be reimbursed as a due-back. In a safe, private location, bartenders count the money in the deposit, and list cash, change, checks, traveler's checks, gift certificates, coupons, credit vouchers, and other forms of income on a cashier's report. They then place the deposit in a deposit envelope along with the cashier's report. They seal the envelope and sign their names across the seal. The deposit envelope is then placed in a drop safe with a witness present. The bartender and the witness sign the drop safe logbook.

Bartenders prepare due-back vouchers for the total amount of money they paid out of their cash bank during the shift. A **due-back** is a receipt for any money that is paid out of the bank. It could cover change or small purchases made with a manager's approval. It might also reimburse the bartender for any cash paid out to staff members for tips on payment cards or house accounts. The cash bank must never be used for personal loans. Most operations will have unannounced audits of cash banks.

The bartender documents due-backs with copies of payment card vouchers, charge tips, and a tips-paid-out voucher signed by each staff member who was paid tips. Bartenders then take the due-backs to the general cashier, along with the backup vouchers, and receive reimbursement for their banks. When the general cashier is not available, they put the tips-paid-out vouchers in the safe-deposit box until the next shift they work. They are then turned in for reimbursement.

Clean and Secure the Bar and Lounge

Bartenders have a number of specific tasks that they must do to help clean and secure the bar and lounge. The exact tasks and procedures will vary among operations, but they generally include:

- Closing out guest checks and point of-sale equipment. This is often the first task in operations connected to a lodging property. It helps the night auditor begin his or her work on time.

- Separating cash bank from shift receipts.

- Washing, sanitizing, and storing all glassware and small utensils.

- Recording all empty liquor bottles (type, size, quantity) on a beverage requisition. Sometimes this task is performed as part of opening duty.

- Storing and locking displayed liquor in the proper cooler or cabinet.

- Storing leftovers. Bartenders discard unusable fruit garnishes, cover fresh garnishes, label and date containers, refrigerate leftover garnishes, and discard unusable mixes.

- Preparing the food requisition for items needed for the next day.

- Cleaning dispensing equipment.

- Emptying trash and washing and relining trash cans.

- Cleaning and sanitizing portable equipment and work areas. The closed bar should be clean and in order.

- Doing a final check of the area.

Specific Beverage Service Procedures

Whether it is the beverage server or the bartender preparing and bringing to the table the drinks, there are certain procedures that apply to different beverages. This chapter will briefly look at the rituals and procedures involved with serving:

- Coffee
- Tea
- Beer
- Wine and champagne

Coffee

Coffee has long been a popular drink in the United States, and specialty coffee drinks are a trend which continues to strengthen. As heated coffee quickly goes bad and can be bitter if improperly brewed, it is important to prepare coffee correctly.

Coffee pots need to be clean before they are used. One common problem is coffee residue. This forms when a stainless steel or glass pot is left on a burner too long. Servers must keep careful eyes on pots as coffee evaporates quickly, scorching the residue. This makes the pots difficult to clean. If an empty pot is left for too long on a hot burner, the pot may explode. Steps for removing coffee residue are to place a scoop of ice in the pot along with a half cup of table salt and a squeeze of lemon juice. The pot must not be hot, or it might explode. The ice is swirled in the pot for several minutes, then the pot is emptied and taken to the dishroom for washing.

To prepare coffee, follow these steps:

- Remove the grounds holder from the coffee maker. If necessary, throw away the grounds and rinse the holder.
- Remove the sanitary wrapping from a pre-measured filter pack of fresh coffee. Shake the filter pack to evenly spread the coffee.
- Place the filter pack in the grounds holder, seam-side down.
- Replace the grounds holder in the coffee maker.
- Place a clean coffee pot under the grounds holder. Use the correct pot for the type of coffee being brewed (regular, flavored, or decaffeinated).
- Pour water into the coffee maker from a measured pitcher or a clean coffee pot. Press the "start" button, if necessary.
- If using an automatic coffee urn connected to a direct water source, press the "brew" button.
- Allow all water to pass through the ground coffee before serving any coffee.
- Turn on the reserve burner. Move the full pot of fresh coffee to the reserve burner.
- Remove the grounds holder and throw away the grounds.
- Rinse the holder and replace it in the machine.
- After each shift, clean the nozzle head on the grounds holder, and the area around the nozzle head.

Coffee strength **layers** as the water passes through the ground coffee. The first third of the pot will be too weak, the second will be too strong, and the last third will be too weak. To get the right flavor, let the full pot drip to blend the layers and arrive at the desired strength.

Coffee begins to go bad immediately after it is brewed. The oils in the coffee break down and a foul odor and taste will develop. Operations should avoid serving coffee that has been held for longer than 30 minutes; it gives off an offensive odor that will spread through the operation. If a coffee pot is one-quarter full or less, most bartenders will start a fresh pot. Do not combine the contents of two partially full coffee pots. This spoils the taste of the coffee.

Anyone serving coffee frequently refills it—typically as soon as a cup of coffee is less than half-full. Coffee cools quickly and guests expect the server to keep their coffee hot and fresh. Most servers will not ask whether guests want a refill but will pour them until guests signal that they have had enough.

Tea

Tea can be made with loose tea or tea bags. When making tea, the water should be at the boiling point when it is poured over the loose tea or the tea bag. The teapot/cup should be kept hot and the tea should be allowed to steep for no more than five minutes. It should be served immediately.

Hot tea is usually brewed by the two-cup pot or by the individual cup. Most guests prefer to place their own tea bags into the hot water. While tea usually takes eight to ten minutes to brew, some guests may prefer more or less time.

Beverage servers typically preheat a ceramic pot by filling it with boiling hot water and letting it stand while they set up the beverage tray. On the beverage tray they put cream, sugar, a spoon, a mug or cup and saucer, a tea bag, and a lemon wedge. They then fill the teapot with hot water from the coffee maker. When using a ceramic pot, they empty the water used to preheat it and then refill it with hot water.

Tea drinkers like refills but are often overlooked. Staff members can show their commitment to superior service by offering to bring more hot water at frequent intervals.

Iced tea is often prepared with one-ounce tea bags immersed in water that has reached the boiling point. The normal proportion is two ounces of tea to one gallon of water. Like hot tea, iced tea should steep for no more than five minutes and then be poured into a glass with ice. When this is impractical, tea should be pre-cooled and ice should be added to the glass when the tea is served. Since ice will dilute the tea, it should be made stronger than hot tea.

Beer

Draft beer is beer that is served from a keg. Servers should hold the glass near its base and then tilt it slightly (about 30 degrees) under the tap so the first few ounces of beer will pour down the side of the glass. Servers should not pour all of the beer down the side of the glass, as a direct pour down the center releases carbon dioxide and will result in a smoother-tasting beer. Servers should open the beer tap dispenser quickly and completely. If they try to hold the tap in a half-open position, they will draw too much air; this creates too much head and changes the taste of the beer.

Exhibit 6   Food and Wine Pairing Guidelines

1. Drink light-bodied wines with lighter foods and fuller-bodied wines with heartier, more flavorful foods.

2. Food preparation methods affect wine pairings. A delicate sauce on a food should be paired with a delicate wine, while a grilled chicken breast might call for a heartier wine.

3. Sweet foods make wines seem drier than they are, so pair them with a sweeter wine.

4. High-acid foods go well with wines that have a higher acidity.

5. Bitter and astringent foods make a wine's bitter flavor more pronounced, so try pairing the food with a full-flavored fruity wine.

6. Taste both the wine and food separately and then together to determine whether it would make a good pairing to recommend.

Servers should tilt the glass to an upright position as it fills. They should pour the beer directly into the center of the glass to form a head about one-half to one-inch thick. If the beer doesn't develop a head, they should change the keg before serving any beer; beer that will not develop a head may have gone bad in the keg. Age or a leaking keg can result in a loss of carbon dioxide and flat beer. It is helpful to check that the carbon dioxide tank is full. Finally, servers should close the tap quickly and completely.

Bottled beer is typically served with a glass—many times a frosted glass. At some operations, beverage servers will pour bottled beer into a glass at the table, while at other operations, guests pour their own beer from the bottle.

Wine and Champagne

Ordering wine and champagne is fun for many people, and staff members can help their guests enjoy it. Over the centuries, rules of etiquette and rituals have been developed concerning the service of wine. There are many guests who will want to have the ritual as part of their dining experience. These rituals include wine and food pairings, glassware, the temperature at which wine is served, how to open bottles, and how to pour.

Selecting Wine. Beverage servers should present the wine list to guests upon arrival. If the wine list is more than one page long, they should open the wine list to the first page before presenting it. Servers should be prepared to suggest one or two wines or champagnes.

The general rule is that white wines go best with white meats and seafood, and red wines go best with red meats and game. Rosé and blush wines and champagnes go with any type of food. Regardless of the general rule, the guest is never wrong in his or her selection of a wine. Good servers allow guests to make their own selections and always support the guest's preference. Some additional guidelines are listed in Exhibit 6. Some websites, such as the Sutter Home Winery (www.sutterhome.com/guide/winewheel.html) have a wine wheel to suggest food and wine pairings.

Exhibit 7   Glassware Shapes

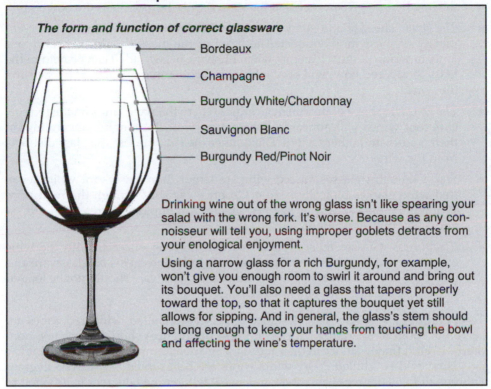

The form and function of correct glassware

Bordeaux

Champagne

Burgundy White/Chardonnay

Sauvignon Blanc

Burgundy Red/Pinot Noir

Drinking wine out of the wrong glass isn't like spearing your salad with the wrong fork. It's worse. Because as any connoisseur will tell you, using improper goblets detracts from your enological enjoyment.

Using a narrow glass for a rich Burgundy, for example, won't give you enough room to swirl it around and bring out its bouquet. You'll also need a glass that tapers properly toward the top, so that it captures the bouquet yet still allows for sipping. And in general, the glass's stem should be long enough to keep your hands from touching the bowl and affecting the wine's temperature.

Many operations will have suggestions for specific wines for each of their main dishes, either printed on the menu or offered to servers during their training. This helps servers make suggestions. Servers can ask guests about their preferences to help them arrive at a suitable choice, and answer any questions about the wines or champagnes on the list. Most operations will have frequent wine tastings for the staff so that staff members can accurately describe a wine's taste and features.

Glassware. Each operation may have several different types of wine glasses. The size and shape of a wine glass can affect how the wine tastes. Some guests prefer a certain type of glass and may request it. These requests should be honored whenever possible. Exhibit 7 shows some of the different glass shapes for different wines. Sparkling wines are often served in crystal glasses; still wines are typically served in transparent glasses so that guests can see the wine properly. Factors that affect glassware include:

- *The stem.* The stem should be long enough so that guests can hold it without having to put their fingers on the bowl. Their hands can change the temperature of the wine if they have to hold it by the bowl. However, the stem should not be so long that it causes the glass to be unstable when wine is poured into the bowl. Many experts say that the stem should be as long as the bowl is tall.

- *The bowl.* The size and shape of the bowl determine the intensity and complexity of the wine's bouquet. The bowl of the glass should be round and long, tapering at the top so that when the wine is swirled, it can be held in the glass. A tapered bowl will also hold in the aroma that is released by swirling the wine.

- *The rim.* The shape of the rim determines where the wine lands on the tongue. Different wines will appeal to different parts of the tongue, depending on their acidity and other factors. The thinner the rim, the less the glass distracts from the wine.

- *Size.* Generally, glasses for red wine are larger than glasses for white wine. Red-wine glasses typically have a 12-ounce capacity, though that will vary. White-wine glasses will be slightly smaller. Champagne flutes will hold six and a half ounces or more.

- *Cleanliness.* Glasses must be clean so that nothing interacts with the wine except air and the glass itself. Sparingly use mild detergents on glassware and either air dry it or dry it with a lint-free cloth. Stemware should not be loaded in the dishwasher with other dirty dishes.

Temperature. White wines are designed to be served chilled, while red wines are served at room temperature. However, guest preferences should always be honored—even if they want ice in their red wine or room temperature white wine.

How cold is "chilled"? Dry white wines are best served between 45 degrees Fahrenheit to 50 degrees Fahrenheit and sweet whites at 40 degrees Fahrenheit to 50 degrees Fahrenheit. It is better to serve a drink slightly colder than needed, as the wine will quickly warm up once it is poured and served.

White wines can be chilled by placing them in a bucket of ice water. There should be enough ice and water in the bucket to cover the shoulder of the bottle. This usually means a server will fill a bucket half full with ice and then pour water into the bucket to just cover the ice. The ice bucket and ice bucket stand are placed to the right of the person who ordered the wine or champagne. A clean linen napkin is often threaded through the ring of the bucket.

Room temperature refers to the wine cellar temperature of most European wine cellars—which is around 64 degrees Fahrenheit. Full-bodied and mature red wines are best at 60 to 65 degrees Fahrenheit, while young reds do better around 55 to 60 degrees Fahrenheit. As most room temperatures are actually warmer than that, many operations will chill a red wine for a few minutes to lower the temperature to a cool room temperature. However, it is not served with an ice bucket unless the guest requests it.

Opening. Wine and champagne service includes rituals that have been handed down for centuries. By following these rules, staff members can impress their most knowledgeable guests and help inexperienced wine and champagne drinkers develop an appreciation for this service. The bottle, wrapped in a linen napkin, is first presented to the guest who placed the order, with the label displayed so the

Exhibit 8   Sample Waiter's Corkscrew

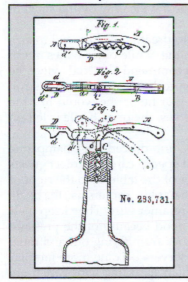

No. 283,731.

Carl Wienke invented the "waiter's corkscrew" and patented it in Germany on May 26, 1882. It was brought to Great Britain and France in 1883. It was nicknamed the "waiter's corkscrew" or "butler's friend" because of how easy it was able to remove and replace a cork. It is still used today by many beverage servers and bartenders.

The drawing on the left was submitted as part of the patent application in the United States in 1883.

guest can read the label. Champagnes and sparkling wines should be held gently with the corks protected, as they are under pressure from carbonation. When the guest approves, the server may proceed.

To open still wines, the wine bottle is set on the edge of the table and the server holds it firmly at the shoulder. Using the blade on his or her corkscrew, the server cuts the foil capsule cleanly around the rim of the bottle. Servers should cut low enough so that the wine won't touch the foil when they pour. The capsule is then removed and placed in their pocket. A clean linen napkin is then used to wipe the lip of the bottle. This also removes any mold or mineral salts that may have accumulated.

The servers insert the tip of the corkscrew slightly off-center of the cork. (A sample waiter's corkscrew is shown in Exhibit 8.) The corkscrew is twisted, with the servers directing it vertically through the center of the cork. They continue twisting until all spirals of the corkscrew have entered the cork. The cork can break if the corkscrew is not deep enough. They stop twisting before the corkscrew comes out of the bottom of the cork. If they insert the corkscrew too far, bits of cork may fall into the wine.

Servers remove the cork by placing the corkscrew lever on the lip of the bottle and holding it firmly with their thumb and forefinger. They never put the bottle between their legs to pull out the cork. With their other hand, they slowly and steadily pull upward to remove the cork. If the cork breaks, they pull out the loose pieces and insert the corkscrew into the remaining cork. They then use the lever to pull up the cork with their free hand until only a half inch of the cork remains in the neck of the bottle. They then grasp the cork with their thumb and forefinger and ease it out of the bottle.

The cork is removed from the corkscrew and placed near the guest who ordered the wine. The server does not smell the cork. The cork is shown to the guest to prove that the wine has been stored correctly. (Wines should be stored on their sides, so the cork should be wet.) You can judge a wine only by the smell of the wine itself—not by the smell of the cork.

Many red wines benefit from the opportunity to breathe (be exposed to air). Younger wines usually need little or no time to breathe, while older wines might need ten to fifteen minutes. Some experts even recommend that red wines be allowed to breathe for 30 minutes to allow oxygen to bring out the wine's full aroma and flavor. Servers should ask the host whether he or she would like the wine to breathe before it is served. If the guest says yes, the open bottle is left on the table and is not poured.

Sparkling wines require a slightly different opening procedure. Champagne service is fun, but it requires attention to details and special care to protect guests from a flying cork. The bottle is placed on the corner of the table or to the right of the host in his or her full view. Working under a linen napkin, servers use the blade of the corkscrew to cut the foil hood just below the retainer wire. They keep their thumb on the cork. The cork is secured by a wire hood because of the pressure inside the bottle. Servers must always protect the cork from flying out and must make sure the cork is never pointed at a guest. As servers become more familiar with the wines on their wine list, they will learn which sparkling wines are more bubbly—and more likely to pop a cork. Servers remove the foil and place it in the trash or in their pocket. They should not place it on the table or in the ice bucket.

Servers then hold the bottle firmly by the neck with one hand with their thumb still securely on top of the wire. They untwist the wire. If they feel the cork moving against their thumb, they keep a napkin wrapped tightly over the cork and bottle until they are sure the bottle is not going to overflow. They then carefully remove the wire and put it in the trash or in their pocket.

The servers then hold the bottle at a 45-degree angle, pointing it away from guests. They grasp the cork firmly and twist the bottle—not the cork. They allow the pressure to force the cork out gently, without popping. Some pressure may be released around the cork to prevent overflow. By tilting the bottle, the server increases the amount of air space within the bottle and reduces the pressure at the small neck of the bottle. They continue to hold the bottle at a 45-degree angle for a few seconds to reduce the chance of the contents foaming out. If the sparkling wine foams to the top of the bottle, the server pours a small amount into the host's glass to prevent a spill.

Pouring. Wine pouring takes some practice, but competent wine service sells wine. Servers should always stand up straight when pouring and pay attention to what they are doing. They should wipe the lip of the opened bottle with a clean napkin to remove any cork pieces or mold. While pouring, they should continue to hold the clean linen napkin in their left hand to wipe the bottle of drips, moisture, or water from the ice bucket.

Holding the bottle firmly by the wide portion, with the label in full view of the guests, servers lower the lip of the bottle to about one inch above each glass. They do not pick up the glasses. They pour a taste (about one-half inch) for the guest who ordered the wine or champagne. The guest may then sniff and taste the wine or champagne and give approval. If the host says the wine or champagne is

Proper beverage service enhances the guests' dining experience. (Courtesy of the Tides Inn, Irvington, Virginia.)

unsatisfactory, the server apologizes, takes it away, and informs his or her supervisor immediately (unless the server is empowered to resolve the complaint). If the host approves, servers pour wine or champagne for women first, then men, moving clockwise around the table and ending with the host. Servers should serve wine or champagne from the right side of each guest, holding the bottle in their right hand.

Depending on the size of the glass, each glass is filled about half-full with wine or champagne. By filling the glasses half-full, guests are better able to smell the bouquet or aroma of the wine.

Champagne and sparkling wines are poured in one of these motions:

- Pour about one-third of a glass and let the foam settle. Then pour more.
- Fill each glass to about half-full.

Servers lift the bottle as they pour so that when they finish, the bottle is about six inches above the glass. They should give the bottle a slight twist as they finish pouring. This will help prevent dripping.

Guests often toast a special occasion with wine or champagne. Servers should step back as soon as they have served everyone so they do not interfere with these festivities. They then place red wine bottles on the table to the right of the person who ordered them. White, blush, rosé, and sparkling wines are placed in the ice bucket, with the server making sure the ice water covers the shoulder of the bottle.

A clean linen napkin often is placed in the ring on the side of the bucket or draped over the top of the bucket.

Servers typically get five or six 6-ounce to 8-ounce glasses of wine from a 750-milliliter bottle. If the party is large and one glass each almost empties the bottle, servers should ask the person who selected the wine or champagne whether they should chill another bottle and have it ready, or open another bottle to allow it to breathe.

As needed, the server will refill guests' wine or champagne glasses. If a guest places his or her hand over the glass, it means they do not want a refill.

When guests order additional bottles of wine, servers should provide a fresh glass for the host to taste the wine from each new bottle. Servers should also bring fresh glasses for everyone if a different wine or champagne is selected. The complete serving ritual should be followed for each bottle served.

Key Terms

cash bank—An amount of cash that a bartender has for making change and performing other business-related tasks.

draft beer—Beer that is served from a keg.

due-back—A receipt for any money that is paid out of the cash bank during a shift.

layers—A term describing what happens with coffee strength when it is brewed. The first third of the pot will be too weak, the second will be too strong, and the last third will be too weak. The full pot must drip to blend the layers and arrive at the desired strength.

reading guests—A process by which a staff member determines what type of service each individual guest desires.

roll-ups—Silverware that is wrapped in linen napkins in advance of service.

sidework checklist—A to-do list that lists sidework tasks and the servers who are assigned to complete each task.

suggestive selling—A sales method that encourages guests to buy additional beverages and food.

upselling—A sales method that suggests more expensive and possibly better quality items to guests.

Review Questions

1. How can beverage servers work as a team with other staff members?

2. What is the difference between suggestive selling and upselling?

3. Why do servers follow an order-taking system?

4. What are the different ways that guests can settle a bill?

5. What are the most important tasks that bartenders perform?

6. How are standard drink recipes developed?

7. What types of incidents might be noted in a bar logbook?

8. How are blended drinks prepared?

9. What reports does a bartender prepare at the end of the shift?

10. How long can coffee be held before serving?

11. What should a bartender or server do if draft beer does not develop a head?

12. What temperature is white wine usually served at? red wine?

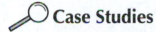 ## Case Studies

Comments, Please!

Louise Crane is the general manager of Harrington's, a 200-seat restaurant that is one unit in a national chain. As she sits at her desk this Monday morning, she thumbs through completed guest comment cards that patrons have left on the table. The morning mail also brought some additional cards.

As she reads through them, she becomes more and more alarmed. While there are two or three that are mildly complimentary, there are several that are highly critical. Here is a sampling of what guests submitted:

- "You charged me $4.50 for a glass of wine and the glass was only two-thirds full. What a rip off."

- "Doesn't anybody in this place ever smile?"

- "There was nobody to greet us when we walked in. We stood there for five minutes."

- "What do you do, put water in the ketchup? It flowed out of the bottle all over the plate."

- "We told the server we were in a hurry and that seemed to slow him down."

- "I don't know who was more surprised, the cockroach or me!"

- "We waited, and waited, and waited for our change. I think the server avoided us hoping we would leave so she could pocket a big tip."

- "Doesn't medium rare mean that the steak should have a pink color in the center?"

- "We asked if we could make a substitution and while the server said okay, she then said you were out of rice."

- "We never did get the ice water we asked for."

Louise was grinding her teeth by this time. She set the comment cards aside and turned on her computer. Among the various e-mails she had received, there were these two comments:

"I'll never go to Harrington's again. My wife's meal was served 10 minutes after mine, and it was cold."

"You really need to have someone check the restroom on a regular basis. It was filthy."

Louise knows that these things cannot continue. "I've got to take action," she says to herself.

Discussion Questions

1. What action should Louise take?

2. Would you share the comments on the cards with your staff?

3. Should you contact the people who wrote the comments? What do you say or do?

This case was taken from William P. Fisher and Robert A. Ashley, *Case Studies in Commercial Food Service Operations* (Lansing, Mich.: American Hotel & Lodging Educational Institute, 2003).

Don't Whine About the Wine!

Dennis Gordon, a nationally known wine consultant, critic, and columnist, has just received a call from Larry Bickford, the president and CEO of Sumptors Restaurant Inc. Sumptors has two nationally known brands that presently make up the organization, but will soon announce that it is developing a new Italian-theme brand by the name Mozzarella's. The concept is to be a full-fare Italian menu (pasta, veal, chicken, beef, and seafood) in an Italian garden setting, with considerable artwork and statuary.

Larry wants to engage Dennis to develop the wine list for the new concept, as he is fully aware that patrons are drinking more wine with their meals. After a short discussion regarding a fee, Dennis agrees.

Dennis jots down some notes of questions he must resolve in his own mind so he can make a proper recommendation to the Sumptors Executive Committee. Some things he is considering are:

*   Should the wine list be domestic wines only, or a combination of domestic and imports?

*   Should California wines be dominant or should wines from other wine producing states such as New York, Washington, and Texas be represented on the wine list?

*   What will be the recommended house wines?

*   Should there be an equal or near equal balance of red wines and white wines? What about blush wines? Champagnes?

*   How should the wine list be structured in terms of pricing? A few low-cost wines, several in the mid-range, a few high-priced wines?

*   Should Mozzarella's arrange to have a private label stock?

*   What will be the recommended price per glass? How many ounces will a glass contain?

- Will wine pairings be suggested on the food menu?

- Should the wine list have descriptive terminology so a patron can have a better idea of what the wine is like?

- What staff training is necessary and who will conduct the training?

Discussion Question

1. If you were Dennis, what would be your answers to these questions?

This case was taken from William P. Fisher and Robert A. Ashley, *Case Studies in Commercial Food Service Operations* (Lansing, Mich.: American Hotel & Lodging Educational Institute, 2003).

 ## References

Adams, Jenny. "Shooting for the High End." *Nightclub & Bar Magazine.* April 14, 2009 24(4): 26–27.

Ante, Spencer E. "The iSommelier will take your order; touch-screen tabletops with interactive menus are coming to wine bars and restaurants near you." *Business Week.* February 25, 2008. 4072: 72

"Bar & Cellar…" *Restaurant Startup & Growth.* April 2008. 5(4): 11.

Berta, Dina. "Restaurants belly up to the bar." *Nation's Restaurant News.* July 21, 2008. 42(28): 35–42.

Brown, Bob. "The seven keys to beverage sales success; simple, smart strategies for a challenging economy." *Cheers.* January–February 2009. 18(2).

"Coffee changes the playing grounds." *Beverage Industry.* December 2008. 99(12): 10–13.

Durocher, Joseph. "Drink to This." *Restaurant Business.* June 15, 2004. 103(10): 64–66.

Elan, Elissa. "Operators uncork 'BYO' wine programs to make sales pop." *Nation's Restaurant News.* April 27, 2009. 43(15): 4.

"The Hit List, Gin Is In." *Beverage World.* December 15, 2008. 127(12): 54.

"Hot F&B Trends." *Expo Magazine.* January 2009. 21(1): 28–29.

Landi, Heather. "The Antioxidant Boom." *Beverage World.* April 10, 2009. 128(4): 72–74.

Licata, Elizabeth. "Staying In For Breakfast." *Nation's Restaurant News.* August 11, 2008. 42(31): 14.

Moore, Sonya. "Perk up beverage sales." *Nation's Restaurant News.* January 26, 2009. 43(3): 42–44.

Perlik, Allison. "Chill Out." *Restaurants & Institutions,* May 20, 2009. 119(5): 34–36.

Ruggless, Ron. "Coffee margins heat up, inspire gourmet-brew binge among QSRs." *Nation's Restaurant News*. May 8, 2006. 40(19): 6.

Thorn, Bret. "Panelists promote premium drinks as reliable profit streams." *Nation's Restaurant News*. November 5, 2007. 41(44): 48.

"Top Ingredient Trends." *Beverage Industry*. May 2009. 110(5): 64–69.

"What's Hot in 2009." *Beverage Industry*. April 2009. 100(4): 39.

White, Geneva. "Wake Up…And Drink Up." *Nation's Restaurant News*. August 11, 2008. 42(31): 6.

Internet Sites

For more information, visit the following Internet sites. Remember that Internet addresses can change without notice. If the site is no longer there, you can use a search engine to look for additional sites. (Many alcohol-related sites require users to be of legal drinking age to enter.)

The Bartender's Foundation
www.bartenderfoundation.org

Bartender Jokes
www.workjoke.com/projoke86.htm

BARTENDER Magazine
www.bartender.com

BartenderZone.com
www.bartenderzone.com

Beer Marketer's INSIGHTS
www.beerinsights.com

Beverage Digest
www.beverage-digest.com

Beverage Information Group
www.bevinfogroup.com

Beverage Marketing Corporation
www.beveragemarketing.com

Beverage World
www.beverageworld.com

CELLARNOTES.net
www.cellarnotes.net

ExtremeBartending.com
www.extremebartending.com

HappyHours.com
www.happyhours.com

iBoozer
www.iboozer.com

Internet Wine Guide
www.internetwineguide.com

IntoWine.com
www.intowine.com

KingCocktail.com
www.kingcocktail.com

Miss Charming.com
www.miss-charming.com

United States Bartenders' Guild
www.usbg.org

The Virtual Bar
www.thevirtualbar.com

The Webtender
www.webtender.com

WineEducation.com
www.wineeducation.com

WineLoversPage.com
www.wine-lovers-page.com

Chapter Appendix: Beverage Trends

Beverage trends are ever-evolving, based on the ever-changing preferences of guests. Servers who keep up with these changing trends can have more success at suggestive selling and upselling.

Bottled Water

Bottled water is a potential upselling item in a food and beverage operation. Rather than asking guests if they want bottled water, it would be better for servers to say: "Would you like Evian still water or San Pellegrino sparkling water this evening?" (This is similar to an upselling question such as "Would you prefer Ciroc or Belvedere vodka this evening?" that a server might ask a guest who orders a vodka martini on the rocks.)

Health, Relaxation, and Beauty Beverages

Many guests today are interested in beverages with perceived health benefits. Health beverages range from enhanced bottled waters to green tea extract to fruit juices fortified with vitamins and minerals. Many health beverages contain phytochemicals (e.g., flavonoids found in fruits and vegetables) and various vitamins (A, B group, C, and E). These antioxidants function by slowing down the damage done to the human body by free radicals, making these types of drinks popular with health-conscious guests.

Super-fruits include açai and pomegranate, as well as acerola, baobab, camu camu, cili (loaded with Vitamin C), gac, goji berries, mangosteen, and yumberry. Blackcurrants are also very high in Vitamin C. "Superfruit smoothies" are being marketed by many food and beverage operations to sell more beverages.

Relaxation beverages often contain one or more of the following "mellowing out" ingredients: chamomile, L-theanine, melatonin, rose hips, and valerian root. These ingredients are added to help calm and quiet the person who is consuming them. Other relaxation ingredients include elderflower, lavender, lemon balm, lemongrass, and valerian root. Relaxation beverages are usually enjoyed at the end of a busy day.

Another category of health beverages, called beauty beverages, feature aloe, antioxidants, biotin, collagen, EGCG, lentin, and omega-3 fatty acids. These beverages are considered to enhance skin care and health, promoting beauty from the inside out.

Coffee

"Energy" coffee drinks are popular with many guests today, such as Starbucks' Doubleshot Energy + Coffee drink that has coffee, B vitamins, ginseng, and guarana. Consumers of energy coffee drinks are looking for an energy boost and other health benefits. Another energy coffee drink, POMx Iced Coffee, is a combination of a pomegranate antioxidant plus Arabica coffee, milk, and sugar. The sugar is organic, the milk is free of hormones, and the coffee comes from Rainforest Alliance Certified farms. All of these product details are selling points that servers can use when employing suggestive selling and upselling techniques.

Sun Shower Super Blends iced coffees, lattes, and teas are fortified with added calcium, magnesium, zinc, and vitamins A, B_3, and E. Again, knowing these details can help servers upsell and suggestively sell these drinks.

Cold coffee drinks are another popular coffee beverage, particularly on warm days in summer. Even many quick-service restaurants now promote iced coffees such as double-whipped iced mochas. Just as they are concerned about the ingredients in their traditional hot coffee drinks, guests are also concerned about where the ingredients in their cold coffee drinks come from. More and more guests are looking for "fair trade" coffees—coffees that are purchased directly from growers and allow for better working conditions and greater profits for the growers.

Smoothies

Another popular drink category that can be upsold or suggestively sold is smoothies. Planet Sunshine features more than fifty different smoothie varieties. In addition to many restaurants, some coffee shops have added smoothies, as have fitness centers. Smoothie flavors have moved beyond strawberry and banana to include such new flavors as chocolate strawberry, apple pear, blackberry, green tea and mango or honey, vanilla lime, and herbal tropical. "Power" smoothies feature an energy booster, fast metabolizer, or whey protein; smoothies can also be fortified with extra vitamins. Guests who like to try new smoothie flavors are prime candidates for upselling and suggestive selling. Smoothies are chilled drinks and, for obvious reasons, chilled drinks are easier to sell in warmer weather.

Frozen Drinks

Like smoothies, frozen drinks are most popular during the hot days of summer. The mojito—a popular drink made from rum, sugar, lime, carbonated water, and mint—can be served frozen. Ingredients such as fresh lemon or lime juice, berry-flavored vodkas, chocolate liqueurs, gelato, ice cream, and ice are usually the starting point of a frozen drink. Of course, frozen drinks should be served in chilled glassware that is very cold. Smaller-size ice cubes are preferred for easier blending.

Spirits

Cordials or cognacs are popular after-dinner drink options. Choices such as Amaretto, Benedictine, Drambuie, Grand Marnier, and Sambuca would add additional sales if guests are encouraged to select them. Of course, servers always have to be concerned about the total amount of alcohol that each guest consumes.

Today's young, affluent guests are choosing to drink gin in greater numbers, and super-premium boutique brands of gin are being produced for these sophisticated guests. Many of these beverages are packaged in unusual bottles to help portray their cool, sophisticated image.

The tendency today is for guests to drink higher-quality cocktails. Shooters (shots of alcohol) have moved from sweet, sticky fruit brandies to shots of Irish whiskey with a pickle-juice chaser. Another shot trend has been labeled "molecular mixology." The Tailor in New York City has created a Gummy Bear shot made from gelatin, sugar, and absinthe, for example. The goal of molecular mixology is to produce drinks with new, unusual flavors that get guests to exclaim, "Wow!" after they put their empty shot glasses down. Younger guests are ordering vodka and Red Bull as a mixed drink.

Wine

"BYOB" in college meant "bring your own bottle" of the alcohol of your choice to a party or other social gathering. In many restaurants, "BYO" now means bring your own bottle of wine to the restaurant to enjoy it with the food you purchase there. A BYO wine program is designed to encourage those who would not normally dine out to choose to dine out, purchasing food items from the food and beverage operation but paying retail for the wine at a store and bringing the wine with them to the operation to enjoy. It makes the overall dining experience more easily affordable. In a tight economy, guests are looking for ways to cut costs, and food and beverage operators are looking for ways to attract repeat guests more frequently. BYO wine also enables guests to bring and consume exactly the wine they enjoy most. Money saved by purchasing the wine elsewhere might be spent at the food and beverage operation on additional food items that guests might not otherwise have purchased, enhancing the guest experience and providing additional revenue to the operation.

Beer

One of today's beer trends is for food and beverage operations to offer micro-brews—that is, beers from breweries that produce less than 15,000 barrels per year. (In contrast, large breweries produce in excess of two million barrels of beer per year.) Brew pubs brew beer on the premises and sell most of their beer for consumption in the pub. Specialty brewers produce specialty beers such as seasonal winter ale for bars and restaurants as well as retail stores. Another trend in beer is for local brewers to use ingredients that are locally grown and sold.

Task Breakdowns: Beverage Service

The procedures presented in this section are for illustrative purposes only and should not be construed as recommendations or standards. While these procedures are typical, readers should keep in mind that each food and beverage operation has its own procedures, equipment specifications, and safety policies.

BEVERAGE SERVER: *Set Up the Lounge for Service*

Materials needed: *An opening duty checklist, a vacuum cleaner, caution signs, cleaning cloths, sanitizing solution, candles or lamp fuel, polish, vases, flowers, table tents, matches, standard tabletop items, guest checks, and a cash bank.*

STEPS	HOW-TO'S
1. Vacuum carpeted areas.	❑ Place caution signs.
	❑ Empty the vacuum cleaner bag if necessary.
	❑ The steps to empty a vacuum cleaner bag vary depending on the vacuum cleaner model. Housekeeping may vacuum and perform cleaning duties in the lounge. Careful vacuuming improves the lounge's appearance and reduces problems with pests and rodents.
	❑ Clean up spills with a damp cloth, followed by a dry cloth. Do not use a linen napkin to clean up spills. Use only designated cloths or cleaning towels.
	❑ Report stained or damaged upholstery or carpeting to your supervisor.
	❑ Unwind the cord and plug the vacuum cleaner into an outlet near the door. Make sure the cord is out of the way so no one trips. To avoid being shocked, do not stand in water when plugging in the vacuum cleaner.
	❑ Begin vacuuming at the far side of the room and work toward the main entrance.
	❑ Move tables and chairs as needed.
	❑ Pay special attention to room corners, carpet edges, high-traffic areas, and areas under booths or banquettes.
	❑ Vacuum booth seats and upholstered chairs if necessary. (Crevices in chair upholstery may collect crumbs.)
	❑ Unplug the vacuum cleaner and carefully wind the cord.
	❑ Empty the vacuum cleaner bag if needed.

(continued)

BEVERAGE SERVER: *Set Up the Lounge for Service*
(continued)

STEPS	HOW-TO'S
	❑ Store the vacuum cleaner to prevent accidents.
	❑ Report carpet or equipment problems to your supervisor.
2. Clean tables and chairs.	❑ Wipe all tabletops with a damp cloth and sanitizing solution followed by a dry cloth.
	❑ Use a second damp cloth to wipe all chairs and stools, never the same cloth used for wiping the table. You may use one cloth if you wipe all tables before you wipe chairs and stools.
3. Check, clean, and refuel table lamps.	❑ Place a new candle in each candle lamp as needed, or refill lamps using liquid fuel. Make sure that wicks are in good condition.
	❑ Be careful refueling lamps. Clean up all spills. Make sure there are no open flames near you when you are filling lamps.
	❑ Make sure lamps are clean and free of chips and cracks. Clean or replace lamps as needed.
	❑ If lamps have brass or silver trim, make sure the trim is free from spots and tarnish. Polish brass or silver trim if necessary.
4. Check flower arrangements.	❑ Check vases for cracks, chips, and fingerprints. Clean or replace vases as needed. Make sure vases are full of fresh water.
	❑ Make sure flowers and greenery are fresh and neatly arranged. Replace wilting flowers.
	❑ Make sure artificial arrangements are free from dust. Use a soft, dry cloth to gently wipe the leaves and petals of artificial flowers and plants. A wet cloth can damage and wrinkle leaves and petals on silk flowers

BEVERAGE SERVER: *Set Up the Lounge for Service*
(continued)

STEPS	HOW-TO'S
5. Adjust drapes and blinds.	❑ Check drapes to be sure they are hanging neatly. Adjust them to give the best appearance. Keeping the blinds adjusted will present a good appearance to guests. ❑ Set blinds based on the angle of the sun to ensure guest comfort. ❑ Report to your manager any food residue or stains on drapes or blinds so cleaning can be scheduled with the housekeeping department.
6. Supply lounge tables with appropriate items.	❑ Put fresh, clean table tents and promotional items on each lounge table. Table tents and displays are sometimes used to promote food and beverage items. ❑ Follow your tabletop specifications for determining what else to place on each table.
7. Get guest checks.	❑ Get guest checks from the host, bartender, or whomever is assigned to issue checks. The point-of-sale equipment may produce a sales check from a tape. If so, no guest checks will be issued. ❑ Sign for enough checks to last throughout your shift, unless your point-of-sale unit produces guest checks. Guest checks help the lounge track its sales and control its income. ❑ Always double-check that you have the correct number of checks. Make sure they are in the correct sequence. You are responsible for every check signed out to you. Some lodging properties do not distribute guest checks for service. ❑ Keep track of every check. Follow your restaurant's check-control procedure.

(continued)

BEVERAGE SERVER: *Set Up the Lounge for Service*
(continued)

STEPS	HOW-TO'S
8. Set up your cash bank if you are responsible for settling guest checks yourself.	❑ The steps to set up your cash bank vary among properties. ❑ Set up your bank in a secure, back-of-house area away from the public.
9. Complete other tasks according to your opening duty checklist.	

BEVERAGE SERVER: *Greet Guests, Take Orders, and Serve Complimentary Food*

Materials needed: Restaurant menus, guest checks or an order pad, a pen, complimentary items, silverware, dinner napkins, beverage napkins, and plates.

STEPS	HOW-TO'S
1. Greet guests as soon as they are seated.	❑ Smile and give a warm greeting. Introduce yourself by name. For example: "Welcome to (name of property). I'm Juan, your cocktail server." ❑ If you are unable to greet your guests within your operation's standard greeting time, stop by the table and let them know you'll be back soon. Apologize for the wait when you return. Many operations have a standard greeting time of two minutes or less. Some have only a 60- or 30-second greeting time. ❑ Tell guests about the specials. ❑ Try to "read" your guests right away. "Reading" guests means determining what type of service they need. Be alert to guests who have been drinking and who may become intoxicated quickly.
2. Verify the legal drinking age of guests who order alcoholic beverages.	
3. Follow an order-taking system.	❑ Place a beverage napkin in front of every guest as you ask for his or her order. This will help you keep track of who has ordered. If guests are not ready to order, leaving a beverage napkin at the table will let other servers know you've checked with the guests. This is another way to use teamwork to provide excellent guest service. ❑ If the beverage napkins have a logo, place each napkin so the logo faces the guest.

(continued)

BEVERAGE SERVER: *Greet Guests, Take Orders, and Serve Complimentary Food* (continued)	
STEPS	**HOW-TO'S**
	❑ Take orders from women first, then men. When you use a standard order-taking system, anyone can serve your guests without having to annoy them by asking who ordered which item.
	❑ Write orders on the guest check or order pad according to how the guests are seated. Follow a clockwise direction. You may be told to write the orders on the back of a guest check, and the point-of-sale equipment will print the orders neatly on the front side.
	❑ Assign a number to each chair at a table. Chair number one at each table is typically the one closest to the door or some other landmark in the lounge. All cocktail servers should use the same reference point as a starting point.
	❑ Write the order for the guest in chair number one on the first line of the guest check or order pad.
	❑ Write the order for the guest in chair number two on the second line of the guest check or order pad, and so forth.
	❑ Use standard drink and food abbreviations.
	❑ Listen carefully to each guest's order, and repeat the order and details.
	❑ Note special requests on the guest check or order pad.
	❑ Find out the guest's preference for service, such as "on the rocks" or "straight up."
	❑ Suggest the most popular call brands when a guest does not specify the brand.
	❑ Suggest a specialty drink if a guest is not sure what to order.

BEVERAGE SERVER: *Greet Guests, Take Orders, and Serve Complimentary Food* (continued)

STEPS	HOW-TO'S
	❑ When offering cocktails, ask guests who don't want a cocktail if they would like a glass of wine or a nonalcoholic drink.
	❑ Always suggest specific alcoholic and nonalcoholic drinks, such as a Bombay Sapphire gin and tonic, a sparkling water, or a mango daiquiri.
4. Bring complimentary food to guests.	❑ Bring popcorn, nuts, bar snacks, or other food provided by the lounge or bar for each group of guests. Some types of food, such as pasta or pretzels, increase the absorption of alcohol into the bloodstream. Foods high in fat, such as fried cheese, slow the absorption of alcohol into the bloodstream.
	❑ Bring two or three service dishes for large parties.
	❑ If complimentary food is offered on an hors d'oeuvres table: • Offer to bring items to the guests. • Select items from the hors d'oeuvres table and place them on a small service plate for each guest. • Bring the appropriate silverware and present it to each guest on a dinner napkin. For serving food in the bar or lounge, silverware may be wrapped in linen napkins in advance These are typically called "roll-ups."
5. Suggest menu items.	❑ If complimentary food is not offered, try to sell appetizers, such as seafood cocktails or nachos, along with each drink order.
	❑ Offer restaurant menus to help guests make selections.
	❑ Provide appropriate silverware for the items ordered.
6. Sell reorders.	

BEVERAGE SERVER: *Place Beverage and Food Orders*

Materials needed: An order pad or guest checks, glasses, a beverage tray, an ice scoop, ice, garnishes, beverage napkins, stirrers or straws, and point-of-sale equipment.

STEPS	HOW-TO'S
1. Pre-ring drink orders using your restaurant's point-of-sale equipment.	❑ The steps to pre-ring drink orders vary among properties. Point-of-sale (POS) equipment varies by restaurant. You will learn to use the equipment at your restaurant.
	❑ Some POS units require you to insert a guest check into the unit's printer. Others print guest checks on a tape that comes out of the unit.
2. Set up glasses for drink orders.	❑ Know which drinks go in which glasses.
	❑ If you follow a calling sequence when ordering drinks, set up the glasses in the order you will call the drinks. Place glasses near the edge of the bartender's side of the service bar.
	❑ Fill glasses with ice for drinks that require it.
	❑ Always use a scoop when putting ice in glasses.
	❑ If drinks are for pool guests, do not use glassware. Use only plastic glasses to avoid injuries.
3. Place drink orders.	❑ In a clear voice, say "Ordering," and then tell the bartender your drink orders, including any special instructions. At your lounge, you may not need to call drink orders.
	❑ The reason for following a calling order is that some drinks take more time to prepare than other drinks, or they do not hold up as well as other drinks.
	❑ Call drink orders for all tables at the same time.

BEVERAGE SERVER: *Place Beverage and Food Orders* (continued)

STEPS	HOW-TO'S
	❑ Make sure you've written each order clearly and correctly on a guest check or order pad. You may need to hand in the written order instead of or in addition to calling out the orders.
	❑ Place written orders in the proper location so the bartender can refer to them.
4. Garnish drinks.	❑ Select garnishes according to the drink recipe or the guest's preference. Garnishes will usually be prepared and placed in the drinks by the bartender. However, you may be asked to help.
	❑ Make sure each garnish is fresh and attractive.
	❑ To prevent splatters, place garnishes after drinks have been poured. Garnishing a drink before it is poured blocks the bartender's sight and causes liquor to splash out of the glass.
5. Set up beverage napkins and stirrers or straws.	❑ Place one beverage napkin on your beverage tray for each glass.
	❑ Make sure napkins are clean and free from tears, folds, and wrinkles.
	❑ Insert stirrers or straws in drinks if needed.
6. Pre-ring and place food orders.	❑ The steps to pre-ring food orders vary among operations.
	❑ Food checks must be rung into the point-of-sale unit before the kitchen will prepare any food.
	❑ These steps to place appetizer orders and entree orders vary among operations.

BEVERAGE SERVER: *Pick Up and Serve Beverages*

Materials needed: A pen, an order pad or guest checks, beverage napkins, beverages, a linen napkin, and a beverage tray.

STEPS	HOW-TO'S

1. Make sure beverages are complete as ordered.	❑ Mixing, pouring, garnishing, and serving drinks the same way every time is the mark of a quality operation.
	
	❑ Check each beverage:
	
	   • Is it the correct beverage?
	   • Is it in the correct glass?
	   • Is the garnish correct?
	   • Have special instructions been followed?
	   • Has anything spilled over the side?
	   • Should it have a chaser?
	
	❑ Take care of any problems right away.

2. Place drinks on the beverage tray.	❑ Line the tray with a linen napkin to improve the look of the tray and to avoid spills and moisture. ❑ Keep an extra pen and extra beverage napkins on the tray. ❑ Center glasses so the tray will be balanced. If possible, put heavy or tall glasses in the center of the tray. ❑ Keep in mind the order in which you will serve the drinks so your tray will be balanced until the last drink is removed.
3. Carry the tray to the table.	❑ Bend at the knees so that your shoulder is below the tray. ❑ Pull the tray with one hand onto the palm of the other hand. ❑ Balance the tray at shoulder level on your fingertips, not on your forearm. If the tray is carried on your forearm, it may tip over.

BEVERAGE SERVER: *Pick Up and Serve Beverages*
(continued)

STEPS	HOW-TO'S
	❑ Keep your back straight as you stand up.
	❑ Steady the tray with your free hand.
4. Serve beverages to guests.	❑ Always serve women first, and the host of the group last. In a "no-host" situation, simply serve women first and men last.
	❑ Place a beverage napkin on the table in front of the guest, unless you've already placed one.
	❑ If the beverage napkins at your operation have a logo, place the napkins so that the logo faces the guest.
	❑ Avoid reaching across guests. Move around the table and serve every guest from his or her right side with your right hand when possible .
	❑ Handle glasses away from their rims or lips. Handle stemmed glasses by the stem or base. Your hands will warm the drink if you touch the outside of a glass. However, you should never put your fingers inside a glass.
	❑ Place the glass on the center of the beverage napkin.
	❑ Follow the guest check or order pad to serve the correct drink to each guest. Do not ask who ordered which drink.
	❑ Repeat the name of the drink and any special requests as you serve each drink to ensure that it is correct.
5. Serve bottled beer to guests.	❑ The steps to serve bottled beer vary among properties. At some lounges, cocktail servers pour bottled beer into a glass at the table, while at other lounges, guests pour their own beer from the bottle.

(continued)

BEVERAGE SERVER: *Pick Up and Serve Beverages*
(continued)

STEPS	HOW-TO'S
6. Serve cordials and ports to guests.	❑ The steps to serve cordials and ports vary among properties.
7. Deny alcohols service to guests who are intoxicated, swimming, or engaging in horseplay.	❑ Tactfully tell guests that you care about their safety and can't serve them alcohol. Alcohol impairs judgment and can lead to serious accidents around the pool. It is better to upset a few rowdy guests than to endanger bystanders or be sued for an accident.
	❑ Do not make accusations, judge the guest, or argue.
	❑ Suggest nonalcoholic drinks and food instead.
	❑ Tell your supervisor whenever you deny someone alcohol service.

BEVERAGE SERVER: *Clean and Secure the Lounge for Closing*

Materials needed: *A closing duty checklist, cleaning cloths, beverage napkins, a bar towel, lemon wedges, a brush, sanitizing solution, a marker, food containers, and trash can liners.*

STEPS	HOW-TO'S
1. Clean throughout your shift to reduce the amount of work that has to be done at closing.	❑ Closing duties are different in different lounges. Your closing duty checklist lists your responsibilities for the end of your shift. ❑ If you are ending your shift but it is not closing time for the lounge, know your responsibilities for turning the shift over to your "relief" person.
2. Clean tables and chairs.	❑ Wipe crumbs from chairs and tables into beverage napkins and throw them away. ❑ Wipe tables and chairs with a different clean damp cloth, followed by a dry cloth. Never use linen napkins for cleaning. ❑ Arrange tables and chairs neatly as guests leave. Pick up paper or debris whenever you see it.
3. Take soiled tableware to the dish room.	❑ Follow standard dish room procedures for scraping and stacking soiled dishes. ❑ Help the bartender put away items and wash glasses.
4. Clean out and store ice buckets.	❑ Remove corks, foil scraps, labels, and other debris from buckets to avoid plugging drains. ❑ Empty ice and water into the appropriate sink. ❑ Return empty wine and champagne bottles to the bar for inventory. ❑ Dry the ice buckets with a bar towel. ❑ Store buckets in the designated side station.

(continued)

BEVERAGE SERVER: *Clean and Secure the Lounge for Closing* (continued)

STEPS	HOW-TO'S
5. Clean service trays.	❑ Wash trays in the kitchen at the end of the meal period. ❑ If the trays are cork-lined, rub the cork with lemon wedges to remove odors. Then let the trays stand for a few minutes before washing. ❑ Spray trays with hot water to remove food residue. ❑ If the trays are cork-lined, use a brush to scrub the cork. Then rinse the trays. ❑ Spray the trays with an approved sanitizing solution. Then stack them upside-down at right angles to allow them to air-dry.
6. Store food.	❑ Date and store food, such as condiments and garnishes, that has not been exposed to contamination. ❑ Throw away food that has been in the Temperature Danger Zone too long.
7. Remove flowers from tables.	❑ Throw away wilted flowers. ❑ Store fresh flowers in a refrigerator.
8. Clean the side station.	
9. Vacuum carpets.	
10. Turn in guest checks at the end of your shift.	❑ Account for all guest checks assigned to you. ❑ Turn in all voided, used, and unused checks.
11. Complete all other duties on your closing duty checklist.	
12. Remove all trash and reline trash cans.	
13. Help the bartender close and secure the bar.	❑ The steps to help close and secure the bar and lounge vary among properties.

BARTENDER: *Inventory and Requisition Bar Stock*

Materials needed: *An inventory form, a beverage requisition, a food requisition, a par stock list, a banquet event order, and a pen.*

STEPS	HOW-TO'S
1. Inventory alcohol.	❑ Count the full bottles of each type of liquor, wine, and beer. Record the amounts on an inventory form. ❑ Estimate in tenths ($1/10 = 0.1$) how much alcohol is left in each open bottle of liquor and wine. Record the amount on the inventory form as 0.1, 0.2, 0.3, etc.
2. Prepare a beverage requisition.	❑ Consult your par stock list to determine how much of each item should be on hand. Par stock lists provide consistent setup and control of the bar operation. ❑ Consult your inventory form to determine how much of each item you already have. ❑ Find out how much to order by subtracting the amounts on the inventory form from the total amounts on the par stock list. Write these amounts on the beverage requisition.
3. Inventory food.	❑ Count whole fruits, vegetables, unopened containers of juice, and dairy products (such as whipped cream) used in drinks. Juice is usually counted as food. ❑ Do not count fruits or vegetables that are already cut, or juices and mixes that are open. ❑ Record the amounts of food on an inventory form.
4. Prepare a food requisition.	❑ Consult your par stock list to determine how much of each item should be on hand. ❑ Consult your inventory form to determine how much of each item you already have. ❑ Find out how much to order by subtracting the amounts on the inventory form from the total amounts on the par stock list. Write these amounts on the food requisition.

BARTENDER: *Prepare Alcoholic Beverages*

Materials needed: Standard recipes, mixes, ice, measuring cups, an ice scoop, a jigger, a bar spoon, shakers, a mixing glass, garnishes, swizzle sticks, straws, service glasses, a blender, and mugs.

STEPS	HOW-TO'S
1. Follow standard recipes.	❑ Standard recipes keep drinks consistent. Make it your goal to memorize standard recipes in your operation.
	❑ Some bartenders think they are doing guests a favor by overpouring. A strong drink is not necessarily a quality drink.
	❑ Read all recipes twice before preparing drinks if you have not memorized the recipes.
	❑ Gather all ingredients and needed equipment. Do not use a mix or garnish that has spoiled or lost its freshness.
	❑ Measure all ingredients every time you prepare a drink. If you use an automated liquor gun for pouring well-brand liquors, the gun will pour a standard shot of alcohol.
2. Select the glass specified by the recipe.	
3. Make sure glasses are free from water spots, lipstick, and chips or cracks.	
4. Use clean ice when preparing and serving drinks.	❑ Clean the ice bin before adding ice each day.
	❑ Handle ice with a clean ice scoop. Do not scoop ice with a glass or with your hands.
	❑ Use cubed or cracked ice for stirred or shaken drinks. Use crushed ice for mists.
	❑ If glass breaks in the ice bin, or anything spills into the ice bin, empty all ice, clean the bin, and refill it with fresh, clean ice.
5. Prepare stirred drinks.	❑ Put ingredients in a mixing glass.

BARTENDER: *Prepare Alcoholic Beverages* (continued)

STEPS	HOW-TO'S
	☐ If several guests order the same stirred drink, prepare the drinks in a batch.
	☐ Stir with a spoon if the beverage is mixed with fruit juices or aromatic. Add a scoop of ice.
	☐ Stir the drink about three to four times to mix and chill it.
	☐ Do not overstir; the alcohol will be watered down by the melting ice.
	☐ Strain the ingredients from the mixing glass into the correct serving glass.
	☐ Strain drinks made in a batch into glasses, filling each glass to the midpoint. Then evenly divide the remainder.
	☐ Garnish appropriately as directed by the recipe.
6. Prepare shaken or blended drinks.	☐ If several guests order the same shaken or blended drink, prepare the drinks in a batch.
	☐ Preparing drinks in a shaker is an opportunity to add flair to your work.
	☐ Place ice in the mixing glass. Add nonalcoholic ingredients first. Add the alcohol last.
	☐ Place a metal shaker firmly upside-down on top of the mixing glass. Hold the mixing glass and shaker securely together.
	☐ Shake the items hard and fast.
	☐ Some bartenders hold the mixing glass and shaker over their head and shake them vigorously to put on a show for guests. This type of showiness works well in a noisy "action" bar, but would be in poor taste in a quiet, intimate bar and lounge.
	☐ After shaking the mixing glass and shaker, strain the drink into the correct glass. Garnish as directed by the recipe.

(continued)

BARTENDER: *Prepare Alcoholic Beverages* (continued)

STEPS	HOW-TO'S
7. Prepare frozen drinks.	❑ Place a scoop of ice in a blender cup and add other ingredients.
	❑ Place the mixture on an electric blender and blend until the ice is crushed and the ingredients are pureed. Pureeing is the process of reducing to a pulp and then rubbing through a strainer.
	❑ Do not over-blend frozen drinks. Pour the drink from the blender cup into the correct glass.
	❑ Garnish as directed by the recipe.
8. Prepare drinks using the build method.	❑ Place ice in the correct serving glass. Add the liquor.
	❑ Add the correct amount of mixer, the garnish, and a swizzle (stir) stick.
	❑ Serve the drink without mixing, stirring, or shaking.
9. Prepare layered drinks by the "float" method.	❑ A layered drink involves pouring each beverage on top of the previous one in layers to form multicolored stripes in the glass.
	❑ Do not use ice.
	❑ Pour heavier ingredients first so that the lighter ingredient will "float" on top of the heavier layer. Some layered drinks have only one alcoholic beverage, and sweet cream (whole cream, not whipped) is "floated" on top.
	❑ If the recipe calls for milk or cream, be sure it is fresh. If in doubt, smell or taste it to be certain.
	❑ If a recipe asks you to float an ingredient off the back of a spoon, pour the ingredient over the rounded part of a spoon into the glass. The spoon method reduces the chance of disturbing the layer below.

BARTENDER: *Prepare Alcoholic Beverages* (continued)

STEPS	HOW-TO'S
10. Prepare coffee drinks.	❑ Pour fresh hot coffee into the correct glass or mug.
	❑ Add the other ingredients called for in the recipe.
	❑ Gently stir the ingredients with a bar spoon.
	❑ Add whipped cream as called for by the recipe.
	❑ Add garnish (such as nutmeg) as called for by the recipe.
	❑ Insert the correct-size straw.

BARTENDER: *Draw Draft Beer and Pour Wine by the Glass*

Materials needed: Glassware, a bar tap, and a corkscrew.

STEPS	HOW-TO'S
1. Choose the correct glasses.	❑ Always examine beer and wine glasses before pouring to be sure they are clean. Glasses with starch or detergent residue can cause a flat beer taste. ❑ Make sure glasses have no spots, lipstick, chips, or cracks. ❑ A glass froster is sometimes used to frost beer glasses or mugs. Make sure glasses are sparkling clean before placing them in the froster.
2. Draw draft beer.	❑ Hold the glass near its base. ❑ Tilt the glass slightly (about 30 degrees) under the tap so the first few ounces of beer will pour down the side of the glass. Do not pour all of the beer down the side of the glass. A direct pour down the center releases carbon dioxide and will result in a smoother tasting beer. ❑ Open the beer tap dispenser quickly and completely. If you try to hold the tap in a half-open position, you will draw too much air. This creates too much head and changes the taste of the beer. ❑ Tilt the glass to an upright position as it fills. Pour the beer directly into the center of the glass to form a head about one-half to one inch thick. ❑ If the beer doesn't develop a head, change the keg before serving any beer. Beer that will not develop a head may have gone bad in the keg. Age or a leaking keg can result in a loss of carbon dioxide and in flat beer. Check that the carbon dioxide tank is full. ❑ Close the tap quickly and completely.

BARTENDER: *Draw Draft Beer and Pour Wine by the Glass* (continued)

STEPS	HOW-TO'S
3. Pour wine by the glass.	❑ Uncork the bottle, using a corkscrew. ❑ Pour the glass two-thirds full. ❑ White wine is normally served in a smaller glass than red wine. However, in bar operations, one standard size may be used for all house wine service. ❑ Recork the bottle to slow the rate at which the wine goes bad. ❑ If your restaurant uses a special vacuum system to reduce spoilage, ask your supervisor to show you how it works.

BARTENDER: *Clean Bartop and Lounge During Service*

Materials needed: *A service tray.*

STEPS	HOW-TO'S
1. Keep the bartop and lounge neat at all times.	❑ Remove glasses, napkins, food plates, and silverware that are not being used.
	❑ Clear empty plates from the guest's right with your right hand.
	❑ Wait to clear glasses and plates until more than one guest at a table is finished, so guests who are still eating or drinking do not feel rushed.
	❑ If a guest appears to be finished with an item, but the glass or plate is not empty, ask the guest if you may remove it.
	❑ Put used glasses and plates onto your service tray.
	❑ Never stack dirty plates in front of guests. Pick them up separately and stack them away from guests.
	❑ Pick up any popcorn or snacks on the floor.

BARTENDER: *Process Drink Reorders*

Materials needed: An order pad or guest checks, a pen, a service tray, and beverage napkins.

STEPS	HOW-TO'S
1. Ask guests if they would like another beverage.	❏ Suggest another beverage when the guest's glass is one-half to three-quarters empty.
	❏ Always count the number of alcoholic beverages each guest has. Remember that a glass of wine, a beer, and a typical mixed drink all have about one ounce of alcohol apiece.
	❏ Provide nuts or other high-fat snacks to slow absorption of alcohol into the bloodstream.
2. Write the second order on your pad or on the guest check.	❏ Draw a line under the first order and write the new orders below the line.
	❏ Write "Repeat" on your order pad or guest check if all guests in a party order the same thing for the next round.
3. Serve additional beverages.	❏ Clear any empty glasses when you serve or before you serve another drink.
	❏ Always bring a fresh glass with a fresh bottle of beer.
	❏ Never put your fingers inside glasses when you are removing them from the bar or lounge tables.
	❏ Put used glasses onto your service tray.
	❏ Place a new beverage napkin in front of the guest.
	❏ Place the new drink on the beverage napkin.
4. Monitor guests closely for signs of intoxication.	
5. Stop alcohol service to intoxicated guests.	❏ Ask a co-worker or manager to watch or help as you refuse to serve alcohol to a guest.

(continued)

STEPS	HOW-TO'S
	❏ Move the guest away from others, if possible.
	❏ Remove all alcohol from the person's reach–even if it is his or her drink.
	❏ Calmly and firmly state your property's policy: "I'm sorry, but I've served you all of the alcohol that I legally can."
	❏ Do not make accusations, judge the guest, or argue.
	❏ Suggest nonalcoholic drinks and food instead.

BARTENDER: *Process Drink Reorders* (continued)

Sources: Adapted from the "Beverage Server Guide" and "Bartender Guide" in the *Hospitality Skills Training Series* (Lansing, Mich.: American Hotel & Lodging Educational Institute, 1995).

Chapter 6 Outline

Competencies

1. Identify legal restrictions and liability issues affecting the service of alcoholic beverages. (pp. 239–244)

2. Describe steps to take when checking identification of guests. (pp. 244–246)

3. Explain the physical effect of alcohol in relation to the strength of drinks and the body's rate of absorption. (pp. 247–249)

4. Identify signs of intoxication and explain how a "traffic light" system is used to monitor and control guests' alcohol consumption. (pp. 249–254)

5. Describe steps to take when stopping alcohol service to intoxicated guests. (pp. 254–255).

6

Responsible Alcohol Service

THROUGHOUT HISTORY, people have used alcohol to celebrate special times. Guests frequent taverns, bars, and other food and beverage establishments and order drinks for many reasons:

- To celebrate special events such as weddings, reunions, and births
- To create a feeling of fellowship among friends
- To make their meals more enjoyable

Unfortunately, people also drink to deal with loneliness, to "drown their sorrows," or to "get wasted." Guests who drink for the wrong reasons are more likely than others to drink too much alcohol. In the wrong hands, alcohol can become a fatal weapon, contributing to traffic accidents and fatalities, boating accidents, drowning deaths, and other mishaps.

Alcohol can also be a fatal poison. Each year many people die from overdoses of alcohol or alcohol in combination with other drugs. When its effects are not fatal, inappropriate use of alcohol can contribute to violent acts as well as serious accidents (slips and falls). It can also interfere with normal fetal development, resulting in fetal alcohol syndrome or other birth defects.

Society is increasingly concerned with alcohol abuse, and courts are increasingly holding establishments responsible for serving intoxicated guests. Groups like MADD (Mothers Against Drunk Driving), SADD (Students Against Drunk Driving), and BADD (Bartenders Against Drunk Driving) are on the rise. Exhibit 1 presents a source for the latest statistics and resources on the effect of drunk driving. Exhibit 2 shows the kind of designated driver and alternate transportation programs promoted by sectors of the beverage industry.

Servers of alcoholic beverages have legal responsibilities. What happens when establishments violate the laws regarding alcohol service?

- Owners, managers, servers, and bartenders can be sued if someone is injured because of irresponsible alcohol service.
- Managers, servers, and bartenders can lose their jobs.
- Establishments can lose their liquor licenses.
- Owners can lose their businesses.

When servers of alcoholic beverages understand their legal responsibilities, they:

- Develop better judgment and confidence when serving alcohol.
- Enhance guest service and safely promote hospitality.
- Reduce injuries and deaths caused by drunk driving accidents.

Exhibit 1   Source for Statistics and Other Information on Drunk Driving

For up-to-date statistics and resources about drunk driving, browse the Mothers Against Drunk Driving website at www.madd.org.

Regardless of legal considerations, bartenders and servers have an ethical duty to see to it that people are not hurt because of the failure to serve alcohol with care.

Alcohol Service and the Law

Under the Twenty-First Amendment of the U.S. Constitution, each state has the right to control the sale of alcoholic beverages within that state. In states that permit the sale of alcoholic beverages, sales are governed by alcoholic beverage control laws, rules, and regulations of the state liquor authority. While alcoholic beverage control boards in each county generally have specific powers and responsibilities, the final control usually rests with the state liquor authority. Every establishment serving alcoholic beverages should have a copy of the rules and regulations of its State Liquor Authority. The laws in every state (and often every county) are different with regard to the on-premises and off-premises sale of alcoholic beverages.

Establishments must be licensed to sell alcoholic beverages and the license must be renewed every year. Applications for a license are made to the local county Alcoholic Beverage Control Board or directly to the State Liquor Authority. Three types of licenses for on-premises consumption are:

Exhibit 2   Designated Driver and Alternate Transportation Programs

Source: Anheuser-Busch, Inc. For more information about responsible alcohol programs, browse the company's endorsed website at www.designateddriver.com.

- Beer license
- Liquor license (includes sale of wine and beer)
- Wine license (may or may not include the sale of beer)

Before granting an on-premises license, the Alcoholic Beverage Control Board inspects and approves the establishment. Once granted a license, the establishment must obtain approval from the Board for any planned increases (or decreases) in the size of the premises or any change in equipment. In many states, no retail licensee for on-premises consumption may deliver or give away any liquors or wines for off-premises consumption.

Alcoholic Beverage Control Boards also regulate the hours of the day during which an establishment may not sell alcoholic beverages. For example, in some areas it is illegal to sell alcohol from 2 A.M. to 11 A.M. It may be illegal to sell alcohol on Sundays in some areas; in others, Sunday sales of alcohol are legal, but only after noon. Some areas prohibit the sale of alcohol on voting days when the polls are open. In a few areas, it is always illegal to sell all or most types of alcohol. These areas are said to be "dry," although they may allow some type of alcohol sales, such as beer with less than three percent alcohol by volume.

State laws usually require every retail licensee for on-premises consumption to maintain records of daily sales and purchases of alcoholic beverages. Purchase records must generally include the sellers' names, license numbers, and places of business.

In some states, a licensed establishment is prohibited from employing any person under the age of 21 as a host, server, bartender, or other staff position whose duties require them to sell, dispense, or handle alcoholic beverages.

Illegal sales of alcoholic beverages may well result in the suspension or revocation of a liquor license. This would cause at least the loss of some jobs and possibly the closing of the business. Alcoholic beverage control laws generally prohibit sales to minors, to habitual drunkards, or to visibly intoxicated persons. It is up to individual states to determine who is a minor (that is, who is too young to drink) and who is legally intoxicated. States classify a person as legally intoxicated based on blood alcohol concentration (BAC). Each state determines a minimum BAC level at which a person in that state is legally intoxicated.

Blood Alcohol Concentration (BAC)

When you drink an alcoholic beverage, some of the alcohol enters your bloodstream. The amount of alcohol in your bloodstream is your **blood alcohol concentration**, or BAC. In most areas, if you have a BAC of 0.08 percent (8/100 of 1 percent), you are legally drunk.

It is important to understand that someone who doesn't look or even act drunk may, in fact, be legally intoxicated. A BAC of 0.10 is equivalent to one drop of alcohol in 1,000 drops of blood. While this may not seem like a lot, a BAC of 0.30 percent may cause a coma, and a BAC of 0.40 percent can cause death.

How can you tell what someone's BAC is? You can't—unless you have special equipment such as a breathalyzer. Bartenders and servers must rely on a guest's behavioral signs and on the amount of alcohol a guest consumes to gauge the guest's level of intoxication.

Liability

Anyone who serves alcohol at an establishment can be sued for injuries or damages caused by illegal alcohol sales. That includes establishment owners, managers, servers, and bartenders. Two basic types of laws determine liability in alcohol sales cases:

- Dram shop acts (legislative acts passed by a state's legislature)
- Common law (negligence)

Dram shop acts are referred to as third-party liability laws. The state legislature enacts them into law. In order to understand how these laws work, you must understand what is meant by the terms "first party," "second party," and "third party." The "first party" is the person buying the alcohol; the "second party" is the person or establishment selling or serving the alcohol; the "third party" is someone outside the alcohol sales transaction. The key statutory words in most states are: the establishment's liability follows the service of alcohol to a minor and/or an obviously and visibly intoxicated individual, who then is involved in a drunk driving accident injuring others.

Liability Under Dram Shop Acts. Under many **dram shop acts**, a plaintiff (the person suing) must prove an unlawful sale of liquor or other alcoholic beverages (beer or wine) to an intoxicated person which causes injury to another party. Dram shop acts date back to the 1800s and were enacted to protect family members from habitual drunkards. Each state has the right to legislate its alcohol liability laws. Bar owners and others should make sure they read the state's dram shop act for their location, as each state's third-party liquor liability statute may differ. For example, the statute in Florida will differ from the statute in New York.

While dram shop acts vary from state to state, they generally provide consistent guidelines about who is responsible when third parties suffer because of an intoxicated person's actions. Let's assume something like this happens in a state where there is a dram shop act:

> A man comes into a bar and drinks four Manhattans in an hour. Even though he is slurring his words and trips over a chair on his way to the bar counter, the establishment serves him two more Manhattans. When the man leaves the bar, he gets into his car and has a head-on collision with a van. He and the woman driving the van are both injured.

Under a dram shop act, the woman in the van (the third party) will probably have a successful suit against the bar. The potential liability of taverns, restaurants, hotels, and other establishments is usually tremendous. The owners may be directly liable to the injured or deceased party or parties for various damages, including medical expenses, property damages, damages for pain and suffering, support for spouse and dependents, lost wages, funeral expenses, and perhaps punitive damages.

All establishments serving liquor should obtain insurance to cover these potentially devastating amounts of recoverable damages. As the frequency and amounts of awards in favor of third parties increase, liquor liability insurance rates rise. Strict adherence to responsible service procedures, documentation of service, and training efforts may help establishments obtain insurance rate discounts—some as high as 15 percent.

The Model Alcoholic Beverage Retail License Liability Act of 1985, or the "Model Dram Shop Act," establishes consistent, equitable, and uniform guidelines for the application of alcohol-server liability. The act created the "Responsible Business Practice Defense" to provide an establishment with a means of protection from liability. The establishment is protected if it can be proven that, at the time of service, a licensee or server was adhering to "those business practices which an ordinary, prudent person would follow under like circumstances." By permitting a defendant to assert a defense of responsible business practices, the act encourages licensees and servers to conduct themselves in a responsible manner toward their guests. The practices and policies cited in the act include:

- Actively encouraging guests not to become intoxicated if they are consuming alcoholic beverages on the premises.

- Promoting alternative, non-alcoholic beverages and making food readily available to guests.

- Actively promoting an alternative, safe means of transportation to prevent guests from driving while intoxicated.

- Prohibiting staff members from consuming alcoholic beverages while on duty.

- Providing a comprehensive, ongoing training program for servers in alcohol awareness, the responsible service of alcohol, and how to effectively interact with intoxicated guests.

Common Law Liability. A person who is injured by the acts of an intoxicated individual may also have the **common law** right to bring a lawsuit against the owners of a restaurant or bar where the person causing the injuries was served intoxicating beverages. Such suits may be based on a common law theory of negligence—independent of any claim under a state's Dram Shop Act. A lawyer representing an injured party in a drunk driving accident case may opt to sue in common law negligence. "**Negligence**," as defined under common law, means the failure to exercise the type of reasonable care used by a prudent person under similar circumstances. "Reasonable care" is a somewhat vague term, but it is crucial to an establishment's defense to be able to show it has exercised reasonable care with alcohol service.

In the earlier head-on collision example, under common law, the woman could argue that the bar was negligent in serving the man, who was obviously drunk. When an establishment is negligent, it means that its staff members failed to do what any sensible person ought to have done under the circumstances: stop service when the man showed signs of intoxication and provide alternate transportation home, possibly a taxi cab. If the drunk is not driving, there is no drunk driving accident. Training should focus on methods to spot the intoxicated guest, and preventing him or her from driving. Stopping alcohol service to the intoxicated guest is not enough.

Checking Identification

Establishments avoid serving alcohol to minors by developing various procedures for staff to follow when checking the identification documents of guests. Some establishments may check identification at the door and not allow minors to enter. Others may allow minors to enter, but use a method (such as hand stamps) to distinguish guests of legal drinking age from minors. Others may have staff check guests' identification as they order alcoholic beverages. Some establishments use an identification register—a book signed by guests who appear to be underage but have identification documents. If a guest's identification is fake and he or she signs the register, liability may transfer from the establishment to the guest.

Typically, a valid identification must have a photograph, statement of age (such as date of birth), and the signature of the person named on the document. Commonly accepted types of identification include:

- Valid driver's license issued by any state
- State-issued identification card

- International driver's license
- United States military identification
- Valid United States passport

Checking guests' identification can be uncomfortable, but it is one of the most important responsibilities staff members of alcohol service establishments face. If the establishment's policy for checking identification is posted at the entrance, guests may be more comfortable showing their identification. For example, a sign could say, "If you look younger than 30 years of age, please be prepared to show identification." If guests see that everyone is treated equally and that it is the establishment's policy to check identification, they may be less likely to object if asked to show identification. Some older guests may even feel complimented.

Regardless of whether an establishment checks identification at the door, a server should always ask to see the identification of anyone he or she suspects is not of legal drinking age before serving the person alcohol. Servers can't ignore good guest relations when checking identification. Ensuring that guests are of legal drinking age is like other services they provide. Servers should always be courteous and polite. Basic procedures include:

- Smile, look directly at the guest, and greet him or her: "Hello. Welcome to the Pub."

- Politely ask to see the person's identification: "May I please see your identification?"

- If the person does not remove the identification from his or her wallet, politely ask: "Could you please remove the identification from your wallet?" Never remove an identification from a person's wallet or purse yourself.

- Look at the birth date on the identification. Is the person of legal drinking age?

- Check whether the photograph appears to be that of the person handing you the identification. Look at the physical description on the document, especially the height and weight. Do they fit the person?

- Check the expiration date to ensure that the identification is valid. All drivers' licenses have an expiration date.

- Check the state seal to ensure that it is the right size and in the proper location.

Sometimes, minors obtain fake identification. When checking documents, you may find one that is altered, counterfeit, or borrowed/stolen from a person of legal drinking age. When checking an identification that you think may be false:

- Feel the surface to make sure a new layer of lamination has not been added.

- See whether the type has been tampered with.

- Examine the official information such as the state seal, number of digits in the driver's license number, borders, and colors.

- Examine the identification with a light behind it to more clearly see any cuts, erasures, or other alterations.

- Look at the picture and physical description on the identification and compare them to the person presenting the document.

If you have any doubts that the person presenting the identification is the legal owner, ask the person questions he or she should be able to answer immediately, such as:

- "What is your address?"

- "What is your middle name?"

- "How do you spell your last name?"

If the person hesitates before answering or behaves in other ways that make you suspicious, ask the person to sign his or her name. Compare the signature to that on the identification. They should match.

If you suspect that an identification is fake, ask for a second identification document. If you still have doubts, you should follow your establishment's procedures and refuse to admit the person or refuse to serve the person alcohol. If you deny someone entrance or service, it's best to be firm and polite, but never pushy or rude. For instance, depending on the establishment's policies, you might say:

- "I'm sorry, but if I let you in without seeing a valid identification, I'll lose my job."

- "I'm sorry, but it's against the law for me to serve you alcohol."

- "I'd be happy to bring you something else, but I can't serve you alcohol."

You should avoid saying anything to embarrass the minor, such as:

- "You're underage, and I'm not going to let you in."

- "Just what are you trying to pull here? I could have you arrested."

- "You're too young to drink alcohol, and I'm certainly not going to serve you any."

Establishments generally have a policy about confiscating false identification documents and also about detaining minors who present them. If a staff member confiscates an identification document or detains a minor, he or she should always complete an incident report as soon as possible after the occurrence. An incident report documents the facts of an occurrence and explains actions taken and the reasons for the particular actions.

Sometimes minors may get alcohol, even if you have refused to serve them. For example, legal drinkers may give alcoholic beverages to minors who are with them and parents may give their children alcoholic beverages. States have differing laws regarding minors who are with of-age guests. In states in which it is illegal for minors to drink no matter whom they are with, most establishments tell servers to call a manager to handle the situations described above. The manager will likely take the legal-age drinker aside and discuss the situation.

Alcohol and Its Physical Impact

True or False?
Alcohol is a depressant.

> True. Alcohol is a depressant that deadens the area of the brain that controls a person's inhibitions. That is why people sometimes seem to be more open and friendly when they drink alcohol. However, as alcohol levels increase, other areas of the brain become numb, and people can quickly become withdrawn and sad or irritable and disorderly.

True or False?
Alcohol decreases body temperature.

> True. Alcohol causes the small blood vessels in the skin to expand and this causes a loss of body heat. A person feels the heat on the skin and thinks he or she is getting warmer, but in fact the body is cooling off.

True or False?
How much you drink—not what you drink—causes hangovers.

> True. Hangovers are caused by how much alcohol a person drinks, not by the type of alcohol consumed. When a person drinks alcohol, the liver cannot perform its regular function of maintaining the body's blood sugar levels. It must instead break down the alcohol. As a result, the sugar level in the blood drops, causing headaches, extreme thirst, and other symptoms of a hangover.

True or False?
Time is the only factor that can restore sobriety.

> True. The only way to increase sobriety is to wait for the liver to break down the alcohol in the body into waste products. Coffee, cold showers, exercise, and other activities do not increase the liver's rate of breaking down alcohol.

True or False?
Alcohol is high in calories.

> True. Alcohol provides more calories per gram than carbohydrates or protein. Therefore, alcohol has more calories than most bread, potatoes, meat, cheese, and other foods that are high in carbohydrates and protein. Alcohol has only slightly fewer calories than pure fat.

Drink Strength

Beer and wine are examples of alcoholic beverages made when certain plants (such as grains, berries, and fruits) undergo a chemical change known as fermentation. Scotch, bourbon, gin, vodka, and rum are examples of beverages made when alcohol is distilled. Distilling alcohol creates stronger, more potent alcohol.

The strength of alcohol is measured in terms of "proof." The percentage of alcohol in a beverage is one-half the beverage's proof. For example, a 100-proof beverage contains 50 percent alcohol.

Exhibit 3   Alcohol Potency

- Most liquors range between 80 and 86.9 proof, except gin, which ranges from 90 to 94.6 proof. Some vodka is 100 proof and some rum is 151 proof.
- Most American beers range from approximately 6.4 to 10.5 proof.
- Imported beers range from about 7 to 26 proof.
- Some American beers made in micro-breweries are also as strong as 26 proof or more.
- Dessert wines and sherry, port, and other aperitifs have a higher percentage of alcohol than other wines.

The following beverages have almost exactly the same percentage of alcohol:

- 12 ounces of beer
- 4 ounces of wine
- 1 ¼ ounces of 80-proof liquor
- 1 ounce of 100-proof liquor

Typically, each of these equals one standard drink and contains approximately one-half ounce of alcohol. Different establishments may use different glass sizes to serve common drinks. For example:

- Some establishments pour four ounces of wine as a standard drink, while others pour six ounces.
- Some establishments use glasses that hold 12 or more ounces of beer, while others use glasses that hold 8 or fewer ounces of beer.
- Some establishments serve beer and other alcoholic beverages by the pitcher.

The same type of alcohol is sold in different strengths. Not all brands of beer have the same percentage of alcohol; not all types of wines have the same percentage of alcohol; and not all brands of the same liquor have the same percentage of alcohol. For example, some vodka is 80 proof while other vodka is 100 proof. Exhibit 3 summarizes the alcohol potency of common types of alcoholic beverages.

Also, the way an alcoholic beverage is prepared can affect its alcoholic potency. For example:

- A drink served over ice is less potent than one with the same amount of alcohol served straight-up (no ice), because, as the ice melts, it dilutes the strength of the alcohol.
- A drink blended with ice, such as a margarita, daiquiri, or other frozen drink, is more diluted and therefore less potent than a drink served on-the-rocks (with ice) or straight-up.
- A "tall" drink, such as a vodka and orange juice (served in a 12-ounce, rather than in a 6-ounce, glass), is less potent than a standard drink. Although the same amount of alcohol is used in both, the taller glass requires more ice and mixer, resulting in a weaker proportion of alcohol to non-alcohol ingredients.

Rate of Absorption

Food has a significant effect on the absorption rate of alcohol. Most food causes alcohol to move slowly from the stomach and small intestine into the bloodstream. This gives the liver more time to break down the alcohol in the body.

Certain types of food slow intoxication more than others. Fatty foods are difficult to digest and therefore remain in the stomach, along with any alcohol present, for a longer time than other foods. However, foods high in carbohydrates, such as pretzels, vegetables, fruits, and pasta, are quickly digested and may actually speed the absorption rate of alcohol into the bloodstream.

An effective way to reduce the rate of alcohol absorption is to eat foods high in fat. High-fat foods to suggest to guests who are drinking alcohol include:

- French fries
- Deep-fried items
- Cheese
- Pizza
- Chips and dip
- Nachos
- Any beef items (hamburgers, meat balls, beef tacos, etc.)

Intervention

Intervention involves more than stopping alcohol service to guests who are intoxicated. It consists of everything servers, co-workers, and managers do to influence guests' attitudes and behaviors as they drink alcohol. In fact, not letting guests become intoxicated is just as important as not serving alcohol to guests who are already intoxicated.

Intervention techniques can help you serve alcohol responsibly, discourage overconsumption, and manage guests who, despite your efforts, become intoxicated. Your first responsibility in intervention is to talk with guests as they arrive. This will establish good guest relations and help you discover who may be more likely than others to become intoxicated.

There are many devices that can help you determine a guest's blood alcohol concentration after drinking certain amounts of alcohol. These devices, similar to the sample shown in Exhibit 4, contain tables that show estimated BAC for various body weights per ounce of alcohol consumed within a specific period of time. However, variables in addition to body weight and the number of drinks consumed affect a guest's BAC. Drink tables and BAC cards have limited practical application, and you should only use them as basic guidelines by which to judge a guest's level of intoxication. Exhibit 5 lists other factors that affect BAC and the impact of alcohol.

One way to monitor a guest's rate of alcohol consumption is to keep track of the number of alcoholic beverages he or she consumes. Some drinks contain more alcohol than others and should be counted as more than one drink. Frequently

Exhibit 4   Sample BAC Card

KNOW YOUR LIMITS

Chart for responsible people who may sometimes
drive after drinking!

Approximate Blood Alcohol Percentage

Drinks	1	2	3	4	5	6	7	8
100	.04	.09	.13	.18	.22	.26	.31	.35
120	.04	.07	.11	.15	.18	.22	.26	.29
140	.03	.06	.09	.13	.16	.19	.22	.25
160	.03	.06	.08	.11	.14	.17	.19	.22
180	.02	.05	.07	.10	.12	.15	.17	.20
200	.02	.04	.07	.09	.11	.13	.15	.18
220	.02	.04	.06	.08	.10	.12	.14	.16
240	.02	.04	.06	.07	.09	.11	.13	.15

Body Weight in Pounds

Influenced   Possibly   Definitely
Rarely

Subtract .01% for each 40 minutes or .03% for each 2 hours of drinking. One
drink is $1\frac{1}{4}$ oz. of 80-proof liquor, 12 oz. of beer, or 4 oz. of table wine.

SUREST POLICY IS . . .
DON'T DRIVE AFTER DRINKING!

This chart is provided for information only. Nothing contained in this chart
shall constitute an endorsement by the Educational Institute of the
American Hotel & Lodging Association (the Institute) or the American
Hotel & Lodging Association (AH&LA) of any information, opinion,
procedure, or product mentioned, and the Institute and AH&LA disclaim
any liability with respect to the use of such information, procedure, or
product, or reliance thereon.

Source: Distilled Spirits Council of the United States, Inc.

used drink recipes should be standardized to help staff members more accurately count drinks. Everyone at the establishment should make these drinks exactly the same way, with exactly the same amounts of alcohol.

What a guest is drinking and how quickly it is consumed are also important items to note. All establishments should have procedures to help bartenders and servers count the number of drinks served to each guest. When guest checks are used, servers can note the time and the person ordering the drink each time an order is placed. When guest checks are not used, drink-tracking records are used (similar to the one presented in Exhibit 6) to count the number of drinks served to each guest and to rate each guest's level of intoxication.

Exhibit 5   Factors Affecting BAC and the Impact of Alcohol

Rate of consumption
Alcohol potency
Rate of absorption
    Food
    Water and carbonated beverages
    Emotional factors
Drugs or medicine
Physical characteristics of the person consuming alcohol
    Body size
    Body fat
    Gender
    Age
Environment in which alcohol is consumed

Signs of Intoxication

In addition to counting drinks, servers can control alcohol risks more effectively by recognizing changes in behavior that may indicate guests' levels of intoxication. When talking with a guest, ask yourself the following questions:

- Does the guest appear stressed, depressed, or tired?

- Is the guest drunk or determined to get drunk?

- Is the guest dieting?

- Is the guest taking any medication or other drugs?

Alcohol may affect guests in any of these situations more quickly or severely than it affects other guests.

Guests can exhibit various signs of intoxication. Exhibit 7 shows four general types of changes in behavior that occur when guests drink alcohol, and provides examples of each type of behavior.

Changes in behavior are more important than the behavior itself. For example, a loud guest may not signal that the guest is intoxicated—the guest may simply be a loud person. However, it may be a sign of intoxication if the guest was quiet and reserved at first and then became loud and rowdy after a few drinks. Similarly, a guest complaint about the strength of a drink may not be a sign of intoxication. However, if a guest complains that his or her drink is weak after drinking one or more of the same alcoholic beverage without complaining, this would be a sign of intoxication, because it indicates a change in behavior.

Traffic Light System

The traffic light system is an easy-to-use method of recognizing and rating guests' levels of intoxication. The system is based upon the colors of a traffic light. When guests drink alcohol, they can change quickly, just like a traffic light. You should

Exhibit 6   Sample Drink-Tracking Record

Table # / Guest #	Drink #	Time		Table # / Guest #	Drink #	Time		Table # / Guest #	Drink #	Time
Table 21 / Guest 1				Table 21 / Guest 1				Table 21 / Guest 1		
Table 21 / Guest 2				Table 21 / Guest 2				Table 21 / Guest 2		
Table 21 / Guest 3				Table 21 / Guest 3				Table 21 / Guest 3		
Table 21 / Guest 4				Table 21 / Guest 4				Table 21 / Guest 4		
Table 22 / Guest 1				Table 22 / Guest 1				Table 22 / Guest 1		
Table 22 / Guest 2				Table 22 / Guest 2				Table 22 / Guest 2		
Table 23 / Guest 1				Table 23 / Guest 1				Table 23 / Guest 1		
Table 23 / Guest 2				Table 23 / Guest 2				Table 23 / Guest 2		
Table 23 / Guest 3				Table 23 / Guest 3				Table 23 / Guest 3		
Table 23 / Guest 4				Table 23 / Guest 4				Table 23 / Guest 4		
Table 24 / Guest 1				Table 24 / Guest 1				Table 24 / Guest 1		
Table 24 / Guest 2				Table 24 / Guest 2				Table 24 / Guest 2		
Table 24 / Guest 3				Table 24 / Guest 3				Table 24 / Guest 3		
Table 24 / Guest 4				Table 24 / Guest 4				Table 24 / Guest 4		

Rating: **g** = green   **y** = yellow   **r** = red

Exhibit 7   Behavioral Changes That May Indicate Intoxication

Relaxed Inhibitions	Impaired Judgment	Slowed Reaction Time	Decreased Coordination
• Personality changes such as a quiet guest becoming overly friendly or an outspoken guest becoming quiet and withdrawn • Anti-social behavior such as leaving a group of friends and drinking alone • Uncontrolled emotional displays or outbursts • Noisy or rowdy behavior such as speaking too loudly or "showing off" • Obnoxious behavior such as suddenly using foul language or making offensive comments	• Complaining about drink strength, preparation, or price after consuming one or more of the same type of drink without complaining • Drinking faster; ordering shots or doubles • Being careless with money by leaving it unattended or offering to buy drinks for strangers or employees • Making irrational or nonsensical statements • Starting arguments or fights	• Glassy, unfocused eyes; dilated pupils • Drowsiness • Loss of concentration such as inability to finish sentences • Altered speech patterns such as slurred speech • Difficulty lighting cigarettes or having two cigarettes burn at once	• Difficulty handling coins or selecting money from a wallet or purse • Clumsiness, such as spilling drinks • Loss of balance, staggering, bumping into people, furniture, walls, etc., falling down • Falling asleep

also be aware that guests may already be in the yellow or red when they enter your establishment.

Green—Go.
The guest is sober. Actions to take include:

- Encourage the guest to order food along with the drinks.

- Explain any designated driver specials (such as free non-alcoholic beverages) that the establishment may provide.

- When a guest asks for a drink served straight-up, bring a glass of water along with it. If it's acceptable at your establishment, serve water with all drinks.

- Serve only one drink at a time to each guest.

- Don't bring a drink to someone who doesn't want one.

Yellow—Caution.
The guest is becoming intoxicated. Actions to take include:

- Take the situation seriously; it's much easier to deal with a guest at this stage than if the guest is in the red.

- Advise a manager about the situation so that he or she can help prevent the guest from moving into the red.

- Strongly encourage the guest to eat something.

- Strongly suggest non-alcoholic or low-alcohol beverages in place of the alcoholic beverages being consumed.

- Wait for the guest to reorder—don't suggest or encourage the purchase of more alcoholic beverages.

- Remove the guests' used glass before bringing a new drink when the guest reorders.

- Ensure that the guest will be safe when he or she leaves by telephoning a taxi, suggesting that the guest telephone for a ride, assuring that someone in the guest's party will drive, or suggesting that the guest stay at an adjacent lodging property.

Red—Stop!

The guest is intoxicated. Actions to take include:

- Get a second opinion from a co-worker or manager before stopping alcohol service.

- Ask a manager or other staff members to help; dealing with guests in the red is a team effort.

- Deny or stop alcohol service by following the establishment's policies and procedures.

Developing a network of staff members that monitor and control alcohol consumption is a responsible business practice that may lower the risk of alcohol-related incidents at an establishment. It's important to train all staff members—including valet attendants, door attendants, cashiers, and others in guest-contact positions—to spot signs of intoxication and to alert a supervisor or manager to the problem.

Stopping Alcohol Service

Denying or stopping alcohol service is never an enjoyable task. However, it is an extremely important one. When dealing with an intoxicated guest, the guest's well-being and the safety of others depend upon the actions you take. General guidelines for denying or stopping alcohol service include the following:

- Ask a co-worker to watch as you refuse to serve alcohol to a guest. You may appreciate the co-worker's help.

- Move the guest away from others.

- Calmly and firmly state your establishment's policy: "I'm sorry, but I've served you all the alcohol that my manager will allow."

- Do not judge the guest, make accusations, or argue. Don't say, "You're drunk" or "You've had too much to drink."

- Repeat your establishment's rules: "We care about your safety, and I can't serve you any more alcohol" or "The local police are really cracking down, and I can't serve you any more alcohol or we'll both get in trouble."

- Remove all alcohol from the reach of the person—even if it is his or her drink.

- Get a doorperson or manager to help you, if required at your establishment.

- Try not to let an intoxicated guest drive away—or even walk away—even if that means calling the police. It's better to risk making the guest angry than to risk lives.

- Make sure the guest has all of his or her personal belongings when he or she leaves.

- Fill out an incident report to describe the situation and record all actions taken.

Other Situations

Some situations require special alcohol service procedures. For instance, banquets, meetings, receptions, and other special events make it more difficult to control alcohol risks effectively.

Lodging facilities face additional challenges, because guests may drink in many hotel areas: guestrooms, hospitality suites, lounges, restaurants, and other areas. Lodging staff members must make sure intoxicated guests do not leave the property. It's not enough to escort an intoxicated guest from the restaurant or lounge to a guestroom. Staff members must then make sure the guest does not later leave the hotel.

In these types of situations, it's extremely important for servers to use the traffic light system and work as a team with other staff members to monitor and control alcohol consumption. Staff members such as guest service representatives, uniformed service staff members, and others must be part of the effort to control alcohol risks effectively.

 ## Key Terms

blood alcohol concentration (BAC)—Expresses the weight of alcohol per unit of blood, usually in grams per 100 milliliters (or per deciliter).

common law—A system of unwritten law not evidenced by statute, but by traditions and the opinions and judgments of courts of law.

dram shop acts—Statutory third-party liability laws that make dispensers of alcohol liable if they dispense alcohol irresponsibly—that is, to minors, to anyone who is obviously intoxicated, or to anyone who becomes intoxicated because of such service.

negligence—As defined under common law, the failure to exercise the type of reasonable care used by a prudent person under similar circumstances.

Review Questions

1. What is the role of state liquor authorities in regulating the sale of alcoholic beverages?

2. What types of licenses do operations need to sell beer, liquor, and wine?

3. What is BAC and how is it determined?

4. Why are Dram Shop Acts referred to as third-party liability laws?

5. How is "negligence" defined under common law?

6. What are the commonly accepted types of guest identification?

7. What actions could servers take if they think that a guest is presenting a fake identification?

8. How is the strength of a drink determined?

9. How is a "traffic light" system used to monitor a guest's consumption of alcohol?

10. What actions could servers take to deny or stop the service of alcohol to intoxicated guests?

 # Case Study

Responsible Alcohol Service: A Rose Between Two Thorny Situations

It was just after 9:00 P.M., at the end of a long Saturday shift, when Rose Wheaton, a server at Vic's Restaurant, noticed a group settling into one of her tables by the bar. Although she had been at Vic's less than a month—and had yet to receive all of her server training—she recognized four of them as some of the restaurant's best guests. There were six people in the group: two older couples that were Saturday-night regulars who she called by name, and a younger man and woman she did not know.

"Hey, Rose!" one of the men called out. "Sure looks busy tonight."

"Never too busy for you and your friends, Mr. Grove," Rose said, smiling as she reached their table. "How are you doing this evening?"

"We're fine. Just waiting for a table." Mr. Grove reached over and put his arm around the young man beside him. "This here's my son, Tommy. He's been away at college, but he's finally going to graduate next weekend. And this is Gwen, his fiancée. We're out for a kind of two-for-one celebration—graduation and engagement."

"That's great," Rose said. "What can I get for you while you wait for your table?"

"I think champagne is in order," Mr. Grove said. "And six glasses."

Rose glanced up from her pad at Tommy and Gwen. She quickly remembered that she had been 22 years old when she graduated from college. And Tommy and Gwen looked young. Were they even able to drink legally?

"I'll bring your champagne right out," she said. She moved around the table toward the younger couple. "Could I please see your driver's licenses?" she asked the couple.

"You've got to be kidding," Tommy said.

"We card everybody that looks really young."

Tommy's face flushed deep crimson as he turned to Gwen. "Do you have yours?"

"I left my purse at your parents' house," she said.

"Along with my wallet," Tommy said, staring back at Rose. "What about a passport? I've got mine out in the car."

Rose shook her head. "It's got to be a driver's license."

"That's crazy. What if we didn't drive a car?"

"Look, I don't make the —"

"I swear, we're both 22. We're getting married, for Pete's sake. Trust us."

"I do trust you, but, you know, it's not up to me. It's my boss's rule. He says that unless you have a driver's license, you can't drink alcohol here. The last thing we need to deal with is a bunch of drunk teenagers!" she said with a laugh.

"What? I—"

"It's okay, son," Mr. Grove interrupted, looking up at her with a smile. "You just bring us four glasses, Rose, and we'll be fine here."

"But, Dad—"

"It's okay," he said with a wink.

Ten minutes later, Rose was picking up a round of beers for a bowling league having a shouting match at table 7 when Gary Hammond, the bartender, called her over. "Did you card those two at table 5?" he asked, nodding toward the Grove party.

"Of course," she said. "They didn't have their I.D.s, but it's okay. They're not drinking."

"You could have fooled me," Gary said. "See for yourself." She looked in time to see Mr. Grove refill four champagne glasses—and two "water" glasses sitting in front of the engaged couple.

Rose shook her head. The bowlers were hollering for their beer. "Gary, I don't have time to play games with these people. Where's Vic?" she asked, referring to the restaurant's owner/manager. When she found Vic overseeing the dinner production in the kitchen, she quickly explained the situation and asked him to come out and talk to the Grove party.

When Vic approached the table, he immediately greeted the four adult regulars by name and asked how they were doing. Everyone seemed to be in especially fine spirits, though he noticed that the young man and woman suddenly weren't drinking their "water."

"May I talk with you for a moment, Ted?" he asked Mr. Grove. The two stepped over to the bar for a private conversation. "Ted," Vic began quietly, "people without a valid photo I.D. cannot be served alcohol here."

"They weren't," Mr. Grove said, his smile starting to fade. "Well, not really, anyway. Rose said you wouldn't allow it, but I didn't see why you couldn't do us a little favor."

"It isn't a matter of favors, Ted, it's a legal requirement for running a restaurant in this state. You know that we trust and respect you and your guests, but this isn't about that. It is simply a matter of obeying the law. Now, I understand you're out for a celebration tonight, and I certainly don't want to rain on that. But, to avoid any further embarrassment, I do have to take the champagne away from your son and his fiancée. I also need to ask that you not give them any more."

"Is that all?" Mr. Grove said glumly.

"Well, no. Because this is a special night for your family and friends, I want to offer you a complimentary appetizer platter. Your table in the dining room should be ready in about five minutes, and I'll have the appetizer delivered hot from the kitchen the minute you all sit down."

"Really? Well, thanks, Vic. I appreciate that." As the two men headed back to table 5, Mr. Grove approached Tommy and Gwen, explained the law, and asked for their glasses. He handed them over to Vic, along with an apology and another "thank you" for the offer of the appetizer platter. Vic took the glasses back to the bar, where Gary was prepping a platter of five 23-ounce beers.

"Nice work, boss," Gary said. "I wish you could handle every problem that comes up like that."

"What do you mean?"

"Look at table 7. Or maybe I should say, listen to table 7. It's the Bolingbrook Bowling League again. They must start drinking at the bowling alley. And for some reason they always come in here with their volume stuck on 10."

"How long have they been here?"

Gary checked his watch. "Forty minutes. And this is round two of large beers."

That meant the five bowlers had each consumed the equivalent of four beers within forty minutes. And who could know how much they may have had to drink before they arrived? "Who's serving table 7?"

"It's Rose's table, but I told her I'd cover during her break. I could be wrong, but I'd say there are a couple people there moving straight into the yellow," he said, referring to the cautionary zone between sobriety (green) and inebriation (red). "Even though they started loud, they seem to be getting even rowdier. And for a while they were telling everyone around them that we're watering down the beer. Unless I'm misreading the signs or they start slowing down, this round will turn the whole table yellow."

"All right. Take five waters along with these beers. You might also ask if anyone would care for coffee. Keep a close eye on them and fill Rose in when she comes off break. I don't think she's ever had to deal with a situation like this before."

"So I'm not cutting them off?"

Vic shook his head. "They're obviously feeling good—and loud—but they still seem to be under control to me."

Fifteen minutes later, Rose was back at the bar with an order for another round of beer for table 7. "That's some wild group," she said, rubbing her temples. "Another round of these and they'll be bowling me across the restaurant."

"That's it, then," Gary said. "You need to cut them off. Offer them coffee, soda, sparkling juice, whatever—but let them know that you cannot serve them any more alcohol."

"Are you serious?"

"Absolutely."

Rose nervously approached the table, but instead of finding five bowlers, she now discovered eight people squeezed around the table.

"Come over here, little lady, and meet some of our new friends!" one of the bowlers said, grabbing her arm and yanking her toward the table.

"Hey," another one spoke up, "where's our brewskies? I succinctly remember ordering another brewskie."

"You did," Rose said, "but it's obvious that you've all had enough. In fact, I'd say it's obvious to every other person in the restaurant. I'm cutting you off. Now, if you'd like something else to drink, or something to eat, I'd be happy—"

"But what about us?" one of the newcomers asked. "We just got here, and we want something to drink."

"'Course you do, buddy," chimed in one of the original five, slapping the man hard across the back. "You got catching up to do. Lots. Nobody's cutting anything off as long as I'm here."

"Are you saying we have to sit here nursing a soda pop or something while our friends are drinking real drinks? You've got to be joking!"

"Look, missy, you're new here, so you probably don't have any idea how much money we spend in this place," another added.

Rose looked up helplessly at Gary behind the bar. Where's Vic now? she wondered.

Discussion Questions

1. What mistakes did Rose make in her handling of the Grove party? the Bolingbrook Bowling League?

2. What steps can a server take to effectively manage someone in the yellow zone?

3. What could Vic have done to better prepare his staff for responsible alcohol service?

Case Number: 3494CA

The following industry experts helped generate and develop this case: Christopher Kibit, C.S.C., Academic Team Leader, Hotel/Motel/Food Management & Tourism Programs, Lansing Community College, Lansing, Michigan; and Jack Nye, General Manager, Applebee's of Michigan, Applebee's International, Inc.

 References

Allen, Robin Lee; Gould, Alan; Koteff, Ellen; and Richard Martin. "Operators That Require Alcoholic-Beverage Training for Workers See Payoff in Protection." *Nation's Restaurant News.* February 7, 2005. 39(6): 21.

Durnal, Randy. "Responsible Alcohol Service Ensures Bar Patrons Get Cut Off Before Reaching Dangerous .08 BAC." *Nation's Restaurant News.* January 21, 2008. 42(3): 21.

Kirkland, Tim. "Join the Team: With the Entire Front-of-House Staff Working Together to Ensure Responsible Service, Everyone Wins." *Cheers*. November– December 2008. 19(9): 66.

Marshall, Anthony. "Responsible Alcohol Service Includes Bartenders, Employees." *Hotel & Motel Management*. September 9, 2004. 219(16): 8.

Meyer, Diana Lambdin. "Don't Bite the Hand That Regulates You." *Restaurant Startup & Growth*. November 2008. 5(11): 38–45.

Chapter 7 Outline

Menu Planning
    Menu-Planning Objectives
    Important Planning Considerations
    Menu Planning and Meal Periods
Types of Menus
Food Categories on Menus
    Appetizers
    Soups
    Salads
    Entrées
    Desserts
    The Planning Sequence
Menu Design
    Electronic Menus
    Menu Design Mistakes
Menu Trends
    Value
    Smaller Portions
    Local Food
    Fresh Food
    Ethnic Food
    Healthy Menu Options
    Environmentally Friendly Food
    Extending Protein Ingredients
    Breakfast
    Vegetarian Menu Items
    Mandatory Menu Labeling
Promotions
Changing the Menu

Competencies

1. Describe the importance of the menu to food service operations, and explain typical menu-planning objectives. (pp. 263–271)

2. Summarize important menu-planning considerations, including menu pricing and rationalization, and describe how the traditional meal periods (breakfast, lunch, and dinner) influence menu planning. (pp. 272–275)

3. List and describe common types of menus, describe typical food categories on menus, and summarize the recommended menu-planning sequence. (pp. 275–278)

4. Explain the importance of menu design, describe menu design elements, discuss electronic menus, and list common menu mistakes. (pp. 278–285)

5. Summarize menu trends, discuss promotions, and identify external and internal factors that can cause managers to change menus. (pp. 285–292)

7

Menu Development

WHEN YOU DINE AT A RESTAURANT, chances are you don't give a thought to the importance of the menu beyond what selections it offers. But if you take time to think about the menu's importance, you can begin to understand how the menu affects almost every aspect of a food and beverage operation. In many respects, a menu is a mission statement; it defines an operation's concept and communicates that concept to guests. Some have described the menu as a restaurant's business card.

A menu is one of the single biggest influences on an operation's development of a loyal guest base and a positive return on its investment of energy, money, time, and other resources. One of the goals of menu development, then, is to influence the behaviors and emotions of the guests reading the menu. From influencing guests to select the most profitable menu items to convincing them to feel good about their menu choices, the menu serves as a statement of the restaurant's theme. As such, a menu should embrace and support the operation's image in addition to describing each appetizer, entrée, and dessert.

As you can see, the menu's role is much larger than just listing the products that are available; the menu serves as a plan for the entire food and beverage operation. Just as the menu serves as a plan, the menu has to be planned, and it has to be planned with guest needs and expectations in mind.

Today's guests are as sophisticated as any in the history of the food and beverage industry. While many enjoy sampling new menu items that add variety and excitement to their experience, others prefer predictable, familiar products. In any case, today's guests are demanding value and are building strong and loyal relationships with operations that provide that value. Value, of course, is directly related to price as well as the tangible products and intangible services the operation provides. A guest's perception of value may be based on any combination of factors, such as the selection offered on the menu, the quality of the products, portion sizes, the style and quality of service, price, and—most importantly—the memories created through the overall experience.

Menu Planning

Any food and beverage operation can be viewed as a system of basic operating activities or **control points,** with menu planning being the initial control point. Each control point is a miniature system with its own identifiable structure and functions (see Exhibit 1).

Exhibit 1   Control Points in a Food and Beverage Operation

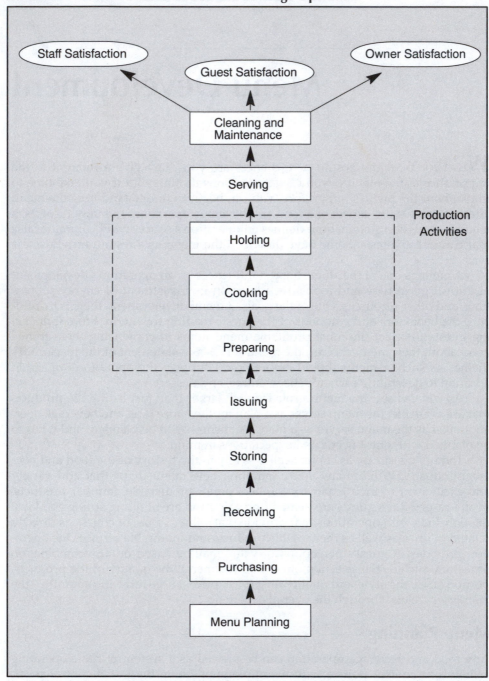

Source: Ronald F. Cichy, *Food Safety: Managing with the HACCP System* (Lansing, Mich.: American Hotel & Lodging Educational Institute, 2008), p. 6.

As Exhibit 1 shows, menu planning is the foundation for the remaining control points: purchasing, receiving, storing, issuing, preparing, cooking, holding, serving, and cleaning and maintenance. The end goal is to satisfy guests, staff members, and owners/investors.

Suppliers can help managers plan a menu. Their input and suggestions can help make a restaurant more profitable (or help managed services and self-operated food and beverage operations keep costs down) while enhancing guest satisfaction. For example, suppliers can offer preparation and merchandising suggestions for various menu items. Excellent food and beverage operations use their suppliers as sources of market trend information, new promotion ideas, and informal competitive analyses.

In addition to influencing the other control points, menu planning affects, and is affected by, the operation's design and layout, equipment requirements, and labor needs. The success of menu planning determines the success of the other basic operating activities.

Menu-Planning Objectives

To produce a memorable menu—one that will please guests and help achieve the goals of the operation itself—there are several objectives that a menu planner must strive to achieve with the menu. These objectives are discussed in the following sections.

The Menu Must Meet or Exceed Guests' Expectations. Because guest satisfaction is the overall goal of food and beverage management, the menu must, above all else, reflect the tastes and preferences of the guests—not those of the chef, the food and beverage director, or the manager. Menu planning is a complex process, but it can be successful when the focus, first and foremost, is on the needs and expectations of guests. All of the factors that go into planning a menu are shown in Exhibit 2. As you can see, guests are listed as the first concern of menu planners.

To plan a menu from the guests' perspective, you must discover exactly what it is that they want. Since the needs and expectations of guests are ever-changing, it is essential that regular input from guests be actively encouraged. Talking with guests, listening to their needs, and acting on this critical input will strengthen an operation's guest-driven reputation. Guests who prefer a fast-casual operation located near a major expressway certainly have different expectations from those having a leisurely dinner in a city hotel's rooftop restaurant.

You can sometimes pinpoint guests' preferences by their ages or socioeconomic status. Whether your operation attracts mostly young families, a singles crowd, or a high percentage of senior citizens, your menu should reflect the kinds of foods and beverages that they enjoy if you wish to continue to attract that particular group.

Another way to identify guest needs and desires is by recognizing what kind of overall appeal your operation has for guests. If your restaurant is part of a "destination property" (a resort, for example) and most of your guests are with you for a week or two, no doubt they would want an interesting, varied diet, and they would be most pleased with either a vast menu or one that changes regularly, even daily.

Exhibit 2   Factors in Menu Planning

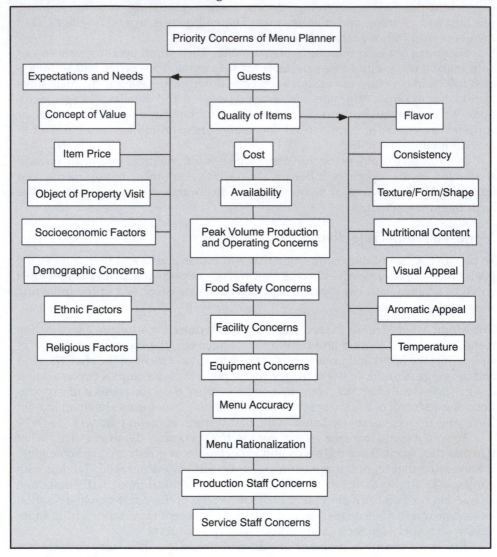

The Menu Must Attain Marketing Objectives. While part of marketing is discovering what guests want, another important aspect is providing for guest needs at convenient locations and times and at prices guests are willing to pay. In some cases, excellent product development, pricing, and promotion will convince guests that you have what they desire—even if they are unaware of what they have been looking for.

Some good examples of specific food items that have been developed and promoted over the years include pizza, specialty hamburgers, fish and chips, a vast array of ice cream flavors, fried chicken, variety pancake and crepe dishes, baked potatoes with various toppings, nachos, and sandwiches made with a variety of artisan breads. When these items first appeared on menus, marketing objectives may have varied from giving the guests a delicious, nutritious, take-away lunch to introducing guests to a new gourmet taste treat. Regardless of the marketing techniques used, the menu must help bring guests back for more visits; guests will not return if their expectations are not met or, better yet, exceeded.

The Menu Must Meet Quality Standards. Quality concerns are closely related to marketing concerns. It is important that you clearly understand all aspects of managing to meet quality requirements and develop menus that incorporate these standards into your food items. If you are planning a menu for a cafeteria line, buffet, or special banquet, for example, you should know that preparation and holding difficulties preclude the addition of such menu items as omelets, unless they are cooked to order—an example of a "made-for-me" customized menu item. If you wish to add a number of prepared-to-order food items (broiled steaks and chops, grilled fish, and stir-fried vegetables) to your menu—and you have a large dining room that regularly has a high guest count—you must determine whether you have the work space and the production staff members needed to prepare a large volume of high-quality, prepared-to-order dishes. Also, you must decide which items are not practical for your operation.

High quality and good nutrition go hand-in-hand. While food and beverage operations in hospitals, schools, and the military must provide nutritionally well-balanced meals on their menus, restaurants have no such requirement—yet. The expert restaurant manager knows that while people want attractive, good-tasting dishes, most are also interested in the nutritional quality of those foods. With trends toward complex-carbohydrate foods and reduced portion sizes, many food service operators have placed more emphasis on nutrition when planning menus. Therefore, a menu that met quality objectives would also offer enough choices to guests so that they could order a nutritionally well-balanced meal. Many menu planners use computer software programs that include nutritional analyses.

Other aspects of food quality include flavor, texture, color, shape, consistency, palatability, flair, and guest appeal. As you plan the menu, remember to balance it so that textures, colors, shapes, and flavors aren't repetitious. Cod in cream sauce, mashed potatoes, and cauliflower—an all-white meal with little variation in texture—is an example of an unbalanced meal. Remember too that some guests cannot eat or do not care for highly spiced or garlic-rich foods, while others cannot get enough of them and would be most unhappy with a menu that offered only bland foods. Because there is a growing trend toward reduced-fat, high-fiber diets, dishes that are both low in fat and high in fiber might attract guests; if these dishes suit vegetarian guests as well, you will add to your potential guest base.

Again, look at your menu from the guests' perspective. What do they want? How can you provide for their needs? Your work is not over until you have produced a menu that not only helps the operation meet quality objectives but also meets the needs of your markets.

The Menu Must Be Cost-Effective. Managed services and self-operated food and beverage operations (also referred to as "on-site" operations) as well as restaurants should plan menus that meet financial goals. Generally, restaurants cannot attain their profit objectives unless their product costs, which the menu often dictates, fall within a specific range. Regardless of the type of operation you are planning for, you must select menu items that are within the operation's budget (its estimate of allowable food expenses).

The Menu Must Be Accurate. Due to rising interest in the subject by guests and legislators, **truth-in-menu regulations** are an increasingly important menu-planning consideration. Although such regulations exist primarily at the state and local levels, more federal regulations are likely in the future.

Truth-in-menu regulations require accurate descriptions of raw ingredients and finished menu items, in addition to other details. Meat that is described as "choice top butt steak" must be graded "USDA choice," for example. Items billed "fresh" must not be frozen, canned, or preserved in any way. A product's point of origin must also be presented accurately; for example, "fresh Lake Superior whitefish" should indeed be fresh whitefish from Lake Superior (a sample list of common points of origin for menu items is presented in Exhibit 3).

The size, weight, and portion advertised on the menu must also be accurate. A bowl of soup should contain more than a cup of soup. Descriptions such as "extra-tall" drinks or "extra-large" salads can lead to guest complaints. "All you can eat" implies that the guest is entitled to exactly that: as much as he or she can eat. For meat items, it is a generally accepted practice to list the precooked weight.

The preparation technique must be accurately described. If there are additional charges for extras (such as substitutions or coffee refills), such charges should be clearly stated on the menu. Any pictures of food products should be accurate. Dietary or nutritional claims, if used, must be precise. "Low-calorie," for example, is vague because it implies that the product is lower in calories but does not specify what the product is being compared to. Servers' descriptions should also accurately portray menu selections.

The Menu Should Blend the Old and the New. Regardless of the type of food service operation, its size, its average check, its guests, or its location, the menu should be a balance between tradition and innovation. The retention of popular and profitable menu items is necessary. Equally important are new additions that give guests something different and fresh. New menu items can be classified into one of two categories: a creative update of a traditional favorite (Caesar salad with spicy shrimp or filet mignon stuffed with smoked garlic, for example), or a radical departure from traditional menu items (pizza topped with ham, coconut, and mango, or fresh pasta served with smoked jalapeño chile peppers, for instance).

Staff Members Must Be Able to Produce and Serve the Items on the Menu. A food and beverage operation's staff members are important to the success of its menu. Before management begins menu planning, the skill levels of production and service staff must be assessed. It may be helpful to consider the production staff and service staff separately, although their functions are closely related in practice.

The production staff produces menu items within the confines of the kitchen. In planning the operation's menu, the objective is to avoid overloading any one

Exhibit 3   Common Menu Representations of Points of Origin

Dairy Products

Danish Bleu Cheese
Domestic Cheese
Imported Swiss Cheese
Roquefort Cheese
Wisconsin Cheese

Fish and Shellfish

Cod, Icelandic (North Atlantic)
Crab
    Alaskan King Crab
    Florida Stone Crab
    North Atlantic Crab
    Snow Crab
Frog Legs
    Domestic Frog Legs
    Imported Frog Legs
    Louisiana Frog Legs
Lobster
    Australian Lobster
    Brazilian Lobster
    Maine Lobster
    South African Lobster
Oysters
    Blue Point Oysters
    Chesapeake Bay Oysters
    Olympia Oysters
Salmon
    Nova Scotia Salmon
    Puget Sound Sockeye Salmon
    Salmon Lox
Scallops
    Bay Scallops
    Sea Scallops

Scrod, Boston
Shrimp
    Bay Shrimp
    Gulf Shrimp
Trout
    Colorado Brook Trout
    Idaho Brook Trout
Whitefish, Lake Superior

Meats

Beef, Colorado
Ham
    Country Ham
    Danish Ham
    Imported Ham
    Smithfield Ham
    Virginia Style Ham
Pork, Iowa

Poultry

Long Island Duckling
Maryland Milk-Fed Chicken

Vegetables and Fruits

Orange Juice, Florida
Pineapples
    Hawaiian Pineapples
    Mexican Pineapples
Potatoes
    Idaho Potatoes
    Maine Potatoes

Source: Ronald F. Cichy, *Food Safety: Managing with the HACCP System* (Lansing, Mich.: American Hotel & Lodging Educational Institute, 2008), p. 75.

person or workstation. A well-planned menu features items that the kitchen staff can consistently produce while maintaining the operation's quality, cost, and sanitation standards.

Management should be realistic in determining what can be accomplished with the existing staff. For example, consider a fine-dining restaurant where every menu item is prepared from scratch. If all meats are received in the wholesale-cut form (which is less expensive than the retail- or portion-cut form), the staff has to do the additional butchering. If the production staff is not properly trained in butchering wholesale cuts into retail cuts of meat, a lot of time and meat will be wasted, and unnecessary sanitation hazards will probably abound. Rather than saving the business any money, this poorly conceived arrangement increases food costs, adds to labor costs, and lowers quality. Such problems can be avoided by organizing the menu-planning function with personnel skills in mind.

The service staff transfers prepared menu items from the production staff to guests. In order to properly serve guests, servers should be ready to answer their questions. Servers should know what items are on the menu, the portion sizes offered, ingredients, how the items are prepared, and the prices. Even if the menu contains all of this information, a server can provide a personal touch by answering guests' questions directly. Servers should also know the meanings of all terms used on the menu so they can explain them to any guests who are puzzled. This is particularly important if the menu includes ethnic foods.

Again, staff training is critical. In addition to thoroughly training servers and production staff, some managers call a five- to ten-minute line-up meeting with all staff members before each meal period. These brief meetings are informal training sessions. They give the chef and the manager an opportunity to explain daily specials, and they give the servers and production staff an opportunity to sample portions of new menu items and ask questions.

Like the skill levels of production staff, the skill levels of service staff must be considered in menu planning. This is particularly true if management is considering menu items to be prepared in the dining room, such as Caesar salads and specialty desserts. Whether an operation uses tableside preparation methods depends, in part, on the image it seeks. Whatever style of service an operation offers, the service staff must be trained in the skills dictated by the menu.

The Menu Must Be Based on the Amounts and Types of Production and Service Equipment Available. Any food and beverage operation must make a large investment in equipment before it can open for business. Naturally, the amounts and types of production and service equipment owned by the operation determines what items it can produce and place on the menu. It is imperative to select equipment based on capacity, skill levels of staff members, maintenance and energy costs (energy-efficient equipment is a must), and initial purchase price. Equipment should be constructed according to nationally recognized sanitation standards or be listed by accredited testing and listing operations such as Underwriters Laboratories and the National Sanitation Foundation. Above all, it is critical that equipment be easy to clean and sanitize.

Adding a new menu item may require purchasing new production equipment. Such purchases should not be made without an analysis of the flow of products and people through the work area. This analysis helps management anticipate where cross-traffic may create safety and sanitation hazards. Many operations use equipment on wheels or casters so it can be moved easily when necessary. In addition to allowing for adjustments to the product and staff traffic patterns, this mobility facilitates cleaning. Before a new menu item is added, the proper equipment should be available to reduce sanitation hazards. For example, if the proposed menu change involves adding a soup bar to the dining room, the kitchen must have adequate steam-tables, steam-jacketed kettles, or range equipment to reach and maintain safe product temperatures when cooking the soup.

A change in menu may also have implications for the operation's service equipment. Again, sanitation hazards and quality standards must be considered beforehand. In the case of the soup bar, for example, the dining room should be equipped with suitable hot-holding equipment before the new soup items are added to the menu.

The Menu Must Be Appropriate for the Operation's Facilities. The physical facilities, both indoor and outdoor, affect the image of a food and beverage operation. The layout and design of the physical facilities are also important considerations in menu planning because they establish the physical limits within which food preparation and service take place. The physical facilities must be adequate for the purchasing, receiving, storing, issuing, preparing, cooking, holding, and serving of every item on the menu. Thus, a major change in the menu may necessitate remodeling the physical facilities. By the same token, a change in facilities may force an operation to revise its menu. This mutual influence can be illustrated by the following examples.

Consider a country club food service operation in which 80 percent of the space is allocated to the dining room and 20 percent to the kitchen. Since the kitchen generally prepares menu items from scratch, the production facilities are often pushed to the limit. The kitchen facilities are almost always overtaxed during the summer, when there are more catered parties and special events. Suppose the country club manager decides to expand the dining and banquet facilities by adding a 90-seat patio service area with a clear glass roof. He is convinced that this area will appeal to guests planning catered events because it offers a breathtaking view of the golf course. However, the manager has not considered the production capabilities of the kitchen; to increase the dining facilities without adding to the production area would be a critical error. Such a decision would likely result in lower productivity and morale among production and service staff. A corresponding reduction in guest satisfaction could be expected to follow.

Suppose that a hotel decides to add in-room dining (room service) in an attempt to generate more revenue. Again, the size and layout of the hotel have an impact on the success of the effort. For example, the kitchen might produce a beautiful and tasty omelet for breakfast, but by the time an in-room dining attendant delivered the order to the farthest wing of the hotel, the product could be cold and unappealing. In-room dining menus must be limited to those items that can be successfully and safely delivered to guests.

Yet another problem occurs when an overly ambitious restaurant sales force convinces meeting planners that special entrées or desserts will add a touch of elegance to their banquets. These salespeople sometimes fail to consider the limitations of the operation's production and service facilities. Likewise, an outdoor barbecue for 500 people in the hotel's gardens may sound like an exciting affair, but if the kitchen or service staff cannot deliver the products, the guests will not be satisfied.

In all of these examples, the unfortunate results can be prevented if managers take into consideration the limitations of their facilities. Managers must design menus around what the physical facilities of their operations can realistically handle.

Important Planning Considerations

Menu planning begins the process of writing the script for creating a positive and memorable experience for guests. Menu planning is based on the fundamental principle that the menu must satisfy the guests that the food and beverage operation is serving. The menu must be planned with guests always in mind.

Many of today's guests are more knowledgeable about food than guests typically were in the past. Guests who are food enthusiasts watch culinary-themed television shows, read culinary books, and are looking to feel a "wow" when it comes to their food and beverage experiences. For these guests, presentation is as important as taste. Variety in the tastes, colors, and heights of the food items on their plates adds to the "wow" factor. The wow factor is also enhanced when a unique sauce is served with a food, or a variety of foods are served in a sampler-size main course. Guests are wowed when they are served fresh seasonal items raised or grown locally. Fresh is best when served on plates that do not appear too cluttered; empty spaces on serving dishes can help accent and frame the food. Garnishes and sauces should not be overdone; they should draw out the character of the main course, not drown it (literally) in a sauce. Food presentations that are too complicated or time-consuming for the kitchen staff to construct will not look good because those responsible for preparing them will not be able to take all the time required. Food presentations must be striking but simple enough that those who must produce them can do so efficiently and effectively time after time.

When planning a menu, a number of other considerations are important. The consistency of preparation as well as presentation must be considered. Consistency means predictability not only for guests but for managers and owners as well, since standard costs are based on standard portion sizes and standard recipes. Consistency helps to deliver the forecasted contribution margin for each particular menu item. This requires careful planning and execution.

Another menu planning consideration is the cost of the food. Food cost is the total cost of all food items sold divided by overall sales revenues for the same time period. Food cost control hinges on standards, beginning with planning standard purchase specifications based on standard recipes. When standard recipes are used, the cost per serving can be calculated, as well as the required selling price for each item.

Ingredient availability for menu items is another menu planning consideration. Ingredient availability depends on the location of the food and beverage operation and, in part, on the season of the year. If the operation is flexible about the source (e.g., country/location of origin) as well as the price of an ingredient, most ingredients today are available year-round. However, if the operation promotes locally grown and harvested tomatoes in Michigan, for example, this requirement can only be met at a certain time of the year.

Menu items should fit with the food and beverage operation's concept. The good news is that today even some of the most eclectic menu choices will fit with most of today's flexible restaurant concepts. New menu items must blend in with the cuisine of the operation, as well as those menu items already being offered for sale.

Labor-intensive menu items are costly to prepare and these labor costs will need to be passed on to guests, meaning higher sales prices. Most guests resist high prices. A high-priced menu item can ruin the overall dining experience of guests, or may not be purchased in the first place because of its cost.

Variety on the menu can be created through the ways that items are put together with different ingredients. For example, a duck main course could be offered on the dinner menu with three different preparations and sauces. Skinless, sliced duck breast could also be featured on the luncheon menu atop a salad. This creates variety—four different choices—using just one main ingredient (e.g., duck in this example).

Will a new menu item satisfy the guest? That is the million dollar question and the most important one, because guest satisfaction is the reason behind all that goes on in a food and beverage operation.

The complexity of planning a menu varies according to the type of food and beverage operation. Obviously, table-service restaurants offer menus that differ from cafeteria or buffet menus. Thus, you need to consider the type of operation you are developing the menu for as well as its check average (the typical amount spent by one person on a meal) and overall marketing concerns. Furthermore, you should consider the items your competitors offer. After all, they are trying to attract the same guests. What are guests purchasing in other restaurants? Why? What can you do to make your products and services special and more attractive to potential guests? If your restaurant has an ethnic theme such as Italian, Mexican, or Thai, or has a distinctive decor such as that of a neighborhood bar and grill or the dining room on a luxury cruise ship, your menu should reflect that theme or atmosphere.

Menu Pricing. Menu pricing is essential to consider as a general planning parameter. Pricing-strategy development requires an understanding of the quality, portion size, and guest service combination as it relates to value. The level of quality has to be based on the requirements of the target markets.

Portion sizes influence the prices charged for menu items; the smaller the portion, the less that needs to be charged for that item to cover ingredient and other costs. Portion sizes are also tied directly to the value perceived by guests. Although many weight-conscious guests are opting for smaller portions, it is not advisable to decrease portion sizes across an entire menu; a better strategy is to offer a choice of portion sizes for a menu item when possible.

It is never a good strategy to lower service standards in order to reduce prices. Most guests are willing to pay for good service. Some restaurants are following the strategy of lowering menu prices or freezing prices at current levels, despite price increases for raw ingredients, to try to build guest loyalty and a base of repeat guests. These operations attempt to make up for the reduced profit margins by increasing the operation's overall volume of business and the frequency of visits by regular guests.

If an operation has no choice but to raise prices, a number of proven strategies might be used. One is to raise prices at the start of a new accounting period to eliminate problems with accounting. Another is to avoid across-the-board price increases and instead raise them only for menu items that are affected by the higher costs. Guests understand that higher quality requires the purchasing of fresh, and often more expensive, ingredients. A third strategy is to think about implementing new menus each month, quarter, or season to respond more closely to market conditions and prices. Above all, it is essential to keep the focus on value as it is perceived by guests. If menu prices far exceed the perceived value of the menu items, guests are unlikely to return.

Menu Rationalization. As mentioned earlier, the menu directly affects a food and beverage operation's purchasing, receiving, and storage requirements. The size of storage areas needed for raw ingredients and finished menu items depends on the menu. One of the primary advantages of a limited menu is that it reduces storage requirements.

In the past, many managers thought the best strategy was to diversify their menus and offer a wide variety of items. Since most items were made on-site, the number and variety of raw ingredients needed increased significantly with each new item. Today the focus is on **menu rationalization:** the creation of a simplified menu for the sake of operational efficiency and guest satisfaction. Although this strategy frequently results in a limited menu, the operation can offer several menu items that use the same raw ingredients (offering several portion-size choices for selected menu items is another way to introduce more variety). The objective of this **cross-utilization** of ingredients is to prepare and serve as many different menu items as possible with a limited number of raw ingredients. This helps streamline the purchasing, receiving, and storing functions.

The decision of whether to diversify a menu is driven to a great extent by guest demands. Guests who dine out frequently are looking for diversity in menu choices. Some food and beverage operators reason that, due to increased competition, they must increase their hours of operation or expand business into new meal periods, diversify their menus in order to build guest loyalty and repeat business, and draw on a wider guest base. However, while a constantly changing menu offers variety, it can cause confusion in the operation and result in lowered overall quality standards. An alternative to making frequent changes to the menu is to promote a different item on the existing menu every week, or supplement the existing menu with a few specials each day.

Proponents of menu rationalization say that a food service operation should discover what it does best and continually refine it. Menu diversification requires additional staff training and additional time for taking orders and answering guest questions. Perhaps the best strategy for most operations is to create a balanced menu that maximizes cross-utilization of ingredients and equipment.

Menu Planning and Meal Periods

The traditional meal periods are breakfast, lunch, and dinner. While the focus on all or some of these meal periods in a specific operation varies (some do the majority of their business at breakfast and lunch, others are primarily dinner houses), some generalities can be drawn.

Breakfast. Breakfast is the most profitable meal period or "day part," according to many food service operators. ("Day part" is a phrase that originated with the use of automated point-of-sale systems that divided a food and beverage operation's day into "day parts.") Breakfast's profitability is the direct result of the relatively low food costs of bakery products and eggs. Often, this relatively high profitability is balanced with fairly low check averages due to generally low prices.

Some food and beverage organizations offer a limited breakfast menu, with relatively inexpensive prices, that is easy to produce and serve. While traditional breakfast items such as eggs, pancakes, and breakfast meats still appeal to many guests, other more healthy menu items are appearing on many menus. These healthier options include multigrain cereals, oatmeal with fresh fruit, and breakfast sausage links made from chicken and apples. Guests are not always consistent in their breakfast choices, however. Some food service operators may discover that their guests tend to choose healthy breakfast items during the week, but choose traditional breakfast favorites on the weekends.

Lunch. While lunch menus vary considerably, most have in common at least one objective—speed of service. Lunch items are usually more complex than breakfast items. Healthy and fresh choices are a specialty of some operations, although these items are often more costly because of the increased costs of raw ingredients. Many food service operators are searching for a balance between healthy and traditional lunch menus.

Traditional lunch menu items include hamburgers and variations, soups, salads, steak sandwiches, and fried chicken. Healthier alternatives include grilled fish, turkey burgers, garden vegetable burgers, pasta, grilled boneless chicken breasts, and a variety of salads.

Dinner. Dinner is viewed by many people as the most important meal of the day. People dine out at dinner for many reasons—to reward themselves, save time, conduct business, or celebrate special occasions such as birthdays or anniversaries. Because dinner is generally the most expensive meal, a good strategy to increase dinner business is to promote value from the guests' perspective.

Food and beverage operators are searching for ways to add variety and healthier alternatives to dinner menus. Traditional favorites on dinner menus include steak, soup, fish and seafood, pasta, Caesar salad, veal, and chicken entrées. Healthier alternatives are entrées prepared by broiling, entrée salads with reduced-fat dressings, steamed fresh vegetables, and fresh fruits for dessert.

Several quick-service restaurant (QSR) chains that primarily serve burgers are searching for ways to build their dinner business. Although adding larger burgers, "value meals" (various combinations of a sandwich, fries, and a drink), fried chicken, espresso, pasta, pizza, and even table service during the evening meal have all been tried, many QSR chains have not been able to increase their share of the dinner market.

Types of Menus

Menus can be classified in many ways—by the type of food and beverage operation in which they appear (coffee shop, fast-casual restaurant, in-room dining, full-service restaurant, and so on); by meal period or day part (breakfast, lunch, dinner); by product (dessert menus, beverage menus); and even by age group (children's menus, for example).

Another way to classify menus is to determine whether they are fixed or cyclical. A **fixed menu** does not change from day to day, although it may feature daily specials in addition to regular items. A **cyclical menu,** on the other hand, changes daily for a certain number of days until the menu cycle repeats itself. This type of menu is usually found in managed services and self-operated on-site food and beverage operations.

Another popular classification is based on the pricing structures of menus. Many restaurants use an **à la carte menu** that offers and prices each food item on an individual basis. Guests may select from a variety of different salads, entrées, vegetables, desserts, and beverages—all individually priced. In contrast, a **table d'hôte** (fixed-price or *prix-fixe*) **menu** generally provides less choice for guests. This menu usually offers an entire meal with several courses at one price, and guests often have little or no choice regarding individual courses. Some full-service operations use this type of menu; banquets are often served table d'hôte.

Some restaurants feature a basic à la carte menu, then combine selections from it to offer a table d'hôte menu as well. Other restaurants feature a semi-fixed-price menu, selling all the basic meal elements for one price to offer guests value for their money, but then offering desserts and beverages à la carte to increase the check averages.

Food Categories on Menus

Traditionally, food on menus is arranged in the following categories: appetizers, soups, salads, entrées, and desserts. Each category has its own unique features and characteristics.

Appetizers

Appetizers begin the dining experience. Many food service operators have realized the power that appetizers have in making a positive first impression with guests. Winning appetizers are large enough to be shared, give good value for the price, and set the tone for the quality to follow in the rest of the meal. Some consumers appreciate smaller appetizers that they can order and consume as their main dish rather than an entrée.

Soups

Soups are traditionally the second course in a meal. More often than not, guests choose familiar soups, particularly if they have "homemade" appeal. Throughout history, soup has served as a comfort food and even as a treatment for the common cold. Soup on a food service menu evokes a nostalgic, old-fashioned mood. Some food service operations report that soup sales are increasing regardless of the season.

Salads

In some food and beverage operations, salads have surpassed sandwiches as the most popular cold luncheon choice. The key to a top-quality salad is to select only the freshest ingredients and then store and prepare them correctly. Restaurants featuring salads prepared fresh from ingredients grown in their own organic gardens are increasing in number. Salads as main courses are becoming more popular, especially those salads that combine grilled chicken, fish, or seafood with fresh salad ingredients.

Many full-service restaurants serve bread just before or just after serving the salad. While, strictly speaking, bread is not a course in a meal, its importance should not be underestimated. Across the country, food service operations are replacing the all-too-familiar dinner roll with unique bread options, such as breads made with jalapeños, sun-dried tomatoes, cheese, or raisins. Bread has been described by some as having "marketing power," since guests are increasingly becoming more choosy and experimental about the breads they eat. The aroma of homemade breads wafting through a restaurant can help differentiate it from competitors.

Entrées

In today's food and beverage operations, menu planners are attempting to balance traditional favorites with innovative items when they choose main courses or entrées. New items are being added to regular main course listings in some instances and are being offered as specials in others. In all cases, what differentiates one operation's set of entrées from another are the signature entrées.

Signature entrées are menu items that guests perceive as special and closely associated with the restaurant promoting them. Signature menu items help build repeat business and guest loyalty. In some cases, restaurants' methods of cooking are being changed to create signature entrées, such as roasting chicken in a wood-fired oven. Slow-roasted, smoked, grilled, and "Wok-seared" are cooking techniques that are becoming more popular. Other "signatures" include relatively small protein portions surrounded and garnished by fresh vegetables or fruits. These accompaniments not only add unique textures and flavors, they also appeal to those who are health-conscious.

Signature vegetarian entrées have become more popular with guests. While fruit salad is still a favorite vegetarian item, a variety of vegetable and grain combinations, pasta main courses, and stir-fry entrées are growing in demand. Many of these main course vegetarian items are adapted from Far Eastern, Indian, and Mediterranean cuisines. Vegetarian entrées provide guests with dining choices that are lower in cholesterol and fat and higher in flavor and fiber. These entrées offer the restaurateur favorable food cost percentages and, therefore, higher profits than meat alternatives. An objective of adding vegetarian menu items is not only to satisfy the needs of guests who are strict vegetarians, but also to appeal to the sometimes-vegetarians who desire a break from their traditional food choices when dining out. (Vegetarians are categorized based on the amount of animal food or products they eat. **Lacto-ovo-vegetarians** eat eggs and dairy products in addition to vegetables, but no fish. **Lacto-vegetarians** will eat dairy products but no eggs or fish. **Pesco-vegetarians** consume dairy products, eggs, and fish as well as vegetables. **Vegans** are strict vegetarians and eat no animal products. As you can see, each group has unique menu needs.)

Desserts

Although guest preferences may have moved toward more healthy fare in main courses, that is not the case with desserts. Chocolate-based desserts are always popular, and if a dessert is cold and creamy, it usually sells well during hot summer months.

Just as an operation can have signature entrées, it can have signature desserts as well. Signature desserts range from simple to complex and are an answer to the public's search for unique, value-filled alternatives. Unique desserts that are in demand include fruit cobblers, larger-than-life cinnamon rolls, sawdust pie (named for its ingredients—coconut and pecans), ice cream–filled puffs, smoothies, berry desserts, specialty chocolate desserts, red velvet cake, key lime pie, and other desserts that promote regional or local ingredients. Once signature desserts are added to the menu, they should be promoted by servers in ways that paint an irresistible mental picture.

For guests who want dessert but with fewer calories, some operations offer fresh fruits and cheeses, served in creative ways. Some top fresh fruits with a light yogurt sauce to create a dessert that is simple, healthy, and refreshing. Frozen yogurt and low-fat, nonfat, and sugar-free frozen desserts are also popular.

The Planning Sequence

When planning a menu, begin with the entrées—the main courses. Keep in mind not only the various types you could offer, but also their cost, their production methods, and, where applicable, their adherence to the theme and atmosphere of your operation.

You can offer a large number of entrées or only a handful. If you feel that you should have something for everyone, you may be faced with some production problems. For instance, you will have to purchase, receive, store, issue, produce, and serve a relatively large number of menu items (especially if the menu is not rationalized), and you will need sufficient equipment and staff to perform all of these activities. Your operating costs will probably increase and production and service problems will likely be more numerous than those for operations offering only a limited number of entrées. The trend in the restaurant industry today is toward a more casual dining experience. Casual-oriented restaurants not only reduce their marketing costs by focusing on a specific segment of the market (guests who desire seafood dishes, for example, or specialty steaks), they also minimize their production and service problems.

After selecting the entrées, determine the complementary items that will fill each of the remaining categories on the menu. A common procedure is to select appetizers and/or soups next, followed by high-starch foods and vegetables (if they are not part of the entrée), then salads. Finally, you should plan the other menu components such as salads served as entrées, desserts, breads, and beverages. Remember that decisions must be driven by the needs and expectations of guests, both current and potential.

Menu Design

Menu design is very important to the success of a food and beverage operation. Menus are sales tools, so they must be designed to grab the attention of guests quickly. One report states that the average guest spends just over 100 seconds (a little over a minute and a half) looking at a menu. In this brief time period, the guest decides on the number of courses, the specific item in each course, and so on. Good menu design steers guests to those menu items that the food and beverage operation wants guests to consider ordering because the items are especially profitable for the operation or for other reasons.

Ideally, the design of a menu achieves an emotional connection between the food and beverage products offered for sale and the operation's guests. Menus that convey the message of relaxation and satisfaction work well in the evening and late-evening hours, because most guests at that time are winding down from a busy, activity-filled day. In contrast, the design of a luncheon menu should be to the point and easy to scan, to help guests in the middle of their busy day quickly order so that they can return to work in a timely manner or continue to conduct business at the table after the luncheon dining is completed.

Positive emotions can be tied to effective menu design. When a guest reads that the operation's tea selection is designed to help the guest relax, feelings of calmness, comfort, and restoration can come to mind for the guest. When a guest selects a healthy menu item, "guilt-free," "physical fitness," "wellness," and other associations can be conjured up in the mind. So too, comfort foods featured on the menu may evoke emotions tied to family, hugs, and smiles.

Menu design must be balanced, with not too few and not too many items in each category. Rather than simply considering the individual menu item's contribution margin, managers should consider the profitability of the entire menu by meal period or day part. High-margin menu items such as beverages should be featured on the menu with distinctive designs that draw attention to them.

Menu design responsibilities vary according to restaurant type (independent or chain, large or small, full-service or limited-service, fine-dining or casual-dining, etc.), restaurateurs' preferences, and organizational structures. Some restaurateurs contract with professional menu designers, advertising agencies, and advertising copywriters. Some do it themselves with the help of managers, chefs, other staff members, and a printer. There are computer software programs available, complete with templates and clip art, that allow restaurant staff to write, format, and print a menu using a personal computer.

Regardless of who is assigned the responsibility of menu design, it is advantageous for all food and beverage managers to be familiar with the process and the considerations involved. Menu design considerations begin with the needs and expectations of guests. When a menu is presented to a guest, a sales transaction begins. A properly designed menu can stimulate sales and increase the guest-check average. Since a menu presents an image of the operation, its appearance should be in harmony with the image the restaurant wants to project, whether it be elegant, businesslike, fun, ethnic, or casual.

Guests are influenced by the menu's visual cues, such as design and layout, artwork, and type styles. As with other communication tools, the way the information is conveyed is as important as the information itself. For example, QSRs offer a limited number of menu items but sell these items in large quantities. Since guests are served at a common sales counter, separate menus are not needed. Most guests are familiar with the standardized menu offerings, so elaborate descriptions are unnecessary; they would only slow down the guests' decision-making

Menu Design's Top Ten

When designing a menu, one of the goals is to create a tool that showcases the personality and virtues of the operation. A well-designed menu communicates the operation's personality and image quickly and effectively. A good menu has been described as a map that encourages easy navigation between hunger and satisfaction. It is also important for the menu to guide guests to the most profitable and distinctive menu items. What follows are the top ten rules for successful menu creation:

1. *Speak plainly.* It is important to use verbiage that is understood by the reader, so carefully select the text to appeal to those who will read it. This is particularly important when the menu features ethnic items.

2. *Say what is important.* This is especially true for menu items that have unique, and perhaps overwhelming, flavors—such as chiles and garlic. It is also important (because of diets, allergies, and aversions) that guests know whether a soup is cream-style, or whether an item includes such ingredients as wheat, pork, nuts, and shellfish, for example.

3. *Do not be afraid to be descriptive.* The use of appealing adjectives, such as "fresh," "crispy," and "crunchy," paints a mental picture of the item in the guest's mind. These descriptors, if used correctly, will also help sell what you want to sell. Note, however, the cautions that follow.

4. *Say it correctly.* Whenever a description or point of origin or government grade or preparation technique or commonly used term (e.g., "marinated") is used on the menu, it must be accurate.

5. *Describe accompaniments.* It is essential to include a description of all items that accompany the main item so that the guest can have a complete understanding of the full dining experience.

6. *Remember, "less is more."* It is best to describe only those ingredients that add significantly to flavor and value.

7. *Maintain a sense of perspective.* If you try to recommend everything, you will end up recommending nothing. It is better to recommend signature menu items, and no more than two or three in each menu category.

8. *Spell it properly.* If you wish to create an image of being the expert, be certain that what you say is spelled correctly and utilizes the correct grammar. When spelling or grammatical inconsistencies surface in print on a menu, they may make guests question the authenticity of the overall experience to follow.

9. *Punctuate properly.* It is helpful, for example, to hyphenate compound adjectives—"chile-roasted flank steak." Using a comma between series items and before "and" or "or" in a series—such as "a combination of breadcrumbs, fresh mushrooms, pasta, olive oil, and fresh parsley"—clarifies what could otherwise be a confusing string of words. Remember that an apostrophe is used in contractions (isn't, aren't) and in possessives (chef's); an apostrophe is not used to indicate plurals (except in certain instances with numbers or letters used individually).

(continued)

---

10. *Follow rules of good typography.* Select paper color, ink color, and type point sizes that can be read in the dining area in the level of lighting maintained during the meal period. Avoid aligning prices near the right margin, since this makes it too easy for guests to compare prices. Leave sufficient blank space between sections and categories to make category identification by the guests easier.

Source: Adapted from Allen H. Kelson, "The Ten Commandments of Menu Success," *Restaurant Hospitality*, July 1994, pp. 103–105.

process. Therefore, most QSRs simply post the names and prices of their products near the sales counter. Enlarged color photographs of menu items show their color and texture and thus may contribute to increased sales. (However, it is important that the items served look like those pictured.) The overall effect is to convey simplicity, speed, and a limited selection of products prepared the same way at every unit.

At the other extreme would be gourmet restaurants catering to affluent, sophisticated guests. These restaurants typically have extensive, elegantly designed menus printed on expensive paper and featuring elaborate, over-sized covers. These menus, with detailed descriptions of a wide range of menu items, offer guests a perception of endless possibilities. Since guests in gourmet restaurants usually seek a leisurely and pleasurable dining experience, taking the time to peruse a complicated menu is usually no problem.

Another element distinguishes the menu of an elegant restaurant from that of a QSR: prices. Prices are sometimes omitted from gourmet menus because of seasonal fluctuations in the cost of some items. Some high-check-average restaurants and clubs provide only the guest paying the bill with a menu that lists prices; the other guests in the party receive menus that list no prices. A major reason for such a service is to let guests select exactly what they want without being concerned about what their host must pay for their choices. Another reason is to allow the host the chance to recommend favorites on the menu without causing guests to feel that price is in any way influencing the recommendation.

Most full-service restaurants provide menus listing items and prices. Usually, a brief description of major items is included. Some menus have photos of the featured items; some use artwork instead of (or in addition to) photos.

The information that is printed on the menu is called "menu copy." It is part of the overall menu design. The menu copy is the menu's reason for being; it communicates to guests what the restaurant has to offer. It is imperative, then, that guests be able to understand the names of food items and the words used to describe them. Information about ingredients is vitally important for guests with health issues such as food allergies. Descriptions of menu items should generate both interest and sales, and they must be in keeping with truth-in-menu regulations. Any general information that the menu provides about the operation must complement the operation's desired image.

Creativity helps make the menu memorable; one creative aspect of any menu is its layout. Exhibit 4 shows examples of menu formats that use different numbers of pages and panels. Once the number of menu items and the sequence that staff

Exhibit 4   Menu Formats

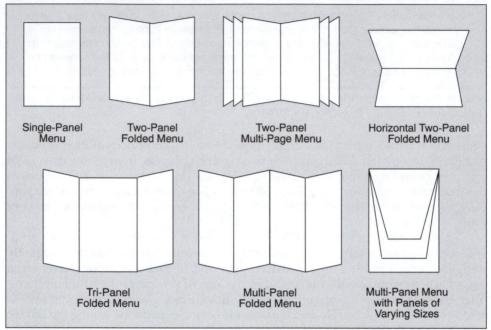

Source: Jack D. Ninemeier, *Management of Food and Beverage Operations*, 5th ed. (Lansing, Mich.: American Hotel & Lodging Educational Institute, 2010), p. 152.

members will follow to take guest orders is determined, the menu size, shape, and fold that is most appropriate can be selected. It is especially important that the menu cover be creative and attractive. It does not need to be filled with information, however; the menu cover simply is an invitation to explore what is inside.

Above all, a menu must be legible—easy to read. The type style and/or lettering used on the menu, and the size, color, style, and background of a menu affect its legibility. Type that is too small or strange-looking is hard to read. It is usually best to use a combination of upper- and lower-case letters rather than all upper-case letters. Because the lighting in many dining areas is much dimmer than in office areas where menus are designed, the proposed type style, size, and color should be tested in the dining area where the menu will be used by guests.

The type of material on which the menu is printed should be in keeping with the food and beverage operation's image. Generally, inexpensive paper is used if guests use the menu only once (a disposable place mat with the menu printed on it, for example). If a menu will be used longer, higher-quality paper should be selected. Durable menu covers, lamination, and treated papers that resist tears and stains help protect menu pages.

Color gives the menu variety. Since production costs increase as colors are added to the menu, it may be important to try to work with only two or three colors. Dark ink on white or light-colored paper usually results in an easy-to-read menu.

The menu should not appear crowded or "busy," with so much going on that it's difficult for guests to choose where to look. Some designers like to reserve almost half of the menu for white or blank space (side borders and space between menu listings).

Common mistakes on menus include type that is too small, lack of descriptions of food items, spelling errors, and limited use of design techniques to set off items that the restaurant wants guests to notice and order.

A good menu has been described as a map that encourages easy navigation between hunger and satisfaction. It is also important for the menu to guide guests to the restaurant's profitable and distinctive menu items so that the guests will have an opportunity to at least consider them. A menu's effect on profitability depends to a great degree on its design.

Frequently, the items at the top of a list in a specific menu division are the most popular (the first meat, poultry, or seafood selections; the appetizers or desserts named first; and so on). Once you know the items you most wish to sell, place them at the head of the list, put a box around them, or otherwise set them apart. Usually, a food and beverage operation will feature one or more specialties—items it is known for. Items on the right-hand page of a two-page, side-by-side menu may sell the best; the middle panel in a three-panel menu is also a good location for food items that you wish to promote. Some operations use clip-ons or inserts in their menus to note daily specials.

If alcoholic beverages are available, say so on the menu; some operations have separate beverage menus that include not only wines but also beers and other alcoholic spirits offered for sale. It is possible, but often not practical, to offer separate menus for each meal period or day part. Some restaurants also offer such separate menus as beverage, dessert, healthy-choice, or children's. To make separate menus more practical, you can use a permanent menu cover and simply insert different menus for the changing meal periods or guests.

You can also use a simple menu and lay it out according to meal periods, listing the time periods during the day that such meals are served. If you use a California-style menu, which allows guests to order any item at any time while the operation is open (often 24 hours a day), you should list items according to type (appetizers, salads, entrées, desserts). Many guests prefer to have the traditional menu headings in their natural sequence, beginning with appetizers and ending with desserts. Nonalcoholic beverages (coffee, espresso, tea, milk, soda) are often placed near the end of the menu.

As just mentioned, some restaurants draw attention to daily specials and highlight signature items by boxing the items on the menu. Another way to increase sales of featured items is to list the items on an illuminated board near the restaurant's entrance. Some restaurants specializing in fresh seafood use a chalkboard to list the flight arrival times of the jet-fresh catch of the day. While this approach sacrifices a degree of elegance, it provides convincing evidence of the freshness and variety of the operation's offerings.

The restaurant's address, telephone number, and hours of operation should appear on the menu somewhere. Some guests may want to take their menus home, which some restaurants allow or even encourage (especially if the menus are inexpensive), and this information will make it easier for guests to return. Restaurants using expensive menus might consider making smaller, take-home versions for guests who request them.

It is better to replace menus than to scratch out old prices and insert new, higher prices. To resolve this problem, menu designers may indicate "market price" on items with fluctuating costs.

No matter how well menus are designed, they must be kept in good condition. Dirty, worn, or stained menus indicate management's lack of concern for the restaurant's image. Because they create a negative first impression, such menus should be discarded. Someone should be responsible for checking the condition of the menus before each meal period begins.

Electronic Menus

With today's ever-changing technology comes menu design challenges. Increasingly, menus today are not just the familiar paper versions that food and beverage operations offer to guests on-site; more and more, menus are appearing on the screens of various electronic devices. Guests today can visit websites to check out an operation's menu, for example, or use their cell phones to access menu information. Electronic menus have even invaded the food and beverage operations themselves. For example, touch-screen menus located at the tables of some restaurants can not only be used to order items but can also accept guest payments via debit or credit cards. When orders are placed by guests, they are transmitted directly to the kitchen; when the food is prepared, it is delivered by a server. These touch-screen menus can include in their design various interactive games that help guests pass the time while waiting for their food to be prepared and delivered.

Electronic menu designs also include menus that talk. When a button is pressed, the talking menu tells guests what is available. For the visually impaired, buttons are identified in braille. In noisy restaurants or for the hearing-impaired, many talking menus offer an earphone option. Talking menus are also available in various languages. If a significant portion of a food and beverage operation's clientele speaks Spanish, for example, a talking menu can be programmed to switch from English to Spanish with the click of a button.

Ordering by text message will be the next big development in electronic menu design. Once a text message is sent to the food and beverage operation to order food, the operation can capture the guest's cell number; this number can then be used to send the guest ads, promotions, special event notices, and other information.

Menu board design has also gone electronic due to the use of big-screen televisions. Digital menus can be displayed on these big TVs and easily changed according to the meal period or day part. For example, a digital menu display system can be programmed to automatically change from a breakfast menu to a lunch menu at 10:45 A.M., and from a dinner menu to a late-night menu at 9 P.M. The menu design on these devices is much more dynamic than with traditional paper-based menus, because digital menus can feature high-definition video clips and high-resolution photos that can be easily changed according to meal period/day part. Digital menu boards will become more prevalent in the future.

Menu Design Mistakes

Many, many mistakes have been made with menu design and continue to be made. One of the top mistakes is not knowing "who are our guests?" and "what do they need, desire, and want?" This knowledge of the guests is essential. Why do guests come back to the food and beverage operation? If first-time guests, what attracted them in the first place?

Another menu design mistake is to line up—right justify—all prices so that they are all together in a single column and can easily be compared by guests. Descriptions help to neutralize some price-point decision-making, but it is better to simply put the price a space or two after the menu item's description ends rather than right-justify it.

Stale menus—those that are not regularly updated—are another mistake. One way to update the menu each day is to offer daily specials. Food and beverage operations that present seasonal menus, based on the freshest, locally obtained ingredients, are being chosen more frequently by guest these days.

Menu Trends

In recent years, several menu trends have had an impact on food and beverage operations. Menu trends, by their nature, change with the tastes and demands of guests. It is critical for food and beverage managers to constantly ask, "Who are our guests?" and "What are their requirements?" By answering these questions, managers can keep their menus fresh and in tune with the needs, wants, and expectations of their guests.

Value

When guests' personal discretionary income is tight, they typically search for more value when dining out. They may be likely to dine out less during the more expensive day parts—e.g., dinner—and dine more frequently at breakfast. Other guests may not order as many side items or courses (e.g., appetizers, desserts). Guests may also be more likely to order sandwiches rather than pricier main courses. When guests are searching for value, food and beverage operators must place more emphasis on value in their main courses and other offerings. Managers should keep in mind, however, that there are more ways to add value than just reducing menu prices. When food and beverage products are improved, value increases; when service is improved, value increases; when the facilities and the ambience are improved, value increases.

Smaller Portions

Smaller portions in supermarket foods prepared to go and on food and beverage menus are increasingly popular with guests. Offering guests smaller portions from which to choose raises the perception of value. If guests wish to consume less than the standard portion, providing smaller portions as options contributes to the guests' perception of customization; they feel that "made-for-me" menu items are available to them.

Bite-size desserts are an example of the smaller portion trend and are great value promoters. Not only do these smaller portions cost less, they also help guests reduce their overall calorie consumption and are perceived as guilt-free "mini-indulgences." Sliders (mini-burgers or mini-sandwiches) are another popular example of smaller-portion menu items at reduced prices.

In response to weight-conscious Baby Boomers and others, food and beverge operations are beginning to downsize or eliminate their "super-sized" portions of sandwiches and soft drinks. For example, Quiznos Sub offers a one-third-size mini-melt in addition to a traditional 16-ounce sandwich. While some guests still enjoy big portions, many others are interested in smaller portions with fewer calories.

Local Food

The "eat local" trend has been increasing in popularity in recent years, as can be seen from the growing number of websites devoted to this topic and the increasing number of food and beverage operations that are making an effort to purchase and prepare foods that have been grown locally. Guests who are interested in eating locally grown foods want information on who grew or raised the ingredients in the menu items they are consuming. For these guests, the closer the growing areas are to the food and beverage operation, the better. "Local" has the connotation of being fresher, which is always a plus with guests, and guests often are interested in consuming locally grown food as a way to support the local economy and reduce the pollution involved in delivering food from faraway locations.

In response to this trend, an increasing number of food service outlets are growing their own fruits and vegetables. Managers of restaurants who want to try this new organic-food approach should be aware that there may be a greater risk of food contamination and loss of temperature control as purchasing frequencies, receiving schedules, storage procedures, and production techniques have to be adjusted. As storage, preparation, and cooking methods change, the skill levels of staff members and managers must also change.

Fresh Food

As just mentioned, for most guests the fresher the food, the better, and fresh is a menu trend that can be incorporated into any menu item made to order, such as salads. Sometimes fresh is coupled with ethnic foods, as in fresh Mexican cuisine. When prepared from local ingredients, three of today's menu trends—local, fresh, and ethnic food—are combined to boost guest satisfaction.

Ethnic Food

Today's guests have developed a taste for ethnic foods because of their increased travel and dining-out experiences. They also have more food information available to them on TV food channels, in magazines geared to food aficionados, in cooking classes offered in local schools, and on the Internet. Ethnic food specialties are no longer just found on restaurant menus; they are also found on the menus of hospitals, college food service facilities, and transportation and recreational food service outlets.

Healthy Menu Options

Healthy menu options appeal to guests who want to choose more foods that are good for them. The opportunity for food and beverage operators is to take healthy foods and make them tastier, more appealing, flavorful, and satisfying. Many guests are avoiding trans-fats, focusing more on complex rather than simple carbohydrates, and choosing protein more carefully. Other guests are changing the way they consume food during the day. Rather than eating three large meals, more guests are choosing to eat a greater number of smaller meals throughout the day, or eat smaller portions during the traditional three meal times and find healthy snacks in between. "Energy beverages" and designer bottled waters continue to gain market share as healthier alternatives to soft drinks. The number of "health food" stores continues to grow, and many supermarkets have added "whole health centers" for health-conscious shoppers. In these centers, consumers can choose "gluten free," "preservative free," "all natural," "free-range," "kosher," and "organic" foods.

It is important that food and beverage operations clearly communicate their healthy menu options to their guests. Healthier-food claims must be backed by facts so that they are believable and embraced by guests. Food and beverage managers must not only do a good job of communicating with their guests but also their staff members. Staff members must be made aware of the operation's healthy menu options and understand how to steer health-conscious guests to these healthier menu choices through staff training programs.

Environmentally Friendly Food

Environmentally friendly food is food that takes into consideration a variety of environmental and social issues that are of importance to a growing number of guests, issues such as animal rights, packaging, organic growing methods, and sustainability. Animal rights include consideration of whether farm animals are treated in a humane way; for example, are chickens raised for food always confined to small cages or are they allowed space to roam around outside in pens for at least part of the day (i.e., are they "free range" chickens)? Environmentally friendly foods are those that do not over-use packaging materials and are produced in manufacturing facilities that are mindful of reducing energy and water usage. Organic foods are produced without pesticides and other chemicals. Sustainability issues include the carbon footprint of distributors and the ways they can reduce their energy usage (e.g., fewer deliveries). Sustainable seafoods are those that have been harvested from environmentally friendly aquaculture farms or from sustainable wild stocks that are not in danger of being over-fished.

Extending Protein Ingredients

Protein ingredients in main courses are being extended by the addition of vegetables, pastas, and sauces, thus reducing the cost of the main courses' raw ingredients. Pasta not only helps minimize costs but helps maximize creativity, given the large array of pasta shapes available. Less expensive cuts of meat that are slow-cooked increasingly are being incorporated into pot roasts, stews, and other main courses.

Breakfast

For some food and beverage operations, breakfast is the fastest-growing meal period of the day. More guests are eating breakfast away from home and are searching for convenient and portable menu options. They also want both standard breakfast menu items and healthier fare. Some of the traditional lunch-menu restaurants (i.e., sandwich shops, delis) have added breakfast as a way to build business. Breakfast burritos, breakfast bowls with biscuits and gravy, breakfast sandwiches, and breakfast bagels, all served quickly and at proper temperatures for reasonable prices, are appealing to many guests.

Vegetarian Menu Items

Vegetarians often are perceived as eating healthier than non-vegetarians. Over half of current vegetarians choose a vegetarian diet because it helps improve their overall health. Some guests choose vegetarian items on menus because they see these items as "more natural" approaches to wellness; other guests choose vegetarian items because of food safety or animal welfare concerns; still others choose vegetarian items because they help them lose weight or maintain their present weight. Vegetarian burgers, desserts made from fresh fruits, and creative vegetarian entrées are all ways that food and beverage operations can cater to the demand for vegetarian menu items.

Mandatory Menu Labeling

Health departments and consumer action groups are increasingly pushing to have mandatory menu labeling laws enacted. Such laws would require food and beverage operations to include on their menus nutritional and other information about the food they serve. This type of legislation is often pushed because of concerns about rising childhood and adult obesity, among other health issues.

Promotions

As part of the overall marketing strategy for all categories of menu items and all types of menus, restaurant **promotions** are designed to build value for guests, excitement for staff members, and profits for owners and investors. Exhibit 5 lists a number of promotion ideas that represent only a sampling of the endless variety of promotions available—limited only by your creativity and the needs of guests.

Organic and sustainable foods are "ripe" to be promoted as featured menu items. Local sources of fruits, vegetables, and cheeses for salads enable even chain restaurants to advertise that they are focused on sustainability. Some restaurants are promoting as the ultimate in sustainability food such as herbs and tomatoes that they are growing on their roofs. There are no distribution costs with these foods, and guests are assured that they are getting the freshest ingredients.

Exhibit 5　Promotion Ideas

Promotion	Components
Culinary History	Tie history of cuisine (such as pasta) to the history of an appropriate wine.
Decorations	Offer posters, T-shirts, or sweatshirts as prizes.
Ethnic Foods	Promote Latin American, Chinese, Italian, Mexican, Korean, Japanese, Peruvian, Greek, Thai, and French cuisines.
Special Events	Build a promotion around a party, craft show, musical, play, or other special event in the community.
Free Items	Offer prospective guests a free menu item (appetizer, dessert) to encourage repeat business.
Sustainable Foods	Promote organic and sustainable fruits, vegetables, meats, and seafood.
Fruit Extravaganza	Feature fresh in-season fruits such as blueberries, cherries, or strawberries. Provide giveaways such as T-shirts or sweatshirts that fit with the theme.
Local and Regional	Showcase foods native to the state or locality; feature those from local farms.
Low-Carb	Promote protein foods, low-carb breads, unique sauces, and Florida SunLite potatoes.
Olive Lovers	Offer menu items that use olives. Tie the theme into giveaways such as photographs, recipe books, olive oils, and other merchandise.
Pasta	Offer a combination of imported and domestic pasta menu items with a variety of red and white sauces, served with freshly baked bread.
Seafood	Add unique seafoods from around the world to build seafood sales.
Specialty Foods	In partnership with suppliers, offer unique specialty foods ranging from regional cuisines to specific menu item ingredients.
Wines and Food	Combine cuisine with wines that are appropriate for new taste sensations.
Beers and Food	Combine food with beer in a complimentary tasting experience.
Flights of Food and Beverages	Bite-size food samplers accompanied by two ounces of an alcoholic beverage (e.g., three or four choices of vodka, each with its own food accompaniment).

Source: Updated and adapted from Cecile Lamalle, "Profitable Promotions," *Restaurant Hospitality,* November 1993, pp. 103–104.

More and more food and beverage operators are promoting prepared "meals to go" to busy guests who just want to relax at home with a pre-cooked meal and a glass or two of their own wine at the end of a busy day. Foods prepared to go can be priced slightly higher than the same foods eaten at the operation, because tips are not necessary and packaging is more expensive. In addition to main courses, soups and desserts make ideal foods prepared to go.

Burgers served with innovative dips are being promoted on some menus, such as a burger with a creamed spinach dip or garlic hummus. Sushi is an item that is easy to promote, but the food and beverage operation must have the expertise to prepare the sushi well. A combination of Japanese and Korean foods fused into new sushi creations with asparagus, avocado, lobster, mushrooms, and shrimp garnished with wasabi is an innovative presentation.

Pairing foods with alcoholic beverages is an old art. A new spin on it pairs the cuisine of a given country with an alcoholic beverage produced in that country. For example, sake, a Japanese rice-based alcoholic beverage, can be paired with various Japanese sushi choices. Wine, cocktail, and beer flights paired with foods that complement these beverages are growing in popularity.

Promoting strictly on price and constantly discounting will condition guests to expect reduced prices all the time. Promotions are often tied to new guests, but food and beverage operations should not ignore their current guests. Promoting only to new guests is a mistake; it undermines guest loyalty and ignores the importance of rewarding repeat customers.

Promotional coupons can help managers with their marketing efforts if the coupons collect guest information such as e-mail and snail mail addresses, birthdays, anniversaries, and so on; such information helps the staff invite guests back to the food and beverage operation to celebrate their special occasions.

Sometimes a food and beverage operation promotes a free food or beverage item, often in hopes of generating enough guest interest to add that item to the regular menu. Guests are given an opportunity to provide feedback after consuming the free item in order to help managers gauge the acceptance of the item.

Food and beverage managers should track all of their promotions to determine how effective and popular they are. Managers must find out if the time and money invested in a promotional campaign was worth it—i.e., there was a good return on investment.

The key to successful promotions is communication to staff members as well as guests. Rather than simply announcing a promotion to staff members, managers should get them involved from the start. By soliciting their ideas regarding what to promote, what sorts of decorations to use, what kind of advertising approach might work best, what changes to current service procedures might help enhance the promotion, and so on, staff members are more likely to take ownership of the promotion. If a new menu item is being promoted, managers should give staff members an opportunity to taste it. With this firsthand knowledge, staff members will do a better job of selling the promoted item to guests.

All staff members, both guest-contact and support, should be given the opportunity to be involved with the promotion. If staff members spend time after-hours decorating the restaurant to fit the promotion's theme, managers should create a festive atmosphere so that staff members can have some fun while putting in the extra work. If the promotion includes giveaways for guests, then managers—rather than giving the prizes away themselves—should let staff members have the fun of giving them away. Some prizes should be given to staff members as well, to further include them in the promotion and recognize their efforts at making the promotion a success. These strategies can help build staff member enthusiasm for promotions.

Last but not least, successful promotions have specific goals—a set sales figure or a targeted percentage increase, for example. Staff members should know these goals in advance.

Changing the Menu

Because market conditions change, a food service operation's menu must also change. Menu changes are influenced by both external and internal factors.

External factors include guest demands, economic factors, the competition, supply levels, and industry trends. Guest demands are the most important factor to consider in changing a menu. Management should first decide which potential markets it wants to attract with a modified menu. The proposed menu change should then be evaluated in light of its potential impact on the current guest markets. Economic factors include the cost of ingredients and the potential profitability of new menu items. The competition's menu offerings can also influence menu decisions. For example, a hotel food and beverage operation located next door to a restaurant offering "the best Thai food in town" might elect not to serve Thai cuisine. Supply levels affect the price and the quality and quantity of the proposed menu items. Supply levels are highly variable for some seasonal raw ingredients, such as fresh fruits and vegetables. Industry trends affect menus as menu planners try to keep current with what's popular with guests.

Internal factors that may result in a proposed menu change are the operation's meal pattern, concept and theme, operational system, and menu mix. The typical meal pattern is breakfast, lunch, and dinner. From time to time management should evaluate whether existing meal periods should be continued or altered. The target markets' expectations directly influence this decision. Any menu change must also be compatible with the operation's concept and theme; for example, a restaurant that is known as the best place in the city for fresh fish and shellfish may do itself a disservice by offering fewer fish and shellfish selections in order to add steak to the menu. An operation's image may also rule out foods that do not match its theme and decor.

Menu changes are also influenced by the operational system. For example, a menu change may raise both food and labor costs to unacceptable levels. Production and service staff members may lack the necessary skills to produce and present the new menu item. If extensive new equipment is crucial to the successful production and service of a new item, the change may be too costly. Many operations deal with this factor by designing flexible kitchens with versatile, multi-purpose equipment. For example, a combination convection oven/steamer can bake, roast, and steam. Tilt skillets can be used for baking, braising, frying, griddling, and steaming.

An operation's existing menu has a certain overall combination or mix of items. This menu mix will be affected by any change in individual items. All of these factors should be evaluated before menu changes are finalized.

The dual goal of any menu should be to satisfy guests and meet the financial objectives of the operation. First and foremost, it is important to know the guests and their requirements. The more you know about your guests, the more likely it is that you will build a menu that will delight them and keep them coming back for more experiences. It is equally important to keep up with trendy foods that should be considered for possible addition to the menu. You should keep in mind the availability of ingredients used to produce the menu items, and remember that variety can be added to the same raw ingredients through the use of additional or new spices and herbs. Remember, too, that it is important for menu items to fit with the production equipment and staff capabilities, the service equipment and staff capabilities, and the operation's concept and theme.

In many respects, menu development is never finished; it is an ongoing process. Menus are dynamic and should never be "frozen in time." Menu development is an evolutionary process of continuous improvement as managers keep a close eye on what their guests want, need, and expect.

 Key Terms ─────────────────────────────────────

à la carte menu—A menu that offers and prices each food item on an individual basis. Guests may select from a variety of different salads, entrées, vegetables, desserts, and beverages—all individually priced.

control points—A system of basic operating activities common to all types of food service operations. Each control point is a miniature system with its own identifiable structure and functions. The control points are menu planning, purchasing, receiving, storing, issuing, preparing, cooking, holding, serving, and cleaning and maintenance.

cross-utilization—In food service operations, a menu-planning strategy that calls for preparing and serving as many different menu items as possible from a limited number of raw ingredients. It is a part of menu rationalization.

cyclical menu—A menu that changes daily for a certain number of days, then repeats the sequence.

fixed menu—A menu that does not change from day to day.

lacto-ovo-vegetarian—An individual who does not eat meat but eats eggs and dairy products (but no fish) in addition to vegetables, fruits, grains, and nuts.

lacto-vegetarian—An individual who does not eat meat but eats dairy products (but no eggs or fish) in addition to vegetables, fruits, grains, and nuts.

menu rationalization—The creation of a simplified, balanced menu for the sake of operational efficiency and guest satisfaction. This approach frequently results in a limited menu, but through cross-utilization an operation can offer several items using the same ingredients.

pesco-vegetarian—An individual who does not eat meat but eats dairy products, eggs, and fish in addition to vegetables, fruits, grains, and nuts.

promotion—All the ways in which a business tries to persuade people to buy its products and services.

signature entrée—A menu item that guests perceive as special and closely associated with the restaurant promoting it. Signature menu items help build repeat business and guest loyalty.

table d'hôte menu—A menu that offers a complete meal with several courses for one price. Also called a fixed-price (or *prix-fixe*) menu. Guests generally have little or no choice regarding individual courses, but there may be two or more complete meals to choose from.

truth-in-menu regulations—Laws requiring accurate descriptions of raw ingredients and finished menu items, in addition to other details.

vegan—A strict vegetarian who eats no animal products whatsoever.

 ## Review Questions

1. What are some common objectives that menu planners should keep in mind when planning a menu?

2. What is "menu rationalization"?

3. What are some considerations menu planners should keep in mind when planning menu items for the breakfast meal period? lunch meal period? dinner meal period?

4. What are some typical menu classifications?

5. What are typical food categories on menus?

6. What are some menu design elements and considerations that menu planners should be aware of when planning menus?

7. What are some examples of menu trends?

8. What are some keys to successful promotions?

9. What are some typical external factors that lead managers to change menus? What are some typical internal factors?

 ## Case Studies

Healthy Specialty Menus

Nancy Thayer has just been appointed as the food service director for the Pounds Away Diet Ranch in the southwestern part of the United States. The facility is a health-oriented resort that targets people who want to lose weight in a relatively short period of time (three to four weeks).

The ranch prides itself on its tasty food service (rather than a spartan diet of bland food) and has several amenities designed to appeal to people who want to return to good physical condition, including two swimming pools, spas, exercise rooms, and outside recreational activities such as bicycle trails, hiking paths, and horseback riding.

Nancy was hired to reinvigorate the menu for the ranch, as it basically has not changed in five years and the ownership is concerned that its reputation is slipping as a mecca for healthy food that tastes good (served in moderate portions, of course) compared to some of its competitors.

Nancy is a graduate of a hospitality program at a notable university where her own situation (she once weighed 300 pounds and is now 140 pounds) caused her to take nutrition courses along with her food and beverage and other hospitality industry coursework.

She thinks, "I'm fully familiar with the four basic food groups, the food pyramid, Recommended Dietary Allowance (RDA), and minerals and vitamins. I think I can make tasty breakfasts, lunches, and dinners by using interesting ingredients."

Discussion Question

1. Pretend you are Nancy Thayer. Prepare two breakfasts, two lunches, and two dinners (a total of six meals), stating the portion size as well as the named item, that will accumulate to less than 1,500 calories for each day. Remember, the meals need to be tasty.

This case was taken from William P. Fisher and Robert A. Ashley, *Case Studies in Commercial Food Service Operations* (Lansing, Mich.: American Hotel & Lodging Educational Institute, 2003).

The Details Are in the Design

Kelly Waldron has just been engaged by the Cornupia Corporation to graphically, artistically, colorfully, and enticingly design a menu for their new restaurant concept named FOOD FASCINATION. She is an independent consultant specializing in the visual impact, artistry, and psychological tantalization of menus to appeal to restaurant patrons.

Kelly is well aware that the menu is the chief marketing tool for a restaurant. FOOD FASCINATION is to be a full-service American-fare restaurant. Entrées will include all the meat groups, poultry, and seafood. Appetizers, soups, salads, and desserts will also be offered. The theme of the restaurant will center on food with artwork depicting tomato vines, fruit bowls, bushel baskets of vegetables, and dissected line drawings of steers, hogs, sheep, etc. Kelly has several things running through her mind. Among them are:

- Should there be a cover for the menu? If so, would it be soft, hard, leather, Naugahyde, or some other material? Would there be any writing on the cover? Or the back cover? What color should it be?

- Should the menu be a two-panel, three-panel, or four-panel menu?

- Should it be a book that would include beverages as well as food items on the interior pages?

- Should the menu start with appetizers, then proceed to soups, salads, entrées, desserts, and beverages (alcoholic and non-alcoholic)? What sequence should be used for best positioning?

- Should there be a different specialty menu? Alcoholic beverages? Coffees? Desserts?

- How will the restaurant's signature items be highlighted? Bold-face print? Italics? A box around the featured item(s)?

- Should menu items have descriptions in addition to the name of the item?

- How will the prices be presented? In a vertical column on the right? Next to the last word in the item description? Should the price be expressed in numerals or written out? Should prices be in even dollars or dollars and cents?

- Should the menu denote heart-healthy items in some way?

- What should be the dimensions of the menu in terms of length and width?

Discussion Questions

1. If you were to discuss these things with Kelly, what would you suggest as answers to her questions?

2. What other suggestions would you have for her to also consider? (Example: photos of products.)

This case was taken from William P. Fisher and Robert A. Ashley, *Case Studies in Commercial Food Service Operations* (Lansing, Mich.: American Hotel & Lodging Educational Institute, 2003).

Anatomy of a Restaurant Promo, or How Seymour Learned to Love Seafood

Schultzie's is a 30-unit casual-dining chain in the heart of the Midwest. Seymour Tidwell, who manages a Schultzie's, likes his job. His unit is clean and attractive, he has lots of regular guests, and he is located in a college town where the pool of workers is relatively large.

Today, however, Seymour is attending a managers' meeting at corporate headquarters, and he's not very happy about it. "I hate these promo roll-outs,"

Seymour whispers to the manager next to him. The promos are part of the chain's new policy of "freshening" its menu with several new items each quarter.

He leans closer to the manager's ear. "My guests come to my restaurant because they like the tried-and-true items. This promo stuff corporate comes up with is just too exotic for them. Like those Tongue-Burner Fajitas—they were just too spicy for this part of the country."

"I don't agree," the manager whispers back. "My guests have been asking for more interesting items. I'm glad corporate headquarters is finally responding."

"Well," Seymour murmurs grudgingly, "I guess everyone has different tastes." But he decides to try to keep an open mind about the new items.

Meanwhile, a corporate vice president is telling the managers, "Our theme for this promo is 'Bounty from the Sea.' Market research indicates that Midwesterners are eating seafood more often. And with Lent coming up, we think these items will be very popular. They're also higher-priced items—something you and your servers might appreciate. We've got three new items you'll be sampling at lunch. The first item is 'Brandied Shrimp from the Barbie,' an appetizer. We've also got a 'King of the Sea' salad and the 'Seafood Puff,' a seafood paté wrapped in a puff pastry with a lemon sauce."

Seymour, who dislikes fish and seafood to begin with, isn't looking forward to sampling the items. But the shrimp isn't bad, he thinks. He reminds himself that he's going to keep an open mind and makes a note to tell his servers that their check averages—and tips—will increase if they are successful at selling the promo items.

As usual, the corporate VP provides a package of training items for managers to use back at their units. There is an introductory video and some quizzes for servers. "We're also sending you back to your units with these special guest comment cards," the VP says. "Please make sure each guest who orders one of the promo items receives a comment card, and send the cards you collect each week back to us. Make sure servers understand that they should not give cards to guests who order substitutions on the promo items."

The next day, Seymour meets with Jennifer, Steve, and Rollo, members of the service staff, to discuss the new menu items. Seymour is running late and decides he doesn't have time to use all of the training materials corporate headquarters provided. He decides to just show the video and have the kitchen make up some sample items. "I don't happen to like seafood myself," Seymour tells the servers, "but these are higher-priced items, so pushing them will help you increase your check averages. The kitchen is making up some sample batches so you can taste them. Oh, and please make sure that guests who order these get one of these comment cards—I have a supply for each of you. If you run out, let me know. Who knows? Maybe the guests will really like this stuff."

Back in the kitchen, the cooks are learning to prepare the new items. "Hey," Mike, the head cook, says to Seymour, "H-Q didn't send any lemon sauce for the puff pastry."

"Well, just put some white sauce on it," Seymour says. "Tell the servers to pretend it's lemon sauce. I'll call and make sure we have the lemon sauce on hand when we roll out the new items to guests tomorrow."

"And we only have two burners for this shrimp, you know," Mike says. "Orders are going to get backed up, and shrimp is so fussy. We've got to turn it right on time or it'll get rubbery. This is going to be a problem if this item is popular."

"Let's not worry about it now. I don't think our guests are going to go for this stuff in a big way," Seymour says.

But Seymour is wrong. When the promos hit the menu at lunchtime the following day, Seymour is surprised to hear guests say, "Oooh, that brandied shrimp sounds good," and, "I'm going to try the 'King of the Sea' salad," and, "I love puff pastry. I'm going to try the 'Seafood Puff.'"

Unfortunately, the servers don't quite understand how to maintain the guests' initial enthusiasm for the new items:

"Is there shrimp in the 'Seafood Puff'? I'm very allergic to it," a guest asks Jennifer.

"Um, I forgot," Jennifer replies. "I tried it this morning and it didn't taste like there was shrimp in it. Want me to ask?"

"No, I'm on my lunch hour and I've only got 45 minutes. Just bring me a burger," the guest says.

"Is the lemon sauce on the 'Seafood Puff' made with cream?" another guest asks Steve.

"I don't know," says Steve. "When I had it, they put white sauce on it."

"Could I have that instead of the lemon sauce?" asks the guest.

"It's not supposed to be served that way," says Steve. "Could I get you something else? Maybe the salad?"

"No, that's okay," says the guest. "Just bring me a burger."

"What kind of dressing do you recommend on the seafood salad?" another guest asks Rollo.

"Gee, I don't know, I really don't like seafood," Rollo says. "We have French, Thousand Island, Bleu Cheese, Ranch, and Italian. Want to try any of those?"

"No, I guess not," says the guest. "I'll have a burger."

Seymour is surprised by the small number of guest comment cards the servers turn in at the end of their shift. "I was afraid these promos wouldn't go over," Seymour says to Rollo.

"Well, I think I could have sold more," Rollo volunteers, "but I just didn't know enough about them. Why didn't we get any fact sheets and quizzes to help us?"

Seymour says nothing, but he decides perhaps he should use more of the training materials for the evening servers. Before the evening shift begins, he not only shows them the video and gives them meal samples, but he goes over the frequently-asked-question cards and quizzes servers about the ingredients. "Gee, it didn't take that long," Seymour says when the training is over. "I should have done this at lunchtime."

Seymour watches the service staff carefully and notices that all of the new items are moving faster than at lunchtime—especially the "Brandied Shrimp from the Barbie." "I wonder if Mike's able to keep up with the orders?" Seymour worries. He goes to the kitchen to find out.

Mike is having problems. "Seymour, I've had to throw out four of these shrimp orders because they got really rubbery, and this stuff isn't cheap. We're doing our best, but we don't have time to watch them like we should. I think we might run out before the night's over. We're also getting behind on some of our other orders because we're backed up with shrimp orders on these burners. The servers are getting cranky with us, and the kitchen staff is really frustrated. This shrimp is nothing but trouble."

"Do what you can for now," says Seymour, "and I'll try to come up with something for tomorrow."

At the end of the evening, Seymour is glad to see many more guest comment cards. Most of the reviews are glowing, especially about the "Brandied Shrimp from the Barbie." "Great stuff! I loved the cocktail sauce." "Cocktail sauce?" wonders Seymour. "The servers must be substituting. Oh well, whatever the guests want. Maybe these promo items aren't so bad after all."

Discussion Questions

1. What did corporate headquarters do right in its introduction of the new menu items? What could it have done to improve the chances for the promo's success?

2. What did Seymour do right with regard to the promo? What did he do wrong or fail to do to help the promo succeed?

3. How could the servers have helped make the promo more successful?

4. What can Seymour do in the next week to make the promo more successful?

The following industry experts helped generate and develop this case: Christopher Kibit, C.S.C., Academic Team Leader, Hotel/Motel/Food Management & Tourism Programs, Lansing Community College, Lansing, Michigan; and Jack Nye, General Manager, Applebee's of Michigan, Applebee's International, Inc.

 References

Abuso, Joseph. "Feast for the Eyes: Food Presentation Basics for Startup Operators." *Restaurant Startup & Growth.* 5(9): 21–26.

Anonymous. "Menu Trends." *Foodservice Director.* April 15, 2008. 21(4): 12.

Brandau, Mark. "Tweak the Menu to Maximize Profits." *Nation's Restaurant News.* January 26, 2009. 43(3): 22.

Butler, Chef Dan. "Chef Training: Can You Spare Some Change? How to Introduce New Menu Items." *Restaurant Startup & Growth.* 5(12): 52–55.

Caranfa, Maria. "Menu Trends Point to a Brighter Future." *Prepared Foods.* December 2008. 177(12): 49–53.

Cobb, Catherine R. "Breakfast Panel: Guests Want Bolder Flavors at Morning Meal." *Nation's Restaurant News.* November 10, 2008. 42(44): 68.

Cobe, Patricia, Cavallaro, M., Lang, J. "50 Great Ideas." *Restaurant Business.* January 2009. 108(1): 21–44.

————. "Can Sustainability Be Profitable?" *Foodservice Director*. September 15, 2007. 20(9): S2.

————. "The Good News –Serve Breakfast." Foodservice Buyer. *Restaurant Business*. December 2008: FSB2.

Coomes, Steve. "Going Small to Gain Big." *Nation's Restaurant News*. April 20, 2009. 43(14): 25.

"Design School." *Restaurants & Institutions*. November 1, 2007. 117(17): 28–29.

"Eight Menu Trends for 2008." *Prepared Foods.* February 2008. 177(2): 87.

Fabricant, Florence. "Shareable Platters Take Over Tables at Every Course." *Nation's Restaurant News*. March 2, 2009. 43(8): 28.

Fernau, Karen. "Food for Thought." *Lansing State Journal*. February 9, 2009: 1C & 4C.

Hoffman, Edward. "Efforts to Push Healthful Menu Items Must Be Heavy on Brand Image." *Nation's Restaurant News*. August 13, 2007. 41(32): 24, 50.

"How Servers Use Coupons to Steal Your Profit (and How to Stop It)." *Restaurant Startup & Growth*. April 2007: 12, 14, 16.

"Insights: Culinary Notes." *Restaurant Startup & Growth.* September 2008. 5(9): 14.

Kruse, Nancy. "Menu Developers Get Creative with Proteins to Control Food Costs and Hook New Diners." *Nation's Restaurant News*. February 16, 2009. 43(5): 34.

Lang, Joan M. "25 Smart Menu Moves." *Restaurant Business*. September 2007. 106(9): 40–49.

Laux, Mark. "10 Costly Menu Mistakes." *Restaurant Startup & Growth*. June 2009: 19–24.

Lockyer, Sarah. "Food Trends." *Nation's Restaurant News*. December 10, 2007. 41(49): S34.

"Make Your Menu Great." *Restaurant Hospitality*. October 1, 2003. 87(10): 35–39.

Perlik, Allison. "24 Big Menu Ideas for '09." *Restaurants & Institutions*. January 2009. 119(1): 24–30.

"R & I Offers an Exclusive Look at the National Restaurant Association's Just Released Menu-Trend Data." *Restaurants & Institutions*. November 28, 2007.

Rule, Cheryl Sternman. "Menu Suggestions." *Restaurants & Institutions*. October 2008. 118(15): 42–44.

Siff, Jay. "10 Smart Promotional Strategies." *Restaurant Hospitality*. June 1, 2005. 89(6):56

Slutsky, Jeff. "Conduct Freebie Promos Wisely to Avoid Giving Away the Store." *Nation's Restaurant News*. April 13, 2009. 43(13): 28.

Strenk, T. H. "The Future of POS: 5 High-Tech Ways to Change the Way Customers Interact with Restaurants." *Restaurant Business.* March 2008. 107(3): 26–29.

"The Verdict: Menu Labeling Is a Must." *Restaurant Hospitality.* May 1, 2008. 92(5): 30.

Thorn, Bret. "Restaurants Face Fresh Competition from Supermarket Meals." *Nation's Restaurant News.* November 10, 2008. 42(44): 64.

"What's Hot & What's Not: Chef Survey." *National Restaurant Association.* October 2007. www.restaurant.org

White, Geneva. "Operators Tap into Breakfast Goldmine." *Nation's Restaurant News.* August 11, 2008. 42(31): S1, 3, 10.

Internet Sites

For more information, visit the following Internet sites. Remember that Internet addresses can change without notice. If the site is no longer there, you can use a search engine to look for additional sites.

American Hotel & Lodging Association SmartBrief
www.smartbrief.com/ahla

The Eat Local Challenge
www.eatlocal.net

Gallup
www.gallup.com

The Menu Advantage
www.menuadvantage.com

Menus that Talk
www.menusthattalk.com

Must Have Menus
www.musthavemenus.com

National Association of College & University Food Services
www.nacufs.org

National Association of Farm Animal Welfare
www.nafaw.com

National Aquaculture Association
www.thenaa.net

National Restaurant Association SmartBrief
www.smartbrief.com/restaurant

Nation's Restaurant News
www.nrn.com

NPD Group
www.npd.com

Organic Trade Association
www.ota.com

Restaurant Associates
www.restaurantassociates.com

Technomic
www.technomic.com

Whole Foods Market
www.wholefoodsmarket.com

Zagat
www.zagat.com

Chapter 8 Outline

Purchasing
  Establishing Quality and Other
    Specifications
  Establishing Par Inventory Levels
Receiving and Storing
Issuing
Controlling
Supplies and Equipment
  China
  Glassware
  Flatware
  Disposables
  Uniforms
  Linens
  Furniture
  Equipment
  High-Tech Equipment
  Sustainable Supplies and Equipment

Competencies

1. Describe procedures and issues involved with purchasing, receiving, storing, issuing, and controlling food and beverage operation supplies and equipment. (pp. 303–315)

2. Summarize purchasing criteria for and characteristics of china, glassware, flatware, disposables, uniforms, linens, furniture, and common equipment items used by food and beverage personnel; and discuss sustainability issues involving food and beverage supplies and equipment. (pp. 315–337)

Food and Beverage Supplies and Equipment

FOOD AND BEVERAGE OPERATIONS of all types require a wide variety of supplies and equipment in order to serve guests properly. This chapter will focus on basic principles that supervisors and managers should practice when purchasing, receiving, storing, issuing, and controlling supplies and equipment. The chapter also provides an overview of the kinds of supplies and equipment that food and beverage staff members typically use, and discusses factors managers should consider when selecting supplies and equipment.

Purchasing

The purchasing of food service supplies and equipment is handled in various ways, depending on the food and beverage operation. If the operation is part of a chain, purchasing is typically done centrally by staff at the chain's headquarters or regional offices. This centralized approach to purchasing attempts to achieve economies of scale by buying in larger volumes and negotiating lower costs per unit. Obviously, managers at operations that are not part of a chain must do their own purchasing.

Purchasing practices have evolved over the years to meet the increasingly challenging economy and the resulting pressure on profit margins. Many more operators today are utilizing a prime distributor for most purchases. Prime distributors can meet 80 percent or more of an operator's purchasing requirements. Another practice that is increasingly popular is to purchase products directly from the manufacturer.

Purchasing is more than just placing an order. Purchasing policies and practices have a direct impact on the operation's cash flow, asset turnover, profitability, return on assets, and return on investment. Purchasing is a key component of a food and beverage operation's control system, coming into play right after menu development and planning. It is very important to purchase the *right* product at the *right* time from the *right* distributor for the *right* price. Planning for the purchase of supplies and equipment begins long before a new operation opens its doors. Before any supplies and equipment are purchased, managers must determine what their guests will want and assess how the operation can best provide for those requirements. The types and quality of supplies and equipment that are used will affect the quality of dining service. Just as you would not use expensive

Purchasing and Prime Distributors

Purchasing activities in a food and beverage operation are designed to reduce costs while maintaining the organization's quality requirements, based on guests' needs. One way to achieve these purchasing goals is to negotiate a relationship with one main distributor, often called the prime distributor. Together, then, the operator and the prime distributor create a strategic alliance that helps the operation stay profitable.

When evaluating a distributor for a possible role as a prime distributor, operators consider a number of factors. Of key importance is whether the distributor can help meet all or most of the operation's product specifications and service requirements. It may not be a 100-percent perfect fit, but do most of the products offered for sale and the services provided meet the operation's requirements? In addition, manufacturers sometimes offer rebate promotions. Does the distributor have a process in place to: (1) let the operator know about the promotions, (2) accurately track the amount of the rebate for each promotion due the operator, and (3) pay the operator on a timely basis? Another valuable service for food and beverage operators is a usage report generated by the distributor showing the volume of products purchased in each category. Sometimes high volumes can qualify the operator for a price reduction per unit, due to the quantity purchased. Without usage reports, the data is not available to track quantities purchased.

Prime distributors will also evaluate the operator. One key consideration is the annual volume of purchases from the operation, and from the entire chain if the operation is a unit in a franchise or multi-unit organization. A second consideration will be the average delivery size (dollars purchased) and the number of deliveries each week. These two directly tie to the distributor's costs. Higher delivery size and less frequent deliveries save costs; these savings may be passed on to the operator. Another consideration will be the product brands required to be in stock. While it is likely that a prime distributor will already stock most of what a operation needs to purchase, there may be some proprietary brands used by the operation that the distributor will now have to stock. Also, the distributor will consider the volume of purchases from the operation. Typically, a prime distributor will look to receive 80 percent of the operation's purchases.

The prime distributor's sales representatives (DSRs) often are the key component in the success or failure of the relationship. Many DSRs are former food and beverage operators and their expertise in operations, coupled with their familiarity with different operations and concepts because of their sales role, potentially makes DSRs valuable consultants for the operation. DSRs try to find the best balance of price, quality, and service for each operator. The consultant role of DSRs is perhaps more important for independent food and beverage operations than for operations that are part of a chain, since chain operations enjoy corporate support that is not available to independent operations.

china in a quick-service operation such as Subway, you would not use plastic flatware and paper plates in a full-service restaurant. Beyond these obvious points, how should managers plan the purchase of service supplies and equipment?

Price and the Purchase Decision

Wise purchasers want to buy products at the lowest possible price. They also know that product quality is a primary factor in determining price. Therefore, they use purchase specifications to make sure that distributors quote prices for products of similar quality. Purchase specifications ensure that price differences between distributors are not likely to be caused by differences in product quality.

Wise purchasers also know that more than just the products themselves are purchased from distributors. Along with dining service supplies and equipment, distributors also provide intangibles such as helping purchasers solve problems or always coming through with timely deliveries. A distributor may give a manager a low price, but if the supplies are not delivered on time, it can cause a lot of problems for the food service operation.

Credit provisions can also cause a manager to choose one distributor over another; having an extended period of time to pay for products might be worth a higher price to a manager. Some distributors offer discounts for volume purchases or timely payments. If a distributor offers a two-percent discount for timely payment on a bill of $5,000, the $100 bottom-line savings is substantial when you consider that a restaurant with a profit margin of 10 percent must generate $1,000 in sales to put $100 on the bottom line.

Wise purchasers consider all of these factors—price, quality, distributor intangibles, and flexible payment plans—when choosing a distributor. Although low prices are desirable, the distributor with the lowest price is not always the best distributor to choose.

Establishing Quality and Other Specifications

It is crucial for managers to consider the requirements and expectations of their guests, as well as applicable operating criteria and the skill levels of their staff, as they set quality requirements for supplies and equipment. At large operations, purchasing department staff can help the general manager and other managers by obtaining information from distributors, discussing alternatives with the distributors, and bringing samples to user departments for further analysis and consideration. Ideas and suggestions from the guests themselves, as well as guest-contact and other staff members, can also help managers establish the right quality requirements for these items.

After managers have a general idea about the level of quality required, they must do research to gain the information needed to make good decisions. Studying brochures, talking with distributors' sales representatives, and reviewing sample products can help them formulate quality requirements. Examining the competition's supplies can also provide them with insight about the practicality of the items they are considering.

Whenever possible, managers should consider manufacturers' brands that are available from more than one distributor. **Open-stock items** are much easier to replace than **custom-made items** produced by a single distributor. If managers decide to purchase a brand carried by only one distributor or a custom-designed item manufactured by only one distributor, they have less leverage to negotiate prices.

When managers are developing a new independent restaurant, it is critical that they consider china and other tabletop items early in the development process so that these items can be matched with the menu, uniforms, and other features of the restaurant's decor. Managers should think about how tabletops that are completely set will appear to guests as they enter the room and as they are seated at their tables. Tabletop items should comfortably fit the size of the tables that will be used in the dining area. Whenever possible, managers should ask distributors to furnish them with samples of tabletop items that they can try out before making a purchase decision. By taking tableware for a "test drive," managers will have a better feel for how each type of ware will fit their needs. The same is true for dining area chairs; managers should sit in a variety of them to determine which chair best meets their needs.

As managers make decisions about quality requirements, they should write the details down in a format similar to the one shown in Exhibit 1. In large operations, information about quality requirements is often sent to a purchasing department. In smaller operations, the general manager him- or herself might use the details to fill out a **standard purchase specification form.** After the form is completed, it should be sent with a cover letter to all eligible distributors. Since the purchase specification form outlines the quality requirements for the products requested, chances are good that all distributors will quote prices for the same quality of product, thus making it easier for the manager to make a selection based on price.

Managers can consult a checklist of food and beverage service accessories similar to the one shown in Exhibit 2 for suggestions for supplies and equipment their operations might need. To help make good purchasing decisions, managers should study advertising brochures available from distributors, review products at trade shows, and draw on their own experiences and those of their staffs.

Questions a manager should consider before purchasing a supply or equipment item include the following:

- Does the operation need the item at this time?
- Will it serve the purpose for which I need it?
- Does it satisfy the unique needs of the operation and its guests?
- Does the item's quality justify the cost?
- Is the item easy to clean (if applicable)?
- Is its appearance and design appropriate to the operation?

And, for equipment:

- Is it safe?
- Will it fit through aisles, doorways, and other areas through which it may routinely be moved?

After receiving bids and making a purchase decision, managers should record the appropriate information on a **purchase record** (see Exhibit 3). Food and beverage managers are very busy; they may not be able to recall the brand, quoted purchase price, and quantity they ordered of an item when it is delivered, sometimes

Exhibit 1   Sample Standard Purchase Specification

Standard Purchase Specification

Royale Room

(Name of food and beverage outlet)

1. *Product name:* Tablecloths

2. *Product used for:* Tables in our full-service restaurant, the Royale Room

3. *Product general description:*
   (Provide general quality information about desired product.)

   To be made of cotton damask, weighing 6¼ oz. per square yard.

4. *Detailed description:*
   (Purchaser should state all factors that help to clearly identify desired product. Examples of specific factors, which vary by product being described, include brand name, color, materials composed of, and style.)

   Material to have approximately 170 threads per square inch; thread count should be 91 (warp) and 79 (weft). Cloth should be 72" x 72" and shrink less than 10% (warp) and 5% (weft). Color to be white, non-fading (see attached sample for color/sheen).

5. *Product test procedures:*
   (Test procedures occur at time product is received and as/after product is used.)

   Sample cloth will be laundered by laundry manager immediately upon receipt to check shrinkage and durability.

6. *Special instructions and requirements:*
   (Any additional information needed to clearly indicate quality expectations can be included here. Examples include bidding procedures, if applicable, labeling and/or packaging requirements and delivery and service requirements.)

   Bids should include price for 150 tablecloths, a sample cloth, and estimated delivery date. (Delivery date to be within 4 months of order.) All bids to be returned in 30 days; chosen bidder to be notified by telephone.

---

weeks or even months after they purchased it. The purchase record documents this information and is useful to the receiving personnel who actually take delivery of the products. (Large operations may also use **purchase orders** as control documents that authorize purchases and detail exactly what is being purchased.) Purchase records and purchase orders are computerized in many operations.

Establishing Par Inventory Levels

Some of the major purchases for any food and beverage operation are such common supply items as china, flatware, glasses and other beverage containers, and napkins. These supplies are maintained at what are known as **par inventory levels** or stock levels. When an independent food and beverage operation uses the par

Exhibit 2   Checklist of Food and Beverage Service Accessories

❑ Menu boards	❑ Pens
❑ Cutting boards	❑ Mobile transport carts
❑ Flower vases	❑ Bus carts
❑ Bottle openers	❑ Utility carts
❑ Condiment holders	❑ Bus boxes
❑ Coffee creamers	❑ Dish storage carts
❑ Sugar bowls	❑ Ice tongs
❑ Napkin holders	❑ Table numbers
❑ Butter dishes	❑ Table stands
❑ Candles	❑ Coffee servers
❑ Salt and pepper shakers	❑ Oil and vinegar cruets
❑ Teapots	❑ Relish dishes
❑ Coffee warmers	❑ Wine cooler stands
❑ Water pitchers	❑ Side stands
❑ Plate covers	❑ Cheese trays
❑ Serving ladles	❑ Check folios
❑ Pie servers	❑ Pastry carts
❑ Napkin dispensers	❑ Wine carts
❑ Silverware bins	❑ Salad carts
❑ Food server trays	❑ Pepper mills
❑ Cocktail server trays	❑ Service plates
❑ Tray stands	❑ Wine decanters
❑ Baby chairs	❑ Food service towels
❑ Booster seats	❑ Menus
❑ Chafing dishes	❑ Utility buckets
❑ Corkscrews	❑ Side towels
❑ Flashlights	❑ Serving utensils

inventory method, its managers must set the par levels and decide the minimum level that each item can be allowed to reach before an order must be placed to build the item's inventory back up to its established par level; this minimum level is called the **re-order point.** (Restaurant chains either mandate or strongly recommend par levels and re-order points for franchisees.) If par levels are set too high and supplies are overstocked, problems with cash flow, theft and pilferage, or wasted storage space can occur. In contrast, if par levels are set too low and there

Exhibit 3   Purchase Record Form for Small Operations

Date: _____   Distributor: _____

Delivery Date: _____   Order Taken By: _____

Freight charge confirmation: _____
(e.g., prepaid, COD, truck shipment)

Item	Purchase Unit	Cost per Purchase Unit	Amount	Total Cost

aren't enough supplies on hand, guest and staff member frustration and dissatis-faction can result.

There are so many different kinds of food and beverage operations that it is impossible to generalize about the specific par inventory levels that should be maintained for a given supply item. The general manager in each independent operation must identify the operation's specific needs, based on the type of opera-tion, the number of seats, the hours of operation, the availability of supplies, the frequency and style of dishwashing, the availability of an on-site laundry (for large on-site food and beverage operations or food and beverage operations that are part of a lodging property), and—first and foremost—the requirements and expectations of guests.

Once the manager of an operation has set par inventory levels for the opera-tion, he or she should re-evaluate them frequently to accommodate any changes in business conditions. There are some rules of thumb in the following sections that can help managers of independent operations establish their own par levels for various supplies. (As mentioned earlier, chain operations often have their par levels set by corporate headquarters.)

Par Inventory Levels for China. Ideally speaking, an operation's china inventory should permit one complete setup in the dining room, one complete setup in pro-cess (in the dish room or in transit), and one complete setup in reserve (storage).

When managers open a new food and beverage operation, the following guidelines can help them establish order quantities for china:

1. Dinner plates—3 times the number of seats

2. Salad plates—3 to 4 times the number of seats

3. Bread and butter plates—3 to 4 times the number of seats

4. Cups—3 to 4 times the number of seats

5. Saucers—3 to 4 times the number of seats

6. Fruit dishes or bowls—2 to 3 times the number of seats

7. Sugar containers—½ to 1 times the number of seats

The cost of each place setting (the items needed for a complete setting at each seat) can vary from $5.95 per three-piece place setting to $300 or more per place setting. As you can see, a tableware purchase can be a significant expense.

Specially made or high-quality china may take extra time to produce and deliver. However, some managers feel that the unique atmosphere and food presentation experiences that can result from the use of such china justifies its high purchase price, as well as the long wait for it. The lead time needed for custom-designed china can be as long as 90 to 120 days.

Par Inventory Levels for Glassware and Flatware. The rule of thumb for flatware is one-and-one-half to three place settings per seat. For glassware, managers should maintain a par of three per seat for each of the most frequently used kinds of glasses, such as water glasses and wine glasses. Obviously, many factors affect the choice of actual pars. For example, if an operation has high breakage (glassware) or losses (flatware), the operation will need higher inventory levels. Par levels also are influenced by how quickly soiled items can be cleaned and sidestations restocked.

Par Inventory Levels for Uniforms and Linens. The service staff's uniforms and the operation's linens (tablecloths and napkins) should be immaculately clean at all times. Many food and beverage operations make three complete uniforms available to each service staff member. With this plan, the staff member can store one, launder another, and wear the third. Managers must make some provision for staff members whose uniforms become soiled during a shift; they may require a uniform change in order to maintain the image and quality requirements of the operation.

Par inventory levels for linens are frequently set higher than those for uniforms. Many operations use a par level of four times the number of tablecloths and napkins used during a busy shift. With this system, one set is in use, a second set is in the laundry, and the third and fourth sets are on the shelf, "resting." Linens need to "rest" or "breathe" between uses in order to maintain their quality and prolong their useful life.

Receiving and Storing

The processes involved in **receiving** and storing food and beverage supplies can be summarized as follows:

1. Check incoming products against the purchase record (Exhibit 3). This document reminds whomever is receiving the shipment of the commitments made at the time of purchase. If, for example, a manager ordered five dozen tea saucers of the Staffordshire style from the Syracuse China Company at a specific price, the purchase record would help the receiving clerk (or other staff

member) check that the proper quantity of these saucers was delivered at the agreed-upon price. (Receivers should carefully count costly items.)

2. Check incoming products against the standard purchase specification form (Exhibit 1). If managers have put quality requirements in writing and given them to distributors, receiving personnel can review incoming products against these quality requirements to ensure that the operation receives the correct type of product.

3. Check incoming products against the delivery **invoice.** The distributor provides a delivery invoice that a representative of the food and beverage operation must sign. Since this document is the basis for the charges from the distributor, it is important that the type and quantity of products the operation receives match those for which the distributor is billing the operation.

4. Record in writing any variances between what has been received and what was ordered. Also record any errors in price. Write credit memorandums for price corrections and unsatisfactory or damaged goods that are returned to the distributor.

5. Remove items to secure storage areas. Items should not be left unattended in receiving areas. Rather, they should be brought under strict storeroom control as quickly as possible to prevent damage, staff member or guest theft, or other problems.

In large operations, it is usually wise to split the responsibilities for product purchasing and product receiving. For example, personnel in the purchasing department can purchase the products, and personnel in the accounting department can receive and store the products. Dividing these duties reduces the possibilities of theft.

Small operations may not be able to assign different staff members to purchase and receive supplies. Frequently, the owner/manager of a small operation will handle both duties. Alternatively, whoever is closest to the back door may do product receiving, as long as they have been trained in the operation's receiving procedures. The complexity of the receiving procedures just outlined suggests that staff members need training to properly receive orders, whatever the size of the operation.

Typically, service supplies are purchased less frequently and in smaller quantities than food and beverage products; service supplies are generally purchased only to restore inventory to par stock levels. Therefore, it may be possible, even in the smallest operations, to keep service supplies in a locked area.

Of course, there is no point to locked storage facilities unless the operation uses key control procedures. Simply stated, only those staff members with a need to use storeroom keys should have access to the keys. Managers do need to ensure, however, that enough staff members are authorized to access keys so that there is always someone available to unlock the storeroom(s). The manager responsible for the storage area should have the keys on his or her person for the entire shift. When he or she is off duty, the operation should keep the keys under lock. Some operations keep keys under lock at all times and use a control form to keep track of who issues the keys and at what times. Locks should be changed when staff

Exhibit 4   Sample Perpetual Inventory Record Form

				Par Levels			
Item: _____				Minimum			Maximum
Specification Number: _____							
Balance Carried Forward: _____				Balance Carried Forward: _____			
Date	In	Out	Balance	Date	In	Out	Balance

members who have had access to the keys leave the employ of the operation. Likewise, keys should not be labeled to identify the locks that they open. Should unauthorized staff members find such keys, the labels would make it easier for them to misuse the keys.

Many food and beverage operations use the "precious room" or "vault" concept for storing expensive service supplies such as china and flatware. This plan entails the use of a locked storage area *within* the locked storeroom, which doubly protects these expensive items from theft.

Entering the quantity of incoming products into a **perpetual inventory** record (Exhibit 4) gives managers a running balance of supplies in stock. This plan is especially important for controlling supplies when managers use par inventory levels and re-order points. A perpetual inventory record shows the quantity of supplies in inventory at any given moment. It also helps determine usage rates by indicating when supplies are withdrawn (issued) from inventory and in what quantity.

Periodically, managers must verify that the quantity of each item listed in the perpetual inventory records is the amount that is actually available. A **physical inventory**—that is, an actual count of the items on hand—serves a dual purpose: it verifies the perpetual inventory figures, and managers can use it to assess the inventory's value. This information is important to producing the balance sheet, which lists the value of an operation's assets, including its service supplies.

Issuing

Service supplies are transferred from storage areas to kitchen and dining areas as they are needed. This process is called **issuing,** and operations should have specific control procedures for managing this process.

Exhibit 5 illustrates an issue **requisition** that staff members can use during the issuing process. Staff members list the items they need on the form, recording

Exhibit 5   Sample Issue Requisition Form

Date: _____		Dept.: _____		
Item	Unit Size	Quantity	Cost per Unit	Total Cost

Authorized By: _____

Issued By: _____

the unit size (for example, a box of 50 candles) and the quantity they need (such as two boxes). Depending on the operation, the issue requisition might be completed by the general manager, an assistant manager, a host or hostess, or another staff member. In large operations, a staff member might complete it and then need authorization from a manager to receive the products from storage.

The use of par inventory levels in the dining area can help staff members assess the quantity of supplies that should be issued to the dining area. For example, managers might determine that, at the beginning of each shift, there should be five boxes of paper goods, one box of sugar packets, and one box of novelties for children available in the dining area. The issuing plan would involve restocking these products in the dining area to the required par levels before each shift begins.

Space for the storage of supplies in dining areas is often scarce. Therefore, managers must ensure that the proper quantities of service supplies—and no more—are available in these areas. Excessive quantities of service supplies waste valuable dining space; service supplies also become more susceptible to pilferage when they are not in central storage areas. When greater-than-needed quantities are readily available, some staff members may have the attitude, "There's plenty; we can waste (or take) a little."

On the other hand, it is not good to have insufficient quantities of supplies on hand. Running out of service supplies will adversely affect service speed and guest satisfaction. The term *mise en place,* which literally means "put in place," applies well to service supplies. While this term is commonly used to refer to the process of setting up tools and assembling raw ingredients for cooking, the concept of *mise en place* is applicable to stocking dining areas with service supplies before the start of service. Maintaining the correct par is a responsibility that should never be ignored.

Controlling

Service supplies are costly; therefore, managers must properly control them. Unlike food and beverage products, which can deteriorate in quality, primary control problems with food and beverage supplies revolve around misuse, waste, breakage, and theft.

Misuse. There are countless ways that food and beverage supplies can be misused. Service staff members who use napkins as pot holders or towels, for example, or who use sugar packets to level wobbly tables are misusing supplies.

Staff members should always have the supplies and equipment they need to do their jobs. Often, creative staff members improvise when they do not have the materials they need to do their work effectively. To help prevent misuse of supplies in dining areas, managers should purchase the proper supplies and equipment, develop procedures to make sure they are available when and where needed, and train and supervise staff members effectively.

Waste. Waste is a serious control problem with service supplies. Throwing away unopened prepackaged condiments such as jelly or mustard, discarding washable supplies because it is easier than sorting them, and accidentally discarding flatware into garbage receptacles or folding it into dirty linen to be sent to the laundry are all wasteful practices. Some staff members may think that the costs of some of these items are so low that wasting them makes no difference; other staff members simply may not care. Regardless of the reason, managers should not tolerate the waste of supplies. Training and supervision can help reduce the problem. Useful techniques to reduce supply waste include developing procedures to improve staff attitudes, motivating staff members to pursue higher standards, and building a team of staff members whose goals are compatible with those of the operation.

Breakage. Breakage of china, glassware, and other service supplies is another potentially serious problem. Managers must train staff members to properly handle breakable items. In most food and beverage operations, 75 to 80 percent of all breakage occurs in the soiled-dish area, so good supervision in this area is essential. Proper stacking of soiled china on trays and clean china in storage areas or on dish carts helps reduce breakage, as does properly handling stemmed glassware and properly dropping off dishes in dishwashing areas. For example, dishwashers can set up a decoy system with dishes of each type; managers can train service staff to stack similar dishes on top of these decoys to help prevent staff members from building unstable stacks of unsorted dishes that often topple and cause breakage.

Theft. Some guests like to take home items that have the operation's logo for souvenirs; some staff members also like imprinted items or just feel that the operation owes them something. Whatever the reason, the result is the same: these stolen items must be replaced, and costs of service supplies increase.

Some food and beverage operations implement inspection programs in which managers inspect all packages that staff members bring into or take out of the facility; such programs help detect staff member theft of service supplies and other items. Managers should check with attorneys to make sure such programs are legal in their localities before implementing them. Managers should also be aware that such programs may create an atmosphere of animosity and distrust between managers and staff members.

To help reduce guest theft, managers should train food and beverage servers to remove empty glassware and other tableware items when they serve a second drink or an additional course. This practice not only helps prevent theft, it gives guests more room and gets tableware to the dishroom faster. A number of food and beverage managers have reduced guest theft by offering service supplies for sale. With this approach, guests who desire these items have a legitimate opportunity to obtain them.

Problems with the control of supplies are especially prevalent in bar and lounge areas. Not only are the beverage products themselves susceptible to theft or misuse, but bar supplies, garnishes, and cash might also be stolen. Many of the same principles presented earlier (creating operating procedures, training staff members, and supervising to ensure that staff members follow required procedures) help minimize these problems. However, because of the increased possibilities of theft in bar and lounge areas, management must give special attention to them.

Supplies and Equipment

There are a number of issues managers must address as they develop purchase specifications for food and beverage supplies and equipment. These range from whether to use disposable napkins to how to select the most suitable chairs for the dining room. Above all, managers should seek value from any purchase. Value relates to not only durability and affordability, but attractiveness and functionality as well; supply and equipment items should enhance the operation's concept, image, interior design, and menu. In the following sections we will discuss supply and equipment items commonly used in food and beverage operations.

China

It can cost many thousands of dollars to purchase an initial china inventory and to replace items as breakage and theft occur. Therefore, it is very important for managers to analyze all factors before purchasing china. The pattern they choose will likely "lock in" their operations for years to come, because the high cost of china makes pattern switching impractical, even if managers later find other products that better meet the operation's quality requirements or harmonize more closely with the decor. Managers who want to change the china in their operations must consider a great deal more than the direct cost:

1. Many orders for new china require a long lead time (typically, three to four months or more).

2. Managers must not discontinue re-ordering replacement items for current stock too soon; if they do, they may face shortages until the new china arrives and can be readied for use.

3. The sizes of the new china items must be compatible with the operation's self-leveling plate-dispensing equipment, storage units (such as sidestations), dishwashing machines, service trays, and plate covers. (Made of either plastic or metal, plate covers keep foods warm and facilitate the stacking of plates for transport to service areas. Obviously, covers need to be the correct size for the china with which they are used.)

4. Food presentation procedures and the placement of garnishes may be affected by new china.

5. New china items frequently become "collectibles," and managers can expect an increased amount of pilferage or theft after the new china arrives, especially when a logo or other identifying mark is imprinted on it.

Many managers prefer to use open-stock, multipurpose china (e.g., a single plate that can be used to serve an appetizer, side dish, or dessert), because by doing so they pay less and have products that are more versatile than special-purpose china.

Since china is expensive, durability is an important selection factor. China of strong construction will last longer than china of lower quality. Commercial-quality china is available that is resistant to breaking, chipping, and scratching. Most food and beverage operations do not use bone china because it is very expensive and very fragile. China with a rolled edge is better reinforced than china without this edge and does not chip as easily. A rolled edge distributes the force of an impact over a larger area than an unrolled edge, so it can absorb more shock than an unrolled edge.

When selecting coffee cups, managers often select thick mugs for low-check-average outlets and graceful cups with comfortable-to-hold handles and matching saucers for full-service operations. Heavy or thick china, which is most often used in fast-service operations, will hold heat more efficiently, but it is not necessarily more durable than other products. It may also make service awkward (because of its weight) and may require extra storage space.

In some operations, traditional, round china is being replaced by china in oval, square, triangular, and other avant-garde shapes that can add interest to the dining experience. Plain white china is giving way to more vibrant colors and intricate patterns. This experimentation is being encouraged by new ethnic cuisines and restaurants seeking a trendy edge.

China should be glazed, with its pattern (if any) under the glaze. To assess the durability of the china's design, managers should test samples of the china they are thinking of buying. Wise managers wash sample pieces of china many times and observe the ability of the samples to withstand standard dishwashing procedures. This helps assure managers that the china's design will not fade or become scratched easily. It can also tell them whether the china itself breaks, chips, or scratches easily.

The color and pattern of china should complement the decor and uniforms in the dining area. When colors are selected for china, managers should accent the

Know the Definitions of Tableware Alternatives

Pottery

The term "pottery" properly applies to the clay products of primitive people or to decorated art products made by unsophisticated methods with unrefined clays. As a generic name, "pottery" includes all fired clayware. As a specific name, "pottery" describes the low-fired porous clayware that is generally colored.

Ceramic products acquire strength through the application of heat. The chemical compositions of the materials used to make a product determine, after heat is applied, the strength, porosity, and amount of glazing of the fired product. Primitive pottery, often baked in the sun and composed of one or more unrefined clays, has little strength and is quite porous.

Earthenware

A porous type of ceramic product fired at comparatively low temperatures, producing an opaque product that is not as strong as stoneware or china and lacks the resonance of those products when struck. The product may be glazed or unglazed.

Crockery

A term, often synonymous with earthenware, used to describe a porous opaque product for domestic use. Because of its permeability, it is normally glazed.

Stoneware

A nonporous ceramic product made of unprocessed clays, or clay and flux additives, fired at elevated temperatures. It is quite durable but lacks the translucence and whiteness of china. It is resistant to chipping and rings clearly when struck. It differs from porcelain chiefly in that it comes in colors other than white. These result from the iron or other impurities in the clay.

Ironstone Ware

A historic term for durable English stoneware. The composition and properties of this product are similar to porcelain, except that the body is not translucent and is off-white. In more recent times, this term has been used to describe a number of other products.

Cooking Ware

A broad term applied to earthenware, stoneware, porcelain, and china designed for cooking or baking as well as serving. It has a smooth, glazed surface and is strong and resistant to thermal shock.

Fine China

A term applied to a thin, translucent, vitrified (fired to produce a nonporous glaze) product, generally fired at a relatively high temperature twice: first, to mature the purest of flint, clay, and flux materials; second, to develop the high gloss of the beautiful glaze. It is the highest-quality tableware made for domestic or retail trade.

(continued)

(continued)

Porcelain

A term used frequently in Europe for china. European porcelain, like china, is fired twice. In the United States, porcelain may be fired in a one- or two-fire process. Porcelain has a hard, nonabsorbent, strong body that is white and translucent. European porcelain is made primarily for the retail market.

Bone China

A specific type of fine china manufactured primarily in England. The body contains a high proportion of bone ash to produce greater translucency, whiteness, and strength. Like fine china, it is made primarily for the retail trade.

Restaurant China

A uniquely American blend of fine china and porcelain, designed and engineered specifically for use in commercial operations. The body was developed in the United States to give it great impact strength and durability, as well as extremely low absorption, which is required of china used in public eating places. Decorations are applied between the body and the glaze, to protect the decorations during commercial use. Most of this tableware is subject to a high temperature during its first firing and a lower temperature during its second. However, some of it is fired in a one-fire operation during which the body and glaze mature at the same time. Like fine china, American restaurant china is vitrified (fired to produce a nonporous glaze).

Source: *Questions and Answers*, American Restaurant China Council, Inc., n.d.

secondary (not dominant) colors of the dining area's carpet, walls, and window treatments. Pastel colors (especially peach and mint) complement lighter, healthier foods; deep, rich, warm earth tones complement hearty ethnic cuisine.

China patterns should also complement the food that is served on the plate. Simple, clean lines are preferred in china as well as in glassware, flatware, and linens. Sometimes china is ordered with lines or bands that provide simple framing for foods. China with floral patterns can provide a soft, warm, elegant feeling. Geometric shapes on china present a bold, dramatic image. However, if an operation wants to focus maximum attention on the food served, the center of the plate should be pattern-free. China patterns include embossed rims on dinnerware, fruit motifs, and hand-painted plates.

While a pattern or logo may look fine on menus or signs, it might lose its appeal on plates or pieces of flatware. However, some managers believe that having the operation's logo or other special imprint on the china enhances the operation's image, and they are willing to pay the typically higher prices for custom-designed products. The type of design (spray-on, print, decal, or hand-decorated) also affects costs.

While the longevity of a china design's production cannot be guaranteed, managers should check with distributors to make certain that the pattern they are considering is not on the verge of being discontinued. Even with the best storage and handling practices, breakage is likely. Because food and beverage operations typically do not mix china patterns (use two or more patterns) in the same dining area, they must be certain that their chosen design will be available for at least the near future.

Additional purchasing considerations for china include how easy it is to clean, how well it holds heat, whether it can be used in microwave ovens, and its rim sizes. Rim sizes on china affect guest perceptions of portion size, value, and the overall presentation. China with wide rims provides maximum framing for the food served on it. Wide rims create an open, spacious feeling, since they put the greatest distance between the food and other tabletop items. Wide rims also make smaller portions appear to be larger, since they focus the guests' eyes on the food presentation. Medium-sized rims provide maximum versatility—they can be used for a formal as well as an informal food presentation. Narrow rims are ideal for larger portions. Rimless plates present foods in the plainest way; however, foods with sauces may not look as appealing on them. Additionally, when servers handle rimless china, they have little material to grip.

Managers can purchase china of almost any quality from domestic or international sources. As a result, an additional selection factor—national pride—may be important in the purchase decisions made at some operations. Although it may have only very subtle image implications for outlets in some areas, overt theft or breakage problems can arise in other areas when certain brands (or patterns) of china stir the emotions of guests or staff members.

Some full-service restaurants use service plates (base plates) to heighten the elegance of their tabletop appointments and their service. These plates frequently are works of art that are custom-designed for each operation. Generally, managers must special-order them, and they require a great deal of care and control to ensure that they are not damaged, broken, or stolen. Typically, staff members wash service plates by hand in the dining or pantry area—rarely in the kitchen's dishwashing machine.

Some restaurants purchase special china specifically for the presentation of one or two signature items from the menu. This strategy is designed to set signature menu items apart from other menu items. By the addition of a different piece of china, managers can create an illusion of serving more food more elegantly. This approach can exceed guests' expectations for food presentation. Some hotel dining rooms, searching for ways to compete with free-standing restaurants, are adding specialty salad, entrée, and dessert china in an effort to set themselves apart. When used with classic white china, a specialty china piece in a bright geometric or flowered design can highlight a signature item.

The quality of china that managers select must be compatible with that of the other food and beverage items they use. It is inconsistent and jarring to use high-quality china with low-quality glassware and flatware (or vice versa). In addition to the need for supplies of similar quality, the total presentation of serviceware, decor, staff, and food must be harmonious; china has an obvious impact on the total appearance of the dining area and must be in step with the area's other elements. Experienced managers know that the appealing presentation of food on the correct china is as important to some guests as the flavor of the food, so the size, shape, thickness, pattern, and color of an operation's china must harmonize with the dining area's atmosphere and theme.

Glassware

Many of the factors important to making purchase decisions about china also apply to the purchase of glassware. Open-stock glassware is less expensive than custom-made glassware; however, just as with china, many operations want their logos or other unique imprints on their glasses, which means the glassware must be custom-made. As is true with china, the selection of glassware has marketing implications, so the glassware must be compatible with the theme and atmosphere of the operation. As with china, breakage occurs with glassware; therefore, managers should consider replacement as well as initial purchase costs. Glassware distributors typically offer a wide range of glassware styles (see Exhibit 6).

The type of glass in which a drink is served greatly affects its presentation. Some operations have begun to use the same style of glassware for several different beverages. This practice reduces the number of kinds of glassware that they must maintain in inventory. However, other operations like the presentation and marketing implications of fancy, special-purpose glassware and use a wide variety of glasses.

Some food and beverage operations are using creative alternatives to traditional glassware. For example, rather than serving a margarita in a traditional margarita glass, some operations are using a frosted, heavy glass mug. Nontraditionally shaped martini glasses with off-center stems can convey a feeling of unique sophistication. Glassware with unusual shapes, textures, or colors can help set a restaurant apart from competitors and provide unique dining experiences for guests. Some operations are using glassware as ways to feature salads, side dishes, desserts, and hot beverages. Oven-safe glassware is gaining in popularity, because it is ideal for baked custards, bread puddings, individual cobblers, and soufflés. This efficient choice uses the same container for preparation and service, reducing the number of dishes needed and the amount of storage space required.

Mass-produced glassware is generally thick and may have imperfections not found in fine, expensive products. However, this type of glassware is quite acceptable in the vast majority of food and beverage operations that consider value important. Rolled edges and rims on glasses reduce problems with chipping and cracking. Selecting glassware with thick glass and certain shapes can also reduce breakage.

Stemmed glassware is very susceptible to breakage, although some designs are harder to tip over than others. Despite its fragility, stemmed glassware should be used if operations serve certain types of beverages. A good wine glass, for example, should have a stem for guests to hold so that the heat of their hands does not affect the wine's temperature.

Some operations are choosing nontraditional wine glasses. Bowl-shaped wine glasses are popular, particularly when they are oversized and made of clear glass. Another trend is the use of colored-stem glassware, particularly in mid-priced food and beverage operations (this type of glassware may not be acceptable in fine-dining outlets). If managers choose this type of glassware, they should make sure that the stem's color accents the colors of plates and other tabletop items.

Many operations have begun to use shatterproof glassware. While shatterproof glasses are initially more expensive than other glasses, their long life usually

Exhibit 6   Types of Glasses Available in One Family of Glassware

Courtesy of Libbey Glass

results in cost savings over the long term. Shatterproof glassware also helps prevent glass particles from contaminating food and beverage products and is very useful in many kitchen and bar areas.

The size of glassware is also important. Some food and beverage operations like to use oversized glasses because they enhance the presentation possibilities and the perception of value. Consider, for example, a colorful cordial in an oversized brandy snifter, or an exotic specialty drink in a large hurricane glass. Some banquet operations use small wine glasses so that one bottle of wine will serve eight guests.

Food and beverage operations that stress quality use crystal. To minimize breakage of expensive crystal, these operations use a racking system; staff members take crystal to and from dishwashing areas in racks to prevent crystal items from coming in contact with each other or with anything else that could cause them to break. When practical, managers should use a racking system for other types of glassware as well.

It is important for managers to think about function as well as form when purchasing glassware. Glassware must not only highlight the beverages served in it, but also withstand the rigors of handling and the dishwashing or glass-washing machine.

Flatware

Washable flatware items such as forks, knives, and spoons are typically made of stainless steel. Genuine silverware is prohibitively expensive for almost all food and beverage operations; however, some elegant full-service operations use "hotel plate" (silver-plated) flatware. Most operations prefer to use stainless steel eating utensils of good quality rather than silver-plated flatware, however, because the plating on the latter can chip and peel. In addition, commercial-grade stainless steel flatware is less expensive and more durable than silver plate; stainless steel is difficult to bend, dent, scratch, or stain; does not tarnish or rust; and does not require replating.

Managers can buy flatware in a wide range of prices and styles to suit almost any requirement. Plain flatware is more popular than patterned because it is less expensive and easier to clean. High-priced flatware generally incorporates alloys of various metals that provide greater durability, grain, and luster than low-priced flatware. A finish can be highly polished, dull, or matte. In addition to the traditional knife, fork, and spoon, a vast array of specialty flatware is available to use with such food items as butter, grapefruit, asparagus, oysters, corn on the cob, lobster, and grapes. To reduce theft, managers must carefully control flatware, especially flatware with logos, or small flatware items such as demitasse spoons and corn-on-the-cob holders.

Managers should choose flatware that is balanced, has good weight, has a simple pattern (or is plain), matches their operation's style of service, and enhances guests' dining experiences. Round and generous flatware forms can convey a feeling of elegance. The most popular flatware today has clean, simple lines and a composition of eight percent nickel and 18 percent chrome. Flatware must be kept clean and shiny. The larger fork that is widely used in Europe is also becoming popular in the United States, because well-traveled guests expect operations to have it available.

Disposables

Some food and beverage operations use disposable dinnerware items in their quick-service, take-out, catering, delicatessen, and other high-volume operations. **Disposables** are a useful alternative in these operations, since they cost less, are consistent with the quality of service these operations provide and their guests expect, and allow guests to consume products off-site. They also reduce the cost of labor needed to clean dinnerware. (However, in some areas of the United States, the cost of sending used disposables to a landfill is about as much as the cost of their initial purchase.)

Because environmental degradation affects all of us and because guests and staff members are increasingly concerned about the environment, managers must also consider the ecological implications of using disposables. With today's increased focus on sustainability, environmentally friendly disposables are much preferred. Managers must be certain that no environmental problems will arise and that no bad publicity or legal or other problems governing the disposal of these products will create difficulties for their operations.

In deciding whether to use disposables, managers should calculate the different costs associated with permanent ware and disposables. But before calculating these costs, managers should ask themselves this important question: "What types of tableware do guests expect in our food and beverage operation?" If the operation's guests clearly expect permanent ware, managers need not perform a cost analysis on using disposables; managers should only take the time and trouble to do a cost analysis when it appears that disposables are potentially appropriate or acceptable to their guests.

Of course, a wide variety of quality levels are available in disposable dinnerware products. Managers should select a type of disposable plate that has minimal ink coverage and a predominantly white background; this combination reassures guests that the plate is a clean and sanitary product. If managers want disposables with a design, they might decide to choose a design that features blades of grass, birds, the sun, trees, waves, or other natural elements in order to encourage guests to not litter when they are finished with the disposables. Two-color contemporary designs with colors that complement the operation's decor add interest and brightness to food and beverage operations. Additionally, disposables offer a fairly inexpensive way to display a logo or other distinctive design.

Uniforms

Uniforms for staff members are an important part of the atmosphere and image of many food and beverage operations. The managers of these operations know that guests view staff members in uniform as more organized, professional, and reliable. These first and lasting impressions help make the dining experience a positive one for guests. The range of uniform styles, designs, colors, and fabrics is almost endless. Many operations feature their logo and name on their uniforms, reinforcing the brand image. Appearance and style are important, but so are such factors as comfort, practicality, durability, and ease of maintenance.

When managers purchase uniforms, they always make trade-offs between aesthetic and practical concerns. Comfort is important because staff members must reach, lift, and stretch to do their work. Because uniform pockets are frequently used to carry pencils, guest checks, and related dining-area necessities, inside pockets are often best; they also present a more "crisp" appearance. Zippers and Velcro strips are more convenient than snaps or buttons. Belts may add to a uniform's appearance, but they are easily lost unless they are attached to the uniform in some fashion. Shoes are seldom if ever part of the uniform; however, managers should give some thought to setting basic footwear guidelines covering such variables as colors, laces, and the toes of the shoes (many operations ban open-toed shoes, for example).

Should uniforms have short or long sleeves? This question raises another criterion for selecting uniforms: safety. Short sleeves can contribute to burn and splash problems. Conversely, long sleeves can get in the way as servers use their arms and can also brush serviceware, food, or heating units, causing sanitation and safety problems. There is no clear-cut answer to the "short sleeves versus long sleeves" dilemma; the managers of each food and beverage operation must make their own determination.

When selecting uniforms, managers should get samples from distributors and ask staff members of all shapes and sizes to try them on. A uniform can look very attractive on some staff members and most unattractive on others; managers should try to find a uniform that makes *all* staff members look good. Managers should also try to find uniforms that staff members can wear year-round. With air conditioning, year-round uniforms are seldom a problem. Managers should involve staff members in the process of selecting uniforms; they are more likely to accept uniforms that they helped select. Some staff members report that they feel better and are more ready to work when in uniform. If staff members like their uniforms and are comfortable in them, they are likelier to have a positive attitude about their work. If they do not like their uniforms, their feelings can have a negative effect on their attitudes and work habits.

Custom-designed uniforms can reflect a unique image that a food and beverage operation wishes to portray; however, the cost of such uniforms can be excessive. Custom designs take a great deal of time to produce for both initial orders and re-orders. On the other hand, customized accessories such as special belts, hats, or scarves and neckties can make open-stock uniforms "special" and create the illusion that they have been customized.

High staff member turnover rates in food and beverage operations generally require the ready availability of a wide range of uniform sizes. Therefore, operations often purchase a large number of uniforms of the most common sizes.

The initial purchase price of uniforms can be significant. Managers should also consider maintenance and replacement costs as they make their selection. Often a uniform service is used to launder staff members' uniforms. Proper laundering is important to the longevity and appearance of uniforms. Uniforms made of permanent-press or other synthetic fabrics will last for a long time if they receive the proper care. Uniforms should be replaced before they look tired and old.

Managers should carefully keep track of uniforms during their distribution, use, and storage. Some food and beverage managers in operations that take care of laundering staff member uniforms suggest that the most satisfactory method of controlling uniforms is to require staff members to turn in a soiled uniform in exchange for a clean one. While further control details are beyond the scope of this chapter, managers should keep in mind that they will incur excessive costs if they do not maintain strict control over uniforms.

Linens

Fabric tablecloths and napkins must be compatible with the operation's design and atmosphere. When managers select **linens,** they must consider quality requirements. Seasoned managers recommend maintaining a wide selection of colored linens to accommodate the varied decor requirements of banquet guests.

Striped or plaid linens are used by many operations today. Above all, managers should select appropriate colors for linens (see Exhibit 7). Linens should also feel good to the user. Cotton and cotton blends are less scratchy and have less of a tendency to slide off guests' laps than synthetics; they are preferred for napkins. Half-polyester tablecloths are becoming more popular because of their durability. Many operations are selecting vibrant colors for their tablecloths, so that when their white tableware is placed on them the color combination really "pops." Deep yellow, cobalt blue, or dark red napkins placed on a simple white tablecloth complement ethnic cuisine well.

Linens can be leased from a textile-rental or linen company. Leases can run as long as five years, although shorter leases are the trend today. Linen leases require the signing of a contract that lists the costs of the products and services the linen company will offer. Linen cleaning charges are usually based on the count or the weight of the soiled items. The contract may include replacement charges for "abused" linen. Sometimes the company will add a delivery or energy/fuel charge, particularly when fuel prices spike. Food and beverage operations that lease their linens must keep accurate counts of linen usage as well as keep track of lost linens and those needing replacement in order to control their costs.

Many managers who undertake cost studies find that on-site laundry facilities would reduce their operating costs. However, these facilities must be sure to maintain the proper quality and cleanliness of linens. Sometimes special procedures and specialized cleaning compounds are needed to remove food and beverage stains. Using linens that contain stains is unacceptable. Some napkin folds require very heavy starch that on-site laundries often find difficult to process.

Furniture

Dining area furniture can help create almost any atmosphere the designer wishes the area to have. However, dining area furniture can be very expensive. Managers must purchase furniture in a price range that fits their operation's budget, while keeping in mind guest expectations, the operation's image, and the need for quality.

When selecting furniture, managers should remember that the comfort of guests is one of the most important factors to consider. (This statement does not apply to quick-service operations such as McDonald's, which typically use uncomfortable seats to encourage fast guest turnover.) The elbow room at tables and the amount of space between tables and chairs are important concerns. When some interior designers select the furniture for a dining area, they allow concerns about the ambience and decor of the facility to have precedence over guest preferences. This should never happen; compatibility with the decor should always take second place to guest comfort. Other factors to consider when selecting furniture include available space and the aisle widths required by fire codes.

Exhibit 7   Color Choices for Linens

Colors have meanings, according to Bibb Hospitality and Leatrice Eiseman, a color specialist the firm hired to select appropriate colors for its line of linens. Here's what they mean:

Brown: The number one association is the deliciousness of chocolate, followed by earthy, rich-warm, woodsy, durable, and rugged connotations.

Beige and Taupe: These are among the most classic of neutrals; they are thought of as soft, warm, earthy, sophisticated basic colors that withstand time and trends.

Pink and Dusty Rose: The ultimate colors of romance; in the lighter tints, associated with sweet scents and sweet tastes. They are seen as soft, soothing, cozy, subtle, classic, and romantic.

Red: Red is always the most stimulating, dramatic, high-energy and happy color. In bright reds and fuchsias, it is often associated with ethnic themes. Berries and burgundies are always associated with wine and are seen as elegant, rich, refined, and classic.

Blue: Shades of blue vary in mood, depending on their intensity. Light to medium blues are calming, restful, fresh, and cool; deep blues are seen as traditional, service-oriented, credible, and classic. Brighter electric blues are as exciting and energetic as red. Teal is seen as the most upscale blue, uniquely pleasing and rich.

Orange: Orange is the hottest of all hues. In the deeper terra cotta shades, orange tones are closely associated with earth or ethnic themes—welcoming, wholesome, country looks. In the lighter values of peach or apricot, it is perceived as sweet, delicious, luscious, inviting, and appealing. The brighter values are happy and playful.

Yellow: Light yellows are seen as mellow, appetizing, lemony, soft, sunny, warm, happy, and sweet, while bright yellows are more luminous and create a cheerful atmosphere. Golden amber yellows and ochers are more closely associated with earth.

Purple: Lavenders are associated with flowers and sweet tastes—soft, delicate, and nostalgic; orchid is more exotic and tropical. Bright purple is flamboyant, sensual, and exciting, while deep-plum purples are seen as expensive, regal, powerful, spiritual, and artistic.

Gray: Gray is the timeless color—a cool classic, always thought of as a quality look. The deeper values are viewed as sophisticated.

White: The essence of purity, white is pristine, airy, cool, and clean. The human eye sees white as brilliant. Cream is a much warmer version of white; it is associated with sweet, smooth, rich tastes—a classic neutral.

Black: Black is the quintessential expression of elegance—basic, bold, dramatic, sophisticated, and, at the same time, magical and mysterious.

Green: Green is the color of leafy, healthy growth; light to medium greens are cool, rich, traditional, and classic. The green to avoid for food service is bright chartreuse—the color of nausea. Blue-greens are the most pleasant, both aesthetically and emotionally—refreshing, cooling, and soothing.

Source: Adapted from John Sanger, "Setting the Course," *Club Management*, July–August 1993, p. 45.

Wood is perhaps the most commonly used material in dining area furniture. Wood is strong, rigid, and able to resist wear and stains. Metals, including aluminum, steel, and brass, are also becoming popular in dining areas, as are plastics, fiberglass, and vinyl. Wood and glass tabletops with metal bases are examples of how manufacturers can use different materials to make attractive, functional furniture. If an operation uses placemats or runners rather than tablecloths, its managers must give careful attention to the tabletops they select. Materials used for tabletops should be easy to clean and long-wearing.

Managers must also make decisions about table size and shape. In general, the table sizes managers are choosing are getting smaller. Tables must match the chairs and provide the proper height between the tabletop and the seat base (usually 30 inches [76 centimeters]). When selecting tables, managers should keep in mind that guests are often more comfortable seated at tables with pedestals rather than legs.

Choosing a variety of table shapes and sizes enhances the dining area's appearance and helps the staff accommodate various group sizes—as long as the shapes and sizes are compatible with each other. For example, if the operation's two-top tables (the term **"top"** is used in the industry to represent a guest; a "two-top" table seats two guests) were the same width as its four-top tables, staff members could combine a two-top and a four-top to accommodate a party of six guests. Of course, when staff members put tables together in this manner, they must ensure the tables are stable. Staff members also need to be certain that no "valley" is created between the two tables when they are placed together, forming an uneven surface where glasses might tip or plates rock.

Round tables frequently have drop sides that make the tables square when the sides are down. Staff members can put the sides up to accommodate large groups when necessary.

Folding tables are essential for banquets and meetings, and they can be purchased in many shapes and sizes. These tables should be easily movable and stackable for convenient storage. Folding tables often have padded tops so that tablecloths can be placed directly on them. However, improper handling during setup and breakdown can damage these pads.

All chairs should be durable, easy to clean, and appropriate for the existing decor. If managers select chairs that contain fabric, they should be aware of potential fire hazards. Some furniture is made of fabrics that burn more quickly than others; some fabrics resist burning but will smolder and give off dangerous fumes. Also, some fabrics wear more slowly and resist stains better than others. When selecting fabric-covered chairs, managers should check to see whether the fabric has been treated with a fire retardant and a stain-resistant or waterproof solution. Because synthetic fabrics can cause perspiration and discomfort, operations with low guest turnover (that is, operations in which guests spend a relatively long period of time seated at their tables) should not use chairs made with synthetic fabrics.

Some chairs are designed more for fashion than for safety or comfort. Therefore, managers should be careful when selecting chairs and avoid choosing chairs, for example, with chair backs and legs that stick too far out into traffic aisles and might trip or hinder guests and staff members. Also, managers should select rigidly constructed chairs with bracing; this can prevent breakage and possible injury to guests. These suggestions apply no matter what type of chair managers select, including stackable or lightweight chairs.

While chairs with arms may be the most comfortable from the guest's perspective, they are likely to take up more space than chairs without arms. At round tables, many operations use chairs with arms. Typically, tables and chairs used for banquets must withstand a great deal of wear and tear; therefore, strength and durability should be central concerns when managers develop purchase specifications for them.

Equipment

Food and beverage service personnel must use a wide range of equipment items that perform such specialized jobs as making ice or holding food at its proper temperature until it is served.* In the following sections we will mention just a few of the most commonly used items:

- Holding tables
- Coffee urns and makers
- Refrigerators and freezers
- Ice machines
- Dishwashing machines

Holding Tables. Holding tables (also called "food warmers" or "steam tables") keep food hot until it is served. They should never be used as a substitute for fast and efficient service, since food that is kept hot for excessive periods of time generally deteriorates in quality and appeal. Holding tables are particularly important in operations serving banquets, buffets, and catered functions. While many models are manufactured and available for purchase, four main categories of holding tables exist: cabinet food warmers, hot-food tables, pot warmers, and radiant warmers.

Cabinet food warmers include mobile food-warming carts and food-warming drawers. In many models, either moist heat or dry heat can be used. Some cabinet food warmers are used to display foods for merchandising purposes, particularly if they contain Ferris wheels, rotisseries, or turntables to keep the food items within them in motion. Lighting is frequently added to further enhance the visual appeal of the food display. Portable cabinet food warmers are either hand-carried or moved on casters. They may be heated by electricity or simply keep food hot through insulation or by canned, gel-type fuel. These warmers are ideal for banquets and off-site catering.

Hot-food tables are popular choices for buffets and use either moist heat (steam tables with *bains marie* or water baths) or dry heat (dry-well hot-food

---

* Some of the following sections on food and beverage equipment were adapted (without citations) from David M. Stipanuk, *Hospitality Facilities Management and Design,* Third Edition (Lansing, Mich.: American Hotel & Lodging Educational Institute, 2006), pp. 343–357.

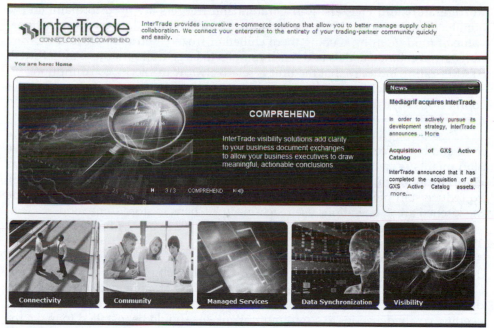

InterTrade (www.intertrade.com) provides an electronic commerce system designed specifically for food and beverage operations and their distributors. (Courtesy of Inter-Trade Systems Corp.)

tables). Some dry-well hot-food tables can also be used to produce moist heat by placing water in the wells and then placing containers of food in the water.

Pot warmers that heat by conduction can be pot-shaped (hence the name) or rectangular or square in shape. They are used to keep chili, soups, sauces, and certain ice cream toppings hot. A feature many operations prefer is a removable stainless steel insert that allows easy access and cleaning. Pot warmers are ideal for displays of hot foods at self-service buffets and may be recessed into tabletops to prevent them from being bumped and tipped over.

Radiant warmers heat food by radiation, using infrared energy provided by alloy, ceramic, or quartz strips or infrared bulbs. These warmers are used for food pickup stations in the kitchen, for buffets in the dining area, or for plating stations. Adjustable radiant warmers, often on tracks, can be focused where the heat is needed most.

Coffee Urns and Makers. A **coffee urn** is a non-pressure-vented water tank heated by electric immersion heaters, gas burners, or steam coils and controlled by a thermostat and relay. Coffee urns range in capacity from 2 to 125 gallons (8 to 473 liters) and have faucets for easy pouring.

Coffee makers are automatic or semiautomatic units that make coffee and dispense it into a coffeepot or into individual cups. Coffee makers are often used when relatively small quantities of coffee are needed, because the quantity and quality of the coffee can be more effectively controlled.

Refrigerators and Freezers. Refrigerators and freezers are used to maintain the quality of stored food. They preserve the color, texture, flavor, and nutritional value of food items by keeping them chilled or frozen. Refrigerators and freezers range from cabinet models and reach-in units to large walk-in units. An ENERGY STAR™ rating indicates that the unit is relatively low in energy consumption.

Cabinet models are small refrigerators or freezers that are located on or under countertops right at a kitchen workstation or dining room sidestation to keep food handy for food preparers or servers.

Pass-through and reach-in refrigerators with glass doors are used in some food and beverage operations to store prepared food such as salads and desserts. Staff members can then take food items from the refrigerators and serve them as guests order them, or the guests may serve themselves (in cafeterias, for example). To reduce staff member trips to walk-in refrigerators (which are usually outside the kitchen area), operations use reach-ins in kitchens to store some food.

Typical upright reach-ins are 78 to 84 inches (198 to 213 centimeters) high and 32 inches (81 centimeters) deep. They commonly come with one, two, or three doors. A one-door unit would be about 28 inches (71 centimeters) wide; a three-door, 84 inches (213 centimeters). Doors are usually self-closing.

Walk-in refrigerators and freezers provide food storage away from the production areas of a kitchen and allow managers to buy food in large quantities, keeping costly deliveries to a minimum. Walk-ins should be installed to make the delivery of food and the movement of food from the walk-ins to production areas as convenient as possible.

Walk-ins are typically built from prefabricated modular panels. Panel sizes vary, and walk-ins can be custom-built. A typical unit measures 8 feet by 12 feet (2.4 meters by 3.7 meters).

A walk-in can be an integral part of a building or a prefabricated room installed in sections within a larger room. Walk-ins can be built outside the building as well. In some cases, outdoor units are installed right next to the main building with a connecting door between them; a door on a different wall is used for deliveries. This saves interior space and allows deliveries to be made easily, without disrupting the normal staff member traffic flow.

Since the ideal storage temperatures for food items vary, an operation may have more than one walk-in. For example, a large operation may have a walk-in refrigerator for vegetables, one for meats, and one for dairy items, as well as a walk-in freezer for frozen items.

Ice Machines. Ice machines make cubed, crushed, or flaked ice. They can be floor models or mounted on a wall. Capacities range from 20 to 800 pounds (9 to 360 kilograms) of ice per day. Machines that allow the first ice made to be the first ice dispensed are desirable. So are machines designed to allow staff members to run cleaning solutions through them during periodic maintenance.

For very large operations, there are machines that make ice in block or bulk form; the ice must then be chipped or crushed. The capacities in these machines run from 40 to 4,000 pounds (18 to 1,800 kilograms) of ice per day.

Dishwashing Machines. Although service personnel do not operate dishwashing machines, they are involved in returning tableware to dishwashing areas and depend on dishwashing machines for clean tableware. There are other types of warewashing machines besides dishwashers—pot and pan, glass, tray, and silverware washers to name a few. But dishwashers are the most commonly used, and we will focus our discussion on them.

When managers must purchase a dishwashing machine, they should take the following factors into account:

- How well the machine cleans and sanitizes ware

- The average and maximum volumes of ware to be washed

- The number of staff members management wants to dedicate to warewashing

- The cost of detergents and other chemicals

- The environmentally friendly nature of cleaning and sanitizing chemicals

- The amount and shape of available floor space

- Budgetary considerations

A dishwashing machine is a long-term investment. Managers should look at the machine they are considering in light of the operation's business volume forecasts and marketing plan. If the operation plans on significant growth and the budget permits it, managers may want to choose a machine that can handle more volume than the operation is now generating. That way, as the operation grows, managers will not need to purchase a new machine too soon.

In the following sections we will briefly discuss door-type, conveyor, and flight-type dishwashers.

Door-type. A **door-type dishwasher**—also called a "single-tank" or "stationary-rack" dishwasher—has a tank holding a solution of heated wash water and detergent. This solution is circulated through spray nozzles above and below the dishes. As with most dishwashers, water for washing is at 150°F to 165°F (66°C to 74°C). Rinse water is circulated through the same spray nozzles. To kill bacteria, rinse water is heated to 180°F (82°C) with a booster heater (most tap water only reaches 140°F to 160°F [60°C to 71°C]). Dishes are placed on racks for cleaning; these racks remain stationary throughout the washing process. Doors may be on one or more sides.

Conveyor. With **conveyor dishwashers,** racks of dishes are placed on a conveyor belt that carries the dishes through the machine. These dishwashers have curtains rather than doors. At one end, a staff member loads the racks of soiled dishes into the machine; after going through the cleaning cycle, the dishes are automatically pushed out onto the clean-dish table at the other end, eliminating the need for a staff member to open a door and manually remove the racks.

The simplest conveyor dishwasher has one tank of hot wash water. After the dishes are washed, they remain in place for the final rinse. In a two-tank machine, the dishes are washed, then moved down the line to a second tank to be rinsed. A three-tank machine has a tank for rinsing off food remaining on the dishes before they are moved to the wash tank and then to the rinse tank. Obviously, the more tanks a conveyor dishwasher has, the longer and more expensive it is.

Exhibit 8   Diagram of a Flight-Type Dishwasher

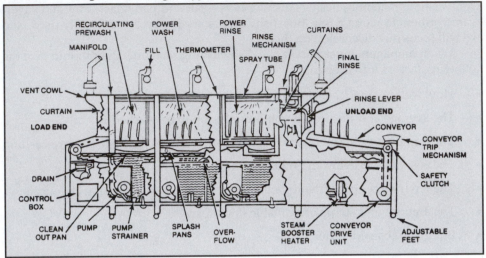

Source: Robert A. Modlin, ed., *Commercial Kitchens*, 7th ed. (Arlington, Virginia: American Gas Association, 1989), p. 259.

Flight-type. In **flight-type dishwashers,** the conveyor is not a belt upon which dish racks are placed; the conveyor itself acts as one continuous rack because it is made up of pegs on stainless steel bars (see Exhibit 8). Plates, pans, and trays are placed between the pegs; cups, glasses, and flatware still have to be racked, however. Flight-type dishwashers are built to handle very large dishwashing demands. They are typically used in large commercial or institutional operations that serve more than 1,000 guests per meal.

High-Tech Equipment

Advances in technology have helped food and beverage operations become more productive and improve service to guests. Three "high-tech" pieces of equipment used by many food and beverage operations are **point-of-sale (POS) systems,** hand-held terminals, and electronic pocket pagers.

POS Systems. POS systems help food and beverage operations take guest orders and process sales transactions more efficiently. Guest check totals, including taxes and service charges (where applicable), are calculated automatically, and payments by credit, debit, or "smart" card can be processed quickly. (A smart card is similar to a credit card and is used in much the same way; however, unlike a credit card, a smart card contains a microprocessor that can read, store, and transfer information.) In addition, POS terminals throughout an operation can be interfaced with food production areas (especially printers in these areas) and managerial and accounting programs to allow quick, accurate transfer of data.

A **cashier terminal** is a POS device that is connected to a cash drawer. A POS terminal without a cash drawer is commonly called a **precheck terminal.** Precheck terminals are used to enter orders, not to settle accounts. For example, a server can

An example of a menu board overlay. (Courtesy of National Cash Register Corporation)

use a precheck terminal located in a dining room sidestation to relay guest orders to the appropriate kitchen and bar production areas, but cannot use the terminal to settle guest checks. Cashier terminals can be used both for check settlement and for order entry.

POS order-entry devices consist of keyboards and monitors. The two primary types of keyboard surfaces are micro-motion and reed style. The micro-motion keyboard design has a flat, waterproof surface, while the reed keyboard design has waterproof keys raised above the surface of the keyboard. More important than the physical design of the keyboard is the number of hard and soft keys the keyboard provides. **Hard keys** are dedicated to specific functions programmed by the manufacturer. **Soft keys** can be programmed by managers to meet their operations' specific needs.

Both keyboard design types can usually support interchangeable menu boards. A **menu board** overlays the keyboard surface and identifies the function performed by each key during the specified meal period. Managers can work with manufacturers to develop the menu boards that will be most useful for their operations.

Touch-screen technology, light pens, card readers, and computer mouse input devices are increasingly popular as input devices for POS systems. With touch-screen terminals, a microprocessor inside a monitor displays "buttons" or graphical representations of functions on the screen. Touching one of the sensitized screen areas produces an electronic impulse that is translated into digital signals that activate programs or make an entry. Staff members can also use a light pen to activate programs or make entries.

Some quick-service operations have installed countertop-recessed touch-screen terminals that guests can use to place orders without interacting with staff members. This new self-service option may improve the accuracy with which guests' special requests and substitutions are transmitted to production staff. It can also reduce labor costs and speed up service, and guests may enjoy the interactivity these systems afford. Overall service may improve as service staff members are freed to focus on guest service.

The digital capture of signatures is also becoming common on precheck POS terminals. Guests sign for payment, whether for checks or payment cards, on a pressure-sensitive pad that "captures" the signature as a digital image that can be stored on disk or verified. Exhibit 9 shows the screen of one signature capture program. Some operations maintain databases of digitized guest photographs to verify guest identities for payment purposes. Such applications can help reduce fraud and problems with overdrawn checks.

Hand-Held Terminals. Hand-held terminals (sometimes called "electronic tablets") reduce unproductive time spent by service staff, particularly during busy meal periods. These terminals help make POS systems mobile. As soon as a server takes an order with a hand-held terminal at a guest's table, the order can be transmitted to the kitchen. Hand-held terminals avoid the wait associated with having servers walk handwritten guest checks to the kitchen (in operations with manual systems) or input orders from an insufficient number of fixed terminal workstations. Hand-held terminals can also free servers to spend more time with guests.

Hand-held terminals may weigh less than one pound (0.45 kilograms) and are battery powered. Some models use buttons; others are activated by using a pen or fingers to touch their screens. Hand-held terminals permit two-way communication between servers and production staff, making it easier for production staff to inform servers when a menu item has been "86'd" (**86** in food service jargon means the kitchen has run out of a menu item). These terminals work very well with food and beverage operations that have heavy rush periods, long distances between the dining area and kitchen or bar, or reduced server staffs (since the terminals improve productivity). Some hand-held terminals have been improved by adding built-in payment card readers and signature capture features.

Electronic Pocket Pagers. First introduced to inform servers when their orders were ready for pickup in the kitchen, **electronic pocket pagers** now are being used to inform guests when their tables are ready in the dining area. When guests arrive at an operation and their table is not yet ready, they can be given a pocket pager. When the table is ready, the manager, host, or hostess telephones the guest's pager number. The pager alerts the guest with flashing lights, a beeping sound, and/or a vibration.

Pocket pagers eliminate the confusion caused by difficult-to-hear public address (PA) systems in crowded operations. By reducing the time it takes to seat guests, pagers speed guest turnover. Pagers also eliminate the need to search for guests when tables are ready, and avoid inaccurate pronunciations of guests' names over a PA system. Guests are free to visit the bar or lounge area and even shop nearby or walk around the grounds of the operation while waiting for their table. Some operations report that once guests register with the host or hostess and are given a pager, they are less likely to leave and go to another operation for their dining. To avoid losing pagers, some operations ask guests to leave a payment card, deposit, or driver's license as security when they are issued a pager. The

Exhibit 9   Sample Screen of a Signature Capture Program

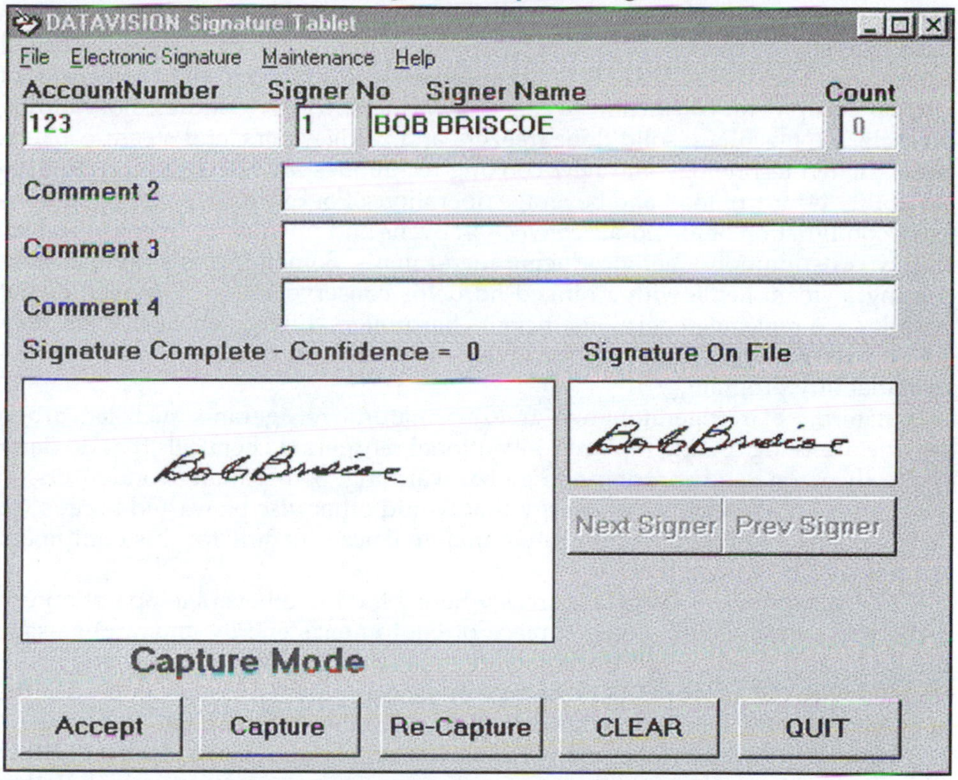

Courtesy of DATAVISION Corporation (www.datavisionimage.com)

name and address of the operation should be written on the pager so that if guests accidentally take the pagers home, they can return them in person or by mail.

Pager signals have ranges of 100 feet to two miles; the strength of the signal can be adjusted on some models. Pagers that vibrate are a great way to communicate with guests who have hearing impairments. Some pagers are waterproof and come with reinforced clips. Pagers operate with batteries that need to be recharged or replaced, depending on the model. Managers should learn about and evaluate any model's features before purchasing pagers of that model in quantity.

Sustainable Supplies and Equipment

Increasingly, food and beverage managers are purchasing supplies and equipment with an eye to their energy efficiency and impact on the environment. "Sustainable" supplies and equipment are ecologically friendly. "Green" equipment uses less energy and may be better for the environment in other ways as well. ENERGY STAR™ certification from the Department of Energy and the Environmental Protection Agency identifies equipment that is at least 20 percent more energy efficient than other equipment in the same category.

Even though commercial kitchens use a considerable amount of energy, there are areas where energy savings can be found. Food and beverage operators can slash their energy costs by 10 to 30 percent each year by purchasing energy-efficient equipment. The ENERGY STAR™ rating currently is applied to eight categories of kitchen equipment: convection ovens, dishwashers, fryers, griddles, hot holding cabinets, ice machines, solid-door freezers and refrigerators, and steam cookers. New kitchen technology and new cooking techniques are also boosting the sustainability efforts of food and beverage operations. For example, some operations use a combination of forced-air convection ovens and microwave ovens to reduce energy consumption when producing menu items. Something as simple as purchasing a steam kettle with a hinged lid helps conserve energy. Grooved or flat griddles are replacing energy-inefficient charbroilers. Energy-efficient dishwashers and recirculating scrappers for table waste also contribute to an operation's sustainability program.

In terms of refrigerators and freezers, natural refrigerants such as carbon dioxide are being used to replace conventional refrigerant chemicals that do damage to the ozone and contribute to global warming. Self-cleaning condensers on these units cut the amount of energy that would otherwise be wasted because of dirty coils by 15 percent. A preventive maintenance schedule for this equipment can potentially save even more.

Energy and water usage are areas where a food and beverage operation can make real sustainability gains. A piece of equipment's energy and water usage should be evaluated over its projected life cycle. Cost savings in energy and water coupled with the improved performance of the equipment can save money for the operation over the long term while being good for the environment.

Water conservation takes many forms. Leaking faucets should be fixed, either with new washers (least expensive) or with new fixtures (most expensive). Rather than automatically delivering glasses of water to guests, servers can offer this service instead. For each glass of water that is not delivered to a table because a guest declines the offer, the operation saves the water in the glass as well as the water and chemicals needed to wash the glass (and saves the accompanying costs). Thawing frozen food under refrigeration rather than under cold running water is another example of saving water. Dishmachines can be fitted with pre-rinse spray valves that cut down on the time that dishes must remain in the machine. Toilets and urinals can be fitted with water-saving devices.

Using biodegradable food and beverage supplies contributes to an operation's sustainability efforts. Purchasing glass bottles that are recyclable and using food waste to create compost are other examples of sustainability practices. Recycling product packaging is one of the most common sustainability practices in the food and beverage industry. Paper is the most frequent item that is recycled, followed by plastic.

Other examples of sustainability practices involving supplies and equipment include the trend to purchase from local distributors whenever possible. This reduces carbon emissions and saves on transportation costs. If on-site food and beverage operations such as those at colleges and universities can eliminate the trays traditionally used by guests of these operations, this will eliminate the need to wash the trays, saving on water and energy. In food and beverage operations that generate a large amount of waste, waste pulping systems can save energy and water. The pulper grinds or shreds waste materials in water; the water is then extracted from the waste by an extractor and recycled to carry more material to the extractor. Most pulpers are built to accept food waste as well as packaging materials and disposable serving materials (e.g., disposable glasses, cups, and tableware).

Key Terms

cashier terminal—An electronic point-of-sale device that is connected to a cash drawer.

coffee maker—An automatic or semiautomatic machine that makes coffee and dispenses it into a coffee pot or into individual cups.

coffee urn—A non-pressure-vented water tank heated by electric immersion heaters, gas burners, or steam coils, and controlled by a thermostat and relay.

conveyor dishwasher—A dishwashing machine in which racks of dishes are placed on a conveyor belt that moves the dishes through the machine.

custom-made items—Supply items (such as china) that are designed specifically for one food and beverage operation and are available only from the distributor that designed them.

disposables—Disposable dishes, cups, flatware, and other supply items; usually made of paper or plastic.

door-type dishwasher—A dishwashing machine in which a rack or racks of dishes remain stationary while heated wash and rinse water is sprayed from nozzles above and below the dishes. Also called a single-tank or stationary-rack dishwasher.

86—A food service code that indicates that the kitchen has run out of a menu item.

electronic pocket pager—A pocket-sized electronic device used to page people or to send them short messages.

flight-type dishwasher—A dishwashing machine in which dishes are placed on a conveyor made of pegs or bars and are moved through several washing and rinsing chambers.

hand-held terminal—A wireless server terminal, also called a "portable server terminal" or "electronic tablet"; performs most of the functions of a precheck terminal and sometimes some account settlement functions; enables servers to enter orders at tableside.

hard keys—Keys on an electronic point-of-sale device that are dedicated to specific functions programmed by the manufacturer.

holding table—An appliance that keeps food hot until it is served. Also called a "food warmer" or "steam table."

invoice—A distributor's transaction statement containing the names and addresses of both the buyer and the seller, the date of the transaction, the terms, the methods of shipment, quantities, descriptions, and prices of the goods.

issuing—The control point at which food products are released from storage; issuing controls ensure that products are only released to authorized staff members in proper quantities.

linens—Table linens such as tablecloths and napkins.

menu board—A keyboard overlay for an electronic point-of-sale device that identifies the function performed by each key during a specific meal period.

open-stock items—Supply items (such as china) that are of manufacturer brands that are available from more than one distributor.

par inventory (stock) level—The standard number of a particular inventory item that must be on hand to support daily operations.

perpetual inventory—A system of tracking inventory that records all additions to and subtractions from stock as they occur and provides a running balance of the quantity and cost of merchandise in inventory.

physical inventory—A count of items in storage.

point-of-sale (POS) system—A network of electronic cash registers and order-entry devices capable of capturing data at point-of-sale locations.

precheck terminal—An electronic point-of-sale device without a cash drawer, used to enter orders and transfer them to food and beverage production areas, but not to settle accounts.

purchase order—A form used for maintaining purchasing control. It contains the details of an order for food or other supplies that is prepared by an operation's purchasing staff and submitted to distributors. A copy is retained to facilitate in-house recordkeeping.

purchase record—A detailed record of all incoming shipments from distributors.

receiving—A critical control point at which ownership of products is transferred from the distributor to the operation. The receiving function involves checking the quality, quantity, and price of the incoming purchased products.

re-order point—The inventory level at which a particular item must be re-ordered to bring supplies back to par.

requisition—A written order identifying the type, amount, and value of items needed from storage.

soft keys—Keys on an electronic point-of-sale device that can be programmed by users to meet the specific needs of their operations.

standard purchase specification form—A form staff members can use to record purchasing guidelines that precisely define the quality, quantity, and other characteristics desired for particular supply and equipment items.

top—A term used in the food and beverage industry (when referring to tables) to represent a guest; a "six-top" table, for example, is a table that seats six guests.

Review Questions

1. What are some important considerations when purchasing supplies and equipment?

2. What types of forms are involved in the processes of purchasing, receiving, and issuing items, and what is the function of each?

3. What role do par inventory levels and re-order points play in an inventory maintenance system?

4. What are the primary control concerns for food and beverage supplies and equipment, and how do operations typically address them?

5. What do purchasers look for when selecting china, glassware, flatware, and disposables for a food and beverage operation?

6. What do purchasers look for when selecting uniforms, linens, furniture, and equipment for a food and beverage operation?

7. What "high-tech" devices are particularly useful in food and beverage operations, and what are their capabilities?

8. How are food and beverage operations addressing environmental concerns when purchasing supplies and purchasing and operating equipment?

Case Studies

Are Suppliers Partners, Friends, or Enemies?

Barbara Nellis and Sandy Watson have just given one another a high five. Close friends and neighbors for several years now, they each recently sent their youngest child off to college. For the past few years they have dreamed of opening a small restaurant so they could re-enter the work force after many years of being stay-at-home moms.

Barbara's husband, a dentist, and Sandy's husband, an electrical engineering contractor, have agreed to finance the new venture for their spouses. They have their name selected—"Delicious Deli"—the concept (a delicatessen), the theme (contemporary fashions), and the location (2,000 square feet in a strip mall).

They are now getting calls, e-mails, letters, and walk-in visits by all sorts of distributors who want their business for the products they sell. Both ladies feel a bit overwhelmed by this. They both come to the conclusion that they need to develop a checklist by which they can evaluate distributors and assist in making the right selections. They have no experience in this regard and ask you to help them. You agree, for a fee.

Discussion Question

1. What will be on the checklist you develop to evaluate suppliers?

This case was taken from William P. Fisher and Robert A. Ashley, *Case Studies in Commercial Food Service Operations* (Lansing, Mich.: American Hotel & Lodging Educational Institute, 2003).

Supplier Assistance!

Sarah Stevens has been in the food service business all her life. Born into a restaurant family, she worked as a young girl in the family restaurant, went to school and majored in hospitality management, and married a classmate. She and her husband, Rick, decided to open the Hancock Farms Inn, a large, old mansion they purchased three years after college.

Hancock Farms seats 160 people in three rooms: the Library, the Sun Porch, and the Sitting Room. All three are on the same level and are served out of the same kitchen. Sarah and Rick keep up with the latest food fads and trends by going to restaurant conventions, reading the trade press, and speaking with other restaurateurs. They also get feedback from their customers, of course.

Sarah and Rick feel that their menu is getting a little tired and it may need an infusion of new ideas. They are also thinking of expanding their wine list, and have recently purchased some new kitchen equipment.

Sarah's responsibilities include the training of employees, and she also feels that it's necessary to keep long-term employees refreshed and challenged so they feel they are developing in their positions and enjoy personal satisfaction.

She begins to wonder if the various distributors to the Hancock Farms Inn could play a larger role in assisting her with employee training and development. She begins to note some things she will ask the distributors.

Discussion Questions

1. In what areas can distributors be of assistance to the operation?
2. Should Sarah invite distributors to be part of the training program?

This case was taken from William P. Fisher and Robert A. Ashley, *Case Studies in Commercial Food Service Operations* (Lansing, Mich.: American Hotel & Lodging Educational Institute, 2003).

Supplies Surprise

"Waitress! Waitress!"

"Yes, sir, may I help you?" Sara asked.

"Take a look at the streaks on my glass. You expect me to drink out of this?"

"No, sir, of course not. I'm very sorry, I'll get you a new one as soon as I can," Sara assured the guest. As soon as I get one from the dish room that isn't stained with lipstick, broken, or too hot to handle, she thought to herself as she hurried away.

• • •

Leroy Rader had been the general manager of Pete's Eats, an independent, mid-scale family restaurant, for a little over a year. The restaurant had recently doubled the size of its banquet facility and had purchased divider walls so smaller parties could be accommodated for banquets simultaneously.

The new banquet room had been open about a month. Leroy had purchased as many new place settings for the banquet room as the owner would allow—which was not enough, in Leroy's opinion. But the owner had told him that the expansion itself had been over budget and that money for new tableware would be limited. Purchases would also have to be minimized for both the dining room and the banquet room for the next few months. Leroy and his assistant manager Eric told each other, "It will just have to do." They consoled themselves with the fact that the tableware would be the same for both facilities, so there would be no danger of mismatching them. They would be able to use reserves from one to cover shortfalls in the other, if necessary.

So far, operations had run fairly smoothly. The dining room had been full for hours on the evening of Valentine's Day, but with only modest banquet bookings that night, Pete's Eats had handled the volume adequately. Tonight, though, the first large banquet was scheduled: a 100-person awards banquet. But the dining room was drawing some attention of its own.

• • •

Leroy looked out across the dining room. It was only 6:15 P.M., and the operation was much busier than anyone had expected. That's weird, thought Leroy. Forecasts called for only an average night. A waiting line was forming and the lounge was filling up.

"Mr. Rader, we're bussing tables as quickly as possible," said Zeke, the senior busperson in the dining room, "but we're not getting clean dishes soon enough."

"What are you running out of the most?"

"Glasses," answered Zeke. "And the ones we're getting are—well, I'm telling the other bussers to look them over carefully before they set them."

"Good," said Leroy. "I'll go talk to Stan in the dish room." Leroy popped in the dish room and asked Stan how he was doing. Then he asked Stan to put the glasses through the dishwashing machine a little faster than usual.

"I usually send racks through only three-quarters full," said Stan, "but I'll start sending them through half full. If we had the right kind of racks, the glasses wouldn't break as much."

"See what you can do to send glasses through faster without breaking any. We're short on those tonight. How are the dishes coming through?"

Stan said, "Okay, I guess. I know that some have been coming through dirty, but bussers have been bugging me for more and more, so I haven't had time to look at them as closely as I usually do."

Leroy thanked Stan for the hard work. Why are we so short on settings? he thought. And so early in the evening? Even with a full banquet room, we shouldn't be so short. Leroy thought about how the chef had approached him earlier that week and asked about renting supplies for tonight because of the large banquet. Leroy and Eric had talked about it and decided it wouldn't be necessary; with only an average night in the dining room, they should be able to handle a large banquet. Better see how the banquet room captain is doing, thought Leroy.

His conversation with the banquet room captain turned up part of the explanation. The full-house banquet had started on schedule with 60 settings to spare—due to a little bit of hoarding by banquet servers—and those were vanishing fast as dining room buspersons brought them to the dining room. Still, 60 settings is not that much extra, thought Leroy.

"Mr. Rader, I've got two guests who would like to speak with you," Sara said out of the corner of her mouth as she moved past Leroy, carrying a platter to a lone diner. "Oooh, please be careful, that plate is hot, ma'am," she told her guest. She turned back to Leroy. "The two guests are over here, Mr. Rader." Sara nodded toward a nearby table.

"Hi, I'm Leroy, the general manager. How can I help you folks tonight?"

"It's like this," growled the male guest. "I was just eating my chicken parmigiana and I found a piece of something fishy stuck to my plate underneath the noodles."

"Something fishy, sir?"

"Yeah, I can't tell what it is, but it smells like fish. What are you trying to push on us?"

"I'm very sorry, sir. I'll see to it that you get a new meal as soon as possible, and this one's on the house."

"Excuse me, Mr. Rader?" Mike, a server, was at Leroy's elbow.

"Please excuse me," Leroy told the guests. "What is it, Mike?" he asked.

"The group at 14 is complaining about chipped plates and dirty glasses. I brought them new ones, but those weren't much better."

"Don't worry, I'll handle it, Mike," Leroy said as he started to head for that table.

"Leroy?"

Leroy turned and found himself face-to-face with Eric. "I need to talk to you, *now*," Eric said. Eric was obviously upset.

Leroy told Eric he'd be with him in a minute. He talked with the guests at table 14, then returned to Eric. "What's up?"

"The dirty dishes are showing up because Stan is having to push racks through faster than the machine normally pulls them through. Dishes are wet because we're out of drying agents for the dishwashing machine. Bussers are short on everything, even though they're practically pulling plates out from under guests, and servers are sometimes bringing guests' food before their drinks, we're so low on glasses. Even the bar is falling short. If we had known the dining room would be so busy, we could have rented more supplies. What do we do now?"

"We'll make it work. I know things aren't perfect, Eric. We've been caught a little off guard. It's times like these when managers have a chance to shine."

"Mr. Rader?" Leroy turned to face a middle-aged woman. "I understand you're the general manager here," she continued. "I'm Mrs. Carey. One of your servers gave me a cracked glass. I didn't notice until I was done with my drink. How does one know if one is bleeding internally?"

Leroy inspected the glass and found a hairline crack. "There are no splinters missing. Are you feeling all right? I'm very sorry this happened to you. I'll correct the problem right away. In the meantime, let me get you a free drink. Would you excuse me a moment?" He pulled Eric aside. "Eric, I'm going to help Mrs. Carey. Go talk to Stan about this, please."

Eric agreed and went to the dish room. As Leroy was serving Mrs. Carey, he heard some sharp voices coming from the dish room. Sara was over there with Eric, and both were speaking heatedly to Stan through the window. Moments later, Eric and Sara rushed up to Leroy.

"Leroy, Stan's walking out!" Sara said breathlessly. "We've got to do something quick! We can't make it tonight without him."

"I know, I know! Where is he?" Leroy asked.

"This way, hurry!" Eric led Leroy to the back of the restaurant.

Discussion Questions

1. How can Leroy and Eric handle the crisis with Stan? What are their options?

2. How can the managers handle the crisis of a shortage of supplies for the rest of the shift?

3. What can be done to prevent this kind of crisis from happening in the future?

The following industry experts helped generate and develop this case: Christopher Kibit, C.S.C., Academic Team Leader, Hotel/Motel/Food Management & Tourism Programs, Lansing Community College, Lansing, Michigan; and Jack Nye, General Manager, Applebee's of Michigan, Applebee's International, Inc.

 References

Abuso, Joseph. "The Chef as Accountant: How the Kitchen Controls Food Costs." *Restaurant Startup & Growth*. January 2009. 6(1):35, 38, 40, 42.

Anonymous. "Paler Shade of Green." *Foodservice Director*. May 15, 2009. 22(5): 24.

Bendall, Dan. "Buying Green Equipment." *Restaurant Hospitality*. April 2008. 92(4): 84, 86.

Erickson, Joe. "The Linen Clauses." Restaurant Startup & Growth. October 2007: 38–42.

Hernandez, Jorge. "Distributor Relationships Are Key to Safe Food Receiving." *Food Management*.

www.foodmanagement.com/business_topics/food_safety/fm_imp_11629/index.html

Jennings, Lisa. "Shrink Your Purchasing Cards. *Nation's Restaurant News*. January 26, 2009. 43(3):78.

Lent, Les, Plotkin, Lee, McGovern, Jim, and Sam Silvio. "Strategies for Working with Your Foodservice Distributors." *Restaurant Startup & Growth.* August 2006: 23, 24, 26–31.

Levin, Amelia. Water Conservation: Saving Money Drop by Drop." *Foodservice Equipment & Supplies.* February 2009. 62(2): 20.

Luebke, Patricia. "Added Value: Getting the Most from Your Vendor Reps." *Restaurant Startup & Growth.* August 2007: 28–32.

Marvin, Bill. "Looking the Part: Setting the Tone for Employee Appearance." *Restaurant Startup & Growth.* September 2007: 45–50.

Perlik, Allison. "Purchasing Power." *Restaurants & Institutions.* March 2009. 119(3): 52–57.

Plotkin, Lee. "If the Shoe Fits…How to Determine If a Primary Vendor Purchasing Program Is Right for Your Startup." *Restaurant Startup & Growth.* May 2008. 5(5): 28, 30, 32, 34.

Schwartz, Bill. "Restaurant Operations: Eliminate Poor Receiving Habits." *Restaurant Operations.* www.restaurantreport.com/management_tips/tip_eliminating_poor_receiving_habits

Schwartz, Stanley. "Waste Pulping Systems for Commercial Kitchens." *PM Engineer.* June 2006. 12(6): 26.

Seelye, Kathleen. "Green Foodservice: Efficient Equipment Selection & Design." *Foodservice Equipment & Supplies.* December 2006. 59(12): 17.

Sommerfeldt, Elise. "Wipes Clean Up the Competition." *Foodservice Equipment & Supplies.* May/June 2009: 10–12.

Teller, Lenny. "A Sustainable Culture." *Foodservice Equipment & Supplies.* July 2008. 61(7): 72.

Thorn, Bret. "Greenwashing Emerges As an Inconvenient Trend." *Nation's Restaurant News.* August 18, 2008. 42(43): 43–44.

"Uniforms Create Positive 'Halos' for Workers." *Restaurant Startup & Growth.* May 2007: 16.

Warner, Melanie. "Supersizing McDonald's Eco-Cred." *Fast Company.* April 2009: 54.

Young, Richard. "Speeding Along the Green Highway." *Foodservice Equipment & Supplies.* December 2007. 60(12): 56.

Internet Sites

For more information, visit the following Internet sites. Remember that Internet addresses can change without notice. If the site is no longer there, you can use a search engine to look for additional sites.

AllHeartChefs.com
www.allheartchefs.com

American Public Health Association
www.apha.org

Centers for Disease Control and Prevention
www.cdc.gov

Chef Depot
www.chefdepot.com

Commercial Food Equipment Service Association
www.cfesa.com

DATAVISION Digital Image Processing
www.datavisionimage.com

The Delfield Company
www.delfield.com

Dietary Managers Association
www.dmaonline.org

Edlund
www.edlundco.com

FoodService Director
www.fsdmag.com

Gasser Chair Company, Inc.
www.gasserchair.com

Hospitality Financial & Technology Professionals
www.hftp.org

Institute of Food Technologists
www.ift.org

International Association for Food Protection
www.foodprotection.org

Jet-Tech
www.jet-tech.com

National Environmental Health Association
www.neha.org

National Restaurant Association
www.restaurant.org

Nation's Restaurant News
www.nrn.com

Professional Chefs Association
www.professionalchef.com

Server Products
www.server-products.com

Supply & Equipment Foodservice Alliance
www.sefa.com

USA Restaurant Equipment
www.amer-rest-equip.com

U.S. Department of Agriculture
www.usda.gov

U.S. Food and Drug Administration
www.fda.gov

U.S. Foodservice
www.usfoodservice.com

Chapter 9 Outline

Competencies

1. Explain the process necessary to plan an effective design for a food and beverage operation, including the role of a planning team and a market analysis; describe trends in food and beverage design; describe how space requirements and traffic-flow patterns affect an operation's overall layout; and discuss how food safety and sustainability affect design. (pp. 347–360)

2. Describe the importance of decor—specifically, color, carpet, wall coverings, decorations, lighting, ventilation, sound, music, furniture, and the exterior—to a successful food and beverage operation. (pp. 360–365)

3. Summarize cleaning issues for food and beverage facilities, including exterior and interior inspections, dining area cleaning programs, and cleaning schedules and procedures. (pp. 365–371)

9

Facility Design, Decor, and Cleaning

A TOTAL DINING EXPERIENCE consists of not only food and beverages but also the food and beverage facility's design and decor. The design and decor must harmonize with the cuisine and the service. Of course, even the most attractive design and nicest decor is negated if the food and beverage facility is not kept clean. Not only is cleanliness an issue of meeting guest expectations, it is also a legal issue; food and beverage facilities must comply with state and local sanitation laws with regard to facility cleanliness. In this chapter we will discuss the importance of facility design, decor, and cleaning to a food and beverage operation's success.

Design

As designers of food and beverage facilities develop design plans from a guest's perspective, they must consider such elements as noise, lighting, color coordination, and use of space. They also must be aware of government regulations concerning safety. These laws govern such factors as emergency lighting, emergency exits, and the maximum number of occupants that public areas may accommodate.

Design also affects service. In a dining area that is laid out properly, guests are comfortable and service staff members are able to do their work efficiently.

The proper design can even help assure guests that they have chosen the right place to dine. One factor that experienced designers take into account is that dining areas should usually appear comfortably full; few things are worse than having just 30 or so guests dining in a large open dining room designed for 200 people. In this situation, the guests start to wonder if choosing to dine at this restaurant was a wise decision, since it appears nearly empty. Once this doubt enters their minds, they tend to start finding fault with the food and service, since (their reasoning goes) if the restaurant was any good, more people would be dining there. To avoid this problem, many food and beverage operations divide their dining area into sections or rooms; they sit guests in one section and fill it up before opening up a second section or room.

In many food and beverage operations, the physical environment where service is created and delivered has shifted from a severely cost-efficient, staid appearance to a high-quality, lifestyle-oriented, comfortable environment. More food and beverage operations are coordinating design elements (e.g., lighting, furnishings) with their menus and uniforms. In addition, guests expect flexibility in the physical environment, for privacy, socialization, quick service, or other desires. The physical environment has a fundamental and dramatic impact on a guest's feeling of comfort and, ultimately, the guest's overall experience.

The design of every food and beverage facility starts with the concept. A small, family-oriented restaurant is a much different concept than an operation that will serve more than 2,000 students per day on a college campus. It's important to develop the concept with the requirements of prospective guests in mind. Part of the concept definition includes the vision (i.e., What do you want to create?) for the operation and all of its components. The proposed menu will dramatically affect the concept. Conceptual planning should also attempt to take into account every detail of the guest's food and beverage experience, which for most operations will begin in the parking lot, may include valet parking, and will continue into the place where guests are first greeted, the lounge, the dining room, the restrooms, banquet facilities, and any other area of the operation that guests may encounter. It cannot be emphasized enough that guest preferences must be taken into account in the design of all areas.

One of the most frequent errors designers and other planners make is to underestimate the amount of space needed, particularly in the kitchen, which must accommodate lots of cooking and preparation equipment, walk-in coolers and freezers, shelving, aisles, and so on. It is tempting for designers to shortchange the kitchen spaces in favor of the dining room, since the dining room is often viewed as a source of revenue while the kitchen is not. However, to do so would possibly hamper the ability of the operation to provide what the people in the dining room (i.e., the guests) need and desire. So there must be a balance in the design between nonpublic space and public space.

Another part of design planning at the conceptual stage is to check out the competition, particularly those food and beverage operations that serve the same guests that the new concept is trying to attract.

Designers must keep in mind that today's guests want a genuine, not a phony, experience, and one that appeals to the entire range of the senses—from seeing and hearing to touching, smelling, and tasting. Seeing includes colors, lighting, and materials in the various spaces. Hearing encompasses the entire acoustic environment, from the background music to the level of excitement generated by the noise made by the various conversations of the guests themselves. (Whether a quiet or a lively atmosphere is desired will drive many design decisions.) Touching is brought into play by the variety of materials and textures used in the guest spaces. Smelling the many odors within a food and beverage operation should reassure guests that the food is fresh and delicious, and the operation is clean. Tasting the food and beverage products completes the guests' tour of the operation via their senses. All of these aspects must be taken into account at the conceptual stage as the proposed operation's owners, managers, and designers work out exactly what the new facility will be like.

Once the design is completed, construction begins. Any changes to the design at this point will be costly, so it is important to get it right initially. Once architects develop a schematic, detailed plan from the conceptual plan and contractors get involved, change orders are expensive and can lead to serious cost overruns. Taking the extra time up front to get the design right is time well spent. This approach to design is less costly in the long run.

Many of the following sections on design pertain mostly to independently owned and operated food and beverage operations. For chain restaurants and other chain food and beverage operations, most if not all design decisions and plans are made by specialists at chain headquarters. However, it is still useful for all food and beverage managers to understand the principles and processes that go into making design decisions.

Planning an Effective Dining Area

Properly designed dining areas require an organized planning process to ensure that:

1. Guest needs and expectations are considered foremost.
2. Dining areas are flexible, to allow changes as guest needs and expectations evolve.
3. Dining areas have the proper appeal and ambience.
4. A maximum return on the investment in space is realized.
5. The layout allows for the efficient flow of staff members and guests.
6. Simplified procedures for performing required tasks are possible.
7. Dining areas provide safe work space for staff members and public access space for guests.
8. Dining areas adhere to the food safety, cleaning, and maintenance standards the operation requires.
9. Dining areas lend themselves to low maintenance costs.
10. Dining areas are energy-efficient and ecologically friendly.
11. Dining areas are designed to support the service staff and efficient operations.

Effective dining area design takes time, and it generally requires the specialized knowledge of several people as the process progresses. These people should form a **dining area planning team.** The owner/manager and the dining area manager should be on the team to help make decisions that affect guest-contact areas. In many instances, an architect is part of the team. The team may also require a food and beverage facility consultant, interior decorator, and other specialized designers. People with backgrounds and experiences ranging from managing operations to designing them are needed to develop the best plan for a dining area.

One of the first steps in the planning process is to determine just what the completed design must accomplish and who it is intended to attract. A high-check-average dining area requires a luxurious ambience, which includes a generous allocation of floor space per guest; the costs of this ambience are included in the prices guests pay. While the atmosphere of a low-check-average dining area must be comfortable and pleasant in order to enhance the dining experience, it does not require elegance or spaciousness. The key is for the design to meet the needs of the guests that the food and beverage operation is seeking to attract. One method the planning team can use to understand the needs of guests is **market analysis**—a detailed study of potential guests and their wants, needs, and expectations.

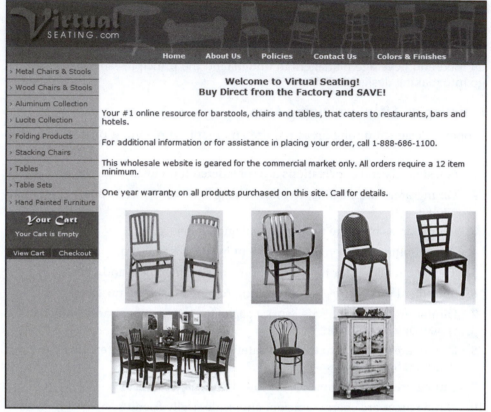

Virtual Seating (www.virtualseating.com) offers an online catalog to restaurateurs and others interested in purchasing chairs or stools for their food service facility. (Courtesy of Virtual Seating, Brooklyn, New York)

Guests care about design, according to a *Restaurants & Institutions* magazine survey of 1,000 restaurant guests. When asked what they would change about the layouts of their favorite restaurants, these guests said, among other things:

- "I'd change the layout of the tables."
- "Put the bar in a more discreet location."
- "More restrooms."
- "Make it bigger, so there's not such a long wait when I go."

Managers contemplating a change to their operation's design should ask their guests for suggestions, then listen carefully to what they say.

In commercial food and beverage operations, economic viability depends on profit. A feasibility study is needed to ensure that an operation's design is cost-effective and has the potential to help the operation be profitable. For example, commercial food and beverage operations base their estimated income on the anticipated turnover of guests and the expected check average. Seating capacities in dining areas affect the number of guests that can be served—and, therefore, affect potential income.

The planning team must also assess cost estimates for dining area plans. Not only is the dining area space itself expensive, but the furniture, fixtures, and equipment necessary to furnish it properly also add to the expense.

Members of the dining area planning team should identify the activities that must be performed to meet the guests' and the operation's objectives, then determine the space and equipment required to perform those activities. In part, this task involves an analysis of the flow of guests and staff through the operation.

Preliminary layout and equipment plans will help the team allocate available space. Preliminary conceptual plans show the proposed arrangement of equipment, traffic-flow aisles, and the relationship of each area to the other. When the team is at the point of examining preliminary floor plans, members can assemble basic cost estimates and make any adjustments needed to bring the project in line with the funds that have been budgeted for it.

When members of the planning team have reviewed, modified, and approved all preliminary conceptual plans, they can produce schematic blueprints for the dining area and prepare specifications for the necessary equipment. They will use these documents to request price quotations and select contractors and distributors for the project. Construction and installation tasks follow, according to a mutually agreed-upon schedule.

The planning process involves many steps and many people. Since a design and construction project usually requires a large commitment of capital funds, a great deal of planning is required to ensure that the project's goals are met without unwelcome financial surprises.

Selecting a Designer

When selecting a designer, managers should allow ample time to review the credentials of several individuals representing a number of design firms. Managers should use the following criteria when selecting a designer:

- *Membership in the American Society of Interior Designers (ASID).* Ideally, the designer should be a member of ASID. Each ASID member has a formal, accredited education and professional experience, and has successfully completed a comprehensive two-day examination. This association stresses high standards of ethical conduct.

- *Education.* Managers should inquire about the degrees that a designer holds, the institutions that granted them, and the designer's major field of study.

- *Experience.* Does the designer have experience in food and beverage design? Is he or she knowledgeable about food and beverage systems? With which food and beverage organizations has he or she worked? Managers should ask for references and contact them.

- *Portfolio.* Professional designers generally have many photographs, drawings, and other information illustrating their creative skills. Managers should examine a designer's portfolio to see if they like what the designer has done in the past.

- *First impressions.* Does the designer appear to be professional? Is he or she a good communicator? Does it appear that the designer understands what the managers want? Do the managers believe the designer can do the job?

- *Contacts.* With which distributors does the designer work? What services will the designer provide and what additional work will others need to do? Do the managers have any problems using the distributors suggested by the designer?

- *Design fees.* What will the designer charge? What additional fees will the managers need to pay to others as a result of the designer's contacts?

- *Budget.* Does the designer think he or she can deliver the design within budget?

These criteria can be modified to address the unique characteristics of any food and beverage organization.

A professional designer will provide a number of ideas for consideration by the design team, but to help a designer come up with good designs, managers must be candid about all details of the organization. Who are its guests and potential guests? What are the organization's menu and marketing concepts? What are its economic concerns? What are the elements that the owner/manager does and does not like in food and beverage design? Effective communication is important.

Trends in Design

Although design trends are numerous and ever-changing, we will consider five trends that will likely have a lasting effect on various types of food and beverage establishments.

Homelike Atmosphere. The designers of many food and beverage operations are attempting to create a homelike atmosphere to attract potential guests away from the comforts of their own homes. They do this by using natural colors and materials to achieve a casual and inviting atmosphere.

Entertainment. Today, dining out often means entertainment. Some theme restaurants use animatronics, antiques, or movie or music memorabilia to entertain, create emotional connections with guests, and build a link between other popular guest interests and dining.

Coupled Areas. A third design trend is the movement toward **coupled areas**— that is, areas that combine the dining area with a distinct bar section and a service space to handle guest overflow. Large dining spaces are being divided into smaller spaces, such as a bar that is more intimate and enclosed, an informal primary dining area, and a flexible atrium space that can be used for breakfast, light lunches, after-dinner business, and overflow from the bar or dining area. The coupling concept provides guests with the opportunity for pre-dinner cocktails in the bar, dinner in the dining room, and after-dinner drinks with entertainment in the atrium. It furnishes a food and beverage organization and its guests with flexibility.

Small Operations. Small food and beverage operations succeed by developing unique identities as intimate gathering places that appeal to very targeted markets. Usually they are also more profitable for their owners/investors. "Small" sometimes also means having more integration between the kitchen and dining area. Exhibition kitchens featuring guest-contact-area pantries, open grills, and rotisseries are designed to appeal to all of the guests' senses, as well as add interest.

As kitchen areas shrink, mobile and multiuse food preparation equipment become more popular. Easily moved equipment creates flexibility in kitchen layouts, increasing efficiencies. Multiuse equipment is flexible enough to meet changing demands. For example, a single deck oven can be used for baking, pizza making, and roasting. Many designers favor multiuse equipment over single-use equipment.

A kitchen workstation analysis prior to final design is recommended. Such an analysis identifies the tasks to be performed in each workstation and details what support is needed from other kitchen areas/workstations. Ideally, the person or people working in a workstation should not have to leave it to accomplish their tasks. Therefore, workstations are being designed to include storage space for tools, tableware, and food supplies.

Accommodating Solo Guests. Designers are coming up with unique solutions to meet the needs of solo guests. Some food and beverage operations feature a special table—known as a "chef's table," "singles' table," or "family table"—that typically seats 8 to 12 single guests, who may or may not know one another. An operation can draw single guests to such a table by serving chef specialties at the table before they make it onto the standard menu or by providing a higher level of service. Some chef's tables feature special themes or tabletop grills that make the dining experience entertaining and unique.

Space Requirements

Determining space needs for dining service is always challenging, since such requirements depend on many factors that are unique to each organization: the number of meals planned, the exact tasks the staff members must perform in dining areas, the equipment staff will use, and the amount of dining space needed for guests. The facility must also have space for storing service supplies, exercising sales income controls, and carrying out various guest-contact activities.

When estimating the total size of a facility, planners often start with the number of seats. Income and profit levels—both of which relate to the number of meals that will be served—determine the feasibility of the organization's design.

Food and beverage managers in the academic market and the business and industry market are able to estimate the number of meals they will serve with relative ease. They base their estimates on past history or, if they are dealing with new facilities, on a percentage that similar facilities have calculated as their averages. The number of meal periods or day parts that the organization will offer will also affect the dining area's seating capacity. For example, if a school has an enrollment of 1,000 students, 80 percent of whom eat three meals a day, and it offers four specific dining periods for each meal, then it must design a seating capacity of 200 for the dining area (80 percent of 1,000 students = 800 per meal; 800 students divided by 4 meal periods per meal = 200 seats per period).

Exhibit 1   Range of Estimated Square Feet for Dining Area Space

Facility	Dining Area Space (Per Person)	
	(Square Feet)	(Square Meters)
Table service	12–18	1.1–1.7
Counter service	16–20	1.5–1.9
Booth service	12–16	1.1–1.5
Cafeteria service	12–16	1.1–1.5
Banquet service	10–12	.9–1.1

Lodging property managers plan the size of their dining areas according to estimates of guestroom occupancy, the extent to which the local community will use their dining facilities, and the number of banquet functions they expect to schedule.

To determine the dining space required for any type of organization, managers must consider the number of guests that will be seated at one time and the total square feet allowed per seat. Exhibit 1 is a base from which specific calculations can be made. Today, designers generally recommend 15 or 16 square feet (1.4 to 1.5 square meters) per seat for casual-dining restaurants. Fine dining is generally designed at 20 square feet (1.9 square meters) per seat. For fine dining with a great deal of tableside service, the recommendation is 22 to 24 square feet (2 to 2.2 square meters) per seat. For bars, the recommendation is 20 square feet (1.9 square meters) per seat. The actual space that must be allowed is determined by the amount of comfort guests desire and by any applicable government regulations that dictate aisle width and space requirements (such as the amount of unobstructed space in front of emergency exits). Design and placement of cashier stations, host stands, sidestations, and salad bars also affect the amount of space a specific facility needs.

Traffic Flow

Traffic flow refers to the movement of staff members, guests, products, supplies, and refuse through an operation. Managers must address issues related to the movement of people and items through support areas as well as through guest-contact areas.

Exhibit 2 is an example of a preliminary drawing developed during the early planning stages of a food and beverage operation. It is not drawn to scale. Instead, it is the kind of drawing that planners make to help them decide how to locate various spaces relative to each other. In the design represented in this exhibit, guests would typically enter the operation through the main entrance (#1). (The operation may find a separate entrance—#2—helpful for banquet guests only.) The location of the emergency exit (#3) will be dictated by local ordinances. Parking areas should be situated on the side of the building near where the entrances are located.

Exhibit 2   Example of a Preliminary Drawing

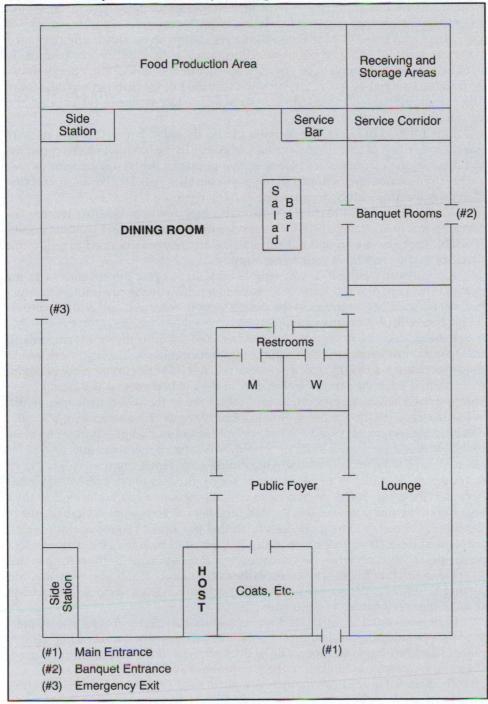

(#1)   Main Entrance
(#2)   Banquet Entrance
(#3)   Emergency Exit

As Exhibit 2 shows, when guests use the main entrance to the facility, they can either go to the lounge or register with the host for service. Some people do not like to go through a lounge to get to the dining room; therefore, a separate entrance to the lounge area is useful. Managers might even design an outside lounge entrance; however, such an entrance might cause problems with sales income control. To avoid the potential problem of guests who "drink and dash," the operation can be designed so that guests must enter and exit the lounge through a public foyer. Upon entering the facility, guests may have access to coat racks, telephones, and restrooms.

In Exhibit 2's drawing, the designer placed the salad bar so that dining room guests and, when practical, small groups of guests in the banquet rooms could use it. Likewise, the restrooms are placed so that guests in the banquet rooms as well as the dining room can use them. (If this plan complies with local municipal codes, it can significantly reduce non-revenue-producing space.)

A service corridor provides service staff quick access to banquet rooms. The service bar is in an area that facilitates service to dining room and banquet guests. (Portable bars also are an option.) Sidestations are in areas designed to reduce the distance that servers must walk to get supplies.

As you study Exhibit 2, you may be able to suggest improvements to the design. This is part of the value of a preliminary drawing. A preliminary conceptual drawing allows members of the design team to react to it and make improvements before final blueprints are prepared.

Exhibit 3 focuses on service staff members and the tasks they must perform. (If the operation requires servers to enter order information on a guest check before they enter the food pickup area, a precheck register [#1] or a similar piece of equipment should be in the servers' traffic flow to the kitchen area, as it is here.) Upon entering the kitchen, servers can unload tableware in the soiled dish area, which is located close to the kitchen's dining room entrance. Planners using a similar design, however, must consider noise control factors so that guests at tables close to the kitchen door are not inconvenienced. Service staff members may also move clean glasses, flatware, and plates to the dining area. However, they will not need to transport clean dishes as frequently as they will need to remove soiled dishes from service areas; therefore, the clean dish storage area can be located slightly away from the traffic flow of service staff members. The clean dish storage area in Exhibit 3 is close to the food service line so that personnel can move clean plates, bowls, and other items to the line as needed, but staff members still have reasonable access to the area when they must transport clean dishes to the dining room.

The operation might use an **expediter** (#2) to coordinate the ordering and plating activities of the service and production staffs. This individual is placed in front of the serving line.

Cold items such as salads or desserts might be available from a pantry area. In some operations, a production staff member retrieves such foods when servers place orders; in others, servers get these items directly. If the latter method is used, the pantry area should be close to the dining room exit.

The planned procedures for income control might require a food checker (#3). This individual might review plate presentations and confirm that items ready

Exhibit 3   Traffic Flow Patterns in Support Areas

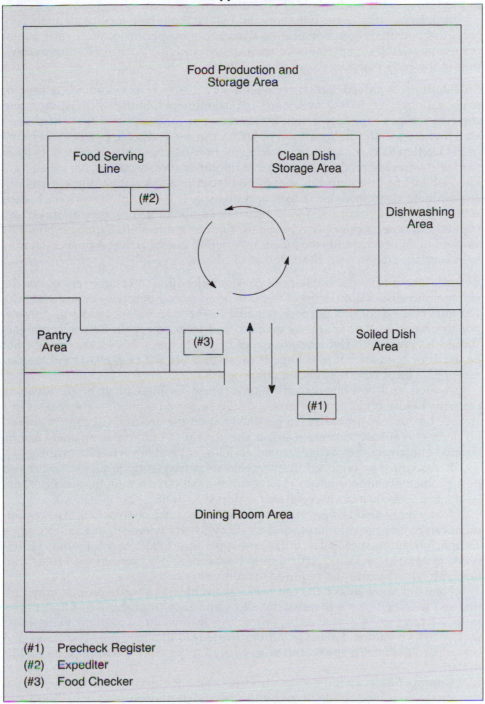

(#1)   Precheck Register
(#2)   Expediter
(#3)   Food Checker

for service have been entered properly on guest checks. Food checkers are usually located close to the kitchen's exit to the dining area.

A drawing such as the one shown in Exhibit 3 can help facility planners consider the potential impact of locating work areas in specific locations. We cannot overemphasize the importance of thoroughly studying such preliminary drawings in the early planning stages of a facility.

Sidestations. A **sidestation** (also called a server station or sidestand) is used to store supplies—including tableware, ice, condiments, butter and creamer, and some beverages—for easy access by servers and others. Sidestations help keep staff members in the dining area, where they can see and serve guests, rather than in the kitchen or in storage areas looking for needed items. It is important to store food and beverage products in ways that minimize contamination. No soiled napkins, tableware, or equipment should be placed in a sidestation; these items can contaminate clean food, beverages, and utensils. It is helpful to stock each sidestation with enough cups and saucers, bread and butter plates, serving trays, tray stands, and other service items to last through an entire shift. Supplies should be stocked in an orderly and convenient way before guests arrive. A busperson may help keep the station neat, clean, and stocked.

Refuse. One additional traffic-flow consideration must not be overlooked: the storage and disposal of refuse. Refuse is often stored outdoors before removal. Containers used for this purpose must be insect- and rodent-resistant, durable, nonabsorbent, leak-proof, easily cleaned, and in good repair. Refuse containers should be lined with wet-strength paper or plastic bags. Bags alone should not be used for outdoor refuse storage because they are not pest-resistant. Outdoor receptacles must have tight-fitting doors or lids.

A food and beverage organization's refuse facilities must be of adequate capacity. Refuse containers not in use should be stored outdoors on a rack or in a storage box at least 18 inches (46 centimeters) off the ground. Containers should be cleaned regularly to prevent insect and rodent infestation. Containers can be cleaned effectively with a combination of detergent and hot water or steam.

Refuse must be removed from service areas frequently to prevent odor and pest problems. Outdoor refuse storage areas must have a smooth, nonabsorbent base (such as asphalt or concrete) that is sloped to drain.

Many large food and beverage operations use trash compactors. Such equipment can reduce the volume of solid waste by up to 75 percent. In addition, some compactors automatically deodorize and apply insecticides to solid waste. Liquid waste generated by a compactor should be disposed of as sewage. Suitable facilities with hot water are also required for compactors.

New developments on the compactor scene include a waste-reduction system that reduces the volume of refuse by 8 to 1 and then produces a moist, compact pulp. All food waste as well as paper refuse is thrown into a partially water-filled tank in which cutting devices grind the waste into fine particles. The water and waste particles form a slurry that is dewatered to produce a damp, popcorn-like material.

Composting is another form of refuse reduction and re-use. Using natural decomposition, biodegradable organic material is transformed into humus, a soil-enriching compound. Composting systems have great potential in food and beverage organizations, which typically have 60 to 80 percent biodegradable waste. Some food and beverage organizations that compost report reductions in landfill fees ranging from 33 to 50 percent.

Recycling has become an important consideration for many food and beverage organizations. Quick-service establishments such as McDonald's and Taco Bell are sometimes accused of generating large amounts of paper, plastic, and polystyrene refuse. Many quick-service chains have responded by reducing the weight and thickness of their containers or by completely changing the materials they use. Many quick-service operations are using recycled paper for cash receipts and place mats.

Other Design Considerations

Other design considerations include food safety and sustainability.

Food Safety and Design. Design plays a part in helping an operation in its food safety efforts. The design of a kitchen, for example, should locate hand sinks where they will be most likely used; easily accessible hand sinks remind kitchen staff and others to frequently wash their hands.

Another example of how good design can promote food safety is when designers take into account the flow of cleaned and soiled tableware, pots and pans, and kitchenware when they are designing kitchen and warewashing spaces, so that cleaned and soiled items are less likely to come into contact with each other. (If they come into contact there is a risk of cross-contamination, leading to a potential foodborne disease outbreak.) Likewise, raw and cooked foods must not come into contact with each other. Therefore, when space allows, designers should design separate refrigerated storage areas for raw and cooked foods.

Sustainable Design. Sustainable design uses the Earth's resources (energy, materials, water) in such a way that the use does not diminish the resources permanently; rather, the resources are replenished and preserved for future generations. Using recycled or reclaimed building materials, reducing energy and water usage during construction, and working closely with local suppliers are examples of sustainable design practices.

LEED (Leadership in Energy and Environmental Design) certification is often a goal of sustainable design. Created by the U.S. Green Building Council many years ago, the LEED certification process employs a rating system and a detailed checklist that encourage designers and builders to create buildings that are "green"—that is, buildings that help sustain environmental and human health by saving energy, materials, and water during their construction and use. When an operation adopts LEED practices and becomes LEED certified, the operation not only saves money over time, it also is able to promote its LEED certification to guests.

Sustainable design calls for energy-efficient equipment. Energy-saving equipment that is given ENERGY STAR™ ratings saves 10 to 30 percent on energy usage compared to nonrated equipment. Some states and localities give a tax break to operations that purchase ENERGY STAR™ equipment.

Changing from traditional to compact fluorescent light bulbs is another sustainable design strategy that can save as much as 75 percent on energy. In addition, the expected useful life of compact fluorescent light bulbs is up to ten times greater than the useful life of traditional bulbs. To promote more energy savings, some operations install occupancy sensors in rooms so that if the room is unoccupied, the lights are automatically turned off.

Decor: Creating the Right Environment

As mentioned earlier, the dining area environment must be compatible with an organization's menu and service style. All too often, owners think yesterday's steak house can become today's pizzeria by simply hanging up a few pictures of the Italian landscape, or believe their Olde English pub can become an 1880s frontier saloon just by changing the uniforms the staff wears. While extreme, these examples point to the tendency on the part of many managers to pay scant attention to the atmosphere created in a dining area. Successful managers do not overlook the fact that details such as fixtures and equipment make their own contributions to dining area decor and ambience. For example, stainless steel and glass no more fit into an Early American theme than heavy wooden furniture fits into a modern twenty-first century motif.

Service staff members themselves contribute to a dining room's atmosphere. Guests in a gourmet dining room find it appropriate, for instance, for the manager to wear a tuxedo; the ambience of a dining room with a Mexican or other ethnic theme is enhanced when servers wear national costumes.

When trying to create the perfect dining environment, managers should not neglect proper function. Furniture, fixtures, and equipment must be easy to clean and durable. Concerns about costs and whether replacement products will be available in the future must be addressed. Managers should purchase products of commercial quality that can withstand the wear and tear to which guests and staff will expose them. Very delicate or rare decorative items should not be used unless they are out of reach and well-anchored. (Unfortunately, it is a fact of life that guests and staff alike may take such decorations for souvenirs if they are not vandal-proofed.) Many people do not treat furnishings in public areas the same way they do in their own homes; furnishings must be able to withstand misuse or mischief.

Color. The colors used in dining areas profoundly affect the atmosphere of those areas. The important consideration for managers is, "What do our guests want?" The answer to that question may be far different from the feelings that an operation's managers or owner has about specific colors and color combinations. For this and many other reasons, it is wise to involve a professional interior decorator in the design of dining areas and to depend on him or her for color-coordination ideas.

Generally, a toned-down color scheme is perceived as being more upscale than vibrant, bright colors. Violets, blues, and light greens are cool colors that tend to make guests feel relaxed; facilities emphasizing leisurely dining may want to use these colors. In contrast, warm colors such as reds, yellows, and oranges are stimulating; they encourage activity. Therefore, these colors subtly encourage fast table turnover.

Rooms that receive little sunlight should have light and warm colors, while those receiving a lot of sunlight should usually balance that by using cool, dark colors. Colors also have an impact on perceived room size. Light colors make a room appear larger; dark colors tend to make a room look smaller. Dark colors also make ceilings look lower than they are. When one wall is a very bright color, the adjoining wall should be more neutral, perhaps in the same shade or tint.

Carpet. Design trends in dining rooms have favored hard floors for the past decade or so. However, there has been a resurgence in the popularity of carpeting in full-service food and beverage operations. This is due in part to the new colors and interesting patterns of modern carpets. Carpeting can be used to reinforce the image and theme of a food and beverage operation; managers should choose a carpet design that complements the rest of the operation's decor. In contrast to the noisy dining rooms of uncarpeted spaces, carpeted dining rooms reduce noise and give guests a more peaceful experience.

Another advantage to carpet is that it is easier on the legs and backs of staff members who spend a lot of time traveling to and fro. Carpeting, if it is installed and maintained properly, also is less likely to contribute to a slip and fall accident for a guest or a staff member. If someone does slip and fall, chances are that the resulting injury will be less than if it had occurred on an uncarpeted floor. There is also a lower risk of tableware breaking if it is dropped on a carpeted floor.

How a carpet is constructed is an important factor because it affects the look as well as the wearability of the carpet. Woven cut-pile construction is preferred because it wears better than loop-pile construction and has a more elegant look. Today's woven cut-pile carpet comes in many color choices and is easy to vacuum and clean.

When making an investment in carpeting, durability is a factor that food and beverage managers should keep in mind. Expensive carpeting tends to be more durable than carpeting that is lower in cost and quality. Designs in less-expensive carpeting are usually not woven in but simply printed on the surface of the carpet; these carpets fade and become tired-looking more quickly.

From a sustainability standpoint, carpeted floors can be produced from recycled, environmentally friendly materials. For example, wool can be utilized to create a woven cut-pile carpet.

Wall Coverings. Choosing a proper wall covering is as important as choosing the right floor covering. As with carpeting, wall coverings can be chosen to reinforce the image and brand of the operation. Also like carpeting, the colors and patterns, flow and sequence of wall coverings affect the guests' overall dining experience.

Painted walls are usually the least expensive. A trend is to use low-VOC (volatile organic compound) paint. Whatever paint is used, it is important that it be washable, because the inevitable spills on the walls will need to be removed quickly. Sometimes paints are applied in a faux finish to mimic a countertop or a tile finish. Paint can also be used to create wall art—a mural, for example, that can bring the focus to one particular wall in the dining area. It is important to consider that if a mural becomes spotted or stained, it may be impossible to clean it without damaging it.

Wallpaper is another option when it comes to wall covering. Here the use of contrasting or complementary textures is possible. Vinyl wallpaper is easy to clean and may be more durable than other wall coverings. Fabric may also be used to cover walls; this gives the space a unique appeal.

Sustainable materials such as wood and bamboo may be chosen as wall coverings. Wood gives walls a feeling of natural warmth; bamboo is growing in popularity along with the sustainable movement. Another wall covering option is laminates produced from metal or plastic. Tiles are yet another option that can be used to create interesting design patterns and flows of colors. Tile is durable and comparatively easy to maintain.

Decorations. Small pictures, wall hangings, and other decorations should be used in small rooms. Large items should be used with care, even in large rooms. When decorations from various periods or with differing styles are selected, a unified effect can be created if their colors are coordinated. Such decorations should be selected carefully if they are to help portray a theme. For example, a nautical theme might include anchors, oars, buoys, fishing nets, seashells, and models of ships. Such items as copper cooking utensils, saloon signs, whiskey barrels, and branding irons might be appropriate for an Old West theme. Of course, a number of popular restaurants have made a theme out of combining mismatched and eclectic decorations. Yet even these apparently haphazard collections of items are chosen with care to appeal to specific, targeted markets. Whatever the theme or style, careful thought and often considerable expense are necessary to decorate dining areas effectively.

Lighting. As with color, the effects that can be created with lighting are endless. Lighting helps create a certain comfort level for guests, contributing to an operation's ambience and mood. Adequate lighting is essential for tasks such as reading the menu. Adequate lighting also improves safety by lessening the chance of an accident for guests as well as staff members.

Light intensity is measured in units called **footcandles**. A footcandle equals one lumen per square foot. (A *lumen* is equal to 0.0015 watts.) Footcandles are measured with a light meter. Most lighting engineers and occupational safety and health inspectors recommend 50 to 70 footcandles of light for dining areas.

While too much light can negatively impact a dining area's ambience and atmosphere, too little is also undesirable. Guests can get annoyed when there is insufficient lighting in dining areas. One solution is to add track lighting or use dimmer switches to achieve flexibility.

Ventilation. Ventilation equipment is designed to remove smoke, fumes, condensation, steam, heat, and unpleasant odors from kitchens and dining areas. Sufficient ventilation also helps to maintain comfortable temperatures and minimizes dust buildup on walls, ceilings, and floors. When ventilation fails or underperforms, the entire dining experience may be spoiled. State and local building codes and, in some jurisdictions, public health officials dictate specific ventilation requirements for each area of a food and beverage operation.

The major food and beverage ventilation problem is the transfer of unpleasant odors and fumes from the kitchen to public areas such as dining, meeting, and

The Psychology of Lighting

More than any other design element, lighting creates the mood of a space. Lighting can also reduce or enhance the effectiveness of all other design elements. Here are some guidelines for lighting:

- Sparkle enhances appetite and encourages conversation. Chandeliers, candles, and multiple pin lights can achieve sparkle. Light bouncing off mirrored surfaces, wet-looking finishes, and shiny tableware also create sparkle.

- Dark shadows appear hostile; small patterns of light appear friendly.

- Brightly lit architectural surfaces tend to move people along and are therefore good for high-volume facilities.

- Light should always flatter people. If lighting makes flesh tones look good, it also tends to make food look good.

- Design lighting in transition zones so guests entering or leaving a facility on a sunny day can still see.

- Use a dimmer switch to permit mood changes:

  - Brightness and cheer for breakfast

  - Restfulness for lunch

  - Animation for early evening

  - Romance for dinner

banquet rooms. This problem usually occurs when the kitchen ventilation system is improperly designed. To avoid ventilation problems, air from the kitchen must be exhausted to the outside and replaced with an equal amount of "tempered" (fresh outside) air.

Sound. While some designers use sound to create a feeling of excitement, some guests are annoyed when the dining area is too noisy. Sound problems can be alleviated by decor changes as well as design modifications. Acoustical panels, carpeting, and draperies can be added to service areas to dampen noise. Items such as padded furniture and fabric wall hangings can be included in the decor to further reduce unwanted noise. Noisy kitchen activities (dishwashing, for example) can be placed in locations farthest from the dining room. This may be particularly important to operations with many older guests, who may wear hearing aids that amplify background sounds.

Music. Operations use music and the volume at which it is played to convey a subtle message to guests. For example, classical music softly played has the effect of telling guests to "relax and take your time," while rock or pop music played at relatively loud volumes conveys the message "hurry up and eat and leave." Music helps put guests into a certain mood or state of mind. When a food and beverage operation provides a sense of privacy and calmness through booths, unobtrusive service, and relaxing music, it encourages guests to linger and enjoy—and also spend more.

Exhibit 4   Recommended Guidelines for Furniture

Chairs

Armrest height: 25 inches (64 centimeters) or less

Seat back angle: 100 to 110 degrees

Seat depth: 20 inches (51 centimeters)

Seat height: 18 inches (46 centimeters)

Seat width: 20 inches (51 centimeters)

Place-Setting Allowances

Minimum width (average): 24 inches (61 centimeters)

Minimum width (fine-dining): 27 inches (69 centimeters)

Minimum width (self-service): 21 inches (53 centimeters)

Tables

Minimum depth allowed for each place setting: 14 inches (36 centimeters)

(Measure from the edge of the table in front of the guest toward the middle.)

Diameters of round tables for comfortable seating:

> 3 guests: 32 inches (81 centimeters)
>
> 4 guests: 40 inches (102 centimeters)
>
> 6 guests: 50 inches (127 centimeters)
>
> 8 guests: 60 inches (152 centimeters)

Height—29 to 31 inches (74 to 79 centimeters)

Furniture. In most food and beverage operations, furniture—chairs in particular—must be comfortable to guests. (On the other hand, some quick-service operations use hard chairs to discourage guests from lingering after their meals.) Dining area chairs should have a slightly more upright back than lounge chairs. While high-backed chairs can be designed to be upright, low-backed chairs should recline a bit. Chair arms should be low enough to easily slide under tables.

Tables must be balanced so that they do not teeter and rock when used, irritating guests. While booths may be part of the decor because they take less space, guests may not like the inability to move their seats closer to or farther from the table. Some guidelines for furniture are presented in Exhibit 4. The goal of a food and beverage operation is to make the right decisions about furniture and other design and decor elements so that guests become loyal repeat guests who tell their friends and associates about the operation and their experiences there.

The Exterior. As with an operation's interior spaces, the design of an operation's exterior should reinforce the operation's concept. The landscaping and physical look of the exterior help set the stage for what is expected in the interior. Guests must be able to read and understand a concept design even before they set foot inside the front door. This sets the stage for a positive, memorable dining experience.

Many food and beverage operations have outdoor dining areas. Not only is outdoor dining in pleasant weather enjoyable to guests, it also changes the statement that the outside of the food and beverage operation makes to guests and prospective guests. An outdoor dining area filled with guests says excitement, there is a crowd here, please join us! If at all possible, the outdoor dining area should be visible from the street so potential guests driving by and guests who have parked in the parking lot and are making their way to the entrance see it. The outdoor dining option should be further reinforced with a question from staff members who greet guests: "Would you prefer outdoor or indoor dining?"

One of the mistakes some designers make in designing and creating an outdoor dining space is purchasing inexpensive furniture (tables, chairs, umbrellas) rather than furniture that is commercial-grade. Commercial-grade furniture is designed for more frequent use and is built to withstand abuse. This furniture is evaluated by the American Society for Testing and Materials (ASTM). Any furniture purchased for outdoor dining should meet ASTM performance and safety standards. Since typically it is not practical to move outdoor furniture indoors each evening (it would be too labor intensive, for one thing, and cause too much wear and tear), outdoor dining furniture must be able to withstand not only the use of many guests but also the abuse of nature—sun, rain, temperature fluctuations, wind, and so on.

Cleaning

Cleanliness is important to food and beverage guests. When the tabletops and items stored there—salt and pepper shakers, condiment containers, and so on—are not clean, it gives the guests the feeling that perhaps other areas of the operation (e.g., the kitchen) are not clean. Cleaning is important not only because of the way that dirty facilities create negative impressions on guests, but also because food safety depends on cleanliness. In addition, the useful life of furniture, fixtures, equipment, and facilities is prolonged through regular cleaning and maintenance.

For cleaning to be effective, cleaning standards and procedures must be put in writing and be part of an orientation training program at the start of a new staff member's career with the food and beverage operation, with ongoing refresher training at regular intervals. Each section or area of a food and beverage operation has unique cleaning requirements. What is essential in the dining room, for example, must be listed on a checklist so it is easy for staff members to follow and use. The same is true for the kitchen, outdoor dining areas, parking lot, restrooms, hallways, receiving and outside storing areas, and all other areas of the operation.

Details are critical in the cleaning requirements. It is not just "clean the oven"; it is "clean, degrease, and shine the exterior of the oven each morning before the oven is lit." All levels in an area should receive cleaning attention. Lighting fixtures and the tops of the stall dividers in restrooms should be cleaned as well as the other restroom areas, for example. The corners where flooring meets the wall must be cleaned. Describing in sequence how these areas should be cleaned is necessary not only for the operation's staff members; it is also necessary if a cleaning service is retained to clean the operation when guests are not present, frequently in the wee hours of the morning.

There are areas in the kitchen where grease buildup is not only unsightly, it is dangerous because it can lead to grease fires. For that reason the exhaust hoods over cooking equipment must be on a regular cleaning schedule. Often this work is contracted out. As with any other contract service (e.g., snow removal, linen rentals) used by a food and beverage operation, it is important that management regularly double check the contractor's performance to evaluate whether the operation is getting its money's worth for the services it is purchasing. A cleaning service, above all, must be trustworthy. The operator wants to trust the service to get the cleaning tasks completed, as well as trust the service with the security of the operation while the service's employees are present in the operation.

Some food and beverage operators hire a cleaning service to do the heavy cleaning (such as cleaning the ventilation hoods) and utilize the operation's staff to do the less-demanding cleaning—sweeping, mopping, polishing, and so on. Whether the cleaning service cleans all areas, or the operation's staff is responsible for doing so, or the cleaning responsibilities are shared by both groups, there must be follow-up by management to determine that the cleaning is actually being done and done correctly. The same is true of equipment and facilities maintenance. The move to systematize the cleaning and maintenance of equipment and facilities makes sense, given the turnover of staff members, supervisors, and managers that is typically seen in a food and beverage operation. When those who have experience doing the cleaning or supervising the cleaning leave the operation, a checklist for each area combined with written requirements will help ensure that regular cleaning and maintenance continues on. Cleaning is a matter of guest satisfaction, contributes to the safety of both staff members and guests, and prolongs the useful life of the operation's assets.

In the following sections we will discuss cleaning issues for food and beverage facilities, including exterior and interior inspections, dining area cleaning programs, and cleaning schedules and procedures.

Exterior

Exterior masonry surfaces are typically brick, concrete block, stucco, stone, or a combination of these materials. These surfaces are porous and attract water, dirt, and scale. Cleaning such surfaces is difficult, but cleaning them is important if an operation is to make an excellent first impression. Cleaning methods vary according to the climate, the type and condition of the masonry, and the design of the building.

Exterior masonry cleaning solutions are frequently applied with spray guns and hoses. During cleaning operations, glass and aluminum exterior surfaces, as well as plants and shrubs, must be protected. Damaged masonry surfaces can be repaired and waterproofed with special chemical compounds. These applications not only enhance the building's appearance, but also prolong its life and increase its value.

Clean parking lots and sidewalks contribute to a positive first impression as guests approach a facility. Ideally, parking lots and sidewalks should be easy to maintain and should not cause dust problems. The type of outdoor cleaning equipment used depends on the area to be cleaned, the type of debris to be removed, the frequency of cleaning, and the financial resources available. There are a number of different types of sweeping machines for parking lots and sidewalks. Air-recycling machines create an air blast to loosen debris; the debris is then pulled up through a hose and deposited in a collection tank. Broom-vacuum machines loosen debris with a rotating broom and deposit it into a hopper. Push-vacuum machines are used primarily to clean large, outdoor surfaces; they function much like standard vacuum cleaners.

Managers deciding when to clean the exterior of a building should begin with a walk-around inspection. This is particularly important for establishments in locations with long, cold, and wet winter seasons. The sides of the building should be inspected for dirt and grease buildup from the kitchen's exhaust system. If the exterior façade needs repainting, timing is critical. In wet climates, for example, damp wood must first be allowed to dry before repainting.

Cobwebs, dead bugs, and other debris should be removed from windowsills. Outside windows can be cleaned with a squeegee dipped in a bucket of water with a drop of dish soap.

Plants and shrubbery should be inspected; damaged parts should be pruned and dead plants replaced. Shrubs can be washed with a mild soap-and-water solution. Spring and summer perennials can add freshness to building exteriors.

Interior

Managers should inspect the interior of the building at the same time as the exterior. In addition to highlighting specific areas in need of cleaning, managers should make a safety check as well. Problems can occur when:

1. Entryways are slippery on rainy or snowy days.

2. Rug edges are exposed (they can trip staff members and guests).

3. Furniture and equipment are highly flammable.

4. Wooden furniture has splinters or metal furniture has sharp edges.

5. Glass doors and windows are neither covered nor marked to prevent people from walking into them.

6. Steps are not lighted and there are no railings.

7. Public areas are so dark that people cannot see as they move about.

8. Furniture is unstable and tips easily.

9. Fixtures or hanging decorations are too low for tall people.

10. The emergency-exit traffic-flow pattern is obstructed.

The list of examples could continue and will vary from organization to organization. However, the point is that managers should be aware of safety issues. When staff members are performing cleaning activities, they should be alert for potential safety problems as well.

Dining Area Cleaning Program

Managers know that dining areas should be cleaned routinely to meet sanitation standards. Furthermore, cleanliness is of paramount importance to guests. Against this need for cleanliness must be balanced the costs involved. For example, the frequency and method of routine cleaning affect how much money must be spent on service supplies.

Managers must develop an effective **cleaning program** and monitor the routine cleaning and maintenance of furniture, fixtures, and equipment in dining areas. They should establish written cleaning procedures for each area and piece of equipment in the organization. The procedures should briefly describe the cleaning task, list the steps in the task, and indicate the materials and tools necessary. Each manager should monitor cleaning procedures in his or her department. This follow-up demonstrates to staff members that management cares about maintaining a clean environment.

Staff members are more likely to follow cleaning procedures if they understand their importance. Training in cleaning procedures must be systematic to be effective. Proper training reduces the risks associated with cleaning. Training should cover cleanliness standards and recommend methods, products, and equipment. Only after proper training should staff members be assigned regular cleaning duties.

Cleaning Schedule

A written **cleaning schedule** further systematizes a cleaning program by indicating who is responsible for each cleaning task and how often the task should be performed. The schedule should be based on a survey of an operation's cleaning needs. If a survey has never been done, managers and staff members should work together to identify cleaning needs for each area in the facility by asking such questions as:

- What needs to be cleaned/maintained?
- Who is responsible for the cleaning/maintenance?
- When is the area or equipment to be cleaned/maintained?
- What safety and sanitation precautions must be observed?
- How should the cleaned item be stored to prevent resoiling (if applicable)?
- Who is responsible for supervising and checking the work?
- What must be done to reduce risks?

Once the survey is completed, a cleaning schedule can be developed.

Cleaning Procedures

Who should perform cleaning activities? Typically, service staff should clean tabletops, the interiors of sidestation refrigerators, and the sidestations themselves. But what about vacuuming floors, washing table bases, cleaning window ledges, and other jobs? The general manager, working closely with other managers who help oversee the cleaning of the facility, should make these decisions. Job descriptions should indicate the specific tasks that staff members in each position are to perform, and cleaning/maintenance schedules should be developed with these activities in mind. It is a good general policy to require all staff members, regardless of position, to clean when they are otherwise unoccupied with guest service activities.

Because differences of opinion often occur over which cleaning procedures are best, managers should obtain advice from experts. Some general guidelines are provided in Exhibit 5. Managers should also consult with manufacturers and distributors of cleaning equipment and supplies for their recommended cleaning procedures.

Curtains, Draperies, and Upholstered Furniture. Careful vacuuming will prolong the lives of curtains, draperies, and upholstered furniture. Some fabrics may be hand-washed when soiled, while others must be dry-cleaned. Because of the variety of fabrics used for these items, it is best to follow the manufacturer's cleaning recommendations.

Use hot-solvent cleaning for silks, crushed velvet, and other fine fabrics. This method minimizes color bleeding and shrinkage. Portable equipment can be used for in-place cleaning.

A dry-foam soil extractor may be used to shampoo and remove spills from upholstery. An extractor can also be used to clean carpeted stairs. Some upholstery fabrics can be made soil-resistant by applying a protective coating after cleaning.

Blinds and Shades. Blinds and shades should be vacuumed or dusted frequently. Some metal and plastic surfaces can be washed with a mild detergent solution and rinsed with clean water. Cloth or fabric materials may require specialized cleaning chemicals and procedures.

Glass. Glass is easy to clean and maintain, and the necessary equipment and supplies are relatively inexpensive. Squeegees come in a variety of sizes; brass models with hardwood handles are more durable than aluminum versions. An ammonia-and-water solution cleans glass effectively. Alcohol may be added to the water as an antifreeze when outside windows are cleaned at temperatures below freezing. Commercial glass cleaners are also effective.

Periodic, scheduled cleaning of glass surfaces is necessary to prevent excessive soil buildup. Some operations contract their outdoor window cleaning to professional companies. This reduces the safety risks for the operation's own staff members.

Floor Coverings. Food and beverage establishments should use floor mats and runners at entrances and in heavy traffic areas to keep carpets clean. Mats and runners also prevent wear, help control noise, and reduce the risk of slip-and-fall accidents. Routine care of mats and runners includes daily light vacuuming, thorough weekly vacuuming, periodic shampooing, and regular deep-cleaning with steam or some other method.

Carpeted heavy-traffic areas and dining spaces where spills often occur may require vacuuming after each meal and shampooing with a dry-foam chemical each night. As is true with hard floors, a wide variety of supplies and equipment

Exhibit 5   How to Care for Materials in Your Establishment

Acoustical Tile

Remove loose dirt or dust with a vacuum or soft brush. A gum eraser will remove most smudges. Soft chalk can cover many small stains. More thorough cleaning can be accomplished with wallpaper cleaners or mild soap cleaners. Excessive water and abrasive rubbing actions should be avoided; using a soft sponge is best.

Aluminum

Wash with a mild detergent solution; avoid common alkalis, which dull the finish. A fine abrasive may be used periodically; rub in one direction, not in a circle.

Bamboo, Cane, Rattan, Wicker

Wash with a mild soap or detergent solution. Rinse with clear water, and dry. Periodic shellacking maintains a natural finish.

Brass

Acidic brass cleaners and polishes are used for unfinished brass. Wash lacquered brass with a mild detergent solution, rinse, and wipe dry.

Carpets

All types of carpets must be vacuumed regularly to extend their useful life. Deep cleaning can be accomplished with impregnated granular cleaners, shampoos, or extraction chemicals with a dry residue to prevent rapid resoiling.

Ceramic Tile

Use a neutral soap or detergent. Remove excess cleaning solution, rinse, and dry thoroughly. Avoid alkalis, salts, acids, and abrasive cleaners. Some soap cleaners may result in a soap-film buildup.

Glass

Wash with a special window-cleaning concentrate dissolved in water. Use a squeegee or chamois to dry glass.

Leather Furniture

Wash with a neutral soap or saddle soap.

Linoleum

Wash with a mild detergent solution; rinse with clear water. Remove water and dry as rapidly as possible. Avoid alkaline solutions.

Painted Surfaces

Immediately remove spots with a cloth wrung from a detergent solution.

Wood Floors

Wood floors must be sealed if they are to be maintained properly. Dust-mopping and damp-mopping sealed floors are usually all that is necessary if a regular maintenance program is followed. Polishing with a floor wax may be required. Some soft woods can be seriously damaged by strong solutions of soap or detergent and water. Oils, grease, and strong alkalis are also harmful. Avoid using excessive water, and always remove water as rapidly as possible.

is available to clean carpets. Managers should contact experts in carpet cleaning to obtain specific information about the best products and procedures to use.

Lighting Fixtures. Lighting fixtures, including lamps and shades in dining areas, should be cleaned routinely by dusting or vacuuming, as dust is the primary cause of reduced light intensity. Bulbs or lamps should be replaced promptly when necessary. Small glass fixtures can be removed for cleaning; large fixtures, including chandeliers, are usually cleaned in place (this difficult job is sometimes turned over to an outside contractor).

Wall Coverings. Because walls in dining areas can be covered with paint, tile, wallpaper, wood, foil, cork, or other materials, managers must be aware of the various methods used to clean these materials.

It is wise to dry-dust walls before washing them. When it is time for washing, staff members should use the cleaning solution recommended by the manufacturer of the wall covering. They should apply a weak solution to a small, hidden part of the wall as a test before cleaning the entire wall. Generally, a water-based cleaning solution—strong enough to be effective without damaging the wall covering in any way—should be used.

Badly soiled areas may need to be saturated with the proper solution. Heavily soiled areas should be rinsed and wiped immediately. Washing marble, ceramic, plastic, metal, acoustic, and papered walls requires special procedures. Seeking advice from an expert is best in these cases.

 Key Terms ———————————————————————————————————————

cleaning program—Formalized cleaning procedures for each area and piece of equipment in a food and beverage operation. The procedures should briefly describe the task, list the steps in the task, and indicate the materials and tools necessary.

cleaning schedule—A written schedule indicating who is responsible for each cleaning task and how often the task should be performed.

composting—Recycling that transforms biodegradable organic material into humus, a soil-enriching compound.

coupled areas—A design trend toward combining the dining area with a distinct bar section and a service space to handle guest overflow.

dining area planning team—A specially selected group brought together to develop an efficient and practical design for a food and beverage interior. The team typically includes the owner/manager and the dining area manager, an architect, a food and beverage facility consultant, an interior decorator, and other specialized designers.

expediter—A staff member who acts as a communication link between kitchen personnel and servers. The expediter must know cooking times, coordinate them to sequentially deliver cooked foods for pickup, and provide leadership during rush periods.

footcandle—A unit of illumination; it is the intensity of light on a surface that is one foot away from a standard candle.

market analysis—A survey or study that depicts the demographic characteristics of the market area to be served by a proposed food and beverage operation. If used in an existing establishment, such a study may report on menu or design changes guests desire.

sidestation—A service stand in the dining area that holds equipment (such as a coffee maker) and service supplies (such as tableware and condiments) for easy access by servers and other staff members. Also called a server station, sidestand, or workstation.

traffic flow—The movement of staff members, guests, products, and supplies through an organization.

 # Review Questions

1. What criteria can help managers select a facility designer?

2. What design trends are affecting food and beverage operations?

3. What are some important design and decor issues for food and beverage establishments?

4. How does color affect guests?

5. How does lighting affect guests?

6. What questions might appear on a cleaning needs survey?

7. How should cleaning responsibilities be assigned and monitored?

 # Case Studies

How Many Supplies? What about Furniture and Fixtures?

Paul Logan, a recent graduate from a hospitality program at the local college, has just gone to work for Apex Restaurant Consultants. The firm specializes in assisting operations to develop and refresh their concepts to generate maximum appeal to their market(s).

Bruce Reed, Paul's supervisor, has assigned Paul to develop a supplies inventory list for the 150-seat Barbary Coast restaurant, which is a new client for Apex. The inventory is to include the optimum number of dishes (all kinds of china), glasses (water, wine, and cocktail), flatware, and linen.

Moreover, Paul must consider the number and types of tables (how many deuces, fours, rounds, squares, etc.), how high they should be, and of what dimensions. Chairs also need to be considered in terms of type (arm, armless, cushioned, etc.), and dimensions (how high, how wide, what is the angle of the back to the seat, etc.). High chairs and booster seats need to be added into the mix as well.

In addition to the 150 seats in the main restaurant, there is a cocktail lounge that has 12 bar stools and six booths; each booth can accommodate four people comfortably. The restaurant has a wine list with 16 wines. The food sales to beverage sales ratio is projected to be 75:25. There are no banquet rooms in the facility.

Discussion Questions

1. If you were Paul Logan, where do you start?

2. Develop a list of the number of supplies (china, glasses, etc.) that should be the opening inventory for the restaurant.

3. Develop a list of the considerations and dimensions for the tables and chairs.

4. What other factors go into this type of decision-making (what is the age of the market you are attempting to attract, what will be pre-set on the table, as that affects table size, etc.)?

This case was taken from William P. Fisher and Robert A. Ashley, *Case Studies in Commercial Food Service Operations* (Lansing, Mich.: American Hotel & Lodging Educational Institute, 2003).

Clean with an In-House Crew or Outsource to a Contract Cleaning Service?

Francesca Almanza was riding a wave of exhilaration after a meeting with her staff members about cleaning the restaurant themselves. For years, Emma's Family Restaurant, a 200-seat independent casual-dining operation, had been cleaned by an outside cleaning company, but Francesca had sold Emma, the owner, on the idea of cleaning with an in-house crew. Emma had asked Francesca to look for ways to cut costs. Francesca told Emma that with the current high level of staff member loyalty at the restaurant, the staff members would care about their cleaning work more than any outside crew would. Perhaps if the cleaning were done in-house, the occasional, mysterious thefts of liquor, food, and dishware would end. Cooks would no longer arrive to find detergents splattered on their prep areas and floors still wet. Tips would increase as guest satisfaction with the restaurant rose, and the predicted savings of $400 per month would eventually have an effect on paychecks, if all went well.

At the meeting with her staff members, Francesca had sold them on the idea, too. Francesca had asked for volunteers for the first work crew, and so many staff members had volunteered that she easily filled the crews for the first two weeks. Staff members had left the room talking about what they would do with their extra pay and how much better the restaurant would look when they had cleaned it. Even some of those who hadn't volunteered talked about the higher tips they'd get from impressed guests.

On the first night of in-house cleaning, Francesca explained in detail the crew's responsibilities. "The kitchen and dish room floors should be swept, soaped down, scrubbed with these deck brushes, and squeegeed dry. The mats should be cleaned with these detergents and brushes, then hosed down. Let me show you how to use these detergent dispensers." Francesca demonstrated their use. "When you're cleaning these areas, make sure you get behind the equipment, down around the legs of tables and machines. All the walls will need to be washed like this." She showed them the methods and materials. "Now, the bar area is going to need at least three of you. Some spills can be pretty stubborn. If you let them soak a while in this detergent, they should come up easier. While you're waiting for those to soak, you can vacuum the carpets and polish the brass in the front of the house. Two of you will work on the bathrooms...." Francesca spent many of the first few nights training and coaching crews on all their tasks.

The first couple of weeks saw success overall in the in-house cleaning program. Francesca, other staff members, and guests all saw a noticeable difference in the appearance of the facility. Francesca even invited Emma in for an extra inspection, and Emma was pleased with what she saw. Emma did notice that the inventory of cleaning chemicals was much lower than it should have been for that time of month. Francesca assured her that she would talk to cleaning crews about how much detergent to use. When Emma asked about thefts, Francesca reported that nothing had been missing since the switch to in-house crews. "That settles that question," said Emma. "If we ever do go back to a contract crew, we won't use that company again."

In the beginning of the third week of the in-house cleaning program, some servers who had not worked on cleaning crews came to Francesca with a complaint. They said that those servers who were on the cleaning crew were not cleaning up their sidestations before they started their night cleaning duties. That Monday, one of the cleaning-crew members called and said he'd be late for work. Two others were late reporting for morning shifts that week, and they also called in sick two nights apiece. The quality of cleaning began to show signs of slipping. When Francesca urged the cleaning crews to be more thorough, she found that some began neglecting their regular duties in the last hour of the regular shifts so they could start cleaning early. And service quality began to sag.

One night Francesca noticed some cleaning crew members using a certain chemical without wearing goggles. She reminded them that goggles were required while that chemical was being used. "I know the goggles can be annoying, but they're for your own safety," she told them.

On Saturday morning of the third week of the program, a cook reported to Francesca that someone had taken two bites out of a dessert in the line cooler, and the bartender reported two bottles of beer missing. Francesca made a mental note to start keeping an eye on the cleaning crews. She was beginning to feel the fatigue of the 15- to 17-hour days she'd been working since the new program began. Cleaning in-house may save money, but it sure doesn't save time and effort in supervision, she thought to herself.

Francesca performed her regular monthly inspection the next week. She noticed that the vents, light fixtures, and blinds that were supposed to be cleaned weekly were not very thoroughly cleaned. At least that's about the same as what the contract crew did, she thought. She asked some staff members how they were feeling about the in-house cleaning program. One server said, "I don't know, I was all excited about it at first, but it's really hard work. And I wonder whether guests will really notice some of the stuff I'm cleaning." Overall, Francesca found that staff members were less enthusiastic about the program than they had been before, but several still thought it was worthwhile. Francesca noted that while crews were using less detergent than they had used initially, they were still using more than they should.

That night Francesca happened to overhear a conversation between two of the cleaning-crew members who were working on the floor of the bar. "Wow, the pay for this cleaning is great. Now I just wish I had time to spend it."

"Yeah, I'm worried that it'll come out equal to my old wages—I'm having to spend more on food, laundry, clothes—"

"Hey, why are you working so hard on those spills? Don't you remember what Francesca said about letting the detergents soak them?"

"Yeah, but—"

"'Yeah, but' nothing. With your back hurting you like it is, you should let the soaking do the work."

"This floor is always disgusting. Sweet-and-sour mix, strawberry daiquiri mix, ice cream, ashes—it just seems like no matter how long you let this stuff soak, you still have to scrub."

"You and I are pluggers: we plug away at this, and we're not afraid of hard work. But one of the cooks was complaining that he's a culinary something-or-other and that it's demeaning for him to scrub walls. I said to him, 'If you don't like it, why did you sign up?' He said, 'I didn't think I'd have to do this kind of stuff.' I don't know what he was thinking, when this is a cleaning crew."

"Well, I'm not afraid of hard work, but just the same, I think I hear my bed calling."

Francesca walked away and thought to herself, This schedule is taking a toll on all of us. I'll go figure out how much we're saving, and I'll tell the staff and Emma about it tomorrow—that will get our spirits up again. Francesca figured out the savings and was shocked to see that, in the first four weeks of the program, they had saved only $50—far less than the $400 she had hoped for. Okay, so the savings haven't hit the target, but what about tips and guest satisfaction? She tallied the month's reported tips and guest satisfaction ratings and found both about the same as what they had been with the contract cleaning crew. Francesca sat back and took a deep breath. Maybe it was time to review the situation.

First, Francesca identified the reasons that savings weren't what they should have been. Then she thoroughly evaluated the in-house cleaning program, examining all the facts at her disposal. Finally, she thought back to the pros and cons of the old contract cleaning arrangement. A couple of hours later, she began preparing a formal report for Emma on the in-house cleaning program.

Discussion Questions

1. What did Francesca learn from the experience of switching from contract cleaners to in-house cleaners?

2. Should Francesca continue the in-house cleaning program or should she recommend to Emma that the restaurant go back to a contract cleaning company? Why?

3. If Francesca decides to recommend contract cleaning, what information should she include in her presentation to Emma to back her position?

The following industry experts helped generate and develop this case: Christopher Kibit, C.S.C., Academic Team Leader, Hotel/Motel/Food Management & Tourism Programs, Lansing Community College, Lansing, Michigan; and Jack Nye, General Manager, Applebee's of Michigan, Applebee's International, Inc.

 References

Alexander, Shawn. "Restaurant Design: Sometimes Great Food and Service Just Aren't Enough." *Restaurant Report*. January 26, 2009. www.restaurantreport.com/departments/biz_eight_design_tips.html

Allen, Aaron. "Restaurant Design." *Restaurant Report*. www.restaurantreport.com/departments/biz_restaurant_design.html

Boss, Donna. "Getting to Great Kitchen Design." *Foodservice Equipment & Supplies*. February 2007. 60(2): 16.

Crowell, Chris. "Flexible Social Spaces Redefine Design Boundaries." Hotel World Network. May 2009. www.hotelworldnetwork.com

Gorodesky, Ron, and Eileen Madigan. "Restaurant Design: Elements of Successful Restaurant Interior Design." *Restaurant Report*. January 26, 2009. www.restaurantreport.com/features/ft_design.html

Katz, Jeff B. "Form and Function: Nine Basic Principles of Good Restaurant Design." *Restaurant Startup & Growth*. August 2007: 43–46.

Levin, Amelia. "Designing a Food-Safe Kitchen." *Foodservice Equipment & Supplies*. March 2008. 61(3): 24.

Lobmeyer, Lori, and Milford Prewitt. "Ambience: Design Key to Attracting Consumers' Palates." *Nation's Restaurant News*. October 4, 2004. 38(40): 68.

Luebke, Patricia. "Clean as a Whistle: Hiring a Cleaning Service for Your Restaurant." *Restaurant Startup & Growth*. December 2008. 5(12): 21–27.

———. "Outside Sales: Buying Furniture for your Restaurant's Outdoor Space." *Restaurant Startup & Growth*. August 2008. 5(8): 49–51.

———. "Rethinking Carpet for Your New Restaurant." *Restaurant Startup & Growth*. July 2007: 8 & 10.

———. "Take It Outside: Big Sales in the Open-Air Market." *Restaurant Startup & Growth*. August 2008. 5(8): 45–47.

———. "Ways to Reduce Your Environmental and Utility Costs Impact Today." *Restaurant Startup & Growth*. March 2009: 19–22.

Lockyer, Sarah. "Designing for Sales: A New Wave of Building Modernizations." *Nation's Restaurant News.* December 10, 2007. 41(49): 14.

Scarpa, James. "Green Operations, Designs Can Lead to Significant Savings." *Nation's Restaurant News.* December 22, 2008. 42(49): 22.

Spaulding, Karen. "If These Walls Could Talk: Making a Statement With Front-of-the-House Wall Coverings." *Restaurant Startup & Growth.* July 2008. 5(7): 44–47.

"Yes, Sustainability Does Affect the Foodservice E&S Community." *Foodservice Equipment & Supplies.* September 2007. 60(9): 24.

Internet Sites

For more information, visit the following Internet sites. Remember that Internet addresses can change without notice. If the site is no longer there, you can use a search engine to look for additional sites.

Aceray LLC
www.aceray.com

American Society of Interior Designers
www.asid.org

American Tables & Seating
www.atsfurniture.com

American Trading Company
www.amtradeco.com

Andy Thornton Ltd
www.andythornton.com

Art Marble Furniture
www.artmarblefurniture.com

Bago Luma
www.bagoluma.com

Carroll Chair
www.carrollchair.com

Chameleon Furniture
www.sundrydesignsolutions.com

Chicago Booth Manufacturing
www.chicagobooth.com

Derry's Ltd
www.derrys.com

DHC Furniture
www.dhcfurniture.com

Ecolab
www.ecolab.com

Ecopreneurist
www.ecopreneurist.com

Emuamericas LLC
www.emuamericas.com

ENERGY STAR Guide for Restaurants
www.energystar.gov/ia/business/
small_business/restaurants_guide.pdf

Factory Direct Wholesale Inc.
www.factorydirectwholesaleinc.com

FHG International Inc.
www.fhgi.com

Foodservice World
www.foodserviceworld.com

Gar Products
www.garproducts.com

Glac Seat Inc.
www.glacseat.com

Grand Rapids Chair Company
www.grandrapidschair.com

Green Restaurant Association
www.dinegreen.com

Grosfillex
www.grosfillexfurniture.com

J. H. Carr & Sons
www.jhcarr.com

Louisiana Contract Furniture LLC
www.louisianacontract.com

National Restaurant Design
www.nationalrd.com

Nation's Restaurant News
www.nrn.com

Pat Kuleto Restaurants
www.kuleto.com

Pavar Inc.
www.pavar.com

Puccini Group
www.puccinigroup.com

Rapids Foodservice Contract and
  Design
www.rapidscontract.com

Restaurant Report
www.restaurantreport.com

ServiceMaster Clean
www.servicemasterclean.com

Trica
www.tricafurniture.com

TriMark Foodservice Design,
  Equipment and Supplies
www.trimarkusa.com

Unichairs Inc.
www.unichairs.com

U.S. Green Building Council
www.usgbc.org

Waymar Industries
www.waymar.com

Whitman Lane Hospitality Consulting
  & Design
www.whitmanlane.com

Chapter 10 Outline

Competencies

1. Describe the critical role of food sanitation in food and beverage operations, summarize the HACCP concept of food safety and other food safety considerations, and describe the role of staff members in ensuring food safety in relation to food handling, personal hygiene, equipment use, and facility cleanliness. (pp. 381–397)

2. Outline preventive steps for workplace safety and the appropriate follow-up and investigation procedures when accidents occur; identify the three common types of fires and how to extinguish them; and list recommendations for handling vandalism, robberies, bomb threats, and bioterrorism. (pp. 398–413)

3. Describe the fundamentals of sound nutrition, how food and beverage operations are addressing guest requests for healthier food options, food allergy issues, and the changing guest attitudes toward smoking. (pp. 413–420)

4. Discuss legal issues of concern to food and beverage operations. (pp. 420–425)

10

Sanitation, Safety, Security, Health, and Legal Issues

ALL SERVICE STAFF must pay close attention to sanitation, safety, security, health, and legal issues. While local, state, and federal laws require food and beverage operations to protect food and beverage products from contamination, prevent guests from being exposed to unsafe procedures and situations, provide no-smoking sections in dining areas, and accommodate guests who have physical disabilities, these and other legal mandates are only the beginning. Professional food and beverage staff members must do everything in their power to ensure that guests' experiences are enjoyable and safe. That obligation goes far beyond the dictates of laws.

In more practical terms, food and beverage managers, staff members, and owners do not want headlines about a food-related illness traced to their operations. Experienced managers know that a kitchen or dining room emergency can adversely affect business, so they ensure that safety and security training is a major part of their standard operating procedures for all service staff. Today's food and beverage operations must find ways to please guests who want nutritious and "heart-healthy" menu items when dining out. And legal issues such as serving alcohol responsibly and sexual harassment cannot be ignored by food and beverage managers and staff. In the following sections we will discuss these and other issues as they affect food and beverage operations.

Sanitation Issues

Imagine a newspaper headline or a radio, TV, or Internet lead story that starts out by stating: "Toxic Tuna Burgers Give Guests Histamine Poisoning," or "Ill Cook Serves *Shigella* to Customers at a Mexican Restaurant," or "Restaurant Chain Pays Each Hepatitis Victim $25,000 to $75,000." Each of these situations actually happened and resulted in media coverage as well as lawsuits against the food and beverage operations that served the food. Large-scale, nationwide recalls of food have made headlines as well. When more than 1,000 people became ill after eating raspberries from Guatemala, Guatemala's crop of raspberries was banned from the United States for the year. A wholesale food supplier recalled 25 million pounds of ground beef because of food safety concerns. A bacteria outbreak almost forced the Jack in the Box quick-service chain out of business after a number of guests died or became seriously ill after eating hamburgers infected with *E. coli* at its restaurants. As you can see, food sanitation issues are high on the list of concerns for guests and owners of food and beverage businesses.

The U.S. Centers for Disease Control and Prevention (CDC) report that millions of people in the United States are stricken with **foodborne illnesses** each year; thousands die from them. Yet the dining public is not fully aware of the scope of potential food dangers.

The source of many foodborne diseases is infectious microorganisms, or pathogens. A foodborne illness also results when food containing toxic or toxigenic (toxin-producing) agents is eaten. The potential problems are getting worse as a result of emerging new pathogens, the increase in imported foods grown and processed under loosely monitored conditions, and the rising number of food and beverage staff members whose training does not impart a basic understanding of personal hygiene and sanitation. Add to these risks hot, humid kitchen production areas, language barriers among food and beverage staff, and high turnover, and you have the potential for dramatic increases in foodborne illnesses. Food and beverage businesses must develop risk management programs to help control sanitation risks.

Food Safety Risk Management Program

A **food safety risk management (FSRM) program** focuses on reducing overall sanitation risks by identifying the risks at each control point in a food and beverage operation. In an FSRM program, standards and procedures for each control point are presented as they relate to the four resources under a manager's control: inventory, people, equipment, and facilities. A resource evaluation is necessary at each control point. The result is a systematic approach to managing risks. Exhibit 1 presents an FSRM diagram for baked chicken. The right side of the diagram indicates the appropriate FSRM actions that reduce risks at each control point.

Inventory is an essential management resource because it is converted into revenue and, ultimately, into profits. Inventory in a food and beverage operation normally consists of food products, beverages, and nonfood items such as table linens and cleaning chemicals. Inventory control is a vital link in an operation's cost and quality control systems; inventory items are assets that must be protected from spoilage, contamination, pilferage, and waste.

Because the hospitality industry is labor-intensive, people are an especially important resource. It is management's responsibility to train staff members in proper sanitation practices. Failing to properly train staff members undermines an operation's FSRM program and jeopardizes the health of guests and staff members, as well as threatens the operation's bottom line.

Equipment selection is important to an FSRM program, as are the proper cleaning and maintenance of each piece of equipment. In addition, facility design and layout have a great impact on the success of an FSRM program. At an FSRM program's core, however, is the FDA *Food Code*.

The *Food Code,* last published by the U.S. Food and Drug Administration (FDA) in 2001 and updated in 2004, represents the FDA's best advice for a uniform system of regulations to ensure that food prepared at retail establishments is safe and properly protected and presented. The *Code* provides guidelines designed to minimize foodborne illness and promote guest and staff member health, manager knowledge, safe food, nontoxic and clean equipment, and acceptable levels of sanitation where food is served. It also promotes fair dealing with guests.

Exhibit 1 Sample FSRM Diagram for Baked Chicken

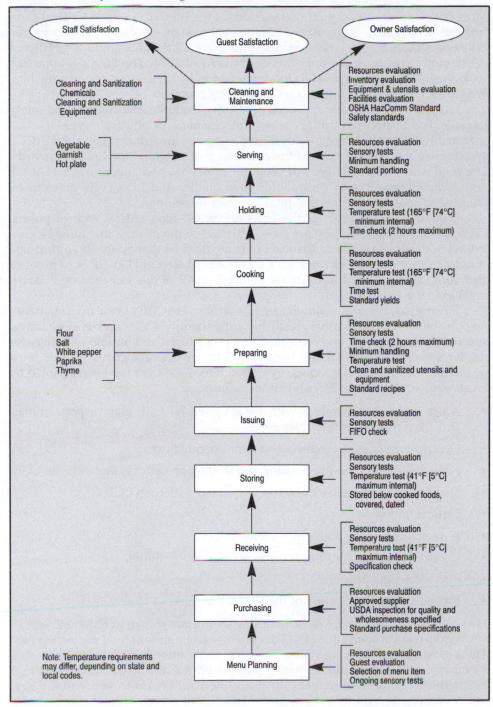

Hazard Analysis Critical Control Point System

Most FSRM programs are modified versions of the **Hazard Analysis Critical Control Point (HACCP—pronounced "Hah-sep") system** developed jointly by the Pillsbury Company, the United States Army Natick Laboratory, and the National Aeronautics and Space Administration (NASA) in 1974. The HACCP approach seeks to eliminate safety risks in food processing by identifying the specific hazards at each important point in a food production system.

HACCP is a systematic approach to identify, evaluate, and control food safety hazards. Food safety hazards are biological, chemical, or physical agents that are reasonably likely to cause injury or illness in the absence of their control. HACCP systems are designed to prevent the occurrence of potential food safety hazards. The food safety risk management program presented here incorporates HACCP and complements it with controls for food quality and food costs that can be adapted to any organization that produces and serves food.

Hazard analysis serves as the basis for establishing **critical control points.** Critical control points (CCPs) are those activities in the process that must be controlled to ensure food safety. Critical limits are defined that establish appropriate standards that must be met at each CCP. The final step in HACCP is to monitor and verify that potential hazards are controlled. All of this information is documented in the **HACCP plan.**

The preparation and maintenance of a written HACCP plan is management's responsibility. The plan must detail hazards, identify CCPs and critical limits, specify CCP monitoring and recordkeeping procedures, and outline a strategy for implementing the plan. An approved HACCP plan and associated records must be on file at the food and beverage operation if the *Food Code* has been adopted by local regulatory agencies. Documents to include are:

- A list of the staff members who are assigned HACCP plan responsibilities, and what their responsibilities are

- Descriptions of food products and their intended uses

- Flow diagrams of food-processing and serving procedures that indicate CCPs

- Hazards and preventive measures associated with each CCP

- Critical limits

- A description of the plan's monitoring system

- Corrective action plans for deviations from critical limits

- Recordkeeping procedures

- Procedures for verification of the HACCP system

HACCP information can be recorded using the format shown in Exhibit 2.

When used properly, the HACCP system is an important food protection tool. The key to success is staff training. For each preparation step they perform, staff members must know which control points are critical and what the critical limits are at these points. Management must routinely follow up to verify that everyone is complying with the critical limits. In a recent survey of food and beverage

Exhibit 2   Sample HACCP Information Reporting Form

Process Step	CCP	Chemical/ Physical/ Biological Hazards	Critical Limit	Monitoring Procedures/ Frequency/ Person(s) Responsible	Corrective Action(s)/ Person(s) Responsible	HACCP Records	Verification Procedures/ Person(s) Responsible

Source: Adapted from the FDA 2001 *Food Code.*

managers, the major obstacles to HACCP training effectiveness were finding suitable training materials, the cost of training, and staff members resistant to change. In HACCP training and practice, the role of staff members cannot be overemphasized, particularly front-line staff members who must understand and implement HACCP principles.

The HACCP system emphasizes the food and beverage industry's role in continuous improvement. Rather than relying on periodic inspections by regulatory agencies to point out deficiencies, food and beverage operations should engage in their own ongoing problem-solving and prevention. The HACCP system clearly identifies the food and beverage operation as the final party responsible for ensuring the safety of the food it sells. It requires analysis of preparation methods in a rational, scientific manner. Management is responsible for maintaining records that document adherence to the critical limits that relate to the identified critical control points. This results in continuous self-inspection. The HACCP system also helps managers and staff determine the operation's level of compliance with the *Food Code.*

An operation's HACCP plan must be shared with local regulatory agencies, which must have access to the CCP monitoring records and other data necessary to verify that the HACCP plan is working. With conventional inspection techniques, a regulatory agency can only determine conditions that exist during the time of the inspection. However, both past and current conditions can be reviewed when a HACCP approach is used. Therefore, regulatory agencies can more effectively ensure that food production processes are under control. Traditional approaches to inspection are reactive; HACCP is preventive.

The Seven HACCP Steps. The National Advisory Committee on Microbiological Criteria for Foods (NACMCF) has developed seven widely accepted HACCP steps.

Step 1: Hazard analysis. Hazard analysis identifies significant sanitation hazards, estimates the likelihood of their occurrence and severity, and develops preventive measures to improve food safety. Hazards can be categorized as biological, chemical, and physical. Biological hazards include bacteria, viruses, and parasites. Chemical hazards may be naturally occurring or may be introduced during food processing. Physical hazards are foreign objects found in food.

In the hazard analysis process step, management must ask and answer a series of questions for each control point in its flow diagrams of food-processing and serving procedures (see Exhibit 3). Once these questions are answered, preventive measures (which may be physical or chemical) can be taken to control hazards. For example, cooking sufficiently to kill pathogens is a physical preventive measure.

Step 2: Identify the CCPs in the food process. A critical control point is a step or procedure at which control must be applied to prevent, eliminate, or reduce to acceptable levels a food safety hazard. Some safety measures used at CCPs are cooking, chilling, recipe control, prevention of cross-contamination, and certain staff hygiene procedures (handwashing, for example). While there may be many control points in a food preparation and serving process (as shown in Exhibit 1), few may be *critical* control points. CCPs differ with the layout of a facility as well as with the equipment, ingredients, and processes used to prepare and serve a particular menu item.

Step 3: Establish critical limits for preventive measures associated with each identified CCP. A critical limit is a boundary of safety. Some preventive measures have upper and lower critical limits. For example, the temperature danger zone has a lower critical limit of 41°F (5°C) and an upper critical limit of 140°F (60°C); potentially hazardous foods should not be held within this range—41°F–140°F (5°C–60°C)—of temperatures.

Consider the cooking of freshly ground beef patties. Critical limit criteria in this instance would include temperature, time, and patty thickness. Each patty should be cooked to a minimum internal temperature of 155°F (68°C) for a minimum of 15 seconds if using a broiler set at 400°F (207°C). Patty thickness should not exceed one-half inch (2.6 centimeters). These three critical limit criteria must be evaluated and monitored regularly. There are other critical limit criteria for cooking freshly ground beef patties as well, including humidity, preservatives, and salt concentration.

Step 4: Establish procedures to monitor CCPs. Monitoring comprises a planned sequence of measurements or observations taken to ascertain whether a CCP is under control. Monitoring procedures should (1) track the HACCP system's operation so that a trend toward a loss of control can be identified and corrective action taken to bring the process back into control before a deviation occurs; (2) indicate when a loss of control and a deviation have actually occurred; and (3) provide written documentation for use in verifying that the HACCP plan is

Exhibit 3   Hazard Analysis Food Process Questions

1. **Ingredients**
   - Does the food contain any sensitive ingredients that are likely to present micro-biological hazards (e.g., Salmonella, Staphylococcus aureus), chemical hazards (e.g., aflatoxin, antibiotic, or pesticide residues), or physical hazards (stones, glass, bone, metal)?

2. **Intrinsic factors of food**
   - Physical characteristics and composition (e.g., pH, types of acids, fermentable carbohydrate, preservatives) of the food during and after the process can cause or prevent a hazard.
   - Which intrinsic factors of the food must be controlled to ensure food safety?
   - Does the food allow survival or multiplication of pathogens and/or toxin formation before or during the process?
   - Will the food allow survival or multiplication of pathogens and/or toxin formation during subsequent control points, including storage or consumer possession?
   - Are there similar products in the marketplace? What has been the safety record for these products?

3. **Procedures used for the process**
   - Does the procedure or process include a controllable step that destroys patho-gens or their toxins? Consider both vegetative cells and spores.
   - Is the product subject to recontamination between production (e.g., cooking) and packaging?

4. **Microbial content of the food**
   - Is the food commercially sterile (as is low-acid canned food)?
   - Is it likely that the food will contain viable spore-forming or nonspore-forming pathogens?
   - What is the normal microbial content of the food stored under proper conditions?
   - Does the microbial population change during the time the food is stored before consumption?
   - Does that change in microbial population alter the safety of the food?

5. **Facility design**
   - Does the layout of the facility provide an adequate separation of raw materials from ready-to-eat foods?
   - Is positive air pressure maintained in product packaging areas? Is this essential for product safety?
   - Is the traffic pattern for people and moving equipment a potentially significant source of contamination?

6. **Equipment design**
   - Will the equipment provide the time/temperature control that is necessary for safe food?
   - Is the equipment properly sized for the volume of food that will be prepared?
   - Can the equipment be sufficiently controlled so that the variation in performance will be within the tolerances required to produce a safe food?

(continued)

Exhibit 3 *(continued)*

- Is the equipment reliable or is it prone to frequent breakdowns?
- Is the equipment designed so that it can be cleaned and sanitized?
- Is there a chance for product contamination with hazardous substances, e.g., glass?
- What product safety devices such as time/temperature integrators are used to enhance consumer safety?

7. Packaging

- Does the method of packaging affect the multiplication of microbial pathogens and/or the formation of toxins?
- Is the packaging material resistant to damage, thereby preventing the entrance of microbial contamination?
- Is the package clearly labeled "Keep Refrigerated" if this is required for safety?
- Does the package include instructions for the safe handling and preparation of the food by the consumer?
- Are tamper-evident packaging features used?
- Is each package legibly and accurately coded to indicate production lot?
- Does each package contain the proper label?

8. Sanitation

- Can the sanitation practices that are employed adversely affect the safety of the food that is being produced?
- Can the facility be cleaned and sanitized to permit the safe handling of food?
- Is it possible to provide sanitary conditions consistently and adequately to ensure safe foods?

9. Staff member health, hygiene, and education

- Can staff member health or personal hygiene practices adversely affect the safety of the food being produced?
- Does the staff understand the food production process and the factors they must control to ensure safe foods?
- Will the staff inform management of a problem that could negatively affect food safety?

10. Conditions of storage between packaging and the consumer

- What is the likelihood that the food will be improperly stored at the wrong temperature?
- Would storage at improper temperatures lead to a microbiologically unsafe food?

11. Intended use

- Will the food be heated by the consumer?
- Will there likely be leftovers?

12. Intended consumer

- Is the food intended for the general public, a population that does not have an increased risk of becoming ill?
- Is the food intended for consumption by a population with increased susceptibility to illness (e.g., infants, the elderly, the infirm, and immuno-compromised individuals)?

Source: Adapted from the FDA 2001 *Food Code.*

working. Examples of measurements for monitoring include sensory observations (observations made via sight, smell, touch), temperature, and time.

Monitoring procedures must be effective to avoid unsafe food. When feasible, continuous monitoring is always preferable. Instruments used for measuring critical limits must be carefully calibrated and used accurately, and calibration records must be maintained as part of an operation's HACCP plan documentation. When it is not possible to monitor continuously, sampling systems or statistically designed data collection should be used. The most appropriate staff member should be assigned responsibility for monitoring each CCP and must be trained to be accurate. If an operation or product does not meet critical limits, immediate corrective action should be taken. All records used for monitoring should be initialed or signed and dated by the person doing the monitoring.

Step 5: Establish the corrective action to be taken when monitoring shows that a critical limit has been exceeded. Although food and beverage operations aim at perfection every time they prepare and serve food, problems or deviations from plan procedures sometimes occur. A corrective action plan determines the disposition of any food produced while a deviation was occurring, corrects the cause of the deviation, ensures that the CCP is back under control, and maintains records of the corrective actions taken.

Specific corrective action plans are required for each CCP. Corrective action procedures should be well documented in the HACCP plan. When a deviation occurs, more frequent monitoring may be required temporarily to ensure that the CCP is under control again.

Step 6: Establish effective recordkeeping systems that document the HACCP system. Recordkeeping is a very important part of the HACCP system. The level of sophistication of recordkeeping depends on the complexity of the food and beverage operation. The simplest effective recordkeeping system is the best.

Step 7: Establish procedures to verify that the HACCP system is working. Typically, there are four phases of verification. The first phase is scientific or technical verification that critical limits at CCPs are satisfactory. (This may be complex and may require expert assistance.) The second phase ensures that the HACCP plan is functioning effectively. It involves frequent reviews of the HACCP plan, review of CCP records, and verification that appropriate risk management decisions and product dispositions are made when production deviations occur. The third phase comprises documented periodic revalidations performed by staff members with HACCP plan responsibilities. The fourth phase is verification by the regulatory authority or authorities that have jurisdiction over the food and beverage operation.

HACCP plan verification procedures may include the following:

- Review of deviations and their resolutions, including the disposition of food
- Visual inspections of operations to observe if CCPs are under control
- Random sample collection and analysis
- Review of critical limits to verify that they can adequately control hazards
- Review of modifications to the HACCP plan

Managers should conduct HACCP verification inspections:

- Routinely as well as on an unannounced basis

- When it is determined that intensive scrutiny of a specific food is necessary because of new information concerning food safety

- When foods prepared at the operation have been implicated as vehicles of foodborne disease

- When consultants request them and resources allow the operation to accommodate the request

- When established criteria have not been met

Routine inspections should be scheduled on an interval based on risk. These inspections are full reviews of the food establishment's operations and facilities and their impact on food safety. Routine inspections include assessing the health of staff members and their knowledge and practice of food safety; food flow, storage, thawing, preparation (including cooking temperatures and times), and post-preparation processes; equipment and facility construction; cleaning and sanitizing processes; water sources; sewage disposal; and vermin control.

Staff training is an important element in the success of a food operation's HACCP system. A HACCP system works best when it is integrated into each staff member's duties and therefore is not seen as an "add-on." The fundamental training goal should be to make managers and staff members proficient in the specific tasks required by the HACCP plan. In addition, the training plan should be specific to the operation.

Other Food Safety Considerations

Guests are very concerned about food safety, and it's no wonder. The CDC estimates that there are almost 50 million cases of foodborne illness each year; of that number, 128,000 are hospitalized and as many as 3,000 cases result in death. The key to lowering these statistics is for food and beverage operations to use a Food Safety Risk Management program based on the HACCP system, with ongoing reminder training and follow-up by supervisors and managers.

Of all the potential food safety problems in a food and beverage operation, one of the greatest concerns is food that is not properly cooked. Proper cooking requires initial staff training and ongoing training in cooking techniques as well as proper holding techniques and other food safety procedures. Servers should be empowered to speak up if they notice that food is being prepared improperly. Another food safety concern of guests centers on staff hygiene. Here again, initial staff training and regular reminder training sessions are essential, as is the careful supervision of staff at the start of each shift and throughout the shifts by supervisors and managers. Food safety procedures are not complicated, but they must be done on a regular basis and become habitual if they are to be effective.

One way to be certain that new staff members follow acceptable food safety practices is to link new staff with seasoned staff members who are familiar with and practicing these techniques. For example, proper handwashing is an essential

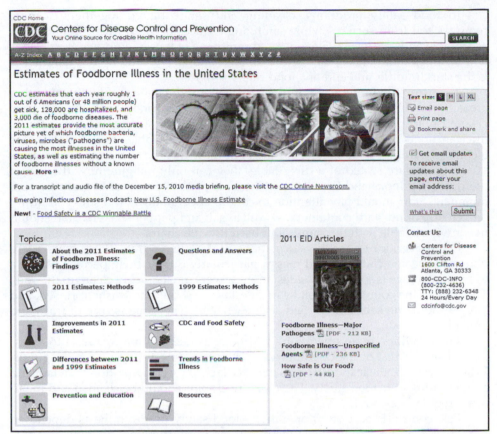

The Centers for Disease Control and Prevention (www.cdc.gov) offer an Internet site with numerous food service sanitation and safety resources. (Courtesy of the Centers for Disease Control and Prevention, Atlanta, Georgia)

food safety procedure. While new staff members should be trained how to wash their hands correctly, reinforcement can come from seasoned staff members in their role as mentors. These mentors can also help remind new staff members to shower or bathe before coming to work, wear clean clothes, and refrain from handling food when ill.

Food safety procedures include the proper cleaning and maintenance of equipment and facilities. The way that a food and beverage operation appears to guests is very important. Dirty, greasy, uncared for facilities and equipment turn guests off, or at least will cause them to think twice about the safety of eating food produced in such an environment. In order to keep equipment and facilities clean, a cleaning and maintenance schedule is required. Cleaning and maintenance activities are called "prerequisite programs" because they must be considered first before building a food safety program. In other words, it is futile to attempt to produce and serve safe food in a dirty facility or with equipment that has not been properly cleaned and sanitized prior to use.

In food safety programs, cleaning and sanitizing go together; cleaning removes soil from surfaces while sanitizing reduces harmful microorganisms to acceptable and safe levels. Cleaning and sanitizing of hands, equipment, surfaces, and facilities should take place before food is handled *and* after food is handled. It is the start, middle, and end of a food safety program.

To ensure food safety, not only the kitchen but the walls, shelving, and other areas in the dining room should be regularly cleaned. Floors must be regularly cleaned not only from an appearance and food safety standpoint, but because unclean floors can be a hazard causing slips and falls. Tables in the dining area technically are not food-contact surfaces but they must have a clean appearance. When guests are seated at a dirty table, they can only imagine how the rest of the operation looks and how little attention is paid to personal hygiene by staff members. Staff should pay attention to condiment containers (no sticky build-up on ketchup or mustard containers) as well as salt and pepper shakers. Staff should never wipe a table with the same cloth used to wipe chairs.

Often overlooked are the sidestations in the dining area. These have a tendency to become cluttered and messy, particularly during busy periods. When a food or beverage is spilled in a sidestation, servers must quickly clean up the spill. The tops of the counters and sinks in sidestations should be washed, rinsed, and have a sanitizing solution applied after each shift. The same is true of trays and bus tubs.

The condition of an operation's restrooms is used by many guests to assess how clean the rest of the operation is. Dirty restrooms are a turn-off for guests. When guests see unclean restrooms they see lack of care, inattention to detail, and no commitment to food safety. Therefore, restrooms should be cleaned and monitored regularly by staff.

Pest control is part of an operation's food safety program. Pests depend on food, water, and places to create their nests, and unfortunately a dining area that is not properly maintained can serve as an ideal location. Floors must be regularly swept and cleaned to remove food crumbs and other debris. When a food and beverage product is spilled, it should be cleaned up immediately and completely to discourage pests from entering the area. When food and beverage operators offer outdoor dining, pest problems can increase, because it is much more difficult to control the presence of pests outdoors. Whether working indoors or outdoors, all staff members should be trained to be on the lookout for pests and report them to management immediately if they are sighted, so the operation's pest management company can be contacted to take care of the problem.

Service Staff Training

Service staff training is the key to reducing sanitation risks and increasing management, staff member, guest, and owner satisfaction. Food and beverage operations should begin with a well-defined training process—focusing on inventory, people, equipment, and facilities—and use the resources of local, state, and national regulatory agencies.

The first phase of staff training should provide information on the history and structure of the operation's food safety risk management program and emphasize specific sanitation goals and objectives. The study of the epidemiology of food-borne illness—including organisms, foods, contributing factors, and all aspects of basic microbiology—is critical. The second phase of training is on-site training conducted by trainers familiar with HACCP inspecting. Trainees should demonstrate expertise in data gathering and analysis before moving to the third phase of training: standardization. In this phase, points of violation are fully discussed and differentiated from similar conditions that are not violations. The final phase of training—lifelong or continuing education—is ongoing. Managers and staff members must remain current in this rapidly changing world, through seminars and workshops offered in person or online by colleges and universities, professional associations, regulatory agencies, and private companies. Food and beverage training programs offer excellent opportunities for acquiring and reinforcing food safety knowledge.

Guidelines for Serving Food

The *Food Code's* specific requirements for the safe display and service of food apply not only to food served from the kitchen but also to items set up for guest self-service at soup and salad bars, buffet tables, and sandwich and dessert bars. The following sanitation guidelines can help an operation control its investment in inventory and reduce its risks at the serving control point.

Potentially hazardous foods must be kept out of the **temperature danger zone (TDZ)** at the serving control point. A **potentially hazardous food** is a food that requires temperature control because it is in a form capable of supporting the rapid and progressive growth of infectious or toxigenic microorganisms; the growth and toxin production of *Clostridium botulinum;* or, in raw shell eggs, the growth of *Salmonella Enteritidus*. Potentially hazardous food includes a food of animal origin that is raw or heat-treated; a food of plant origin that is heat-treated or raw seed sprouts; cut melon; and garlic-in-oil mixtures that are not modified in a way that results in mixtures that do not support growth. The TDZ is the temperature range defined by the U.S. Public Health Service as the range in which most pathogenic activity takes place and food spoilage can occur. It is typically 41°F–140°F (5°C–60°C), although the TDZ may vary from locality to locality; managers should check with their state and local regulatory agencies. Hot food should be served on heated plates, cold food on chilled plates; this practice helps to keep product temperatures outside the TDZ and enhances product quality.

Milk and milk products served as beverages should be served in unopened, commercially filled packages of one pint (.47 liter) or less or drawn from a commercial milk dispenser into a cleaned and sanitized glass. Dairy and non-dairy coffee creamers should be individually packaged, drawn from a refrigerated dispenser, or poured from a covered pitcher. If stored at a sidestand, milk or cream must be refrigerated. Individually portioned coffee creamer that has been ultra-high-temperature pasteurized, aseptically filled, and hermetically sealed is the only liquid dairy or non-dairy coffee creamer exempted from refrigeration requirements. It has a shelf life of 120 days at room temperature.

Dressings, seasonings, and condiments such as chutney, mustard, and relish that are placed on tables or self-service stands must be presented in covered containers, dispensers, or single-serving packages. Ketchup and other sauces may be served in their original containers or in pour-type dispensers. Generally, the refilling of original containers is prohibited. Sugar on tables should be in either individual packets or pour-type dispensers.

Ice for guest consumption should be handled with ice-dispensing scoops or tongs or dispensed by an automatic ice machine. Guests should serve themselves only from automatic dispensers. Utensils for dispensing ice should be stored in a sanitary manner between uses.

Staff members should use utensils or gloves when dispensing food to guests. In-use dispensing utensils can be stored in the food with the handles extended, or under running water, or clean and dry. Production staff or servers should never dispense food (biscuits or rolls in a buffet line, for example) with their hands unless wearing single-use gloves; likewise, guests should use utensils and not their hands when serving themselves.

Leftover food returned to the kitchen must not be re-served. For example, crocks of cheese or butter should be served only once. The exception to this rule is packaged, non-hazardous food in sound condition. Self-service guests should not reuse tableware when they return to the service area for additional food; however, they may reuse beverage glasses and cups. Unpackaged food on display should be protected from guest contamination by easily cleaned food shields (sneeze guards).

Guidelines for Servers

Servers, like all food and beverage staff members, must practice good personal hygiene and cleanliness. Standards of personal hygiene should be adapted to the individual operation and presented to all staff members during orientation and training. Proper handwashing is extremely important. Servers should wash their hands before starting work and frequently throughout the shift. It is also important that they wash their hands immediately after touching hair or skin, sneezing, coughing, using a handkerchief, smoking, visiting the restroom, handling raw food products, or handling soiled containers or tableware.

In addition to proper handwashing, the following sanitation standards apply to all servers:

- Do not chew gum or eat in the dining area or kitchen.

- Never serve food that has left the plate or fallen to the floor.

- Replace dropped tableware with clean items.

- Use recommended utensils and store them in a sanitary manner when they are not in use.

- Avoid touching food with your hands. Dishes, cups, glasses, and flatware should only be handled in places that will not come into contact with food or with the guest's mouth. Dishes should be held with four fingers on the bottom and the thumb on the edge, not touching the food. Cups and flatware should be touched only on the handles. A glass should be grasped at the base and placed on the table without touching the rim.

- Never carry a service towel or napkin over your shoulder or under your arm.

- Be certain the bottom of a piece of tableware is clean before placing it on the table. Remove all soiled tableware and return it to the dirty-dish station to prevent its reuse.

- Keep the tops, bottoms, and sides of serving trays clean to prevent unnecessary soiling of uniforms, tableware, and tablecloths.

- Maintain a clean and professional appearance.

- Work carefully and always keep standards of cleanliness in mind.

Guests expect their dining experiences to be pleasant and safe. If servers violate the standards of personal hygiene or cleanliness with unsanitary practices, disease agents may be transmitted to guests. In addition, physical foodborne contaminants, such as hair or glass fragments, can result in an unpleasant dining experience or even guest injury.

When placing orders in the kitchen, the server's timing is critical to the rapid flow of products to the dining area. Properly timed orders are plated and served almost simultaneously, thus maintaining product temperatures and reducing sanitation risks. In some operations, an expediter acts as a communication link between the kitchen staff and servers. Servers give their orders to the expediter, who calls the orders to the appropriate kitchen stations. The expediter must know cooking times, coordinate them to sequentially deliver cooked foods for pickup, and provide leadership during hectic rush periods. He or she should be a member of the management team.

In some operations, servers are responsible for a few production and portioning tasks, such as portioning beverages, soups, or desserts; adding dressings to salads; garnishing plates; and obtaining food accompaniments such as sauces. In all cases, servers must follow the operation's sanitation and portioning standards.

Servers should load serving trays carefully to reduce the likelihood of accidents. Once food is served, servers should return frequently to the table to remove dirty dishes and refill water glasses. After guests leave, the table should be cleared and reset with clean items. Whoever performs this duty—a server or a busperson—should wash his or her hands after handling soiled tableware and before resetting the table with clean items.

Servers need not wash their hands every time they handle money. Although money is often thought of as "dirty," the FDA has determined that currency does not support enough microorganisms to be a source of contamination. However, guests generally do not like to see servers handle money and then serve food.

Equipment, Furniture, and Supply Guidelines

Serving equipment must be cleaned, sanitized, stored, and handled in a manner that prevents contamination.

Preset tableware must be wrapped or set no sooner than one meal period before use. Presetting should not be a substitute for proper utensil storage. Extra settings of tableware should be removed from the table when guests are seated. This not only helps protect the sanitary quality of tableware, but also prevents needless washing, rinsing, and sanitizing of clean tableware. Sneeze guards and proper serving utensils are required on self-service food bars in the dining area.

Self-service food bars, if not properly maintained, can be perceived as messy and unsanitary. Some outbreaks of foodborne illness have been traced to salad bars. However, certain procedures can help reduce risks. The conditions and temperatures of the food and the salad bar should be checked every 10 to 15 minutes. Spills should be wiped up and utensils replaced when necessary. To ensure freshness and quality, food in salad bars should be placed in relatively small containers, replaced frequently, displayed on crushed ice or in cold inserts, and protected by properly designed sneeze guards. Sneeze guards should extend the length and width of the bar and be positioned 10 to 12 inches (25.4 to 30.5 centimeters) above the food. Display stands for unwrapped food must be effectively shielded to intercept the direct line between the average guest's mouth and the food being displayed.

Soup and dessert bars call for similar procedures. Equipment should be capable of properly maintaining food temperatures. Covers, but not food shields, are required for self-service soup containers. The covers do not have to be hinged or self-closing. It is a good idea to display small amounts of each food item and replenish items frequently. Constant supervision of all types of food bars is crucial to risk reduction and should be part of every server's responsibilities.

Tables and chairs should be dusted or wiped to remove food debris before the operation opens each day. The cloths used to clean table tops should not be used to wipe chairs or the benches in booths. Servers should inspect tables and chairs frequently throughout their shifts for cleanliness and proper setup.

Items placed on tables must be kept clean. This is often a part of the server's sidework. Sugar dispensers and salt and pepper shakers should be wiped clean at least once a day. If glass dispensers or shakers are used, they should be periodically emptied, washed, rinsed, dried, and refilled. The volume of business affects the amount of sugar, salt, and pepper used at each table and, therefore, the frequency of refilling. Some operations use disposable dispensers and shakers to reduce the labor costs associated with maintaining these items.

If syrup or condiments are placed on tables, the exteriors of the containers should be cleaned regularly. They can be wiped with a damp cloth to remove fingerprints and drips. Original condiment containers designed for dispensing (like ketchup bottles) should not be washed and refilled. Wide-mouth condiment or syrup bottles can easily become contaminated and should not be used in the dining area.

Napkins are usually folded before service. They should be stored so as to prevent soiling. Paper napkins should be discarded from tables after service, even if they look clean. Cloth napkins must be properly laundered after each use and should never be used to wipe flatware, glasses, or cups. Servers should check their service trays before beginning work to make sure the bottoms, tops, and sides of the trays are free from grease, food, and other debris.

One item frequently neglected during sidework is flatware. Soiled, spotted eating utensils are both unsightly and unsanitary. Soiled flatware may require soaking before being washed in the dishwashing machine. After washing, all flatware should be checked to make sure it is clean.

Plate and platter covers allow servers to carry more orders on a tray. They also help maintain a menu item's serving temperature if the item is placed on a heated (for hot items) or chilled (for cold items) plate in the kitchen. Covers also help guard against contamination during transportation from the kitchen to the guest. Plate and platter covers must be regularly cleaned, sanitized, and stored in such a manner as to prevent contamination before their next use.

Take-out service requires additional equipment to hold hot and cold packaged foods. Some holding units have clear covers or doors to display the selection of hot and cold items to guests. Equipment selection is based on the menu items offered for take-out. Holding equipment should be able to maintain proper temperatures and relative humidities. It should be cleaned and sanitized regularly.

Care should be exercised in handling all equipment and supplies used for serving. Waste and breakage can be costly to the operation. Each time a server carelessly soils linen, wastes supplies, or throws away or breaks tableware, the operation's costs increase. If fragments of glass find their way into guests' food and beverages, safety is sacrificed and the operation's reputation and revenues will suffer.

Guidelines for Facilities

The cleaning, repair, and maintenance of the operation's facilities are essential at all control points. These activities are particularly important at the serving control point, because the dining area environment directly affects guest satisfaction. A clean and pleasant dining area enhances the operation's image and makes a positive first impression on guests.

The dining area supervisor should inspect the facilities with all the lights turned on before service begins. This daily inspection is part of the overall preparation for service. The supervisor should check floors, walls, and ceilings to see if they need to be cleaned or if any maintenance or repairs are necessary. In addition, tables, chairs, and booths should be inspected for cleanliness. If the dining area has windows, the ledges should be dusted. Menus should be inspected to ensure that daily specials are attached. Dirty or damaged menus should be removed from circulation. The inspection should include food displays and sidestands. If there are pieces of equipment in sidestands (coffee makers or small coolers, for example), they should be checked to make sure they are functioning properly.

After the inspection, the dining area supervisor should adjust the lighting levels to create the proper ambience. The ventilation system should be designed so that the dining area does not become stuffy while guests are dining.

While wood is sometimes used to create a cozy dining atmosphere, untreated wood is subject to decay caused by bacteria and fungi. This process is accelerated by alternating periods of moisture and dryness. Wood for holding and displaying fresh fruits, fresh vegetables, and nuts in the shell may be treated with a preservative approved for such use.

One additional sanitation consideration is important for serving facilities: animals. Although there are some exceptions, animals are not generally allowed in food and beverage operations in the United States. One notable exception is guide dogs; they are permitted in dining areas to accompany guests with visual impairments.

Workplace Safety Issues

Workplace safety should be a top concern of all food and beverage managers and staff members. Attention to workplace safety will pay off for food and beverage operations, since most food service accidents and injuries are preventable. Critical workplace safety issues we will discuss in this section are accidents, injuries, and fires.

Accidents and Injuries

The National Safety Council notes that the most frequent accident in a food and beverage operation is a fall in either the kitchen or service area. (The Occupational Safety and Health Administration is another agency that closely monitors food service safety and safety violations.) These accidents cost employers more than $200 million each year in workers' compensation payments to injured staff members. Slippery floors, often the result of unattended spills, cause most of these falls. A well-designed safety training program can reduce such accidents.

The Importance of Training. Safety training should be a part of every staff member's regular job training and should center on the *prevention* of accidents and injuries. In food and beverage operations, learning solely by experience may be dangerous. In addition to a lack of training, accidents and injuries may also be

---

Accident Investigation and Prevention

When an accident occurs, investigation should occur immediately and focus on determining the accident's cause in order to prevent future accidents. The following steps will help general managers make the most of their investigations:

1. Be objective. Resist the temptation to speculate on what caused an accident.

2. Consult with managers and supervisors responsible for the area where the accident occurred.

3. Investigate immediately after the accident is reported. This is particularly important in incidents involving guests. Conditions and opinions change with time and discussion. Only delay an interview if the subject needs time to regain composure or is undergoing medical treatment. Take photographs of the accident scene whenever possible.

4 Interview all witnesses. Establish a relaxed, nonthreatening atmosphere. Don't ask leading questions (for example, "Did John seem distracted today?"). Ask open-ended questions, such as "What exactly did you see?"

5. Record all significant information. Detailed notes can suffice as a permanent record of an interview. Collect information first; edit and review your notes later. Be sure the facts collected and recorded are pertinent to the investigation.

6. Provide a definite recommendation and schedule of corrective action.

7. Be aware of state reporting requirements. Each state sets requirements for adequate and timely reporting of accidents. Fines for violating these requirements can total $1,000 in some states.

caused by unsafe equipment or conditions. It is management's responsibility to periodically conduct in-house safety inspections to identify and correct hazards.

Successful safety training involves a combination of defining precise techniques and operating procedures, teaching staff these techniques and procedures, assigning specific jobs, carefully supervising staff, and properly maintaining the facilities and equipment. Staff members will show an interest in safety if management emphasizes its importance during initial training and then regularly reminds them about safety. Posters, displays, and other visual aids can help remind staff members to take safety precautions every day.

Preventive Measures. Typical injuries occurring within food and beverage operations include burns, cuts, and injuries caused by lifting improperly or falling. Exhibit 4 presents some safety rules designed to prevent common accidents.

Staff members should know how to operate equipment safely before they use it. Equipment should be regularly inspected and well maintained. Malfunctioning equipment should be reported to the department supervisor, who should then contact the maintenance department so repairs can be completed as soon as possible. Staff should wear the appropriate protective gear when using potentially dangerous machinery or chemicals.

Floors should be kept clean and dry. Spills should be wiped up immediately. Aisles and passageways should be kept clean, uncluttered, and unobstructed.

Hot pans or utensils should be handled only with dry cloths, mitts, pot holders, or towels. Staff members should know how to avoid steam burns (for example, when lifting the lid from a pot of boiling soup or some other hot liquid, tilt the lid away from you, not toward you).

Glass breaks easily if handled carelessly. Broken glass should only be picked up with a broom and a dustpan—never with bare hands. Staff members must be trained to be very cautious when handling glass, especially during dishwashing. Trays or racks of glass items must be handled carefully. Personal drinking glasses should not be allowed in food service areas.

Sharp objects such as knives must also be handled with care. Several manufacturers are marketing cut-resistant, lightweight, seamless knitted gloves for food and beverage staff members to use when cleaning knives and slicers.

As alluded to earlier, improper lifting can cause injuries. Staff members must be trained to assess the weights, sizes, and shapes of objects before lifting them. They should also be trained to lift properly—keeping a straight back and lifting with their legs. They should know when and how to use mechanical lifting devices. Heavy objects should be stored at least 12 inches (30.5 centimeters) off the floor to avoid causing strains when lifted.

Strains or falls may occur when staff members stretch or over-reach to obtain objects overhead. Staff members should always use a ladder to reach items on high shelves; chairs, boxes, or containers are not safe substitutes for ladders. Carried boxes should be stacked squarely so they will not fall and should not be stacked higher than eye level; staff members must be able to see where they are going. Caution should be exercised to avoid collisions when moving around corners and through congested areas. When carts or other types of equipment on wheels need to be moved, they should be pushed, not pulled.

Exhibit 4   Safety Rules for Food and Beverage Operations

Burn Prevention

1. Maintain traffic and workflow patterns in production and service areas.
2. Maintain adequate working space around hot holding and cooking equipment.
3. Use a clean, dry cloth or pot holder when handling hot dishes, pans, and equipment.
4. Follow the manufacturer's recommendations when operating equipment.
5. Use coffee urns with care. Do not talk or turn away while filling coffeepots or cups. Look before turning with coffeepots in your hand.
6. Do not leave empty coffeepots on heating units.
7. Carry only as many cups of coffee at one time as you can manage safely.
8. Turn off all electrical equipment immediately after you are finished using it.
9. Keep the range and surrounding areas grease-free to prevent fires and burns.
10. When lifting covers from pots and pans on the range, tilt the covers away from you, not toward you, to allow steam to safely dissipate.
11. Keep pot holders and towels away from open flames.
12. Maintain safety and sanitation precautions at all times.

Cut Prevention

1. Do not use any cutting, slicing, or grinding equipment without learning how to operate it properly.
2. Be sure all safety devices are in place before using dangerous machinery such as slicers and grinders.
3. Use the right tool for each kitchen job. For example, do not use knives to open bottles or cans.
4. Keep knives and cutting tools sharp and in good condition.
5. Do not turn away from your work while handling knives.
6. Do not pick up a knife by the blade. Never try to catch a falling knife.
7. Handle glass with care to avoid breaking it.
8. Discard all chipped glasses and dishes promptly and safely.
9. Wear protective gloves and be careful when putting your hands in water containing knives or glassware.
10. Use a broom and dustpan to pick up all broken china and glass. Do not use your hands.
11. When using steel wool, protect your hand with a cloth or glove.
12. Remove or bend down nails and pieces of metal protruding from barrels and boxes.
13. Clean and sanitize knives after use and store them away from other utensils.
14. Do not use your fingers to push the end of an item through a moving slicer blade.

Exhibit 4 *(continued)*

Fall Prevention

1. Keep all floors dry around workstations.

2. Wipe up spilled food, water, oil, and grease immediately.

3. Keep all aisles and work areas clear and free of obstructions. Do not leave drawers or doors open.

4. Do not leave debris or boxes where other staff members might fall over them.

5. When you drop something on the floor, pick it up as soon as possible.

6. Avoid blocking passageways when bending down. Make sure no one is coming along with hot food.

7. Do not stand in a doorway or otherwise block the flow of traffic.

8. When you walk, place your feet firmly on the floor. Do not run.

9. Wear shoes with good soles and heels. Wear full-leather shoes with anti-skid soles in the kitchen.

10. Load trays carefully and distribute the weight evenly.

11. Pass to the right of others when carrying trays.

12. Say "Passing on the right" when carrying trays through congested traffic areas.

13. Allow others the right of way when they are carrying trays.

14. Set trays, dishes, pots, and pans away from the edges of surfaces. Do not allow serving spoons or pot handles to stick out into aisles.

15. Do not use chairs or boxes to reach high shelves; use a solid ladder.

16. Use grates or anti-skid mats on floors in areas where spills are likely.

Lifting Injury Prevention

1. Before lifting, get a firm grasp on the object.

2. When lifting, keep your back straight and bend only your knees. Use your leg muscles—not your back—to lift heavy objects.

3. Lift with a smooth action, keeping the object close to your body. Never jerk a load.

4. If necessary, shift your footing, but do not twist your body while lifting.

5. Exercise caution to prevent fingers and hands from getting pinched.

6. Obtain help when lifting bulky or heavy objects. Never try to lift a load you know is too much for you. The probability of injury increases as the weight of the object approaches 40 pounds (18.16 kg). When in doubt, ask for assistance.

7. Use available lifting and moving equipment (such as dollies and hand trucks).

8. Maintain clean, dry, and uncluttered floors in areas such as storerooms where lifting is necessary.

The operation's outdoor areas present safety issues as well. These areas should be well-lighted and regularly cleaned and maintained. This includes entrance-ways, sidewalks, parking lots, trash areas, and so on. Trash buildup is not only unsightly, it is unsafe and should not be permitted. Sidewalks and parking lots should be kept free from ice and snow during cold months to minimize the threat of someone slipping and falling outside.

For obvious reasons, staff members and managers should not work under the influence of alcohol or illegal drugs. New staff members should be informed that any person working under the influence of alcohol or illegal drugs is subject to immediate disciplinary action. Legal drugs can be problematic as well, as some prescription drugs come with warnings that individuals should not operate equipment when taking them.

Even with all of these preventive measures and precautions, an accident or injury may occur. If so, each staff member, supervisor, and manager must be trained in advance to know how to respond.

Handling Accidents and Injuries. Every food and beverage operation should have a clearly stated policy on how to handle emergencies such as injuries to staff members or guests. If an accident occurs, staff members should notify their supervisors immediately. After appropriate medical attention has been secured, management is responsible for investigating the incident. Once the causes of an accident are identified, corrective action can help eliminate further accidents. Managers can use an accident reporting form (see Exhibit 5) to record and analyze accidents.

Any staff member may provide first aid *if properly trained*. Immediate first aid treatment could mean the difference between life and death to a severely injured person. At least one staff member trained in first aid techniques should always be on duty. All staff members should know where the first-aid supplies are stored and how to use them to treat minor injuries.

Every operation should have at least one conveniently located first aid kit. First aid kits are available in three basic types: unit, bulk, and combination. Unit first aid kits are compact and contain compresses, splints, tourniquets, and triangular bandages. Bulk first aid kits usually contain adhesive tape, bulk cotton, and elastic and plastic bandages. Combination first aid kits contain a mixture of both unit and bulk kit supplies. In addition, combination kits usually contain antiseptic sprays, antacids, aspirin, burn sprays, cold treatments, eye solutions, and special bandages. A supervisor should be responsible for checking first aid supplies each month and restocking them when necessary. Refills can be obtained from manufacturers, distributors, or drugstores.

When an accident involves a guest, staff members should avoid discussing similar accidents with the injured guest. Regardless of who might be at fault, staff members should never be discourteous or argue with a guest. On the other hand, staff members should not admit that the operation is at fault when an accident occurs; there should be no discussion of insurance claims or settlements. Guest injuries must be recorded on an accident report; the form shown in Exhibit 5 can be adapted for this purpose.

Staff members and supervisors should notify top management of a guest injury as soon as possible. The supervisor should attempt to get as much

Exhibit 5   Accident Reporting Form

Food and Beverage Operation: Address:

Supervisor: Name of injured:

Department: Position:

Date of accident: Time of accident:

Place of accident:

Nature of injury:

Type of treatment received:

None   First aid   Medical doctor   Ambulance
Hospital   Other (specify):

Medical attention necessary:

Action of injured at time of accident:

Conditions in the environment contributing to the accident:

Corrective action necessary to prevent further accidents:

Date corrective action taken:

Staff member's   Supervisor's
signature: signature:

Date: Date:

Exhibit 6   Procedures for Aiding Choking Victims

1. Send someone for help, but don't wait for it to arrive.

2. Ask the victim if he or she can talk. If the victim is conscious but unable to make a sound, you can be reasonably sure he or she is choking.

3. Using a napkin to get a firm grip, pull the victim's tongue forward as far as possible. This should lift the obstruction into view.

4. Using the index and middle fingers like tweezers, grasp the obstruction and pull it out.

5. If this fails, use the Heimlich maneuver. Stand behind the victim and wrap your arms around his or her waist, allowing the head and arms to hang forward.

6. Make a fist with one hand and clasp it with the other hand. Place your hands against the victim's abdomen just above the navel and below the rib cage.

7. Press in forcefully with a quick upward thrust. Repeat several times. This pushes the diaphragm up, compressing the lungs, and may force the object out of the windpipe. (Measures 5–7 may be used on children and adults. Infants and toddlers should be held upside down over the arm of the rescuer and struck between the shoulder blades.)

8. After the obstruction is removed, restore breathing by artificial respiration if necessary. Keep the victim warm and quiet. Seek medical help.

information as possible about how and why the accident occurred. It is a good idea to have emergency numbers (ambulance, doctor, hospital, fire, police) conveniently posted, so a telephone call for assistance can be made quickly. When in doubt about an injured person's condition, it is best to leave treatment to a trained professional.

Because of the nature of the business, food and beverage staff members must be prepared to handle incidents involving choking. Choking is a leading cause of accidental death in the United States, responsible for more than 3,000 deaths each year, many of which could be prevented. Food and beverage staff members must be trained to recognize choking symptoms and respond rapidly with acceptable techniques.

If the victim is able to talk or cough, he or she is not choking and staff members should not intervene. A person who is choking is unable to breathe or make a sound but may look very alarmed. The victim may attempt to stand up and may clutch at his or her throat. With no intervention, the victim will eventually turn blue and lose consciousness. Death may occur in a matter of minutes. Therefore, fast action is necessary.

There are two generally accepted techniques for saving a choking victim (see Exhibit 6). Some rescuers attempt to remove the obstruction directly, usually with their fingers or with plastic tongs. The other technique is called the **Heimlich maneuver**, an action that forces trapped air out of the victim's lungs and often expels the obstruction from the throat. Regardless of which method is used, treatment must begin immediately if the victim is to survive.

Artificial respiration is necessary when a person's heart or lungs have stopped functioning. In most cases, a fatality can be avoided if prompt action is taken.

Cardiopulmonary resuscitation (CPR) is a technique used to provide artificial circulation and breathing to the victim. The American Red Cross regularly conducts CPR courses consisting of lectures, demonstrations, and student practice. This valuable training usually takes only eight hours and could save a person's life. It is a good idea to have at least one person certified in CPR on duty at all times.

Fires

A fire can destroy a food and beverage operation's property and, more tragically, injure or kill staff members and guests. A comprehensive fire safety program can help managers reduce this tremendous risk.

Some fires in food and beverage operations are ignited intentionally. Cases of arson have been traced to owners attempting to collect insurance money, angry or recently terminated staff members, vandals, guests with unsatisfied complaints, and mentally unbalanced individuals. Good security—locked doors, proper key control, bright outdoor lighting, and burglar alarms—can help prevent arson.

Faulty electrical wiring also causes many fires; managers should have the operation's wiring periodically checked. Proper grounding is essential, as is strict adherence to all electrical safety codes. Faulty electrical appliances also cause fires. Equipment should always be used according to the manufacturer's recommendations.

Most cooking fires are caused by grease or fat on hot surfaces or in equipment. To prevent these fires, equipment and exhaust hoods and filters must be kept clean. Appliances must be cleaned daily to prevent bonded dust (a potentially flammable film of grease and dust) from accumulating on their surfaces. Grease drippings in broiler and griddle drip pans should be emptied daily. Spills of fats, oils, sugar sauces, and other flammable foods should be wiped up immediately.

Exhaust-duct fires can be prevented with regular maintenance. The ducts should be cleaned and inspected at least quarterly (more frequently, if necessary) by a qualified service contractor. An exhaust-duct fire is very dangerous because it can smolder unnoticed for hours and then rapidly burn out of control.

Heating and air conditioning equipment also must be regularly inspected and maintained. Inspections should include chimneys, flues, filters, and air ducts. Whenever replacement parts are necessary, the correct sizes and types should be installed. This is particularly important for fuses and circuit breakers.

Flaming drinks, desserts, and entrées are forbidden to be served in restaurants in some parts of the United States because of the fire risk. Accidents with flaming foods occasionally occur that cause property damage as well as personal injury to guests and staff. Municipal codes may regulate whether a food and beverage operation can flame foods, or they may specify the type and maximum amount of fuel that can be used. If a restaurant does flame food items, staff members must know what they are doing, and fire safety concerns must be reflected in procedures. For example, because carrying flaming items from the kitchen to guest tables is especially dangerous, some operations have rules forbidding this in crowded dining areas. When flaming is allowed, the proper types of fire extinguishers should be readily available.

Exhibit 7   Fire Classifications

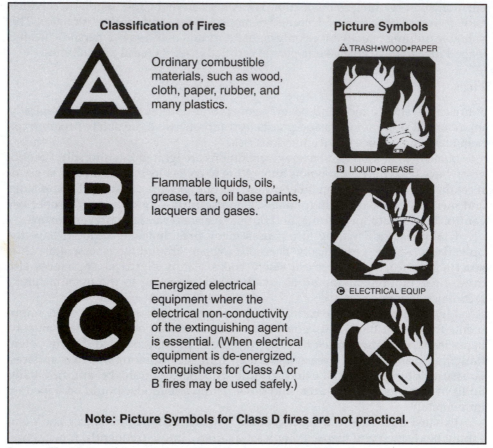

Source: The National Association of Fire Equipment Distributors.

Smoking by staff members should be restricted to designated outside areas during their meal times or breaks. Smokers should never throw their cigarette butts on the ground but should always discard them in a proper receptacle.

Types of Fires and Extinguishers. According to the National Fire Protection Association, there are three major classifications of fires (see Exhibit 7). **Class A fires** involve ordinary combustibles such as wood, paper, and cloth. These fires can be extinguished by water or the cooling action of water-based or general-purpose fire-extinguishing chemicals. **Class B fires** involve flammable liquids such as grease, gasoline, paints, and other oils. They are extinguished by eliminating the air supply and smothering the fire. **Class C fires** are electrical and usually involve motors, switches, and wiring. They are extinguished with chemicals that do not conduct electricity. (Fires classified as Class D, caused by combustible metals, are rare.)

Never use water on a Class B or C fire. A grease fire may be smothered by simply covering it with a tight-fitting lid. Salt may also put out a small grease fire. In the United States, all state fire codes require both hand-held portable fire extinguishers and fixed automatic fire suppression systems in food and beverage operations. Automatic systems must be installed in exhaust hoods and duct work, and over charbroilers, upright broilers, fryers, and griddles. Portable extinguishers and automatic fire suppression systems should be checked regularly by an expert. The local fire department usually provides this service.

Fire Safety Programs. Staff training is the key to fire safety. Initial orientation and training should stress fire prevention. Additional training should cover specific staff duties in the event of a fire. Without proper training, staff members are likely to panic if a fire breaks out. Fire safety should also be reviewed periodically at staff meetings. Fire departments, hotel/motel associations, and restaurant associations may offer in-house training sessions.

Advance planning is necessary to control a fire emergency. Staff members and managers should know what to do if a fire is discovered. They should call the fire department immediately and then calmly evacuate guests. Attempting to be secretive about a fire could endanger everyone in the building. Each server should be responsible for the guests in his or her station. The dining area manager or host should check other public areas to ensure that everyone has been evacuated. Kitchen workers should also have an evacuation plan. It is more important to protect human lives than to stay and fight an overwhelming fire.

A fire safety checklist can be used during regular inspections of the property. A team approach to fire safety inspections (involving both supervisors and staff members) is beneficial because it raises the fire safety consciousness of the entire staff. Most fires are preventable if management and staff members are aware of fire hazards, exercise caution, and use common sense.

Security Issues

Food and beverage managers must be prepared for any emergency. Only intensive preparation can help ensure that they will handle emergencies in a professional manner with a minimal threat to both staff members and guests. In this section we will talk about security issues that food and beverage operations might experience.

Vandalism

While perhaps not a top-of-mind security issue for many food and beverage managers, vandalism is a form of workplace security breach. A vandal often does damage to the facility by leaving graffiti on walls or other surfaces. Breaking windows is another form of vandalism. If vandalism takes place, it is important to remove the signs of it quickly so that other vandals are not encouraged to do similar acts of damage. Additionally, guests, staff members, and members of the surrounding community will appreciate it if signs of vandalism are removed promptly. When an act of vandalism occurs, management should contact the local police as well as the operation's insurance provider. The police will want to investigate the incident in order to apprehend the vandals if possible. The operation's insurance company may want to begin its own investigation before reaching a settlement to fund all or part of the repairs necessary to restore the facility.

Robberies

Food and beverage operations can be targets for robberies. After an operation closes, a manager or supervisor normally prepares the daily deposit paperwork and reconciles cash and noncash sales before depositing the receipts in a financial institution. A thief may try to sneak in or break in after hours or wait outside to rob a manager of these receipts before they can be deposited. In addition, during business hours a food and beverage operation has cash on hand for transacting business and as a result of sales throughout the day. At any time while an operation is open a thief may confront a staff member or a guest and demand money or other valuables.

Managers need to carefully think about and develop procedures to follow during robberies. As an operation considers robbery precautions, its paramount concern should be the safety of staff members and guests. While sales income is obviously important, concern for everyone's personal safety has a much higher priority.

When a robbery attempt is made, staff members can benefit by following procedures such as the following:

1. Do not make any sudden moves and cooperate in every respect with all requests made by the criminal. Do not say or do anything that would jeopardize your safety. Cooperation reduces the possibility of injury or violence.

2. Give the robber cash, food, beverages, or anything else he or she demands.

3. Do not attempt to deceive, lie, resist, or be uncooperative in any way.

4. Do not volunteer unsolicited information.

5. Attempt to observe everything possible about the criminal, if you can do so without provoking him or her, including:

   - Gender.

   - Height. One easy way to gauge relative height is to note whether the criminal's eyes are above or below your line of vision.

   - Skin color.

   - Eye color.

   - Hair. Note the length and color of the criminal's hair. Also, is there any facial hair?

   - Facial characteristics, such as size of nose, scars, and so on.

   - Weight.

   - Voice. Is it high- or low-pitched? Does the criminal talk fast or slow? Is there an accent?

   - Right- or left-handedness: In which hand is the weapon?

- Weapon. What kind is it?

- Clothing. Is the clothing new or old? What is the color, type, and style of each item? Is the criminal wearing any unusual item, such as a special belt buckle or designer's logo?

- Miscellaneous items. Any distinctive personal characteristics, such as earrings, elaborate rings, or other jewelry? Tattoos? Piercings?

6. Do not follow the criminal out of the building. If the operation has a window or other safe viewing place, you may be able to note the criminal's mode of transportation. If possible, note the license plate number, the color and type of the vehicle, and any rust, dents, or other special characteristics of the vehicle.

7. Try to determine the direction the robber took when he or she left.

8. As soon as the criminal leaves, notify the police, then notify the general manager (if he or she is not already on the scene). Even before the police arrive, staff members should begin to write down all that they can recall about the criminal and his or her personal characteristics. Each staff member should make notes without talking to other staff members. Items that were touched by the robber should not be moved or handled.

9. Encourage guests who were witnesses to remain until the police arrive.

10. Give police officers your full cooperation as they attempt to obtain relevant information about the robbery.

11. Do not discuss the robbery with people not involved in the incident or who are not investigating the incident. Never have a conversation about the robbery with a member of the media unless you are given permission to do so by management.

There are several procedures a food and beverage operation can use to reduce the impact of robberies. For example, the manager can remove large sums of money from the cash register(s) during each shift and place the money in a safe or other secure place. This procedure reduces the amount of sales income that someone can take during a robbery, since most robbers would not know how to open a safe on the premises. Making frequent bank deposits can help reduce the amount of cash on the premises. Some operations employ such anti-theft measures as silent alarms, bullet-proof cashier cages, and on-site guards. Finally, closed-circuit television can be used to monitor cashier areas; the obvious presence of a camera may deter some robbers.

Additional precautions are necessary to protect sales income that is in transit to a bank for deposit. Operations with large amounts of sales income should consider the use of an armored car or bonded messenger service. Managers who make bank deposits should avoid routines when making them—for example, they should leave for the bank at varying times and should not always use the same exit when leaving the building. A few trusted staff members can take turns making deposits. If staff members use their own cars to make bank deposits, they should park them as close as possible to the door they will use to exit the building. If a manager makes a night deposit after the facility closes, the manager should exit through doors within the public's view rather than through back doors that may not be visible to passing cars or pedestrians. Managers can contact local police for additional, specific suggestions that can help reduce the possibility and magnitude of losses from theft.

Bomb Threats

Unfortunately, the possibility of a bomb threat is real for just about every type of food and beverage operation. Managers have the responsibility to develop written procedures for handling these threats and training staff members in these procedures. The number of bombs or other potentially dangerous devices that are found as a result of threats is much lower than the actual number of threats. Nevertheless, experienced managers treat bomb threats as real announcements of potential death, injury, and extensive damage.

If threats are received by mail (regular, e-mail, or fax), they should immediately be referred to the local police. In addition, when the United States mail service is involved, postal inspectors and the Federal Bureau of Investigation (FBI) should be notified.

Many bomb threats are communicated by telephone. Therefore, management should train staff members in advance to solicit as much information as possible from the caller. For example, if it is the policy of the operation, the staff member who receives the bomb threat should:

1. Attempt to keep the caller talking. If possible, alert another staff member who can listen on another telephone.

2. Attempt to discover when the bomb will explode, where it is located, what type of device it is, and what it looks like.

3. Listen to the voice. Is the person male or female, sober or intoxicated, rational or irrational? Is it someone you know? Does the speaker have an accent or speech impediment? Is the voice that of a child, teenager, or older person?

4. Listen for any identifiable noises in the background (e.g., factory, nightclub, or street sounds).

5. Note any additional information, such as an explanation of why the caller placed the bomb and if the caller has any demands.

6. Note the time the call was received and the time the caller hung up.

7. Attempt to recall the exact words the caller used.

8. Notify local police immediately.

Frequently, if a caller is serious, he or she will provide information helpful in finding the bomb. If the caller is incoherent, obviously intoxicated, or sounds as though he or she thinks the telephone call is a joke, the call is probably a hoax. Even so, the staff member who phones the police should carefully follow any advice they provide.

If the top manager on duty did not take the call, he or she should be notified. If the operation has an internal security department, its staff members should also be notified, according to company guidelines.

Time cannot be wasted when an operation receives a bomb threat. Yet, managers and staff members must not panic; advance training in security procedures can help keep everyone calm.

Police and other personnel who are looking for the bomb may request the aid of staff members who know the work areas being searched and who would more readily notice anything out of the ordinary. Staff members should call attention to anything out of place or unusual, such as a bag, box, case, or package that should not be in the area. Police may allow staff members to make a preliminary search before officers arrive. If anyone notices an unusual package or other item whose presence cannot be explained, no one should attempt to move, touch, examine, or in any other way disturb it. Rather, all staff members should leave the area, and the police should be notified about the suspicious object's exact location.

While the factors surrounding every situation are unique, many authorities suggest that it is generally unwise to evacuate a facility before a search confirms that a bomb or suspicious device is present. However, if you have a strong feeling that the threat is real, an immediate, calm evacuation is in order. Again, closely follow the advice of police officials regarding the need to evacuate the premises.

Generally, guests evacuating a building during a bomb threat should leave through the fire exits. Staff members should exit according to plans that enable the operation's management to account for them. All evacuation plans should ensure that absolutely no one remains in the building.

If an evacuation is in order but no imminent danger exists, managers should lock all equipment containing cash. Doors should remain unlocked in order to facilitate the search for the bomb. If police do not object, equipment can be turned off and other precautions taken to protect the facilities.

After an evacuation is complete, no one should return to the building and grounds until the police declare the areas safe. Staff members should then return to their assigned work areas to await instructions from their managers.

Bioterrorism

Bioterrorism takes place when harmful biological substances are intentionally used by terrorists to injure or terrorize others. Sometimes these substances are introduced into food. There is a real concern in the United States and elsewhere that terrorists might be seeking ways to contaminate the food supply using biological or chemical agents. Biological agents include anthrax and ricin. Anthrax is a serious disease caused by *Bacillus anthracis,* a bacterium that forms spores. Anthrax was used as an agent of bioterrorism in 2001 when it was deliberately spread through the U.S. postal system via contaminated letters. Ricin is a toxin found in the seeds of the castor bean plant; this toxic protein is so deadly that just one milligram can kill an adult. Chemicals that can contaminate food include pesticides, mycotoxins, heavy metals, and other acutely toxic chemicals such as cyanide. These harmful substances and many others can be introduced into food anywhere along the food chain between farm and table by terrorists. Imported food could be tainted with biological or chemical agents before it even enters the United States, or toxins might be introduced at a domestic food-processing plant.

There has already been one terrorist attack in the United States involving food. In 1984, members of a religious commune in rural Oregon tried to influence a local election by poisoning the salad bars of several restaurants with salmonella bacteria to sicken voters. The group hoped to take over county government by preventing local citizens from voting. Although no one died, 751 people became ill.

Food Safety and Security. Food safety and security fall under the jurisdiction of several centers and offices within the FDA, including the Center for Food Safety and Applied Nutrition and the National Center for Toxicological Research. The FDA is responsible for the safety of about 80 percent of the U.S. food supply; the exceptions are meat, poultry, and processed egg products, which are under the jurisdiction of the U.S. Department of Agriculture (USDA). FDA oversight includes the safe production, processing, storage, and holding of domestic and imported food. If a terrorist-related incident involving the deliberate contamination of food occurred in the United States, the FDA would work closely with federal, state, and local authorities to identify the problem, investigate, and get the contaminated food products off the market quickly.

After the terrorist attack of September 11, 2001, the FDA conducted food supply vulnerability assessments and later issued guidelines on security measures that the food industry could take to minimize terrorism risks. A critical component of controlling threats from deliberate food contamination is the ability to rapidly test large numbers of samples of potentially contaminated foods for a variety of biological, chemical, and radiological agents. The FDA has worked closely with the Centers for Disease Control and Prevention and the USDA to establish the Food Emergency Response Network (FERN)—a national network of laboratories ready to respond to a food security emergency.

Under the authority of the Public Health Security and Bioterrorism Preparedness and Response Act of 2002, the FDA developed some new regulations for the food industry. Owners and operators of foreign or domestic food facilities that manufacture or process, pack, or hold food for human or animal consumption in the United States must submit information to the agency about the facility, including emergency contact information. The FDA must now receive prior notice of imported food shipments before the food arrives at a U.S. port. (The FDA expects to receive about 25,000 notifications about incoming shipments every day.) Food manufacturers, processors, packers, importers, and others are required to keep records that identify the source from which they receive food and where they send it. Lastly, the FDA now has the authority to detain any food for up to 30 days if there is credible evidence that the food poses a serious threat to humans or animals.

An *Emergency Management Guide for Business & Industry* is available from the Federal Emergency Management Agency (FEMA). This guide includes a four-step planning process, covering how to:

1. Establish a planning team
2. Analyze capabilities and hazards
3. Develop the plan
4. Implement the plan

Additional emergency management considerations, hazard-specific information, and sources for more information on emergency management can also be found in the guide, which can be downloaded from the FEMA website.

For more information about food safety, you can call the FDA's toll-free consumer information line at 1-888-SAFEFOOD or visit the website at www.foodsafety.gov. Typing in "Terrorism and Food" into an Internet search engine can lead you to the latest government articles and other information relating to this topic.

Health Issues

Health issues discussed in this chapter cover four broad areas: nutrition, healthier menu options, food allergies, and smoking. With the trend toward more healthy menu items and food and beverage operation concepts, a basic knowledge of nutrition, healthier menu options, and food allergies is valuable for all managers and staff members. Similarly, the move toward elimination of smoking from public areas in buildings requires a fundamental knowledge of smoking issues on the part of all individuals who work in food and beverage operations.

Nutrition

Americans are increasingly making lifestyle choices and changes that contribute to healthier living. Food and beverage operations are selling less alcohol today than a decade ago. More guests are choosing smaller portion sizes and demanding foods that are low in fat, sodium, cholesterol, and sugar than in years past. Vegetarian menu items are appealing to a growing number of those who consume meals away from home. Nutrition and health issues are not fads, but trends that are expected to grow in importance with the graying of America.

Nutrition Basics. An understanding of the fundamentals of nutrition is a foundation for exceeding guests' expectations. Food consists of its building blocks: nutrients. The kinds and qualities of nutrients, along with their order and arrangement, determine the characteristics of a food product.

Much of the nutrient content of food is determined by the genetic makeup of the plant or animal. Nutrient quality is also influenced by the kind of fertilizer or feed. Once the food is harvested, however, its nutrient profile changes. Some changes are out of a food and beverage operation's control; others can be managed, to an extent. For example, the operation controls:

- How foods are received
- Storage conditions—including light, temperature, time, and relative humidity
- Handling conditions—whether the product is thawed, frozen, or canned
- How the food is prepared and served

The objective should be to avoid losing any more nutrients than necessary.
The six nutrient classes are:

- Proteins
- Carbohydrates
- Lipids (fats and oils)

- Vitamins
- Minerals
- Water

Of these six, four are organic—proteins, carbohydrates, lipids, and vitamins; minerals and water are inorganic. An organic compound contains the element carbon, which can chemically bond with many other elements. The word *organic* is often misunderstood. Some believe that "organic" signifies quality. For example, some believe that organic vitamin C taken from oranges is better than synthetic vitamin C manufactured in the laboratory. The truth is that the nutrient profile of both vitamins is exactly the same. While the vitamin C in both cases is the same, additional nutrients (vitamin A, potassium) present in the orange would not be found in the pure vitamin C from the laboratory. *Inorganic* simply means that the nutrient does not contain carbon.

The three nutrients that provide energy to the human body are proteins, carbohydrates, and lipids. Weight for weight, both proteins and carbohydrates have equal energy values (4 kilocalories per gram), while lipids have over twice as much energy (9 kilocalories per gram).

Proteins. Proteins are large molecules that consist of approximately 500 amino acids chemically linked together. Proteins serve several critical roles. They function as enzymes to speed up the rate of chemical reactions in the body. They are used for transportation and storage of other components of the body; for example, oxygen is transported in the blood by the protein hemoglobin and is stored in muscles in myoglobin, another protein. Proteins help produce antibodies, which recognize and control foreign substances such as viruses and bacteria. Proteins generate and transmit nerve impulses in the body. Finally, proteins can be used as a source of energy. However, using protein for energy is like using expensive, handmade furniture for kindling wood. Since proteins have so many more important functions in the human body, carbohydrates and lipids are preferred for energy sources.

The recommended daily intake of proteins varies based on a person's age. Relative to body weight, children need a higher amount of protein than adults. This is reasonable, since children are growing and need the extra protein for building body tissues. Protein requirements increase during the last six months of pregnancy for women and during lactation. The daily intake of protein is also affected by a person's activity; active people require more protein than sedentary individuals.

Important sources of protein include meat, poultry, fish, seafood, milk and milk products, legumes (e.g., dried beans and peas), soybeans, and nuts. The quantity and quality of protein found in each of these foods will vary, based on the amounts and kinds of amino acids present in the foods. Most U.S. adults are in little danger of getting an inadequate amount of protein in their diets.

Carbohydrates. Carbohydrates are classified into three broad categories: monosaccharides, disaccharides, and polysaccharides. Both monosaccharides and disaccharides are known as sugars.

Monosaccharides are the simplest of the three categories and include glucose, fructose, and galactose. Glucose is the primary source of energy within the human body. It is found in some fruits and vegetables (e.g., grapes, young peas, and carrots). Fructose, the sweetest of all sugars, is present with glucose in many fruits; it also is found in honey and is used as a sweetener in some processed foods. Galactose is normally only found linked to glucose.

When two monosaccharides bond together, they form a disaccharide. Disaccharides include sucrose, lactose, and maltose. Sucrose is common sugar, and it also gives fruits their characteristic sweet taste. Lactose is the only carbohydrate found in milk. Maltose is produced in malted grains and is important in the production of alcoholic beverages.

Polysaccharides are the most complex carbohydrates. They include starches, cellulose, glycogen, pectin, agar, and alginate. These carbohydrates are useful in cooking, improve the "mouth feel" of certain foods, and help the digestive process.

There are no recommended daily allowances (RDAs) for carbohydrates, although the average adult human needs about 100 grams (roughly 3.5 ounces) per day. This amount is less than one-third of the amount consumed daily by most adult Americans, although the kinds of carbohydrates consumed in the average American diet could be changed for the better. A healthy diet emphasizes complex carbohydrates that are high in fiber (e.g., vegetables, fruits, and whole grains) rather than sugary foods.

Lipids. Fats and oils are collectively known as "lipids" and are made up of fatty acids and glycerol. Although we group them together, there are differences between fats and oils. Fats are usually found in animal products, while oils are usually extracted from vegetable sources. Fats are solid at room temperature and contain a large amount of saturated fatty acids. Oils, on the other hand, are liquid at room temperature and contain more unsaturated fatty acids.

Fats or oils and water generally do not mix. However, when a substance known as an emulsifying agent is added, the mixture stabilizes and does not separate, because an emulsion is created. Milk and ice cream are examples of fat-in-water emulsions, butter is an example of a water-in-fat emulsion, and margarine is a water-in-oil emulsion. Some other important food emulsions include mayonnaise, hollandaise sauce, cream soups, salad dressings, and sauces. Some of these foods contain egg yolks, which are natural emulsifiers.

Nearly all meats contain considerable fat. You can reduce your intake of fat by trimming away all of the visible fat, but the resulting meat may be far from fat-free. There can remain a considerable amount of fat within the tissue of the meat, a characteristic known as "marbling." The one common food of animal origin that can be made virtually fat-free is milk; skim milk has less than 1.6 percent fat, allowing it to qualify for "fat-free" labeling.

Fats and oils are concentrated sources of energy, so they take longer to burn once consumed. Fats and oils contain nine kilocalories per gram, more than double the energy value of equal weights of proteins or carbohydrates. Excessive calories (whether in the form of lipids, carbohydrates, or proteins) are converted into fat by the body and stored in adipose tissue cells. The adipose tissue acts as an energy reserve and helps protect vital organs of the body, such as the kidneys. Fats and oils are also a source of the fat-soluble vitamins A, D, E, and K.

There are a number of sources of fat in the diet. The fat content of meat can vary from animal to animal and from one part of the animal to another. Some fish, particularly salmon and trout, are relatively high in fat content compared to other fish. Butter can contain as much as 80 percent fat, while margarine may have just as much oil. Unless they are specially produced, products made from milk and milk products—including yogurt, sour cream, and cheese—contain fat. Fat typically plays an important role in the preparation of pastries and breads.

Most foods of plant origin, such as grains, fruits, and vegetables, are low in fat when harvested. (One notable exception is the avocado.) For example, only one-thousandth of the weight of a potato is fat. But when a potato is prepared by frying or by adding sour cream, butter, margarine, and/or cheese, the fat content can easily be one hundred times the original. Potatoes are not fattening, but the extra ingredients add considerable calories and fat.

There is no recommended daily allowance for fat, since the average adult American is in little danger of consuming too little. In fact, the situation is just the opposite. One estimate states that adult Americans consume, on average, 40 percent of their total energy needs in the form of fats and oils.

Vitamins. Vitamins are complex organic compounds required by the body to maintain health. These essential nutrients are found in foods in very small amounts, but their importance is great. Vitamins help speed the release of energy from proteins, carbohydrates, and lipids. (By themselves, vitamins are not nutrients, since they cannot be used by the body for energy.)

Vitamins are either water-soluble or fat-soluble. Water-soluble vitamins dissolve in water and include the vitamin B complex of vitamins and vitamin C. Excessive amounts of water-soluble vitamins are eliminated by the body through urination. Fat-soluble vitamins, on the other hand, dissolve in fats or oils. They include vitamins A, D, E, and K. Excess amounts are stored in the body.

The vitamin content of food changes as it is harvested, processed, shipped, stored, prepared, cooked, and held for service. For example, when wheat is refined into flour, many of the B vitamins present in the original bran are lost. In addition, heat, light, and oxygen can have devastating effects on the vitamin content of food. Water-soluble vitamins are lost when food is soaked or cooked in excessive amounts of water for long periods of time.

Minerals and Water. Minerals and water are similar in that they are both inorganic yet are critically important to human nutrition.

Minerals are chemical elements other than carbon, oxygen, hydrogen, and nitrogen. In general, they make up between four to six percent of total body weight. Compared to other nutrients, minerals are incompletely absorbed; therefore, the amount required in your diet is greater than what is actually needed by your body. Excess minerals exit the body through urine, perspiration, and blood. Minerals are lost from food when they dissolve in the water used to soak or cook food products. However, they are generally much more stable than vitamins when exposed to heat, light, or oxygen. Minerals important to the human body include calcium, iron, sodium, chlorine, potassium, phosphorus, iodine, and magnesium.

Water is essential to life, and all living organisms contain it. It is the vehicle in which chemical reactions take place. It also transports nutrients to cells and carries waste products away from cells and out of the body.

Water is available from three sources: liquids, solid foods, and—internally—through oxidation. (Oxidation forms water inside cells as a by-product of chemical reactions.) Soda, beer, and fruit juices contain a large percentage of water. Fruits and vegetables are largely water; melons are as much as 94 percent water, while cabbage contains roughly 90 percent water.

The average adult eliminates about two quarts of water per day. This amount increases when an individual exercises—or works in a hot environment—and loses water in the form of perspiration. This lost water must be replaced for metabolism to continue. The amount of water taken into the body is influenced by habit and social custom as well as by thirst. It is a good idea to consume at least eight glasses of water per day.

Dietary Guidelines. A healthy diet can be sustained by following these guidelines:

- Eat a variety of foods
- Choose foods low in fat and cholesterol
- Include foods with adequate starch and fiber
- Limit high-sugar foods
- Avoid foods high in sodium
- If you drink alcoholic beverages, do so in moderation

Debates continue to escalate over which foods are "good" for you and which foods are "bad." Whether the subject is fats, calories, antioxidants, vegetarian or vegan diets, or various ethnic cuisines, mountains of conflicting data usually do little more than confuse the public. When in doubt regarding the soundness of nutrition advice, it may be best to consult a registered dietitian.

Marketing and Merchandising Nutrition. Marketing and merchandising nutrition is paying large dividends for many food and beverage operations. While strategies differ, the key to using the nutrition issue to improve business is to focus on nutritious menu items, perceived quality, and value.

Whether promoting more nutritious menu items makes sense is a decision that depends on an operation's guests and potential guests; it is important to correctly identify guests' needs, preferences, and expectations. Many guests have preferences for foods that are lower in calories, fat, salt, and sugar. These same guests want information to help them identify nutritious items on the menu and sort out menu options.

Guest feedback is absolutely essential when it comes to evaluating and planning ongoing and future nutrition programs. Surveys might precede the addition of new menu items; a good strategy is to use food samplings with guests or daily specials to test items for possible inclusion on the menu. Tasting parties can be held to evaluate new recipes. Nutritious or healthy options should be presented in every menu category—from appetizers, soups, and salads to entrées and desserts. Condiments and side dishes that are lower in calories, fat, salt, and sugar should also be presented.

On the menu, boxed sections or graphic indicators (for example, a heart logo) can draw guest attention to healthy choices. Guests should also be invited to request nutrition information from service staff. Some menus clearly state: "Ask your server how we can prepare this menu item without salt or fat." Cooking procedures should be described to convey healthy preparation and cooking methods ("broiled without butter," "garnished with lemon and herbs"). As an alternative, a separate menu or menu insert can be used to feature nutrition information.

Many food and beverage operations are already offering more nutritious fare; these items should be clearly promoted on the menu. Other items may need only slight modifications to meet the needs of guests concerned about nutrition. When menus are rewritten, a larger number of nutritious options can be added.

The entire staff should be included in promoting nutrition. Fact sheets, food tastings, and staff discussions can help prepare staff members to match nutrition-minded guests with the meals they would most appreciate and enjoy.

Healthier Menu Options

While a growing trend is to offer healthier menu options in food and beverage operations, some operators resist doing so, and some guests do not choose lighter, healthier options even when they are featured on menus. Perhaps it is the occasional food and beverage guest that is less interested in healthier menu offerings than the more frequent guest, because the less frequent guest may see a dining-out experience as an opportunity to splurge and forget about personal diet issues, while the more frequent guest watches his or her diet more closely when dining out out of necessity. In any case, food and beverage operations of all types are focusing on providing healthier menu options. One way to do so is to use concentrated flavors rather than fats to add the extra taste desired by guests. Most guests do not object to food items with less fat, provided that there is little or no loss in flavor. In addition to concentrating flavors, having a variety of textures in a single menu item is another way to add interest to healthier menu choices.

One way some guests try to eat more healthfully while still ordering more traditional main courses is to order healthier side items such as salads or steamed vegetables. For these guests, it may not be necessary for a food and beverage operator to completely revise a menu to make it healthier. Rather, it may be enough to simply add healthy side items and a few lighter main courses to appeal to guests who want healthy choices, while continuing to keep the more traditional menu choices for the bulk of the menu to attract other guests.

In the future, food and beverage operators may have less choice in whether they offer guests healthier menu options. Some local and state governments are considering laws that ban trans fats on menus and require operators to include calorie counts for menu items. Legislators are considering requiring this across the spectrum of food and beverage operations, from quick-service restaurants to full-service restaurants. So it may be in every operator's best interest to consider some menu changes in advance of this legislation. Some changes are not that difficult to make. For example, reduced calorie counts are achievable simply by reducing portion sizes or offering different portion-size choices for current menu items.

In addition to reduced calorie counts and reduction of trans fats, sodium is an ingredient that may see more regulation in the future. The focus on sodium reduction is in keeping with the push by some consumers and regulators to focus on single ingredients in processed foods and/or menu items. Some health and dietary experts advise against this single-item focus, urging instead that everyone involved look at the complete picture and take a more balanced view. Another ingredient-based focus may be on gluten, as more and more consumers are diagnosed with gluten allergies.

Reducing sodium in food may help guests with hypertension and high blood pressure, but salt is often used as a preservative and a contributor to the flavor of menu items. Sodium is a naturally occurring ingredient in foods, and is it fair to those not suffering from a sodium-related health issue to reduce sodium in foods? These and other questions will have to be sorted out as the debate about diet, health, and the public interest continues.

Food Allergies

Food allergens are ingredients in foods that cause those who consume the foods to have an allergic reaction. It's estimated that more than 300 million people worldwide are on special diets because of food allergies. This has the potential to negatively affect the revenue of food and beverage operations, because if guests with food allergies do not trust food and beverage staff members to be knowledgeable about food allergies or food ingredients, they may dine out less. Therefore, it would be wise for food and beverage operators to study food allergies and ways they can make available menu choices designed to accommodate guests with allergies. As an example of just one resource, the Food Allergy & Anaphylaxis Network's website at www.foodallergy.org includes articles about food allergies, staff training tips, food-labeling information, case studies, and practical suggestions for accommodating guests with food allergies.

Smoking

Not all that long ago, restaurant seating was typically divided 75 percent smoking and 25 percent no-smoking. Today, that ratio is reversed in many restaurants, and, in some locales, smoking in restaurants is banned completely. People in the United States have changed their attitudes about the acceptability of smoking in public places, including the dining areas of food and beverage operations.

One of the turning points came in 1993, when the Environmental Protection Agency (EPA) classified secondhand smoke as a Class A carcinogen. As such, it was linked to lung cancer and other respiratory diseases, and it was put in the same category as such cancer-causing substances as asbestos, benzene, and radon. Based on the EPA's report, the Working Group on Tobacco (an organization of 18 state attorneys general) recommended that all quick-service chains voluntarily ban smoking in their restaurants. McDonald's was one of the first to do so, issuing a no-smoking policy for its 1,400 corporate-owned restaurants. The National Council of Chain Restaurants (NCCR), representing 40 of the nation's largest chain restaurant companies, went on to support the Smoke-Free Environment Act of 1993. Many other food and beverage operations have banned or severely restricted smoking.

In the spring of 1993, Vermont became the first state to outlaw smoking in public places. In 1995, California banned smoking in most indoor workplaces, including the nonbar areas of restaurants; in 1998 the 35,000 previously exempt bars, casinos, and restaurants in the state were required to ban smoking as well.

Since that time, other states have enacted laws banning or restricting smoking in restaurants and other public places. But the fight isn't over; owners and managers of food and beverage operations on both sides of the issue are pressing for legislative changes.

The economic effects of no-smoking laws on food and beverage operations are still undetermined and vary based on the type of operation, its location, and its guests. The situation is not black-and-white. Some operations in states that still allow smoking in food and beverage establishments have voluntarily become smoke-free and report increased business from former guests and new guests who had been avoiding smoky environments. On the other hand, some food and beverage operations that have banned or restricted smoking as a result of local or state ordinances report that this has led to lost guests, lost revenues, and staff cutbacks. Each food and beverage operation will have to decide for itself how best to meet the needs of its guests and staff members while complying with existing laws. Increasingly, these laws are banning smoking entirely in food and beverage operations.

Legal Issues

Several issues that affect the legal responsibilities of a food and beverage operation have already been presented. Additional legal issues that will be discussed at some length in this section include risk management, sexual harassment, the Americans with Disabilities Act, minimum wage and immigration reform, health care reform, and AIDS and herpes. Each has a real or potential impact on food and beverage operations.

Risk Management

Earlier in the chapter, the fundamentals of a food safety risk management (FSRM) program were presented. Recall that the goal of an FSRM program is to reduce sanitation risks, as well as address key quality and cost control issues. Risk management, as it relates to legal liability, has surfaced as an area of acute concern in the food and beverage industry. Often, liability issues are raised because service to guests did not meet guest expectations.

Alcohol service is an area of particular concern when managing risk. Some states have modified their dram shop laws to make drinkers of alcoholic beverages more responsible for their actions. These states have outlined in detail the procedures that operations should follow to provide responsible alcohol service. When an intoxicated guest leaves the premises and is involved in someone's injury or death (and a subsequent lawsuit), some states now require proof that the provider or seller of alcoholic beverages knew the guest was intoxicated when the guest was served and that the intoxication was the direct cause of the injury or death. It is essential for food and beverage managers to stay current on the laws that affect them, their staffs, and their operations in the areas of alcohol service and liability.

The goal of food and beverage operations is to move toward an ideal level of service. As service moves toward this level, the sales potential (as well as tip income and guest loyalty) increases, while the liability potential is reduced. By lowering legal exposure and liability while meeting or exceeding guests' expectations, managers of an operation can create a win-win situation for guests, staff members, and the operation.

Sexual Harassment

Sexual harassment has no place in any food and beverage operation. It is illegal, immoral, and potentially devastating to the lives of everyone involved. In more practical terms, sexual harassment interferes with an operation's efficiency, and sexual harassment complaints have the potential to cost an operation a great deal of money. It's been estimated that legal fees for defending a civil case in court average over $250,000, and judgments in sexual harassment cases routinely exceed $1 million. Even food and beverage operations that are never taken to court are affected. The U.S. Department of Labor estimates that U.S. businesses lose about $1 billion annually due to workplace problems caused by sexual harassment.

Title VII of the Civil Rights Act of 1964 protects staff members from sexual harassment. However, until 1991, victims who had lost their jobs were allowed only to collect back pay and lost wages and be reinstated. In 1991, Congress amended the Civil Rights Act to allow sexual harassment victims to receive compensatory and punitive damages.

The Equal Employment Opportunity Commission (EEOC) guidelines define sexual harassment as "unwelcome sexual advances, requests for sexual favors, and other verbal or physical conduct of a sexual nature." Title VII defines two forms of sexual harassment that might occur in the workplace. The first is *quid pro quo* harassment. This form of sexual harassment occurs when a staff member's employment status is directly linked to whether the staff member is willing to participate in unwanted sexual activity. A "hostile work environment" is the more common form of sexual harassment. A hostile work environment is one that unreasonably interferes with a staff member's ability to work or creates an offensive workplace.

Prohibited sexual harassment includes, but is not limited to:

- Sexual assault or otherwise coerced sexual intercourse

- Propositions or pressure to engage in sexual activity

- Sexual innuendo, suggestive comments, insults, threats, or obscene gestures

- Inappropriate comments concerning appearance

- Leering or ogling in a sexually provocative manner

- Sexual or sexually insulting written communications or public postings, including those that appear in electronic media or e-mail

- Display of magazines, books, or pictures with a sexual connotation

- A pattern of hiring or promoting sex partners over more qualified persons

- Any harassing behavior, whether or not sexual in nature, that is directed toward a person because of the person's gender—including, but not limited to, hazing workers employed in nontraditional work environments

It is essential that every food and beverage operation create policies that make it clear that the operation will not tolerate sexual harassment. These policies should also clearly state how a staff member can file a complaint and get a complaint resolved. Sexual harassment policies should be communicated to everyone in the operation and to new staff members as they are hired. The EEOC encourages employers to "take all steps necessary to prevent sexual harassment from occurring, such as affirmatively raising the subject; expressing strong disapproval; developing appropriate sanctions; informing staff members of their right to raise, and how to raise, the issue of harassment under Title VII; and developing methods to sensitize all concerned."

Americans with Disabilities Act

The **Americans with Disabilities Act (ADA)** makes it unlawful to discriminate against workers with disabilities in employment and related practices, such as recruitment, selection, training, pay, job assignments, leave, benefits, layoff, promotion, and termination. There are an estimated 43 million Americans who have some type of disability. Based on the ADA, they are qualified for employment if they can perform the essential functions of a position with or without reasonable accommodation. "Reasonable accommodation" refers to what the employer must do to make the work environment accessible to those with disabilities. The act also addresses design considerations for public areas, to make sure these areas are accessible by individuals who have disabilities. For example, high-contrast colors for doors and walks in public areas can assist guests in locating doorways. Doors must be fitted with push or levered handles. Textural differences on floors not only are appealing, but allow those with visual impairments to sense when they are moving from one kind of space to another. Deep pile carpeting and uneven floors should be eliminated.

Wheelchair accessibility presents additional challenges. Steps should be removed between lobbies and dining areas and replaced with ramps. Dining area seating should be spaced wide enough to permit wheelchair access. Buffets, salad bars, and other bar setups can be constructed to be low enough for people who use wheelchairs to access, yet still be comfortable for other guests. Restrooms may need to be remodeled to accommodate everyone's needs. Where steps are present in addition to ramps, they should be equipped with lighted strips to indicate level changes. Elevator doors must operate with slow timers so that guests with disabilities who are entering or exiting are not rushed. Gift shops and other public areas can be designed with access in mind. Vending machines should be accessible to all guests. Tax incentives in the form of deductions may help offset the costs associated with ADA compliance.

Thorough staff training is a key to complying with the ADA and making all guests feel comfortable. Information can be adapted from existing sources or developed using input from people with disabilities or advocacy groups for the disabled.

Minimum Wage and Immigration Reform

The minimum wage was implemented in 1934 because Congress believed that paying less than "decent" wages was illegal. In recent years, however, there has been increasing debate among business owners, workers, and legislators over what constitutes a "decent" minimum wage. As the figure rises every few years, each increase directly affects food and beverage operations, which typically rely on large numbers of entry-level, minimum-wage-earning staff members.

Minimum wage opponents firmly believe that food and beverage operations cannot simply pass wage increases on to guests through higher prices. Guests have alternatives; they can dine at home or purchase take-out food from a supermarket, for example. In addition, opponents cite more than two dozen studies that indicate higher minimum wages may shrink the number of entry-level jobs by as much as 2.5 percent for every 10 percent rise in the minimum wage. Yet minimum-wage positions can provide staff members with basic job skills that are transferable to other positions in other industries. The Employment Policies Institute has reported that:

- 93 percent of current and former food and beverage staff members said they were glad to have had the experience of working in a hospitality job for tips.

- 80 percent said the experience helped them develop important work skills useful for future employment.

- 79 percent would recommend such work to others.

Because of a shortage of qualified hospitality workers in many areas of the United States, many food and beverage operations are already paying entry-level workers more than the minimum wage. However, if minimum wages continue to rise, they may negatively affect the employment opportunities for entry-level food service workers, since operations may have to cut staff or hire fewer workers.

The **Immigration Reform and Control Act (IRCA)** was passed to control the hiring of illegal aliens in the United States and to prohibit discriminatory hiring practices. Fines for violations range from $100 to $10,000 and may include back pay, legal fees, and reinstatement of staff members.

Compliance with IRCA is not simply a matter of checking for correct documentation and completing the government's I-9 Employment Eligibility Verification Form. Discrimination can take the form of "citizenship status discrimination," "document abuse," and "national origin discrimination." While employers must verify that potential staff members are legally authorized to work in the United States, employers should not ask for additional information (e.g., work-status documentation) unless they ask everyone for such information. Otherwise, they might be accused of discrimination.

Several community-based organizations are educating immigrants regarding their workplace rights. Others are encouraging immigrants to fight discrimination in hiring. For these and other reasons, food service managers should be fully aware of IRCA and its ramifications for their businesses. Enforcement of IRCA provisions is expected to increase.

Health Care Reform

Food and beverage operations have joined other service and manufacturing businesses in their concern over proposed health care reform mandates. The Business

Roundtable, an association of 200 chief executive officers representing some of the largest U.S. companies, has spoken out against specific legislation that would determine the scope of employer-provided health care. The National Restaurant Association (NRA) also is opposed to health care as an employer-paid option. According to their promotional material, "The National Restaurant Association will fight against employer mandates and for medical malpractice reform, increased deductibility for the self-insured, voluntary employer purchasing groups, and medical savings accounts." Food service managers should track proposed health care legislation and stay well informed on health care reform issues.

AIDS and Herpes

Although AIDS and herpes simplex are *not* foodborne according to current scientific information, they are topics of concern for owners, managers, staff members, and guests of food and beverage operations.

AIDS—acquired immune deficiency syndrome—is caused by HIV, a virus that attacks a person's immune system. As the virus reproduces in the body, it reduces the body's natural ability to resist infections. The virus can survive in the human body for years before actual symptoms appear. AIDS is transmitted in the following four ways:

- Sexual contact with a person infected with the AIDS virus

- Sharing drug needles and syringes with a person infected with the AIDS virus

- Blood-to-blood contact involving infected fluids

- Perinatal transmission from mother to child during pregnancy or transmission through breast-feeding

There is no medical evidence that proves the AIDS virus can be transmitted through saliva, tears, perspiration, or mosquito bites, or by using drinking fountains, toilet seats, toothbrushes, or other items used by someone with AIDS. The Centers for Disease Control and Prevention (CDC) have stated: "All epidemiologic and laboratory evidence indicates that bloodborne and sexually transmitted infections are not transmitted during the preparation or serving of food and beverages." The CDC guidelines on AIDS in the workplace state, "Food service workers known to be infected [with the AIDS virus] need not be restricted from work unless they have evidence of other infection or illness for which any food service worker should be restricted." Perhaps the best way for food and beverage managers to handle AIDS is to initiate an educational campaign that clearly presents the facts to staff members.

Although it has been overshadowed by the AIDS virus, **herpes simplex virus (HSV)** is also receiving attention because of its increasing incidence. HSV consists of two different but closely related viruses: HSV-type 1, which causes approximately 90 percent of ocular and oral (fever blisters and cold sores) herpes infections; and HSV-type 2, which causes about 85 percent of genital herpes infections.

HSV can be transmitted when any part of a person's body directly touches active HSV or sores containing active HSV. Mucous membranes and broken or damaged skin are easy points of entry into the body. Even though HSV cannot survive very long outside of the human body, recent information suggests that HSV might be able to survive in warm, damp towels.

HSV is not known to be transmitted by food or drinking water, through the air, by water in hot tubs and swimming pools, or by toilet seats. HSV is not transmitted by food-contact surfaces or equipment. Nevertheless, it is critical for all staff members to practice good personal hygiene and personal cleanliness procedures, including proper handwashing, while at work.

Other Legal Issues

A relatively new legal issue facing food and beverage operators today is that of guests who claim that their long-term consumption of food and beverage products has resulted in weight gain to the point of becoming obese. For example, several vending operators have been asked to eliminate carbonated sodas and other beverages from vending machines in schools because of weight gain by children that may or may not be directly linked to consumption of those products. Quick-service restaurants have been a target of obesity lawsuits. The issue is not clear-cut, but one point *is* clear. Whether to purchase and consume a food and beverage product is a choice; individuals are not forced to purchase or consume certain products. However, obesity is a serious health issue in the United States, and obesity lawsuits remain a potential legal concern for some food and beverage operators.

Menu labeling is another legal issue. To pre-empt the proliferation of menu labeling requirements, some individual operators and chain restaurants are choosing to voluntarily provide nutritional information to their guests, such as information about calories, carbohydrates, sodium, cholesterol, and the fat content of menu items. One food and beverage chain tied its information about special diabetes-friendly menus to the Diabetes Research Institute and National Diabetes Month. Another chain has developed a special menu for guests with celiac disease. When guests identify themselves as being interested in ordering from this special menu, the chef comes to the guests' tables to answer questions.

You may not think of guest complaints as a potential legal issue, but there is a legal side to some guest complaints, such as those involving discrimination or food safety. It is a fact that complaints that are not handled properly are more likely to result in lawsuits to resolve them. Therefore, food and beverage operators should have in place a process to handle guest complaints, including, if necessary, procedures for gathering facts, taking remedial measures, dealing with the media, and interacting with advocacy groups. When dealing with the area of discrimination, as a first step an operator should have a written personnel policy or staff member code of conduct addressing the acceptable treatment of staff members and guests. The sooner that guest complaints that touch on legal issues are addressed and resolved, the less likely that litigation will take place.

 **Key Terms**

acquired immune deficiency syndrome (AIDS)—A disease affecting the immune system, caused by a virus that can be transmitted through bodily fluids.

Americans with Disabilities Act (ADA)—Legislation passed by the U.S. Congress that requires commercial operations to remove barriers to persons with disabilities in the workplace and to provide facilities for guests with disabilities.

bioterrorism—The intentional use of harmful biological substances to injure or terrorize others.

cardiopulmonary resuscitation (CPR)—A technique used to provide circulation and breathing to a victim whose heart or lungs have stopped functioning.

Class A fire—The burning of ordinary combustibles such as wood, paper, and cloth. A Class A fire can be extinguished with water and water-based or general-purpose fire-extinguishing chemicals.

Class B fire—A fire involving flammable liquids such as grease, gasoline, paint, and other oils. It can be extinguished by eliminating the air supply and smothering the fire.

Class C fire—An electrical fire, usually involving motors, switches, and wiring. It can be extinguished with chemicals that do not conduct electricity.

critical control point (CCP)—A point or procedure in a food preparation or serving process where loss of control may result in an unacceptable health risk.

Food Code—A model code last published by the U.S. Food and Drug Administration (FDA) in 2001 and updated in 2004. It represents the FDA's best advice for a uniform system of regulations to ensure that food sold at retail establishments is safe and properly protected and presented.

foodborne illness—An illness caused either by germs in food (known as "food infection") or by germ-produced poisons in food (known as "food poisoning").

food safety risk management (FSRM) program—A program that identifies food-safety risks and implements procedures for reducing those risks.

HACCP plan—A written document that delineates formal procedures for following the Hazard Analysis Critical Control Point principles.

Hazard Analysis Critical Control Point (HACCP) system—A system that identifies and monitors specific foodborne hazards. The hazard analysis identifies critical control points (CCPs)—those points in the food preparation or serving process that must be controlled to ensure food safety. CCPs are monitored and verified in subsequent steps to ensure that risks are controlled. All of this information is specified in an operation's HACCP plan.

Heimlich maneuver—A generally accepted technique for saving a choking victim by squeezing the trapped air out of the victim's lungs, forcing the obstruction out.

herpes simplex virus (HSV)—A term used for two different but closely related viruses: HSV-type 1 causes the majority of oral and ocular herpes infections; HSV-type 2 causes the majority of genital herpes infections. HSV can be transmitted when any part of a person's body directly touches active HSV or sores containing active HSV. It is not known to be transmitted by food or drinking water or by food-contact surfaces or equipment.

Immigration Reform and Control Act (IRCA)—Federal legislation designed to regulate the employment of aliens in the United States and to protect staff members from discrimination on the basis of citizenship or nationality.

potentially hazardous foods—Any foods or ingredients in a form capable of supporting (a) the rapid and progressive growth of infectious or toxigenic microorganisms; (b) the growth and toxin production of *Clostridium botulinum;* or (c) in raw shell eggs, the growth of *Salmonella Enteritidus.* Potentially hazardous food includes a food of animal origin that is raw or heat-treated; a food of plant origin that is heat-treated or raw seed sprouts; cut melon; and garlic-in-oil mixtures that are not modified in a way that results in mixtures that do not support growth.

temperature danger zone (TDZ)—The temperature range of 41°F–140°F (5°C–60°C), defined by the U.S. Public Health Service as the range in which most pathogenic activity takes place in food and food spoilage can occur.

 # Review Questions

1. What is the HACCP system and how is it implemented in food and beverage operations?

2. How can servers help ensure food safety?

3. What preventive measures can be taken to help reduce workplace accidents?

4. What are the differences between Class A, B, and C fires?

5. What steps can be taken in the event of a robbery? a bomb threat?

6. What nutritional information is increasingly important to guests?

7. What does the Americans with Disabilities Act mean for food and beverage operations?

8. Why are AIDS and herpes simplex topics of concern for food service managers?

 # Case Studies

Did Food Poisoning Happen Here?

Luis Diaz, the food and beverage director of the Herndon Hotel, is in a cheerful mood at 10:30 A.M. this Thursday in September. The hotel has just finished serving a 1,000-seat kickoff breakfast to the United Way Campaign leadership and volunteers. The annual campaign is about to start, and Chris Chambers, the general chairman (and local bank president) wanted a particularly elegant breakfast to instill optimism in and inspire the audience.

Luis and Chris worked on the breakfast together, choosing the menu, the color of the linen, the table setting, etc.

The menu consisted of eggs Benedict, hash brown potatoes, asparagus spears with hollandaise sauce, a fruit compote, rolls (both bread and sweet), and the usual juices and other beverages. At the breakfast, Chris gave a rousing speech, and at the conclusion of his remarks asked Luis, Eduardo (the chef), and all the kitchen staff to enter the dining room for applause by the audience.

Luis smiled and thought to himself, "I think we can put this one in the 'win' column."

At 2 P.M. on that Thursday, the buoyant spirit Luis had felt earlier was rapidly disappearing. Chris Chambers had called him to say that he had been hearing from others at the breakfast that they were becoming ill, experiencing stomach cramps and nausea, and some were vomiting. Chris himself was experiencing a cold sweat and had visited the restroom with greater frequency than normal.

As he was finishing his conversation with Chris, Linda Berry, the hotel's general manager, came into Luis' office and said, "I've just had four calls in the last 20 minutes from people who said they were at breakfast this morning and are now ill. They think it had to be something they ate at the breakfast."

At that moment, Patricia, Luis' secretary, appeared in the doorway and said that a county health official was on the phone and wanted to come over immediately. Luis took a deep breath and said, "Let me speak with him."

Discussion Questions

1. If you were Luis, what would you say to the health official at this point?

2. If it is determined that food poisoning was evident at the breakfast, what do you do now, to overcome the current situation and to keep it from ever happening again?

This case was taken from William P. Fisher and Robert A. Ashley, *Case Studies in Commercial Food Service Operations* (Lansing, Mich.: American Hotel & Lodging Educational Institute, 2003).

How Special Is the Luncheon Special Caper

Mary Chang is the chef/owner of Chang's Chinese Restaurant, a 102-seat restaurant in an ethnic Chinese area of a major U.S. city on the West Coast. The restaurant has been in business for a little over two years and has experienced a growing patronage at both lunch and dinner.

Mary always has a special of the day that many of her regular customers look forward to.

On this Monday morning, Mary is debating what her specials will be for the week. The sweet and sour chicken over fried rice has been popular recently and she decides that that will be the Tuesday special.

Mary knows the standardized recipe calls for the rice to be cooked off the day before for the fried rice. In other words, the rice had to be cooked off today. She finished it at 10 A.M. She placed the rice in a covered steam table pan and placed it on the kitchen counter to cool. At 6:00 P.M., eight hours after it was cooked, she placed the pan of rice in a refrigerator at 38 degrees Fahrenheit.

The next day, Tuesday, Mary started production of the rice dish at 9 A.M., mixing in other ingredients to make the stir-fried rice. Checking the standardized recipe, she brought the mixture to 165 degrees Fahrenheit for a minimum of 15 seconds. She then placed the rice in the steam table at 10:30 A.M., one hour before lunch service began.

Later, Margaret Chow, the restaurant's hostess, tells Mary that a luncheon customer is on the phone complaining that he has been vomiting and has had diarrhea since 1 P.M., shortly after he had lunch. Margaret says the customer wants to talk to the owner. Mary picks up the phone.

"This is Mary Chang, how may I assist you?"

The customer says, "I had lunch at your restaurant today and I now feel awful. I can't keep anything down."

"What did you eat?" Mary inquires.

"I had the luncheon special, it was sweet and sour chicken with fried rice. It tasted wonderful at the time, but something has hit me and I thought you ought to know about it," the customer said.

Discussion Questions

1. If you were Mary, what would you say or do?

2. Was there a problem in the kitchen? If so, what is it?

3. What remedial procedures should be undertaken?

This case was taken from William P. Fisher and Robert A. Ashley, *Case Studies in Commercial Food Service Operations* (Lansing, Mich.: American Hotel & Lodging Educational Institute, 2003).

Safety Is No Accident!

"I've got some bad news I'm afraid," Brad Morris tells his friend and client Ken Alter. Brad is an insurance agent who has handled all of Ken's insurance requirements since Ken first opened his restaurant seven years ago. The restaurant, Ken's Korner, has 280 seats and employs 130 people, full or part time.

"It's your worker's compensation premium, Ken. It has more than doubled this year. I called the company and asked them to check their calculations, thinking they may have made a mistake. They didn't. It's all those injury and accident claims that have got their attention, Ken. They even mentioned that they came close to canceling the policy altogether."

Ken knew that there had been a number of incidents over the past year that resulted in lost time for some of his employees, but he thought it was just a run of back luck and that everything would work itself out in the long run.

"That's money right out of my pocket!" Ken exclaimed. "Is there anything I can do?"

"Well, Ken," Brad began, anticipating such a question, "we've got to eliminate or drastically reduce the number of accidents in the future that you've experienced in the past. If you don't have a safety checklist, you better put one together and make sure all your employees read it and heed it. It should be part of your training program and a standing agenda item for your staff meetings."

Discussion Questions

1. If you were Ken, what items would you include on the safety checklist?

2. How do you inspire a safety first attitude in your employees?

This case was taken from William P. Fisher and Robert A. Ashley, *Case Studies in Commercial Food Service Operations* (Lansing, Mich.: American Hotel & Lodging Educational Institute, 2003).

The Health Inspector Is at the Door!

Jim Carlisle is the owner/manager of the Pinnacle, a 240-seat fine-dining restaurant. In addition to the 40-seat cocktail lounge, there is a banquet room that can accommodate up to 80 guests. The menu is traditional American fare, and the signature item is the Pinnacle cut of roast beef, a 24-ounce bone in rib cut. Jim inherited the business from his father three years ago. The restaurant is open six days a week for lunch and dinner.

On a Friday at 10 A.M., Jim is in his office reviewing the labor schedule for the upcoming busy weekend. One of Jim's servers stops by his office to tell him that a Mr. Hedges, who says he is with the county health department, is in the foyer, accompanied by a young lady. Mr. Hedges wishes to speak with the manager.

Jim rises from his chair and goes to the front of the restaurant. The gentleman introduces himself as Bob Hedges from the health department and announces he is here to inspect the premises. He introduces his companion, Sally Rodgers, who is a department trainee. Mr. Hedges asks Jim if he will consent to having Sally accompany him on the inspection.

Jim asks to see authorizing identification from both visitors, which they present and which is in order. Ordinarily, Jim is reluctant to have surplus visitors in the back-of-the-house areas due to safety and security precautions. However, the Pinnacle has had good relations with the health department, and Jim agrees to the inspection.

Discussion Questions

1. If you were Jim Carlisle, what would you do at this point?

2. If you were Bob Hedges, what are the key areas that you would bring to the attention of Sally Rodgers as being the most critical areas or the most frequently violated food safety standards?

3. If the restaurant receives a passing score, what do you say to your employees?

4. What are the levels of repercussion if the restaurant does not receive a passing score?

This case was taken from William P. Fisher and Robert A. Ashley, *Case Studies in Commercial Food Service Operations* (Lansing, Mich.: American Hotel & Lodging Educational Institute, 2003).

 References

Allen, Robin Lee. "The Fries, They Are a-Changin', and the Public's Call for Healthful Food Presents a Chance to Grow Sales." *Nation's Restaurant News.* September 1, 2008. 42(34): 19.

Bee, Lisa and Gerald L. Maatman, Jr. "Is the Customer Always Right on EPL?" *National Underwriter.* February 16, 2004. 108(6): 24.

Bowman, Quinn. "Legal Grounds: A Look at Some of the More Prominent Legislative Issues Facing the Quick-Service Industry." *QSR Magazine.* December 2005. www.qsrmagazine.com/issue/84/legal.phtml

Butler, Chef Dan. "Lighten Up! How to Cut Fat from the Menu." *Restaurant Startup & Growth.* August 2007: 51–52.

Frumkin, Paul. "Industry Heads Back to Regulatory Salt Mines as Lawmakers Turn Attention to Sodium Levels in Food." *Nation's Restaurant News.* March 16, 2009. 43(10): 21.

———. "Make Menu Labeling Work for You by Beating Mandates to the Punch." *Nation's Restaurant News.* January 26, 2009. 43(3): 38–39.

———. "Nutrition Groups Set Sights on Sodium as Next Menu Battleground." *Nation's Restaurant News.* June 30, 2008. 42(26): 3.

Glazer, Fern. "NPD: Consumers Seek Out Restaurants with Healthful Options." *Nation's Restaurant News.* August 11, 2008. 42(31): 16.

"Health and Sanitation...Table for Two, Hold the Roaches." *Restaurant Startup & Growth.* July 2008. 5(7): 15–16.

Hernandez, Jorge. "Sanitation Standards Savvy." *Food Management.* October 2001. 36(10): 78.

Hume, Scott. "Basics Training." *Restaurants & Institutions.* September 1, 2005. 115(16): 85.

Johnson, Beth. "Uniform Menu-Labeling Standards Would Help to Limit Costs, Confusion." *Nation's Restaurant News.* March 23, 2009. 43(11): 18–19.

Licata, Elizabeth. "Healthy Menu Options Can Eliminate Veto Votes from Guests." *Nation's Restaurant News.* March 23, 2009. 43(11): 29.

Luebke, Patricia. "About 80 Percent of Diners Eat Out Less Frequency Due to Food Allergies and Celiac Disease." *Restaurant Startup & Growth*. October 2008. 5(10): 8.

———. "Loss Prevention Starts Small for Big Results." *Restaurant Startup & Growth*. February 2008. 5(1): 8.

———. "Poll Suggests Consumers' Greatest Concerns When Dining Out." *Restaurant Startup & Growth*. February 2008. 5(1): 8–9.

———. "What to Do When You Hear 'I Got Sick at Your Restaurant.'" *Restaurant Startup & Growth*. August 2007:8–9.

Meyer, Diana Lambdin. "Don't Bite the Hand That Regulates You." *Restaurant Startup & Growth*. November 2008. 5(11): 38–45.

"Nutrition Labeling, Jobs Creation Are Top Concerns." *Show Daily: Restaurant Hospitality & Food Management*. May 24, 2010: 1, 6.

Runk, David. "State Promoting Healthy Eating." *Lansing State Journal*. May 30, 2010: 6B.

"Welcoming Guests with Food Allergies." *Restaurant Startup & Growth*. January 2009. 6(1): 12.

"What to Do if You Are Robbed." *Restaurant Startup & Growth*. July 2008. 5(7): 10.

Wilson, Stanford G. and William A. Pinto, Jr. "May the Force Be With You: Improving Restaurant Security by Working With Local Law Enforcement." *Restaurant Startup & Growth*. April 2008. 5(4): 45–47.

Internet Sites

For more information, visit the following Internet sites. Remember that Internet addresses can change without notice. If the site is no longer there, you can use a search engine to look for additional sites.

ADA Home Page
www.ada.gov

AllergyFree Passport
www.allergyfreepassport.com

Celiac Disease Foundation
www.celiac.org

Centers for Disease Control and
  Prevention
www.cdc.gov

Food Allergy & Anaphylaxis Network
www.foodallergy.org

FoodSafety.gov
www.foodsafety.gov

GlutenFree Passport
www.glutenfreepassport.com

Institute for Biosecurity
www.bioterrorism.slu.edu

Institute for Food Laws and
  Regulations
www.iflr.msu.edu

International Food Information
  Council Foundation
www.ific.org

MeatPoultry.com
www.meatpoultry.com

National Restaurant Association
www.restaurant.org

Nation's Restaurant News
www.nrn.com

Nutrition Navigator
http://navigator.tufts.edu

OSHA
www.osha.gov

U.S. Food and Drug Administration
www.fda.gov

Chapter 11 Outline

Labor and Revenue Control Considerations
Establishing Labor Standards
    Developing a Staffing Guide
Forecasting Sales
    Moving Average Method
    Weighted Time Series Method
    Forecasting for Lodging Properties
Preparing Work Schedules
Analyzing Labor Costs
Revenue Control Systems
    Manual Guest Check Systems
    Point-of-Sale Guest Check Systems
    Accepting Personal Checks
    Processing Payment Cards
    Point-of-Sale Settlement Devices
Revenue Collection
    Server Banking System
    Cashier Banking System
    Protecting Cash after Collection

Competencies

1. Discuss labor and revenue control and explain how food and beverage managers develop labor standards for service positions. (pp. 435–439)

2. Identify factors food and beverage managers consider when constructing a staffing guide, and distinguish between fixed and variable labor in relation to food and beverage service positions. (pp. 439–442)

3. Forecast food and beverage sales using the moving average and the weighted time series methods, and discuss sales forecasting for lodging properties. (pp. 442–446)

4. Explain how food and beverage managers use staffing guides to prepare work schedules and analyze labor costs. (pp. 446–452)

5. Describe revenue control procedures for manual guest check systems and for computer-based guest check systems, discuss policies for accepting personal checks, summarize guidelines for processing payment cards, and describe point-of-sale settlement devices. (pp. 452–460)

6. Distinguish the server banking system from the cashier banking system and explain how managers protect cash after collection. (pp. 460–464)

Labor and Revenue Control

Every dollar in excessive labor costs represents a dollar subtracted from the bottom line. Consider a restaurant operation that consistently exceeds its standard labor costs by $100 a week. During the course of a year, this would drop $5,200 off the bottom line. How much revenue would the restaurant have to generate to restore that amount to the bottom line? Much more than $5,200! If the restaurant's profit margin is 12 percent (.12), the restaurant would have to generate $43,333 in gross sales to make $5,200 in profit ($43,333 × 12 = $5,200 [rounded]). Clearly, when actual labor hours exceed standard labor hours, the restaurant must pull in a substantial amount of additional revenue to make up for the additional labor costs.

This chapter presents a systematic approach to labor cost control. The system begins with defining the quality of service offered by an operation and then determining labor standards. Labor standards indicate the number of labor hours required to deliver quality service at various volumes of business. Using a labor staffing guide and sales forecasts for various meal periods or day parts, managers are able to match up the required labor hours to the forecasted volume of business. Labor hours are then scheduled on the basis of labor standards and sales forecasts. Variances between actual labor hours and standard labor hours are analyzed for each meal period/day part and plans for corrective action are implemented to complete the cycle of labor cost control.

This chapter also addresses revenue control procedures. Obviously, a dollar of lost revenue also has an impact on the bottom line. Revenue control begins with establishing standards—the amount of revenue the operation expects to collect for specific meal periods. This chapter demonstrates how revenue standards are established by operations with manual guest check systems and by those with computer-based, point-of-sale guest check systems. In addition, sections of the chapter present procedures designed to help ensure that the actual revenue collected corresponds with established revenue standards.

Labor and Revenue Control Considerations

Labor and revenue controls and control systems vary in complexity, usually with the size and revenue volume of a food and beverage operation. Independent, privately owned operations often face challenges in labor and revenue control that larger operations that are affiliated with chain food and beverage organizations do not have to address. This is because chain operations have support (and revenue and labor control systems) from the chain's corporate headquarters; in contrast, independent operators are on their own to establish and monitor control systems.

Controls are nothing more than tools to help food and beverage managers monitor and evaluate the results of operations. Controls for revenues are designed to build sales and keep the sales revenues that are realized without an "evaporation" of these hard-earned revenues due to theft or carelessness. Accurate tracking and recording of sales are necessary if the operator is to know precisely the level of revenues. Similarly, detailed controls for labor and other operating costs help the operator plan for a profit (in a commercial food and beverage operation) or a surplus (in an on-site food and beverage operation) in order to stay in business.

Labor expenses in both the kitchen and service areas are really investments in the guests' overall dining experience. Given the labor requirements in a food and beverage operation and the percentage of total expenses that labor typically represents in an operation, labor standards and staffing guides are critical to maintaining control for the operator.

As a general trend, labor costs per hour have been rising in food and beverage operations due in part to rising minimum wages mandated by law. Higher labor costs also may mean that the operation is attracting and retaining more qualified and productive staff members. So higher labor costs can be a function of some good things happening at the operation, such as reduced staff member turnover and better staff member training.

Another labor control issue is the amount of staff member overtime. Overtime is not necessarily negative, as it may indicate that initial staff member scheduling was closely tied, and accurately compared, to the forecasted level of business. If the level of business increases beyond the forecast, overtime may be necessary and justified. When no overtime is ever being paid, it may indicate that staff member scheduling is "padded"—that is, too many staff members are being scheduled.

Labor costs may be able to be controlled in other ways that do not negatively affect guest satisfaction or profitability. Rather than cutting steaks in the operation's kitchen or preparing salad ingredients, pre-cut steaks or ready-to-serve salad ingredients may be purchased from distributors. Even though these steaks and salad ingredients may be more expensive to purchase (since they have "built-in" labor), they will likely reduce the operation's labor costs (as well as reduce portion control problems). The kitchen staff that used to cut the steaks and prepare the salads with raw ingredients may now be assigned to other responsibilities, or their labor hours may be reduced altogether.

It is difficult for food and beverage managers to achieve the proper level of staffing—not too low or too high. If staffing levels are usually too low, which means staff members feel overworked and are unable to properly perform the responsibilities of their positions, they will likely feel demoralized and are more likely to leave the operation, increasing the turnover rate, which increases labor costs. Just as it is more cost-effective to retain current guests than find new ones, it is more cost-effective to retain current productive staff than to continuously be looking for new staff members.

In contrast, if staff levels are too high—for example, if too many servers are scheduled for the number of guests—this leads to reduced shifts per server and fewer tips. Unproductive shifts force staff members to stand around, sometimes for long periods; then, if the operation gets busy, it is sometimes difficult for staff to pick up the pace of service and provide positive, memorable dining experiences for guests.

So it is the responsibility of the operation's managers, when scheduling staff members, to achieve a balance among the needs of the staff (adequate wages and a feeling of "this is a good place to work"), guests (delivering the expected levels of service and experiences), and the owner/operator (controlling costs to ensure profitability).

Establishing Labor Standards

All work should have a standard against which actual performance can be measured. Managers develop **labor standards** by determining the amount of time required to perform assigned tasks. Some managers know how long it should take to perform a particular task in a manner that meets the operation's service quality requirements. In this case, it is only necessary to formalize the knowledge by putting it in writing. However, in many operations, managers do not have this detailed knowledge. Perhaps no one has analyzed the job recently, perhaps work procedures have been changed since the last **job analysis**, or perhaps the management team is new to the unit.

Exhibit 1 suggests how to develop labor standards that incorporate service quality requirements. Let's assume that the manager (working with the host as well as with selected servers and other staff members) has established quality guest service levels in the dining area for the lunch period. This would entail defining the tasks performed by servers and outlining those tasks in a sequence of activities such as greeting the guests; approaching the table; providing beverages, salad, entrée, and dessert; and so on. An observation period is then set up during which the service staff follows all policies and procedures. The manager supervises the service staff during this period and assesses job performances by closely observing better-than-average servers. During the assessment, the manager answers such questions as:

- Is the server providing the required level of service?
- Does the server seem rushed or overworked?
- Could the server do more work and still maintain the required level of service quality?
- How many guests were served?
- How many more guests could be served, or how many fewer guests should be served in order to meet the required level of service quality?
- Are there any changes that can be made to improve the efficiency and effectiveness of the server?
- How long should it take for a new server to perform at the same skill level as an experienced server?

In the case of Exhibit 1, the manager observed a server over five lunch shifts. For each shift, the manager recorded the number of guests served and hours worked. For example, 38 guests were served during a four-hour work period on

Exhibit 1   Position Performance Analysis Form

Position Performance Analysis

Position: _____ *Service* _____   Name of Employee: _____ *Joyce* _____

Shift: _____ *A.M.—Lunch* _____

	4/14	4/15	4/16	4/17	4/18
No. of Guests Served	38	60	25	45	50
No. of Hours Worked	4	4	4	4	3.5
No. of Guests/Labor Hour	9.5	15	6.3	11.3	14.3
Review Comments	Even workflow; no problems	Was really rushed; could not provide adequate service	Too much "standing around"; very inefficient	No problems; handled everything well	Worked fast whole shift; better with fewer guests

General Comments

Joyce is a better than average server; with all the tasks that service personnel must do in our restaurant, approximately 10 guests per labor hour can be served by one server. When the number of guests goes up, service quality decreases. When Joyce really had to rush, some guests waited longer than they should have had to. When the number of guests per labor hour dropped and Joyce was not busy, there was a lot of unproductive time.

Suggested Guests/Labor Hour   10   *W. Brown*
(for this position):   _____   Performance Review by: _____

                                                        Restaurant Manager

---

April 14. That means 9.5 guests were served per labor hour (38 guests divided by 4 hours of work).

Before calculating a labor standard for this position, the manager would have completed worksheets for several trained servers who worked similar lunch shifts. In our example, the manager determined a labor standard of 10 guests per labor hour. That is, in the manager's view, trained servers should be able to serve 10 guests for each hour worked without sacrificing quality requirements.

With slight alterations, Exhibit 1's format can be used to determine labor standards for other positions in the operation. A performance analysis should be completed for each position and meal period or day part. This is because labor standards for positions are often different for each meal period/day part due to the different tasks required by the various menus and service styles. Also, if a business (such as a hotel, for example) has more than one food and beverage outlet, separate studies should be conducted for each outlet.

A labor standard functions as a productivity rate. Determining productivity rates by position and shift yields more useful information than determining an overall productivity rate for the entire operation. For example, suppose that, after carefully studying the operation, a manager determines that a productivity rate of

15 meals per labor hour is a desired efficiency level. Let's assume that productivity rates for cooks, dishwashers, and service staff were not considered separately. After a given meal period, the manager discovers that the actual productivity rate was only 13 meals per labor hour. Since the productivity rate was established without considering positions separately, the manager cannot pinpoint the cause of the lower overall productivity. If, however, the manager had known that the labor performance standard for servers was 10 guests per labor hour, while the actual productivity rate during the meal period or day part was only 8, then at least part of the problem could have been immediately traced to the service staff.

Developing a Staffing Guide

A staffing guide answers the question, "How many labor hours are needed for each position and shift to produce and serve a given number of meals while meeting minimum quality requirements?" The **staffing guide** incorporates labor standards and tells managers the number of labor hours needed for each position according to the volume of business forecasted for any given meal period. By converting the labor hour information into labor dollars, the manager can also establish standard labor costs. The staffing guide serves as a tool for both planning work schedules and controlling labor costs. When the number of actual labor hours significantly exceeds the standard labor hours identified by the staffing guide, managers should analyze the variance and take corrective action.

A staffing guide can be developed either for each department within the food and beverage operation or for each position within each department. If the staffing guide is developed for a department as a whole, first analyze and summarize each position within the department (such as cook, assistant cook, and kitchen helper in the food production department). Then, average the required labor hours. Developing a staffing guide for each position within each department provides more useful labor control information because it enables the schedule-maker to plan the number of labor hours needed for each position. If actual labor hours exceeded standard labor hours, it becomes obvious which position incurred the additional hours.

When constructing staffing guides, managers should keep in mind the following points:

- Each operation must set specific labor standards. Standards developed by another operation are generally meaningless, unless both operations are part of a chain offering uniform products and services.

- Labor standards should reflect the productivity rates of better-than-average staff members.

- As staff members become more efficient through experience, work simplification, or other efficiency measures, managers should change the staffing guide to reflect the higher productivity rates.

- The standard labor hours of a staffing guide need to be converted to labor dollars to ensure consistency with labor costs permitted by the operating budget.

Fixed and Variable Labor. Fixed labor refers to the minimum labor required to operate a food and beverage operation regardless of the volume of business. This minimum amount of labor must be considered and incorporated into the staffing guide as the minimum staffing level. For example, if the dining area is open from 6:00 A.M. to 11:00 A.M. for breakfast, there must be at least one server on duty no matter how slow the period may be. One server may work the entire five-hour shift or may work until 9:30 A.M., at which time another server takes over until 11:00 A.M. Regardless of the schedule pattern, in this example there is a fixed labor requirement of five labor hours for the server position during the breakfast shift. Up to a certain volume of business (a point determined by management), no additional servers are necessary. Above this defined level, however, additional labor is needed. This additional labor is referred to as **variable labor**, which varies according to the volume of business activity. As more guests are served or as more meals are produced, additional service and production labor is needed.

Exhibit 2 provides a sample staffing guide format for positions in a food and beverage operation. The hours noted in the staffing guide include the fixed hours required regardless of business volume. Examine the position of food server. When 50 dinners are forecasted, 8.5 food server labor hours should be scheduled. The 8.5 labor hours represent this operation's standard of meals served per labor hour, based upon its analysis of the food server position. That is, the labor standard (8.5 labor hours) equals the total hours this operation allows to serve 50 meals. The boxes also indicate the recommended number of servers to schedule (2 when 50 to 75 meals are forecasted, 4 when 100 to 150 meals are forecasted). The manager must decide which food servers to schedule, based on their abilities and availability.

The shifts listed in each box represent a staff schedule that takes into account typical peaks and valleys in business volume for each shift during the dinner period. In the first box, for example, the first server works a 5:00 P.M. to 9:30 P.M. shift, the second works a 7:00 P.M. to 11:00 P.M. shift, so that both servers are working during the peak dinner hours of 7:00 P.M. to 9:30 P.M. These shift times are based on patterns of business volume, reservation records, and other information suggesting times during which a specific number of servers are needed during the meal period. Also, note that the staffing guide in Exhibit 2 incorporates economies of scale. That is, the efficiency per unit of output increases as business volume increases. The exhibit shows that 16 server labor hours are scheduled when 100 or 125 meals are expected to be served.

Because the amount of fixed labor significantly affects the labor control program, if a business has more than one food and beverage outlet (a hotel or resort, for example), fixed labor requirements should be established for each outlet. While a manager designates the amount of fixed labor judged necessary, the assessment is always open for review. Factors such as changes in service quality requirements, menus, service styles, operating procedures, and guests' expectations influence the amount of fixed labor required. Careful analysis of work performance ensures that staff members are as productive as their situation permits. For example, on an average slow shift (when most labor is fixed), how much of the staff members' time is spent on work normally expected of the position? As the amount of idle time increases, it is important for managers to reconsider the hours of operation. Perhaps the outlet can open later or close earlier. Or managers might consider

Exhibit 2   Sample Staffing Guide

Standard Labor Hour Staffing Guide: Dinner				
Number of Meals				
50	75	100	125	150
Position Food Server				
8.5 5:00-9:30 7:00-11:00	9.5 5:00-9:30 6:30-11:30	16.0 5:00-9:30 6:30-10:00 7:00-10:00 7:30-12:30	16.0 5:00-9:30 6:30-10:00 7:00-10:00 7:30-12:30	19.0 5:00-10:00 6:00-11:00 6:00-11:00 7:30-11:30
Bartender				
9.0 4:00-1:00	9.0 4:00-1:00	9.0 4:00-1:00	9.0 4:00-1:00	9.0 4:00-1:00
Cocktail Server				
6.5 4:30-11:00	6.5 4:30-11:00	6.5 4:30-11:00	6.5 4:30-11:00	6.5 4:30-11:00
Cook				
7 4:00-11:00	14 3:00-10:00 5:00-12:00	14 3:00-10:00 5:00-12:00	14 3:00-10:00 5:00-12:00	16 3:00-11:00 4:00-12:00
Steward				
6.5 5:00-11:30	6.5 5:00-11:30	9.0 3:00-12:00	9.5 3:00-12:30	9.5 3:00-12:30
Busperson				
—	2 7:30-9:30	4 7:30-9:30 7:30-9:30	5 7:00-9:30 7:30-10:00	7 7:00-9:30 7:30-10:00 7:30-9:30
Host (Manager serves as host on slow evenings)				
—	3 6:00-9:00	3.5 6:00-9:30	4.0 6:00-10:00	4.0 6:00-10:00

NOTE: Labor hour standards are used for illustrative purposes only. Information must be developed for a specific operation based upon factors that influence worker efficiency within that food service operation.

adding tasks for the fixed-labor staff members to perform. Servers performing additional duties during slow times could reduce the amount of labor needed during subsequent shifts.

Salaried labor costs do not increase or decrease according to the number of guests served. One manager, paid at a predetermined salary rate, represents a fixed labor cost. Normally, salaried personnel should be scheduled to perform only the work their job descriptions require. Managerial tasks should be scheduled during slow times during the day. During busy times, managers must be available to perform supervisory and operational duties. However, during slow meal periods or day parts, salaried staff could be assigned duties normally performed by hourly staff members. For example, an assistant restaurant manager might be stationed at the host stand, seating guests and taking reservations. However, salaried staff should not be used indiscriminately to reduce hourly labor costs. It is often wise to develop responsibilities, tasks, and the volume of work for salaried staff first;

then schedule variable-labor staff to perform the remaining tasks. Although managers should know how to perform all the tasks in the operation, salaried staff should not be the first chosen to replace hourly staff members who fail to report to work. Efficiency, attitude, and ability all decrease as the length of the workweek increases. Turnover in management positions can often be traced to overwork.

Operations with unionized work forces must incorporate a wide range of other restrictions into the staffing guide. It is not uncommon, for example, for a labor contract to stipulate the minimum and maximum hours that a server can work per shift. Some unionized operations have a specific ratio of seats or guests that one staff member can serve. Overtime restrictions for unscheduled labor hours and the number and timing of work breaks may also need to be considered. Another basic part of many union contracts is the exact definition of tasks that union members in each position can and cannot perform. For example, if food and beverage servers cannot clear tables, the variable staffing guide should exclude the time required to perform this task from the server's labor hours and include it only under the labor hours required for buspersons.

Forecasting Sales

There are no industry standards for food and beverage managers to refer to when forecasting sales, since sales forecasts are unique to each food and beverage operation because of its clientele, location, menu, service style, and other variables. Therefore it is up to each operation's managers to create reliable sales forecasts.

Sound sales forecasts are crucial to many areas of a food and beverage operation. Production staff use sales forecasts to purchase, receive, store, issue, and produce menu items in sufficient quantities to serve the estimated number of guests. Forecasting sales involves more than just predicting sales volumes in terms of dollars. To schedule the right number of production and service staff, managers must know approximately how many guests to expect, what they are likely to order, and when they are likely to arrive. This is all part of forecasting sales as well.

Forecasts are a form of predicting the future, and prediction—by its very nature—is inexact, because the future is rarely a mirror image or simple projection of the past. Forecasts are usually based on historical averages for each meal period or day part and then adjusted to account for current conditions. For example, if the road in front of a restaurant is partially closed for construction now, and it was not under construction last year during the same week, the forecasted number of guests may be reduced for the current week. In contrast, if the operation is advertising a special menu promotion this week that was not offered during the same week in the previous year, managers may decide to bump up forecasted guest counts. It is important that the person doing the forecast keep in touch with current events that may influence the operation's guest counts, events either in the operation itself (special promotions, for example) or in the local community (such as a convention).

Usually, it is valuable to not only forecast by meal period or day part, but to have an idea of which hours will be the busiest within a meal period/day part. For example, if an operation defines its lunch day part as 11:30 A.M. to 2:30 P.M., and most guests who come to lunch at the operation want to dine between noon and

Exhibit 3 Hourly Revenue Report

Through Time	Revenue	Guests	Checks	Labor Hrs	Labor $$	Lbr/Rev
8:00 AM	0.00	0	0	0.00	0.00	0.00%
9:00 AM	0.00	0	0	0.13	0.70	0.00%
10:00 AM	0.00	0	0	5.52	27.46	0.00%
11:00 AM	0.00	1	1	10.28	47.68	0.00%
12:00 PM	100.45	12	5	16.30	65.98	65.68%
1:00 PM	93.40	7	8	17.78	67.81	72.60%
2:00 PM	139.05	14	13	18.00	67.81	48.77%
3:00 PM	76.80	6	10	18.00	67.81	88.29%
4:00 PM	615.89	86	56	17.67	64.42	10.46%
5:00 PM	240.55	7	12	25.17	85.85	35.69%
6:00 PM	609.85	48	28	39.73	137.82	22.60%
7:00 PM	1,319.29	141	89	45.42	160.94	12.20%
8:00 PM	1,573.40	167	131	52.70	190.49	12.11%
9:00 PM	1,815.77	92	169	56.95	213.66	11.77%
10:00 PM	1,376.40	67	213	57.50	229.18	16.65%
11:00 PM	1,317.80	159	237	51.53	203.61	15.45%
12.00 AM	1,281.95	34	237	47.18	181.08	14.13%
1:00 AM	1,220.30	22	231	38.62	152.32	12.48%
2:00 AM	791.30	122	161	32.97	128.98	16.30%
3:00 AM	2,575.50	3	3	20.90	78.13	3.03%
4:00 AM	0.00	0	0	6.73	11.67	0.00%
5:00 AM	0.00	0	0	0.00	0.00	0.00%
6:00 AM	0.00	0	0	0.00	0.00	0.00%
7:00 AM	0.00	0	0	0.00	0.00	0.00%
Total	15,147.70	988	1604	579.08	2,183.40	14.41%

Source: Ibatech, Inc., Aloha Hospitality Software, Hurst, Texas.

1:30 P.M., the noon to 1:30 P.M. time period will be when the most staff is required during the lunch day part.

Reliable forecasting helps managers ensure that staff members and workstations are ready for guest service at the start of each service period. The number of guests that is forecasted helps managers know how many supplies to stock in service areas, for example. In many operations, food servers perform some preparation duties, such as filling portion containers with condiments, preparing butter chips, slicing bread, portioning sour cream, preparing iced tea, and wrapping flatware in napkins. The forecasted number of guests obviously affects the quantity of these items that service staff must make ready for service. Some restaurants find a correlation between the total number of guests they expect to serve and the number of two-person, four-person, and other-sized groups. Forecasts help them determine how to set up dining area tables to accommodate these different groups.

When guests typically arrive is important information for managers to know when scheduling staff. Electronic **point-of-sale (POS) systems** can provide useful historical data for forecasting guests and labor needs. Exhibit 3 presents a sample report itemizing the revenue, number of guests, number of guest checks opened in the system, and number of labor hours and dollars, as well as the labor/revenue ratio for each hour of operation during a single day. By analyzing a number of

Exhibit 4   Dinners Served on Tuesdays

Previous Weeks	Dinners Served
1 (most recent)	285
2	270
3	260
4	290
5	280
6	290
7	300
8	275
9	285
10	295
	2,830

these hourly sales reports for the same day over several weeks, managers can identify the hours during a meal period that require the greatest number of servers and determine the best beginning and ending times for shifts during breakfast, lunch, dinner, and other day parts.

Forecasting techniques vary from relatively simple intuitive methods to extremely complex mathematical formulas. For our purposes we will look at two commonly used methods: the moving average approach and the weighted time series method. These approaches to forecasting are based on historical data and mathematical formulas and their projections must be tempered by a variety of other factors, such as holidays, the weather, and community activities, as well as the ongoing and special advertising and promotional activities of the food and beverage operation.

Moving Average Method

The **moving average method** of forecasting is based on averaging historical sales data and is expressed mathematically as follows:

$$\text{Moving Average} = \frac{\text{Activity in Previous } n \text{ Periods}}{n}$$

where n is the number of periods in the moving average. Exhibit 4 lists the number of Tuesday dinners sold over a 10-week period. Using a 3-week moving average, the estimated number of dinners for the coming Tuesday would be 272, determined as follows:

$$\text{3-Week Moving Average} = \frac{285 + 270 + 260}{3} = 272 \text{ (rounded)}$$

As new weekly results become available, they are used in calculating the average by adding the most recent week and dropping the oldest week. In this way, the calculated average is a "moving" one because it is continually updated to include only the most recent data for the specified number of time periods.

More than 3 weeks could be used to determine the forecast for the upcoming Tuesday. For example, a 10-week moving average of the data in Exhibit 4—"dinners served on Tuesdays"—would forecast 283 meals, determined as follows:

$$\text{10-Week Moving Average} = \frac{\begin{array}{c}285 + 270 + 260 + 290 + 280 \\ + 290 + 300 + 275 + 285 + 295\end{array}}{10} = 283$$

The more periods averaged, the less effect random variations will have on the forecast. However, a serious limitation to the moving average method is that it gives equal weight to each of the data gathered over the specified number of time periods. Many managers would agree that data from the most recent time periods contain more information about what might happen in the future and, therefore, should be given more weight than older data used to calculate the moving average. A forecasting method that counts recent data more heavily than older data is the weighted time series method.

Weighted Time Series Method

The **weighted time series method** of forecasting allows for placing greater value on the most recent historical data when forecasting sales. For example, if we are forecasting the number of next Tuesday's dinners, we could base our projection on data from the five most recent Tuesday dinners shown in Exhibit 4 (Weeks 1, 2, 3, 4, and 5). For purposes of this example, assume weights of 5, 4, 3, 2, and 1 for the prior Tuesdays, with 5 assigned to the most recent Tuesday, 4 to the next most recent Tuesday, and so on. To forecast the number of dinners for the upcoming Tuesday using the weighted time series method, the following steps are taken:

1. Multiply each week's number of dinners sold by its respective weight and total the values:

   (285) (5) + (270) (4) + (260) (3) + (290) (2) + (280) (1) = 4,145

2. Divide the computed total by the sum of its weights. This will yield the weighted forecast:

$$\frac{4,145}{5 + 4 + 3 + 2 + 1} = \frac{4,145}{15} = 276 \text{ (rounded)}$$

Electronic point-of-sale systems and hospitality computer software provide forecasting programs that quickly analyze data and make mathematically correct projections. These programs forecast on the basis of stored data, manually inputted data, or data transferred from point-of-sale systems within the operation. The forecasts help managers plan production and purchase supplies, as well as schedule labor hours.

Forecasting for Lodging Properties

Additional factors affect food and beverage sales forecasts in lodging operations. Since the number of guests staying at a lodging property affects its level of food and beverage business, the occupancy forecast developed by the property's rooms department influences forecasts developed in the food and beverage outlets. Food and beverage outlets within a hotel or resort also depend on timely and accurate information from the sales and catering departments. For example, food and beverage managers need to know what events the banquet or catering department has scheduled and whether the events are for local attendees or for hotel guests. A hotel's restaurant and in-room dining (room service) operation would expect less business than normally anticipated at a certain occupancy level if the banquet department is serving breakfast, lunch, and/or dinner to a group of guests staying at the property.

Preparing Work Schedules

The staffing guide and sales forecasts are the tools managers use to schedule staff members. For example, if 150 meals are expected to be served during the evening shift on Thursday, and the staffing guide indicates that 19 food server labor hours are needed to handle this volume of business, then 19 food server hours are scheduled. If less than 19 hours are scheduled, the quality of service is likely to suffer, since the staff probably will be rushed. If more than 19 hours are scheduled, the staff will not work efficiently, labor costs will increase, and productivity will be lower than labor standards permit.

In most food and beverage operations, the work flow is rarely constant throughout a shift. There is usually a mixture of rush, normal, and slow periods. Therefore, it is generally not a good idea to have all staff members begin and end workshifts at the same time. By staggering and overlapping workshifts, managers can ensure that the greatest number of staff members is working during peak business hours. For example, one server might begin work an hour before the dining room opens. The server can use this time to check or set up tables and perform other miscellaneous tasks. A second server could be scheduled to arrive one-half hour before opening to perform other preopening duties. Both staff members can begin serving when needed. Staggered ending times are also encouraged to ensure maximum worker efficiency. The first staff member to check in might be the first to leave. Of course, it is necessary to comply with the operation's policies as scheduling decisions are made.

Two of the most useful scheduling tools are the manager's past experience in putting together work schedules and the manager's knowledge of the staff's capabilities. In many food and beverage operations, the pattern of business volume stabilizes, creating a recognizable pattern of labor requirements. The more experience the manager acquires in relation to a specific operation, the easier it becomes to stagger work schedules, balance full-time and part-time staff members, and effectively use temporary workers. Similarly, the better the manager understands the capabilities of the staff, the easier it becomes to schedule the right staff members for particular times and shifts. For example, some servers may work best when they are scheduled for the late dinner shift. These factors can be taken into account when planning work schedules.

Some managers find it convenient to schedule required labor hours during the midweek for the next workweek (Monday through Sunday). Others may develop work schedules for longer or shorter time periods. In any case, the important point is to establish a routine scheduling procedure. Whenever possible, managers should consider staff members' preferences, because this will improve staff morale and retention. Staff members can be given schedule request forms to indicate which days or shifts they want off. These requests should be submitted by staff members several weeks in advance and honored by management to the maximum extent possible. Once the working hours for each staff member are established, they should be combined in a schedule and posted for staff member review and use. The posted schedule attempts to provide staff members with the best possible advance notice of their work hours. Many food and beverage managers tell staff members that once they are scheduled to work, they are expected to do so, and if for some reason they cannot work their scheduled hours, they are responsible to find suitable replacements from among their co-workers.

Of course, schedule plans do not always work. Staff members might phone in sick or fail to show up without warning. Also, the number of actual guests and the volume of meals might be lower or higher than expected. Therefore, it is often necessary to revise posted work schedules. Having staff members who are willing to come in on short notice helps protect the operation when personal problems of staff members result in a reduced number of workers on a given shift.

Once the schedule has been finalized, a projected labor cost can be calculated. This is a simple matter of multiplying the hourly rate for each individual on the schedule by the scheduled number of hours, then totaling the amounts. Rather than making these calculations with pencil, paper, and calculator, increasingly operators rely on computerized scheduling systems (that may or may not be linked to the operation's point-of-sale system) or web-based software.

Analyzing Labor Costs

Using the department's staffing guide and a reliable sales forecast to develop work schedules does not guarantee that the hours staff members actually work will equal the number of hours for which they were scheduled to work. Managers must monitor and evaluate the scheduling process by comparing, on a daily and weekly basis, the actual hours each staff member works with the number of hours for which the staff member was scheduled to work. Automated time-clock systems and electronic point-of-sale systems enable managers to monitor and verify the number of hours each staff member actually works.

Many operations use a **computerized time-clock system** that records time in and time out for staff members. Exhibit 5 shows a sample time card from one of these systems. When the time-clock system is interfaced to a host computer system, data may be transferred each day to the back office payroll system and the previous day's pay calculated for each staff member. Many of these systems can be programmed to handle several job codes for a single staff member. This is an important feature for food and beverage managers, because a single staff

Exhibit 5   Sample Electronic Time Card

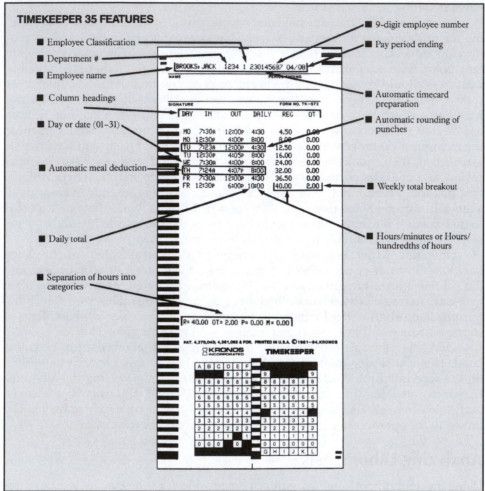

Source: Kronos Inc., Waltham, Mass. You can visit this company's website at www.kronos.com.

member could work at different jobs (each with different pay rates) over a number of workshifts.

When time clocks are used, it is important for managers to clearly communicate to staff members the operation's policies regarding punching in and out. For example, many operations have policies requiring staff members to get approval from their managers before they punch in prior to their scheduled shifts or remain "on-the-clock" after their scheduled shifts end. Also, most operations clearly define the disciplinary action that will be taken against anyone who punches in or out for another staff member.

Automated point-of-sale systems generally include a labor management module that incorporates a time-clock function. Staff members are issued pass codes or staff member numbers and, as they log into terminals, their time and attendance records are developed. The **labor master file** of a POS system contains one record for each staff member and typically maintains the following data:

- Staff member name
- Staff member number
- Social Security number
- Authorized job codes and corresponding hourly wage rates

This file may also contain data required to produce labor reports for management. Each record in the labor master file may accumulate:

- Hours worked
- Total hourly wages
- Tips
- Credits for staff member meals
- Number of guests served
- Gross sales

Data accumulated by the labor master file can be accessed to produce a number of reports. A labor master report contains general data maintained by the labor master file. Managers generally use this report to verify a staff member's hourly rate(s), job code(s), or Social Security number. A daily labor report, such as the one shown in Exhibit 6, typically lists the staff member numbers, hours worked, wages earned, and wages declared for each staff member on a given workday. A weekly labor report contains similar information and may be used to determine which staff members are approaching hour totals beyond which they must be paid for overtime.

A weekly labor hour and cost report, such as the one shown in Exhibit 7, enables managers to identify variances between standard labor hours (dictated by the staffing guide) and actual hours worked by the staff. Since variances will almost always exist, management generally specifies either dollar or percentage amounts to define significant variances that warrant explanations and may trigger corrective action.

When budgeted labor costs are based on the same labor standards as the staffing guide, it is relatively easy for managers to keep labor costs in line with budgeted goals. When this is not the case, managers must ensure that labor hours permitted by the staffing guide remain within budgeted labor costs. To ensure consistency with budgeted labor costs, the standard labor hours of a staffing guide must be converted to labor dollars and forecasts of guest counts must be expanded to include revenue forecasts for meal periods. These conversions allow a direct comparison because labor costs are generally expressed as dollars and budgeted as a percentage of revenue. If the comparison shows that the staffing guide yields higher labor costs than were budgeted, then several courses of action could be taken. One would be to revise the budget accordingly. If costs could not be reduced

Exhibit 6   Sample Daily Labor Report

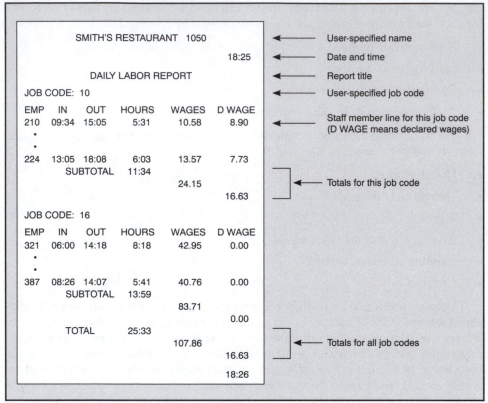

Source: International Business Machines Corporation, White Plains, New York.

in other expense areas, or if revenue could not be increased, profit expectations would have to be lowered. Another course of action would be to revise the quality requirements and increase the productivity rates on which the staffing guide is based.

If managers can explain the variances that occur, there is generally little or no need for corrective action. For example, recent turnover in the dining room may have resulted in several new servers who are at various stages of training and not yet performing to standard. Since these servers would handle fewer tables, additional servers would have to be scheduled. Therefore, actual labor hours would exceed standard labor hours until the new servers are fully trained. Also, a sales forecast could significantly differ from the number of meals actually served for a given meal period. A forecast that was too high would help explain some overstaffing; a forecast that was too low would help explain some understaffing.

On the other hand, a problem exists if actual labor hours vary from standard labor hours and managers cannot explain or defend the variance. The next step would be to discuss possible causes and potential solutions with other managers, the immediate supervisor, and affected staff members. Managers must then

Exhibit 7   Sample Weekly Labor Hour and Cost Report

Week of: _____7/14/XX_____

Department: _Food Service_   Supervisor: _____Sandra_____

Shift: _____P.M._____

Actual Labor Hours Worked

Position/ Staff Member	Mon 7/14	Tues 7/15	Wed 7/16	Thurs 7/17	Fri 7/18	Sat 7/19	Sun 7/20	Total Labor Hours Actual	Total Labor Hours Standard	Hourly Rate	Total Labor Costs Actual	Total Labor Costs Standard
1	2	3	4	5	6	7	8	9	10	11	12	13
DINING ROOM												
Jennifer	7	—	7	6.5	7	6	—	33.5	31.0	$5.00	$167.50	$155.00
Brenda	—	7	6.5	7	6.5	6.5	5	38.5	38.5	5.15	198.28	198.28
Sally	—	5	8	7	8	10	—	38.0	36.0	5.25	199.50	189.00
Patty	8	6	6	4.5	—	—	6	30.5	31.0	5.10	155.55	158.10
Anna	4	4	6.5	—	4.5	—	5	24.0	22.0	5.10	122.40	112.20
Thelma	6	5	5	5	5	—	—	26.0	24.0	5.40	140.40	129.60
Elsie	6	—	—	6	6	8	8	34.0	34.0	5.05	171.70	171.70
								224.5	216.5		$1,155.33	$1,113.88
COOK												
Peggy	4	4	4	4	4	—	—	20.0	20.0	11.00	220.00	220.00
Kathy	4	4	4	—	—	4	4	20.0	20.0	11.15	223.00	223.00
Tilly	4	—	—	4	4	4	4	20.0	18.0	11.50	230.00	207.00
Carlos	—	4	4	4	4	4	—	20.0	20.0	11.00	220.00	220.00
Sam	4	4	—	—	—	—	4	12.0	12.0	11.10	133.20	133.20
								92.0	90.0		$1,026.20	$1,003.20
DISHWASHING												
Terry	—	—	6	6	6	—	—	18.0	18.0	6.50	117.00	117.00
Andrew	6	6	—	—	8	5	5	30.0	30.0	6.25	187.50	187.50
Robert	8	8	8	8	—	—	6	38.0	38.0	6.55	248.90	248.90
Carl	5	—	5	5	5	6	—	26.0	26.0	6.50	169.00	169.00
								112.0	112.0		$722.40	$722.40
											$2,903.93	$2,839.48

identify where the problem is actually occurring, assess the options, and select a course of action from the alternatives to resolve the problem. When developing a corrective action plan, managers should consider the following:

- *Probability of success.* How successful will a particular alternative be in reducing the variance?

- *Cost.* What costs are involved in implementing an alternative? Do the benefits of an alternative outweigh the costs of implementing it?

- *Guest impact.* How will guests be affected by the corrective action plan? Guests' needs and expectations must be evaluated in relation to the proposed action.

- *Past experience.* What actions were taken in the past to address similar problems?

- *Feasibility.* Is it really possible to successfully implement the chosen alternative? While this may seem obvious, some managers waste time wishing things were different instead of accepting the situation as it is and working within its constraints.

- *Compromise.* The best plan to resolve a labor control problem is often a compromise between two or more possible solutions.

- *Experimentation.* Sometimes it is best to test a solution before fully implementing it throughout a department or operation. For example, one staff member or one shift could evaluate proposed revisions to procedures.

- *Learning from others.* A study of similar food and beverage operations, a review of hospitality literature, and conversations with managers with similar responsibilities may help identify ways to reduce labor costs.

The success of labor control efforts is often dependent on the reactions of staff members to corrective actions. Managers must carefully and regularly communicate with staff members so that everyone clearly understands what is expected. When corrective action entails new work procedures, managers must implement additional training, reinforcement, and on-the-job coaching. Some staff members may resist changes and defend the status quo. Managers can best address these situations by clearly explaining the need for change and, when possible, detailing how staff members will benefit from the change. After implementing corrective action, managers must evaluate the results to ensure that the variance between actual labor hours and standard labor hours has been appropriately reduced and to ensure that revised procedures have not created spin-off problems in other areas.

Revenue Control Systems

Guest check systems are designed to ensure that food production areas produce only items actually ordered and that revenue is collected for all items served. As electronic point-of-sale technology becomes more affordable, fewer food service operations use manual guest check systems. However, when automated systems crash, the manager who knows how to implement a backup, manual guest check system can save the day. The following sections describe fundamental features of both manual and computer-based guest check systems.

Manual Guest Check Systems

A basic revenue control procedure for manual systems requires that servers neatly write all food and beverage orders on guest checks. Servers generally use pens, not pencils, and mistakes must be crossed out rather than erased. In many operations, the server must have a supervisor initial a guest check that has items crossed out or voided. Before initialing, the supervisor makes sure that the deleted items were not prepared by kitchen or bar staff.

Before food or beverage items are produced, servers must provide appropriate production staff with **requisition slips**. The server lists items on a requisition slip and also records his or her name (or staff member identification number) and the serial number of the corresponding guest check. Some operations use a **duplicate**

guest check system for food orders. With this system, each guest check has at least two parts. The server turns in the duplicate copy to the kitchen and keeps the original copy for presentation to the guest. When the guest is ready to pay, the guest check is tallied. A calculator with a printer that produces a tape is sometimes used. The tape is stapled to the check for the guest's review of charges.

Requisition slips or duplicate checks are useful for routine guest-check audit functions. At the end of a meal period, the manager (or a designated staff member) can match requisition slips (or duplicate copies of guest checks) turned in to the kitchen with the corresponding guest checks for which revenue has been collected. This procedure identifies differences between what was produced and what was served. Routine audits of guest checks may also reveal mistakes made by servers in pricing items on guest checks or in calculating totals. These mistakes should be brought to the attention of the responsible staff members. By conducting routine audits of guest checks, management indicates to staff members its concern about effectively controlling the operation's revenue collection system.

Several other procedures apply to revenue control with a manual guest check system. Guest checks should be unique to the property. If guest checks are purchased from a local restaurant supply company, anyone—including a dishonest staff member—can buy them. In this situation, guest checks can be used in the operation with no record of who has them or from whom revenue is due. Therefore, it is best to order specially printed, hard-to-duplicate guest checks. Unused checks should be securely stored, not left unsecured in the manager's office or at the host stand.

Guest checks should be sequentially numbered and a record kept of which checks are given to which server. Beginning and ending serial numbers for all checks issued to each server should be listed on a guest check number log. Servers accepting the checks should sign the log to verify receiving the checks for which they will be held accountable.

All checks issued to each server must be accounted for at the end of a shift. Checks will be either used and turned in with revenue, unused and turned in as part of the server's closing duties, or kept in use and transferred to another server. All transfers of guest checks should be approved by a supervisor. Requisition slips or duplicate guest checks are helpful when a check is unaccounted for. If a requisition slip (or the duplicate guest check) corresponding to a missing guest check has been turned in to the kitchen, management knows that the missing guest check has been used, that items listed on it have been served, and that revenue is due from the server. According to property policy and in accordance with applicable wage and hour or other laws, penalties may be applied when checks are unaccounted for at the end of a server's shift.

Point-of-Sale Guest Check Systems

Some automated systems use preprinted, serially numbered guest checks like those used in manual guest check systems. Before entering an order, the server "opens" the guest check within the system by inputting his or her identification number and the paper guest check's serial number. Once the system has recognized the server and opened the electronic guest check, orders are entered and relayed to remote printers at food or beverage production areas. This eliminates the need for the requisition slips or duplicate paper checks used in manual guest check systems and also reduces the number of trips servers make to production areas—which gives servers more time to provide direct guest service. The same menu items (with their selling prices) are printed on the server's guest check.

Once a guest check has been opened, it becomes part of the system's **open check file**. For each opened guest check, the open check file may contain the following data:

- Terminal number where the guest check was opened

- Guest check serial number (if appropriate)

- Server identification number

- Time guest check was created

- Menu items ordered

- Selling prices of items ordered

- Applicable tax

- Total amount due

A server adds orders to the guest check at the terminal by first inputting the guest check's serial number and then entering the additional items.

There are many variations of this automated system. Some systems use guest checks with bar codes corresponding to the preprinted serial numbers. This eliminates the need for servers to input the guest check's serial number when opening a guest check or when adding items to guest checks already in use. When the guest check is placed in the guest check printer, the system reads the bar code and immediately accesses the appropriate file.

Receipt-printed check systems eliminate the traditional guest check altogether. These systems maintain only an electronic file for each open guest check. A narrow, receipt-like guest check may be printed at any time during service, but is usually not printed until after the meal when the server presents it to the guest for settlement. Since no paper forms are used during service, the table number often is the tracking identifier for the order. With some systems, seat numbers are used for tracking multiple checks per table. When presenting these checks to guests for settlement, the receipt-like guest checks can be inserted in high-quality paper, vinyl, or leather presentation jackets.

Some systems feature a receipt-like guest check that also serves as a payment card voucher. This reduces the time it takes servers to settle guest checks. Instead of presenting the guest check, collecting the guest's payment card (credit card, debit card, or other payment card), printing a payment card voucher, transferring information from the guest check to the voucher, and then presenting the voucher to the guest to sign, servers are able to present the guest check and the payment card voucher simultaneously.

POS technology simplifies guest check control functions and eliminates the need for many time-consuming manual audit procedures. Automated functions

Exhibit 8   Sample Server Check-Out Report

```
                        MRS

                 DEMONSTRATION

Server:  ANNA

   Date:  11/20

         In Time     Out Time   Total
         12:36       15:23      02:47
         15:25       15:26      00:01

   Total Hours Worked:  02:48

              Persons    Tables    Net      Tips
   Lunch:       19         6      290.55    39.71
   Dinner:       0         0        0.00     0.00
   Total:       19         6      290.55    39.71

                 Tips on Credit Cards:      39.71
                 Credit Card Surcharge:      1.99

                        Net Total Tips:     37.72

                           Balance Due:     37.72
```

Source: Genlor Systems, Inc., Northport, New York.

eliminate mistakes servers make in pricing items on guest checks or in calculating totals. When items must be voided, a supervisor (with a special identification number) accesses the system and deletes the items. Generally, automated systems produce a report that lists all guest checks with voided or returned items, the servers responsible, and the supervisors who voided the items. At any point during service, managers and supervisors can access the system and monitor the status of any guest check. This check-tracking capability can help identify potential walkouts, reduce server theft, and tighten guest check and revenue control.

The status of a guest check changes from open to closed when payment is received from the guest and is recorded in the system. Most automated systems produce an outstanding-checks report that lists all guest checks (by server) that have not been settled. These reports may list the guest check number, server identification number, time at which the guest check was opened, number of guests, table number, and guest check total. This makes it easier for managers to determine responsibility for unsettled guest checks. Exhibit 8 presents a sample server check-out report. Note that the report lists time in, time out, hours worked, number of guests served, tables attended, net sales, and the amount of tips to be paid to the server from guest charges during the shift.

Accepting Personal Checks

Some food and beverage operations allow guests to pay by personal check, while others have a strict policy against accepting personal checks. Although an operation has no obligation to accept personal checks, it cannot refuse to accept a check on the basis of a person's race, sex, or other grounds that would constitute illegal discrimination.

Operations that accept personal checks should require proper identification. Many operations request at least two pieces of identification (such as a driver's license and a major credit card), one with a photograph. The guest's driver's license number, address, and telephone number should be recorded on the face of the check. Bank stamps and clearinghouse imprints will often appear on the back of the check.

Common guidelines that protect operations from accepting fraudulent personal checks include:

- Accept checks only for the amount of the purchase.

- Require that personal checks be made payable to the food and beverage operation, not to "Cash."

- Do not accept checks marked with "For Deposit Only," "For Collection Only," or similar terms.

- All checks should be legible and not have smudges, erasures, or other signs of tampering.

- Do not accept undated or postdated personal checks—that is, checks carrying no date or a future date instead of the current date.

- A guest should sign the check in the presence of a manager or designated staff member.

- Upon acceptance, personal checks should be marked with the operation's stamp "For Deposit Only."

Most food and beverage operations will not accept second- or third-party checks. A second-party check is one made out to the guest presenting the check. A third-party check is one made out to someone who has in turn signed the check over to the guest presenting it. Accepting such checks may create collection problems, especially if the writer of the check has registered a "stop payment" order on the check.

Some operations may choose to use a personal check guarantee service. When such a service is available, a manager or designated staff member telephones the service and provides data from the tendered check and the amount of the transaction. The check guarantee service, in turn, determines the check writer's credit history and either guarantees or refuses to support payment. Since these services charge a fee for each transaction, staff members should only accept checks that are written for the exact amount of the purchase. Otherwise, the operation is simply advancing cash to guests while paying a fee to provide the service.

Exhibit 9   Suggestions for Resolving Guest Payment Problems

> **When a payment card company refuses to authorize a transaction:**
>
> - Discuss the matter with the guest in private.
> - Use care when describing the guest's unauthorized transaction (for example, do not call the guest's payment card "bad" or "worthless").
> - Offer the use of a telephone to help resolve the matter with a payment card company representative.
> - Allow the guest a chance to provide alternate, acceptable means of payment.
>
> **When a guest's personal check cannot be accepted:**
>
> - Explain the operation's check-cashing policy.
> - Remain friendly and cooperative.
> - Discuss alternative methods of payment with the guest.
> - If local banks are open, direct the guest to a nearby branch, or extend the use of a telephone.

Processing Payment Cards

Authorization and verification of payment cards are important revenue control functions. Food and beverage operations usually compile a set of steps for processing payment card transactions. In addition, payment card companies often require specific procedures in order to ensure payment. Local banks may also provide procedural guidelines. It's often a good idea to have a legal review of the operation's payment card procedures to be sure of adherence to state and federal laws and to the specifications contained in payment card company contracts. Exhibit 9 provides some suggestions for resolving payment problems with guests. The following sections summarize basic guidelines for processing payment card transactions.

Expiration Date. When a guest presents a payment card, the staff member handling the transaction should immediately check the payment card's expiration date. If the date shows that the card has expired, the staff member should point this out to the guest and request an alternate method of payment. Since payment card companies are not required to honor transactions made with an expired card, accepting an expired card may lead to uncollectible charges.

Online Authorization. After checking a payment card's expiration date, the staff member should make sure the payment card isn't listed as stolen or otherwise invalid. Many operations validate payment cards through an online computer service accessed through a direct telephone connection. Once the connection is made, the required payment card and transaction data may be spoken, entered on a touch-tone key pad, or automatically captured through a magnetic strip reader. On the basis of the entered data, the payment card verification service consults an account database and generates either an **authorization code** or a **denial code** for the transaction. Online authorization services often charge a transaction-processing fee.

Cancellation Bulletins. In operations without online payment card authorization, the staff member should validate a payment card by checking the payment card company's current cancellation bulletin. Expired cancellation bulletins should be stored and filed in case a dispute eventually arises between a payment card company and the operation. The operation can refer to previous cancellation bulletins to prove that a payment card number was valid at the time the payment card was accepted for payment.

Invalid Card. Staff members should follow procedures established by the operation and by the payment card companies when a payment card appears to be invalid. The card may appear to be invalid because it has been tampered with or the signature on the payment card does not match the signature the guest writes on the voucher. Normally, it is appropriate for staff to politely request an alternate form of payment.

Imprinting the Voucher. Staff members imprint approved, valid payment cards onto payment card vouchers for the guest's signature. The imprinted voucher should be carefully checked to ensure that all card numbers are properly imprinted. If they are not legible, the first voucher should be destroyed and the procedure repeated, or the card numbers should be written in ink clearly on the hard copy of the voucher. Some operations require staff to circle the card's expiration date and initial the validation number on the imprinted voucher as proof that procedures have been followed. It's also wise to have the guest sign applicable guest checks as well as the payment card voucher.

Tableside Processing. Whenever a payment card is taken from a guest and processed out of sight of the guest, the possibility for fraud increases. When a payment card number is used by a staff member in an unauthorized way, invalid charges are made to that card. This results in a blow to the image and reputation of the food and beverage operation through negative publicity and word-of-mouth.

Consider this scenario: a guest phones a restaurant to place a take-out order. When the guest arrives at the restaurant to pick up the order, the guest gives a server a payment card and the server walks to another part of the restaurant to process the payment and, at the same time, surreptitiously record the guest's name, the payment card number, the card's expiration date, and the security code on the back of the card. The server returns with the payment card slip for the guest to sign, gives the guest the payment card and the take-out food, and thanks the guest. To the guest, all appears to be normal.

The next day, the payment card holder receives a telephone call from the credit union that issued the payment card, asking the individual if charges on the card from businesses in another state (i.e., a tire store, gas station, grocery store, and department store) were legitimate charges. The payment card holder is shocked to learn of these unauthorized charges, and the credit union suggests that the account be closed immediately and the unauthorized charges contested. The next day, the individual has to sign a notarized statement attesting that the charges in the other state were unauthorized, and then go through the process of setting up a new payment card account. Because of this case of identity theft, the guest has never returned to the restaurant *and* has told many friends and acquaintances about this negative experience.

One method that some food and beverage operators are implementing to combat this kind of fraud is to provide servers with handheld devices that can capture payment card information tableside in front of the cardholder guest, thus eliminating the need for servers to walk to a location that is out of sight of the guest. (These handheld devices can also be used to take guest orders and send them to the kitchen, thus speeding service.) In addition to helping to prevent identity fraud and all of the subsequent negative experiences for guests, these handheld devices also make the processing of transactions tableside more efficient and less time-consuming. They can greatly increase the comfort level of guests who are worried about identity theft and improve their satisfaction with their overall dining experience.

Point-of-Sale Settlement Devices

POS technology offers several labor-saving settlement devices. A **magnetic strip reader** is an optional device that connects to a cashier terminal. These readers do not replace keyboards or touch-screens; they extend their capabilities. Magnetic strip readers are capable of collecting data stored on a magnetized film strip typically located on the back of a payment card or house account card. This enables a POS system to process payment card transactions. Some operations also distribute plastic, bar-coded identification cards to staff members who use them to log into the POS system. Managers may be issued specially encoded cards to access ongoing transactions and perform strictly managerial functions with POS system data.

Processing payment card transactions is simplified when a **power platform** is used to consolidate electronic communications between the operation and a payment card authorization center. A POS power platform connects all POS terminals to a single processor for settlement. This eliminates the need for individual telephone lines at each POS cashier terminal. Power platforms can capture payment card authorizations in three seconds or less. This fast data retrieval helps reduce the time, cost, and risk associated with payment card transactions.

The two most common payment cards are debit cards and credit cards. **Debit cards** differ from credit cards in that the cardholder must deposit money in a personal account in order to establish value. The cardholder deposits money in advance of purchases through a debit card center. As purchases are made, the balance in the debit account is adjusted accordingly. For example, a cardholder who has deposited $300 to a debit card account has a value of $300 available for settling transactions. As the cardholder makes purchases, the money is electronically transferred from the guest's account to the account of the business where the purchase is made. A debit card is similar to an automatic-teller-machine (ATM) card in that the purchaser must have cash on account to complete a transaction successfully.

Restaurants may also accept ATM card payment through specially designed equipment at cashier stations. After the amount of payment is entered into an electronic cashier terminal, a display on the back of the terminal asks the guest to swipe the ATM card through a card reader. The guest then enters his or her personal identification number on a numeric keypad that is out of the cashier's sight. Usually within seconds, cash is transferred from the guest's checking account to the restaurant's bank account.

Revenue Collection

In food and beverage operations, revenue collection may be a duty assigned to individual servers, or it may be a function centralized at designated cashier stations. Whenever feasible, operations generally use cashiers because this ensures a **separation of duties**—a single staff member is not responsible for an entire series of transactions: order entry, delivery, collection, and reconciliation.

Staff members responsible for revenue collection are issued **cash banks** at the starts of their shifts. Generally, the staff member counts the opening bank in the presence of a manager. The cash bank should always contain the same amount of money and the minimum amount of each type of currency required for making change. In some operations, staff members sign a receipt form certifying that they received the cash bank and that they accept responsibility for it during their shifts.

Server Banking System

With a **server banking system**, servers (and bartenders) use their own banks of money to collect payments from guests and retain the collected revenue until they check out at the end of their shifts. In some operations, locking cash boxes are provided for each server to store collected revenue, payment card vouchers, and other sales materials.

After all checks are accounted for at the end of a shift, the amount of revenue due the operation is determined by tallying the totals from all guest checks assigned to each server. The tally is made by the manager (or cashier) in conjunction with the server. Totals from guest checks settled by payment card vouchers, personal checks, and house account charges are subtracted from the tally to arrive at the amount of cash to be collected from the server. The remaining cash represents the server's opening cash bank and any cash tips earned. After the actual revenue collected by the manager (or cashier) balances with the tally of totals from all guest checks assigned to the server, charged tips (as recorded on payment card or house account vouchers) are paid out to the server.

In nonautomated operations, these closing procedures can be very time-consuming. POS technology speeds up the process by producing a report at the end of a shift that automatically tallies the total revenue due from each server. These reports generally identify transactions opened by the server and itemizes each of them in terms of:

- Table number
- Number of covers
- Elapsed time from opening to closing of the transaction
- Totals for food and beverage revenue

Exhibit 10   Sample Daily Transactions Report

Date	8-30												
Time	5:31 A.M.			DAILY TRANSACTIONS									

Guest Check	Tabl/ Covrs	Employee	ID	Time In	Time Out	Elapsed Time	Food	Bar	Wine	Guest Total	Tax	Tip	Settlement Method	Settlement Amount
11378	2-2	Jones	4	8:23	9:00	0:37	13.75	0.00	3.50	17.25	0.87	2.00	CASH	20.12
11379	2-1	Jones	4	8:25	9:00	0:35	2.35	0.00	0.00	2.35	0.12	0.00	COMP 1 0004	2.47
11380	3-3	Jones	4	8:32	9:01	0:29	13.15	0.00	5.50	18.65	0.93	0.00	CASH	9.58
													COMP 2 0033	10.00
11381	4-4	Jones	4	8:34	9:16	0:42	9.05	0.00	0.00	9.05	0.47	0.00	MC	9.52
11382	3-2	Jones	4	8:40	9:18	0:38	6.20	0.00	5.50	11.70	0.60	0.00	Cancelled	
11383	3-2	Jones	4	8:41	9:19	0:38	4.35	0.00	0.00	4.35	0.22	0.00	COMP 1 0004	4.57
11384	4-4	Jones	4	8:43	10:16	1:33	33.80	11.00	0.00	44.80	2.25	0.00	AMEXPRESS	47.05
11385	4-2	Jones	4	8:46	10:17	1:31	0.00	9.75	0.00	9.75	0.49	0.00	VISA	10.24
11386	4-5	Jones	4	8:51	10:17	1:26	0.00	18.50	0.00	18.50	0.91	0.00	MC	19.41
11387	8-2	Jones	4	8:54	10:18	1:24	14.65	2.50	0.00	17.15	0.85	0.00	COMP 1 0004	18.00
11388	4-3	Jones	4	9:23	10:17	0:54	4.70	3.00	0.00	7.70	0.39	1.00	CASH	9.09
11389	2-2	Jones	4	9:34	10:16	0:42	4.60	0.00	0.00	4.60	0.24	0.00	CASH	4.84
11398	3-2	Jones	4	12:09	12:10	0:01	11.35	0.00	0.00	11.35	0.57	0.00	CASH	11.92
11399	3-2	Jones	4	12:20	12:21	0:01	10.25	2.00	0.00	12.25	0.61	0.00	CASH	12.86
21615	3-2	Jones	4	11:39	11:41	0:02	13.15	0.00	0.00	13.15	0.65	0.00	CASH	13.80
21616	1-2	Jones	4	11:40	11:41	0:01	7.90	0.00	3.50	11.40	0.58	0.00	CASH	11.98
	Total cancelled			11.70										
**** Totals							143.05	46.75	12.50	202.30	10.15	3.00		215.45

Source: American Business Computers, Akron, Ohio.

- Tax
- Tips due
- Settlement method

Exhibit 10 shows a sample daily transactions report that can be generated at any time during or after a shift. This type of report summarizes all major transactions by server and enables managers to trace and analyze revenue variances by guest check, server, time of day, food and beverage category, tips paid out, or settlement methods.

Cashier Banking System

With a **cashier banking system**, guests pay the cashier, the bartender, or the food or beverage server (who then pays the cashier or the bartender who has cashiering duties). Upon receiving a guest check for settlement, the cashier keys each item listed on the check into the register. The register tallies each item and imprints the total on the check for verification with the server's handwritten total. The cashier (or bartender) then retains the money and the accompanying guest checks. With most POS systems, the cashier does not to have to key each item from every guest check into the system. The cashier's terminal simply accesses the transaction number opened by the server, and the cashier closes it by collecting and recording the revenue.

At the end of a shift, each cashier completes a report that establishes the amount of revenue that should have been collected and compares this revenue standard with the amount of revenue actually collected. The revenue standard is the total of items such as:

- Food revenue—net system readings (subtracting the opening system reading at the start of the shift from the ending system reading at the close of the shift for this keyed item)

- Beverage revenue—net system readings

- Sales tax—net system readings

- Tips charged—tips that guests entered on payment card vouchers or house account drafts

- Guest collections—payments received from guests to be applied toward prior charges on house accounts

- Cash bank—the cashier's initial funds for making change

After the cash bank is restored to its original amount and types of currency (a certain number of pennies, nickels, dimes, quarters, one-dollar bills, five-dollar bills, and so on), the actual revenue collected is the total of the following items:

- Cash for deposit—cash, personal checks, and traveler's checks

- Payment card charges—Visa, MasterCard, American Express, Diners Club, and other charge cards

- Purchases paid out—vouchers and receipts for incidentals paid from the cash drawer during the shift

- Tips paid out—payments for tips that guests entered on payment card vouchers or house account drafts

- Guest charges—charges made by guests on their house accounts

The total of cash funds and amounts represented on supporting documents should reconcile with the revenue standard, except for minor cash shortages or overages. Minor variances are generally due to errors in processing numerous cash transactions throughout the shift. Any significant variances should be investigated. Electronic POS systems can combine elements of cashier reports from several stations during the same shift. Exhibit 11 is a sample settlement methods report that indicates the amounts due (standard revenues) from four beverage cashier stations in the form of payment card vouchers, house account charges, and cash.

If at all possible, only one cashier or one bartender should be assigned to a register. To do otherwise makes it difficult if not impossible to determine who is responsible for that register's shortage or overage. Additionally, the manager on duty should be the only one able to void register mistakes (for example, a bartender entering $20.00 for a beverage sale that was $2.00). If, due to the high-volume nature of the food and beverage operation, a manager is not always available to void mistakes, then each individual's overages and shortages for each shift can be recorded and aggregated by week and by month.

Exhibit 11 Settlement Methods Report

Ring Off #22	—2:52 A.M.	1/06			
Accumulators Cleared	—8:00 A.M.	1/05			

Settlement Methods	STATION 1 SALES	STATION 2 SALES	STATION 3 SALES	STATION 4 SALES	TOTAL SALES
Cash	1548.65	1560.20	1368.00	683.65	5160.50
Visa/MC	.00	10.75	.00	.00	10.75
Diners	179.70	.00	.00	.00	179.70
Amex	52.25	.00	96.60	24.25	173.10
Promo	.00	.00	.00	.00	.00
Company	.00	.00	.00	.00	.00
Discovery	.00	.00	.00	.00	.00
Direct Bill	.00	.00	.00	.00	.00
Total Settlements	1780.60	1570.95	1464.60	707.90	5524.05

Source: American Business Computers, Akron, Ohio.

Another effective cash control procedure is for managers to require a receipt to be printed and presented to each guest for each transaction. This makes it easier for managers to identify whether the bartender, cashier, or server is accurately recording each sale. This must be required for all transactions and all staff members if it is to work properly.

Mystery shoppers are sometimes retained by food and beverage managers to visit the operation posing as guests to observe staff members as they perform their cashiering duties. These shoppers then write reports for management that not only detail staff members' cashiering activities but also may include observations about the quality of food and beverages served to them, the service they experienced, and their impressions of the operation as a whole from a guest's perspective.

Protecting Cash after Collection

Revenue control procedures must address issues related to revenue collection, preparation of bank deposits, and the actual transportation of funds to the bank. All revenue collected should be deposited in the operation's bank account on a daily basis. Some operations may make several daily deposits. Moreover, all revenue should be deposited intact. This means that bills should not be paid with cash from daily revenue; they should be paid by check. This policy makes it easier to trace the flow of revenue into the operation, on to the bank, into the proper account, and back out again through proper disbursement procedures in paying bills.

Separating duties is critical to protecting revenue collected. When possible, different staff members should collect revenue, audit and account for guest checks, and prepare the tallies of daily revenue. These staff members should not normally be involved in preparing bank deposits or paying bills. Specific practices that can help control revenue at the time of deposit include the following:

- Staff members should compare the amount of each bank deposit with records of daily revenue collected.

- Staff members who open mail should not make bank deposits. This reduces the possibility of staff members diverting revenue from checks received that should be deposited.

- All staff members who handle large sums of cash, assess bank deposits, and make cash disbursements should be bonded.

- The staff member who prepares a bank deposit should not be the staff member who actually makes the deposit—unless the owner/manager takes responsibility for these tasks.

- All personal checks should be marked "For Deposit Only," preferably at the time they are received. Local banks should be instructed to not issue cash for any personal checks made payable to the operation.

Two final rules are important for handling revenue receipts. First, the combination of the operation's safe should be changed periodically, and as few staff members as possible should know how to open the safe. Second, all cash-handling staff members should be required to take uninterrupted annual vacations. This way, another staff member can assume the duties and may uncover improper practices.

 ## Key Terms

authorization code—A code generated by an online payment card verification service, indicating that the requested transaction has been approved.

cash bank—An amount of money to make change that is given to a staff member with cashiering duties at the start of each workshift.

cashier banking system—A revenue collection system in which all revenue is collected at cashier stations and accounted for by cashiers.

computerized time-clock system—Records time in and time out for staff members as they enter and leave the work area; when interfaced with an automated payroll system, relevant data can be transferred each day and the previous day's pay calculated for each staff member.

debit card—A plastic card similar in size to a credit card. The cardholder deposits money in advance of purchases through a debit card center; as purchases are made, the balance on the debit card falls.

denial code—A code generated by an online payment card verification service, indicating that the requested transaction has not been approved.

duplicate guest check system—A control system in which the server turns in a duplicate copy of the guest check to the kitchen and keeps the original check for presentation to the guest.

fixed labor—The minimum amount of labor required to operate a food service facility regardless of the volume of business.

job analysis—The process of determining the tasks, behaviors, and characteristics essential to a job.

labor master file—A file maintained by electronic point-of-sale systems containing one record for each staff member with data such as staff member name, staff member number, Social Security number, authorized job codes, and corresponding hourly wage rates.

labor standard—A time and productivity standard against which a staff member's actual work performance can be measured.

magnetic strip reader—An optional input device that connects to a point-of-sale system terminal and is capable of collecting data stored on a magnetized film strip that is typically located on the back of a payment card or house account card.

moving average method—A method of forecasting in which historical data over several time periods are used to calculate an average; as new data become available, they are used in calculating the average by adding the most recent time period and dropping the earliest time period. In this way, the calculated average is a "moving" one because it is continually updated to include only the most recent data for the specified number of time periods.

open check file—An electronic file maintained by automated point-of-sale systems that records information for each guest check used, such as terminal number where the guest check was opened, guest check serial number, server identification number, time guest check was opened, menu items ordered, prices of menu items ordered, applicable tax, and total amount due.

point-of-sale (POS) systems—A network of electronic registers or terminals capable of capturing data at point-of-sale locations, transferring data to other terminals, and integrating data for management reports.

power platform—Consolidates electronic communications between a hospitality establishment and a payment card authorization center; helps reduce the time, cost, and risk associated with payment card transactions.

requisition slips—Slips provided by servers to production staff before items are produced; the slips indicate items for preparation, the server's name or identification number, and the serial number of the corresponding guest check.

separation of duties—An element of internal control systems in which different staff members are assigned the different functions of accounting, custody of assets, and production; the purpose is to prevent and detect errors and theft.

server banking system—A revenue collection system by which servers (and bartenders) use their own banks of change to collect payments from guests and retain the collected revenue until they check out at the ends of their shifts.

staffing guide—A labor scheduling and control tool that outlines labor standards and tells managers the number of labor hours needed for each position according to the volume of business forecasted for any given meal period.

variable labor—Labor requirements that vary according to the volume of business activity; for example, as more guests are served or as more meals are produced, additional service or kitchen labor is needed.

weighted time series method—A forecasting method that places greater value on the most recent historical data when forecasting sales.

Review Questions

1. Why must managers consider quality requirements before developing labor standards?

2. How can managers use a position performance analysis to determine labor standards for each position and shift?

3. What are some factors managers must consider when constructing a staffing guide?

4. How is fixed labor different from variable labor?

5. How can managers evaluate a staffing guide in relation to budgeted goals?

6. How are requisition slips or duplicate guest checks useful in determining standard revenue for nonautomated food operations?

7. In what ways do electronic point-of-sale systems simplify guest check control functions?

8. What procedures should operations adopt to help ensure payment of payment card charges?

9. What elements distinguish a server banking system from a cashier banking system?

10. How is a daily cashier's report used to compare standard revenue and actual revenue collected?

Case Studies

Will We Ever Get It Right?

Andrea Cabot is the new food and beverage manager at the Windsor Hotel, a family owned and operated property in the upper Midwest. The previous manager was the nephew of the owner and never really had his heart and mind on those responsibilities. Consequently, food cost was erratic month to month, the kitchen experienced frequent crises due to unanticipated excessive business demand coupled with lack of preparation. Complaint letters were being received with great frequency. The owner/manager and the nephew mutually agreed to part ways, which resulted in the opening that Andrea has now filled.

After reviewing all the financial records for the past 12 months, the purchasing records, labor schedules, guest satisfaction (and dissatisfaction) comments, she begins to get a feel for the problems and decides she can get things under control quickly.

One critical piece of continuing information is missing, however, and she can't find it anywhere. "Where are the daily meal forecast forms that project the level of business we expect?" she asks herself. She goes to the executive chef and asks him about the daily forecast sheets.

He laughs and says, "We're lucky to get a weather forecast in this place. I've been asking for forecasts for two years and people just give me a blank stare. I hope you are going to develop a forecast system so we can get things right once in a while!"

Andrea smiles, for she knows that the forecast is the cornerstone that drives all the other elements of food production and service.

Discussion Questions

1. What are the elements that go into constructing a forecast for a hotel property?
2. How does a free-standing restaurant develop its forecast?
3. How does a club develop its forecast?
4. Do external factors such as weather conditions, road construction, holidays, etc., affect forecasting?

This case was taken from William P. Fisher and Robert A. Ashley, *Case Studies in Commercial Food Service Operations* (Lansing, Mich.: American Hotel & Lodging Educational Institute, 2003).

Dom's Dilemma: Dealing with Staff Member Theft

Unfortunately for owners and managers, restaurants present plenty of opportunities for staff members to steal, in ways both large and small. Just a few examples can reveal the scope of the problem:

- Every Friday night at the Gourmet Eatery and Pub, a group of five men sit in the same five seats at the bar, tell stories, and drink for a couple of hours before going home. The head bartender makes sure their drinks are extra strong, and "Rusty's Regulars," as they are informally known, make sure that the head bartender's tips are extra generous.

- At Barnaby's Steakhouse, the assistant manager is closing on the first Sunday night of the month when he decides to take $100 worth of unsold gift certificates, scribble a signature on them, and put them in with the bank deposit. He then pockets $100. He knows that the restaurant only audits gift certificates at the end of the month, and he plans on giving his two-week notice tomorrow.

- At Tweedledee's Grill, a cook "accidentally" overcooks a steak during the lunch rush. "Hey, boss, can I take this home? It'd be a shame to waste it."

- At the White Knight Restaurant, servers maintain a cash bank during their shifts and "cash out" at shift's end. One day, after Michelle, a server, cashed out and left the restaurant, the manager goes into the computer system and voids off one of Michelle's $20 checks as a "complimentary meal," which changes the end-of-day report. After manipulating the numbers in the computer, the manager pockets $20. Varying the day of the week, the shift, and the server, he has pocketed $10 to $20 a week in this way for almost a year now.

- Phil is a server at Richard's Bistro. He has become friendly with Mr. Ramos, a guest who comes in once or twice a week. A few months ago, Phil accidentally forgot to include Mr. Ramos's salad on his guest check and noticed that he got a larger tip. Since then, Phil has given Mr. Ramos either a free salad or a free dessert every time Mr. Ramos comes in, and Mr. Ramos has left a very large tip each time.

In most cases of income or product theft, restaurant managers know exactly what course of action to take with staff members. In some cases, however, the best way to handle a situation is not so clear cut.

$$\bullet \qquad \bullet \qquad \bullet$$

All Dom could think as he watched Rebecca run out of his office Friday morning, crying, was: Not again. This can't be happening again so soon. Within one week, first Joshua, and now Rebecca—the last person he would suspect of stealing.

Dominick's is a 75-seat, fine-dining restaurant that Dom started five years ago. The first few years had been a struggle, but in the last year the restaurant had really caught on and Dom was beginning to hope that being the owner/operator of a small independent restaurant was not a sure road to bankruptcy and divorce after all. The long hours and hard work were paying off at last.

Even in the early, especially stressful days, Dom had always tried to make working at his restaurant as fun as possible. He wanted staff members to enjoy working at Dominick's and, partly due to his "we're all one big happy family" approach, many staff members had stayed with him for years—some had even been with him for the entire five years.

Losing staff members when they left voluntarily was bad enough; it was especially hard for Dom when he had to fire someone. Luckily, he hadn't had to fire that many people. In fact, not counting Joshua, it had been almost two years since he had fired anyone—that was one of the reasons why firing Joshua Monday night had been especially hard. But Dom had felt he had no choice.

Joshua was the son of Wendy Morris, one of Dom's best day cooks. Wendy had told Dom that Joshua needed a job, and Dom had hired him as a busperson. During Joshua's 60-day probationary period, there had been problems with his performance: he showed up late for work several times, he had broken quite a few dishes, and he wasn't friendly with the rest of the staff. As Helen, Dom's assistant manager, put it, "He has kind of a snotty, know-it-all attitude." Despite these problems, Dom kept Joshua on staff after his probation was up, giving him the benefit of the doubt because of Wendy. And then four nights ago—just two weeks after Joshua's probationary period was over—a server, Gail, had come up to Dom and said, "I think Joshua just stole some tips."

"You're kidding," Dom said. "Are you sure?"

"Well, the last time I checked table four to see if anyone wanted more coffee after their desserts, there was a lot of money in the middle of the table, but when I went back to pick it up after the guests left, it was gone. Sheila saw me looking around and came up to me and whispered that she saw Joshua stuff some money in his pocket while he was bussing the table."

"Sheila's sure about what she saw?"

"She seemed to be."

"Where is she now?"

"Last time I saw her, she was heading for the kitchen with a tray."

"Okay, I'll handle it."

Dom started off for the kitchen to find Sheila and confirm the story, but halfway there he saw Joshua loitering near the doorway to the staff breakroom, and something about Joshua's furtive reaction when he saw Dom coming down the hallway changed Dom's mind about the need to talk to Sheila.

"Hi, Joshua," Dom said. "Let's go to my office for a minute. I want to talk to you about something."

When they got to the office, Dom shut the door and got right to the point. "Someone just told me that some tips have disappeared. Do you know anything about that?"

Joshua said, "No," but there was something guarded in his eyes and his cheeks flushed a sudden red.

"Are you sure?"

"Yes I'm sure. I didn't take anything!"

Dom just looked at him and let the silence build.

Joshua blushed an even deeper red under Dom's gaze. Finally Joshua pulled some wadded bills from his pocket and threw them on Dom's desk.

"You took that money from Gail's table?"

Joshua nodded sullenly.

"Well, Joshua," Dom said, "stealing is a serious matter, so I think it's best that we end our relationship right now. I'll punch out for you—you can go on home."

"I don't care," Joshua said, "this job stunk anyway."

Dom let that pass. "I'm not going to tell your mother what happened, but I'm sure she's going to find out sooner or later, so I suggest you tell her before she hears it from someone else." Maybe having to break the news to Wendy would really drive this painful lesson home to Joshua.

"Can I go now?" Joshua snarled.

Dom nodded, and Joshua left without another word.

That was Monday night. During the next few days, everyone on staff but Wendy had come up to him and said he'd done the right thing—"that kid was just trouble waiting to happen" was how one staffer put it. But now, this morning, it had been Rebecca's turn to stand shame-faced in his office—Rebecca, who for five years had never given him even a moment's trouble and had long since become more friend than worker to him. Rebecca had been a hostess/cashier since opening day. In her late thirties with two children to support, she was the kind of staff member restaurant managers dream of: dependable, mature, hardworking. She always had a smile and a kind word for everyone. Not only was she nice to the restaurant's guests, she also went out of her way to be nice to the restaurant's staff. She remembered everyone's birthday with a card and was an adopted-mom figure to many of the teenagers on staff because she listened sympathetically to their dating troubles and their stories about shots at the buzzer that wouldn't fall at the end of basketball games. In short, she was a vital part of the Dominick's "family."

That's what made what Rebecca had done so hard to accept. After Dom had locked the restaurant's doors last night and was making up the bank deposit for the next day, he had counted down Rebecca's till over and over, but it always came up the same: $50.08 short. It was rare for any till in the restaurant to balance to the penny, but a shortfall of $50 definitely raised a red flag.

When Rebecca passed his office doorway that morning on her way to hang up her coat, Dom had called out to her to come see him when she had the chance. When she came in a few minutes later, she said good morning, but instead of her usual sunny smile, her eyes looked strained and she stood defensively in front of his desk instead of sitting down. Dom's heart sank, but he put a smile on his face and tried to sound matter of fact. "Something weird came up last night and I just wanted to talk to you about it. I couldn't get your till to balance—in fact it was fifty dollars short. Do you remember anything unusual about last night?"

There was a silence, then Rebecca's lower lip began to tremble and her eyes filled with tears. "I'm sorry," she said finally, so softly that Dom barely heard her. She cleared her throat and went on more strongly: "I took one of the fifties out of the drawer when no one was looking. I don't know why—I just did. Maybe it's because I've been under a lot of stress lately. My boyfriend just lost his job, my little one's sick and I've got to take her to the doctor, my tips have been down all week, and—I don't know—all of a sudden I just slipped it into my pocket. I'm really sorry," she said again, sniffing and wiping her eyes.

Dom pushed a box of tissues across his desk and she took one gratefully. "I don't know what to say," Dom said finally. "I'm sorry Samantha's sick, but—" his voice trailed off. Suddenly he thought of the time last year when his mother, who was in a wheelchair and couldn't get out much anymore, had come to the restaurant with the rest of the family to celebrate her 80th birthday. Rebecca had fussed over her all evening, making her feel important and telling her how proud she should be of her son and the success he had made of Dominick's.

Dom came out of his thoughts to see Rebecca looking at him expectantly, waiting and scared. "I don't know what to say," he said again, and sighed. "I guess the best thing right now is for you to go home. We both need a chance to think about this." Dom stood up to signal Rebecca that the meeting was over. The gesture seemed uncomfortably formal, given their close relationship, but somehow appropriate under the present circumstances. "Go home and try not to be too upset, and when you come in tomorrow I'll have a decision for you."

"All right," Rebecca said. "I'm so sorry, I'll give the money back. I'd do anything if I could live last night over again."

Dom just smiled sadly and watched as Rebecca ducked her head and ran from the room. He didn't even see her go past on his way out after retrieving her coat—she must have left the restaurant the back way.

Dom was still at his desk an hour later when Helen stuck her head through the doorway. "I just can't believe the news about Rebecca!" she said breathlessly.

Dom waived her to the chair across from his desk. "Who told you?" he asked.

"Tom saw her leave through the kitchen, crying and all upset, and called her when she got home. She told him the whole story."

"So everyone knows?"

"Yep. No one can believe it, though. Everybody's wondering what you're going to do. They think you should give her a second chance."

"Even Wendy?"

"Wendy's not here—she asked for the day off."

"Oh, right—I forgot."

Helen stood up to leave. "Rebecca's so good with guests, and you know how much everybody loves working with her—it would seem really strange not to have her around anymore. Are you going to let her go?"

Dom sighed. "I don't know. I told Rebecca I'd sleep on it. It'll be tough, but I'll have a decision for her when she comes in tomorrow."

Discussion Question

1. Should Dom fire Rebecca? Why or why not?

The following industry experts helped generate and develop this case: Christopher Kibit, C.S.C., Academic Team Leader, Hotel/Motel/Food Management & Tourism Programs, Lansing Community College, Lansing, Michigan; and Jack Nye, General Manager, Applebee's of Michigan, Applebee's International, Inc.

 # References

Erickson, Joe. "Which Systems Do I Want in Place First?" *Restaurant Startup & Growth*. March 2009. 6(3): 25–31.

———. "Wired for Success: How to Take Advantage of Online Tools for More Effective Restaurant Management." *Restaurant Startup & Growth*. November 2008. 5(11): 21–27.

Laube, Jim. "Eyes in the Back of Your Head: Internal Control Essentials for New Restaurant Owners." *Restaurant Startup & Growth*. July 2008. 5(7): 21–27.

———. "Right on Schedule: Labor Scheduling Basics Right From the Start." *Restaurant Startup & Growth*. August 2006: 42–47.

Liddle, Alan J. "Latest Transaction Tech Gains Traction as Operators Explore POS Possibilities." *Nation's Restaurant News*. April 13, 2009. 43(13): 4.

Ninemeier, Jack. *Planning and Control for Food and Beverage Operations*, Seventh Edition. Lansing, Mich.: American Hotel & Lodging Educational Institute, 2009.

Pavesic, Dave. "How Low Can You Go?" *Restaurant Startup & Growth*. January 2009. 6(1): 48–51.

Ruggless, Ron. "Preventing Employee Theft Safeguards Bottom Line, Ensures a Stronger Staff." *Nation's Restaurant News*. November 24, 2008. 42(46): 38.

Shea, Erin J. "Creative Control." *Restaurants & Institutions*. July 1, 2005. 115(2): 137–138.

Tripoli, Chris. "Good Medicine: A Guide to Assessing the Health of Your Restaurant's Operation." *Restaurant Startup & Growth*. August 2008. 5(8): 21–29.

Tsai, Daw. "At-Table Payments Can Reduce Fraud." Nation's Restaurant News. November 10, 2008. 42(44): 32.

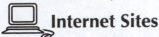

Internet Sites

For more information, visit the following Internet sites. Remember that Internet addresses can change without notice. If the site is no longer there, you can use a search engine to look for additional sites.

Bureau of Labor and Statistics
www.bls.gov

Nation's Restaurant News
www.nrn.com

CMS Hospitality
www.cms-hospitality.com

NCR Corporation
www.ncr.com

Comtrex Systems Corporation
www.comtrex.com

Newmarket International
www.newmarketinc.com

Lodging
www.lodgingmagazine.com

POSitouch
www.positouch.com

Lodging Hospitality
www.lhonline.com

Restaurant Hospitality
www.restaurant-hospitality.com

MICROS Systems, Inc.
www.micros.com

System Concepts, Inc.
www.foodtrak.com

Part II

Chapter 12 Outline

Casual-Dining Restaurants
    Casual-Dining Markets
    Menu Considerations: Food
    Menu Considerations: Beverages
    Value
    Guest Feedback
    The Dining Environment, Supplies,
       and Equipment
    Getting Ready for Service
Other Types of Restaurants
    Fast-Casual Restaurants
    Quick-Service Restaurants
    Hotel Restaurants
    Fine-Dining Restaurants

Competencies

1. Describe casual-dining restaurants. (pp. 475–500)

2. Discuss fast-casual, quick-service, hotel, and fine-dining restaurants. (pp. 500–503)

12

Restaurants

It is not the strongest of the species that survives, nor the most intelligent that survives. It is the one that is the most adaptable to change. —Charles Darwin

T**HE QUOTE** from Charles Darwin applies to the evolution of species in the animal kingdom, but it also can be applied to the restaurant industry. Relentless growth in the competition requires that restaurant operators make a choice—evolve or fail. The rate of change in restaurants is accelerating with each passing year due to a number of reasons, the most significant being the enhanced experience and sophistication of guests. Guests demand choice, quality, value, and a dining experience that fits their needs for the moment—they may desire a thirty-minute dinner before a movie one night, a two-hour lunch with a favorite uncle the next week, mojitos and tapas with friends on a Friday, followed by a vegetarian family dinner out on Saturday. New restaurants open daily that offer guests new and exciting food and beverages in a way that they hope will more closely match the guests' needs, wants, and expectations.

There are many different types of restaurants, divided into categories based on their menus, food preparation methods, service styles, prices, and other variables. This chapter discusses casual-dining, fast-casual, quick-service, hotel, and fine-dining restaurants, with most of our focus on casual-dining restaurants, since this is a dominant segment within the restaurant industry.

Casual-Dining Restaurants

For many years, the term "casual dining" was used to define a broad array of restaurants that generally offered table service, alcoholic beverages, and a variety of menu items at prices much lower than fine-dining restaurants. The casual-dining concept was born in the late 1960s/early 1970s as a response to the needs of a rapidly growing population of Baby Boomers who wanted restaurants that would meet their needs and fit their lifestyle. Often these restaurants had themes that were designed to attract people in pursuit of an entertainment/escape atmosphere while dining out. Staff members, dressed in costumes or gimmicky uniforms, would serve guests in restaurants decorated to resemble a British railway station, a Hollywood movie set, or even a tropical rainforest. While some of these concepts still exist (the Hard Rock Café chain is still quite successful, for example), most did not survive.

Today's **casual-dining restaurants** typically offer full menus of both foods and beverages in an informal service environment. A chain of mid-priced steakhouses is an example of a casual-dining food and beverage operation. In such a chain, there will likely be no tablecloth on the table, paper dinner napkins may be used, and the ambience may be indicative of a log cabin in the Wild West, complete with animal-head trophies and vintage firearms hanging on the walls. This more casual environment may include servers and managers dressed in open-collar shirts with the operation's logo. Featured beverages may be draft beer by the glass or in a pitcher, and wines by the glass. Another example of a casual-dining restaurant is a bistro-style food and beverage operation that features an eclectic menu of food choices, perhaps the cuisines of selected countries, with a wine and beer selection to match so that the food and beverage pairings are more easily done.

Typically, family-focused food and beverage operations are found in the casual-dining segment. These family-friendly operations often compete for the guest's discretionary income with quick-service restaurants (QSRs) and grocery stores that sell foods prepared to go. In the past, family-dining operations targeted Baby Boomers and their families. As the Baby Boomers have aged, some family-dining operations have tried to attract new markets by updating their decor, providing new menu items and faster service, and promoting alcoholic beverages more frequently. Others have expanded their children's menus and changed their server uniforms to project a more casual, family-friendly atmosphere. More diverse menus give family-dining operations the feel of independent rather than chain restaurants. Menus that vary with the locality or region and feature specialties of a local chef are seen as more guest-focused and appealing by guests who are trying to avoid the same old dining experience.

"Family-dining" is just one way to categorize casual-dining restaurants. The casual-dining segment of the restaurant industry has evolved into many smaller segments based on consumer demands. For example, "entertainment casual-dining" concepts such as Dave & Buster's and Fox & Hound Sports Bar & Grill provide interactive fun while guests enjoy micro-brewed beers and grilled turkey burgers; "varied-menu casual dining" concepts such as Applebee's, Chili's, and Ruby Tuesday's strive to offer something for everyone; "specialty casual-dining" concepts—LongHorn Steakhouse, Olive Garden, and Red Lobster, for example—hope to attract guests by serving superb food in an "escape" environment; and "polished casual-dining" concepts such as The Cheesecake Factory, P.F. Chang's, and Houston's offer food and atmospheres that mimic fine-dining levels, but with more approachable service and more reasonable menu prices.

Competition in the casual-dining segment is fierce. Providing guest-driven service in such a competitive environment is not just a "should" but a "must." One of the few ways to build guest demand is to create and deliver guest experiences that will differentiate a restaurant from the clutter of its competition. Managers of casual-dining restaurants should keep a marketing perspective in mind as they develop, implement, and evaluate plans that affect guest service. Managers of casual-dining restaurants must (1) know who their targeted guests are, and (2) know what these guests want and expect. The ultimate goal is to consistently increase sales through building a loyal base of frequent guests.

Family Restaurants

Family restaurants are a large and important subcategory of casual-dining restaurants. As the name implies, family restaurants take extra care to appeal to guests with children.

While children often influence where families dine, obviously it is the parents who pay the bill. If parents sincerely believe that their children's as well as their own needs and expectations are being met, the payoff for the restaurant will be increased sales, repeat guests, positive word-of-mouth referrals, and a good image for the restaurant in the marketplace.

Although guests with children are the primary focus of family restaurants, there are other markets and submarkets as well—senior citizens, for example, who are drawn by a family restaurant's moderate prices. And, of course, each market may consist mostly of guests from the local area or guests who are traveling, depending on the restaurant's location and marketing thrust.

Many family restaurants offer a children's menu, either included on the regular menu or printed as a separate menu. Children's menus may or may not reflect the restaurant's regular menu. For example, a seafood restaurant's children's menu may offer such items as spaghetti, grilled cheese sandwiches, pizza, and hamburgers instead of seafood.

Comfort is critical for families, especially those with small children. Lighting plays an important role in family restaurants. Generally, bright lighting is preferable because children like it and it connotes cleanliness to many parents.

Some family restaurants are transforming empty banquet rooms and private dining rooms into places where children can eat and be entertained by staff members while parents enjoy their meal in the regular dining area. Separate areas with child-size furniture and children's reading materials and games also can occupy children while their parents finish their meals.

One feature is essential for family restaurants: diaper-changing stations, whether located in restrooms or some other area. Locating changing stations in both men's and women's restrooms indicates that the restaurant is in tune with the times. Changing stations, like highchairs, must be fitted with safety belts and cleaned regularly.

As is true in any service organization, managers of family restaurants set the tone for the style and quality of service delivered to guests. A family restaurant manager who directs a server to take care of "the table with the two rug-rats" does not set the right tone for guest-driven service to families.

Some food service professionals say that managers and staff members who are parents themselves provide family-friendly service better than those who are not parents, perhaps because they have firsthand knowledge of how children can behave when dining out. In any case, one of a manager's most important tasks in a family restaurant is to train staff members to be sensitive to the needs and expectations of guests with children. Servers especially must be trained to pay special attention to children, for it is often the server who makes or breaks a family-dining experience.

Tips for Serving Guests with Children

It is generally advisable to seat parents with young children—especially toddlers—in a section with other families with young children. The presence of others with

(continued)

(continued)

children usually eases the parents' nervousness about how their children will behave and whether they will negatively affect the dining experiences of others.

In some restaurants, after guests with children are seated, servers are instructed to greet the children first, kneeling down so they are speaking at the children's level. Forks, knives, and glasses can be dangerous in the hands of toddlers, so servers should remove these items soon after toddlers are seated. Some restaurants provide plastic cups with lids and straws for toddlers. Servers also must be sensitive to parental needs for assistance with booster chairs, highchairs, or cushions.

Since children have relatively short attention spans, it is important to quickly give them something that keeps them occupied and happy. Many restaurants present children with place mats and small packages of crayons to color figures and complete puzzles and mazes on the place mats. Some give children inexpensive toys or other giveaways. (Children who take these giveaways home may be reminded to ask parents for a return visit to the restaurant.) Many restaurants serve crackers, bread, or rolls immediately to keep children content. Restaurants might also provide children with a cup of ice to chew on while waiting for their meals. In any case, these distractions should be distributed as soon as children are seated.

Servers should request that the kitchen staff rush the orders of families with small children—especially the children's orders. (Families dining with children are generally not looking for a leisurely experience.) When serving families with infants, servers should be attentive to the need to heat formula bottles or jars of baby food. Some parents may want to share their food with small children rather than order from the children's menu.

Once service is completed, servers should clear plates quickly and deliver the check promptly. Parents may want to leave before their children get restless. And if the children have been active and boisterous, parents will want to leave quickly to avoid further disturbing other guests.

Servers and other staff members should offer departing parents a genuine thank-you and a reassuring comment about children being welcome. This helps reduce the anxiety that many parents feel about dining out with children and may convince them to return and to tell others about the restaurant.

Casual-Dining Markets

There are casual-dining restaurants for virtually every market imaginable. There are ethnic restaurants; restaurants that appeal to senior citizens; restaurants that feature certain foods (e.g., chicken on the bone) or certain food preparation methods; and restaurants that appeal to sports fans, theater-goers, video game buffs, romantics, health and fitness enthusiasts, and people who just enjoy good food in a comfortable setting.

Characteristics of Selected Markets. It would be impractical to attempt to describe every casual-dining market—there are local markets, visitor markets, single markets, family markets, and more. What follows are key characteristics of some of the major markets—Generation Y, Generation X, and Baby Boomers are demographic descriptors of markets, while terms such as "influentials" and "affluent" are psychographic descriptors of markets. (Keep in mind that there are many

Gift Cards　Locations　Contact

DARDEN.

English | Español

OUR COMPANY　OUR BRANDS　OUR COMMITMENTS　INVESTORS　MEDIA　CAREERS

Darden is the world's largest full-service restaurant company.

The Darden family of restaurants features some of the most recognizable and successful brands in full-service dining: Red Lobster, Olive Garden, LongHorn Steakhouse, The Capital Grille, Bahama Breeze and Seasons 52. Our brands are built on decades of learning from our guests. Their culinary inspirations come from the fishing villages of Maine, the family tables of Italy and the American West – icons that reflect the rich diversity of those who visit our restaurants.

In fact, it's no exaggeration to say our biggest brands have become icons themselves. Since opening our first Red Lobster restaurant in Lakeland, Fla., in 1968, Darden has grown to become the world's largest full-service restaurant company. Through subsidiaries, we own and operate 1,800 restaurants, employ approximately 180,000 people and serve more than 400 million meals a year.

How It All Began

Generation Commitment

100 Best Companies to Work For

Recent News

Darden Restaurants to Present at Barclay's Capital 2011 Retail and Restaurants Conference
Tue, 19 Apr 2011

Darden Restaurants Reports 14% Increase in Third Quarter Diluted Net Earnings Per Share and Announces Quarterly Dividend of 32 Cents

According to Darden's website (www.darden.com), Darden is the world's largest full-service restaurant company; its brands include Red Lobster, Olive Garden, and Long-Horn Steakhouse.

market overlaps; for example, an influential might also be a Baby Boomer and might also be one of the affluent.)

Generation Y. Generation Y (also known as the Millennial Generation or Millennials) is made up of those born sometime between the late seventies/early eighties to the mid-1990s. The Generation Y population is three times larger than Generation X and is destined to dominate the marketplace in much the same way that the Baby Boomers have done. This demographic group was the first to grow up with the Internet and has never known a world without cell phones, CDs, DVDs, cable TV, and personal computers. As you might suspect, individuals who are part of Generation Y are technologically savvy and expect immediate gratification. They have little or no brand loyalty and are generally suspicious of traditional advertising methods. Some of the best ways to reach Generation Y are through social media outlets (Facebook, Twitter, Foursquare), grass-roots marketing, and sponsorship of extreme-sports events.

Generation X. Generation X (often defined as those born between 1965 and 1981) is made up of smart, value-conscious consumers. They tend to be less driven than their Baby Boomer parents when it comes to work. Generation X watched their parents put in long hours to advance their careers, often at the expense of their families; this has led most Gen-Xers to be self-reliant (there is a high percentage of entrepreneurs in this generation) and somewhat distrustful and cynical about big companies, big government, and authority in general. They look at advertising claims closely and do their homework (often via the Internet) before making a purchase. Those trying to sell to Gen-Xers should appeal to their desire for immediacy, independence, and innovation. They respond to restaurant concepts promoting excitement, entertainment, and group interaction.

Baby Boomers. Baby Boomers, those born sometime during the years 1946 to 1964, make up roughly one-third of the U.S. population. Younger Baby Boomers have busy lifestyles and are likely to have dual-career families, while older Baby Boomers tend to eat less while still desiring to eat out often. If the past is an indicator of the future, when Baby Boomers enter their fifties and their peak earning years, the discretionary dollars they spend on food away from home should increase. Unlike Generations X and Y, Baby Boomers respond well to target marketing. Compared to Generation Y, Baby Boomers are easier to accommodate and satisfy. Baby Boomers are more likely to choose moderately priced restaurants over QSRs, but have shown a growing preference for fast-casual restaurants.

Influentials. "Influentials" is a market designation for those who are deemed leaders—people whose opinions on a variety of subjects are valued. If a restaurant can impress an influential by exceeding his or her expectations through a positive, memorable experience, the resulting word-of-mouth referrals could make the difference between long-term profit or loss. By exceeding the expectations of influentials, a restaurant can connect with a large social network.

One of the most popular leisure activities of influentials is dining out, particularly on weekends. Influentials prefer full-service restaurants and report that they dine out often because it is fun. Influentials with children dine out to combine entertainment with family time. They value attentive, anticipatory service and have little tolerance for poor service. Influentials also are more likely to enjoy food in moderation and practice a healthy lifestyle than the general public.

Influentials who are subcategorized as "intellectually curious" are lured by restaurants offering a combination of education and entertainment to create intrigue, excitement, and positive memories. To attract the "intellectually curious" market, some restaurants feature teaching chefs who offer cooking tips and classes. Other restaurants offer "theme dinners" during which guests can learn about the history of the unique menu items they are eating and how the ingredients are grown and prepared. If a special wine is part of the dinner, sometimes distributors will co-sponsor the dinner and provide speakers who are knowledgeable about wines.

The affluent. The affluent market is composed of U.S. adults who earn $100,000 or more a year. The affluent can afford to sample and enjoy the best that money can buy. In general, the affluent seek out exceptional service, and the quality of service is a big factor in whether they decide to return to a given restaurant. They like to be pampered and at the same time feel they are getting value for the time and money they are spending. Fresh foods, regionally grown, are favorites of this market.

Menu Considerations: Food

Menu changes at casual-dining restaurants have taken place in response to (1) more sophisticated guests with an interest in fresher and lighter dining with greater variety; (2) more talented chefs attracted to this segment who have introduced innovative menu selections, more sophisticated ingredients, and an overall upgrade of food quality; and (3) guest demands for more sustainable and healthy menu choices, including low-sodium, trans-fat-free, and gluten-free items. There is a trend toward synthesizing foods from many cultures by adding creative twists. For example, menus have evolved to include such innovative menu items as wasabi salmon sliders; curry mango crème brûlée; Kobe beef cheeks; Kona-crusted flat iron steak; chestnut flour pasta with arugula, kalamata olives, and capers; coconut buns with pork belly; macadamia-crusted ono with ginger lime sauce; and basil-infused sea bass. The "miniaturization" trend has grown at many restaurants by chefs responding to guest request for smaller portions. Seasons 52 restaurants offer tiny dessert "taster" portions, while the tapas-style approach of offering a variety of smaller tasting-style portions has grown considerably in popularity. There is a growing trend for restaurants to offer fresh, local, and/or sustainable food products. For example, Chipotle Mexican Grill uses organically grown pork, the Silver Diner chain in Maryland has partnered with local farmers to support sustainable agriculture, and Andrew Weil has partnered with noted Phoenix restaurateur Sam Fox to create True Food Kitchen that offers great-tasting food with a strong orientation toward healthy eating.

Breakfast has traditionally only been served until the next meal period—lunch—begins, but today more and more food and beverage operators are offering breakfast selections at any time of the day. Eggs along with traditional accompaniments such as bacon are viewed by many guests as comfort foods to be enjoyed throughout the day. Traditional breakfast menu items are being offered alongside ethnic breakfast items such as huevos rancheros and scrambled eggs with chorizo sausage. The breakfast burrito is just one example of a seemingly endless number of breakfast sandwiches. Other breakfast items that are more frequently seen on food menus are smoked fish, crab cakes, and other seafood choices. With health consciousness growing among many guests, fresh fruits are popular choices for breakfast as well.

Some guests at lunch or dinner are now ordering an appetizer or selection of appetizers as a replacement for the main course. To promote sharing, appetizer combination plates and platters have been promoted to guests. Mini-salads as appetizers are popular with those who are looking to reduce their intake of calories. Tapas, the "little dishes of Spain," are bite-sized appetizers served on salad plates to be shared with others at the table. Japanese versions of tapas are served in food and beverage operations called *izakayas* (Japanese taverns). Known for value-priced small plates, *izakayas* are popular with guests who are looking for a

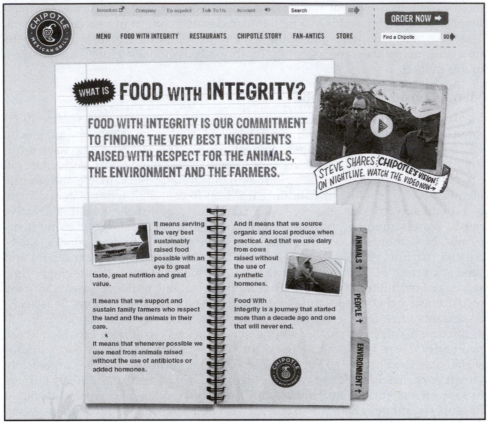

Chipotle is committed to serving "food with integrity," which means, among other things, that it strives to serve the best sustainably raised food possible and uses organic and local produce when practical.

unique food and beverage experience. The small plates mean reduced prices for guests; several small plates can replace a main course.

Another menu trend is to use organic and fresh locally or regionally grown produce. Small vegetables (e.g., mini-squashes, baby carrots) are being utilized on main course plates as the vegetable. Exotic fruit (e.g., dragon fruit, guava, and passion fruit) and the so-called super fruits (e.g., acai, goji berries, mangosteens) are appearing on more menus.

Main items on menus have experienced a transformation as well. There has been a growing use of less-expensive cuts of meat, such as the bone-in veal chop, Denver steak, flat iron beef, or pork steak. In the pork and poultry category, free-range products are preferred by some guests since they mean that the animal was not confined to an extremely small space while being raised. Non-traditional fish such as barramundi (also called Asian seabass) are more popular today than just a few years ago. Asian noodles, such as udon, ramen, and laksa, served in a chicken, beef, vegetarian, or fish stock are appearing on more menus and may be ordered as appetizers or main courses.

Comfort foods include main courses that evoke in the minds of guests a less stressful, more relaxed and comfortable time in their lives. Traditional comfort foods such as macaroni and cheese are being revamped with new noodle options and the addition of two, three, or sometimes four different varieties of cheese. Pasta and meatballs, turkey with dressing, and meatloaf are other examples of popular comfort foods.

Turkey legs prepared with Asian or Italian seasonings, and spicy to mild chicken wings are being added to menus. The traditional hamburger is being served in smaller portions (e.g., rather than a six-ounce single patty, three two-ounce patties are served on specialty breads or rolls). Some hamburgers are being topped with pickled vegetables, sausage, thick-cut smoked bacon, and fried eggs, to name just a few of the endless toppings available. Of course, these are offered to guests at higher menu prices, but, once again, they provide a unique experience.

Side dishes and starches represent another menu category, sometimes referred to as go-withs or accompaniments. Some guests are opting to order these side dishes as main courses after sampling an appetizer or two or enjoying a small salad and soup combo. One of the most popular side dishes is mashed potatoes. Variations on mashed potatoes are endless but include redskin potatoes with fresh garlic, mashed potatoes with pureed vegetables, mashed potatoes with a selection of different cheeses, mashed potatoes with bacon, or mashed potatoes with a variety of additional flavorings such as capers or fresh ginger. Additional starches that are being added to menus include couscous, lentils, polenta, quinoa, and various forms of pasta made with different grains and in different shapes. Ancient grains such as amaranth, buckwheat, and spelt are also being used for unique starch menu selections. Grilled and steamed vegetables have replaced vegetables with cream sauces. Mini-versions of vegetables when served in a medley provide a beautiful color complement to main courses.

Other ingredients being added to food menus are artisanal breads and cheeses, usually produced in small quantities by local manufacturers. Popular breads today are the flatbreads, including lavash, naan, pita, and tortilla. These flat breads are being served as accompaniments to salads and soups.

Salt as a menu-item ingredient has been criticized for raising blood pressure; however, various forms of specialty salts are being marketed to guests as flavorings for main courses, side dishes, and starches. Beyond the Shaker, a company specializing in unique premium gourmet salts, promotes Windy City Celery, Truffle Wet Salt, Hawaiian Black Lava, Citrus Wet Salt, Himalayan Pink Salt, Hot Habanero Blend, and other gourmet salts. The company has a website (www.beyondtheshaker.com) that includes all of its gourmet premium salts, as well as a salt guide and messages from the Salt Scribe.

Desserts have taken on a new look on food menus. Keeping with the theme of "mini," samples of desserts that are bite-sized are being promoted as a sweet but healthier indulgence at the end of meals. Dessert combinations, sharing platters, and any dessert with chocolate as an ingredient have become more popular. Cocoa, the main flavor ingredient in chocolate, is being promoted as a source of anti-oxidants and a way to lower blood pressure.

Healthy menu items seem to be growing in popularity as Baby Boomers age and experience more dietary restrictions. Look for smaller portion sizes, fruit and vegetable chips to replace potato chips and french fries, yogurt with complex carbohydrates (fiber) and added protein, ginger-flavored and green tea sodas to replace higher-calorie traditional soft drinks, juices from rain forest super fruits (e.g., acai, goji, guava, mangosteen) promoted for their antioxidant contents, and ice creams with green tea. Preparation methods for food items are also heading in a healthier direction. Braising and grilling are replacing frying, and sautéing has become more popular.

Menu Considerations: Beverages

One of the most pressing menu considerations for managers of casual-dining restaurants is how to grow beverage sales. Across the United States, restaurant guests are ordering fewer alcoholic beverages than they ordered in years past. Industry experts attribute the drop in alcoholic beverage sales to a number of circumstances:

- Baby Boomers are drinking less as they age.
- There is rising interest in fitness and health.
- Drunk-driving laws and penalties have been made tougher in almost every state.

Many managers have come up with strategies to prevent this drop in alcoholic beverage sales. Creating unique-tasting, visually appealing **signature drinks** is one strategy. Dylan's in Manhattan offers chocolate martinis; the Spice Market restaurants promote their ginger margarita; and bacon-infused Bloody Marys are growing in popularity.

Premium beverage options can also be promoted successfully. Premium wines by the glass are appealing to guests who want less than a full bottle of wine to accompany dinner. Fleming's restaurants offer one hundred wines by the glass, and the Two Urban Licks restaurant in Atlanta offers forty signature wines straight from the barrel. With today's focus on quality—and in light of the fact that some guests order only one drink—premium brands make a great deal of sense. Beverage distributors typically offer a wide range of promotional items (such as banners, table tents, and displays) to help restaurateurs sell these beverages.

And finally, brew pubs are helping to increase beer's popularity in the United States. Featuring on-premises brewing and often a variety of micro-brews, some brew pubs offer **signature menu items,** others feature fine-dining and upscale menus, and still others sell "pub-grub"—casual menu foods such as burgers, nachos, ribs, and seafood.

Beverage Selection. Beyond their concerns with building alcoholic beverage sales, restaurateurs need to make decisions about which types and brands of beer, wine, and liquor to offer.

Many casual-dining restaurants use three or more classifications for spirits. The three commonly used classifications are house, call, and premium. **House brands** (also called well brands) are served when the guest does not specify a particular brand of spirits when ordering a drink (a martini, for example); house brands are usually priced lower than call brands. Likewise, house wines are served when the guest does not specify a label. **Call brands** are spirits that guests request (or "call") by brand name (a Bombay Sapphire martini, for example). **Premium brands** are costlier call brands requested by guests (a Ketal One or Ciroc vodka martini, for example). In addition to premium spirits, there are premium beers and wines.

Attitudes of managers about house brands range from "do not use anything you would not be proud to display on the back bar" to "use the least expensive; let the people pay extra for premium brands." Many managers use neither the least nor the most expensive brands for their house brands; rather they shop for value with an emphasis on what their guests desire.

It is generally not possible (nor, for that matter, desirable) to offer every available brand of spirits. A better approach is to stock call brands that guests most frequently request. If a specific brand is not available, most guests will order another. Obviously, if a number of guests frequently order an unavailable call brand, it should be added to the product list. Servers and bar staff can help managers identify which brands guests are requesting.

Beverage Trends. One beverage trend that is here to stay is locally brewed craft beers, often produced in relatively small quantities in microbreweries. These beers often take the form of specialty beers that have fruit added, or herbs and spices added during the brewing process.

Similarly, artisanal micro-distilled alcoholic spirits from local and regional areas are being featured on menus. These spirits, when paired with local or regional food items, make great combinations that provide guests with a unique dining experience. Organic wine is another menu choice that is often regionally or locally produced and paired with food menu items.

New cocktails are being prepared for guests using a number of interesting ingredients. For example, there is a move from traditional martinis to flavored martinis; there is even a chocolate-flavored martini called a "chocotini." Bartenders have combined alcoholic beverages with energy drinks to make new and interesting cocktails, although there are some concerns about mixing alcohol with caffeine-loaded energy drinks. Creative bartenders will prepare a guest's choice of cocktails made with rain forest super fruits, cocktails flavored with herbs (e.g., basil, lavender, rosemary), cocktails with a base of a freshly produced vegetable puree, or cocktails made from fresh blackberries or strawberries that reportedly raise the antioxidant levels of the beverage.

Value

"Value" is the watchword for today's guests. The search for value is important to all categories of guests, including affluent guests. Guests are better educated in terms of what they want in their food and beverage experiences. When they get what they want and expect, relative to the price they pay, they perceive value, which in turn generates loyalty.

Casual-dining restaurants need to emphasize and reinforce the value they offer. Value can be part of any number of promotions, including:

- Daily specials
- Reduced-price menu items

- Seasonal specials and local regional food tastings

- Senior citizen discounts, often offered as part of early-bird dinner prices

- Social media enticements via Facebook and e-commerce

- Frequent-diner programs

The list can go on and on, as long as the promotions match what current and potential guests want and expect.

Several independent restaurants and full-service restaurant chains are promoting high-quality prepared foods to go. These restaurants are providing value by blending convenience and high quality for people on the go. A growing number of people want high-quality elaborate foods at home, but they cannot or will not take the time to prepare them. In addition to traditional items such as baby back ribs, lasagna, and rotisserie chicken, unique items such as four-grain salads, sushi, kona-rubbed ribeye steaks, veal entrées, and holiday specialties are being featured by restaurants. The prepared-foods-to-go or home-replacement-meals concept is driven largely by value. Restaurant-quality meals can be consumed at home where there are no service charges and consumers can dine as casually as they want.

Some people view brunch as a value option. Brunch today in casual-dining restaurants often differs from the unlimited buffets that were popular in the recent past, featuring instead an á la carte menu that includes at least a few light items. Some interesting brunch items are omelets made with herbs, beans, chili peppers, and vegetables; pancakes and waffles topped with apples, bananas, kiwi, mangos, or raspberries; French toast made from brioche, raisin bread, or sourdough bread and flavored with almond extract or liqueurs; skillet eggs scrambled with a variety of cheeses and vegetables; and crepes filled with protein (chicken, lobster, or shrimp) or sweet fruit fillings. These unique brunch items add value by exceeding guests' expectations.

Many experts agree that the food is the number-one reason that guests choose a restaurant initially, but that it is service and the overall experience that largely determine whether they will return. A restaurant's combination of food, ambience, and service, along with menu pricing, create the guest's perception of value. Because service is so important in the value equation, casual-dining restaurant operators are studying and adapting the service expertise of fine-dining restaurants to their operations. Their goal? To create and deliver what is perceived by the guest as a $40 guest-check-average dining experience at an $18 guest-check-average casual-dining restaurant. To achieve this goal, many restaurant operators investigate the food, service, and decor components found in more upscale restaurants and adapt what can be implemented in their operations. One of the elements of success in chains such as The Cheesecake Factory and P.F. Chang's is their ability to deliver on this goal.

Sometimes a fine-dining element is easy to implement, such as upgrading uniforms or encouraging servers to make eye contact with guests within sixty seconds after guests have been seated. Other components require more work and expense, such as providing servers with continuous training so they have a more thorough knowledge of menu items and beverage selections, or introducing linen napkins and tablecloths to the restaurant. Some casual-dining restaurants have

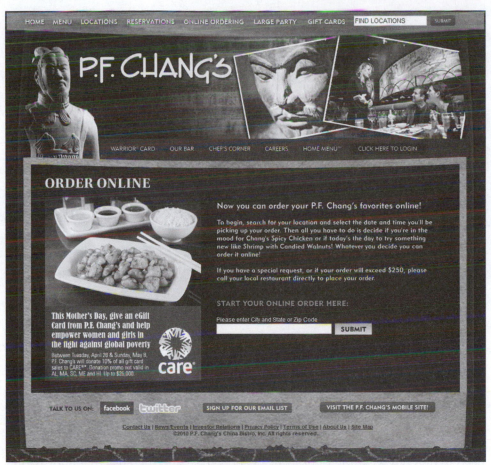

P. F. Chang's, founded in 1993, is a casual-dining restaurant chain that seeks to deliver an upscale dining experience at affordable prices.

introduced or upgraded their wine service; this lends a fine-dining feel to the casual-dining experience and can increase the perception of value in the eyes of guests. Other casual-dining restaurants have focused on training servers to better use observational skills so they can discern the varying expectations of guests and then customize their service style and menu suggestions for each guest. Additional lessons learned from fine-dining restaurants and adapted to casual-dining operations include scheduling an additional server during busy meal periods to assist with service, or using a team-based service style in which one server never leaves the dining room and is present at all times to take drink and appetizer orders and give immediate attention to guests. It all boils down to managers who are passionate about delivering value to guests and approach their responsibilities with enthusiasm, working closely with their staff members to constantly improve their restaurants and increase guest loyalty.

Exhibit 1 Shopper's Report Form for Wine Service

	Strongly Agree				Strongly Disagree
A. The food server suggested a wine to complement the meal.	5	4	3	2	1
B. The wine was properly presented before opening.	5	4	3	2	1
C. The wine was opened properly (e.g., the server used a knife to cut the foil just below the bulge).	5	4	3	2	1
D. The glass selection was an excellent choice for the type of wine served.	5	4	3	2	1
E. The host was poured a sample of the wine.	5	4	3	2	1
F. The bottle was twisted at the completion of the pour.	5	4	3	2	1
G. The wine was filled to the proper glass level (e.g., no more than half full for red wine, three-fourths full for white).	5	4	3	2	1
H. The wine was served at an appropriate temperature (e.g., white wine chilled—50°F (10°C); red wine at cellar temperature—65°F (18°C).	5	4	3	2	1
I. Comments regarding your wine service: _____					

STANDARD POINT SCORE FOR WINE SERVICE 40   ACTUAL POINT SCORE _____

Guest Feedback

Casual-dining restaurants are constantly evolving to keep pace with the needs and expectations of guests. For that reason, managers and staff members of these restaurants must continually evaluate their products and services. To do so, they need to find out what their guests need and expect and then use that information to create a dining experience that guests desire. Guest feedback is only helpful if it is used properly.

Managers and staff members should seek guest comments on an ongoing basis. Guest comment cards, questionnaires, Internet surveys, focus groups, social media queries, telephone surveys, guest interviews, and other means to discover information about guests can be used to determine guest needs and expectations and whether they are being met. One restaurant phones guests two or three days after a private party to solicit feedback. Another sends a text message to guests who have visited asking for feedback. A number of successful restaurant chains offer guests a discount on their next visit provided they fill out an online evaluation of their recent dining experience.

Some restaurants use a **shopper's service** (also known as a "mystery shopper" service) to evaluate a restaurant's service from the guest's perspective. A sample shopper's service report form is shown in Appendix A at the end of the chapter. This form can be adapted as necessary to suit a specific restaurant.

Exhibit 1 is a sample shopper's service report form for evaluating wine service. It can be used in dining areas in conjunction with food service shopper forms.

Guest Pet Peeves

A reporter for the *Detroit Free Press* asked readers to share their pet peeves (that is, their biggest gripes) about restaurants. The top five things that irritated these restaurant guests the most were the following:

1. Being addressed as "you guys"

2. Being asked by servers, "Do you need change?" when they are picking up a guest's check that has been paid with cash

3. Presenting a guest's check too soon

4. Wiping tabletops and chair seats with the same cloth

5. Having to tolerate music at high volume

Let's discuss these guest pet peeves in order and see how food and beverage managers can take simple steps to address them.

The top gripe was related to the inappropriately casual ways that servers address guests, as in: "How are you guys?" and "Are you guys ready to order?" Guests, in general, do not know servers as casual friends. The "you guys" phrase comes across to guests as not business appropriate, at the least, or as disrespectful or insulting at the worst. SOLUTION: Substitute a simple, polite greeting, such as "How are you?"

Gripe number two ("Do you need change?") appears to the guest to be presumptuous on the part of a server. Even though the server may simply be trying to avoid an additional trip back to the table with the guest's change in cash, it comes across to many guests as, "I'm trying to keep the change and get a larger tip from you." Some guests are irked enough to then leave a smaller-percentage tip. SOLUTION: Rather than say, "Do you need change?" a server can say, "I will return with your change." This gives guests the option to say "We're all set" if they indeed intend to let the server keep the change.

The third gripe—getting the guest check too soon—leaves guests with the impression that the server is indicating "your dining was finished after you wolfed down that main course. Time to leave. Hurry." This action by the server may make guests feel that ordering dessert or a cup of coffee would be too much of an imposition on the server or the restaurant. SOLUTION: Servers should wait until guests are finished with the main course, offer dessert and coffee, and then present the check.

Gripe number four relates to how clean the guest perceives the restaurant to be and the restaurant's overall food safety practices. If a cloth is used to wipe tables, it should be cleaned and rinsed frequently. To not do so gives guests the impression that the same dirty cloth is used for wiping tables and chairs (and who knows what else). SOLUTION: Regularly rinse the cloth in a sanitizing solution and do not use the same cloth to wipe the table and the chairs.

Gripe number five is about music that is too loud. Guests do not want to shout when trying to have a conversation. It is not just loud music but also multiple TV screens in sports bars that can mar a dining experience for guests. Loud music or televisions at high volumes may energize servers, but they are likely to upset guests. SOLUTION: Turn down the music and the television volume.

(continued)

(continued)

> As you can see, these gripes can be solved quite easily. Food and beverage managers are well advised to communicate with their guests to discover what irritates them and what they want from their dining experiences. Managers should not assume that they know what their guests want. Managers who do not communicate with their guests run the risk of reading about their guests' complaints in the morning paper, on a reporter's blog, or on Facebook or some other social media outlet. Such negative guest feedback casts the food and beverage operation in a bad light and may convince others to adopt these same negative opinions about the operation without ever setting foot on the premises.

Note that Exhibit 1 refers to specific procedures; for example, the hypothetical restaurant that uses this form requires that red wine be poured so that glasses are no more than half full, and white wine so that glasses are no more than three-fourths full. Exhibit 1 can be adapted as necessary to suit a specific restaurant's needs. Restaurants that use shopper services should use the reports as training tools, sharing them with all staff involved.

The Dining Environment, Supplies, and Equipment

Design and decor play a major role in shaping a casual-dining restaurant's ambience—a fusion of design, decor, image, and service that is one of the most important factors in many guests' restaurant selection. By definition, design and decor are paramount in theme restaurants.

Whether subtle or eclectic, low-key or flashy, there are casual-dining restaurants for seemingly everyone's tastes. Some designs call for display kitchens and bakeries, some for furnishings reminiscent of neighborhood restaurants. Some restaurants feature a nautical decor with a seafood theme; some, music of the 1950s and '60s with a diner theme; and others, original artwork displayed with a gallery theme. Some restaurants spotlight sports memorabilia for an athletic theme, fresh pasta and garlic for an Italian theme, rustic furnishings for a steakhouse theme, or even tropical live and robotic animals for a rain forest theme.

The supplies and equipment that dining area staff members need in order to fulfill their responsibilities are not the same in every casual-dining operation. There are differences based on markets, restaurant image and size, level of service, check average, location, and other factors. For example, some restaurants have service bars where servers can pick up their beverage orders; in others, servers may be required to go to the bar or lounge area. Casual-dining restaurants typically have assortments of beverage glassware, and servers need to know which glassware is used for which drinks. Tablecloths, cloth napkins, and full tableware service may be used in some of the more upscale casual-dining restaurants, and servers may even need to learn special napkin-folding techniques.

For all restaurants, it is imperative that supplies and equipment be clean and presentable and in good, usable condition. Spotted, chipped glassware and tableware; bent flatware; messy condiment containers; and noisy, rusty, dented, or dirty

As you might imagine, Mitchell's Fish Market restaurants feature nautical/seafood decor in keeping with their overall theme. The company is "obsessed" with serving fresh seafood and is also involved in seafood conservation efforts.

pieces of equipment are simply not compatible with any dining atmosphere and do not exhibit a concern for food safety. Health officials can close food and beverage operations that are not operating with food safety practices.

Getting Ready for Service

Independent restaurants and restaurant chains should develop their own service methods and procedures. Generally speaking, casual-dining restaurants use plate service techniques with a casual approach based on their guests' desired levels of comfort. Whatever service methods and procedures a restaurant develops, they should be followed consistently. For instance, if the house rule is to have the ends of flatware handles an inch away from the table edge, staff members should set all of the tables in the restaurant that way. (While there is no universal standard that applies to flatware placement, flatware handles should always be set back from the table edge to some degree so that guests do not knock flatware off the table while being seated.) Similarly, whether the menu is already on the table when guests are seated or the host or server hands menus to guests after they are seated depends more on the rules of the house than on rules of etiquette. The point is that all of a casual-dining restaurant's service procedures should be consistently followed and enforced.

Another consideration in getting ready for service is quality standards. Based on guest requirements, a casual-dining restaurant's management team defines the quality standards that service staff members must meet as they get ready for service, actually serve guests, and perform a wide range of duties, including operating equipment, using income control procedures, placing and picking up food orders, and interacting with bar staff. Guests evaluate many factors other than food and beverages while in the dining room; therefore, managers and staff members must pay close attention to all details to ensure cleanliness and the compatibility of atmosphere and service with the quality of the products offered.

The restaurant's manager is ultimately responsible for all these details and for ensuring that the restaurant's standard operating procedures incorporate a concern for quality guest-driven service.

Training. Training for casual-dining restaurant service should focus on menu knowledge and sales skills as well as courtesy, consistency, efficiency, and teamwork.

Providing menu information to guests is one of the most important services servers perform. In order to sell menu items, servers must know the menu and the house policies and rules about what they can and cannot do (allowing substitutions, for example). In order to do their jobs properly, servers must:

- Be thoroughly familiar with the menu.

- Know how to pronounce each menu item.

- Know the daily specials and the restaurant's signature items along with their prices.

- Know how every item is prepared, including ingredients. (Some guests must avoid certain ingredients because of food allergies or other health considerations.)

- Know how to describe every item properly. Truth-in-menu laws in many states prohibit misrepresenting menu items and ingredients. For example, servers should not try to pass margarine off as butter or describe frozen foods as fresh.

- Know portion sizes and what side dishes or garnishes are included.

At times, guests will ask servers to describe how an unfamiliar item tastes. Some restaurants provide tasting sessions for service staff so that servers can describe how an item tastes; the chef or a cook can attend these meetings to provide information about the item. Likewise, wine-tasting and beverage-tasting sessions can boost the staff's beverage sales skills. Bartenders and bar staff can provide information about specialty drinks.

Once servers know the menu, they will be able to use selling techniques that can increase not only guest satisfaction, but also the guest check, to the benefit of both the servers and the restaurant. (Since tips are usually based on the check total, a larger total generally means a larger tip.) **Suggestive selling** involves encouraging

Serving Special Guests

Although in one sense all guests are special and should be treated that way, servers sometimes find themselves serving guests who require out-of-the-ordinary attention. For example, staff members in family restaurants are trained to focus special efforts on children—one category of "special guests." What follows are other categories and considerations.

Guests with Special Dietary Needs

Servers should know which menu items do not contain sodium and which items are available for vegetarians. Servers should know menu item ingredients in case guests have questions concerning food allergies. Servers should be able to suggest low-calorie menu items to those guests who request such information; however, low-calorie items should not be suggested unless a guest asks about them, lest the server anger a guest or hurt his or her feelings. People with special health concerns may need to speak to the manager or chef to ensure that their concerns are properly addressed.

Senior Citizens

Some older guests like light meals and tend to eat more slowly than other guests. They may prefer foods that are soft and bland rather than chewy and spicy. Some seniors are on a limited budget. Servers should know which items senior guests might enjoy and, if asked, recommend them.

International Guests

Non-English-speaking guests should be spoken to slowly, not loudly. Servers should ask them if they have any special food preferences. Servers should try to put themselves in the guests' place and ask themselves, "How would I like to be treated if I were a visitor in another country?" Menus with pictures help communicate the identities of items.

Guests with Disabilities

Guests who have visual impairments should be welcomed in a normal tone of voice and asked whether they would like assistance, if they are not accompanied by guide dogs. (If a guest is accompanied by a guide dog, no one should attempt to feed, pet, or otherwise interact with the dog while it is "working.") If a guest who has a visual impairment desires assistance, the host should offer his or her arm and walk while informing the guest of steps, level changes, and crowded areas. Guests with visual impairments should be asked whether they prefer to receive a braille menu (if one is available) or to have the menu read. The host or server should use the positions of numbers on a clock to describe locations of glassware, food on plates, and other tabletop items.

When welcoming guests who have hearing impairments, it is important to remember not to shout at them. Rather, since many can read lips, the server should face them directly and speak slowly and distinctly. Alternatively, the server can offer a pad of paper and a pen so the guest can write requests.

Guests in wheelchairs should be asked if they would like assistance. These guests should be seated at tables with sufficient space to comfortably accommodate the wheelchairs.

guests to order such extras as appetizers, cocktails, wine, desserts, and after-dinner drinks. **Upselling** means suggesting more expensive (and often better-quality) items than those that the guest first mentions. If a guest orders a scotch on the rocks, for example, the server might say, "Would you prefer a premium scotch such as Chivas Regal or Johnny Walker Blue?" Servers should be trained in suggestive selling and upselling on an ongoing basis to help the restaurant build revenues and promote guest satisfaction. However, suggestive selling and upselling should be done judiciously. Servers should be sensitive to the needs of guests, and never oversell or cajole or trick guests into ordering expensive items that they cannot afford. Exhibit 2 gives additional selling tips.

Server training also should address timing and its effect on the **table-turn rate**—the average amount of time that a table is occupied. If a dining area seats 150 guests and staff members serve 300 guests during a specific shift or day part, the table-turn rate is 2 (300 guests divided by 150 seats equals 2). In other words, each chair accommodated an average of two guests during the day part. Servers like to maximize table turns to enhance their tips (more people served in the same amount of time usually means more tips). Likewise, managers like the table-turn rate to be as high as possible for financial reasons. But as rates increase, it is important to ensure that the quality of service guests receive does not decrease. All other factors being equal, a high table-turn rate has a tendency to reduce levels of service. It is a balancing act to maximize both table turns and guest satisfaction. The timing of both production and service affects table turns. It is essential to time the entire dining experience so that guests do not feel rushed, yet the financial needs of the food and beverage operation are met.

Servers in casual-dining restaurants should be trained to provide personalized service. For example, some restaurants use technology to record information about regular guests, including favorite foods and beverages, preferred table in the dining area, and preferred server. During preshift lineup meetings, this information can be reviewed when these repeat guests have made a reservation. This personalized service helps the restaurant exceed guest expectations.

And finally, servers in casual-dining restaurants that serve alcohol need special training in how to serve alcoholic beverages responsibly. They should know the legal ramifications of serving alcohol to underage guests or to those who should not consume any more alcohol. (In states that have dram shop laws, servers and restaurateurs can be held liable for injury to a third person caused by an intoxicated restaurant guest.) Servers need to learn how to check identification to see that guests are of legal drinking age, and how to monitor guests' alcohol intake and handle alcohol-related problems.

Dining Service Staff Positions. Standard titles for dining service staff positions do not exist. For example, servers may also be called *salespersons* or *waitpersons,* buspersons may also be called *busers* or *food service attendants* or *assistants,* and the person in charge of the dining room may be called a *manager, host, captain,* or some other title. Which titles are used depends on the restaurant's type of service and degree of informality, as well as management's preferences.

Likewise, the number of staff categories varies from restaurant to restaurant; in addition to those described in the following sections, there may be others—expediters and wine stewards, for example.

Exhibit 2   Tips for Effective Selling

Suggestive selling and upselling require tact and good judgment. If guests know exactly what they want, don't try to change their minds. However, you shouldn't hesitate to suggest additional items that will improve guests' meals. And learn to pick up on when guests want suggestions.

Suggestive selling might make you nervous. If so, it's probably because selling reminds you of a pushy salesperson you've known. Using suggestive selling and upselling techniques, however, is not being pushy. These techniques are part of providing good service.

The key to effective selling is knowing the menu. You should know all of the menu items your restaurant sells. When you are completely familiar with the menu and how each item is prepared, you can suggest dishes confidently and professionally.

Here are some tips for effective suggestive selling and upselling:

- Develop a "selling attitude."

- Be enthusiastic. It's easier to sell something you're excited about.

- Make food sound appetizing. Use words like "fresh," "popular," and "generous" when describing menu items.

- Ask questions. Find out if guests are really hungry or just want something light; whether they like chicken or beef; or if they feel like having something hot or cold.

- Suggest specific menu items. Don't simply ask: "Would you like soup with your meal?" Instead, point out: "A hot bowl of tortilla soup would go nicely with your salad on a cold day like this."

- Suggest your favorites. Try as many menu items as you can, and tell guests you've tried them: "You'll like the Crispy Calamari. It's one of my favorites here." But be honest—don't say that something is your favorite when it isn't.

- Offer a choice: "Would you like a slice of our famous cheesecake or our homemade pecan pie for dessert?"

- Suggest the unusual. People dine out to get away from the routine fare they have at home. And most people don't know what they want to order when they arrive.

- Suggest foods and beverages that naturally go together—soups and sandwiches, bacon and eggs, steak and baked potatoes, coffee and dessert.

- Compliment guests' choices. Make guests feel good about their choices even if they don't order what you suggest.

Remember to always ask for the sale. After you suggest and describe an item, ask if the guest would like it. A good way to do this is to describe several items and ask which the guest would prefer: "A glass of cabernet sauvignon or the lighter merlot would go very well with your six-cheese lasagna. Which would you prefer?"

Source: Adapted from the "Restaurant Server Guide" in the *Hospitality Skills Training Series* (East Lansing, Mich.: American Hotel & Lodging Educational Institute, 1995).

Bartenders and possibly cocktail servers and assistant bartenders will also be employed at many casual-dining restaurants. A head bartender typically supervises bar staff members and, depending on the restaurant's size, reports to the restaurant's general manager, beverage manager, or food and beverage director. Even so, there is interaction between dining room and bar staff (just as there is between dining room and kitchen staff), and managers need to foster cooperation and team spirit among these staff members.

In the following sections we will discuss typical dining service staff positions in casual-dining restaurants—servers, buspersons, hosts, cashiers, and dining room managers—and the work staff members in these positions typically perform.

Server. In many casual-dining restaurants, servers perform the bulk of the food and beverage serving duties, assisted by buspersons. Servers typically present food and beverages to guests and perform a wide range of other tasks before, during, and after service. For example, in some restaurants, servers help with some food preparation—adding dressings to salads, portioning soups, and dishing up desserts from serving equipment located behind counters or in sidestations. Servers are also usually responsible for a number of service-related but non-guest-contact tasks that are called **sidework.** Sidework typically includes making coffee, folding napkins, refilling condiment containers, end-of-shift activities, and other responsibilities. Since servers can earn tips only when serving guests, they frequently view sidework with disdain. However, these tasks are an extremely important part of a server's responsibilities.

The kind of service required in casual-dining restaurants suggests special concerns that managers must address as they select staff members. For example, servers must be able to work quickly yet carefully. They must be able to do several tasks during one trip through the dining area, such as carry food to one table, present a guest check to another, and remove used dishes from a third. Servers must show genuine concern for guests' schedules and provide especially timely service to those guests who are in a hurry. Servers working morning shifts may have to deal with guests who are easily irritated early in the day. A friendly "Good morning" accompanied by prompt, attentive service can really make a difference in a guest's attitude toward the server and the restaurant.

It is difficult to discuss the specific order-taking and food delivery duties of a server in a casual-dining restaurant because of the enormous variety of such restaurants. For example, in some operations, the server takes the guests' orders but **runners** deliver them. This approach keeps servers in the dining room and in contact with guests, thus speeding up service. In other casual-dining restaurants, servers take guests' orders and give them to the production staff, but whichever server is available when the order is ready delivers it. This type of service is known as the "first-available-server" concept. In such cases, servers must be especially careful in writing order information on guest checks so that "who gets what" is clearly indicated for another server. In traditional operations, where servers are responsible for delivering the orders they have taken from guests, servers also have to be careful about clearly indicating to themselves "who gets what" so they will be able to provide smooth service.

Busperson. Typical duties of a busperson include clearing tables after guests depart and taking soiled tableware to the dish room, and stocking and replenishing supplies required in sidestations. It is also common for buspersons to perform pre-opening duties such as setting tables, filling ice bins with ice, and moving tables.

During service, buspersons perform a wide array of tasks designed to help servers provide better service to guests. Depending on the restaurant, such tasks may include pouring water, refilling coffee and tea cups, taking bread and butter to the table, clearing tables, and even serving food and beverages during busy periods. Cleaning tables and chairs (including highchairs and booster chairs) and resetting tables with fresh linens, clean serviceware, and glasses are all jobs that buspersons often perform.

A busperson's closing responsibilities usually include cleaning and restocking sidestations, cleaning and resetting dining area tables, emptying and cleaning food preparation carts, cleaning the coffee urn and the bread warmer, and returning soiled linens to the laundry.

Since buspersons typically have entry-level positions, it is important that managers take an active interest in them, show them the possibilities for career advancement, and provide them with training so that they can be ready to move to higher-paying and more responsible positions if they so desire.

Host. The person carrying out host responsibilities may be called a *host, greeter, receptionist, captain,* or *dining room manager,* depending on the extent of his or her responsibilities. (Some restaurants use the term *hostess* for a female host, but *host* is acceptable for both men and women.) In restaurants that also have a dining room manager, the host's responsibilities usually are limited to welcoming guests, providing menus, and performing other guest services such as confirming the number of guests in a party and leading guests to seats in the appropriate section of the restaurant. The host is sometimes responsible for inviting guests to comment on the food, beverages, and service, and is usually responsible for thanking guests and inviting them to return as they are leaving.

Cashier. In some casual-dining restaurants, a cashier collects payments of guest checks from servers or guests, and is responsible for providing an accurate accounting of all transactions, collections, and disbursements. A cashier's responsibilities may overlap with those of a host. Cashiers who have guest-contact responsibilities should be friendly and courteous. Cashiers must follow income control procedures at all times.

Dining room manager. The manager in charge of dining room service has a wide variety of responsibilities and tasks (see Appendix B), which can differ from one operation to another. For example, in small restaurants, the dining room manager may perform the responsibilities of host and manage the entire restaurant as well as the dining room. In large restaurants, the dining room manager may have one or more hosts who report to him or her, and may in turn report to a general manager who manages the restaurant as a whole—in which case the dining room manager's responsibilities are more narrowly defined and consist mainly of managing the dining room and service staff.

Typically, dining room managers have had extensive education, training, and experience and have worked their way up in the restaurant to assume this position. While some operations may not use the "manager" designation, they do employ individuals who are given managerial responsibilities designed to ensure that guests receive the proper quality of service.

Lettuce Entertain You Enterprises began as a single restaurant in 1971 and now owns, licenses, or manages more than eighty establishments throughout the United States.

Closely checking and delivering on guests' expectations, helping everyone in the operation understand that creating and delivering a positive, memorable dining experience for each guest is critical to the restaurant's success, and encouraging repeat business are among the primary responsibilities of dining room managers today. These managers monitor guest expectations by soliciting guest feedback as well as feedback from staff members. One of the ways managers can meet guest requirements and ensure guest satisfaction is by enabling and motivating staff members to deliver the quality service that guests expect. Dining room managers can encourage repeat business in many ways. Some managers make a note of local residents' celebrations (birthdays, anniversaries, and similar special events) held in the restaurant throughout the year. As the special event approaches the next year, they write to the guest who hosted the previous year's celebration to ask if the restaurant can again help make the occasion special. Or managers can send frequent guests a letter thanking them for their visits and enclose a card for a complimentary drink, dessert, or a "two meals for the price of one" discount.

Dining room managers have a number of preopening, operating, closing, and miscellaneous responsibilities that vary according to the restaurant. Before

Buffalo Wild Wings Grill & Bar is one of the fastest-growing restaurant chains in the United States; it features fourteen signature sauces for its wings and a "fun, edgy, high-energy" atmosphere.

the dining room opens for guest service, managers inspect table settings, chairs, lamps and lampshades, tablecloths, napkins, place settings, glassware, condiment containers, candles, and any other tabletop items. They also check sidestations to see that they are adequately stocked. Managers also look for safety problems such as loose tabletops and wobbly chairs or tables. They also might look for rough spots on furniture that could snag guests' clothing. Some dining room managers use a preopening checklist similar to the one shown in Appendix C, which may be adapted to any operation.

Dining room managers may perform other miscellaneous tasks, such as checking that menus are in good order and are not dirty, worn, or torn. Since the menu represents the image, quality standards, and reputation of the restaurant and is something that every guest pays attention to, managers should frequently check the menus to make sure they are in good shape.

Supervising dining service staff members during the performance of their duties is a major responsibility of the dining room manager. Dining room managers make specific table assignments and conduct preopening meetings to inform the staff about daily specials, menu changes, VIP guests, special events, and any potential difficulties. These managers should make certain that service flows smoothly, that water glasses are refilled, and, in general, that the desires of guests are anticipated and provided for by all. Dining room managers must know safety and food safety procedures and ensure that staff members follow them.

Handling guest complaints and guest-related problems may be the dining room manager's responsibility, but more managers today empower staff members to take care of most of these matters and provide them with guidelines for doing so. For example, what should be done for a guest who complains about the flavor of her entrée? Enlightened managers empower servers to take care of this type of situation, typically suggesting that the best way to address it is to offer another choice to the guest, as well as a complimentary dessert.

After the dining room closes, dining room managers supervise staff members as they perform miscellaneous closing duties. They ensure that staff members properly set the tables for the next meal period, clean and fill all condiment containers, replace soiled tablecloths, and reset tabletops. Managers should also make sure that sidestations and sidework areas are clean and restocked, and they should confirm that dining area tables are in the proper configuration for the next shift.

Other Types of Restaurants

Other types of restaurants that we will address in the remainder of the chapter are fast-casual, quick-service, hotel, and fine-dining restaurants.

Fast-Casual Restaurants

Fast-casual restaurants are a relatively new and growing concept. Unlike casual-dining restaurants, they do not offer full table service; rather, customers typically pick up their food at a counter and can often see their food being made via an open kitchen. The average check falls into the $8–$15 range, and alcohol may be served. Fast-casual restaurants saw increases in sales during the recent economic downturn. Fast-casual dining operations have, on average, a younger guest base than casual-dining restaurants, yet they also tend to attract guests with higher incomes. The appeal of fast-casual operations is that they combine the best of casual-dining and QSR concepts, bridging the gap between casual-dining restaurants and QSRs in pricing, atmosphere, and food quality (many fast-casual operations are known for their healthier menu choices). Some examples of fast-casual concepts are bakery cafes in which fresh-baked products are served along with salads, soups, and sandwiches; operations featuring Mexican and Italian foods; operations featuring meat-filled and vegetarian wraps; operations with Asian and noodle-based menus; and operations that feature chicken menu items. The most popular meal period or day part of the fast-casual segment is usually lunch, although more fast-casual operations are expanding into the breakfast day part with bagels, specialty pastries, quiche in a variety of choices, and breakfast burritos. Well-known fast-casual chains include Chipotle Mexican Grill, Noodles & Company, and Panera Bread.

Quick-Service Restaurants

Quick-service restaurants (also known as fast-food restaurants) feature limited menus and affordable prices with an emphasis on speed of service; there is minimal or no table service. QSRs are typically franchise operations that are part of a chain. McDonald's, KFC, and Taco Bell are well-known QSRs.

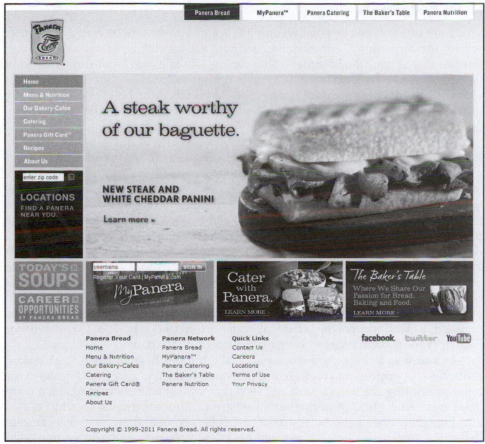

Panera Bread is a fast-casual restaurant chain of "bakery-cafes" that feature fresh bakery products.

Quick-service restaurants have undergone some dramatic changes in concepts and menu offerings recently. Examples include QSRs that have expanded their operating hours into the late-night day part, added premium coffee and tea beverages, put pizza or freshly made deli sandwiches on the menu, expanded their beverage selections to include energy and sports drinks, and added fresh salad choices in an effort to appeal to a larger and more diverse guest base. Some QSRs have re-engaged with their core values of quality, cleanliness, and service. Most have a renewed focus on pleasing their guests.

Today's QSR guests are searching for a less expensive, more value-driven food and beverage experience. Operators have responded with menu changes, decor upgrades, and staff members trained and empowered to enhance the guest experience. QSRs have increased their number of drive-through lanes, added big-screen televisions in dining areas, and provided WiFi service for guests. Additional equipment upgrades have included latte and cappuccino machines, and equipment to produce smoothies.

Hotel Restaurants

There are many types of hotel restaurants for guests to choose from, sometimes within the same hotel. For example, a single full-service hotel may have a restaurant that is considered either a fine-dining, upscale, or casual-dining concept (which used to be referred to as "the main dining room"); another restaurant that today is considered fast-casual (which used to be called the hotel's "coffee shop"); in-room dining (which used to be called "room service"); and a bar with dining options.

Hotel dining has experienced declining popularity in many markets during the recent economic downturn. There are fewer guests in many hotels, and fewer of those guests dine in. Some hotel dining operations have trimmed their hours of operation in response to declining revenues. For example, a hotel's fast-casual operation may only be open for breakfast and lunch, while its full-service restaurant may only be open for dinner or only on those weekdays when there is close to a full house in the hotel. Alternatively, a hotel may choose to have both types of restaurants open but served from a single kitchen to reduce labor and other operating costs. If two hotel food and beverages operations that serve dinner tend to attract the same group of guests, perhaps only one is needed and the other should be closed. To make these decisions, hotel food and beverage managers are evaluating actual and potential revenues, forecasted guestroom occupancy, and local demand, as well as tracking a fully allocated profit and loss (P&L) statement for each operation, often broken down by meal period/day part.

In addition to keeping a close eye on the bottom lines of their hotel restaurants, hotel operators are emphasizing sales and the importance of everyone in the hotel promoting the hotel's food and beverage options. The answer from a front desk agent to a guest inquiring about where to dine for dinner should be, first and foremost, one of the hotel's food and beverage operations, not a restaurant down the street. The hotel's food and beverage operations should be marketed in the local community as well. Special food and beverage offerings (e.g., Sunday brunch), special occasions (e.g., anniversary or birthday celebrations, Mother's Day breakfast or lunch), as well as more casual menu options in the hotel's bar are popular with patrons from the local community.

Hotel restaurants have also changed their concepts. Some now have attracted talented chefs who specialize in a certain type of cuisine (Asian, Italian, seafood, and so on). Kitchens have been opened to guests so they can observe the preparation of the foods they are about to enjoy. This not only attracts guests who are staying in the hotel, it also attracts patrons from the local community. The goal of these hotel restaurants is to have guests perceive them as destinations rather than simply food and beverage outlets for hotel guests only. These operations offer menu variety and an experience that entertains guests and creates positive memories.

Hotel bars also provide food and beverage experiences, typically in a more casual setting. Some hotel bars that serve food are the local "happening place," featuring trendy music, specialty cocktails, and menu items intended to be shared by guests at a table. Other hotel bars are located on the top floor of the hotel specifically to give guests a breathtaking view of the city as part of the dining experience. Still other hotel bars have the look and feel of a large living room, where guests are encouraged to enjoy their favorite alcoholic beverage, dine on a variety of sampler-size menu offerings, and engage in conversation after a busy day of meetings and other business activities. In addition to attracting hotel guests, hotel bars need to draw people from the local community. Some hotel bars do this by using specialty drinks, unique food menu items, and distinctive decor and ambience.

It should be noted that some hotels have chosen to outsource their restaurants and have entered into business agreements that allow non-affiliated restaurants to operate inside the hotel. Many of these alliances provide value for guests by offering them a familiar place to eat and drink. For example, Starwood Hotels has partnered with the BR Guest restaurant company; Kimpton Hotels has successfully partnered with notable independent operators such as Wolfgang Puck; and Budgetel Inns has alliances with Applebee's and Bob Evans.

Fine-Dining Restaurants

Fine-dining restaurants are full-service restaurants that prepare and serve high-quality, artfully presented food to discriminating patrons within an elegant atmosphere. Servers are usually highly trained and wear more formal attire than servers in other types of restaurants. Fine-dining restaurants typically are independent operations with one or just a few locations. The reason that these food and beverage operations are called fine-dining or upscale is because of the overall high-quality experience they provide for guests.

In some operations and markets, the number of guest visits to fine-dining restaurants has declined due to a loss of discretionary income as the economy has taken a downward turn and personal incomes have dropped, retirement accounts have diminished, and entertainment reimbursed by businesses has been eliminated or severely curtailed. But in some fine-dining restaurants, patronage has remained steady and menu prices have actually increased, as guests less affected by the economic downturn seek out experiences that others cannot afford.

Some fine-dining operations have moved toward being more casual because more and more of their guests are arriving without a coat and tie. Managers must take care not to make the atmosphere too casual, however, as many of these same guests still enjoy being served by a formally dressed server and seeing the manager of the operation dressed in a coat and tie or a smart suit. In any event, guests of fine-dining operations expect top food quality, anticipatory service, a selection of premium brands in alcoholic beverages, and an ambience and decor that reflect these top levels of products and services.

🔑 Key Terms

call brand—A brand of liquor that guests request by brand name (a Beefeater martini, for example).

casual-dining restaurant—A segment of the full-service restaurant classification. There are many types of casual-dining restaurants, most of which serve alcoholic beverages and have moderate to moderately high guest-check averages and informal dining environments.

house brand—A brand of liquor a restaurant carries for use when guests order cocktails (a martini, for example) without specifying the use of any particular brand; also called well brands, they are usually priced lower than call brands.

premium brand—A costly call brand of liquor specified by guests when they order cocktails (a Grey Goose or Belvedere vodka martini, for example).

runner—A staff member who delivers guests' orders to the table, allowing servers to remain in the dining room and in contact with guests, thus speeding up service.

shopper's service—An agency that restaurants can employ to evaluate how guests' needs and expectations are being met. Shopper's services use shoppers (also called "mystery shoppers") who pose as guests in order to review a restaurant's service from the guest's perspective and complete evaluation reports.

sidework—Preparatory, service-related tasks such as making coffee, folding napkins, refilling condiment containers, restocking stations, and performing end-of-shift activities.

signature drink—A beverage that guests perceive as special and closely associated with the restaurant promoting it. Signature drinks help boost beverage sales.

signature menu item—A menu item that guests perceive as special and closely associated with the restaurant promoting it. Signature menu items help build repeat business and guest loyalty.

suggestive selling—A technique by which servers can increase guest satisfaction and sales by encouraging guests to order such extras as appetizers, cocktails, wine, desserts, and after-dinner drinks.

table-turn rate—The average amount of time that a table is occupied. For example, if two separate parties are seated at the same table within a 120-minute period, the table-turn rate is one time per hour.

upselling—A technique by which servers can increase sales by suggesting more expensive (and often better-quality) items than those that the guest first mentions.

Review Questions

1. What are the characteristics of a casual-dining restaurant?
2. What is a house brand? call brand? premium brand?
3. How do casual-dining restaurants deliver value to guests?
4. How do casual-dining restaurants solicit feedback on how successfully they are serving guests?
5. What are some typical training issues for casual-dining restaurants?
6. In a casual-dining restaurant, what are the typical duties of a server? busperson? host? cashier? dining room manager?
7. What are the characteristics of a fast-casual restaurant? a quick-service restaurant?
8. How are hotels changing the way they provide food and beverage service?
9. What are some characteristics of fine-dining restaurants?

 Case Studies

There Is a Problem at Table Sixteen!

Janice Zaretzky has a worried expression on her face as she approaches Joe Molina, the general manager of Pattina's, a 220-seat fine-dining restaurant. Janice is an experienced server and has worked at this restaurant for eight years. She prides herself on her professionalism in greeting guests courteously, being warm and friendly when interacting with them to take orders, and having a sixth sense as to when to return to her tables to check back, being sure not to interrupt conversations or hard-sell coffee and desserts. She has excellent food knowledge and is a frequent recipient of compliments from the restaurant's patrons.

Tonight appears to be an exception. She tells Joe, "There is a problem at table sixteen!"

Joe responds with surprise, as his view of things is that the evening is progressing smoothly. "What's happening, Janice?" Joe asks.

"It's a party of four, two couples, and they want to see the manager. Things started out okay, but after cocktails things have gone downhill. One gentleman complained that we serve only four shrimp for the shrimp cocktail appetizer and that for $6.95 the shrimp are too few and too small. One of the women complained that her lobster bisque was cold, so I took it back for replacement. They all complained about their salads being served on warm plates. I just brought them the wine they ordered, and the man who tasted it said it's sour. He wants to see you. I haven't put in their entrée orders yet, as nothing seems to be right in their view. You better get over there."

Joe takes a deep breath. "What did they order for entrées?"

"One roast beef medium rare, one medium, one Dover sole, and one swordfish," she replies.

"Go place the orders," Joe directs. "I'll go speak with them now. Ask Lillian if you can switch one of her tables with this one so you won't have to face them anymore. Perhaps an approach by a different server can diffuse the discontent that may be building up."

"All right, let me know if I can help in any other way," Janice says, somewhat relieved.

Joe Molina approaches table sixteen.

Discussion Questions

1. How should Joe Molina introduce himself when he arrives at table sixteen?
   a. "Good evening, I am the general manager."
   b. "Hello, I'm Mr. Molina, the general manager."
   c. "Hi there, I'm Joe Molina, the general manager."
   d. "I'm the general manager. You wanted to see me?"

2. Should Joe let the guests do most of the speaking at first, or tell them he is already aware of the situation, reciting what Janice told him?

3. Should Joe pull up a chair and join the party of four, or remain standing?

4. Should Joe taste the wine to be sure it is spoiled, or should he accept the opinion of the guests?

5. What can, or should, Joe do right now to ameliorate the situation?

6. Would you have switched Janice and Lillian as the server responsible for table sixteen?

7. Once the entrées are served, should Joe do anything more in relationship to the guests?

This case was taken from William P. Fisher and Robert A. Ashley, *Case Studies in Commercial Food Service Operations* (Lansing, Mich.: American Hotel & Lodging Educational Institute, 2003).

Terry Tackles Turnover

Fargo's is a casual-dining restaurant chain that was started just ten years ago. There are 70 units in the chain; each unit has 250 to 300 seats, with an average lunch check of $7 and an average dinner check of $13. Revenue per unit ranges from $2.5 to $3.1 million per year. Each unit employs about 35 to 40 servers, depending on the mix of full- and part-time staff members. Annual turnover per unit for the chain is from 80 percent on the low end to 160 percent on the high end. Until last year, the average turnover rate held steady at around 100 percent. However, when the chain grew from 50 to 70 units over the past 12 months, the average rate shot up to 138 percent, which raised a red flag for Terry Dickinson, the chain's new vice president of human resources.

When Terry was hired thirty days ago, one of his first goals was to come up with chain-wide selection tools that would help Fargo's managers choose wisely from among the many job applicants they interviewed. Fargo's is pursuing an aggressive growth strategy, with 20 more new units planned for next year and 10 to 15 planned for the next few years after that. Turnover will only get worse unless Terry can develop an effective selection guide.

Terry decided to meet with three unit managers representing different locales and turnover rates: Kate Pullum's unit, at 84 percent annual turnover, had one of the lowest turnover rates in the chain; Lisa Ragalado's turnover rate, at 125 percent, was about average; and Joe Eldrige's, at 156 percent, was one of the highest. Terry hoped to get an idea of how Fargo's managers, who so far had been left to their own devices, were actually selecting applicants. More importantly, Terry hoped these managers would help him come up with selection criteria that would be useful for managers throughout the chain.

Terry stood and began the meeting with one of his beloved sayings. "At the risk of sounding trite, I thought I'd start off with some 'words to live by' that a college professor of mine drummed into my head many years ago: 'Better hiring means less firing.' I've brought you together to help our company solve a chain-wide problem: high turnover—specifically, high turnover among our servers. Solving this problem will make your job and every manager's job at Fargo's easier in the long run. I don't have to tell you about all the headaches that high turnover causes—you experience it on the front lines every day." The managers around the table nodded and smiled ruefully. "Of course, this is also a financial issue," Terry went on. "Operating margins are dropping chain-wide, due in part to the high turnover.

"Kate, congratulations on having one of the lowest turnover rates in the company. You must be doing something right. Why don't you start us off and outline some of the things you look for in a job candidate." Terry sat down and picked up a pen to take notes.

"Well, I don't know that I have a secret formula or a magic wand," Kate began slowly. "Like most people, one thing I always look for in a job candidate is experience."

"That's nice if you have that luxury," Joe interjected, his fingers tapping nervously on the table. "But in my labor market, it's rare to find someone with experience. Heck, it's rare to find someone, period! Most of the time I end up taking anybody I can get."

Lisa smiled sympathetically. "The warm body syndrome."

Joe nodded. "Exactly."

"What kind of experience do you look for?" Terry asked.

"I look for 8 to 12 months of experience in a high-volume, full-service, chain restaurant," Kate said. "I used to take people with other types of experience—for example, if someone told me she worked in a small independent restaurant, I would take a chance on her. But I've found that those people usually can't adjust to the high-volume, high-pressure, fast pace of my restaurant. Either that, or they bring a lot of bad habits with them that are hard to break.

"Of course, hiring experienced people sometimes can cause problems, too," Kate continued. "You can run into the problem of someone who is *too* experienced. By that I mean they've worked for several restaurant chains and they know the system so well they can get around it when they want. For example, I've hired servers with a lot of experience who knew how to manipulate the ordering system and sneak free desserts to their regular guests to build up their tips. I'm especially careful with bartenders, because that's the easiest area for an unscrupulous staff member with some experience to rip you off. With bartenders I almost prefer to hire an 18- or 19-year-old college kid with no experience who doesn't know the control systems inside and out."

Lisa nodded in agreement. "I like to hire college students when I can, too, simply because they tend to be responsible and goal-oriented," she said. "That's the good news. The bad news is that the college in our town is small—just 2,000 students—and the students tend to belong to the same clubs and want to go to the same events. I constantly face the problem of half my staff wanting the same night off to go to the game, or the dance, or whatever. I've tried to combat that problem by spreading the students out throughout the restaurant—putting one in the host position, one in the kitchen, only one or two student servers on a particular shift—that kind of thing."

"Let's focus on the interview process itself," Terry said. "What do you do to make sure that an applicant is willing to work certain shifts, or won't leave right after you've spent months training them?"

"Yes, I'd be interested in some help with that," Joe said. "Time after time I've had people let me down that told me all the right things when I interviewed them. Just last week I had a guy quit on me after six months—nice guy, seemed mature, had some restaurant experience—and I had asked him all the right questions when I interviewed him: 'Are you willing to work at least two lunch shifts during the week?' 'Yes.' 'Are you willing to work Saturday nights?' 'Yes.' 'Do you plan on staying in the area for at least two years?' 'Yes.' 'Can you live on $300 a week?' 'Yes.' After I hired him it turns out he can only work one lunch shift a week, he can't work Saturday nights after the first month, and last Tuesday he tells me he's graduating and transferring to another school to get his master's degree."

Kate turned to Joe. "One thing I've learned about interviewing is to try not to ask too many yes-or-no questions. Instead of asking college-age applicants if they're going to be around for a year or two, I'll ask them to tell me where they are in their schooling. If they tell me 'I'm a freshman' or 'I'm starting my sophomore year,' I know that chances are they'll be around for a while. That's one hurdle that people have to jump before I get serious about hiring them—for me, they've got to be around for at least a year.

"Another hurdle is finding out what shifts they can work—but again, I don't ask yes-or-no questions. I'll say something like, 'What hours are you available to work?' or 'What's your class schedule like next term?' Some people will literally show me their class schedules. That tells me whether they are available to work some lunch shifts for me. But if I had just asked them a yes-or-no question—'Are you willing to work a lunch shift?'—they might have said 'yes' just to get the job.

"Another hurdle," Kate continued, "is: 'What are your financial expectations?' I like to find out what the applicant is expecting in terms of take-home pay. With my restaurant's volume, the average server can expect to take home about $300 a week, so if a guy says, 'I can't work for less than $500 a week'—he's got kids, maybe, or a big car payment—that tells me he's not a good fit for my restaurant. On the other hand, if someone mumbles, 'Gee, I can get by on $100 a week'—that's not always a good situation either. That tells me this person probably isn't very ambitious or self-confident."

"One of my 'hurdles,' as you call them," Lisa smiled at Kate, "is: 'How *many* shifts can you work in a week?' Unless they say 'four or five,' at minimum, I tend to move on. And I've taken a hard line on lunch shifts, too. I don't have to tell you how hard it is to get people to work lunch shifts, especially experienced people, because you only need them for a couple of hours, the work is intense, and the tips don't compare to what they can make on a 6- or 8-hour dinner shift. But now I tell people flat out, 'You'll be a more attractive candidate if you can give me two lunch shifts a week.' In fact, I don't hire people anymore unless they can pull at least one lunch shift for me.

"I also look for clues as to how responsible an applicant is," Lisa went on. "Did they graduate from high school or did they drop out? Are they going to college now, or pursuing some other goal? Do they have any obligations that would encourage them to take their job seriously? If someone is buying a house, or has children, or is paying for college, he or she is less likely to quit for some frivolous reason."

"You can get that kind of information from an applicant by using the 'lantern principle' when you interview," Kate said. "Remember how the old-fashioned kerosene lanterns started out narrow at the top, then opened up where the flame was, then narrowed down again at the base?" Kate traced a lantern shape in the air with her hands. "When I interview, I start out with the narrow-scope, basic yes-or-no questions. 'Are you a student?' might be one of my first questions, and—depending on how desperate I am—I might end an interview with, 'Can you start tomorrow?'" Terry and the other managers laughed appreciatively. "But in the middle part of the interview I try to ask open-ended questions. Instead of asking someone, 'Are you ambitious?' or 'I'm looking for someone with a lot on the ball—are you that kind of person?'—because they're going to tell you what you want to hear, right?—I'll ask a question like, 'Where do you want to be in five years?' That gives people a chance to talk about themselves. If they tell me, 'I want to be lying on the beach without a care in the world,' that tells me maybe I'm not talking to a real go-getter. But if they say something like, 'In three years I'll have my teaching degree, so I hope I'll be teaching somewhere' or 'I'm a working mom, but what leisure time I have I devote to a local theater group and I hope to be the president of the group someday,' then I know maybe this person will be someone who can be counted on to take the initiative at my restaurant."

"Wow," Joe said to Kate, "I can't believe you spend so much time with applicants. I don't have time to have a long conversation with people—I'm usually so desperate I want to hire them on the spot and put them to work."

"Well, you learn a lot just by letting people talk," Kate said. "Sometimes it's not so much what they say as how they say it. So much of our business depends on communication—between server and cook, manager and host, server and bartender, staff member and guest—that it's important to pay attention to an applicant's communication style. For example, I once had someone interview for a server position who wouldn't stop talking! After I said hello I literally could hardly get a word in. That told me she would probably not let her guests get a word in, either, or would place an order in the kitchen and then spend ten minutes telling the cook how to prepare it."

"You also learn from the mistakes of others," Lisa added. "One of my restaurant-manager friends, a brilliant guy, used to hire college students just because they had a high grade-point average. 'Do they know anything about working in a restaurant?' I'd ask him. 'No, but they're smart,' he'd say. Most of the time they didn't work out, but he had to learn that lesson the hard way."

"Some managers only hire people who are like themselves," Kate agreed. "I used to work for a manager who was like your friend when it came to hiring, but just the reverse. He never went to college; he worked his way up from the bottom and took great pride in 'graduating from the school of hard knocks,' as he always put it. So he didn't want to hire college students."

Terry put his pen down with an air of satisfaction. "This has been a great learning experience for me," he said. "From what you've told me, I think I can generate five basic guidelines that all of Fargo's managers can use when hiring new staff members. They won't be anything fancy or complicated, but they'll hit key issues and be something that managers throughout the chain can benefit from. Thanks for meeting with me today."

Discussion Questions

1. What five basic guidelines can Terry pull from what the managers discussed that might be helpful to other Fargo's managers?

2. One of the things Kate talked about was the need to ask open-ended questions. How can you turn the following closed-ended questions into open-ended questions that can help you get more of the information you want?

    "Can you work Sundays?"
    "Can you work five shifts a week?"
    "Can you live on $300 a week?"
    "Do you think you will still be in this area a year from now?"

The following industry experts helped generate and develop this case: Timothy J. Pugh, Regional Manager, Damon's—The Place for Ribs (Steve Montanye Enterprises, East Lansing, Michigan); and Lawrence E. Ross, Assistant Professor, Florida Southern College, and owner of Sago Grill, Lakeland, Florida.

References

Berta, Dina. "Chuy's: Guest-Centric Culture Keeps Turnover Down, Sales Up." *Nation's Restaurant News*. March 16, 2009. 43(10): 4, 18.

Cobb, Catherine R. "Ecofriendly Chains Get Healthy Business via Emphasis on Taste, Green Practices." *Nation's Restaurant News*. July 16, 2007. 41(28): 4.

Colchamiro, Jeff. "Cozy Up: Hotel Bars Are Getting Bigger, Better, and More Comforting." *Lodging Magazine*. March 2010. 35(6): 36–39.

———. "Value Meals: How Hotels Are Adjusting F&B Operations for a Rough Economy—Without Leaving Their Guests Hungry for Better Service." *Lodging Magazine*. July 2009. 34(11): 38, 40, 41.

Coomes, Steve. "Upscale Restaurants Don't Discount the Danger to Reputations as They Turn to Bargain Promos." *Nation's Restaurant News*. December 8, 2008. 42(48): 18.

Hamstra, Mark. "Family Chains Heed Casual-Theme Rivals, Adopt New Service, Ambience Upgrades." *Nation's Restaurant News*. July 24, 1995. 29(29): 45–48.

Jameson, Jonathan. "Restaurants' Secrets to Success Are Written in Their 'Brand DNA'." *Nation's Restaurant News*. April 6, 2009. 43(12): 16.

Licata, Elizabeth. "MenuMasters Panelists: Innovation Key to Attracting Diners." *Nation's Restaurant News*. March 23, 2009. 43(11): 27.

Martin, Andrew. "The Happiest Meal: Hot Profits." *The New York Times*. Sunday Business Section. January 11, 2009: 1, 8–9.

Rector, Sylvia. "Hey Guys: Here Are the Top 5 Restaurant Gripes." Life Section. *Lansing State Journal*. May 16, 2010: 5C.

"Restaurant & Hotel Food Trends." *The 2009 Restaurant, Food & Beverage Market Research Handbook*. 2009: 49–59.

Rowe, Megan. "Trendspotting: What's Hot for '09." *Restaurant Hospitality*. January 2009. 93(1): 24–27.

Schneider, John. "Fine-Dining on Paper Is Not Fine." LSJ Blogs. *Lansing State Journal*. www.lsj.com/schneiderblog

"Trends in Casual-Dining." *The 2009 Restaurant, Food & Beverage Market Research Handbook*. 2009: 157–161.

"Trends in Fast-Casual Dining." *The 2009 Restaurant, Food & Beverage Market Research Handbook*. 2009: 166–167.

"Trends in Fine-Dining." *The 2009 Restaurant, Food & Beverage Market Research Handbook*. 2009: 154–156.

Vermillion, Len. "Dinner Engagement: These Hotel Restaurants Are Giving Guests Something to Talk About." *Lodging Magazine*. April 2009. 34(7): 26–30.

"What's Hot." *The 2009 Restaurant, Food & Beverage Market Research Handbook*. 2009: 45–48.

"What's Hot: 20 Restaurant Trends." State of the Industry 2008. *Restaurant Hospitality*. February 1, 2008.

Internet Sites

For more information, visit the following Internet sites. Remember that Internet addresses can change without notice. If the site is no longer there, you can use a search engine to look for additional sites.

American Culinary Federation
www.acfchefs.org

Applebee's
www.applebees.com

Beyond the Shaker
www.beyondtheshaker.com

Bob Evans
www.bobevans.com

Brinker International
www.brinker.com

Bugaboo Creek Steak House
www.bugaboocreek.com

Burger King
www.bk.com

Cameron Mitchell Restaurants
www.cameronmitchell.com

Capital Grille
www.thecapitalgrille.com

Champps
www.champps.com

Cheesecake Factory
www.thecheesecakefactory.com

Chick-fil-A
www.chickfila.com

Chili's
www.chilis.com

Chipotle Mexican Grill
www.chipotle.com

Cracker Barrel Old Country Store
www.crackerbarrel.com

Denny's
www.dennys.com

Einstein Bros.
www.einsteinbros.com

Famous Dave's
www.famousdaves.com

Four Seasons
www.fourseasonsrestaurant.com

Frankenmuth Bavarian Inn
www.bavarianinn.com

Golden Corral
www.goldencorral.com

Harley-Davidson Cafe
www.harley-davidsoncafe.com

Joe's Stone Crag
www.joesstonecrab.com

Joseph Baum & Michael Whiteman
  Company
www.baumwhiteman.com

KFC
www.kfc.com

Kimpton Hotels & Restaurants
www.kimptongroup.com

Lettuce Entertain You
www.leye.com

Levy Restaurants
www.levyrestaurants.com

Long John Silver's
www.longjohnsilvers.com

LongHorn Steakhouse
www.longhornsteakhouse.com

Maggiano's
www.maggianos.com

Max & Erma's
www.maxandermas.com

McDonald's
www.mcdonalds.com

Mitchell's Fish Market
www.mitchellsfishmarket.com

National Restaurant Association
www.restaurant.org

Nation's Restaurant News
www.nrn.com

Noodles & Company
www.noodles.com

NPD Group
www.npd.com

Olive Garden
www.olivegarden.com

On the Border Mexican Grill & Cantina
www.ontheborder.com

Outback Steakhouse
www.outbacksteakhouse.com

Panda Express
www.pandaexpress.com

Panera Bread
www.panerabread.com

Perkins Restaurant & Bakery
www.perkinsrestaurants.com

P. F. Chang's
www.pfchangs.com

Qdoba.com
www.qdoba.com

QSR
www.qsrmagazine.com

Rainforest Cafe
www.rainforestcafe.com

Red Lobster
www.redlobster.com

Restaurant Associates
www.restaurantassociates.com

Restaurant Briefing
www.restaurantbriefing.com

Restaurant Marketing Group
www.rmktgroup.com

Ruth's Chris Steak House
www.ruthschris.com

Salty's Seafood Grills
www.saltys.com

Sandleman & Associates
www.sandelman.com

Sbarro
www.sbarro.com

Scarborough Research
www.scarborough.com

Smith & Wollensky Restaurant Group
www.smithandwollensky.com

Smokey Bones Barbeque & Grill
www.smokeybones.com

Subway
www.subway.com

Taco Bell
www.tacobell.com

TAO
www.taolasvegas.com

Technomic
www.technomic.com

Texas Roadhouse
www.texasroadhouse.com

T.G.I. Friday's
www.tgifridays.com

III Forks
www.iiiforks.com

Top of the World
www.topoftheworldlv.com

Waiter.com
www.waiter.com

Wendy's
www.wendys.com

Which Wich
www.whichwich.com

Zagat Survey
www.zagat.com

Appendix A

Shopper's Service Report

Name of Property (Dining Outlet) _____
Address _____
Date of Visitation _____ Meal Period _____ Time _____
Manager/Supervisor on Duty _____

ITEMS PURCHASED:

Beverages: Food:

#	ITEM	PRICE	#	ITEM	PRICE
___	_____	_____	___	_____	_____
___	_____	_____	___	_____	_____
___	_____	_____	___	_____	_____
	TOTAL	_____		TOTAL	_____

Total Price _____

Please respond to each statement using the following scale:
5—Strongly Agree
4—Somewhat Agree
3—Neither Agree nor Disagree
2—Somewhat Disagree
1—Strongly Disagree
NA—The statement does not apply.
To Score: Total all points and compare the actual score with the Standard Point Score. (When statements are not applicable, change Standard Point Score correspondingly.)

TOTAL STANDARD POINT SCORE _____   TOTAL ACTUAL POINT SCORE_____

GREETING

A. You were greeted immediately upon entering the dining area.	5	4	3	2	1
B. The host/hostess moved away from the stand.	5	4	3	2	1
C. The host/hostess asked your name and/or made a friendly/gracious comment.	5	4	3	2	1
D. Comments regarding your greeting:_____					

_____

_____

STANDARD POINT SCORE FOR GREETING __15__   ACTUAL POINT SCORE_____

SEATING

A. You were asked whether you preferred to be seated in the nonsmoking or the smoking section.	5	4	3	2	1
B. When you were ready to be seated, you were immediately led to your table.	5	4	3	2	1
C. The host/hostess was attractively dressed.	5	4	3	2	1

Appendix A *(continued)*

D. The host/hostess was neat and clean.	5	4	3	2	1
E. The selection of your table location showed good judgment.	5	4	3	2	1
F. The chair/booth was comfortable.	5	4	3	2	1

If uncomfortable, in what way? _____

_____

G. The host/hostess distributed menus when you were seated.	5	4	3	2	1
H. The host/hostess informed you of special or additional menu items.	5	4	3	2	1
I. The host/hostess informed you of the name of your server(s).	5	4	3	2	1
J. The host/hostess left with a pleasant message.	5	4	3	2	1
K. The host/hostess seemed happy about his/her job and interested in you.	5	4	3	2	1

L. Comments regarding your seating: _____

_____

_____

STANDARD POINT SCORE FOR SEATING __55__   ACTUAL POINT SCORE _____

CLEANLINESS

A. The dining area was clean.	5	4	3	2	1
B. The table was clean and free of crumbs.	5	4	3	2	1
C. The chair/booth was clean.	5	4	3	2	1
D. Dirty dishes were completely cleared from the table as soon as they were empty.	5	4	3	2	1
E. The flatware and dishes were clean.	5	4	3	2	1
F. The glasses were clean.	5	4	3	2	1
G. The carpet was clean.	5	4	3	2	1
H. The restrooms were clean.	5	4	3	2	1
I. Rank the overall cleanliness.	5	4	3	2	1

J. Comments regarding cleanliness: _____

_____

_____

STANDARD POINT SCORE FOR CLEANLINESS __45__   ACTUAL POINT SCORE _____

ATMOSPHERE

A. The dining outlet was conducive to conversation.	5	4	3	2	1
B. The lighting was appropriate.	5	4	3	2	1

If not, what was wrong? _____

_____

C. There was no noticeable kitchen noise.	5	4	3	2	1
D. The background music was peaceful.	5	4	3	2	1
E. The following were in agreement with the outlet's theme:					
Decor	5	4	3	2	1
Menu	5	4	3	2	1
Uniforms	5	4	3	2	1
F. The experience was what you expected.	5	4	3	2	1

(continued)

Appendix A *(continued)*

G. Comments regarding atmosphere: _____

_____

_____

STANDARD POINT SCORE FOR ATMOSPHERE __40____   ACTUAL POINT SCORE _____

SERVICE

	5	4	3	2	1
A. A server made contact with you within three minutes after you were seated.	5	4	3	2	1
B. The server provided water during his/her first contact.	5	4	3	2	1
C. The server had a pleasant greeting.	5	4	3	2	1
D. The server's hands and fingernails were clean.	5	4	3	2	1
E. The server's posture was good.	5	4	3	2	1
F. The server was cordial, smiled, and created a pleasant atmosphere.	5	4	3	2	1
G. The server was familiar with the menu items.	5	4	3	2	1
H. The server used suggestive selling and was courteous without being pushy.	5	4	3	2	1
I. The server could answer all your questions about the property.	5	4	3	2	1
J. The lady's order was taken first.	5	4	3	2	1
K. The server did not use his/her tray as a writing platform.	5	4	3	2	1
L. Beverage items were served promptly.	5	4	3	2	1
M. Food items were served promptly.	5	4	3	2	1
N. The timing between courses was appropriate.	5	4	3	2	1
O. The server knew which items to serve to each guest.	5	4	3	2	1
P. Beverages were served from the right.	5	4	3	2	1
Q. Food items were served from the left.	5	4	3	2	1
R. The server returned to the table within five minutes to provide additional assistance.	5	4	3	2	1
S. Water glasses were refilled promptly.	5	4	3	2	1
T. Empty dishes were removed promptly.	5	4	3	2	1
U. Dirty dishes were removed from the right.	5	4	3	2	1
V. Dirty ashtrays were properly removed (capped) and replaced.	5	4	3	2	1
W. It was not necessary to summon the server during the meal.	5	4	3	2	1
X. The server seemed to enjoy his/her job.	5	4	3	2	1
Y. The server did an excellent job.	5	4	3	2	1

Z. Comments regarding the service: _____

_____

_____

_____

_____

_____

STANDARD POINT SCORE FOR SERVICE __125__   ACTUAL POINT SCORE _____

FOOD

(Please indicate suggestions to improve the quality of any item under "Additional comments.")

	5	4	3	2	1
A. The food items corresponded with their menu descriptions.	5	4	3	2	1

Appendix A *(continued)*

	5	4	3	2	1
B. All items ordered were available.	5	4	3	2	1
C. The hot foods were served hot.	5	4	3	2	1
D. The cold foods were served cold.	5	4	3	2	1

APPETIZER (Name_____)

E. The appetizer:

looked appetizing,	5	4	3	2	1
was fresh,	5	4	3	2	1
had excellent coloring,	5	4	3	2	1
had an excellent flavor, and	5	4	3	2	1
was seasoned well.	5	4	3	2	1

BREADSTICKS

F. The breadsticks:

were fresh and	5	4	3	2	1
were seasoned perfectly.	5	4	3	2	1

G. Additional comments regarding the appetizer or breadsticks: _____

_____

_____

_____

_____

SALAD (Name_____).

H. The salad:

looked appetizing,	5	4	3	2	1
was neatly plated,	5	4	3	2	1
was appropriately portioned,	5	4	3	2	1
had excellent coloring,	5	4	3	2	1
was fresh,	5	4	3	2	1
had a dressing that complemented it, and	5	4	3	2	1
was of excellent quality.	5	4	3	2	1

I. Additional comments regarding the salad: _____

_____

_____

ENTREE (Name _____)

J. The entree:

looked appetizing,	5	4	3	2	1
was neatly plated,	5	4	3	2	1
was appropriately portioned,	5	4	3	2	1
had excellent coloring,	5	4	3	2	1
was fresh,	5	4	3	2	1
was seasoned well,	5	4	3	2	1
had an excellent flavor, and	5	4	3	2	1
was of excellent quality.	5	4	3	2	1

K. Additional comments regarding the entree: _____

_____

_____

_____

(continued)

Appendix A *(continued)*

VEGETABLE (Name————————————————————————)					
L. The vegetable:					
was appropriately portioned,	5	4	3	2	1
had excellent coloring,	5	4	3	2	1
was fresh,	5	4	3	2	1
had the correct texture,	5	4	3	2	1
was seasoned well, and	5	4	3	2	1
had an excellent flavor.	5	4	3	2	1

M. Additional comments regarding the vegetable: _____

_____

STARCH (Name ————————————————————————)					
N. The starch item:					
was appropriately portioned,	5	4	3	2	1
was fresh,	5	4	3	2	1
was seasoned well, and	5	4	3	2	1
had an excellent flavor.	5	4	3	2	1

O. Additional comments regarding the starch item: _____

_____

DESSERT (Name ————————————————————————)					
P. The dessert:					
was appropriately portioned,	5	4	3	2	1
was fresh,	5	4	3	2	1
was served at the correct temperature, and	5	4	3	2	1
had an excellent flavor.	5	4	3	2	1

Q. Additional comments regarding the dessert: _____

_____

R. Each of the following items corresponded with its menu description:					
Appetizer	5	4	3	2	1
Salad	5	4	3	2	1
Entree	5	4	3	2	1
Dessert	5	4	3	2	1

S. Additional comments regarding the overall food quality: _____

_____

_____

_____

_____

STANDARD POINT SCORE FOR FOOD _220_   ACTUAL POINT SCORE _____

MENU

A. The menu was clean and free from spots.	5	4	3	2	1
B. The menu fit the theme of the dining outlet.	5	4	3	2	1
C. The menu was well organized.	5	4	3	2	1
D. The menu was clearly written.	5	4	3	2	1
E. Descriptions were appetizing.	5	4	3	2	1

Appendix A *(continued)*

F. The number of items available was appropriate.	5	4	3	2	1
G. Specials were available.	5	4	3	2	1
H. Vegetarian menu items were available.	5	4	3	2	1
I. The menu was an effective marketing tool.	5	4	3	2	1

J. Comments and changes you'd like to see regarding the menu: _____

_____

_____

_____

STANDARD POINT SCORE FOR THE MENU __45__   ACTUAL POINT SCORE _____

GUEST CHECK (BILL) HANDLING

A. The guest check arrived at the appropriate time.	5	4	3	2	1
B. The check was readable.	5	4	3	2	1
C. The check correctly reflected what had been served.	5	4	3	2	1
D. The check was correctly totaled.	5	4	3	2	1
E. The server informed you that he/she would return for your payment when you were ready.	5	4	3	2	1
F. The server said thank you after he/she received your payment.	5	4	3	2	1
G. The server took the payment directly to the cashier.	5	4	3	2	1
H. The server brought your change directly from the cashier.	5	4	3	2	1
I. You received the correct change.	5	4	3	2	1
J. You received the check stub.	5	4	3	2	1
K. The server invited you to return.	5	4	3	2	1

L. Please list restaurant check number _____ Total _____ Tip (if charged) _____

M. Comments regarding check handling: _____

_____

_____

STANDARD POINT SCORE FOR CHECK HANDLING __55__   ACTUAL POINT SCORE _____

Appendix B
Typical Duties of a Dining Room Manager

OPENING DUTIES

Make sure the dining room temperature is comfortable.

Check the light level and all light bulbs. (Some operations have a policy that guests should be able to read a newspaper at the table. Other operations have discovered that guests wish for very subdued lighting.) Make sure lamp shades are straight.

Make sure pictures are straight and lighted.

Check table locations and room setup.

Inspect the dining room for cleanliness and safety. Check restrooms.

Communicate information regarding reservations (numbers and arrival times) to production personnel. (Put special emphasis on large parties.)

Check the schedule to confirm adequate staffing.

Gather as much information as possible about guests who are VIPs (Very Important Persons).

Check the menu items and the conditions of menus.

Make sure the music level is appropriate.

Check the sound system (if you use one).

Discuss special instructions with the staff.

Plan table arrangements according to group reservations.

Ensure that precheck and/or other registers and/or sales income control equipment are set for the beginning of the new dining period.

Make sure each food server is properly groomed.

Check each food server station's checklist to ensure that the dining room supplies are at proper inventory levels.

Meet with the service staff to discuss special guests, special menu items, daily specials, etc.

OPERATING DUTIES

Greet and seat guests.

Make recommendations and provide information about foods, wines, and spirits.

Ensure courteous and efficient service.

Make sure that the guests are satisfied, and follow up on any complaints.

Discreetly take care of intoxicated or hard-to-handle guests, or those who have disabilities. (It may be necessary to get assistance from another supervisor.)

Enforce procedures to detect fraudulent guests. (Also, ensure that dishonest service staff cannot steal from guests.)

Appendix B *(continued)*

OPERATING DUTIES *(continued)*

Enforce safety regulations.

Relay any special instructions to the kitchen.

Maintain a pleasant atmosphere in the dining room.

Maintain the reservation book.

Take appropriate action in the case of an accident to guests or staff members.

Follow up on special requests.

Supervise food service.

CLOSING DUTIES

Inspect for fire hazards (especially look in waste containers and linen receptacles for lighted cigarettes).

Turn off lights and adjust the air conditioning to the proper level.

Lock all doors.

Leave written information concerning any items requiring correction and any other information that will help the dining room manager who opens the room for the next dining period.

Follow the procedures for processing cash and charge vouchers.

Report any maintenance problems.

Review the next day's schedule and menus if possible.

Be sure to communicate to the appropriate personnel any guest complaints or comments.

Close precheck and other registers; follow required closing procedures.

Inspect for safety and sanitation.

Turn in the required reports to the appropriate officials.

MISCELLANEOUS DUTIES

Conduct training sessions for dining service staff members.

Participate in food and beverage, safety, and other meetings.

Plan reservations. (This is a key element in efficient service flow.)

Review menu items for their sales popularity.

Interview prospective staff members.

Maintain staff-member time records.

Develop effective operating procedures for dining service with a special focus on periods of high business volume.

Prepare weekly work schedules according to forecasted guest demand.

Issue maintenance orders.

Adjust work assignments and schedules.

(continued)

Appendix B *(continued)*

MISCELLANEOUS DUTIES *(continued)*

Authorize overtime, vacation time, and time off for dining room staff according to established practices.

Conduct accident/incident investigations and hold weekly training meetings, monthly safety meetings, and fire drills as required.

Implement and enforce safety regulations and house rules.

Coordinate cost control, purchasing, and maintenance duties with the assistant food and beverage director.

Order and requisition special-occasion cakes from the bake shop.

Prepare requisition sheet for operating supplies.

Observe and record staff member performance.

Make recommendations regarding staff member promotions.

Make complete dining room inspections at least weekly.

Source: Adapted from the *Dining Room Manual* of Hotel du Pont, Wilmington, Delaware.

Appendix C

Sample Preopening Checklist

	Required Quantities						
	M	T	W	TH	F	S	SU
1. Serving Supply Areas A. Prestock with all necessary service supplies							
tablecloths							
place mats							
napkins							
knives							
forks							
teaspoons							
soup spoons							
cocktail forks							
steak knives							
juice glasses							
water glasses							
coffee cups							
salad plates							
side dishes							
bread/butter plates							
dessert plates							
soup cups/bowls							
coffeepots							
water pitchers							
wine brackets/stands							
candles							
doilies							
bus tabs							
doggie bags							
sanitizing solution (to wipe tables)							
other:							
B. Prestock with food supplies:							
salt							

(continued)

Appendix C *(continued)*

	M	T	W	TH	F	S	SU
pepper							
sugar							
sugar substitute							
steak sauce							
ketchup							
mustard							
Worcestershire sauce							
preserves							
butter							
cream							
milk							
sour cream							
crackers (saltine and/or oyster crackers							
decaffeinated coffee							
horseradish							
tea bags (variety of flavors)							
lemons							
filled ice bins							
other:							
2. Public Areas							
reception area clean							
foyer clean							
public restrooms clean							
entry clean							
exterior areas clean							
dining room areas clean							
other:							
3. Service Staff							
clean and proper uniforms worn							

Appendix C *(continued)*

	M	T	W	TH	F	S	SU
preopening meeting held							
stations assigned							
daily specials reported							
run-outs reported							
out-of-stock items reported							
groups/reservations discussed							
guest checks dispensed							
other:							
4. Dining Room							
table decorations (flowers, candles, etc.)							
lighting							
regular and emergency exits							
air conditioning							
sound system							
no-smoking signs							
other:							
5. Service Stations							
tables steady							
tables set							
chairs clean							
napkins folded							
candles lit							
centerpieces fresh looking							
salt/pepper/etc. available							
ashtray/matches available							
table tents available							
table arranged for size of group reservation							
tray stand ready							

(continued)

Appendix C *(continued)*

	M	T	W	TH	F	S	SU
other:							
6. Reception Stand							
reservation book							
menus (food/wine/beverage)							
pencils							
flashlights							
credit card authorization machines							
other:							

Chapter 13 Outline

Competencies

1. Describe how banquets and catered events are sold—through identifying markets, employing sales strategies to sell to prospective clients, and making offers. (pp. 529–544)

2. Explain how banquets and catered events are booked and planned, and describe function books, contracts or letters of agreement, and function sheets. (pp. 545–549)

3. Summarize how banquet and catering operations get ready to provide service to clients during an event, from setting up function rooms to scheduling staff members and preparing, plating, and storing food. (pp. 549–558)

4. Describe different styles of food service; explain various beverage payment plans for banquet/catered event clients; list examples of protocol issues that banquet and catering staff members must be aware of; and describe "after service" issues for banquets and catered events, including controls, gathering guest comments, and using guest feedback in planning. (pp. 558–569)

13

Banquets and Catered Events

PROFESSIONAL BANQUET AND CATERING MANAGERS know that having a first-class **banquet and catering operation** can enhance the overall image of their food and beverage operations within the community. For many guests, their first contact with a given food and beverage operation occurs when they attend a banquet or catered event. If a guest's experience is positive, he or she may very well return to the operation with family and friends. Some banquet guests may also be the future organizers of similar functions for other groups. If these guests have already experienced a banquet that exceeded their expectations, they may simply return to the operation with their groups to experience the same kind of menu and service that delighted them previously.

Banquets and catered events can represent a substantial amount of revenue for food and beverage operations and hotels; in the United States alone, banquets and catered events generate billions of dollars each year. Banquets and catered events are part of many office events, meetings and conferences in hotels, and special events such as weddings, graduations, anniversary celebrations, bar and bat mitzvahs, retirement parties, and so on. When comparing the return on sales of a banquet (typically in the range of 20 to 30 percent) to return on sales in an à la carte dining room (typically 4 to 10 percent), one realizes that banquets and catered events have the potential to greatly add to a food and beverage operation's bottom line.

One reason for the greater return is that banquet and catered events are more predictable. These activities typically require a guarantee to the food and beverage operation, have predetermined and set menus for beverages and food, and may include room rental fees on top of the food and beverage charges. The hours of the banquet or catered event are agreed to in advance. Typically a service fee is charged to the guest booking the banquet or catered event. In addition, the amount of staff member and management labor required is predetermined by agreement. Another advantage to a banquet or catered event is that it may be used to promote the rest of the operation and therefore may generate future business.

A banquet and catering operation can be an independent business, part of a larger commercial or noncommercial food and beverage operation, or a department within the food and beverage division of a lodging property. In all of these various forms, a well-run banquet and catering operation can generate substantial profits, for several reasons:

1. Banquets and catered events allow flexibility in pricing. Prime rib priced at $30 on a food and beverage operation's restaurant menu may bring $40 on the banquet menu, for example. (Part of this increase is due to the cost of erecting and tearing down the banquet setup.)

2. Food costs for banquets and catered events are lower due to volume preparation and low food waste (because the number of guests is known).

3. Beverage costs can be controlled through pricing flexibility and volume purchasing.

4. Labor costs are lower. Since banquet servers can be supplemented by part-time workers on an as-needed basis, the regular banquet/catering service staff can be kept small. (The cost of restaurant staff members, in contrast, is largely fixed; restaurants must maintain a regular staff even during slow periods.)

5. Additional income can be generated from outside vendors such as photographers, entertainers, bakeries, florists, and printers. Some banquet and catering operations work with preferred vendors who pay them a commission for business generated from banquet clients.

In this chapter we will identify groups that typically book banquets or catered events and discuss strategies for selling to them. The process of booking and planning banquets and catered events will be the subject of the next section. We will then discuss getting ready for banquet or catering service, delivering service, and issues of concern after service.

Selling Banquets and Catered Events

Commercial food and beverage operations face stiff competition for banquet and catering business—not only from each other, but from businesses outside the commercial sector. According to *Food Management* magazine's survey of on-site (noncommercial) food service managers, 87 percent of those responding said they offer catering services. Forty-one percent of these same managers have an on-site building or banquet rooms devoted to accommodating catered events. Supermarket chains and independent grocery stores also compete aggressively in the lucrative banquet/catering arena via foods-prepared-to-go concepts.

Markets

Banquet and catering operations in commercial food service handle a wide variety of functions, including beverage service, snack service, special-event catering with a **buffet** or table service, and meal service delivered to guests off-premises. Other opportunities for banquet and catering operations include barbecues, conferences, hospitality suites, receptions, theme parties, wedding receptions, and sports banquets. Appendix A at the back of the chapter lists potential markets and some of the typical functions they plan. Banquet and catering managers should remember that each guest they serve is typically involved with many groups; a favorably impressed convention attendee might subsequently book social gatherings or business meetings with the operation, for example. The more delightful and memorable the service and the more personal attention staff members give to guests, the more likely it is that guests will generate new business leads for the operation.

A food and beverage operation's potential markets for banquets and catered events will vary based on where the food and beverage operation is located. For example, if the food and beverage operation is located in a state capitol that has a number of trade associations located within it along with a university, three likely markets have been identified: government agencies, trade associations, and the university. Additional markets may include law offices, lobbying organizations, and member organizations of the trade associations. Food and beverage operations in smaller cities may focus on service clubs (e.g., Kiwanis, Rotary) not only as organizations that may book regular meetings and banquets, but also as organizations that have members who may be interested in booking a banquet or catered event.

While there is countless variety in the types of banquets and catered events that are planned and executed, the markets for such events usually come from just three major sources: associations, corporate and business groups, and social groups.

Associations, or professional and special-interest groups, may include fewer than a hundred members to tens of thousands of members. Annual meetings and other events may feature simultaneous meetings and a wide range of food and beverage functions, such as coffee breaks, hospitality suites, cocktail parties, and banquets.

Corporate and business groups are composed of business associates and number from a handful of people to many hundreds. These groups may require food and beverage service for meals and coffee breaks, and have the potential to produce high revenue for food and beverage operations that offer banquet and catering services.

Social groups also can range from a handful of people to hundreds. Social groups' functions include private parties arranged by individuals for such family events as weddings, anniversaries, graduations, and bar and bat mitzvahs. Civic and political events, award or testimonial dinners, and fund-raising events are more examples of social-group events that often require banquet or catering services. Event planners for social groups are usually amateurs and may need extra help with planning their events.

The needs of associations and corporate groups are different from the needs of social groups. Associations and corporate groups normally require exhibit space and services, audiovisual equipment, office services, or other special equipment or services that social groups usually do not need. Managers of independent banquet and catering firms will feel market pressure to offer more than just food and beverage services if they target associations and corporate groups. Independent firms that cannot provide all of the services that these groups require sometimes partner with outside suppliers or hotels that can supply these services.

The regularity with which associations and corporate groups meet makes them prime prospects for a banquet and catering operation. Whether independent or part of a larger food and beverage organization, a banquet and catering operation usually should book non-annual events only after it has booked all of the annual events it can, because of the long-term value of accounts that hold annual meetings. Almost all associations and corporate groups hold annual meetings, and many hold smaller, more sporadic meetings as well.

A large association usually books its annual national convention in a different city each year and often selects the city years in advance of the convention's date. Corporate meetings are held wherever it is most convenient, often near corporate headquarters or a field office. Training seminars, management meetings, and other corporate meetings often are not rotated among various locations. This lack of a geographic pattern opens the door for almost any banquet and catering operation, no matter what its location or size, to book corporate meetings business. Business from social groups typically comes from clients who live in the local area.

Association meeting planners usually plan conventions one or more years in advance. Corporate meetings have no particular "time cycle"; most corporate meetings are scheduled as needed and may occur at any time throughout the year, so lead time for these meetings is far more variable than for association meetings. The annual sales meetings of corporations are usually planned a year or more in advance, but training meetings and seminars may be set three to six months in advance, or with even less lead time if the meeting is called to deal with a crisis. Executive conferences and board meetings also may be called on short notice. Weddings, family reunions, award banquets, retirement parties, and other events sponsored by social groups are usually planned a year or less in advance.

Whether event planners are experienced professionals planning events for thousands, or brides-to-be or other individuals planning small-scale social events for the first time, event planners always prefer to deal with people who take the time to understand their needs. They also appreciate working with one representative of the banquet and catering operation from the beginning of negotiations to the end of their events—someone who both sells the operation's services to them and helps coordinate the actual event for them.

Sales Strategies

To be competitive, food and beverage operations must aggressively sell their banquet and catering services. While detailed procedures for selling banquets are beyond the scope of this chapter, the general principles are the same from operation to operation. Likewise, certain basic tasks must be performed regardless of who performs them. Depending on the type and size of the operation and the titles used, the person responsible for banquet and catering sales may be the general manager, the food and beverage director, the director of sales, a banquet and catering director, or a salesperson.

Depending on local zoning laws, it may be possible to create an outdoor display, banner, or sign to market the operation's banquet and catering facilities. Menu inserts and table tents in the dining room are another way to promote sales. Fliers sent to the businesses and homes of current guests or included when prepared food-to-go is picked up are other marketing ideas. Prerecorded messages can be placed on the operation's telephone message system that describe the operation's banquet and catering facilities; callers can listen to them when they are put on hold. Newsletters sent to current guests and potential guests are another way to market banquets and catered events.

Selling to clients who have booked banquets and catered events in the past is a good idea, particularly if they indicated that they had a positive experience. Businesses in office buildings located within a five-mile radius of the food and beverage operation are other likely prospects. Nonprofit organizations, associations, and service clubs may be interested in booking banquets or catered events.

Hosting weekly or monthly meetings for these nonprofits and donating to their fundraising activities in return for publicity may lead to banquet and catered-event business. Direct contacts with the leaders of nonprofits via the telephone, personalized letters, or face-to-face conversations may be just the spark that stimulates them to book a banquet or catered event.

Local convention and visitors bureaus (CVBs) are knowledgeable about meetings and conferences that are coming to the area in the future. Referrals from these CVBs may be a source of untapped event bookings. The key is to pursue all options and all day parts. For example, a pharmaceutical firm may want to host an event at breakfast for local physicians; a financial institution may want a catered luncheon at its location for staff members who are attending a day-long professional development program; and a law office may want to book a banquet for one of its partners who is retiring. Networking with local churches and ministers and attending bridal shows in the community may generate wedding bookings. In a college town, reaching out to fraternities, sororities, and other student organizations may result in special parties or wedding bookings for the food and beverage operation.

Direct marketing to targeted groups often requires the development of a cover letter from the appropriate manager at the food and beverage operation and a brochure or folder that includes options for theme banquets and catered events, sample menus, and a list of special services available (e.g., audiovisual equipment, specialty cakes and pastries). Personal sales calls can help salespeople develop relationships that can result in banquet and catering business leads and bookings. Some operators deliver sample-size food items to prospective clients along with their direct marketing materials. Another strategy is to give the decision-maker in the business or nonprofit organization a gift certificate for dinner for two to come try the operation's products and services. The key to selling banquets and catered events is to target prospective customers, not simply send brochures and gift certificates to just anyone.

Targeting present guests requires a database as part of the food and beverage operation's guest relationship management (GRM) system. You must start to assemble the database at some point, so begin to gather guest information as soon as possible. The ability to offer banquets and catered events can also be marketed within the four walls of the operation through posters, fliers, big-screen displays, and word-of-mouth promotions by servers and managers. The sales message is best delivered through multiple media and on multiple occasions. Additional marketing can be done through the operations website and may include testimonials from satisfied guests and photos/videos of banquets and catered events.

It is important for the operation's managers to sell the strengths of the operation to prospective clients. It may be the operation's spectacular view that would be ideal for a wedding setting, or the operation's unique theme, or the ability to accommodate a wide variety of special event celebrations, or a talented pastry chef who understands how to exceed expectations with specially designed birthday or anniversary cakes. Whatever the strengths of the food and beverage operation, those should be promoted to potential clients.

Selling a variety of banquets and catered events very much depends on the flexibility of the meeting space in the food and beverage operation. Large rooms that can be easily subdivided into smaller spaces, flexible serving layouts for buffets, the proper tableware as well as serving equipment (e.g., chafing dishes, spoons, tongs, portable bain-maries) are all essential if the operation is to serve a buffet, a sit-down banquet, a coffee break with snacks, or any other of a variety of banquets and catered events.

One of the most effective sales strategies for banquet and catering operations is building a tradition of excellent service by creating positive, memorable experiences. It is much easier to sell banquets to people who are aware of the operation's fine reputation—or better yet, to those people who have had previous delightful experiences at the operation—than to people who know nothing about the operation. An operation that has an unimpressive reputation, or that tries to sell banquet and catering services to prospective clients who have had problems with events catered by the operation in the past, has a difficult, if not impossible, sales job.

To sell banquets and catered events effectively, banquet and catering managers must segment the event market into groups and know what potential guests in those groups require, how the operation can best meet those requirements, and how to negotiate a contract to provide the right products and services at the right price.

Prompt attention to prospects' inquiries about banquet/catering services demonstrates to prospects that the banquet and catering operation is efficient and has a concern for meeting the needs of clients and guests. This good first impression is something the operation can build on as it forms relationships with clients.

In addition to responding to inquiries, managers and salespeople in the banquet and catering area may also initiate contact with prospects, through telephone calls, direct mail letters, **sales blitzes** (personal visits to many prospects within a relatively small geographic area), or interaction with community organizations, convention centers, the local chamber of commerce, and tourist organizations. The Internet is also a useful sales tool. Whether salespeople or prospective guests make the initial contact, salespeople must convey to prospects that the food and beverage operation is interested in their business.

If a client books a convention or large corporate group's meeting with the operation several years ahead and will require many diverse food and beverage products and services, the salesperson should try to attend that group's meeting the year previous to when the group will arrive at his or her operation. The salesperson's attendance at the convention or meeting will enable him or her to meet the client and learn details of the group's food and beverage needs. This approach could help ensure that the salesperson books all of the ancillary food and beverage functions connected with the event the following year.

Inexperienced planners of national conventions may base their budgets for next year's food and beverage functions on the previous year's costs—often with a small increase to cover inflation. This is a mistaken approach, because it overlooks such variables as differences in the cost of living for different geographic locations throughout the country. So that the planners of national conventions will not begin negotiations with unrealistic expectations, banquet/catering salespeople should contact them many months ahead of time, before the planners finalize their budgets.

Effective salespeople can sometimes find new clients by visiting competitors. Dropping in on the competition and looking at their bulletin boards and "reader boards" (the area below a hotel's outdoor sign that is devoted to spelling out temporary messages) are good ways for salespeople to learn about which groups are booking where. Then the salesperson can work on finding out who the event planners are for the groups and convincing them to book with his or her operation in the future.

To help generate sales from these and other prospects, a salesperson might offer **familiarization tours** or "fam" tours. These tours involve showing prospects the operation's banquet/catering facilities and function rooms, providing prospects with supplemental information to help them plan their events, providing complimentary food and beverages, and providing complimentary lodging (if the banquet and catering operation is part of a hotel) as a sample of what the operation has to offer.

Many banquet and catering salespeople also use **presentation books,** laptops, or tablet computers to help them sell clients on their operation. These presentation aides can illustrate the possible eating and table arrangements within banquet and meeting space, contain photographs of past events, and display options for table settings. Presentation books can showcase outstanding past events and provide useful ideas to clients; laptops and tablet computers can display videos and slide shows depicting special events, which are especially effective sales tools. This type of information is also available online for clients and prospective clients to access at any time.

Now we will take a closer look at the two elements of a banquet and catering operation's services that are of most importance to clients: the operation's function rooms and its menus.

Function Rooms. From the client's standpoint, choosing the right function room is very important, because it must comfortably accommodate the number of people expected, and its atmosphere must complement the event. The floor plans of function rooms can be very helpful to clients who need certain kinds of lighting, electrical outlets for equipment, or space that is free of pillars or other obstructions. (The floor plan for each function room can be included in an operation's presentation book, in files used on laptops and tablet computers, and on the operation's website.)

Association and corporate meeting planners sometimes want **breakout rooms** available near the main function room. Breakout rooms are small meeting rooms used when a large group session divides into smaller sessions for discussions and group work. Breakout rooms are especially suitable for training meetings or seminars.

In order to present clients with workable function room alternatives, salespeople and managers must know the capacities of all of the rooms for each kind of seating arrangement. Chair and table sizes should present no surprises when staff members set up function rooms in the way the salesperson has promised the client. While this may seem like a minor point, tables or chairs that are just a few inches larger than others can significantly reduce the number of guests that a room can accommodate. Every bit of space counts.

In addition, the following factors should be considered when a salesperson is helping a client decide on a particular function room:

1. Does the room have enough space to accommodate everything the client's event requires? In addition to a specific number of guests, it may be necessary to provide space for portable bars, buffet tables, entertainment bandstands, dance floors, and staging areas.

2. Does the event require guest seating? Function rooms can accommodate many more people for a stand-up reception than for a sit-down banquet. (A rule of thumb is ten square feet [.9 square meters] per person if guests sit, and nine square feet [.8 square meters] if they stand.) Similarly, the space requirements for theater-style and classroom-style seating differ significantly. Managers should develop charts that illustrate for clients the seating arrangements and capacities of each function room under each setup. (Copies of these charts should also be given to the person in charge of setting up function rooms.) Exhibit 1 shows commonly used function room setups; Exhibit 2 shows a sample chart of seating capacities for various function rooms under various setups.

3. Are any events planned for the function room immediately before or after the event under consideration? For example, if staff members must break down a function room that held exhibits before they can set up for the next event, they will need much more time to prepare the room for the next event than if the room had been set up for a theater-style meeting or a stand-up reception.

4. Are any events planned for the function room(s) next to the function room the client is thinking of booking? Noise from one room's meeting, setup, or cleanup/breakdown can disrupt a neighboring event that is happening simultaneously.

5. What occupancy limits are set for the room by municipal codes and ordinances? Fire or other safety codes might limit the number of people that may occupy a room.

6. Is the function room accessible to guests with disabilities? Rooms accessible only by stairs are undesirable; managers should use them only when no other appropriate space is available.

What should a salesperson do if a client wants to book a party of 20 into a room that can seat 50 guests? Obviously, if the client is booking the event a year in advance, the salesperson should make a serious effort to convince him or her of the benefits of a smaller room so that the salesperson can put the larger room to its optimal use with a future booking. However, if the client's party is only two weeks away and the room is available, the salesperson is more likely to fulfill the client's request, because the salesperson cannot easily sell the room within the next two weeks anyway.

Most operations set a minimum number of covers (meals served) for each banquet room, but if a client whose dinner doesn't meet the minimum

Exhibit 1   Sample Function Room Setups

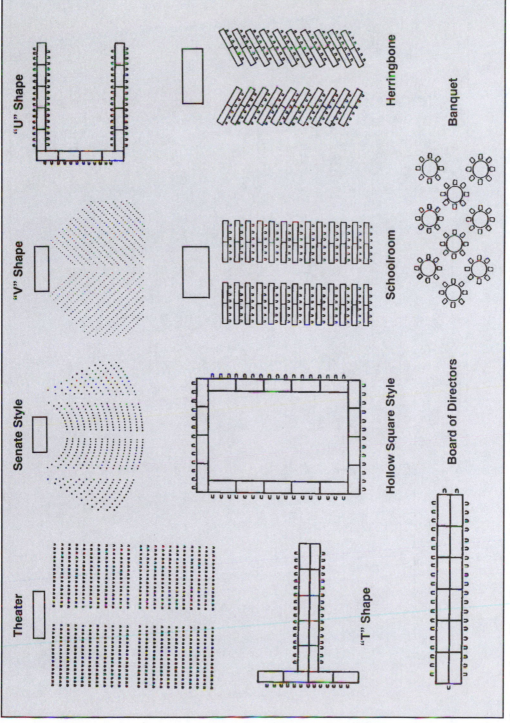

Source: Adapted from Convention Liaison Council, *The Convention Liaison Council Manual*, 7th ed. (Washington, D.C., 2000).

Exhibit 2 Sample Function Room Capacities and Dimensions

CAPACITIES AND DIMENSIONS*

ROOM	CAPACITIES						EXHIBITS		SQUARE FEET	DIMENSIONS	
	THEATRE	SCHOOL ROOM	BANQUET	RECEPTION	U-SHAPE	HOLLOW SQUARE	8x10	10x10		DIMENSIONS	CEILING HEIGHT
GRAND SALON	–	–	640	1,373	–	–	28	28	9,612	178'x54'	12'
GRAND BALLROOM	4,556	1,008	3,340	4,556	–	–	307	254	50,112	270'x150'	22'-16'
ADELPHI ROOM	1,896	1,008	1,020	1,929	–	–	85	74	13,500	150'x90'	22'-16'
BROADWAY ROOM	1,120	735	650	1,286	–	–	52	52	9,000	150'x60'	22'-16'
CAPITOL ROOM	1,120	735	660	1,286	–	–	52	52	9,000	150'x60'	22'-16'
RIALTO ROOM	1,120	735	600	1,286	–	–	52	52	9,000	150'x60'	22'-16'
RIALTO 1	150	84	120	264	52	65	–	–	1,850	45'x37'	22'-16'
RIALTO 2	150	84	120	264	52	65	–	–	1,850	45'x37'	22'-16'
RIALTO 3	150	84	120	264	52	65	–	–	1,850	45'x37'	22'-16'
RIALTO 4	150	84	120	264	52	65	–	–	1,850	45'x37'	22'-16'
REGISTRATION OFFICE	–	–	–	–	–	–	–	–	350	14'x25'	10'
GOLDWYN BALLROOM	5,000	3,400	3,400	5,200	–	–	291	237	44,600	180'x240'	10'-23'6"
GOLDWYN OFFICE	–	–	–	–	–	–	–	–	1,221	37'x33'	10'
GOLDWYN FOYER	–	–	–	–	–	–	–	–	1,232	22'x56'	12'
PALACE ROOM**	–	–	340	462	–	–	24	24	5,082	–	10'
PALACE 1	65	40	40	113	22	34	–	–	792	22'x36'	10'
PALACE 2	96	63	50	113	32	40	–	–	792	22'x36'	10'
PALACE 3	280	154	170	280	70	85	–	–	2,112	32'x66'	10'
PALACE 4	76	54	50	99	32	40	–	–	693	21'x33'	10'
PALACE 5	76	54	50	99	32	40	–	–	693	21'x33'	10'
PALACE 6	84	45	50	102	32	40	–	–	713	23'x31'	10'
PALACE 7	84	45	50	102	32	40	–	–	713	23'x31'	10'
DIRECTOR'S ROOM	Permanent Conference Table Seats 22								1,189	41'x29'	12'-10'
GROUP INFORMATION BOOTH	–	–	–	–	–	–	–	–	196	14'x14'	9'
ASSN. OFFICE 1, 2, 3, 4	–	–	–	–	–	–	–	–	108	9'x12'	9'
CELEBRITY ROOM	Permanent Seating for 1,499								2,640 Stage Dimensions Only	60'x44'	26'
ZIEGFELD ROOM	Permanent Seating for 1,096								5,016 Stage Dimensions Only	88'x57'	30'

Source: Bally's Casino Resort, Las Vegas, Nevada.

requirement requests a large banquet room that will otherwise go unsold, the client will usually get it. Managers must consider heating, air conditioning, and other fixed costs when they establish minimum covers for their banquet rooms.

Most operations set **cutoff dates** for tentative reservations (or "holds") of rooms—dates by which clients must either confirm or cancel their tentative reservations. Managers often set cutoff dates for either two weeks after the hold was placed or 30 days before the date of the event. By doing so, they add urgency to the negotiations between the salesperson and the client, and they also guarantee that the operation will have some time to sell the space if the client decides to cancel.

While a room is on hold, the salesperson and the client are often involved in negotiations over prices and other variables concerning the event. The willingness of salespeople to make price and other concessions will depend on the extent to which they desire the business. As alluded to earlier, if a room will go unsold if the negotiations with a client fall through, the salesperson may offer an additional service or upgrade a menu without additional cost to close the deal. However, if there is a good chance that the salesperson can sell the space to someone else, obviously the salesperson is less likely to make concessions.

Menus. Most banquet and catering operations create standard banquet menus to help salespeople give prospective clients an indication of what is available within specific price ranges. Most clients find standard menus acceptable. However, some clients have special desires or needs—they might want an especially extravagant meal, for example, or might require kosher foods (see Appendix B for information on kosher service). Managers should decide in advance whether they will accommodate such requests. If managers are willing to let clients design their own menus, then salespeople must be knowledgeable enough about the operation to be able to point out to clients such details as the costs of the menu items they want and the projected effect their nonstandard menu will have on the speed of service. Therefore, allowing clients to customize menus or ask for special services may mean giving salespeople more training. In any case, salespeople should encourage clients to keep ease and speed of service in mind when choosing menu items for a custom menu, since all guests at most banquet or catered events should be served at about the same time.

Production concerns may limit options for customized menus. When a client requests melon balls, for example, the salesperson should point out how labor-intensive, and thus how expensive, their preparation will be. The salesperson might suggest using melon cubes or an entirely different option instead. Of course, before the salesperson makes any promises to a client, he or she should discuss the customized menu with the chef and others to ensure that it is practical from production, service, and financial standpoints.

If managers create a variety of tempting standard menus, clients are less likely to want to customize. When developing standard menus, managers should strive for a balance of colors, textures, shapes, and temperatures in addition to nutritional content. Today's clients tend to eat lighter and healthier, so items that are broiled, baked, or poached should be offered in addition to sautéed or fried dishes. Appetizers and desserts that are low in fat, cholesterol, and salt are also popular, but managers should watch out for the "food fads" trap; blackened fish and chicken, for example, died quickly in most areas of the United States. Instead, managers should investigate long-lasting trends in food and beverage preferences among the operation's target markets.

Managers and chefs at successful banquet and catering operations are always looking for new ideas for menus. There are many resources for menu ideas, including competitors' menus, suppliers, industry periodicals and other publications, and the Internet (see Exhibit 3).

When planning a standard menu, managers should select entrées first, then hot food accompaniments such as high-starch items and vegetables. The accompaniments' colors, textures, flavors, costs, and other factors must fit in with the entrées. After managers have selected hot foods, they should select salads. Finally, managers should choose desserts and beverages that complement the other food items.

When managers plan menus for banquets and catered events, they must take into consideration the resources available to the operation. Managers must recognize the following constraints as they plan menus:

- *Facility layout/design and equipment.* The operation must have the space and equipment to produce all of the items offered on the menus.

- *Available labor and skills.* Managers must have staff members with the skills required to produce and serve all of the items on the menu. If staff members do not have the skills to prepare certain menu items, managers must implement training programs, hire additional staff members, purchase pre-made or ready-prepared items, or reconsider including such items on the menu. (Often, banquet and catering managers employ part-time or temporary staff members to support full-time staff.)

- *Ingredients.* Before managers make final decisions about which menu items to include on banquet/catering menus, they should look at the standard recipes that production staff will use to prepare the menu items so they can make certain that all of the ingredients required by each recipe will be available during the life span of the menus. Managers should choose menu items whose ingredients are always available. If managers select items that require such seasonal ingredients as strawberries and asparagus, they must realize that they will have to pay premium prices for those ingredients during the off-season.

- *Quality levels.* Managers must know what level of quality their clients expect and how to incorporate quality requirements into the food items offered on the menu. If for any reason the operation cannot provide a certain proposed menu item with the desired degree of quality, managers should not include it on the menu. Staff members' skills and knowledge, the capabilities of the operation's food-holding equipment, and the availability of certain ingredients all affect food quality.

- *Marketing implications.* Clients' preferences should be a primary concern when managers plan banquet and catering menus. Even though certain menu items may be especially practical to serve from the operation's standpoint, if the operation's clients do not care for them, managers should eliminate them from further consideration.

Exhibit 3   Sample Internet Source of Menu Ideas

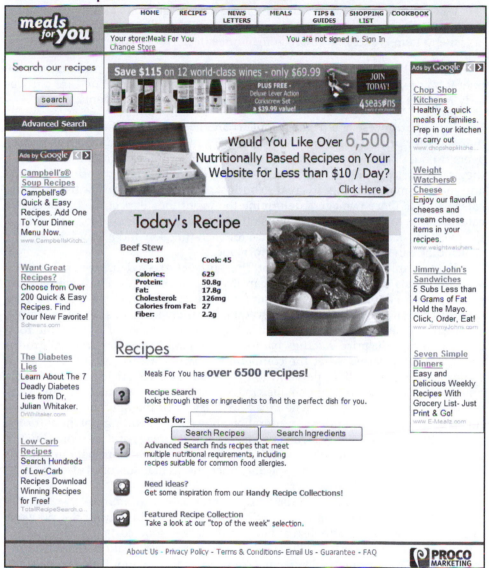

"Meals For You" and other Internet sites can provide many new menu ideas to banquet and catering managers and chefs. At this site, when you pick a recipe, you can select how many servings you wish to prepare (the range is typically 1–300 servings), and the recipe instructions and ingredient amounts are adjusted accordingly.

- *Meal period.* Another menu planning concern deals with the meal period involved. Typically, breakfast and lunch menus focus on nutrition and fast service. Dinner menus, however, are designed to offer more leisurely dining, because most dinner guests prefer a relaxed and festive experience.

- *Costs.* Food items that are expensive to produce and serve should be priced at levels that compensate for their high costs. Managers must know the costs of preparing specific menu items and their possible selling prices. If the cost of a menu item is excessive, management may decide not to offer it.

Most of these criteria also apply to menu items selected for inclusion on the operation's regular restaurant menus. However, these considerations are particularly important when planning menus for banquets or catered events.

Pricing. What prices should salespeople charge clients? Salespeople look to their managers for pricing guidelines. Unfortunately, many banquet and catering managers do not objectively consider the relationship between profit and price when they set up pricing guidelines. To help them arrive at appropriate prices, banquet and catering managers should create a budget or "profit plan" for the banquet and catering area. Once managers determine the profit they expect the banquet and catering area to generate, they can use the projected costs expressed in the budget to establish both a base selling price for each function and a standard against which they can measure financial performance.

For example, if the banquet and catering budget projected income of $1,000,000 and food costs of $250,000 for the year, managers could develop a simple base markup for food: banquet and catering food income ($1,000,000) divided by banquet and catering food costs ($250,000) equals a base markup of 4. In this example, managers or salespeople could sell functions for an average of 4 times the food costs, adjusting the pricing somewhat for each function according to what groups are willing to pay and what the competition charges. However, this is only an example; it is up to each operation to determine its own pricing system. Some managers may want to use a smaller markup to generate business during slow periods, or a higher markup when they are busy or (if the operation is part of a hotel) when the group under consideration shows low spending potential for the hotel's other revenue centers (such as guestrooms, lounges, and in-room dining). Managers could use a menu markup factor to price both standard banquet menus and special menus developed for specific functions. Managers could also use similar procedures to price beverages.

In addition, managers can use budget information to monitor the financial performance of the banquet and catering area. Using figures from the previous example, managers can establish a standard (or target) food cost percentage as follows: budgeted food costs ($250,000) divided by budgeted banquet and catering income ($1,000,000) equals 25 percent. Managers can study monthly income statements knowing that the banquet and catering food percentage must be approximately 25 percent in order for the banquet and catering area to attain its budget goals.

Determining a menu's selling price is more difficult with buffets than with other service styles that allow the operation more control over guest selections. Some operations develop buffet pricing plans based on the anticipated number of guests for an event. For example, if an operation expects 200 guests at a buffet and it wants approximately $4,000 in revenue from the function, it might charge $20 per person for the buffet. Most food and beverage operations allocate a specific

Buffets for Banquets and Catered Events

Many banquets and catered events feature buffets. There are many production and serving considerations that go into creating an attractive, guest-pleasing buffet. Keeping hot foods hot and cold foods cold is a prime example. There are many tricks of the trade that production personnel can use to maintain the quality of buffet food. For example, for breakfast buffets that include scrambled eggs, sour cream can be added to the eggs to prevent them from drying out so quickly while being held hot on the buffet line. Sometimes it is preferable to batch cook in small batches those food items that do not hold well hot on a buffet. This is true of cooked vegetables, for example, which tend to deteriorate quickly. Small batch cooking is the answer.

Glazes or broths on meats for a buffet not only add flavor, they also prevent the items from drying during holding. Grilled vegetables or main courses (e.g., meats, seafood) can be marked with the grill marks first, refrigerated, then brought to proper serving temperature in a combi-oven. Preparation of fish may be best done by poaching it first, then finishing it in an oven. Fresh vegetables that are steamed, tossed with seasoning ingredients, then finished in a combi-oven retain more of their moisture, which prevents drying and preserves the color of the vegetables.

A general guide is to set up a buffet line for every 100 guests. A buffet line that is accessible to guests on both sides can serve 200 guests. When a carved meat item is part of a buffet, the carver should set up at the end of the buffet or at a separate station to improve traffic flow for guests. Main course items on the buffet should be in smaller portion sizes than the portions typically served in à la carte service, since there are many more food options on the buffet for guests to choose from.

Usually, the lower-cost-per-portion foods (e.g., salads, vegetables, fruits) are placed on a buffet at the beginning of the line, with the higher-cost items (e.g., meats, seafoods) placed last. In a setup where there are multiple buffet lines due to the number of guests to be served, the lines can be consolidated when most of the guests have been served or when the amount of food left is down to 25–35 percent of the total food prepared for the buffet.

Whenever canned heat is used to keep foods at proper serving temperatures on the buffet, staff should keep a careful watch to be certain that the canned heat is not used up before the buffet is finished. If it is used up, then it should be replaced so the hot foods are maintained at the right temperatures. Some operations equip serving and kitchen staff members with two-way radios so that kitchen staff can more promptly be notified that food on the buffet is in need of replenishing.

The proper presentation of food products on a buffet is critical to eye appeal and guest satisfaction. As was already mentioned, the less-expensive foods should be placed first on the buffet, right next to where guests will find clean plates, and the most expensive food items should be placed last. Attractive presentation of room-temperature foods (e.g., cheeses, grilled vegetables, fresh fruits, salads) in non-metal, colorful ceramic containers add to eye appeal.

In many cases the color appeal comes from the food itself, as in a salad prepared with a variety of colors, so for these foods placement in a plain white container works perfectly. Main courses can be presented on a bed of vegetables for added appeal (this will also help prevent these courses from drying out). Food items placed at different heights or in contrasting serving containers, roll-top chafers, mirrors, and garnishes all add to the appeal of a buffet.

(continued)

(continued)

> When kitchen staff or servers serve food from a buffet, it may increase labor costs, but these costs may be more than offset by reduced food costs due to better portion control. This is true for traditional buffets as well as carving and dessert stations.
>
> The costs of food on a buffet are generally four to six percent higher than à la carte table service because leftovers and waste usually increase. But labor costs are typically less, since guests do their own self-service.
>
> The equipment needed to properly deliver a buffet, including decorative dishes and platters, chafing equipment to keep foods hot, ice bins to keep foods cold, and equipment for carving stations, is an investment whose return is realized only after a number of buffets have taken place.

percentage (usually 50 percent) of their buffet income to cover the buffet's food costs. Using this information, the menu planner can select food items for the buffet menu within the range of the operation's allowable costs. Other food and beverage operations plan their buffet menus first, calculate their estimated costs, then set a selling price based on a markup factor. For example, if an operation felt that food costs should be 50 percent of the buffet income, the menu planner would first determine the per-person food costs of the buffet menu, then double that figure to determine the per-person selling price.

Of course, managers must consider other costs besides food costs when they are calculating prices. Labor is another big cost factor. Labor costs for a buffet include the cost of "runners" or other staff members that attend to the buffet throughout the meal period to keep it looking fresh and wholesome during service. Other buffet labor costs include staff time for setting the buffet up and breaking it down, and additional cleaning time required when some food preparation is done on the buffet line. Labor costs for table service are even higher than for buffet service.

The Offer

Once negotiations have reached the point where a salesperson makes an offer, the salesperson should draft a proposal letter for the client that summarizes the offer and includes preliminary prices. This written summary helps eliminate misunderstandings that could affect the success of the negotiations.

Salespeople must be very careful when negotiating with clients and writing offers. The annual banquet business is very competitive. A cost difference of $2 or less per guest can make the difference between a client's choice of one banquet and catering operation over another. Some operations have lost the revenue from a dinner for 2,000 people over the price of a salad or side dish. When a banquet and catering operation loses a sale, managers or salespeople should record information about the loss, such as the estimated value of the event, the reasons for the loss, and the names of the client, the group, and the event. Careful study of information about lost business can help banquet and catering managers revise sales strategies to minimize future business losses.

Booking and Planning Events

Three documents play a primary role in booking and planning banquet and catering events: the **function book,** sometimes called the daily function room diary; the **contract** or letter of agreement; and the **function sheet,** which is also called a banquet event order (BEO). Electronic versions of these documents are typically used today.

The Function Book

Managers and salespeople use the function book to determine if a certain room is available for a particular function at a particular time. The function book is also used to reserve a room after an event is sold so that no one else will commit the room for another function covering the same time period. The function book lists all of the operation's function space available for sale, and has a daily time log for each space to facilitate the recording of sold blocks of time. The function book's size and format depend on the size of the banquet and catering operation and the number of available function rooms. Some operations need less information in their function books than others, but entries typically include the group's name; the client's name, title, and phone number; the estimated attendance; the name of the event; and the type of event (for example, hospitality suite, lunch, or meeting). See Exhibit 4 for a sample screen from a computerized function book.

Typically, at operations without a computerized function book, one person is responsible for making entries into and otherwise maintaining the function book. This individual must notify banquet and catering managers and salespeople of any duplicate bookings or other conflicts concerning space in the book. Exhibit 5 is a sample **function room reservation form,** which is what a salesperson in an operation that uses a manual system would give the coordinator of the function book to tentatively or definitely reserve a room. At operations with computers, there is no need for a function book coordinator. Salespeople and managers can make entries into or consult the function book quickly and easily, since the book is computerized and accessible via their computers. Because staff members can access the book instantaneously and simultaneously, there is less chance of selling the same room for the same time period to two different groups, and therefore less need for one-person oversight of entries.

Using a function book to accurately keep track of sold and unsold space is very important to the operation as well as to clients. Managers view function space as a potentially profitable commodity. Space that goes unsold represents lost income that can never be recuperated. That is why managers cannot afford to trust oral agreements with clients or make mistakes in making entries into the function book.

If negotiations are successful and a client decides to book with the operation, the function book coordinator (in operations with manual systems) or the salesperson (in operations with computerized systems) will officially enter the event into the function book. A copy of the salesperson's proposal letter that the client has signed, a confirmation letter from the client, or a function room reservation form may serve as official authorization for the event. A confirmed reservation

Exhibit 4   Sample Computerized Function Book

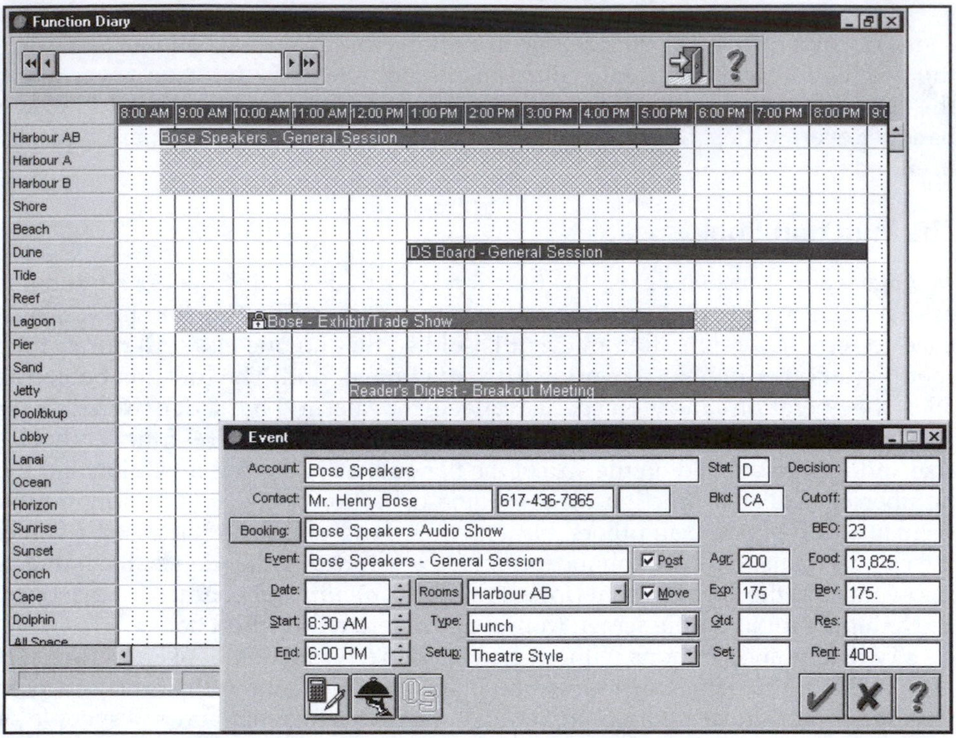

Source: Delphi 7/Newmarket Software Systems, Inc., Durham, New Hampshire.

indicates to the salesperson that it is time to generate a contract or letter of agreement that outlines the client's and the operation's obligations.

Contracts or Letters of Agreement

As just mentioned, after the salesperson and client have agreed on terms, the salesperson should draw up a contract or letter of agreement. Every detail that the two parties have discussed and agreed upon should be covered in the contract.

It is important to estimate attendance figures at the time the contract is signed. However, if the event itself will be held months or even years later, the operation might not require an attendance estimate on the signing date. Some operations contact the client approximately two weeks before the event to get an update on the expected number of guests. Of course, if the event is large or requires special purchases, the operation will make this inquiry a month or more in advance of the function; operations may also contact the client for attendance updates more and more frequently as the date of the function approaches. In some cases (such as with conventions, which have optional attendance), ticket sales fluctuate so much from the original proposal that the group may need a larger or smaller room than was originally booked. On a date that is a certain number of days or weeks before the event and is specified in the contract (two days before the event for

Exhibit 5   Sample Function Room Reservation Form

RMI   EXAMPLE

TIME: _____2:35 P.M._____   SALES MANAGER: ____SS____

DATE: _____3/9/XX_____

CATERING INQUIRY

ORGANIZATION: ___Carter/Hale Wedding_____

ADDRESS: ___1414 E. 14th St., Anywhere___   STATE: __AZ__   ZIP: __81414__

NAME: ___Mrs. Andrew Hale_____   PHONE: __262-2626_____

TITLE: ___Mother of the Bride_____

BUSINESS POTENTIAL

TYPE OF FUNCTION: ___Wedding Reception_____   TIME: __7 P.M.–12:30 A.M.__

NO. OF PERSONS: ____175_____   DATE: __8/22/XX_____

ALTERNATIVE DATE: _____None_____

GUEST ROOMS: _____5_____   ROOM RATE: ____(current rack)____

Have you ever used the Ramada Anywhere?   No, but neighbor
Where are/were functions held? _____   had her reception here last year

ACTION: ____X_____   TENTATIVE BOOKING

_____   DEFINITE BOOKING

_____   FUTURE BOOKING

MENU ACTION:

TO BE MAILED: YES __X__   NO _____   MENU: ___Wedding package_____

OTHER: _____

FOLLOW-UP BY: _____3/18_____   HOLD SPACE UNTIL: ____4/9_____

REPORT ON FOLLOW-UP—LOST DUE TO (check one)

SPACE RELEASE POLICY _____

PRICE _____   NO SPACE _____   SPACE NOT SATISFACTORY
                                                                    (reason below)

OTHER _____

NO EXPLANATION GIVEN _____

CHECK LIST

ENCLOSURES REQUIRED FOR LETTER(S) CHECKED-OFF:

BUSINESS CARD	__X__
CATERING MENU BROCHURE	__X__
MENU PRICE LIST ONLY	_____
LETTER	__X__
CREDIT APPLICATION	_____
RACK BROCHURE	_____
AIRPORT TRANSPORTATION BROCHURE	_____
A/V SHEET	_____
WEDDING INFORMATION	__X__

Catering Administration Manual

Source: James R. Abbey, *Hospitality Sales and Marketing*, Fifth Edition (Lansing, Mich.: American Hotel & Lodging Educational Institute , 2008), p. 558.

small-scale events is typical), the client must state the final number of attendees that are expected. This number is the **guarantee.**

A food and beverage operation may apply a variance percentage to guarantees. For example, if the client guarantees an attendance of 240 guests, the operation might allow a five percent variance; since five percent of 240 is 12, the client would have to pay for at least 228 guests and at most 252, and the operation would prepare portions and set places for a maximum of 252 guests. Of course, if the menu is unusual or difficult to prepare, or if the estimated attendance is large, the variance percentage may be smaller. The larger the estimated attendance, the smaller the percentage of guests over the guarantee for which the operation should prepare. If an operation uses a five percent variance for an estimated attendance of 240, for example, it might prepare for only three percent over the guarantee for groups of 350 or more.

Unless the food and beverage operation receives satisfactory credit references from the client, the contract often requires the client to pay a specific portion—as much as 100 percent—of the estimated cost of the function at least two weeks in advance of the event's date; clients usually pay any remaining balance within 30 days after the event. Food and beverage operations generally reserve the right to cancel an event if the client has not established proper credit or made the required advance payment.

The contract must indicate the exact products and services that will be provided to the client's group. The food, beverages, labor, and other direct costs incurred to produce and serve the items required by the contract are included in the total price the operation charges for the event, as are rental charges (if any) for the function rooms. Some operations charge clients a room rental fee if the cost of the event does not exceed a specific amount; others require a room rental payment from clients whose events do not include dinner. Typically, the following services are included in room rental rates:

1. Setup labor for normal meetings (tables, chairs, tablecloths, and ice water)

2. Movement of large furniture in the room to other locations

3. Removal of carpets

4. Public address system and microphones

5. Easels, chart boards, movie screens, tables for projectors, and extension cords

The following services are often *not* included in room rental rates but are charged separately:

1. Electrical layouts, plumbing, or other services for exhibits

2. Computers for PowerPoint presentations, VCRs, DVD players, slide projectors, overhead projectors, tape recorders, screens, and flipcharts (these items may be available from the operation for an additional charge, or the operation might obtain them from an outside supplier and charge the client a fee that reflects a markup for the operation)

3. Table decorations

4. A dance floor

5. Service staff, including audiovisual, electrical, or other technicians

Once the contract is signed, the salesperson must generate a function sheet to inform the rest of the banquet and catering staff about the event.

Function Sheets

A function sheet lists all of the details that apply to the function—everything any-one at the food and beverage operation might need to know about the function to prepare for it and provide service during it (see Exhibit 6 for a sample function sheet). The salesperson who books the event completes the function sheet, then makes as many copies of it as necessary to distribute to the banquet/catering office, the manager who will schedule staff for the event, the beverage department (which schedules staff and orders the necessary products), the accounting department (which prepares the billing), the convention service or floor manager (if the beverage and catering operation is part of a large hotel; the convention service or floor manager is the person in large hotels who arranges function room set-ups), the kitchen storeroom, the kitchen banquet staff, the kitchen's pantry area, the kitchen commissary, and the kitchen's bakeshop. Software programs make it easier to generate function sheets.

Coordination is critical to the success of any banquet or catered event. Typically, representatives from such areas as the sales, accounting, and food and beverage departments will meet regularly to discuss the function sheets for upcoming banquets and catered events. The client may also be asked to attend these meetings. For very large and other special events, detailed planning begins months in advance. Some functions are annual events, so detailed planning that leads to a successful event can help secure repeat business the following year. (Managers should not assume that clients who choose their operation to host annual functions will stay with the operation forever. If their events are not serviced properly, clients will quickly take their business elsewhere.) Participants in event-planning meetings should study the function sheets closely to ensure that they clearly understand what is required for the event. This will help eliminate potential problems.

Getting Ready for Service

Getting ready for service for banquets and catered events includes setting up the function room(s); scheduling staff members; and preparing, plating, and storing banquet food.

Setting Up Function Rooms

The design and decor of function rooms, like the food and beverages that are served in them, can take many forms. A simple coffee break may be served in an undecorated, theme-less room, while an elaborate reception featuring foods from around the world may be served in a function room that has complex decorations to fit the theme. The type of function room chosen and how it is decorated are largely dictated by the needs and expectations of the client.

Exhibit 6   Sample Function Sheet

NOGA HILTON GENÈVE

BANQUETING DEPARTEMENT

Address		Date:
		Master N°:
		Telex:
		Telephone:
Name of the client:		Reservation N°:
INFORMATION BOARD		Client:

Time	Type of Function	Rooms	N° Pers. guaranted	CONFERENCE SET UP	Fr.
				Room rental	
				Table set up	
				School / Cinema Style.	
				Minerals	
				Writing pads / pencils	
				Flip chart.	
				Head table . . . . pers.	
				Stage.	
MENU:			Fr.	Speaker desk	
				Welcome desk	
				LUNCH / DINNER	
				Table set up	
				Host table . . . . pers.	
				Candlesticks.	
				Table numbers	
				Stage.	
				Dance floor.	
				ORCHESTRA by hotel.	
				by client	
				Police authorization by hotel . . . . h.	
				by client . . . . h.	
				TECHNICAL EQUIPMENT	
				Video.	
				Screen.	
				Overhead projector	
				Film / Slide Projector	
				Large / small control center	
				Telephone.	
				Microphone	
				Technician from . . . . to	

COFFEE BREAK	Fr.	LUNCH / DINNER	Fr.	**MENUS**	Fr.
. . . .		Minerals		Simple print by our self	
. . . .		Wines		Double print by our self	
Croissant. . . . . Cake.				Print by client	
				Title :	
BAR / APERITIF				. . . .	
Chips, peanuts, olives				**FLORAL DECORATIONS**	
International bar.				Round and long terrine	
Simple bar (without whisky, gin,				Arrangement	
wodka)				Green plant.	
		Liquors		By the client	
		Cigars		**WARDROBE ROOM**	
		Drinks		Stander.	
				. . . . personne(s)	

NH 6206   **IMPORTANT: SIGNATURE AND CONDITIONS ON THE REVERSE SIDE OF THIS PAGE**

Courtesy of Noga Hilton Genève, Geneva, Switzerland

Frequently, managers come up with layouts for function rooms to help setup crews carry out instructions on the function sheet. Some clients have strong preferences about the layout of function rooms, and those might be expressed in unusual or creative layouts. Managers should carefully plan the location of such room elements as bars, food buffet stations, ice carvings, garden and tree decorations, and stages for speakers or entertainers. The location of these elements affects the guests' experiences in the room. The need for staff members to pay close attention to the details listed on the function sheet and illustrated on the layout is just as important for small events as it is for large, elaborate events.

Adequate space for display tables, guest tables, and other room elements (for example, stages and lecterns) is an important setup consideration for banquets and catered events. Crowded, hot rooms make for an unpleasant dining experience. Adequate space also allows for more efficient movement of inventory and people.

The client is usually responsible for reviewing any seating charts that the event may require. However, the manager can assist the client with that task and indicate the staff's preferences regarding seating arrangements.

As noted earlier, Exhibit 1 portrays several commonly used function room setups. Procedures for setting up function rooms vary according to the needs of the client and his or her group. The following is a partial list of activities and items that might be involved in setting up a function room:

1. Place runways, carpets, and pianos.

2. Place dinner tables, meeting tables, and head tables.

3. Place chairs, sofas, and other seats.

4. Place bars, buffets, and cake tables.

5. Place the registration, gift, and display tables.

6. Place the video screen, projector table, projector, and extension cords.

7. Place chalkboards, easels, and any other display equipment.

8. Place microphones, lecterns, and flags.

9. Place linens, sugar containers, salt and pepper shakers, tableware, and other tabletop items (see Exhibit 7 for one place-setting option).

10. Place cakes, candle holders, fountains, flowers, and decorations.

11. Place table numbers or reservation cards on tables, if necessary.

Because guests at banquets and catered events must be served quickly, service stations should be set up to allow for maximum staff efficiency. Equipment requirements vary with the type of function and the menu, but function-room service stations may have the following:

- Microwave ovens

- Flatware

- Glassware

Exhibit 7   Sample Place Setting

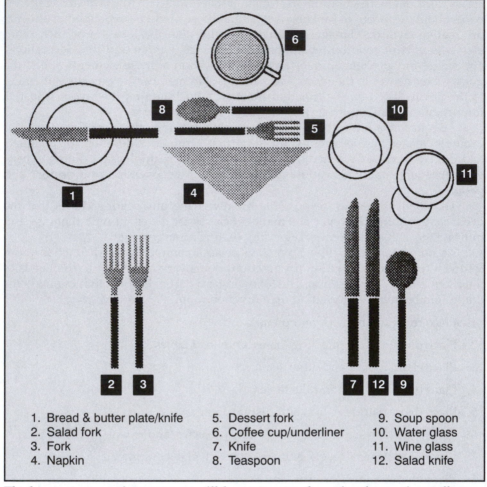

1. Bread & butter plate/knife	5. Dessert fork	9. Soup spoon
2. Salad fork	6. Coffee cup/underliner	10. Water glass
3. Fork	7. Knife	11. Wine glass
4. Napkin	8. Teaspoon	12. Salad knife

The banquet or catering manager will lay out a sample setting for service staff members to follow during setup. A typical place setting is shown here. Whatever setting is used, staff members must be consistent and pay attention to detail. Source: Adapted from the *Better Banquets: Basic Service Skills* video (Lansing, Mich.: American Hotel & Lodging Educational Institute, 1997).

- Water, coffee, and tea
- Cream, sugar, and stirrers
- Place mats and napery
- Candles, flowers, or other table decorations
- First aid kits
- Salt, pepper, and other condiments

Prior to opening the function room's doors and allowing guests to enter, the manager overseeing service for the event must ensure that the room setup is complete. Whenever practical, the manager should meet with the client immediately before the event to inquire about the latest guest count or any last-minute changes to the plan for the event. The manager should walk through the function room (or assign someone else to do so) to make a safety check. No cords should be positioned where someone could trip on them; supports for platform panels, acoustical shells, table leaves, and risers should all be secure; chairs and tables should not wobble, and all their legs should be sturdy; and hallways and doorways (especially fire exits) should not be obstructed.

The manager in charge usually holds a brief meeting with all service staff (and sometimes kitchen staff) to review details and give final updates just before the event begins.

Scheduling Staff Members

Managers must schedule the proper number of staff members and types of staff positions for each banquet or catered event. What follows are position titles and responsibilities covering staff members who might work in a large banquet and catering operation.

The *banquet* or *catering director's* primary responsibilities are the sales and administrative aspects of the banquet and catering operation. The director is also responsible for the cost-effectiveness of the department and works closely with other people (purchasing agents, chefs, and salespeople, to name a few) to ensure that the operation falls within budget guidelines while still providing excellent service to clients and their groups.

The *banquet* or *catering manager* is responsible for overseeing food and beverage functions and supervising service personnel (see Exhibit 8 for a sample job description for a catering manager). He or she may be directly involved in setting up, cleaning up, and breaking down function rooms (at large convention hotels, however, setup duties are often handled by a convention service manager, head houseperson, or floor manager). Banquet or catering managers also schedule personnel, prepare payrolls, and work with the banquet or catering director on special functions.

Salespeople actively solicit business and follow up on written, telephone, Internet, and walk-in inquiries. Salespeople must know the proper procedures to follow to develop leads, process paperwork for an account, and follow up with clients after their functions. Knowledge of what types of business to book and when is also important. For example, hotel catering salespeople should avoid booking a social function such as a bridge tournament luncheon in the ballroom on a weekday. Such a booking could prevent someone from booking a four-day corporate meeting with rooms business and breakfast, lunch, and dinner business each of the four days.

Clerical staff members maintain the paperwork generated by salespeople, handle routine inquiries, and follow up on accounts. In large properties, an administrative assistant may help the director with administrative duties or manage the banquet/catering office.

Exhibit 8   Sample Job Description: Catering Manager

1. *Basic Function*

   To service all phases of group meeting or banquet functions; coordinate these activities on a daily basis; assist clients in program planning and menu selection; solicit local group catering business.

2. *General Responsibility*

   To maintain the services and reputation of Doubletree and act as a management representative to group clients.

3. *Specific Responsibilities*

   a. To maintain the function book and coordinate the booking of all meeting space with the sales department.
   b. To solicit local food and beverage functions.
   c. To coordinate with all group-meeting or banquet planners their specific group requirements with the services and facilities offered.
   d. To confirm all details relative to group functions with meeting or banquet planners.
   e. To distribute to the necessary inter-hotel departments detailed information relative to group activities.
   f. To supervise and coordinate all phases of catering, hiring, and training programs.
   g. To supervise and coordinate daily operation of meeting/banquet setups and service.
   h. To assist in menu planning, preparation, and pricing.
   i. To assist in referrals to the sales department and in booking group activities.
   j. To set up and maintain catering files.
   k. To be responsive to group requests or needs while in the hotel.
   l. To work toward achieving Annual Plan figures relating to the catering department (revenues, labor percentages, average checks, covers, etc.)
   m. To handle all scheduling and coverage for the servicing of catering functions.

4. *Organizational Relationship and Authority*

   Is directly responsible and accountable to the food and beverage manager. Responsible for coordination with kitchen, catering service personnel, and accounting.

This is the job description used for catering managers at Doubletree Hotels. (Courtesy of Doubletree, Inc.)

The *function book coordinator* (in operations that use a manual, noncomputerized booking system) is the single person who makes entries into the function book and is responsible for ensuring their accuracy. (In operations that do not have this position, the banquet and catering director or manager is usually responsible for the function book.)

Service personnel serve food and beverages, set up function rooms, and maintain banquet areas and equipment. Service personnel include hosts or captains, food servers, buspersons, and housepersons or setup crews. During events, food servers and buspersons are either supervised directly by the banquet or catering manager or by a banquet host or captain. (Operations that can simultaneously host several groups are more likely to have mid-level supervisors such as hosts and captains.)

Based on the number of special functions scheduled each day, the banquet/catering director or manager must schedule staff members to set up and break down function rooms, as well as schedule service staff to perform all of the guest-contact service and related tasks involved in the events themselves.

The number of servers and other personnel that are scheduled for an event varies from operation to operation and from event to event. Among top private clubs, for example, the ratio is usually one server for every 10 to 15 guests. A greater than usual number of servers and other personnel will also be needed for an event if a client asks for special services. **Synchronized service,** for example, requires the entire service staff to enter the function room through one set of doors to serve each course. In unison and using precise movements, servers place the courses in front of guests. Often wine service is also synchronized. Obviously, this style of banquet service requires a great deal of training, rehearsal, skill, and additional staff.

Training. The pressures inherent whenever food is served to guests are greater when large numbers of guests must be served in a relatively short period of time. Under these circumstances, mistakes can happen very easily if staff members are not well trained in service procedures.

Training staff members to be banquet servers requires that trainers have a fundamental knowledge of all service styles and skills that might be used at events that the operation hosts. Rehearsals in which service actions are repeated a number of times are often the best way to help servers internalize service styles and skills. Special styles of service as well as the details of the "script" (the function sheet) should be reviewed during practice sessions. The goal of training is to present consistent service styles to guests at banquets and catered events.

Banquet and catering service personnel also must be trained to realize that, as guest-contact staff members, they give guests first and last impressions of the operation. In successful banquet and catering operations, staff members understand and follow the operation's service philosophy.

Some guests at banquet and catered events may have unique service needs. For example, international groups may have unique cultural customs that cannot be ignored. Business banquets are popular in Chinese culture; they end promptly after the host rises and gives a toast. Children from Asian countries such as Thailand and India should never be patted on the head—a common American way to show friendliness, but one that should be avoided in this instance—because in certain Asian countries the head is considered sacred and should never be touched. Even interpretations of facial expressions and hand gestures differ from culture to culture. Staff members who will serve guests at international functions should be trained to be sensitive to the guests' customs.

Exhibit 9   Possible Setup for Plating Banquet and Catered-Event Meals

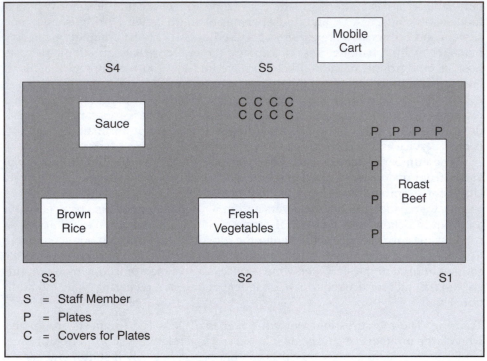

Managers must be on their toes as well. In China, for example, someone named "Liang Cheng-wu" should be addressed as "Mr. Liang"; "Cheng-wu" is a compound of the man's first and middle names and it would be socially incorrect to use it. Some international clients may present a small gift to the banquet or catering manager, who should be prepared to give a modest gift in return.

If the banquet and catering operation is part of a larger food and beverage operation, it is wise to cross-train dining area staff members in banquet and catering service procedures. Then, if a function room needs to be set up in a hurry, properly trained dining area staff members can help the banquet and catering staff.

Preparing, Plating, and Storing Food

Banquet and catering managers must be sensitive to the concerns of the chef and other personnel who prepare food for an event. Managers must never overlook the fact that the chef should be an integral member of the planning team. When the input of the chef and other food production staff members is used to develop menus for banquets and catered events, few, if any, production problems should arise when the staff prepares these menus.

Some banquet and catering operations that handle events with large numbers of guests use an automated assembly line to portion meals. More commonly, however, operations use a manual plating process. Exhibit 9 shows one arrangement of people, equipment, and supplies that can be used to plate and set up one kind

"Every Plate Represents a Person"

In a banquet setting, it is important for staff members to remind themselves that "every plate represents a person"—a person who is waiting to be impressed. Individual guests do not really care that the banquet staff produced perhaps 800 other perfect plates; they only want their plates to be perfect, and, if they are not, the banquet experience is disappointing from their point of view.

How can hotel food service operations deliver perfect plates more efficiently? Some operations use plate-stacking systems that permit plates to be set up (that is, have the food placed on them) in advance of service and locked between pegs in a mobile-stacking rack system. This saves space in refrigerators and allows the plates to be rolled right up to the area where the banquet will be served. Less handling means there is a greater likelihood that the plates will be perfect then they are placed in front of guests. Some units have a plate-lock rack that can be rolled into a warming cabinet.

Small electric mobile steam tables can be set up next to narrow tables to create a plating line with two sides. For larger banquets and catered events, conveyor belts can be used to move plates along so that production staff can plate food faster and more efficiently.

All of these types of improvements are being implemented by food and beverage operations because, fundamentally, guests determine whether a banquet or catered event was satisfying based on the quality of the food, how the food was presented/plated, and the quality of service provided by the service staff.

of meal. As illustrated in Exhibit 9, one person (at "S1" or Station 1) carves and places roast beef slices on plates, then passes (slides) the plates along the table to a second staff member, who portions the fresh vegetables. A third staff member portions the brown rice and slides the plates across the table to a fourth staff member, who places sauce on the meat. A fifth staff member puts covers on the plates and loads the plates onto a mobile cart. Using this system, five staff members can plate food for 300 people in approximately 45 minutes. (If the client wants the meal to be served in less time, a second plating line could be set up.) If the client had requested a plate garnish, the process would have required another staff member to provide it.

In banquet and catering service, time and temperature control for food is critical. It is virtually impossible to prepare hundreds of individual plates as service progresses. Therefore, foods are usually preplated for large banquets or catered events and then stored hot or cold in holding cabinets. Refrigerated mobile storage units must maintain internal product temperatures of 41°F (5°C) or less; mobile hot storage cabinets must maintain a minimum internal product temperature of 140°F (60°C). This keeps held food out of the temperature danger zone (TDZ) of 41°F (5°C) to 140°F (60°C). (Because the TDZ may be defined slightly differently in various areas of the country, managers should check with local and state health authorities to make sure they are in compliance with all food safety codes.)

For holding cold products, ice is usually an acceptable means of maintaining chilled temperatures. However, food must not be directly exposed to ice or melted water; instead, it must be held in bowls or containers embedded in the ice.

Hot food can be kept hot in a number of ways. Chafing dishes powered by electricity or canned heat are usually used to hold hot foods on a buffet table. Large roasts, hams, and turkeys that are to be carved in the function room should be displayed under infrared heat lamps. Sneeze guards or other equipment to prevent contamination of displayed food may be required by local or regional health regulations.

Outdoor service presents unique holding challenges. Food must be protected from dust and other contaminates, so staff members may need to use special coverings for food and beverage products to protect them between production and service. Outdoor food preparation involves other holding problems as well (such as maintaining foods at proper temperatures). It is a good idea to check with state or local authorities for laws governing the outdoor cooking and serving of food before planning such functions.

Delivering Service

Because of all the planning and other preparatory work that goes into every banquet or catered event, you might think that a banquet or catering manager would only need to supervise staff members from a distance during the event itself. In reality, last-minute issues and challenges often occupy the manager throughout an event. Because challenges arise, the manager in charge should either be present at the event or easy to reach, both by staff members and the client. The following are examples of challenges that managers and staff members may face just before or during an event:

- Supply shortages
- Staff members who phone in sick or become ill during the event
- The arrival of an unexpectedly large number of extra guests
- Equipment malfunctions
- Guests who need assistance to operate equipment
- Conflicts between staff members
- Large or dangerous spills
- Injuries, choking, and other medical emergencies
- Angry guests
- Inebriated guests
- Speakers or entertainers who show up late or not at all
- Power outages
- Fire alarms
- Natural disasters

Wise managers have contingency plans in place for the most common challenges.

Kitchen Considerations for Banquets and Catered Events

If a food and beverage operation wants to be in the banquet and catered-event business, it is critical that its kitchen be designed to provide adequate space for serving a banquet or catered event efficiently. Rather than pacing service over a three- or four-hour day part, as is the case with à la carte food and beverage service, banquet and catered-event service takes place in a much more compact time frame. A banquet for 1,000 guests, for example, will require that all 1,000 main courses be plated and served in a 20- to 30-minute period.

In the design of a kitchen, it is preferable to have a dedicated space where banquets and catered events are staged. This space has to contain the right equipment. More often today, combi-ovens are being installed in operations that enjoy a high volume of banquet and catered-event business, since this equipment is so versatile. The combi-oven is capable of low-temperature cooling and holding, drying, grilling, poaching, roasting, steaming, and thawing – all in one piece of equipment. Whenever space is limited in a kitchen, equipment such as a combi-oven provides maximum flexibility.

Another vital piece of equipment is a range with open burners as well as a flat top to place bain-maries. (A bain-marie is a pan containing hot water in which smaller pans may be set to cook food slowly or keep hot foods hot.) The base of the range should be a convection oven (again, because of its versatility).

Refrigeration equipment and countertops are also required in the banquets and catered-events kitchen space. Heated plate-storage units, sinks, warmers, mobile tables, and a full assortment of portioning and serving equipment are necessary in this space as well.

Food Service

If a client wants table service at his or her event, it is usually one of four common types:

- **Plate** or American service—a service style in which fully cooked menu items are individually portioned, plated, and garnished in the kitchen, then transported to each guest.

- **Family-style** or English service—a service style in which servers take food on large platters or in large bowls from the kitchen and deliver it to guest tables; guests at each table then pass the food around their table, serving themselves.

- **Cart** or French service—an elaborate service style in which menu items are prepared on a cart beside guest tables by specially trained staff members.

- **Platter** or Russian service—a service style that requires servers to take platters of fully cooked food to tables, present the food for the guests' approval, then plate the food from the platters at tableside and serve it to the guests.

In the United States, guests at most banquets featuring table service are served using the plate service style. With plate service, a server's main responsibility is to deliver the plated courses to the guests as quickly and efficiently as possible.

Sometimes a client prefers buffet service rather than table service. By attractively arranging a seemingly endless array of food, a food and beverage operation can delight guests who enjoy being able to choose whatever they like in the quantities they prefer. Buffet service also provides staff members with the opportunity to create food displays and showpieces. Ice carvings, vegetable and fruit sculptures, flowers, or other decorations often enhance a buffet's presentation. Buffets may also offer novelty foods chosen to fit the theme of the buffet (e.g., Rocky Mountain oysters for a Western theme).

Sometimes events feature a combination of table service and a buffet—the appetizers are displayed in a buffet during the cocktail hour and the rest of the meal is provided via table service, for example, or servers deliver beverages, bread and butter, and desserts directly to guest tables but the guests help themselves to main-course items from a buffet.

Whether the food is served through table service, a buffet, or a combination of the two, managers in the banquet and catering area must see to it that service personnel follow the operation's rules for serving food properly and graciously. A list of basic service rules for banquets or catered events that feature plate service can be found in Exhibit 10. Service rules vary from operation to operation, but all are founded on the basic principle that guests should be given an enjoyable service experience and inconvenienced as little as possible.

Beverage Service

Managers must carefully plan procedures for providing beverage service to guests at banquets and catered events. Just as lounges and bars must do, banquet and catering operations must observe liquor laws. Age limits and legal hours for beverage service are among the most important beverage laws that affect banquet and catering operations. In some localities, laws may require clients to obtain permits to serve alcoholic beverages to private groups in function rooms during certain hours. If this is the case, banquet/catering managers or salespeople must make this known to clients and tell them how to obtain the special approvals or permits. In addition, managers may need to curtail the service of alcoholic beverages on election days in some states.

The banquet and catering operation is responsible for preventing underage drinking in its function rooms; the operation's managers cannot delegate this responsibility to clients. Because of this, it is wise for a banquet or catering manager to closely monitor beverage service when underage guests attend an event.

Many operations use one or a combination of the following popular beverage plans to provide beverage service at banquets or catered events.

Cash Bar. At a **cash bar,** guests pay cash to the bartender or purchase tickets from a cashier to pay for drinks prepared by the bartender. With a ticket system, the cashier may be issued numbered tickets of various colors, which represent different drink prices. Guests pay the cashier for the drinks they want and are given tickets of the appropriate colors that they can present to the bartender. The banquet/catering manager or salesperson generally specifies the drink prices in the contract; the prices can be the same as or different from normal selling prices. Frequently, managers or salespeople will reduce beverage prices from the normal lounge rates in order to attract group business.

Exhibit 10 General Service Rules for Banquet and Catered-Event Service

1. All servers must carry a napkin or side towel at all times.
2. All food must enter the room on a tray with a cart unless otherwise specified.
3. All liquids (hot or cold) must be on trays with spouts facing inward.
4. When placing plates in front of guests, servers must place them so that the operation's logo is at the top.
5. Used plates, glasses, and flatware must leave on properly stacked trays.
6. Leftover foods must be placed on a tray and set under the cart.
7. Servers should always pick up glasses by the base, flatware by the handle, and plates by the rim.
8. Serve all plated food from the right. Serve anything that is actually passed by the guests from the left.
9. Serve all beverages from the right.
10. Serve the head table first.
11. Serve ladies first.
12. Clear all dishes and glasses from the right.
13. Do not stack dishes or scrape plates in front of guests.
14. Place appetizers on the tables before service begins, unless they are hot items that must be served after the guests are seated.
15. Set salads on tables unless they are served as a separate course.
16. Clear the empty appetizer plates.
17. Serve the main course.
18. Serve coffee and/or wine.
19. Serve more water if needed.
20. Clear entrée plates, bread and butter plates, butter, melba toast, rolls, salt and pepper, and any flatware not needed for dessert.
21. Serve the dessert.
22. Serve more coffee if needed.
23. Clear dessert plates and any empty wine glasses and coffee cups. Remove napkins. If a meeting follows food and beverage service, leave water glasses and partially filled coffee cups on the table.

Host Bar: Charge by the Drink. A **host bar** that charges the host by the drink uses a system to keep track of the number of each type of drink served (through tickets turned over to the bartender by guests, transactions recorded by a point-of-sale system, or marks on a tally sheet). Guests do not pay anything. Managers will frequently reduce the prices of the drinks from the normal charges in order to obtain the host's business.

Host Bar: Charge by the Bottle. This plan involves charging for beverages consumed on the basis of the number of bottles used or opened. The difference

Off-Site Catered Events

Off-site catered events can range from a simple luncheon or breakfast to a cocktail party with heavy hors d'oeuvres to a formal sit-down dinner event. Off-site catered events may take place in a variety of locales, such as at a place of business, a private residence, or a facility that is specifically designed for such events (say a hall in the basement of a church) but does not have catering equipment and other capabilities in-house.

Drop-off catering is an off-site catering option that is popular with guests on a budget. One example of drop-off catering is a catered luncheon at the client's place of business during an all-day staff meeting. A predetermined menu is prepared—including a main course of perhaps sandwiches or a selection of wraps, one or two salads, a vegetarian option, and non-alcoholic beverages. The sandwiches could be pre-made or a make-your-own-sandwich luncheon may be featured. In any case, the caterer simply drops the items off, has the decision-maker sign the bill, and comes back later to retrieve the serving utensils, platters, and dishes. (If these items are disposable, there is no need for the caterer to return after the event.) Using drop-off catering as a way to test the catering market and enter the business is highly effective to assess the level of interest in the local community without having to make a huge investment in permanent catering equipment.

Another off-site catering option is to sell complete meals-to-go on holidays such as Thanksgiving or Easter. All the client needs to do is specify the number of guests to be served and choose a main course (e.g., turkey for Thanksgiving, ham for Easter), side items, bread, and desserts from a list of options. The food and beverage operation does the rest and has the complete meal ready for the client to pick up at a predetermined time during the holiday.

A third off-site catering option is providing food and beverages for a party—a birthday, anniversary, post-game celebration, etc.—that a client wants to throw in his or her home. Foods and beverages can be prepared and simply dropped off by the operation's staff, or selected staff members can remain to serve and clean up after the event. Of course, this extra service costs more for the client, but it may provide exactly the type of worry-free, enjoyable catered event that the client wants.

One of the challenges operations face when providing off-site catered events is to maintain food safety through proper temperature control. In other words, these events add an additional control point—transportation—between holding and serving. The operation has to have the proper holding equipment in order to safely transport the food and beverages ordered so that food safety and quality is maintained. Otherwise, the reputation of the operation and—more importantly—the health of the operation's clients and their guests are at risk.

between the number of bottles of each type of liquor, beer, or wine in the beginning inventory and ending inventory at the function room's portable bar represents the number of bottles used. An agreed-upon price for each bottle opened is assessed to the host (who is, in effect, purchasing the beverages that remain in open bottles but were not consumed by guests).

Host Bar: Charge by the Hour. This pricing plan charges hosts a fixed beverage fee per person per hour. This plan involves estimating the number of drinks guests will consume each hour. While estimates are not easy to make that will apply to all groups (health- or weight-conscious groups will probably consume less than fraternities, for example), a rule of thumb used by some banquet and catering managers is three drinks per person during the first hour, two the second, and one-and-a-half the third. Managers who want to price drinks for special events on a per-person, per-hour basis can use this formula to estimate the number of drinks each person will consume during the event. They must then multiply the number of drinks per person by an established drink charge to arrive at the hourly drink charge per person. As managers use the hourly charge system, they should maintain their own statistics on consumption; these statistics can assist them in more accurately setting hourly charges for future events.

Wine Service. When banquets or catered events involve wine service, service staff may circulate with bottles of several wines (red and white, dry and semi-dry) so that they can offer guests a choice. Of course, these staff members must be trained to serve wine properly. (So that staff members will be knowledgeable about the wines they serve, managers should tell them about the wines during the briefing prior to the event.) Other operations set up a portable bar in a nearby area so that bartenders can prepare glasses of wine (and other drinks) as needed.

Wines that should be chilled before service might be handled in one of the following ways:

- The bottles might be moved to refrigerators in the banquet serving kitchens close to the time of service.

- The bottles might be maintained for small groups using ice in totes or other containers.

- The bottles might be chilled in remote walk-ins and quickly transported to the banquet site when they are needed.

Portable beverage service equipment makes the tasks of providing beverages at banquets and catered events much easier. Most portable equipment is on wheels; it can be stored in remote areas and wheeled to the point of use as needed.

Protocol for Special Banquets and Catered Events

Every banquet or catered event is special to the guests who attend it, and banquet and catering staff members must always be courteous and exercise common sense to make the guests' experiences as enjoyable as possible. However, there are some "special" banquets and catered events in which staff members must also understand **protocol**—the formal rules of etiquette used for ceremonies of state, military functions, and other special events.

While the details of protocol are beyond the scope of this chapter, banquet and catering managers should be aware that there are rules that dictate the proper way to do things when very special guests are served. Managers and service personnel who will come in direct contact with special guests must understand and be able to practice protocol. The following examples illustrate the types of issues that can come up.

Exhibit 11   Protocol for Seating Guests at the Head Table

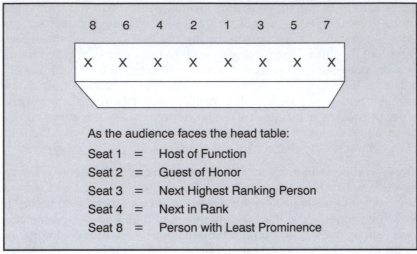

As the audience faces the head table:

Seat 1 = Host of Function

Seat 2 = Guest of Honor

Seat 3 = Next Highest Ranking Person

Seat 4 = Next in Rank

Seat 8 = Person with Least Prominence

At formal events, the seat of honor at the head table is to the right of the host. The second seat of honor is to the left of the host. If another seat of honor is required, it is the second seat on the right of the host. The rest of the seats at the head table should be allocated according to the rank or prominence of the guests. These guests should be assigned seats by alternating from the right to the left of the host out from the center of the head table (see Exhibit 11).

Flag display is also important in protocol. In the United States, for example, at a cocktail party, a standing gathering, or an event with theater seating for which flags must be positioned before the guests arrive, the U.S. flag is placed on the left side of the front of the room, as viewed from the dining area. If a five-place arched flag stand is used, the U.S. flag takes the center (highest) position. Other flags are placed to the left and right of the U.S. flag in order of importance: the second most important flag is placed in the hole immediately to the left of the U.S. flag, from the audience's perspective; the third most important flag goes immediately to the right of the U.S. flag; and the next most important flag goes in the hole furthest to the left, leaving the hole furthest to the right for the least important flag.

When flags are used behind a podium, the national colors are placed on the physical right of the speaker as he or she addresses the audience. When displayed behind the speaker's platform without a pole, the flag must be flat against its display surface and must have its longest dimension parallel to the floor, directly behind and slightly above the podium.

Staff members should never use the flag of any country as a table cover, drape, rosette, or any other type of decoration. To decorate with bunting that has the national colors of the United States (red, white, and blue), staff members should place the color blue uppermost, then white, and finally red as the lowest of the three colors.

Exhibit 12   Checklist for Post-Event Duties

Banquet/Catered Event

- ☐ Clear all tables of china, glass, and flatware.
- ☐ Remove all linens.
- ☐ Straighten legs on all tables.
- ☐ Rearrange all chairs around tables neatly.
- ☐ Store salt and pepper shakers, sugar bowls, water pitchers, and other tabletop items.
- ☐ Clear all remaining carts and lock them.
- ☐ Remove candles and any melted wax from candelabras and return to storage.
- ☐ Check out with supervisor on duty.

Banquet/Catered Event Supervisor

- ☐ Supervise the banquet/catered event service staff.
- ☐ Turn off public address system.
- ☐ Collect microphones and cords and return to proper storage area(s).
- ☐ Collect projectors and other audiovisual equipment and return to storage.
- ☐ Search area for valuable items left behind.
- ☐ Check cloakroom and restroom areas.
- ☐ Secure any items found and turn them in to the Lost and Found the following day.
- ☐ Inspect for fire hazards.
- ☐ Turn off lights.
- ☐ Lock all doors. (If a band is moving out, remain until the move is completed).
- ☐ Leave written information regarding any maintenance problems or items helpful to the supervisor who will open the room the next day.
- ☐ Leave written information on the manager's desk regarding any guest complaints or serious problems among staff members.
- ☐ Lock, secure, and turn off lights and air conditioning units in all other function rooms.

After Service

After the completion of food and beverage service at an event, the manager in charge must perform several after-service tasks. One such task is supervising staff members to ensure that they complete their clean-up and breakdown duties properly. Exhibit 12 is a checklist for many of these required tasks. Staff members must clean up the function room(s) and break down temporary structures (such as a dance floor or stage). Managers must evaluate how well the operation handled the banquet or catered event. The experience gained from each event can help with the planning of other events.

During the cleanup and breakdown of the function room(s), control efforts must occur to ensure that both the client and the operation attain the goals established for the event. Guest comments must also be sought to provide guest input into continuous quality improvement.

Controls

Managers must establish systems of control for the food and beverages served in banquets and catered events.

Food Controls. Payments may or may not be collected from clients at the time of the banquet or catered event; the contract for each event specifies the payment terms that the operation and the client agreed upon. However, when the banquet actually occurs, the operation must count the number of guests served to determine if payment is due for guests served in excess of the original estimate.

How do managers determine how many guests were served? If a buffet is planned in which no one can go back for seconds and therefore guests only use one plate, managers can take a plate count. The number of plates on the buffet line at the beginning of service plus any plates that were put on the line during service minus the number of plates on the buffet line at the end of service equals the number of guests served.

At buffets where guests go through the line more than once or at table service events, the manager must personally count the number of guests served. Typically, the manager takes a count that he or she confirms through separate counts taken by other supervisors in charge of specific function room areas or through counts of meals served by individual food servers. Another way to take a count is to count the number of empty seats and subtract that number from the total number of chairs set up; this gives the manager the number of guests served. In some operations, the guests receive tickets from their host that they turn in either as they enter the function room or after they are seated.

At stand-up receptions, a representative of the operation might be stationed at the entrance of the reception area to count guests as they arrive. To avoid recounting guests who leave and return, a ticket system could be used; the count of guests served would then be based on the number of tickets turned in.

At coffee breaks and similar functions, the price charged to the client usually is based on the volume of products used to set up the event, such as gallons of coffee or dozens of pastries. If, however, a coffee break's price is determined by the number of people served, a manager should count the number of guests seated in the meeting immediately before the start of coffee service.

The responsibility for determining the number of guests served, no matter what type of service or counting method is used, rests with the manager in charge of the event. Having more than one count performed is a good way to ensure accuracy. It is often a good idea to involve the client in the process of counting guests or supplies, too. Managers try to avoid disagreements over counts, and when the client monitors or is otherwise involved in determining the count, he or she is less likely to dispute it later.

Exhibit 13   Portable Bar Setup Sheet

Function Order Number ___1007-F___   Number of People ___25___

Name ___Anne Helmstead___   Date 5/2/XX

Room ___Blue___   Time 5:00-6:00 P.M.

Number of Bottles or Drinks

Name of Item	Size	Setup	Add'l.	Add'l.	Add'l.	Total	Full	Empty	Partial	Net Use
								Returns		
House Scotch	liter	5	3	1	1	10	1	8	.5	8.5
House Bourbon	liter	3	1			4	1	3	0	3.0
Call Scotch	liter									
Call Gin	liter									
Vodka	liter									

Beverage Controls. Revenue control for beverages is just as important in managing cash bars at banquets and catered events as it is in managing dining and lounge areas. In some respects, however, managers can simplify the control procedures, since fewer kinds of alcoholic beverages are generally available at banquets and catered events. For example, if only two types of vodka (house and premium) are available, management can easily reconcile the amount of alcohol sold with the amount of income collected.

The amount of alcoholic beverages issued to a portable bar (both initially and during service) can be recorded on a form similar to the one in Exhibit 13. (Managers should remember to count partial bottles as whole bottles in the "Net Use" column on the far right if the payment plan is "charge by the bottle.") By conducting a beginning and an ending inventory, the amount of each product actually used can be determined. In a by-the-drink payment plan, the amount of income that the servers should have generated from a particular product can be determined by converting the figure in the farthest right column of Exhibit 13—"Net Use"—into standard portion sizes and then converting that into the number of drinks sold (Exhibit 14 illustrates this process). The form works reasonably well when the same price for all drinks of one type (house or call) is charged. However, if different prices are charged for drinks that are of the same type but that have different

Exhibit 14   Sample Calculation of Potential Income

For Scotch:

8.5 liter bottles (Net amount used)	×	33.8 oz. per liter (Ounces/Bottle)	=	287.3 (Total oz. used)
287 (rounded) (Total ounces used)	÷	1.5 oz (Average portion size)	=	191.33 (number of drinks sold)
191 (rounded) (number of drinks sold)	×	$4.00 (Average sales price)	=	$764.00 (Potential income)

Typically, bartenders pour (measure) liquor on the basis of ounces; however, they purchase liquor bottles in metric units. Managers can calculate potential income from sales of a particular beverage as follows:

1. Calculate the number of ounces actually used. (In Exhibit 13, you will note that 8.5 one-liter bottles of scotch were used at the banquet. Since each liter contains 33.8 ounces, approximately 287 ounces of scotch were actually used.)

2. Determine the approximate number of drinks sold. (Divide the total ounces used by the portion size: 287 oz. ÷ 1.5 oz = approximately 191 drinks sold.)

3. Estimate the potential income. (Multiply the number of drinks sold by the selling price: 191 drinks × $4.00 selling price = $764).

amounts of spirits (e.g., a double), the average number of ounces of liquor per drink must first be calculated. The calculation must also be adjusted when different drinks have different amounts of the same ingredient. For example, a martini that contains two ounces of house gin might be sold for $5, while a gin and tonic that contains one-and-a-half ounces of house gin might be sold for $4.

You can see the difficulty in assessing standard income per bottle that arises in complex cases. Many managers resolve the problem by tracking drink sales, ounces used, and income generated in order to arrive at average rates that they can easily include in the calculation in Exhibit 14. The same process is used to reconcile the amount of beverage sold with the income generated by all other types of beverages listed on the setup sheet in Exhibit 13.

Guest Comments

After major functions, the client usually meets with the operation's managers to give feedback and settle accounts as much as possible. After small functions, the review process may be more modest: the manager in charge may give the client an evaluation sheet and ask him or her to fill it out and return it. A telephone call to the client a day or two after the event provides the manager with an opportunity to thank the client and ask for additional feedback. This reinforces for the client the operation's commitment to guest service. It also helps communicate to clients that their future business is desired. Online surveys are also helpful, especially if clients provide detailed comments.

Using Feedback in Planning

Planning is a critical activity for banquets and catered events, and feedback about past events can help managers plan future events. Regardless of whether an operation holds a review meeting with the client after an event, managers should hold such a meeting with all staff members who were involved in providing service during the event. These meetings are particularly helpful when mistakes that guests noticed occurred. Such mistakes may happen again if managers do not take the time to review them and discuss possible solutions. Managers and staff should relay to each other any comments from guests or the client. This exchange should lead to action plans to correct problems that were mentioned most often by guests. Continuous quality improvement is the key to the development of a profitable and guest-pleasing banquet and catering operation.

 ## Key Terms

banquet and catering operation—An operation that sells and plans food and beverage functions for meetings and special events. As a hotel department, a department within the food and beverage division that arranges and plans food and beverage functions for (a) conventions and smaller functions, and (b) local events booked by the sales department.

breakout rooms—Small meeting rooms used when large group sessions divide into smaller ones for discussion and group work.

buffet—A typically large assortment of foods attractively arranged for self-service by guests.

cart service—A table-service style in which specially trained staff members prepare menu items beside the guests' tables using a cart; the food is prepared and plated on the cart, then served to the guests. Also called French service.

cash bar—A beverage setup for a banquet or some other special event in which each guest pays for each drink as it is ordered. Also known as a C.O.D. bar or an à la carte bar.

contract—A document listing the services, space requirements, and products that the food and beverage operation promises to provide the client and the client promises to pay for at an agreed-upon price; it becomes binding when it is signed by both parties. Sometimes called a letter of agreement.

cutoff date—The designated date when the client must either book or release the function room(s) being tentatively held for him or her.

familiarization ("fam") tour—A reduced-rate or complimentary trip or tour, designed to acquaint potential clients with the food and beverage operation's products and services.

family-style service—A table-service style in which servers take food on large platters or in large bowls from the kitchen and deliver it to guest tables; the guests at each table then pass the food around their table, serving themselves. Also called English service.

function book—The master control of all function space, broken down by function room and time of day.

function room reservation form—A form a salesperson submits to the function book coordinator to reserve or determine the availability of a certain function room for a certain event at a certain time. These forms are used at properties with manual booking systems.

function sheet—A document that includes all of the details about a function's requirements. Also called a banquet event order (BEO).

guarantee—Prior to an event, the figure the client gives the food and beverage operation for the number of persons to be served. Payment is made on the basis of the guaranteed number or the total number actually served, whichever is greater.

host bar—A function-room bar setup where drinks are prepaid by the host. The price, agreed upon ahead of time, may be determined by the drink, by the bottle, or by the hour.

plate service—A table-service style in which fully cooked menu items are individually produced, portioned, plated, and garnished in the kitchen, then carried to each guest directly. Also called American service.

platter service—A table-service style in which servers carry platters of fully cooked food to the dining room and present them to guests for approval. Servers then set hot plates in front of each guest and place food from the platters onto the plates. Also called Russian service.

presentation book—A book of pictures, diagrams, menus, and other promotional materials that salespeople use to sell their operation's products and services to clients. Many operations now make their presentation books available online or have created enhanced electronic versions for the Internet.

protocol—Sets of formal guidelines or rules for the conduct of business, dining, and entertaining.

sales blitz—A concentrated campaign of personal sales calls to prospects in a selected geographic area.

synchronized service—A type of service in which servers enter the function room through one set of doors to serve each course; they serve all of the tables in unison, using precise movements.

 Review Questions —————————————————————————————

1. What should catering salespeople know about associations and corporate groups to effectively sell banquets and catered events to them?

2. What are the major records, documents, and forms used to book and plan banquets and catered events, and how is each used?

3. Which types of table service are commonly used in banquets and catered events?

4. What factors should banquet and catering managers keep in mind when developing standard menus?

5. What positions are typically found in a large banquet and catering operation?

6. What kinds of skills and knowledge do service personnel need to provide service during banquets and catered events?

7. What are some common beverage service payment options for banquets and catered events, and how do they work?

8. How do banquet and catering managers obtain and use feedback to improve operations?

Case Studies

The Typographical Error

Jessica Alexander smiles as she walks out of the Hotel Granada's catering office. "This is going to be a great banquet," she muses.

Jessica has just finished meeting with Whitney Casir, the catering manager of the hotel. Jessica is the social chair for the Senior League, a women's volunteer organization that takes on various community projects. She has just completed arrangements for the group's annual recognition banquet. This is the second year she has been in charge of arrangements and she was so pleased with the results of the evening last year that she made it a point to return to the Hotel Granada. "The 400 women who will be attending will surely like what we're doing this year," she thinks.

Whitney Casir prepares the banquet event order (BEO) based on her conversation with Jessica. An undiscovered error creeps into the BEO. Instead of inserting 400 on the number-of-guests line, the number 300 is inserted.

Inexplicably, this typographical error is not noticed by anyone right up to the start of the opening reception. Jessica didn't pay any attention to the confirmation she received, "because the hotel did such a good job last year." All the purchasing, flower centerpiece counts, linen supply, and related items were based on the incorrect count of 300.

When Jessica enters the Ballroom 30 minutes before the doors open, she thinks, "This looks small." So she takes a count. There is a head table for ten, and 31 rounds with ten seats at each table for a total of 320. (The hotel has an over-set policy of setting 5 percent more than the guarantee to provide for last-minute emergencies.)

Jessica spots Whitney across the room. "Whitney! Whitney!" she nearly screams. "Why are there only 320 seats? We have 400 women in the foyer." Whitney checks the BEO and it says 300. "What are we going to do? What are we going to do, Whitney?" Jessica asks, near tears.

Whitney realizes she has to move quickly. She needs to check with housekeeping and the kitchen right away.

Discussion Question

1. If you were Whitney Casir, what would you do?

This case was taken from William P. Fisher and Robert A. Ashley, *Case Studies in Commercial Food Service Operations* (Lansing, Mich.: American Hotel & Lodging Educational Institute, 2003).

What Do We Do with the Leftovers?

Darlene Alden is gritting her teeth and shaking her head. Darlene is the catering manager for the Chanticleer Hotel. Due to an abrupt cancellation of the guest speaker, only 250 people have arrived for a 500-seat banquet. The guarantee was for 500, and all the purchasing, thawing, and preparation has been done in the kitchen in anticipation of serving 500 people.

Darlene knows that the hotel is protected financially, given the guarantee in the contract, although she expects that Norm Raffleson, the group's contact, will want to discuss the matter. However, she is not going to think about that now.

She's thinking of all the food that is left unconsumed, cannot be refrozen, etc.

"It would be a terrible waste to throw out perfectly good food," she comments to herself. "What do we do with the leftovers?" After a moment's thought, she decides that she has several options.

Discussion Questions

1. What are Darlene's options?
2. Which option would you choose?

This case was taken from William P. Fisher and Robert A. Ashley, *Case Studies in Commercial Food Service Operations* (Lansing, Mich.: American Hotel & Lodging Educational Institute, 2003).

Who Scheduled Those Banquets?

The Highlander Hotel has a problem. Five days from today there are three banquets scheduled that have remarkably similar menus. The 1,000-room hotel will also be at 100-percent occupancy due to a convention that is in town. The hotel's main kitchen will be able to handle the normal traffic in the property's three dining establishments, but will not be able to assist the banquet kitchen. The three banquets consist of the following groups:

1. A 1,000-seat dinner for the Horatio Alger award honoree.

2. A high school senior prom that will have 400 young men and women, age 17 to 18, dressed in their finest.

3. A World War II aviator's reunion, which guaranteed 300 people. Several special menu requests were noted for this group (low sodium, vegetarian dishes, etc.).

The banquet event order (BEO) for each of these groups displays the following:

- Horatio Alger—fruit compote, Caesar salad, beef tenderloin (4 oz.) and fillet of salmon (3 oz.), twice-baked potato, snow peas, and crème d'menthe parfait.

- High School Seniors—filet of sole with lemon sauce (appetizer), garden salad, roast prime rib of beef (8 oz.), au gratin potatoes, green beans and slivered almonds, and raspberry sherbert.

- Aviators—Shrimp cocktail, Caesar salad, veal chop (bone in), mashed potatoes, garden peas, and strawberry mousse.

- Each group has the usual assortment of rolls, beverages, etc.

These banquet events were booked after one catering manager left and before a new one arrived. Kathy Daniels is the new catering manager, and now realizes what the hotel is facing. She places a call to Pierre DuBois, the banquet chef, and asks to meet with him immediately. She tells him she is concerned with the large volume of meals that must be plated within an hour's time and wonders how Pierre is going to schedule production. The banquet kitchen has:

- Six convection ovens
- Two ranges
- Three broilers
- Three steam-jacketed kettles
- Several preparation tables
- Adequate freezer, refrigerator, and dry goods storage spaces
- Several heat lamps
- Adequate small equipment (pots, pans, scoops, etc.)

Discussion Question

1. If you are Pierre DuBois, how do you organize and schedule the food production for the four banquets that will occur five days from now?

This case was taken from William P. Fisher and Robert A. Ashley, *Case Studies in Commercial Food Service Operations* (Lansing, Mich.: American Hotel & Lodging Educational Institute, 2003).

Banquet Gone Bad

It was a beautiful Saturday morning at the club. In his office, Foster Neuman moved reluctantly from the window, sat down at his desk, and pulled out the banquet event orders (BEOs) for the weekend. His meeting with the general manager, Susan Truscott, was in ten minutes and he wanted to make sure he was familiar with all the details of the weekend's events.

Foster had been hired as banquet manager for the High Hills University Club two weeks earlier. He spent his first week reading the employee manual and reviewing club policies. The second week had been spent meeting staff members and learning where things were kept in the club. This weekend, Susan was going to work with him on each banquet, training him in the club's policies and procedures for banquets.

Just as Foster finished scanning the first BEO, his phone rang. "University Club, Foster Neuman speaking. How can I help you?"

"Hello, Foster, this is Susan."

"Susan, hello! Where are you? I can barely hear you through all the background noise."

"I'm at the airport. My father is in the hospital, and I'm taking the next flight to London so I can be with him. You'll have to take care of the banquets this weekend by yourself. But don't worry, it shouldn't be too bad. It's just a baby shower this afternoon, the Woodstone wedding this evening, and a poker tournament tomorrow afternoon. The wedding is a big one, but Mrs. Woodstone is a long-time member of the club and is very supportive of the staff."

"No problem, Susan, don't worry about a thing. I'll have everything under control. I hope everything goes well with your father. We'll be thinking about you."

"Great, Foster, I knew I could count on you. If you need anything, you have a very talented staff to help you. Good luck," Susan said as she hung up.

Foster smiled as he replaced the receiver. He'd left his previous position because there were few challenges; this weekend was just the sort of opportunity he needed to prove his talent. He picked up the BEO for the wedding and had just begun studying it when his phone rang again. "University Club, Foster Neuman speaking. How can I help you?"

"Good morning, Mr. Neuman, this is Mrs. Woodstone. Cindy at the switchboard said I should talk to you about the wedding tonight."

"Yes, ma'am, I'm the new banquet manager. Ms. Truscott was called out of town at the last minute. What can I do for you?"

"I'm afraid that, with all of the wedding preparations, my daughter's been a little absent-minded. She forgot to give me 28 names of people who told her they'd be coming to the reception tonight."

Foster scanned the BEO quickly. Two days ago, Mrs. Woodstone had guaranteed the reception for 300 people. Cornish hens were being served, and Foster was fairly certain that exact orders had been placed for the meal. At any rate, there wouldn't be enough for a 10 percent increase. Valetta, a long-time, experienced banquet captain, walked into Foster's office and smiled at him as she moved past his desk and pulled one of the banquet order binders off his bookshelf.

"I'm sorry, Mrs. Woodstone," Foster said, "but it says here that on Thursday you confirmed the reception at 300 guests, and the club requires a 48-hour notice for changing the guest count and other major items on an event order." Valetta looked at Foster in surprise. "We have that rule because it gives the club the best chance to prepare properly and give members what they want and expect."

"What I want, Mr. Neuman," Mrs. Woodstone replied icily, "is for my daughter's reception to be perfect. That means that we're not going to call her friends and tell them they can't come. I know my club is capable of serving an extra 28 people. Surely it's not a big deal to add them now. You have all day to prepare."

"I'm sorry, but rules are rules," Foster said. Valetta began waving frantically at him to get his attention. "Could you hold for just a moment, Mrs. Woodstone?" Foster asked as he hit the hold button. "What is it, Valetta?"

"Mr. Neuman, you can't say 'no' to Mrs. Woodstone!" She glanced at her watch. "It's only a little after eight. Tell her we'll find a way to fit in the extra people. Just make sure you tell the chef about it."

Foster looked at Valetta narrowly. He didn't like having a banquet captain telling him how to do his job, but he supposed she knew the members better than he did. "Thank you, Valetta, I'll tell her. Now, do you need anything else?" Valetta shook her head. "Then please leave so I can finish this phone conversation uninterrupted."

Valetta frowned and left his office. Foster punched the hold button again. "Mrs. Woodstone, thank you for waiting. I've just spoken with my staff and told them that we must do our best to accommodate you. Is there anything else we can do for you?"

Foster and Mrs. Woodstone reviewed the remaining details of the banquet. When they hung up, Foster basked in Mrs. Woodstone's profuse gratitude. He then began putting together a diagram for the evening's setup. Foster had noticed that very few BEOs had seating diagrams with them; that was one thing he planned on changing as the new banquet manager. He quickly sketched out where all the tables would go to fit 328 people in the ballroom.

He then went in search of Valetta. He found her pulling deep-purple table skirting and tablecloths from storage. "Hello, Valetta. What an awful color!"

Valetta gave him a half-smile. "It's the wedding's color. Unusual for summer, but if the bride wants it, it's what we'll do."

"No accounting for taste," Foster said. "I've diagramed how the tables need to be set up tonight. Please pass this along to your setup staff."

"Yes, sir," Valetta replied. "Have you spoken with Chef Cohen about the additional guests yet?"

"No, but I will. I'll be in my office later if you need me." Foster went to the kitchen and poked his head in the door. He didn't see Chef Cohen, and decided he could return later to talk to him. In the meantime, he was going to go meet a friend for lunch downtown.

Several hours later, Foster returned to the club and went to the ballroom to see how the setup was progressing. He glanced at the tables, frowned, and reached into his shirt pocket and pulled out a copy of the diagram he had sketched earlier. He was dismayed to see that the table setup didn't match his diagram. He spotted Valetta at the far end of the ballroom and hurried over for an explanation.

"What's the meaning of this?" Foster demanded, indicating the tables with a sweep of his hand.

"I beg your pardon?" Valetta responded. "We're setting up for tonight's wedding."

"You're not following the diagram I gave you. Why not?"

"Oh, that," Valetta shook her head. "You weren't around when I looked for you to talk about it. If we set it up your way, it would be too cramped. What we have to do in this room is—"

"Are you the banquet manager?" Foster interrupted. "It's not your job to decide how to set these tables up. I know what I'm doing. Tear down these tables and set them up according to the diagram I gave you." Foster briefly wondered if Valetta was trying to sabotage him, make him look bad just because he was the new guy. Maybe she'd applied for his job and hadn't gotten it. He made up his mind to lay down the law with her from now on, so she wouldn't get him into trouble.

Valetta had been standing with pursed lips, but now she spoke up again: "I've helped set up banquets at this club for 15 years. I know what this room is capable of. Your way doesn't work."

"Listen, you do it my way, or you're fired."

"Oh yeah? Well, let me save you the trouble," she retorted. "I quit! And when Ms. Truscott gets back, I'll tell her exactly how you've behaved."

"Oh, going to run and tattle to Mommy like a five-year-old?" Foster said, his voice rising angrily. "This isn't kindergarten anymore, lady. We have a job to do, and if you're not going to do it right, we don't need you here."

Valetta's face flushed with anger. She jerked her apron and name tag off, flung them toward a table, and stalked out without another word.

Oblivious to the growing number of banquet staff members who had stopped working and gathered around to listen to his tirade, Foster shouted at Valetta's back: "And don't bother coming back! And you!" he barked at a nearby staff member. "Follow little miss 'I'm-too-good-to-do-as-I'm-told' and make sure she doesn't steal anything on her way out!"

The staff member stared at him incredulously for a moment, then ran for the door. Foster was too angry to hear her call out, "Mom, wait!" He had already turned to the remaining staff members, all of whom were staring at him, uncertain what to do. "Who's worked here the longest?" Foster asked.

Pierre stepped forward. "I haven't been here as long as Valetta, but I've been here over ten years."

"Well, hopefully you're not as rigid as her, either. Here's the way these tables are supposed to be set up." Foster shoved his diagram into Pierre's hands. "Take care of it and do it right. This banquet's too important to screw up." With that, Foster stormed out of the ballroom. On the way back to his office, he remembered that he still hadn't gotten in touch with Chef Cohen about the extra wedding guests. Oh well, he thought, wedding counts never match the guarantee anyway. It won't be a problem.

By the time the wedding guests began to arrive, Foster had calmed down and was again looking forward to the banquet. He walked down to the club's lobby when he saw the limousines pull up with the bridal party. He stood at the top of the stairs as the door attendant opened the door for the guests. Foster quickly spotted Mrs. Woodstone (he had looked up her photo in the club's files so that he'd know what she looked like). He approached her with a smile and introduced himself to her and her husband. He then escorted them to the ballroom and pointed out the head table.

Mrs. Woodstone told him she was thrilled with the decorations and especially appreciated him making the arrangements for their extra guests. "The next time I see her, I'll be sure to tell Susan what a wonderful job you're doing," she said as she left him to join the receiving line.

Foster smiled and headed for the kitchen. He complimented one of the banquet servers on the plate presentation as she passed by, then joined the service line in the kitchen, where the chef and other staff members were frantically plating orders. Foster had only been helping for a few minutes when one of the servers rushed over to him. "Mr. Neuman, we have a problem. The tables are so crammed together we can't get between them to serve the drinks. And the groom is complaining because his aunt's wheelchair can't make it to her table. Could you come talk to them?"

Foster hurried out to reassure the groom and help find a place for his aunt. In the meantime, another server came into the kitchen looking for Foster. Not finding him, she hurried over to Chef Cohen. "Chef, there aren't enough tables for the guests. There are a bunch of people without seats."

Chef Cohen, bent over the serving line, put a hand to his back and straightened up slowly. His face turned red and there was an angry look in his eye. Those who recognized the warning signs of his notorious temper quickly found somewhere else in the kitchen that they desperately needed to be. "That fool of a banquet manager!" the chef snorted. "He doesn't have a clue about what he's doing! I'll have to take care of it myself or it'll never get done right. You!" Cohen pointed at a cowering server. "Go get me a head count of how many people don't have seats. Linda!" He turned to another server. "You have half a brain—take Phil and Tom and go set up another table on the dance floor. We may need more than one, but get started now and we'll let you know if we need more. I'll send Sonya out with some additional place settings in a few minutes."

The staff members scurried to do the chef's bidding. Chef Cohen turned to his assistant and shook his head. "For Foster's sake, I hope he just forgot a table and there aren't that many extra guests. Because if there are, they'll have to go hungry. I only made 12 extra servings."

Meanwhile, Mrs. Woodstone joined Foster and the groom, who were having a tense conversation in the corner. The groom was telling Foster exactly what he thought about the table setup, and Foster was working to keep the defensive edge out of his voice. Foster turned to Mrs. Woodstone with a smile, hoping she had come over to defend him and take her new son-in-law back to the wedding festivities. His smile faded as he saw the anger in her eyes. "Mr. Foster, what's the meaning of *that!*" She pointed a trembling finger toward the dance floor, where three aproned staff members had set up a table and were putting a bright yellow tablecloth on it.

"Um, I'll be happy to find out for you," he stammered.

"Well, let me inform you of what your staff members have told me. They said that there weren't enough seats for everyone, so they're having to set up extra tables. And those atrocious yellow tablecloths are the only clean linen you have available! My husband is telling *everyone*—" Mrs. Woodstone paused to catch her breath, her voice heaving with emotion—"that my daughter's wedding reception"—another gasp for breath—"is starting to look like an L.A. Laker's awards banquet!" She closed her eyes at the horror of it all, then managed to collect herself. "I called you this morning and told you we would have extra people. We even had six no-shows and you *still* seem utterly incapable of responding appropriately to the simplest requests. I hope you have a good explanation for this!"

Discussion Questions

1. What did Foster do wrong?

2. What should Foster do now?

3. How did Susan's actions contribute to the failure of the event? What should she do now to make things right?

The following industry experts helped generate and develop this case: David Brown, CCM, General Manager, The Heritage Club, Mason, Ohio; and Sara J. Shaughnessy, Clubhouse Manager, Somerset Country Club, Mendota Heights, Minnesota.

Banquet Ballyhoo at the Brunswick

The annual member's meeting and banquet at the Brunswick Club was only three days away, and dining room manager Alex King was a little worried. He had just hired five new servers, but he wasn't completely convinced they could handle the job. The selection process had been dismal: the applicants with experience didn't want to work for the hourly wage the club was offering, and the five applicants who would accept $7 an hour had less-than-stellar work histories. But he had been forced to hire all five of these latter applicants, despite his misgivings. One had been fired from a previous job, one had only quick-service restaurant experience, and another seemed to move from job to job. Still, warm bodies were better than no bodies at all, he figured.

Alex was swamped with the final preparations for the banquet and was counting on his experienced servers to give the new staff members enough of an orientation to get them through this first big affair. Then he could take the time to train them thoroughly. For now, he planned to quickly review the employee manual with the new servers, go over some basic club procedures, and have them shadow the veteran servers during the lunch and dinner shifts between now and the banquet. It was only two days. Alex crossed his fingers and hoped for the best.

On Saturday evening, the dining room gleamed with crystal and candlelight. Alex strode through the room, straightening a centerpiece here, pushing in a chair there. At the back of the dining room he found the club's senior servers—Charlotte, Margie, and Alfred—giving the five new servers some final instructions. Wait, there were only four new servers.

"Where's Tammy?" asked Alex. He turned as the young woman rushed in, hair billowing around her shoulders. As she brushed her hair out of her face, her bright red fingernails caught Alex's eye. When he explained that her hair would need to be pulled back and that bold nail polish was *not* part of the server's uniform, she said sullenly, "No one told me." "Well, you've been told now," he replied. Alex hoped this incident wouldn't set the tone for the evening.

For a while, things seemed to progress without a hitch. Then Alex spotted Miranda, another new server, pop a canapé into her mouth as she mingled among the club members with her tray. I hope nobody else saw that, he thought, scanning the faces of nearby members. Then he saw Phil, the bartender, apologizing as he handed over a drink to Mr. Finley, who was obviously perturbed. Alex hurried over to see if he could help.

Phil explained that Mr. Finley was the fourth member who had complained about a botched drink order. "Didn't anyone tell these new kids how to place drink orders?" Phil asked. "Mr. Finley only drinks Dewar's scotch, but I didn't know it was his order and made the drink with our house scotch. If I'd known we had so many new servers, I would've given them a crash course in member service and bar procedures. They sure need it."

Kevin, another of the new servers, approached the bar. Phil pointed him out as the server who had messed up the drink orders. When Alex asked Kevin why he didn't specify the brand of liquor the member had requested, Kevin looked amazed. "Scotch is scotch, right?" he shrugged. Phil groaned and rolled his eyes.

Alex turned from the bar just in time to see a disaster—Tammy and Miranda colliding with full trays of salad. After a stunned silence, the young women began giggling as they grabbed for the scattered plates. Two busboys came over to help them get the mess cleaned up. Charlotte and Margie had witnessed the disaster and, veterans that they were, had hurried back to the kitchen to get more salads so that the club members seated at Tammy and Miranda's tables wouldn't go hungry.

The beleaguered dining room manager continued to "put out fires" throughout the evening. He brought the board president and his wife a new bottle of merlot when they pointed out to him that their server, Kelsey, had brought their first bottle in an ice bucket. "When we asked about the wine, she told us there was red and white—and she called me 'sweetie,'" the president harrumphed. At the muffled sounds of arguing from the kitchen, Alex excused himself from the president's table and entered the kitchen, where he found the chef shouting at Alfred.

"What's the problem here?" asked Alex, surprised that two veteran staff members would be arguing where members might hear them.

The chef was upset because entrées hadn't been picked up and delivered to tables. Alfred was upset because he was working as fast as he could—serving his tables *and* Kevin's tables.

"Where's Kevin?" asked Alex. His question was answered by a furious Charlotte, who explained that she was scrambling to cover for two other new servers—Kelsey and Dakota. "They're all outside having a cigarette break!" she fumed. "It's not fair—we're having to do all the work. Don't they know what kind of service we give at the Brunswick Club?"

"Well, they've been shadowing you for the past two days. Didn't you tell them that our members expect superb service?" Alex retorted. "Don't they know better than to take a break now?"

"That's right, blame me!" Charlotte exclaimed. "I've tried to teach those kids, but I can't make a silk purse out of a sow's ear, not in two days. That Dakota thinks every meal ought to come with fries and a prize, and the rest of them aren't much better. It's not my job to turn burger-flippers into club servers. Come to think of it, it's *your* job!"

Alex knew she was right. As he headed outside to haul in the smoking servers, he caught sight of the general manager headed his way. He knew the look on her face. Looks like I'd better make some time in my schedule for a meeting tomorrow. A long meeting, he thought ruefully.

Discussion Questions

1. What did the new servers do wrong at the members' banquet?

2. What five training topics should Alex have covered with the new servers in the two days before the banquet?

3. What should Alex acknowledge as his mistakes when he meets with the general manager?

4. What steps should Alex take after the meeting?

The following industry experts helped generate and develop this case: David Brown, CCM, General Manager, The Heritage Club, Mason, Ohio; and Sara J. Shaughnessy, Clubhouse Manager, Somerset Country Club, Mendota Heights, Minnesota.

 References

Abbey, James R. *Hospitality Sales and Marketing,* Fifth Edition. Lansing, Mich.: American Hotel & Lodging Educational Institute, 2008.

Astroff, Milton T., and James R. Abbey. *Convention Management and Service,* Eighth Edition. Lansing, Mich.: American Hotel & Lodging Educational Institute; and Cranbury, N.J.: Waterbury Press, 2011.

Attias, Michael. "B2B: Building a Banquet Business with Business and Organizations." *Restaurant Startup & Growth.* April 2007: 21–27.

———. "Profit Through Catering." *Restaurant Hospitality.* October 1, 2008. 92(10): 33.

"Banqueting Basics." *Hospitality Ireland.* September 2007. Issue 40: 54–55.

Bensky, Gary. "Banquet Catering a Boon to Business, But Setup Is Key." *Nation's Restaurant News.* February 16, 2004. 38(7): 18.

Friedland, Ann. "45 Tips for Better Buffet Service." *Food Management*. March 2004. 39(3): 48–56.

Luebke, Patricia. "Why Many Independents Are Focusing on Catering and How to Do More In Your Restaurant. *Restaurant Startup & Growth*. November 2008. 5(11): 10.

Pavesic, Dave. "Don't Get Eaten Alive at the Buffet." *Restaurant Startup & Growth*. March 2007: 38–47.

Internet Sites

For more information, visit the following Internet sites. Remember that Internet addresses can change without notice. If the site is no longer there, you can use a search engine to look for additional sites.

CATERWARE Inc.
www.caterware.com

Convene
www.pcma.org/convene.htm

CuisineNet
www.cuisinenet.com

Food Network
www.foodnetwork.com

GoLeads
www.goleads.com

Hilton
www.hilton.com

Hyatt
www.hyatt.com

The Food Channel
www.foodchannel.com

Marriott
www.marriott.com

Meeting Professionals International
www.mpiweb.org

M&C Online
www.meetings-conventions.com

Newmarket International
www.newmarketinc.com

Professional Convention Management Association
www.pcma.org

Sheraton Hotels
www.sheraton.com

Successful Meetings
www.successfulmeetings.com

Westin Hotels & Resorts
www.westin.com

wine.com
www.wine.com

zapdata
www.zapdata.com

Appendix A

Potential Banquet and Catering Markets

Markets/Submarkets	Lead Source	Possible Functions
Hospitals		
Auxiliary	Public Relations or Administrative Office	Luncheon fashion shows, evening fund-raisers, art auctions, etc.
Medical Staff	Medical Staff Secretary	Quarterly or annual dinners/dances, graduation dinners (interns)
Volunteer Functions	Director of Volunteers	Lunches
Staff Recreation Club	Personnel Office	Holiday parties, seasonal parties, dinners/dances
Staff Awards Dinner	Personnel Office	Usually midweek dinners
Credit Union	President of Credit Union	Annual dinner/dance or meeting
Colleges & Universities		
Alumni	Alumni Office, University Affairs Office, or individual schools	Recruiting parties, annual dinner/dance, class reunions, fund-raisers, alumni functions related to athletic events
Sororities and Fraternities	Panhellenic or Inter-Fraternity Council or social chairperson of each sorority or fraternity University Affairs Office	Founders day luncheons, formal installations, dinner/dances
Ceremonial Events	University Affairs Office	Groundbreaking, dedication events
Athletics	Athletic Department, Business Manager, Athletic Director	Awards dinner/alumni events
Department Functions (e.g., Math or English department)	Department Head	Dinner meetings
Graduation Parties	Affairs Office for graduating classes/schools	Weeknight & weekend dinner functions
Faculty & Staff Functions	Faculty Club President, Personnel or Business Office	Dinners
High School		
Proms	School Office for names of class officers	Friday night dinners

Appendix A *(continued)*

Markets/Submarkets	Lead Source	Possible Functions
Reunions (past years) 10 year, 25 year, etc.	School Office	Weekend dinner/dance
Athletic Dinners	Athletic Office	Annual banquets
Faculty Events	Faculty Club President	Annual banquet
Churches/Synagogues		
Anniversary Events	Pastor's Office, Rabbi's Office, Church or Temple Business Manager	Annual dinner, usually weeknights
Women's Council or Auxiliary	Church Office	Fashion show luncheon
Choir	Musical Director or Church Office	Annual dinner
Budget/Finance Committee	Church Office	Dinner meetings
Banks		
Staff Member Clubs (25/50 yr.)	Personnel Office	Midweek dinners, holiday parties
Stockholders Meeting	Administrative Office	Annual meeting, various meal functions
Friends of the Bank	Corporate Development Office	Dinners/meetings
Local Corporations		
Long-Term Staff Member Clubs	Personnel Office	Dinners & dinner/dance
Retirement Dinners	Personnel Office	Weekday dinners
Credit Unions	Credit Union Office	Annual meeting or dinner/dances
Staff Member Groups	Personnel Office	Holiday parties
Charitable Groups, Service Clubs & Miscellaneous Organizations		
Charitable Groups (e.g., American Heart Assn., Cerebral Palsy)	Chamber of Commerce, Public Library	Fund-raising banquets
Men's Club, Women's Assn. (e.g., Rotary, Lions, etc.)	Chamber of Commerce	Midweek luncheons, evening functions

(continued)

Appendix A *(continued)*

Markets/Submarkets	Lead Source	Possible Functions
Professional Associations		
State/Local Bar Assn., Medical Assn., Homebuilders Assn., etc.	Chamber of Commerce, Public Library	Monthly luncheon or dinner meetings, annual dinner/dance
Miscellaneous Markets		
Weddings	Newspapers	Receptions & dinners, rehearsal dinners
Bowling Leagues	Secretary of League, Manager of Bowling Alley	Weeknight awards dinner (low budget)
Political Organizations	Local Party Chairperson	Dinners
Major Department Stores (Long-Term Staff Member Clubs, Store Anniversaries)	Personnel Office	Midweek/weekend dinner functions, holiday parties
Cultural/Musical Organizations (Opera, Ballet Society, etc.)	Chamber of Commerce	Weekend evening dinners
Local Youth Sports Groups (e.g., Little League, Adult Softball Leagues)	Little League Regional Headquarters (for names of local groups): County, City or Town Recreation Department (has names of all leagues)	Awards dinner (low budget)

Courtesy of Resorts International Hotel and Casino, Atlantic City, New Jersey

Appendix B

Preparing for Kosher Service

Many hotel food and beverage operations enjoy extensive kosher catering and banquet operations. Other facilities could expand into this market if they knew more about kosher laws and how they apply to menu planning and other aspects of food and beverage operations. The following questions and answers provide background information on this subject.

What is the definition of kosher? Kosher is a term that means "fit or proper"; it applies to foods that meet the specifications and requirements established by Jewish dietary laws. These laws are extremely rigid, do not permit deviation, and mandate many aspects of the purchase, preparation, and service of food.

What meat, fish, or poultry are edible by kosher law? Meat from those animals that have split hooves and chew their cud may be eaten. Pigs have split hooves but do not chew their cud; that is why pork is not eaten. (Some people erroneously believe that health reasons prohibit the consumption of pork; this is not correct.) Specifically, those animals that may be eaten are cattle, sheep, goats, and deer (Leviticus 11:10). Only fish that swim and have easily removable scales and fins may be eaten. Shellfish and mollusks are forbidden, which eliminates lobster, shrimp, crab, clams, oysters, and mussels from the menu. Only domestic birds such as chicken, duck, goose, turkey, and Cornish hen can be eaten. Neither birds of prey, nor scavenger birds, nor those used in the hunt are permitted. Only specific portions of permitted animals and food may be consumed. There are, for example, certain nerves, veins, and fats that cannot be eaten and must be removed before eating.

Are there restrictions on eating certain fruits and vegetables? No. There is no prohibition against anything that grows on the land. All fruits, vegetables, and edible grasses (e.g., oats, wheat) are permitted by kosher law.

What rituals are involved in the preparation of kosher food? The rituals of preparation basically apply to the slaughter of animals and how they must be treated immediately after slaughter, being prepared for eating. Meat for any kosher food production must be slaughtered and "kashered" by an authorized "shocket." Meat and poultry are "kashered" by the following process: within 72 hours of slaughter, the meat or poultry must be soaked in cold water for one-half hour in vessels kept specifically for soaking purposes. The meat is then rinsed with cold water, sprinkled with coarse (kosher) salt, and placed upon a grooved board that is tilted to allow the blood to flow from the meat. The meat must then remain on the board for one hour, at which time it is again washed and finally readied for use. Meat may not be frozen for future use unless it is first kashered. Only meat from the forequarters may be eaten. The hindquarters may be used if certain textured fat and all veins

(continued)

Appendix B *(continued)*

have first been removed. (Unfortunately, the process of removing those veins and fat is entirely too labor-intensive to make it commercially feasible.) After meat is prepared according to this procedure, it may be ground, frozen, or processed in any desired manner.

Are there any exemptions to this rule? Yes. Meat used for broiling need not be kashered it is used within 72 hours of slaughter. Livers need not be kashered and may be frozen for preparation later. However, when livers are ready to be processed, they must be completely thawed, washed, sliced, broiled, sprinkled with salt while broiling, rinsed, and prepared for eating.

Are there other regulations governing kosher food? Yes. All meat and meat products may not be cooked with any dairy product or dairy derivatives. For instance, you cannot serve chicken à la king or creamed chipped beef at a kosher function. Dairy food may not be served at a meal where meat is being used. For example, butter may not be served at a steak dinner. In addition, coffee may not be served with cream; however, a nondairy substitute may be used. The pots and pans in which meats have been cooked and the dishes upon which they are served may only be used for meat products. The same is true of pots, pans, and dishes used for dairy food preparation and service. If these utensils are used incorrectly, they must be discarded. Drinking glassware need not be changed as service moves from meat to dairy products; however, glass dishes used for service of hot food require a separation of meat and dairy items.

Do fish have to be kashered? No. Fish may be used in its entirety and requires no salting after cleaning. Fish dishes may be combined with dairy foods, but must not be combined with meat dishes. Fish may, however, be eaten separately at a meat meal as an appetizer (separate forks should be set).

Do vegetables require special handling or ritual? Vegetables and fruits may be combined with either dairy or meat dishes. If the vegetables are used with meat dishes, they must be cooked in pots and pans used for meat service. All fruits and vegetables, including vegetable oils, and all cereals and derivatives (as well as eggs) are called "parve."

What is meant by milchik and fleshik? "Milchik" refers to milk-containing foods, including milk, milk derivatives, and any product that contains milk in any proportion. "Fleshik" refers to meat products and includes any item containing meat, its byproducts, or derivatives.

Is there a term used to denote forbidden foods? Yes. "Trefe" is used to denote all forbidden foods.

Do these rules apply all year? Are there times when they may be relaxed or modified? These rules are never relaxed. They become even more stringent during the eight days of Passover. During Passover, for instance, unleavened bread is the only bread that may be eaten. Also, the separate cooking and serving of meat and dairy products is done with special pots, pans, and china set aside for use only during Passover. Specific utensils are also used only for Passover and are stored for the remainder of the year.

Appendix B *(continued)*

What are the rules for the preparation of kosher foods? Since it is not possible to mix meat and milk, separate sets of utensils become necessary. Most kosher caterers prepare only meat dinners and eliminate the need to maintain two sets of utensils. Some hotels with extensive kosher business maintain two separate kitchens, one for the preparation of meat and one for dairy products, and use color codes to distinguish the utensils used in each unit.

Kosher regulations prohibit the cooking of kosher food in nonkosher equipment; similarly, kosher food cannot be served in nonkosher serving utensils. (The reason is that hot food can absorb traces of nonkosher food from a nonkosher dish even if the utensil is clean.) Therefore, utensils used in hot food preparation and subsequent service must be used for kosher purposes only.

In contrast, since cold foods do not absorb food traces from utensils used to handle them, solids that contain kosher ingredients can be eaten from nonkosher dishes.

Utensils, equipment, and flatware can be made kosher even if they were previously used for handling nonkosher items. Techniques include immersing them in boiling water, passing them through a flame, or putting them into the soil. However, these techniques must be performed with a mashgiach (a trained supervisor) or rabbi in attendance.

Utensils made of porcelain, enamel, and earthenware cannot be made kosher, since they are porous and absorbent. Solid flatware made of a single metal piece can be made kosher; items made with a plastic or bone handle or with uncleanable crevices or grooves cannot.

Is supervision required during preparation, service, and cleanup? Since some kosher laws are very technical and complex, the supervision of a mashgiach is required. The food service operation offering kosher food must ensure that all aspects of the function are in accordance with kosher dietary laws.

What are alternatives for kosher catering in a hotel? Hotels make various provisions for kosher catering. For example, as previously mentioned, some hotels maintain separate kosher kitchens in which hotel personnel prepare the food. In contrast, others contract with an external kosher caterer who does catering exclusively for kosher functions at the property. Still other hotels rent their kitchen facilities to one or more kosher caterers. The subcontracting of facilities for kosher events is frequently justifiable due to the extensive amount of thorough cleaning required to render utensils and equipment items kosher.

Sometimes kosher food is ordered only as needed for a specific function; no separate storage areas for meat are then required. In contrast, dry products can be stored in a central storeroom as long as they do not come into direct contact with nonkosher products.

(continued)

Appendix B *(continued)*

Exactly how is kosher food preparation undertaken? Under the supervision of a mashgiach, the kitchen area must be thoroughly cleaned and then koshered. Ovens and stoves can be koshered by sterilizing the interior surfaces with a propane torch. Or, salt can be spread inside an oven that is then heated to its highest temperature for 30 minutes.

Hotels with extensive kosher business frequently purchase dishes especially for this business. Since solid flatware made of one metal piece can be koshered, it is not usually necessary to purchase separate flatware for kosher functions. However, since items to be koshered cannot be used for 24 hours prior to the koshering process, a larger supply of silverware may be needed. The koshering process for flatware involves immersing it in a pot of boiling water, removing it, and then rinsing it in cold water.

Sometimes the hotel supplies kosher caterers with all the necessary equipment; in other instances, caterers provide their own utensils. It is necessary to mark all utensils with an identifying feature when the caterer and the hotel mix equipment so that each business can identify its own utensils.

Dishwashing machines can be made kosher; the soaps used should be of vegetable or chemical origin. All areas in the immediate vicinity of the kosher preparation, even if they are not used by the kosher caterer, must be covered with paper or aluminum foil. Exact procedures may vary with the particular equipment and should be done only by rabbinic authority and under the careful supervision of a mashgiach.

Should a contract be used when an external caterer uses the hotel's facility? Yes. Typically a formal agreement is necessary to ensure that misunderstandings do not arise. Frequently, revenues are split according to an agreed-upon formula between the hotel and the caterer. In addition, the hotel includes the costs of the foods it provides. A hotel may, for example, prepare such parve foods as melons and fruit cups, raw vegetables, salads, and coffee. Typically, the hotel is responsible for liquor service, but—because of restrictions placed upon wine—wine service is frequently the caterer's responsibility.

The hotel should charge for the space used, the dishwashing costs, and the labor expenses. Most often, service personnel are provided by the hotel; members of the kitchen staff are provided by the kosher caterer.

The menu is conceived jointly by the caterer and the hotel. While menus are starting to reflect a trend toward lighter and more healthful foods, traditional products are still very popular. Typically the hotel will establish the selling price of the kosher event. Occasionally the caterer will bill the client and reimburse the hotel for the prearranged costs; however, it is generally more advantageous for the hotel to contract with the caterer, add its costs and profit margin, then bill the client directly.

How can kosher functions be classified? There are two basic types of kosher functions: commercial activities, such as fund-raising events and awards programs, and social or family functions, such as weddings and bar and bat mitzvahs.

Appendix B *(continued)*

> **Is the kosher catering business seasonal?** Generally, kosher catering is not seasonal, but that depends in part on the scheduling of community activities. Usually there are no catered kosher functions during Jewish holidays or during brief periods that are designated as times of mourning. Cooking is prohibited on the Jewish Sabbath (from sunset on Friday until after sunset on Saturday). Therefore, most kosher functions are not routinely scheduled for Saturday evenings during the summer months, since the Sabbath ends late in the evening.
>
> **What conditions are necessary for the success of a kosher catered event?** In order for kosher catering to be successful, all individuals participating in the catered affair must be aware of their specific responsibilities. Trust is also important. Clients trust the caterer to provide the kosher meals that have been arranged. Likewise, the caterer trusts that the mashgiach and the hotel will provide necessary services.

Source: Some of this material was adapted from Marianna Desser, "Kosher Catering: How and Why," *Cornell Quarterly*, Vol. 20, No. 2, pp. 83–91.

Task Breakdowns: Banquet Service

The procedures presented in this section are for illustrative purposes only and should not be construed as recommendations or standards. While these procedures are typical, readers should keep in mind that each food and beverage operation has its own procedures, equipment specifications, and safety policies.

BANQUET SERVER: *Follow Banquet Event Orders and Change Orders*

Materials needed: *Banquet event orders (BEOs) and change orders (if any).*

STEPS	HOW-TO'S
1. Review banquet event orders for functions that you will serve.	❑ Note the following information: • The room the function will be held in • The number of guests expected • Table setup specifications (including the sizes, types, and colors of tablecloths and table skirts) • The menu for the function (including beverages, number of courses, and dessert) • The time guests will arrive • The time food should be plated (put on plates) • The time to serve each course • The type of function • Special requests ❑ Always make sure the BEOs are in order, with the first function of your work shift at the front.
2. Review change order for changes that will affect service or room setup.	

BANQUET SERVER: *Take and Serve Beverage Orders*

Materials needed: *A guest check, a pen, a service tray or beverage tray, clean linen napkins, beverages, beverage napkins, and a tray jack.*

STEPS	HOW-TO'S
1. Take beverage orders.	❑ The function's host will have selected the beverages when booking the function. The beverage choices will be listed on the banquet event order. If a guest asks for a beverage not included on the BEO, know whether there is an extra charge, and tell the guest what the charge is.
	❑ Tell guests which beverages are available.
	❑ Ask if guests would like to order beverages.
	❑ Write orders on the guest check according to how guests are seated.
	❑ Assign a number to each chair at a table. Chair #1 is typically the one closest to the door or other landmark in the room. All banquet servers should use the same reference point.
	❑ Write the order for the guest in chair #1 on the first line of the guest check.
	❑ Write the order for the guest in chair #2 on the second line of the guest check, and so forth.
	❑ Take orders from women first, then men. For instance, if the guest in chair #2 is the only woman at the table, take her order first and write it on the second line of the guest check.
	❑ Continue to take orders clockwise around the table.
	❑ Use standard drink abbreviations.
	❑ Listen carefully to each order. Repeat the order and any special requests. Find out the guest's preference for service, such as "on the rocks" or "straight up."
	❑ Check the IDs of guests who order alcohol if they look underage.

BANQUET SERVER: *Take and Serve Beverage Orders*

(continued)

STEPS	HOW-TO'S
2. Place beverages on a cork-lined tray.	❑ Line the tray with a clean linen napkin to improve the look of the tray and to absorb spills and moisture. You'll likely use service trays—not beverage trays—to serve drinks at banquets. ❑ Center glasses so the tray is well-balanced. Put heavy or tall glasses in the center of the tray. ❑ Place a stack of beverage napkins on the tray.
3. Carry the tray to function room and place it on a tray jack near your guests.	
4. Serve beverages.	❑ Serve each beverage from the guest's right with your right hand. ❑ Place a beverage napkin on the table in front of each guest. ❑ If the beverage napkins at your property have a logo, place the napkins so that the logo faces the guest. ❑ Handle glasses by their stem, base, or handle. Place each glass on the center of each beverage napkin. ❑ Follow your guest check to serve the correct beverage to each guest. Do not ask who ordered which drink. ❑ If pouring a beverage from a pitcher or bottle, pour into the glass or cup without picking it up. ❑ When pouring, use a folded linen napkin as a splash guard to protect guests.

BANQUET SERVER: *Serve Each Course at Sit-Down Banquets*

Materials needed: Service trays, tray jacks, and condiments.

STEPS	HOW-TO'S
1. Prepare the table for each course before serving it.	❏ Clear any empty plates or glasses from the guest's right with your right hand. Always ask guests if they are finished. ❏ Never stack dirty plates in front of guests. Pick them up separately and stack them away from guests. ❏ Bring all condiments and accompaniments to the table before serving the order. ❏ Only bring full—not partially full—condiment bottles to guests. ❏ If you will be serving an item that guests will share, bring a plate for each guest.
2. Pick up each course.	❏ The banquet manager or captain will signal when to serve each course. ❏ You will typically serve courses in the following order: • Appetizers • Soup • Salads • Entrees • Dessert • Cordials • Coffee ❏ Check the order before you take it out of the kitchen: • Does the food look fresh and appealing? • Have all preparation instructions been followed? • Is the presentation garnished? • Have all special requests been met? • Is the plate clean? • Is hot food hot and cold food cold?

BANQUET SERVER: *Serve Each Course at Sit-Down Banquets* (continued)

STEPS	HOW-TO'S
	❑ Ask the cook to make any corrections necessary to meet the operation's high standards.
	❑ Notify your supervisor immediately of any problem in the food preparation so that he or she can speak to the guests and correct the situation.
	❑ If you are having trouble meeting guest needs, ask your supervisor or another server for help until you can catch up.
	❑ Don't let the guests suffer because you're busy.
	❑ Thank the kitchen staff for their cooperation.
3. Deliver each course.	❑ Carry loaded service trays to tray jacks in the function rooms.
	❑ Serve the children first, women next, then men, and the host last.
	❑ Serve food from the guest's right side with your right hand whenever possible. Don't reach in front of guests.
	❑ Place the plate with the first course on top of the base plate, if a base plate is included in the table setting.
	❑ Place the entree plate so that the main item is closest to the guest.
	❑ Place side dishes to the left of the entree plate.
	❑ If a guest asks for something extra, deliver it as quickly as possible so that the meal does not get cold.
	❑ Ask if guests would like you to bring or do anything else for them at this time.
	❑ Remove empty beverage glasses as needed.

BANQUET SERVER: *Maintain Buffets*

Materials needed: *Pitchers of water, cans of gel-type fuel, matches, pitchers of ice, dishes, serving utensils, and food-safe cleaning cloth.*

STEPS	HOW-TO'S
1. Keep hot items hot.	❑ If there is less than one quarter of an inch of water in the liners of hot chafing dishes, use a pitcher of water to refill the liners. ❑ If the chafing dishes are heated by canned, gel-type fuel, make sure the cans stay lit, and replace them when they become empty. ❑ Replace the lids on serving dishes when guests are not in the buffet line.
2. Keep cold items cold.	❑ Use pitchers to add ice to the buffet as needed to keep the containers holding cold items surrounded by ice. ❑ Remove ice that gets into the food containers, and replace any items that become waterlogged.
3. Refill food.	❑ When a container is less than one-quarter full, get a full container from the kitchen. ❑ Remove the old container and replace it with the full one. Do not combine food from the old and new containers. ❑ Bring the old container to the kitchen and give it to the appropriate person.
4. Maintain serviceware.	❑ Restock dishes when there are fewer than ten dishes in a stack. Never let a stack get below five dishes. ❑ Make sure each container has an appropriate serving utensil. ❑ Return serving utensils to the correct containers. ❑ Replace utensils that fall on the floor with clean utensils from the kitchen.
5. Use a damp, food-safe cleaning cloth to wipe spills on the buffet table.	

BANQUET SERVER: *Set Up and Maintain Hors d' Oeuvres for Receptions*

Materials needed: *A banquet event order (BEO), change orders (if any), tables, tablecloths, table skirts, flounces, food or flower displays, equipment for hot and cold food, ice, water, cans of gel-type fuel, bread-and-butter plates, matches, beverage napkins, cocktail forks or picks, knives, small plates, linen roll-ups, and serving utensils.*

STEPS	HOW-TO'S
1. Place tablecloths on tables.	
2. Skirt and flounce tables.	
3. Decorate tables with food or flower displays as specified by your supervisor or the banquet event order (BEO).	
4. Set up equipment for hot and cold food.	❏ Make sure all equipment is clean and polished. Return soiled equipment to the dish room.
	❏ Set up ice beds for cold items. (The steps to set up ice beds vary among properties.)
	❏ Set up chafing dishes or electric warmers for hot items.
	❏ Make sure there is enough water in the liners of chafing dishes to prevent scorching equipment and burning food.
	❏ If the chafing dishes are heated by canned, gel-type fuel, place one can on a bread-and-butter plate under a half-size chafer and two cans under a full-size chafer. Light the cans of fuel 10 minutes before putting the food in the chafing dishes.
5. Put silverware and napkins on the table.	❏ Arrange stacks of beverage napkins on the table.
	❏ Place cocktail forks or picks, knives, and small plates on the table.
	❏ Place linen roll-ups on the table if they are requested on the BEO.

(continued)

BANQUET SERVER: *Set Up and Maintain* *Hors d' Oeuvres for Receptions* (continued)

STEPS	HOW-TO'S
6. Bring food from the kitchen 10 to 15 minutes before the guests are expected.	❑ Place cold food containers on the beds of ice. ❑ Place hot food in the chafing dishes. ❑ Place the appropriate serving utensils in the serving dishes.
7. Maintain the hors d'oeuvres table.	

BANQUET SERVER: *Provide Service for Cocktail Receptions*

Materials needed: *Beverage trays, linen napkins, beverage napkins, food and beverages, and a cleaning cloth.*

STEPS	HOW-TO'S
1. Prepare trays.	❑ Only use trays that are clean (and polished if necessary). ❑ You typically will use a 12-inch beverage tray to serve cocktails and hors d' oeuvres at cocktail receptions. Sometimes silver or glass trays are used. ❑ Line trays with linen napkins. ❑ Place a stack of beverage napkins on each tray. ❑ Place food or beverages on the trays. Center items so each tray is balanced.
2. Serve beverages to reception guests.	❑ At large cocktail receptions, the banquet event order may specify that servers will pass trays of food and trays of the most popular beverages to speed service. ❑ Balance a tray of beverages on your fingertips and hold it in front of your chest. Do not try to hold beverage trays above your shoulder. ❑ Approach guests and offer them a beverage from your tray. ❑ Pick up a beverage napkin and beverage and hand them to the guest with your free hand. If guests try to remove a beverage from your tray, politely ask them to let you serve them so you don't upset the balance of your tray. ❑ Refill your tray as needed. ❑ As you return to the bar to refill your tray, collect empty glasses and place them on your tray.

(continued)

BANQUET SERVER: *Provide Service for Cocktail Receptions* (continued)

STEPS	HOW-TO'S
	❑ Place dirty glasses in the dirty glass racks in the service bar.
	❑ Wipe spills from your tray and from tables using a clean, damp cloth.
3. Serve food to reception guests.	❑ Carry a tray of food on your fingertips above your shoulder. Move among the guests, and offer the food.
	❑ Lower the tray and present it at chest level to the guests. Try to avoid interrupting conversations. Usually if you approach a group, they will pause to pick up a food item.
	❑ Refill your tray as needed.
	❑ As you return to the kitchen or other area to refill your tray, place empty plates on the tray and bring them to the dish room.
	❑ Wipe spills from your tray and from tables using a clean, damp cloth.
4. Suggest courtesy transportation or a taxi to guests who have had too much to drink.	

Source: Adapted from the "Banquet Server Guide" in the *Hospitality Skills Training Series* (Lansing, Mich.: American Hotel & Lodging Educational Institute, 1995).

Chapter 14 Outline

Competencies

1. Describe typical markets for in-room dining and techniques for reaching these markets, summarize considerations for planning and creating in-room dining menus, and describe in-room dining variations and alternatives. (pp. 603–611)

2. Explain considerations for preparing for in-room dining, including organization, typical duties of in-room dining staff members, forecasting and staffing, facility design, inventory and equipment management, and preparations for service shifts. (pp. 611–619)

3. Describe typical procedures for taking, routing, preparing, delivering, cleaning up after, and following up on in-room dining orders; and explain how in-room dining provides wine service and special amenities. (pp. 619–629)

4. Summarize in-room dining income control procedures, ways to gather guest comments, and typical guest complaints about in-room dining; and describe the use of feedback in planning. (pp. 629–632)

14

In-Room Dining

MANY LODGING PROPERTIES provide their guests with the opportunity to order and enjoy food and beverages in the privacy of their own guestrooms or suites. Some guests enjoy in-room dining as a way of adding a special touch to a special occasion. Others see it as a status symbol, and still others appreciate it simply for its convenience.

In this chapter we will take a look at in-room dining issues, including markets, marketing, menus, and in-room dining variations and alternatives. We will then discuss the in-room dining cycle: getting ready for service, delivering service, and attending to various responsibilities after the service has been delivered.

In-Room Dining Issues

In-room dining in hotels is considered by many experts to be the most expensive service that a full-service hotel can provide. Despite its expense, most hotels offer in-room dining, because many of their guests expect it and are willing to pay for it. In-room dining can help a hotel build guestroom occupancy numbers and justify higher guestroom rates. Upscale in-room dining can transform an ordinary lodging stay into a memorable and luxurious experience. When the food and beverage products are properly presented in the guest's room, feelings of satisfaction result from the comfort and security that accompanies in-room dining.

Many people, when they see an in-room dining menu for the first time, are surprised at the relatively high prices. Even more surprising is the fact that few in-room dining operations make a significant profit, despite these prices. Why, then, do full-service hotels bother with in-room dining? It is because, as just mentioned, enough of their guests want it and are willing to pay for it. In a guest survey by *Lodging Hospitality*, in-room dining breakfast was found to be the number one guestroom amenity for which respondents were willing to pay extra, out of a list that included video movies, Internet access, an in-room microwave oven, and in-room coffee. Professional hospitality managers have guest satisfaction as their goal. These managers know that when in-room dining is well managed, it can give their property a competitive edge, enhance guest satisfaction, and enhance the property's public image.

From the perspective of guests, the key elements of well-managed in-room dining include the following:

- Prompt and courteous responses when guests call to place orders
- Correctly filled orders

- Efficient and quick delivery of orders to guestrooms

- Tact and courtesy from staff members who deliver and serve orders

- Staff members who strictly adhere to rules of safety when using equipment that involves liquid fuels or open flames

- Hot and cold foods and beverages that are at the correct temperatures when they are served

- The prompt removal of trays and other equipment when guests have finished their meals or snacks

In-room dining should be designed to meet the needs of guests, but it should also be designed with the property's human and material resources in mind. Managers should consider the extra resources required before implementing a new in-room dining program: new facilities might have to be built, new equipment purchased, and additional staff members hired. Many properties add a surcharge to in-room dining menu items to cover some or all of these costs, although the industry trend is toward pricing in-room dining menus at the same levels as dining room menus. For example, Wyndham Hotels & Resorts has eliminated in-room dining surcharges and views in-room dining as if it were simply another restaurant in the hotel.

Twenty-four-hour in-room dining is much easier when one or more of the hotel's restaurants are also open around the clock; in-room dining generally costs much more than it brings in if a separate production facility must be maintained for it. For this reason, in-room dining at some lodging properties ends whenever the restaurant closes for the night. Some properties use separate production facilities for in-room dining and transfer the production responsibilities from the in-room dining kitchen to a restaurant or coffee shop kitchen only during slow times.

Increasingly, because of the growing number of alliances between hotel companies and chain or independent restaurants, hotel food and beverage departments that have not traditionally offered in-room dining have added it to the amenities they offer, but they have their affiliated restaurants provide it. For example, a Radisson hotel with a T.G.I. Friday's restaurant may provide its in-room dining via the restaurant. This kind of arrangement gives the hotel the cost-effectiveness of quantity cooking that most stand-alone in-room dining operations cannot achieve.

Some hotels do a large volume of **hospitality suite** business, offering food and beverage service for small group meetings, corporate meetings, organizations entertaining guests during conventions, and other occasions. These properties are able to increase the productivity of their in-room dining operations by placing the responsibility for hospitality suites with in-room dining rather than with the banquet or catering department. In-room dining then provides all food and beverage service in any hotel room, including suites, for any number of guests. Since food and beverage sales in hospitality suites usually produce a profit, they can help offset losses accrued from offering traditional in-room dining.

Markets

Few guests rely on in-room dining for the majority of their meals. Most hotel guests eat in one of the hotel's restaurants or make other arrangements for meals rather than use in-room dining. When guests do choose to eat a meal in their rooms, it is most often breakfast.

Limited-service properties rarely offer in-room dining. In contrast, luxury hotels that cater to executive business travelers, convention groups, and the upscale leisure market typically offer 24-hour in-room dining. Guests who are traveling on birthdays, anniversaries, or holidays may be more willing to consider ordering in-room dining. When targeting these kinds of markets, managers may want to protect the novelty or prestige factor of in-room dining by keeping in-room dining menu prices higher than dining room prices and offering items that enhance the special image of in-room dining, such as escargot.

On the other hand, managers may attempt to position in-room dining as an amenity that can be enjoyed as much for its functional merits as its symbolic merits. Its functional merits include the privacy of eating in the guestroom, solitude for those who prefer to eat alone, security, and the convenience of not having to leave the guestroom for a meal. If managers position in-room dining this way, they should keep menu prices low and choose menu items that are nutritious and attractive but inexpensive and easy to prepare.

Whichever route managers choose for positioning in-room dining, business travelers are a viable in-room dining market for most operations. While some business travelers view in-room dining as a status symbol, others appreciate it for its functionality. Business travelers typically are not as price-conscious as leisure travelers, but they are often more concerned about saving time. Some of their discussions during a meal concern very sensitive issues, so they are often willing to pay for the extra privacy and security that in-room dining affords. Personal security motivates some business travelers to order in-room dining. Women business travelers, for whom personal security plays a strong role in hotel selection, are more likely to select hotels on the basis of extended-hour or 24-hour in-room dining than their male colleagues. (Security concerns can work against in-room dining, too. Some guests do not like to admit strangers into the privacy of their guestrooms, even when the "strangers" are in-room dining staff members.)

Among sports teams, football teams usually eat as a group in the dining room or in banquet halls, but baseball and basketball players are usually on their own when it comes to meals. These players appreciate 24-hour in-room dining and a variety of menu options. Many motorcoach tours cater to older travelers who like the convenience of in-room dining. International travelers may use in-room dining if they are not comfortable enough with the hotel staff's language to dine in a hotel restaurant. Such travelers especially appreciate in-room dining menus that make extensive use of photographs. (The management of the Grand Hyatt in New York designed a unique in-room dining menu that is, for all intents and purposes, a picture book. The menu, which is left open on the desk in each guestroom, features a photograph of the finished dish on the page opposite from the page that has a description of the dish and its ingredients.) Families with young children, travelers with visual or mobility impairments, and other guests for whom leaving the guestroom is especially inconvenient are markets a hotel's in-room dining department might pursue.

Marketing

Ongoing marketing to hotel guests is the key to building steady demand for in-room dining. In-room dining managers should see their marketing efforts as part of those of the whole property. Large in-room dining operations may have a separate marketing plan, but it should be in harmony with the hotel's overall marketing plan. It is counterproductive for in-room dining staff to market to prospects who are not also being targeted by the property's other revenue centers.

A lodging property's salespeople should have access to information about the kinds of service and menus the in-room dining operation offers. Most often this communication takes place through the property's **fact book**—a book salespeople use to familiarize themselves with and remind themselves about the property's products and services. The in-room dining department's hours of operation and menu(s) should be included in this important publication. In-room dining managers should check regularly to ensure that telephone salespeople, front desk agents, and all other guest-contact staff members have the same information about in-room dining and that their information is complete, accurate, and up-to-date.

The external aspect of in-room dining marketing involves using in-room dining as an attraction to help convince prospects to choose the property for a stay. To this end, the property can entice prospects through both rack and convention brochures. In these brochures, properties should not merely mention in-room dining; they should use photographs, testimonials, abbreviated menus, or examples of the kind of in-room dining prospective guests can expect to receive. A property's video brochures, video magazines, CD-ROMs, faxes, and Internet site can all be used to promote in-room dining as well.

Once prospects become guests, they may forget some of the amenities that first attracted them to the property. Some of the biggest obstacles to in-room dining success are unawareness that it is offered and ignorance of the kinds of menu items and services offered and their prices. **Internal selling,** especially cross-selling, can help overcome these obstacles. Staff members who practice internal selling create awareness of in-room dining by regularly reminding guests that in-room dining is available. A short segment on the property's guest-services television channel or fliers placed in strategic spots throughout the hotel can tell guests about in-room dining specials and menu items.

Hotel operators must know the number for in-room dining if they are to be good internal sellers of this amenity. In properties that operate in-room dining out of an in-room dining kitchen during busy hours and out of other production facilities at slower times, the operator should know which in-room dining telephone number to give guests at any given time: it could be the in-room dining department's order-taker's number during busy periods, the "theme" dining-room cashier's number when the dining room is open, or the family-dining restaurant operator's number during still other periods.

Cross-selling involves staff members or advertisements in one hotel area promoting the products or services of another revenue center in the hotel. For example, an in-room dining staff member might remind a guest that the gift shop has souvenirs or personal hygiene items for sale, or a front desk representative might encourage a registering guest to try the property's in-room dining. In the area of advertising, tent cards promoting in-room dining that are placed on tables near the swimming pool are also examples of cross-selling.

Personal cross-selling can take place as part of routine interactions with guests, such as the following:

- Taking guest orders for wake-up calls, for cribs or extra blankets, and other services

- Making wake-up calls

- Checking in or checking out

In the case of a front desk representative making a wake-up call, the representative, rather than simply saying, "Hello, it's seven o'clock" might say, "Good morning, Ms. Ricker. It's seven o'clock. Would you like in-room dining to bring you a fresh pot of coffee and a Danish?" Cross-selling keeps in-room dining in the forefront of guests' minds and also helps keep it in the minds of staff members.

In-room dining managers should advertise in-room dining with prominently displayed menus, posters, fliers, and tent cards. Just as with any in-house advertising, managers should choose locations that receive a lot of traffic. Elevators, lobbies, and stairways are usually high-traffic areas in hotels. In-house promotions can tie in-room dining revenues to other revenues. Managers may choose to offer a discount on one in-room dining order for guests who stay at the property for three days or more, for example. A sample of in-room dining could be built into familiarization ("fam") packages that the property offers to meeting planners or travel intermediaries.

Menus

Menu design is closely related to in-room dining marketing, in that both should match the operation's products and services with guest needs and expectations. The following sections discuss considerations for planning and designing an in-room dining menu.

Menu Planning. Menu planning for in-room dining should take place at the same time the marketing plan for in-room dining is created, because menu items must meet profitability criteria as well as quality criteria. Too many in-room dining managers set themselves up for failure when they plan menus that cannot fulfill budgetary goals. In-room dining menus must also reflect the positioning of the property and appeal to its target markets. As mentioned earlier, managers should consider the property's needs as well as the needs of guests when planning an in-room dining menu. The people who can best represent these two perspectives should be involved in the menu-planning process: the in-room dining manager, the food and beverage manager, the chef, and possibly the director of sales.

In-room dining menus generally offer more expensive food items and frequently provide less variety than dining room menus. Often, managers build an in-room dining menu with items from the operation's restaurant menu(s) that can maintain their quality during transportation to guestrooms. In other instances, managers plan special in-room dining menus featuring items not found on the restaurant menu(s). Some properties use both their dining room and coffee shop menus as sources for the in-room dining menu, then add fast-service items.

Regardless of the approach used, managers must be sure that the items on the in-room dining menu will meet guest and property quality requirements. Such items as french fries may become soggy, cold, or otherwise suffer a loss of quality if they are held for long time periods between production and subsequent service in guestrooms. Likewise, egg soufflés are a poor choice for most in-room dining menus. Other items, such as a chicken breast in a wine sauce, tournedos, or beef sauté à la Deutsch could require tableside preparation that in-room dining attendants may not be able to perform.

More and more properties are limiting their in-room dining menus to only those items they can prepare and deliver best. Some properties have seen increased profitability by using specialty kitchens that offer a single item, such as pizza, fried chicken, burgers, or sandwiches. In-room dining managers might also focus on a single meal, such as breakfast (35 percent of the breakfast business at some upscale properties is generated by in-room dining).

For most in-room dining operations, breakfast is the easiest meal to sell and the most difficult to deliver properly. Many breakfast combinations that feature eggs simply do not maintain product temperatures during transportation. It is also difficult to deliver toast to guestrooms at proper temperatures. A limited breakfast menu that lists only menu items that will survive the trip from the kitchen to the guestroom may be a good alternative to an extensive menu. Specialty pastries, for example, may be offered instead of toast; scrambled eggs may be preferable to eggs Benedict, because hollandaise sauce is highly perishable.

During the week, breakfasts are usually served through in-room dining for business travelers. Additionally, business meetings in function rooms may include breakfast. In general, these breakfasts are light and quick, since these are two features that business guests most often request. For example, the Omni Hotel in Houston, Texas, has introduced a "Simply Healthy" breakfast featuring freshly squeezed orange juice, fresh in-season fruits, vanilla bean yogurt made on the premises, granola, and a selection of "healthy" muffins such as carrot-raisin bran and seven-grain. The "Simply Healthy" breakfast is a popular in-room dining choice, since it provides convenience and value (a healthy breakfast alternative) for guests.

Many properties use **menu engineering** to select and monitor the success of restaurant menu items; in-room dining managers should consider applying menu engineering to the in-room dining menu as well. Menu engineering involves analyzing both the demand and the profit contribution margin for each item on the menu, then adjusting prices and adding or subtracting menu items as necessary.

In summary, managers should consider the following factors when planning an in-room dining menu:

- What are the requirements and preferences of the hotel's target markets?
- What types of food and beverages should we offer?
- How many menu items should we offer?

- How long does it take to prepare each menu item? (Complicated menu items or items that for other reasons take a long time to prepare are not suitable for the in-room dining menus of most properties.)

- Will each menu item be reasonably popular?

- Can the quality of each menu item survive the transport to the guestrooms farthest from the in-room dining department's food preparation areas?

- Can we make a reasonable profit on each menu item? That is, are guests willing to pay the price we must charge to cover the costs of purchasing and preparing the menu item, plus a reasonable markup?

Menu Design and Presentation. An in-room dining menu's design and presentation should reflect the property's positioning and the requirements and preferences of its target markets. Guests should be able to easily understand the information on the menu and easily find what they're looking for. Because guests should be able to easily locate the telephone number for in-room dining, for example, this number should be in a conspicuous location on the in-room dining menu. Of course, the menu itself should be placed in the guestroom so that guests can easily find it.

In hotels that cater to international guests, in-room dining menus are frequently written in several languages. This feature is important, since guests who are alone in their rooms do not have service staff available to help them, as the guests in public dining areas do. As mentioned earlier, to help international guests, some in-room dining menus include many pictures. Some hotels offer special menus in braille (in domestic as well as international versions) for guests with visual impairments. Hotels who serve a lot of international guests also may employ multilingual in-room dining operators.

Designing menus in a way that highlights the products with the highest contribution margins (food income minus food and labor costs) is just as important to in-room dining as it is to any other food and beverage outlet. Uniquely designed in-room dining menus can influence guest purchases in much the same way that restaurant menus do. Menu designers should first determine which menu items they most want to sell (such as those items with the highest contribution margin), then provide good descriptions of those items and use boxes, pictures, or other techniques to focus attention on them. For most properties, all items available through in-room dining should be included on their in-room dining menus. However, some in-room dining departments at upscale properties sometimes include a notice on their menus that invites guests to inquire about unlisted items.

In addition to menus, some properties put tent cards on the guestroom dresser, television, nightstand, or other piece of furniture to promote in-room dining as well as other food and beverage services. Some properties offer a nightly turn-down service in which housekeepers prepare the guest's bed, tidy up the room, provide additional linens if necessary, and place a flower, candy, or a cheerful note on the guest's pillow; housekeepers may also place a breakfast **doorknob menu** on the guest's pillow. Other properties may always have a breakfast doorknob menu available in every guestroom for guests to complete and hang on the doorknobs outside their rooms. Staff members then pick up these menus during the early-morning hours. Guests indicate on the menu not only which items they want, but the approximate times at which they would like their breakfasts to be served as well. (Some flexibility, such as one-half hour, should be built into the delivery time, since the time that a guest prefers could be a very busy period for the in-room dining staff.) A doorknob menu expedites in-room dining, since guests can place orders and in-room dining staff can prepare and deliver them without involving the order-taker during the breakfast rush.

Variations and Alternatives

In-room dining is undergoing dramatic changes at some properties. Because it is a costly amenity in a time when labor is scarce and maintenance and overhead costs are high, some hotels are opting for lower-cost alternatives. To avoid the risks and costs of providing in-room dining themselves, many economy/limited-service and all-suite hotels have added food to guestroom minibars, placed combination microwave-oven-and-refrigerator units in guestrooms, added pizza delivery service from nearby pizzerias (one hotel chain marketed this option as "Vrroom Service"), or outsourced in-room dining to nearby restaurants. Other properties feature delicatessens where guests can pick up their favorite foods and consume them in their guestrooms.

Many properties are giving guests an alternative to paper in-room dining menus by offering in-room dining via **video ordering.** Guests can turn on the television in their guestrooms, select the in-room dining option from a menu of hotel services, and order food and beverages using their television's remote control. Managers must make video ordering an easy process if they expect guests to use this option, however. One guest commented on the complexity of one property's video ordering service by saying, "Only a computer nerd can use it." Video ordering has the potential to reduce mistakes in in-room dining orders, but it must be guest-friendly.

The Sheraton New York Hotel in New York City augments its regular in-room dining menu with a supplemental in-room dining menu. This menu lists popular menu items from three neighborhood ethnic restaurants: China Regency, New York's Stage Deli, and San Leone. Overall, there are about 100 menu items from which to choose. Menu prices are the same as guests would pay if they actually went to these neighborhood restaurants (there is also a nominal delivery charge). The supplemental menu has the same delivery promise that is printed on the regular in-room dining menu: "If the order is not delivered in 30 minutes or less, the order is free." This creative strategy gives guests a wider selection, builds strategic alliances with neighborhood restaurants, and can enhance the guest's stay significantly.

Other out-of-the-ordinary in-room dining options include the "movie-and-a-snack" package offered by the Park Hyatt Chicago. For $15, guests can order a DVD from the hotel's extensive library for delivery to their room, along with a snack such as chocolate chip cookies and milk or fresh, warm pretzels and a soda. At another full-service hotel, the hotel's "ice cream man" will visit guestrooms in costume with all the fixings for ice cream sundaes. Guests create their own sundaes using vanilla or chocolate ice cream and such toppings as chocolate and other syrups, bananas, Gummi bears, and so on. Targeted at guests with children, this service is priced at just $6 per person; parents can book the ice cream man at check-in or at any time during their stay. The Peninsula Hotel in Chicago delivers a full-fledged afternoon English tea to the guestrooms of interested guests, featuring freshly baked scones with clotted cream and jam, specialty miniature pastries also baked at the hotel, savory quiche, finger sandwiches, and a choice of black, green, white, or herbal tea.

The Mirage Hotel in Las Vegas, Nevada, has eight elevators assigned to the in-room dining department. Two of the elevators are designed to deliver one of three kinds of breakfasts in ten minutes or less. Guests in the hotel's suites receive extra attention. As soon as they order breakfast, a first service of coffee, Danish, juice, and a newspaper is delivered immediately; breakfast follows shortly thereafter. Throughout the hotel, a 20-minute-delivery guarantee for in-room dining is stressed. Behind the scenes, the actual goal is 15 minutes or less.

Holiday Inn Express limited-service hotels give guests a free continental breakfast to complement their in-room coffee makers. Another hotel chain presents guests with complimentary continental breakfasts in plastic bags that are hung on the guestrooms' outside door handles; the breakfast consists of a four-ounce container of orange juice and a wrapped muffin or sweet roll. This limited type of in-room dining adds value for guests, particularly those traveling with children.

Finally, some properties are offering in-room dining options that have nothing to do with food and beverages. For example, the Four Seasons Hotel in London offers in-room tailoring services by the master tailors of Saville Row. Several hotels in the Detroit area, including The Ritz-Carlton and River Place Inn, have entered into agreements with a local company called "Hotel Doctor" that sends doctors on "house calls" direct to hotel guestrooms. The company averages about 100 calls per week; doctors arrive at the hotels complete with white hospital jacket, dress shirt and tie, photo identification, and black bag, and treat everything from common colds to serious ailments. A similar program is offered in major cities across the United States by InRoomMD.

Other non-food in-room dining options offered at upscale hotels and resorts include the following:

- Beauty services such as hairstyling and manicures
- Psychological consultations (in addition to traditional therapists for people, some hotels even offer "pet therapists" who will counsel owners of travel-traumatized pets)
- Yoga sessions
- Fitness training
- Massages
- Acupuncture treatments

Getting Ready for In-Room Dining

Getting ready for in-room dining includes attending to staffing requirements as well as gathering the inventory and equipment necessary to provide excellent in-room dining. In-room dining managers must give careful thought to staffing.

InRoomMD (inroommd.com) offers medical services to travelers.

A limited-service property may have ten or fewer in-room dining staff members, while full-service properties may have large in-room dining departments. The inventory and equipment required for in-room dining ranges from simple trays for delivering continental breakfasts, to the carts, candles, special tablecloths and napkins, and other items involved in serving an elaborate candlelight dinner.

Staff member knowledge of the in-room dining menu will enhance a guest's enjoyment of the property in general and in-room dining in particular. At the very least, all in-room dining staff members should know the following:

- Proper pronunciation of the names of menu items

- Menu specials of the day

- Signature or featured menu items

- In-room dining menu items that are in or out of season

- Ingredients and preparation methods
- Prices
- Alcoholic and other beverages that are available and that go well with certain menu items

In-room dining staff members must also be prepared to suggest items that may be prepared and delivered quickly to guests who are in a hurry, and menu items that are not on the menu but may be prepared for a guest who is on a special diet.

Staffing Requirements

Managers of a new in-room dining department or a department that is reorganizing need to decide how to allocate their staff members. What tasks need to be performed, which position should perform which tasks, and what are the standards by which performance should be measured for each position are just some of the questions managers must ask themselves. The answers to these and other questions affect the hiring, training, and evaluation of staff members.

To answer these questions, managers should first create a task list for each position. The tasks on task lists are arranged roughly in the order in which they should be performed. Tasks are not described in depth on a task list; detailed descriptions of how to do the tasks appear in separate job breakdowns for each task on the list (see Exhibit 1 for a sample job breakdown). A job breakdown supplies all the information and instructions a staff member needs to perform the task being described. To figure out what training a staff member needs, in-room dining managers can complete a training needs evaluation form similar to the one shown in the chapter appendix. Finally, managers should construct a training schedule to plan their training (see Exhibit 2 for an excerpt from a sample training schedule).

While titles and duties vary from property to property, most of the duties listed under the position descriptions that follow must be performed at every property that offers in-room dining.

In-Room Dining Manager. The **in-room dining manager** has a large number of management responsibilities, ranging from planning and executing the department's operation to enforcing its rules. He or she is responsible for organizing the in-room dining staff and often selects, orients, trains, and schedules staff members. Handling problems with food and beverage orders and delivery, controlling costs, and ensuring that staff members collect all sales income due the operation are additional duties.

When guests plan hospitality suites and if in-room dining is responsible for these functions, the in-room dining manager becomes an important member of the hospitality-suite planning team. Furthermore, the in-room dining manager must handle complaints from guests, staff members, and others; ensure that in-room dining equipment is properly maintained; and order equipment and supplies. In-room dining is labor-intensive, so supervisory duties form a significant part of the in-room dining manager's work.

Assistant In-Room Dining Manager. In large properties that have an **assistant in-room dining manager**, this individual performs some of the tasks that would

Exhibit 1   Sample Job Breakdown

Place the In-Room Dining Order	
STEPS	**HOW-TO'S**
1. Turn in the food order to the kitchen	❑ At some properties, in-room dining attendants hand-carry orders to the kitchen. Other properties use point-of-sale equipment that automatically transmits orders to the kitchen.
2. Let the cook or expediter know about any guest request.	❑ Guest requests may include the degree of doneness for eggs and steaks, a fat-free preparation, extra sauce, etc.
3. Place beverage orders.	❑ When food orders are almost ready, place the beverage orders with the bar.
	❑ Do not place bar orders too early—the ice will melt and water-down the drinks.
	❑ Timing in-room dining drink orders is important. Food must stay at the correct temperature, and the ice in beverages must not melt and water-down the drinks.

Source: Adapted from the "Room Service Attendant Guide" in the *Hospitality Skills Training Series* (Lansing, Mich.: American Hotel & Lodging Educational Institute, 1995).

otherwise be the responsibility of the in-room dining manager. Frequently, the assistant in-room dining manager supervises staff members, undertakes many of the daily or routine decision-making tasks associated with special functions, solves operational problems, and completes departmental records and reports.

In-Room Dining Captain. During a specific shift, the **in-room dining captain** is in charge of the department's order-takers, in-room dining attendants, and buspersons. Captains help the assistant in-room dining manager ensure that staff members follow all operating procedures and maintain performance standards. They also issue guest checks, ensure that in-room dining supply areas are adequately stocked, and personally supervise functions in hospitality suites. When VIPs order in-room dining, the captains themselves may prepare and deliver the orders to these guests.

In-room dining captains may also expedite in-room dining when special problems arise, such as an unexpectedly busy period. Rescheduling or reassigning

Exhibit 2   Excerpt of a Sample Training Schedule

Day 1:

Department Orientation

Knowledge for All Staff Members:

- Quality Guest Service
- Bloodborne Pathogens
- Personal Appearance
- Emergency Situations
- Lost and Found
- Recycling Procedures
- Safe Work Habits
- Manager on Duty
- Your Property's Fact Sheet
- Staff Member Policies
- The Americans with Disabilities Act

The Task List for In-Room Dining Attendants

Day 2:

Review Day 1 (Plan additional training time, if necessary)

Knowledge for All Front-of-House Food and Beverage Staff Members:

- Telephone Courtesy
- Safety and Security
- Alcoholic Beverage Terms
- House Brands and Call Brands
- Liquor Brands and Categories
- Beverage Prices

Knowledge for In-Room Dining Attendants:

- What Is an In-Room Dining Attendant?
- Working as a Team With Co-Workers and Other Departments
- Key Control
- Property Floor Plan
- Par Stock System
- In-Room Dining Equipment Terms
- VIPs

The Job Breakdowns for Tasks 1–4:

Task 1 Perform Beginning-of-Shift Duties
Task 2 Preset In-Room Dining Trays and Carts
Task 3 Process Express Breakfast Orders
Task 4 Deliver VIP Amenities

Source: Adapted from the "Room Service Attendant Guide" in the *Hospitality Skills Training Series* (Lansing, Mich.: American Hotel & Lodging Educational Institute, 1995).

in-room dining attendants is an example of how they could expedite in-room dining. Captains may make inspection rounds to ensure that buspersons remove in-room dining equipment and dishes promptly from guestrooms and hallway floors. The captain may also check incoming orders to ensure that order-takers are taking them in a timely fashion and that in-room dining attendants are delivering them quickly. When in-room dining attendants are preparing to leave the kitchen area, captains may serve as checkers to confirm that orders are correct. Properties with heavy in-room dining demand (such as resorts) may assign a captain to an in-room dining area or pantry on each floor. Overall, captains help ensure that the in-room dining operation runs smoothly.

In-Room Dining Order-Taker. The **in-room dining order-taker** or in-room dining operator is a critical guest-contact position. An order-taker's shift begins when he or she takes possession of numbered guest checks; learns about any problems, substitutions, or other concerns related to the menu; and ensures that in-room dining attendants are on duty as assigned. As guests place in-room dining orders, the order-taker must record their orders on the guest checks according to hotel procedures, see that the orders get to food production areas, and, in many properties, enter the check into a precheck register or another data machine. An in-room dining order-taker may also serve as a food checker to confirm that orders that are about to be removed from the production area match the items listed on their corresponding guest checks.

The order-taker's role during initial contacts with guests is much like that of a food or beverage server with dining room guests; that is why suggestive selling and knowing the menu are among this staff member's responsibilities. The order-taker is really a salesperson rather than someone who simply takes orders.

In-Room Dining Attendants. **In-room dining attendants** accept orders from production areas, ensure that all items listed on the guest check are on the food tray or cart, permit the order-taker or captain to double-check the order if procedures require it, deliver orders to designated guestrooms, and serve guests in their guestrooms. (At some properties, they also take in-room dining orders from guests.) They may also perform station setup and breakdown tasks in the in-room dining area and do the work of buspersons during busy shifts. Procedures for delivering in-room dining orders will be discussed in more detail later in the chapter.

It is absolutely essential for in-room dining attendants to be thoroughly familiar with the property's layout and the location of each guestroom and suite. Time lost while an attendant looks for a guestroom affects not only the quality of that guest's service, but also the service of subsequent guests who will receive their orders later than expected. The quality of food deteriorates as the length of time between production and service increases during transportation.

In lodging properties that are spread over many areas and buildings (many resorts fit this description, for example), in-room dining attendants often deliver orders in motorized vehicles such as golf carts. In-room dining managers at resorts must often meet the needs of very demanding guests and should ask for input from in-room dining attendants to help them develop creative methods to ensure that those needs are met.

In general, in-room dining attendants function like food and beverage servers; they not only serve food and beverages to guests, but also ensure that the guests are completely satisfied with the items and the service.

Buspersons. Buspersons may help set up in-room dining stations in food production areas, assemble items for an order, deliver small orders, pick up in-room dining equipment and dishes from guestrooms and hallways, take used serviceware to dishwashing areas, clean in-room dining tables and trays, and perform miscellaneous tasks that increase the efficiency of in-room dining attendants. Buspersons may help set up hospitality suites by placing tablecloths on tables and delivering serviceware and food and beverage supplies to the suites.

Forecasting and Staff Member Scheduling

In-room dining managers must plan carefully when scheduling staff members. Unfortunately, this task is not easy, because it is difficult to assess all of the factors that have an impact on in-room dining demand. Some of these factors include (1) occupancy levels (experienced in-room dining managers can estimate from the house count the approximate number of guests who will desire in-room dining); (2) the number of guests who are traveling on an expense account; (3) the number of convention and business groups in-house (front desk and catering department staff can help in-room dining managers forecast how many people will require in-room dining based on the estimated attendance of organized meal functions); and (4) the number of guests whose room rates include a continental breakfast, a fruit basket, or similar in-room amenities (obviously there will be a direct correlation between these guest counts and in-room dining needs).

Some lodging properties transfer service staff back and forth between dining areas and the in-room dining department as volume fluctuates in these areas. When this system is used, all service staff members must be well trained in all of the service procedures that apply to each area. Properties that do not use this system have a much greater need to accurately forecast the volume of business anticipated for in-room dining, since slow service is likely to result if the estimates for in-room dining staff are inaccurate and not enough staff members are scheduled. (And if too many in-room dining staff members are scheduled, labor costs are unnecessarily high.) In-room dining business that is arranged in advance (such as cocktails and appetizers in hospitality suites or small group dining in guestrooms) is not as difficult to staff. The schedule planner will need to study the applicable **function sheets** that provide detailed information about in-room dining staff needs in those areas.

Facility Design

In-room dining production and order-assembly areas must be designed to use space efficiently and facilitate the prompt delivery of in-room dining orders to guestrooms. It may be worthwhile for managers to conduct a motion study on in-room dining food and beverage preparation procedures and examine in-room dining areas (or hire a consultant to do so) to see how design improvements could improve service speed.

Guestrooms must also be designed for efficiency. In some properties, all of the items needed for in-room dining, including a mobile dining table, are rolled into the guestroom when the order is delivered. Designers must make certain that the chairs already present in the guestroom are compatible in design (particularly in height and width) with in-room dining tables. At some properties, in-room dining orders are delivered on trays to guestrooms. In this case, there must be a comfortable eating surface in the guestroom, such as a table or desk.

Inventory and Equipment

In-room dining varies greatly from one lodging property to the next, but there are some inventory and equipment items that almost all properties use.

Carts are used to transport food to guestrooms and hospitality suites. These carts may be equipped with electrically heated hot boxes or canned, jellied alcohol fuels that are lit by the in-room dining attendant. Some properties use a two-piece pellet system; in-room dining staff members place a preheated pellet in a base and put the plate in or on the base, then place a second hot pellet on the cover.

A wide variety of equipment and supplies should be available in appropriate quantities in in-room dining areas. Storing equipment close to where it will first be used can improve transportation time. While some small in-room dining departments may require only a cart, shelving units, or one or two shelves on a wall to store their supplies, larger departments require more storage space. Setting par stock levels and keeping a log of supplies and equipment will help in-room dining managers know when more items need to be ordered. In some properties, inventory maintenance for in-room dining may be handled by housekeeping or the food and beverage department. Equipment repair should be coordinated with the property's maintenance and engineering department.

The number of in-room dining orders will differ by day and by shift. For example, if a lodging property caters primarily to business travelers, its weekday occupancy rates and in-room dining breakfast volumes will be higher than those on weekends. Therefore, the property will require a different quantity of in-room dining equipment and supply items at different times. The checklist shown in Exhibit 3 allows for variations between busy and slow shifts.

Preparations for Service Shifts

In well-run in-room dining departments, in-room dining attendants have completed preparation work during slow times or prior to the beginning of a service shift so they have only a minimum number of these tasks to perform during peak business hours. For example, they will have preset in-room dining carts or trays (they make certain the cart or tray is clean; they place a place mat, tablecloth, or other covering on it; and they set it properly with tableware, napkins, and appropriate condiments). Preset carts and trays are generally stored in out-of-the-way aisle areas where in-room dining attendants can conveniently obtain them. To ensure that attendants have an adequate number of items at the beginning of their shifts, some managers use a checklist similar to the one in Exhibit 3.

Before in-room dining attendants begin work, they should be briefed about any special functions occurring at the property, the amount of forecasted business,

Exhibit 3   Checklist of In-Room Dining Equipment and Supplies

Items	Amount Required			
	Day/Shift	Day/Shift	Day/Shift	Day/Shift
	Weekday (A.M.)	Weekend (A.M.)	Weekday (P.M.)	Weekend (P.M.)
Service Trays				
Tables				
Tablecloths				
Cloth Napkins				
Paper Napkins				
Bread Baskets				
Place Mats				
Coffee Cups				
Saucers				
Juice Glasses				

any unavailable menu items, specials of the day, a list of VIPs and groups of people staying at the hotel, and any other information that will enable them to provide superior service to guests. Order-takers should be well-informed about menu item ingredients and production techniques so they can answer guest questions.

Delivering In-Room Dining

Now that you understand the roles of the various positions associated with in-room dining, it's time to consider how in-room dining actually operates. What follows is an overview of in-room dining procedures, first for food and beverage orders, then for wine service and special in-room dining amenities. (Sample job or task breakdowns for typical tasks performed by in-room dining personnel are included at the end of the chapter.)

Procedures

In-room dining procedures involve taking the in-room dining order, routing the order, preparing the order, delivering the order, and clean-up and follow-up.

Taking the Order. Order-takers should follow the specific procedures developed by their lodging property as they take orders from guests. Order-takers should answer all telephone calls promptly and offer an apology if the phone rings for a long period of time. Many properties require the telephone to be answered within three rings.

The order-taker should identify him- or herself and indicate that the caller has reached in-room dining. The order-taker should use a cheerful voice to convey a spirit of hospitality. Caller identification systems that identify guests' names for order-takers enable them to provide personalized service. Most guests are impressed when an order-taker uses their names when the guests haven't identified themselves yet. Some computerized systems create guest lists that can be printed at the front desk and taken to the in-room dining department; other systems display the guest's name and room number on a screen when the phone rings. Order-takers should ask for the guest's name and guestroom number immediately if they are not already available.

Order-takers in automated in-room dining operations can input orders at point-of-sale (POS) systems. They typically use the same type of POS system used by catering or other food and beverage departments at the property. Lodging properties without POS systems use manual guest check systems; as the guest recites the order, the order-taker fills out a paper guest check with a pen or pencil (see Exhibit 4). Frequently, duplicate guest checks are used. Guest checks are usually prenumbered and assigned to specific order-takers; all guest checks must be accounted for at the end of each order-taker's shift. When order-takers use manual systems, it is very important that they write legibly, since production staff, service personnel, the guest, and in some cases a cashier all may need to read the check. Order-takers should also use standard menu abbreviations to help prevent misunderstandings.

The order should be repeated to the guest to confirm its accuracy. Order-takers should also give callers an estimate of the delivery time, particularly during rush periods when several orders may be in line for preparation and delivery. Some guests may be in a hurry and will not want to wait for an in-room dining order. If it later becomes clear that it will be impossible to deliver in-room dining orders within the originally estimated time, the order-taker should call the guests and let them know when to expect delivery.

Order-takers can sell by suggestion. The same procedures that servers use in the dining room apply here. **Suggestive selling** gives guests the opportunity to order something extra. This helps guests enjoy the best that the property has to offer, helps the property receive higher revenues, and helps in-room dining staff earn more tips. Everyone wins. Guests may forget to order beverages, appetizers, or desserts if order-takers do not specifically ask about these kinds of items. Informing guests about specials, describing item preparation and presentation,

Exhibit 4   Sample Guest Check

	Table	Guest
		1
	Server	Room Number
	Ed	330
	Date	Check Number

❶ *Cutler*

Holiday Inn ®

Room Service

❽ 7:30   8:15 ❾

❹ 1	Zoe/BAC	$X.XX
2		
3		
4		
5		
6		
7		
8		
❺ 9	Lg OJ	$X.XX
10	Cof	$X.XX
11		
12		
13		
14		$X.XX ❼
	Tax	$X.XX
	Sub Total	
	Tip	
	Total	

❻ *Charge*

Signature_____ Room No. __330__

Address_____

❶ Ask for guest's name and write on check.

❷ Ask for the room number and write on check.

❸ Ask the guest how many settings they would like.

❹ Request and write the entrée using standard abbreviations. Ask for and write details (i.e., rare, medium, well for steaks, choice of salad dressing, etc.).

❺ Upsell side orders, larger portions, desserts, and beverages. Advise guest of any "specials."

❻ Ask if the order will be cash or charged to the room. Check the prepaid list to verify the guest has charging privileges. If not, write "prepay" on the check so the server knows to collect cash.

❼ Price the items, total the check, and tell the guest the amount.

❽ Tell the guest the time and write it on the check.

❾ Advise the guest of the approximate time of delivery.

Note: When separate bar checks are used, transfer the total of the bar check to the front of the food check. As a reminder to include bar totals, write the word "BAR" on the food check when taking the bar order.

Source: *Room Service* (Memphis, Tennessee: Holiday Inns, Inc.—U.S. Hotel Operations, 1981), p. 20.

suggesting high-contribution-margin items, and asking **open-ended questions** (as opposed to closed-ended questions, to which guests can answer "yes" or "no") or **forced-choice questions** such as "Which of our two excellent desserts would you like, Mr. Marshall?" are all techniques that can increase in-room dining sales. Good order-takers learn to gauge how well callers know what they want. Suggestive-selling techniques should not be used on guests who seem to know exactly what they want, since they might become annoyed. When the order-taking process is completed, order-takers should always thank the guest.

Some properties use a voice mail or tape-recorded message system for in-room dining; the guest phones the in-room dining number and places the order without talking to a staff member. Other properties use this system only during very slow periods when an order-taker is not on duty. For example, during slow periods an in-room dining attendant may serve as the order-taker as well; guests leave a taped message when the attendant is away from the station, delivering an order. The impersonal service and the possibility of confusion about the guest's exact needs are two potential disadvantages to this system. The in-room dining manager must ensure that the advantages of faster service and reduced operating (labor) costs offset these potential problems before using a voice mail or other message system.

Telephone etiquette may be a matter of common sense to most in-room dining staff members; nevertheless, all staff should receive initial as well as refresher training on the rules of telephone etiquette. In-room dining attendants, though they typically spend much less time on the phone with guests than order-takers, should be familiar with telephone etiquette so that when they do phone guests, answer guests' calls, or substitute for order-takers, they are prepared. Whoever answers the phone should stop talking with others before picking up the receiver. Because guests should not have to hear unnecessary noise and background conversations, and to help ensure accurate order-taking, nearby staff members should not converse among themselves while another staff member is speaking to a guest on the phone.

Putting callers on hold the right way is a part of good telephone etiquette. When two phone calls are coming in or when a phone call comes in while the order-taker is on the line with another guest, the order-taker should put guests on hold using the following procedures:

- Ask Caller #1 if you may put him or her on hold to answer another line.

- Ask Caller #2 to please hold while you complete another order.

- Return to Caller #1, apologize for the delay, and finish taking the first order.

- Return to Caller #2, apologize for the delay, and take the order.

- If you think Caller #2 will be on hold for too long, or if a third call is received, apologize to Caller #2 and offer to call back for the order. Take the guests' orders as soon as possible.

- Anytime you must interrupt the conversation, explain the reason to the guest.

Exhibit 5 summarizes telephone etiquette guidelines and order-taking procedures for in-room dining personnel.

Exhibit 5   Telephone Etiquette and Order-Taking Procedures

1. Answer the telephone promptly—within three rings when possible.

2. Identify yourself and your department with a friendly greeting. For example, a property may specify that from 7:00 A.M. to noon an order-taker named Carla should say, "In-Room Dining, Carla speaking, good morning"; from noon to 6:00 P.M., "In-Room Dining, Carla speaking, good afternoon"; from 6:00 P.M. to 9:00 P.M., "In-Room Dining, Carla speaking, good evening"; and from 9:00 P.M. to closing, "In-Room Dining, Carla speaking, may I help you?"

3. Politely ask for the guest's name and room number (if the in-room dining department doesn't use a caller identification system or receive guest lists from the front desk).

4. Use the caller's name whenever possible, being certain that it is pronounced correctly. Ask the caller how to pronounce his or her name if necessary.

5. Use a cheerful voice throughout the conversation.

6. Obtain a complete order by asking the guest about appetizers, entrées, desserts, beverages, and special preparation instructions.

7. Use suggestive selling to encourage guests to order something extra and help them make sure that they remember all they want to order. If it is clear that the guest knows exactly what he or she wants, make fewer suggestions or none at all.

8. To help eliminate errors, repeat the order the guest has placed.

9. State the approximate time that the guest can expect the order to be delivered. State a range of time, depending on the amount of business that in-room dining is currently handling. If the guest has ordered items that require extra preparation time or that are usually prepared at tableside, inform the guest about this to confirm that the order will be ready when the guest wants it.

10. Thank the guest for calling. Allow the guest to hang up the phone first.

Routing the Order. After the order-taker receives a guest's order, he or she must route it to the appropriate food or beverage production area. There are several methods of doing so:

1. The order-taker may carry the guest check to the production area by hand. This system may work well when a separate in-room dining kitchen and service bar are located close to the order-taker's telephone stand or when the order-taker is a cashier or receptionist in the dining room.

2. The order-taker may give the guest check to an in-room dining attendant, who then takes it to the production area.

3. The order-taker may use a precheck register or POS system with a remote printer. With this equipment, the order-taker automatically transmits the order to production staff members as he or she enters the information into the precheck register or POS system. This technology can dramatically speed service.

Exhibit 6   In-Room Dining Order Form

Date: _____						
Room #	Guest Name	Time Order	Delivery Time	Order	Tray	Cart

Courtesy of Hotel du Pont, Wilmington, Delaware

Order-takers using a manual system must then enter information from the guest check onto an **in-room dining order form** (see Exhibit 6). Properties use this form to record information about each order, such as the room number, the guest's name, and the time the order was placed. The order-taker must also make an entry on the **in-room dining control form** (see Exhibit 7), which keeps track of all guest checks. It indicates the person responsible for delivering the order, the time required to prepare the order, and the total amount of cash and charge sales generated by in-room dining. A POS system can automatically generate reports covering the information recorded on both of these forms, since the system can maintain all of the information related to each order.

Procedures for transmitting in-room dining orders to production personnel become more complicated when order-takers must give copies of orders to two kinds of production stations (those at which hot food is produced and those at which cold food is produced, for example) as well as to the service bar. One operation solves this problem by using a five-part order ticket. The order-taker writes the entire order on this ticket; one copy goes to the cashier, another goes to the hot food station, a third goes to the cold food station, a fourth goes to the service bar, and the fifth copy goes to the in-room dining attendant so that he or she can put the order together on a tray or service cart. Automation would drastically improve service in in-room dining operations at which orders are prepared in several different areas.

Exhibit 7   In-Room Dining Control Form

Food & Beverage Department
Room Service Control

①

Day_____ Date_____ Cashier_____ Shift_____

LOCATION **②**

Guest Name	Server	Order taken ⑤	A.M./P.M.
Check No. **③**	Amount $ **④**	Tray out	A.M./P.M. **⑥**
Room No.	No. Served ( ) paid ( ) charge **⑧**	Tray in	A.M./P.M. **⑦**
Guest Name	Server	Order taken	A.M./P.M.
Check No.	Amount $	Tray out	A.M./P.M.
Room No.	No. Served ( ) paid ( ) charge	Tray in	A.M./P.M.
Guest Name	Server	Order taken	A.M./P.M.

① Complete the heading at the beginning of the shift.

② Write the guest's name and room number. This information should be checked with the front desk to verify:

- The guests are registered
- The correct room number
- The guest's credit standing

③ Write the guest check number and obtain the server's signature. This signals a change of responsibility from the order taker to the server for the proper use of guest check.

④ Write the dollar amount of the order and the number of guests served.

⑤ Record the time the order was taken.

⑥ Record the time the tray is taken out for delivery.

⑦ Record the time of day the tray is returned to the kitchen.

⑧ Record the form of payment (cash or charge).

NOTE: Charged tips should be recorded on a tip tally form.

Source: *Room Service* (Memphis, Tennessee: Holiday Inns, Inc.—U.S. Hotel Operations, 1981), p. 30.

Preparing the Order. In-room dining attendants should be aware of the orders being prepared by production staff so they can do any additional setup work. For example, attendants may prepare or portion salads and desserts while production staff members prepare other parts of the order. If necessary, attendants should cover these salads and desserts with plastic wrap or store them in protective containers to help maintain quality. In-room dining attendants could also obtain beverages, typically from a service bar located close to the in-room dining area. Attendants must give the bartender a copy of the in-room dining order indicating the beverages they need.

In properties with a central beverage storeroom, a manager issues full bottles of alcoholic and other beverages from the central storeroom to the in-room dining beverage storage area. The manager can use a standard issue requisition and then transfer the costs of issued beverages to the in-room dining department. If guests request full bottles from in-room dining, in-room dining attendants at some hotels may obtain bottles from the in-room dining beverage storeroom. In-room dining managers must always have controls in place to keep track of beverage inventory, supply accounting information, and protect inventory from theft or quality deterioration.

When food orders are ready, the in-room dining attendants pick them up, cover them with lids or some other insulated material, and, at some properties, present them to the order-taker, food checker, or another designated staff member for inspection (at other properties, the in-room dining attendant is the final inspector). At some properties, in-room dining attendants put caps or covers on cups to prevent spills. The entire cart or serving tray should be covered with a washable cloth or disposable clear plastic cover. The food and beverages are now ready for one final inspection and then rapid delivery to the guest.

Why is each order checked so thoroughly before it is delivered? A frequent guest complaint is that condiments or other items are missing from in-room dining orders. Because guestrooms can be a long way from the kitchen, an error found by a guest takes more time to correct and creates more problems than it would if the error had been discovered in or near the kitchen by a staff member.

Delivering the Order. It is imperative that in-room dining attendants deliver orders as quickly as possible. The fastest route to the guestroom should be used; attendants and other in-room dining staff members must know the layout of the property extremely well. Hot food should still be hot, and cold food should still be cold when it gets to the guest. Time and temperature are the most important elements in in-room dining delivery, because as product holding times increase, so does the likelihood of contamination and loss of quality. Some properties offer **split service,** which means that in-room dining attendants deliver courses separately. Split service helps maintain food quality and safety; each course can be portioned and served when it is ready, eliminating short-term holding in the kitchen. The disadvantage of split service is that it takes more staff to deliver courses separately, and therefore is more costly.

Some lodging properties use **dumbwaiters** (small service elevators) to expedite order delivery. Using dumbwaiters to move products between floors may work well when continental breakfasts (coffee, juice, and rolls) are offered to all guests or when standard breakfasts are offered to VIPs and guests in guestroom suites. Some properties designate one or more freight or passenger elevators for in-room dining use during busy periods. **Flying kitchens**— well-equipped elevators that enable service staff to prepare a limited number of menu items as they move between floors—are sometimes installed. An in-room dining attendant could be assigned to one or more floors during peak business periods; after the carts are transported to each floor, they can be transferred to the attendant assigned to the floor, who then delivers the orders. From time to time, managers should brainstorm ways to keep service timely with in-room dining staff.

In-room dining managers should develop procedures for delivering in-room dining orders. For example, all in-room dining staff members should know that when entering or exiting elevators with an in-room dining cart, the cart should be pulled rather than pushed. Why? Pulling gives the staff member more control over the cart and there is less chance that a guest or another staff member will bump into it. Other procedures might include delivering orders approximately in the sequence in which they were received, using a uniform greeting and method of alerting guests that their orders have arrived, greeting the guest warmly, and verifying the guest's name and room number when the guest opens the door. At some lodging properties, in-room dining attendants ask guests for permission to enter their guestrooms, then ask them where they prefer their orders to be placed—on a table, left on the cart, or elsewhere. Hot foods should be left in warmers for the guest's self-service unless he or she indicates otherwise. If the order requires table-side preparation, attendants may be required to tell guests how long the order will take to prepare and to ask if they may begin the preparation.

Normally, in-room dining attendants ask guests to sign a copy of the guest check to verify that they received the order. It is a good idea to give the guest the guest check and a pen before setting up the order. This will eliminate an awkward time lag while the guest reviews and signs the check. Usually, the guest's signature is sufficient; however, cash payments are required in certain circumstances, such as when the guest paid cash for the room and has no guest folio set up with the front desk.

The in-room dining attendant should use discretion in the guest's room. It is critical to respect the guest's privacy and not disturb any of the guest's personal items. If it is absolutely necessary to move items to serve the order, the attendant should politely ask the guest for permission to do so. The attendant should offer to pour beverages for the guest. When serving food on the in-room dining cart, the attendant should check the supporting braces of the cart extensions to be certain that they are secure and will not collapse. If the in-room dining cart has a heating element, it should be extinguished by the attendant according to the property's procedures. Guests should be cautioned about handling plates that are hot.

Before leaving, in-room dining attendants should offer additional assistance to the guest and remind the guest about cart or tray pickup procedures. Attendants may give the guest a number to dial for additional service or to request tray pickup; this information might also be provided on a courtesy card left on the tray or cart. The attendant should always thank the guest and wish him or her an enjoyable meal.

Clean-Up and Follow-Up. Properties should have a system in place for removing used in-room dining trays and carts quickly. On their way back to the in-room dining area after delivering an order, in-room dining attendants should pick up any trays or take care of any carts left in hotel corridors. Some properties offer bonuses to staff members for taking care of carts or trays left in hallways.

Coordination and effective communication between housekeeping personnel and the in-room dining staff are essential. Housekeepers could phone in-room dining staff to remove in-room dining equipment from guestrooms, or housekeepers could move used in-room dining items to a central location, or (as just mentioned) a card left on the tray or cart could ask guests to phone in-room dining or the housekeeping department when they wish in-room dining equipment to be removed.

If time permits, order-takers or other in-room dining staff members should phone guests after their orders are delivered to ask them how they are enjoying the meal and to offer additional assistance. Many guests appreciate this extra service.

Providing Wine Service and Special Amenities

Guests may order table or sparkling bottled wines from in-room dining; therefore, in-room dining attendants should know the proper ways to uncork them. In-room dining attendants may also be responsible for delivering fruit baskets, cheese trays, and other special amenities for guests; therefore, management should develop standard procedures for preparing, arranging, and delivering these items. In addition, if special amenities require cloth napkins, flatware, or plates, the attendants must ensure that those supplies accompany the orders. A form like the one shown in Exhibit 8 can be used whenever a hotel executive or a friend, relative, or business associate orders a special in-room dining amenity for a guest. Often, these amenities are a good source of revenue for the in-room dining department. (When a hotel executive provides a special amenity for a guest, he or she should credit in-room dining for at least the cost of the item. The executive can charge the item to a sales promotion account.)

Frequently, a welcome card accompanies special in-room dining amenities, and the in-room dining attendant is often responsible for ensuring that it is in place. Managers design or write welcome cards simply to welcome a guest and to wish him or her a pleasant stay. This special touch can be instrumental in gaining the favor of a VIP. In cosmopolitan hotels, welcome cards may be available in many languages. Room attendants must make sure the guest receives a card in his or her language.

Guests frequently order bar setups through in-room dining. Typical items in a bar setup are alcoholic beverages, cocktail napkins, stir sticks, glasses, a pitcher of water, a bucket of ice, and appropriate garnishes. In addition to alcoholic beverages, the guest requesting a bar setup may order mixers such as tonic water, club soda, or bottled water. Depending on the guestroom's location, attendants may bring ice to the guestroom from the in-room dining area or from an ice machine that is close to the guestroom.

Some properties offer executive coffee service. Guests who are staying on special VIP floors, specific guests identified by management, guests paying the full rate for expensive rooms, and others may receive this extra in-room dining amenity. This complimentary morning coffee service may consist of juice, pastries, hot beverages, and a morning newspaper. Special order forms for executive coffee

Exhibit 8 **Order Form for Special In-Room Dining Amenities**

NR: **1555**

Special Room Service Order

For Mr./Ms.: _____   Room: _____

Delivery Date: _____   Cost Code: _____

From: ☐ _____   ☐ _____

☐ _____   ☐ _____

☐ _____

☐ $XX.XX **Large deluxe fruit tray with one bottle of wine**
(Selection of fruit and chocolate, presented on a silver tray including one bottle of wine, white or red)

☐ $XX.XX **Large deluxe fruit tray**
(Selection of fruit and chocolate, presented on a silver tray)

☐ $XX.XX **Small fruit mirror with cheese and $1/2$ bottle of wine**
(Selection of fruit, cheese, and chocolate presented on a small mirror with $1/2$ bottle of wine)

☐ $XX.XX **Small fruit mirror with cheese and chocolate**
(Selection of fruit, cheese, and chocolate presented on a small mirror)

☐ $XX.XX **Fruit arrangement in a wicker basket**
(Assorted fruit in a basket)

☐ $XX.XX **Presentation of chocolate cups with 2 small liquor bottles**
(Presented on a blue plate with chocolate cups and flowers)

☐ $_____ Champagne Domestic _____ Import _____

Name: _____   Total Cost: $ _____

Courtesy of Hotel du Pont, Wilmington, Delaware

service typically supply the information that in-room dining staff members need to provide this amenity.

After In-Room Dining

After in-room dining has been delivered, issues important to managers include income control procedures, guest comments, and funneling feedback about in-room dining into planning activities.

Income Control Procedures

While many of the income control procedures used in the in-room dining department mirror those used in public dining areas, some are unique to in-room dining operations. Control procedures to collect payment for all orders served through in-room dining begin at the time order-takers write orders on guest checks or enter orders into a POS system. In manual systems, order-takers enter information about an order and the amount of income it will generate on the in-room dining control form (see Exhibit 7). After service, attendants return copies of guest checks that guests have signed to the order-taker. The order-taker then enters information about the payment (cash or charge) into a log. At the end of the shift or at another time designated by management, order-takers must carry the in-room dining control form and the signed guest check copies to the front desk for posting into **guest folios**. Hotels increasingly are using POS systems rather than manual systems in their in-room dining departments. When in-room dining uses POS equipment, guest charges are electronically transferred to guest folios at the front desk.

Because most guests wish to have their in-room dining charges billed to their guestroom accounts, procedures to accommodate these requests should be developed. Sometimes, however, charges are not possible. For example, a guest may have paid for the room in advance with cash, or guests may have reached or exceeded their lines of credit. The front office should regularly report guests who are on a cash basis to the in-room dining department so that order-takers can note the need for cash payments on the guest checks of these guests. In addition, order-takers should inform these guests that the in-room dining attendant will require cash when he or she delivers their orders. Some properties provide in-room dining attendants with a payment card imprinter and appropriate supplies in anticipation of guests who wish to use their payment cards. Policies and procedures regarding the acceptance of payment cards and checks must comply with those developed by the lodging property for use in other property areas.

Guest Comments

Guest comments and complaints about in-room dining span a wide range of topics. High prices are the main reason that guests do not use in-room dining. Guests may resist tipping staff members because of perceived high menu charges; some hotels add an automatic gratuity percentage to in-room dining charges for that reason. In general, business travelers are not as price-conscious as pleasure travelers, most likely because their in-room dining charges are often paid by their companies.

Some guests focus on the quality of the food and beverages served or the quality of the service rather than price. Guests dislike slow service. They often expect their meals to arrive no more than 20 minutes after they order. Some properties' in-room dining order-takers cannot speak the native language well, so communicating with guests can be difficult. Even without the language barrier, guests who use in-room dining often complain that the items that were delivered were not what they ordered, were delivered at improper temperatures, or were presented poorly. Many guests complain about dirty dishes left in hotel hallways from in-room dining deliveries.

Guests sometimes complain that there is not enough variety on in-room dining menus. Today's guests often expect a selection of fresh fruits and the option to design their own meals to suit their preferences or dietary restrictions. Clearly, guest expectations of in-room dining today are high, and it is worthwhile for in-room dining managers to familiarize themselves with the expectations of their property's target markets.

Managers may obtain guest comments by asking guests for feedback in person or recording comments that guests made to service staff. They may also ask guests to complete comment forms that cover all areas of their hotel stay. In-room dining should be included on this form as a way to obtain additional feedback for planning.

Another strategy for obtaining detailed, timely guest feedback is to have the in-room dining manager regularly phone a sampling of guests who have used in-room dining. Specific details about menus, staff member service styles, and the overall in-room dining experience can be obtained if the right questions are asked. As an incentive, managers could offer a slight reduction in the hotel's guestroom rate to guests who provide this valuable feedback.

Using Feedback in Planning

Information obtained during and after in-room dining can be a valuable source of feedback for in-room dining planners. In-room dining menus must continue to evolve, based on the needs and expectations of guests. Guests today are generally in search of high-quality menu items, served in smaller quantities, at affordable prices. These three criteria translate to value for guests.

Suppose that a property surveys its guests concerning in-room dining and discovers that their complaints are (in order):

1. High prices

2. Slow service

3. Food not as hot/cold as it should be

4. Don't like eating alone

5. Limited hours

6. Insufficient variety

7. Inadequate menu

How could managers at the property improve in-room dining to make it more guest-driven? First, the managers should consider reducing in-room dining menu prices, since that was the top complaint. Next, the managers should evaluate how in-room dining is delivered at the property, because slow service and food not at its proper temperature are the next highest complaints. To alleviate these service-related problems, managers should make sure in-room dining staff members are properly trained and have the inventory and equipment it takes to deliver quality food and beverages to guests. Managers cannot do anything about the fact that some guests do not like eating alone, but they can look into doing something about the limited in-room dining hours and insufficient variety on the in-room dining menu, and do more investigating to find out why guests think the menu is "inadequate." Of course, managers must keep budget constraints in mind as they think about making improvements to in-room dining.

In a guest-driven in-room dining operation, the needs and expectations of guests come first. In-room dining staff must be trained to embrace the philosophy that when they deliver an in-room dining order, they are really bringing the dining room to the guest's room. By respecting the guest's privacy and providing prompt and attentive service, in-room dining staff members can delight guests. Positive in-room dining experiences can help give guests a good impression of the property, enhance the property's reputation, and increase revenues for all of the property's revenue centers.

 **Key Terms**

assistant in-room dining manager—An assistant to the in-room dining manager who assumes some of the responsibilities that would otherwise be the in-room dining manager's, such as supervising staff, making daily or routine operational management decisions, and completing records and reports.

busperson—A staff member who helps set up in-room dining stations in the kitchen, assembles items for an order, delivers small orders, picks up in-room dining equipment and tableware from rooms and hallways, takes used serviceware to dishwashing areas, cleans in-room dining tables and trays, and otherwise supports in-room dining attendants.

cross-selling—In internal selling, a sales technique in which hotel staff members working in one hotel area suggest that guests take advantage of the products and services of other hotel areas. Cross-selling can also be accomplished with advertising media.

doorknob menu—A type of in-room dining menu that guests use to select what they want to eat and the time they want it delivered; they then hang the menu outside the guestroom door on the doorknob. Later, staff members collect the menus so that the orders can be prepared and sent to the rooms at the indicated times.

dumbwaiters—Small service elevators that can be used to deliver in-room dining orders.

fact book—A book salespeople and others at a lodging property use to familiarize themselves with and remind themselves about their property's products and services.

flying kitchen—A well-equipped elevator that enables in-room dining staff members to produce a limited number of menu items as they move between floors.

forced-choice question—A question that seeks to limit the respondent to choosing from the alternatives presented by the questioner.

function sheet—A document that gives a detailed breakdown of items, people, and tasks needed to prepare for, provide service during, and clean up after a special event. Also called a banquet event order (BEO).

guest folio—A file (electronic or paper) containing all of a guest's charges during the guest's stay at a lodging property.

hospitality suite—A guestroom, suite of guestrooms, function room, or parlor that guests use for entertaining (for example, by throwing a cocktail party).

in-room dining—The department within a lodging property's food and beverage division that is responsible for delivering food and beverages to guests in their guestrooms. May also be responsible for producing the food and beverages.

in-room dining attendant—A staff member who accepts orders from the kitchen, ensures that all items listed on the guest check are on the food tray or cart, permits the order-taker to double-check the order if procedures require it, delivers orders to designated guestrooms, and serves guests in their rooms. May also take orders from guests, return carts, trays, and dirty dishes to the in-room dining area, and perform other duties to help the department run smoothly and deliver quality service to guests.

in-room dining captain—A staff member who oversees order-takers, in-room dining attendants, and buspersons for a particular area or shift. In-room dining captains typically report to the in-room dining manager or assistant in-room dining manager.

in-room dining control form—An accounting form that keeps track of guest checks and indicates the person responsible for delivering each order, the time required to prepare each order, and the total amount of cash and charge sales generated by in-room dining.

in-room dining manager—The head of the in-room dining department, responsible for organizing, selecting, orienting, training, and scheduling in-room dining staff; handling problems with food and beverage orders and delivery; controlling costs and ensuring revenue collection; and monitoring department operations. Reports to the lodging operation's food and beverage director or assistant director.

in-room dining order form—A form used to record information about each in-room dining order, such as the room number, the guest's name, and the time the order was placed.

in-room dining order-taker—A staff member who answers guest phone calls for in-room dining, takes guest orders, fills out logbooks and accounting forms, and acts as an intermediary between guests and in-room dining staff members.

internal selling—Specific sales activities of staff members used in conjunction with an internal merchandising program to promote additional sales and guest satisfaction once guests have arrived at the establishment.

menu engineering—A menu management technique that analyzes the profitability and popularity of menu items.

open-ended question—A question that cannot be answered with a "yes" or "no."

split service—An in-room dining delivery method in which staff members deliver courses separately. Split service helps maintain food quality because each course can be portioned and served when it is ready, eliminating short-term holding in the kitchen.

suggestive selling—The practice of influencing a guest's purchase decision through the use of sales phrases.

video ordering—A means of ordering in-room dining through the guestroom television, usually with the television's remote control.

 Review Questions ———————————————————————

1. From the guest's perspective, what are the key elements of a well-managed in-room dining department?

2. What should managers keep in mind when planning and designing in-room dining menus?

3. What are the responsibilities of typical in-room dining positions?

4. How do in-room dining staff members usually prepare for an individual service period?

5. How do in-room dining staff members take orders, route them, prepare them, deliver them, and perform cleaning tasks after orders have been delivered?

6. What is in-room dining's role in providing wine service and special in-room dining amenities?

7. What income control procedures are used in in-room dining?

8. What are typical guest comments and complaints about in-room dining? How can this feedback be used in planning?

 References ———————————————————————

Brecht, Adam. "U.S. Hotels Reduce Food and Beverage Service, Lodging Research Network Reports." *Hotel Online Special Report* (November 4, 1998), www.hotel-online.com.

"Dial for Luxury." *U.S. News & World Report,* January 26, 1998.

Flint, Jerry. "Room Service." *Forbes,* April 29, 1991.

"Ideas." *Innkeeping World,* September 1994.

Olvera, Jennifer. "Eating In at Hotels Can Be as Exquisite as Dining Out." *Chicago Sun-Times,* June 29, 2005.

Payne, Kirby D. "Room Service, or Is It Food Delivery?" *Hotel Online Special Report* (August 9, 2003), www.hotel-online.com.

Rowe, Megan. "Volume Feeding à la Vegas." *Lodging Hospitality,* April 1991.

———. Rowe, Megan. "What It's Worth." *Lodging Hospitality,* December 1997.

Straus, Karen. "Dial-A-Breakfast." *Restaurants & Institutions,* June 15, 1993.

Wolff, Carlo. "Roomservice Blues." *Lodging Hospitality,* December 1992.

Internet Sites

For more information, visit the following Internet sites. Remember that Internet addresses can change without notice. If the site is no longer there, you can use a search engine to look for additional sites.

American Culinary Federation
www.acfchefs.org

CATERWARE
www.caterware.com

CuisineNet
www.cuisinenet.com

Food Network
www.foodnetwork.com

The Food Channel
www.foodchannel.com

The Global Gourmet
www.globalgourmet.com

Newmarket International
www.newmarketinc.com

wine.com
www.wine.com

Appendix

Sample Training Needs Evaluation Form for In-Room Dining Attendants

How well are your current staff members performing? Use this form to observe and rate their work.

Part I: Job Knowledge

Rate the staff member's knowledge of each of the following topics:	Well Below Standard	Slightly Below Standard	At Standard	Above Standard
Knowledge for All Staff Members				
Quality Guest Service				
Bloodborne Pathogens				
Personal Appearance				
Emergency Situations				
Lost and Found				
Recycling Procedures				
Safe Work Habits				
Manager on Duty				
Your Property's Fact Sheet				
Staff Member Policies				
The Americans with Disabilities Act				
Knowledge for All Front-of-House Food and Beverage Staff Members				
Telephone Courtesy				
Safety and Security				
Kitchen Safety				
Alcoholic Beverage Terms				
House Brands and Call Brands				
Liquor Brands and Categories				
Standard Drink Abbreviations				
U.S. Alcoholic Beverage Laws				
Responsible Alcohol Service Procedures				
OSHA Regulations				

Rate the staff member's knowledge of each of the following topics:	Well Below Standard	Slightly Below Standard	At Standard	Above Standard
Knowledge for All Front-of-House Food and Beverage Staff Members *(continued)*				
Beverage Prices				
Restaurant Menus				
Basic Food Preparation Terms and Timing				
Correct Plate Presentation and Garnishes				
The Restaurant Reservation System				
Tipping Policies				
Heimlich Maneuver and First Aid				
Sanitation				
Health Department Regulations				
Point-of-Sale Equipment				
Community Services				
Knowledge for In-Room Dining Attendants				
What Is an In-Room Dining Attendant?				
Working as a Team With Co-Workers and Other Departments				
Superior Performance Standards				
Key Control				
Property Floor Plan				
Special Guest Situations				
Guestroom Safety				
Suggestive Selling				
In-Room Dining Equipment Terms				
Glassware Types and Use				
China				
Silverware				
Linens and Napkin Folding				

(continued)

Rate the staff member's knowledge of each of the following topics:	Well Below Standard	Slightly Below Standard	At Standard	Above Standard
Knowledge for In-Room Dining Attendants *(continued)*				
Standard Drink Ingredients and Garnishes				
Standard Tray and Cart Setups				
Standard Portable Bar Setup				
Standard Place-Setting Arrangement for Small Group Dinners				
Standard Setup for Small Receptions and Buffets				
Standard Setup for Coffee Breaks				
Par Stock System				
VIPs				
Part II: Job Skills				
Rate the staff member's skills in performing each of the following tasks:				
Perform Beginning-of-Shift Duties				
Present In-Room Dining Trays and Carts				
Process Express Breakfast Orders				
Deliver VIP Amenities				
Use the Point-of-Sale Equipment				
Take and Record In-Room Dining Orders				
Handle Special In-Room Dining Requests				
Place the In-Room Dining Order				
Perform Pantry Prep for In-Room Dining Orders				
Prepare Coffee				
Prepare Hot Tea				
Prepare Hot Chocolate				
Prepare Iced Tea				
Set Up Bottled Wine or Champagne for Service				

Rate the staff member's skills in performing each of the following tasks: *(continued)*	Well Below Standard	Slightly Below Standard	At Standard	Above Standard
Assemble the Beverage Order and Food Condiments				
Pick Up the In-Room Dining Order				
Deliver the In-Room Dining Order				
Serve the In-Room Dining Order				
Serve Coffee or Hot Tea				
Check IDs				
Open and Serve Wine or Champagne				
Present and Settle the Guest Check				
Retrieve Trays and Carts				
Close Out the Guest Check				
Follow Up with Guests				
Respond to Dissatisfied Guests				
Clear and Reset Trays and Carts				
Handle Soiled In-Room Dining Linens				
Set Up Portable Bars in Suites or Guestrooms				
Set Up and Serve Small Group Dinners and Receptions				
Set Up and Serve Small Buffet Banquets				
Set Up and Serve Coffee Breaks				
Maintain In-Room Dining Side Stations				
Pick Up and Restock In-Room Dining Supplies				
Perform Closing Shift Duties				
Make Shift Deposit and Collect Due-Backs				
Use the In-Room Dining Logbook				

Source: Adapted from the "Room Service Attendant Guide" in the *Hospitality Skills Training Series* (Lansing, Mich.: American Hotel & Lodging Educational Institute, 1995), pp. 15–17.

Task Breakdowns: In-Room Dining

The procedures presented in this section are for illustrative purposes only and should not be construed as recommendations or standards. While these procedures are typical, readers should keep in mind that each food and beverage operation has its own procedures, equipment specifications, and safety policies.

Preset In-Room Dining Trays and Carts

Materials needed: *In-room dining trays and carts, tray and cart setup charts, lemon wedges, a brush, cleaning cloths, sanitizing solution, tablecloths, hot boxes, and canned, gel-type fuel.*

STEPS	HOW-TO'S
1. Ask your supervisor for the tray and cart setup charts for each meal.	
2. Clean service trays.	❑ Wash trays in the dish room.
	❑ If the trays are cork-lined, rub the cork with lemon wedges to remove odors. Then let the trays stand for a few minutes before washing.
	❑ Spray trays with hot water to remove food residue.
	❑ If the trays are cork-lined, use a brush to scrub the cork. Then rinse the trays.
	❑ Spray the trays with an approved sanitizing solution. Then stack them upside-down at right angles to allow them to air-dry.
3. Clean in-room dining carts.	❑ Remove all equipment and supplies from the carts.
	❑ Use a clean cloth and a sanitizing solution to wipe the carts, including the shelves, legs, and wheels.
	❑ Polish the carts with a clean, dry cloth.
	❑ Replace equipment and supplies.
	❑ Report any squeaky wheels to maintenance staff members or stewards immediately, so they can fix the carts quickly.
4. Place tablecloths neatly over in-room dining carts.	
5. Organize and preset trays and carts before the meal period begins.	❑ Make sure you have the number of carts and trays requested on the tray and cart setup charts.

(continued)

Preset In-Room Dining Trays and Carts (continued)

STEPS	HOW-TO'S
	❑ Items you may place on a tray or cart include salt, pepper, ketchup, mustard, mayonnaise, sugar, and artificial sweetener.
	❑ Make sure each item is clean before placing it on a tray or cart.
	❑ Wipe containers with a clean cloth if necessary.
	❑ Follow the tray and cart setup charts to place items on trays and carts.
	❑ Spread the weight of the items evenly across the tray. Place heavy items in the center and lighter items around the edges.
6. Replace cans of gel-type fuel in hot boxes.	❑ Carefully open the hot box door.
	❑ Remove the empty can.
	❑ Place a new can in the box. Never place a new can in a hot box containing a can that is in use.
	❑ Close the hot box door.
	❑ Wash your hands right away. Canned, gel-type fuel is poisonous.
7. Position preset trays and carts where they won't be in the way.	

Take and Record In-Room Dining Orders

Materials needed: *Guest checks, a pen, point-of-sale equipment, in-room dining menus, the cash-only list, a telephone, and a time-date stamp.*

STEPS	HOW-TO'S
1. Greet callers warmly.	❑ Pick up the telephone within three rings.
	❑ Identify your department and introduce yourself by name.
	❑ Ask how you may help. For example: "Thank you for calling in-room dining. This is Lily, your in-room dining attendant. How may I help you?"
2. Use good telephone etiquette.	
3. Ask the guests for their names and room numbers.	❑ Always use the guest's last name with a courtesy title during the conversation: "Good morning, Ms. Soda."
	❑ Even if your computerized telephone system displays the guest's name and room number, confirm that you are talking to the registered guest.
	❑ Neatly write the guest's name and room number on the guest check. (With automated point-of-sale equipment, the system will record room numbers on the check.)
4. Determine whether guests have approved credit accounts at the front desk.	❑ As soon as you have the guest's name and room number, check the cash-only list to see if the guest's name is on that list.
	❑ If the guest's name and room number are on the list, politely explain that the guest will have to pay for the order when it is delivered.
	❑ If the guest's name and room number are not on the cash-only list, take the order without discussing payment.

(continued)

Take and Record In-Room Dining Orders (continued)

STEPS	HOW-TO'S
5. Use suggestive selling.	❑ Suggest appetizers, soups, salads, specials, profitable entrees, desserts, wine, and other products. Suggest premium-brand alcoholic beverages.
	❑ Recommend specific items to enhance the meal. For instance, say, "Would you like stuffed mushrooms or shrimp cocktail to begin your meal?"
	❑ Describe the daily specials. Always give the prices of specials. Your descriptions help guests "see" the items, and the guests may be more likely to order items they can picture.
	❑ Describe the ingredients and preparation in an appealing way.
6. Take orders.	❑ Pay attention to orders, and know the menu thoroughly.
	❑ Ask questions to find out the guest's choices or preferences for service, such as how he or she would like an item cooked or prepared (medium rare, "on-the-rocks," etc.). Ask the guest for his or her choice of salad dressings and for any special requests such as fat-free preparation, etc.
	❑ Write down all information clearly. Highlight special requests.
	❑ Ask how many guests will be eating and write the number on the guest check. You (or another in-room dining attendant) will set up trays or carts based on these numbers.
	❑ Record the time the order was taken on the check, or stamp the check with a time-date stamp.
	❑ Be prepared to suggest one or two appropriate wines or champagnes.

Take and Record In-Room Dining Orders (continued)

STEPS	HOW-TO'S
7. Help guests select a wine.	❑ In general, white wines go best with white meats and seafood, and red wines go best with red meats and game. Rose, blush, and sparkling wines go with any type of food.
	❑ White wine is served chilled, and red wine is served at room temperature (about 68°F or 20°C).
	❑ Guests are never wrong in their selection of wines, regardless of the general rules.
	❑ Answer any specific questions about the wines or champagnes at your property.
	❑ Never argue with a guest over the selection of a wine or the pronunciation of a name.
	❑ Allow the guest to make his or her own selection. Always support the guest's preference.
8. Politely read the order back to guests and repeat all details.	
9. Tell guests how long delivery will take.	
10. Thank guests for the order.	
11. Tell guests what the total charges will be, including tax and the service charge or automatic tip.	
12. Combine bar and in-room dining checks.	❑ If your property uses separate bar checks for in-room dining orders, transfer the bar check totals to the front of in-room dining checks. This will allow you to present one check to guests.

Perform Pantry Prep for In-Room Dining Orders

Materials needed: *A guest check, a service tray or in-room dining cart, foil, foodservice film, lids, napkins, straws, an ice bucket, ice, and an ice compote.*

STEPS	HOW-TO'S
1. Set up a service tray or in-room dining cart so the order can be delivered as soon as the food is ready.	❑ Set up the tray or cart according to the items listed on the guest check. Double-check every detail. ❑ Make sure all china, glasses, and silverware are clean and free from chips, cracks, water spots, and food residue. ❑ Throw away chipped or cracked china or glasses. Return soiled or spotted items to the dish room. ❑ Handle china, glasses, and silverware by the edges, and do not touch anywhere food or a guest's mouth will touch. ❑ Arrange items attractively on the tray or cart.
2. Prepare beverages, salads, crackers or bread and butter, and desserts.	❑ Cover dishes with foil, foodservice film, or lids. ❑ If the order includes food for children, include straws and extra paper napkins.
3. Get an ice bucket.	❑ If bottled beer or wine is to be served, pick up a filled ice bucket. ❑ If ice buckets were not prepared during opening sidework, fill a clean bucket two-thirds full with ice and pour enough water to cover the ice. ❑ Put a clean linen napkin through the ring of the bucket and drape it over the top of the bucket.
4. Set up an ice compote.	❑ Rest dishes filled with items that need to be kept cold in a bed of ice to keep the items from warming or melting during delivery.

Assemble the Beverage Order and Food Condiments

Materials needed: Beverages, glasses, food condiments, an ice scoop, ice, beverage containers, teapots, underliners, cream, lemon wedges, hot chocolate garnishes, a cleaning cloth, foodservice film or lids for glasses, and a service tray or in-room dining cart.

STEPS	HOW-TO'S
1. Preheat containers that will be used to carry hot beverages to the guestroom.	❑ Fill each container with hot water from the drip coffee maker and allow it to stand for three to five minutes. ❑ Preheating ensures that a cool container won't cool the hot beverage while you're delivering it. You will preheat teapots when you prepare hot tea.
2. Pour cold beverages without ice into the correct glass when the hot food is nearly ready.	
3. Pour hot drinks into preheated containers.	❑ Hot drinks include coffee, hot tea, and hot chocolate. ❑ Empty the water from the preheated container. ❑ Immediately fill the container with the hot drink. ❑ Make sure coffee is fresh. Never serve coffee that is more than 30 minutes old.
4. Pour drinks with ice.	❑ If glasses were previously filled with ice, drain off any water from melted ice before adding the beverages. ❑ If the glasses were not filled with ice, use a clean ice scoop to fill each glass. Then add the beverage.
5. Place beverages on a service tray or in-room dining cart.	❑ Place preheated containers of hot chocolate and coffee on the tray or cart. ❑ Place teapots full of hot tea on underliners and place them on the tray or cart. Wide-based teapots may not need underliners ❑ Place cold beverages on the tray or cart.

(continued)

Assemble the Beverage Order and Food Condiments
(continued)

STEPS	HOW-TO'S
6. Cover all glasses with foodservice film or lids to prevent spills.	
7. Place cream, lemon wedges, hot chocolate garnishes, and other appropriate items for beverage service on the tray or cart.	
8. Place the appropriate food condiments on the tray or cart.	❑ Make sure condiment containers are full and free from food residue. ❑ Wipe containers with a clean cloth if necessary.

Pick Up the In-Room Dining Order

Materials needed: *Foodservice film or lids for glasses, a service tray or in-room dining cart, aluminum foil or plate lids, a hot box, and canned, gel-type fuel.*

STEPS	HOW-TO'S
1. Pick up the beverage order from the bar.	❑ Check that the order is complete.
	❑ Check that the drinks have been prepared correctly.
	❑ Check that the drinks have been garnished correctly.
	❑ If there is a problem with the beverage order, work with the bartender to resolve the problem right away.
	❑ Cover all glasses with foodservice film or lids to prevent spills. The steps to place beverages on a service tray or in-room dining cart vary among properties.
2. Pick up the food order as soon as it is ready.	❑ The steps to pick up food orders from the kitchen varies among properties.
3. Check the food order.	❑ Make sure the order includes all entrees and side dishes.
	❑ Check the food before you take it out of the kitchen.
	• Does it look fresh and appealing?
	• Have all preparation instructions been followed?
	• Is the presentation garnished correctly?
	• Have all special requests been met?
	• Is the plate clean?
	• Is the hot food hot and the cold food cold?
	❑ If the food does not meet your property's standards, bring it to the attention of the cook or your supervisor. Do not deliver substandard food to guests. Thank the kitchen staff for their cooperation.

(continued)

Pick Up the In-Room Dining Order (continued)

STEPS	HOW-TO'S
	❑ Immediately notify your supervisor of any problems with the food preparation so he or she can speak to the guests and help correct the situation.
4. Place cold food on the tray or cart. 5. Cover hot food with aluminum foil or plate lids. 6. Place hot food in a hot box.	❑ Light the canned, gel-type fuel in the hot box if this type of fuel is used. Gel-type fuel is poisonous. Proper safety precautions should be taken when handling it. ❑ Wash your hands immediately. ❑ Place the hot box on an in-room dining cart, then place covered plates in the hot box.

Deliver the In-Room Dining Order

Materials needed: A service tray or in-room dining cart with a complete order.

STEPS	HOW-TO'S
1. Double-check the order to make sure nothing is missing, damaged, or soiled.	❑ Check everything carefully before leaving the kitchen to save unnecessary return trips to pick up items that were missed. ❑ Check the following: • Serviceware • Linens (napkins and tablecloth as appropriate) • Condiments • Bread and butter • Cold food (salad, cold appetizers, etc.) • Hot food • Garnishes • Hot beverages • Cold beverages • Beer or wine • Cocktails • Guest check in a check folder • Pen • Corkscrew (if needed) • Ice bucket (if needed) • Matches • Extra napkin for cleaning up spills
2. Lift and carry the in-room dining tray.	❑ Lift the tray carefully, using your legs for leverage. ❑ Bend at the knees to pick up the tray. Pull the tray with one hand onto the palm of your other hand. ❑ Balance the tray on your palm or fingertips at shoulder height. ❑ Use your free hand to steady the tray as you stand. ❑ Keep your back straight as you stand.

(continued)

Deliver the In-Room Dining Order (continued)

STEPS	HOW-TO'S
	❏ Watch where you are going. Be aware of opening doors and wet spots on the floor.
	❏ Use correct entrance and exit doors and pass to the left of people walking toward you.
	❏ Say "behind you" to let people know when you are behind them and to avoid a collision.
3. Carefully move in-room dining carts.	❏ Ease carts over uneven surfaces, such as where carpets meet tile floors.
	❏ Pull carts into and out of elevators. This allows you to see where you are going.
	❏ Avoid running into walls, guests, or co-workers.
	❏ Do not push more than one cart at a time.
4. Go directly to the guestroom.	❏ Know where the guestroom is before you leave for the delivery. Know the best way to get to the guestroom.
	❏ Use stairwells, service elevators, and halls to speed delivery time. Avoid congested areas such as public elevators, lobbies, function areas, and restaurant entrances.
	❏ Do not stop along the way. The food will get cold, the drinks will be watered down by melting ice, and the guest will grow impatient.
5. Enter the guestroom.	❏ Knock firmly three times with your knuckles and announce, "In-room dining." Do not use a key or any other hard object to knock on the door.
	❏ If there is no answer, knock and announce again. The guest may be in the shower or the bathroom.

Deliver the In-Room Dining Order (continued)

STEPS	HOW-TO'S
	❑ If the guest still does not answer, check the room number. If the room number is correct, call the in-room dining department and tell your supervisor about the situation.
	❑ When the guest opens the door, greet the guest by name in the form of a question, to verify that you have the right room: "Mr. Johnson?"
	❑ As soon as the guest acknowledges that you are at the right room, follow up with a greeting, such as: "Good morning. I have your breakfast."
	❑ If you are at the wrong room, apologize for disturbing the guest, and go to the correct room or call your supervisor right away.
	❑ Do not enter the room until the guest acknowledges you and invites you in. Remember that the guestroom is the guest's "home away from home." Just as you wouldn't barge into someone's home, you don't want to enter the guestroom unless you're invited.

Serve the In-Room Dining Order

Materials needed: A guest check and a service tray or in-room dining cart with a complete order.

STEPS	HOW-TO'S
1. Set up the order in the guestroom.	❑ Offer to place the order on the table, desk, or credenza, whichever the guest prefers. ❑ If using an in-room dining cart, fold out the wings of the table and spread out the tablecloth. ❑ Place the linen napkins and silverware on the table.
2. Serve food.	❑ Remove the hot food from the hot box or service tray and place it on the table. ❑ Place entree plate so that the main item is closest to the guest. ❑ Place side dishes to the left of the entree plate. ❑ Remove the foil or plate covers from the hot foods. ❑ Place condiments within the guest's reach, but out of his or her way.
3. Serve beverages.	❑ Place beverages, beverage napkins, glasses, mugs, cups, and saucers to the right of the entree plate. ❑ Handle glasses, mugs, and cups by their stems, bases, or handles. ❑ Remove foodservice film or lids from glasses. ❑ If wine or champagne is included, offer to open and serve it.
4. Place cream, sugar, spoons, and other appropriate items on the table.	
5. Present and settle the guest check.	

Serve the In-Room Dining Order *(continued)*

STEPS	HOW-TO'S
6. Ask if the guest would like you to bring or do anything else at this time.	
7. Ask the guest to call the in-room dining department for any further service and when he or she is ready for the tray or cart to be picked up.	
8. Thank the guest for the in-room dining order.	

Retrieve Trays and Carts

STEPS	HOW-TO'S
1. Go to the guestroom.	❑ Before you leave to retrieve a service tray or in-room dining cart, know where the guestroom is located, and know the best way to get to the guestroom. You will pick up trays or carts when a guest calls you to retrieve them and whenever you see trays or carts in guestroom corridors.
	❑ Use stairwells, service elevators, and halls to speed delivery time. Avoid congested areas such as public elevators, lobbies, function areas, and restaurant entrances.
	❑ Trays and carts in guestrooms and corridors are hazards. A guest could trip over these items. Also, soiled dishes and equipment in corridors are unsightly and indicate a poorly run in-room dining department.
2. Enter the guestroom.	❑ Knock firmly three times with your knuckles and announce, "In-room dining." Do not use a key or any other hard object to knock on the door.
	❑ If no one answers, knock and announce again. The guest may be in the shower or the bathroom.
	❑ If the guest still does not answer, check the room number. If the room number is correct, call the in-room dining department and tell your supervisor about the situation.
	❑ When the guest opens the door, greet the guest by name in the form of a question, to verify that you have the right room: "Ms. Martin?"
	❑ If you are at the wrong room, apologize for disturbing the guest, and go to the correct room or call your supervisor right away.
	❑ If you are at the right room, let the guest know that you are there to pick up the tray or cart.

STEPS	HOW-TO'S
	❏ Do not enter the room until the guest acknowledges you and invites you in. Remember that the guestroom is the guest's "home away from home." Just as you would not barge into someone's private home, you don't want to enter the guestroom unless you're invited.
3. Retrieve an in-room dining tray.	❏ Place serviceware, glasses, used linens, and trash on the tray. ❏ Bend at the knees to pick up the tray. Pull the tray with one hand onto the palm of the other hand. ❏ Balance the tray on your palm or fingertips at shoulder height. Use your free hand to steady the tray as you stand.
4. Retrieve an in-room dining cart.	❏ Secure soiled items inside and in the center of the cart and fold down the leaves of the cart. ❏ Pull—don't push—the cart into the hallway.
5. Thank the guest and leave the room.	
6. Retrieve trays and carts whenever you see them in guestroom corridors. If your hands are full, note where the trays and carts are and go back for them as soon as you can.	
7. Return to the in-room dining area quickly.	❏ Use stairwells and service elevators. ❏ Be careful and watch where you are going when carrying a tray or moving a cart.

Source: Adapted from the "Room Service Attendant Guide" in the *Hospitality Skills Training Series* (Lansing, Mich.: American Hotel & Lodging Educational Institute, 1995), pp. 15–17.

Retrieve Trays and Carts (continued)

<table>
<tr><td>Chapter 15 Outline</td><td>Competencies</td></tr>
</table>

Chapter 15 Outline

Major Market Segments of the On-Site
  Food and Beverage Industry
    Self-Operated and Contract
      Management Options
    Branded Food Options
Business and Industry Food and Beverage
  Operations
    Reducing Subsidies from Host
      Organizations
Health Care Food and Beverage Operations
    Going Healthy, Local, and "Green"
    Reinventing the Cafeteria
    Tray Service—Hospitality Style
    Spoken Menu Concept
    On-Demand In-Room Dining
    Chef Visits
College and University Food and Beverage
  Operations
    Flexible Meal Plans
    Serving Policies
    Menu Planning
    Encouraging Healthy Food Choices
    Sustainability Issues
    Summer Promotions
    Smart Card Technology

Competencies

1. List major market segments of the on-site food and beverage industry and the types of organizations within them; list contract management companies and distinguish self-operated food and beverage facilities from those operated by contract management companies; and summarize the advantages of including branded foods and food outlets in on-site food and beverage operations. (pp. 659–666)

2. Describe the business and industry food and beverage segment and explain how on-site food and beverage operations can reduce the subsidies they receive from their host organizations. (pp. 666–670)

3. Discuss health care food and beverage service and summarize issues important to this segment of the on-site food and beverage industry, including the trend to go healthy, local, and "green" and the drive to reinvent the cafeteria. (pp. 670–673)

4. Describe the college and university food and beverage segment, including issues ranging from flexible meal plans and serving policies to summer promotions and smart card technology. (pp. 674–681)

15

On-Site Food and Beverage Operations

Managing food and beverage services within larger host businesses or other organizations has changed dramatically over the past few decades. On-site food and beverage operations used to be characterized as "institutional" or "noncommercial," but these terms carried negative connotations. "Institutional" suggested regimented menus and impersonal service; "noncommercial" implied inefficient operations that survived only through subsidies from the host organization. Overall, on-site food and beverage operations were depicted as somehow substandard or second-rate when compared to freestanding, profit-oriented food and beverage operations.

Today's on-site food and beverage operations can be as varied, innovative, and successful as any restaurant or catering company. From menu planning and service delivery to cost control systems and the design of facilities, on-site food and beverage operations have implemented concepts, processes, and practices that have truly modernized this segment of the food and beverage industry.

For example, the menus of on-site food and beverage operations have undergone evolutionary and revolutionary changes. Ethnic cuisines (e.g., Thai and Pacific Rim, Indian, Peruvian, Mediterranean, Middle Eastern, Caribbean, Cuban, and Nuevo Latino) have been added to complement traditional Asian, Italian, and Mexican cuisines. These menu options and varieties, long the domain of commercial food and beverage operations, have driven changes in staff selection as well. More executive chefs, sous chefs, and pastry chefs have joined on-site food and beverage operations. In many instances recruited from fine-dining or casual-dining restaurants, these professionals often conduct culinary training for other staff members to upgrade their skills through in-house seminars, workshops, and demonstrations. Some on-site food and beverage operations even hold annual culinary competitions to further emphasize their more commercial approach to operations.

Display cooking and exhibition kitchens have risen in popularity with the arrival of professional culinary staff in on-site operations. Food stations featuring a variety of menu items (e.g., made-to-order sandwiches, freshly baked pizza, main courses of the day, make your own salad, soup selections, grab-and-go sandwiches and salads, desserts) have replaced the limited-choice cafeteria lines of yesteryear.

One of the economic forces affecting on-site food and beverage operations today is the rising cost of food and beverage ingredients. As the costs of these ingredients go up, on-site operations have had to evaluate menu prices, menu choices, portion sizes, and labor costs. Some operations have increased the required number of bids from distributors in an effort to find that distributor who can provide a menu ingredient at the lowest possible cost. Others have shifted from disposable tableware to reusable tableware, which over time reduces the cost of the tableware to the operation as well as reduces the amount of items that must be recycled (an additional cost savings). Switching menu items from more expensive proteins (e.g., beef) to less expensive proteins (e.g., pork and chicken) has also helped reduce costs. Purchasing products with built-in labor (e.g., precut vegetables, bakery products purchased ready-to-serve, and so on) has lead to savings in labor costs (though these savings are offset in part by higher food costs).

This chapter describes the types of services offered by on-site food and beverage operations. These services range from self-service vending facilities in staff member dining areas to full-service, restaurant-style food and beverage service in executive dining rooms. Depending on the needs of the host organization, on-site operations may include traditional forms of food service such as table service, banquet service, and even in-room dining (room service), but the focus of this chapter is on the unique service features of on-site operations. The chapter also explores the challenges of managing food and beverage operations in three of the major on-site markets—business and industry, health care, and college and university. An appendix at the end of the chapter presents sample job descriptions of line-level, supervisory, and managerial positions associated with on-site food and beverage operations.

Major Market Segments of the On-Site Food and Beverage Industry

An **on-site food and beverage operation** is part of a larger **host organization** whose primary business is not that of providing food and beverage products and services. Some of the major market segments for on-site food and beverage operations are:

- Business and industry
- Health care
- College and university
- School
- Military
- Correctional institution
- Sports and entertainment facility
- Transportation

The business and industry segment includes manufacturing and industrial plants, commercial centers, office complexes, financial institutions, and government

Exhibit 1   The Importance of On-Site Food and Beverage Service to Responding Organizations

Senior or middle management positions (i.e., senior vice president or vice president) of the client organizations were asked to rate the overall importance and the importance of 10 specific attributes of on-site food service to their organizations, using a 5-point scale (1=very unimportant to 5=very important). When asked how they would rate the overall importance of on-site food service to their organizations, the average rating was 4.32. Thus, overall, senior management perceived on-site food service to be important to their organizations. The following table ranks the average ratings on each of the 10 importance attributes.

Importance Attribute	# of Respondents	Average Rating
1. Convenience	147	4.43
2. Employee morale	148	4.41
3. Productivity	148	4.22
4. Multi-purpose facility	148	3.74
5. Employee networking	148	3.69
6. Recruitment/retention	148	3.67
7. Less entertaining costs	147	3.53
8. Employee health	148	3.52
9. Employee benefit	146	3.28
10. More revenue potential	147	2.58

For more information about the business and industry segment of on-site food and beverage services, access other areas of the Society for Foodservice Management's Internet site at www.sfm-online.org.

agencies. The health care segment includes hospitals and eldercare facilities specializing in extended care and assisted living. Post-secondary educational institutions make up the college and university segment; on-campus food and beverage operations and activities include food service for catered events and conference centers, dining halls, and food courts. The school segment covers day care centers as well as elementary and secondary schools. Sports and entertainment facilities include stadiums, convention centers, recreational facilities, and park systems. Airports, in-flight catering, trains, and cruise ships are within the transportation segment.

While the types of organizations within these segments have very different primary functions, on-site food and beverage services play important supportive roles in fulfilling their overall missions. For example, in the business and industry segment, organizations often approach food services as an investment. As a return on this investment, on-site food and beverage operations are expected to help achieve organizational goals. The Society for Foodservice Management (SFM) surveyed managers at host organizations in the business and industry segment on the importance of ten characteristics (or attributes) commonly associated with on-site

Exhibit 2   Important Features of On-Site Food and Beverage Service to Correctional Institutions

For more information about the food and beverage needs of correctional institutions, access ARAMARK's Correctional Services Internet site at www.aramark.com.

food service. As indicated in Exhibit 1, the three most important attributes were the added convenience for the organization's staff members, the positive impact on staff member morale, and the potential for increased staff member productivity.

Important characteristics in relation to food and beverage services for correctional institutions differ tremendously from those identified for the business and industry segment. Correctional institutions operate under many regulatory restrictions and other rules. For example, the American Correctional Association upholds the U.S. Recommended Daily Allowance (RDA) standards and insists that on-site food and beverage operations in correctional facilities meet or exceed these standards while, at the same time, containing costs and offering the greatest amount of control and security possible. Exhibit 2 discusses the features and benefits of the program offered by ARAMARK's correctional services.

Clearly, the priorities of on-site food and beverage operations change as the nature of the host organization changes. Sophisticated dietary and nutritional programs are critical features of a health care organization's primary mission to care for patients. However, on-site health care food and beverage operations are also expected to attract and cater to the needs and tastes of staff members and visitors by offering low-cost, nutritious meals in a variety of food service formats. Similarly, the primary function of colleges and universities is to educate students. An on-site food and beverage operation in a college or university residence hall contributes to its school's mission by providing meals to students living and studying in the residence hall. However, these on-site operations are also expected to contribute to the learning environment by offering flexible meal plans and dining options that meet the needs of students with irregular class and study schedules.

Self-Operated and Contract Management Options

Self-operated food and beverage services are on-site operations whose managers and staff members are employed by the larger organization within which the food and beverage operation resides. Host organizations can also outsource their food and beverage operations to **contract management companies** (also referred to as "managed services"). Some host organizations have both types of food and beverage operations. For example, a large university might outsource its vending operations and the operation of a food court to a contract management company, but retain other food services as self-operated departments.

While self-operated on-site food and beverage operations can be very successful, the market share captured by contract management companies has grown over the past few decades as more and more businesses have adopted strategies to outsource functions that do not directly relate to their core business. Some contract management companies have become appealing outsource alternatives by offering a wide range of managed services such as laundry, housekeeping, and facilities management in addition to their food and beverage services.

There are scores of contract management companies throughout the United States, including:

- ARAMARK Managed Services
- Sodexo
- Compass Group
- Bon Appétit Management Company

Exhibit 3 explains the food service philosophy of Compass Group, which claims on its website to be "the world's leading provider of food and support services."

In addition to operating on-site food and beverage facilities, a contract management company may operate different types of commercial, freestanding food and beverage units as well. This breadth of experience enables contract management companies to create synergies that are beyond the scope of many self-operated on-site food and beverage operations. By cross-training on-site food and beverage managers at commercial operations, a contract management company can create a culture of guest-driven service that builds guest loyalty and repeat business for the company's on-site operations. New menu items, new design and decor concepts, and creative service styles can be developed, tested, and refined in the

Exhibit 3   Compass Group Website

For more information about Compass Group, access other areas of the company's website at www.compass-group.com.

commercial sector before being implemented at on-site operations. Also, company-wide professional development and training programs bring managers from on-site market segments and managers from commercial operations together for a regular exchange of best practices, successful promotions, and operating strategies.

Self-operated on-site food and beverage operations obtain financial, technical, and managerial benefits through membership in various nonprofit associations. These associations help self-operated food and beverage programs achieve economies of scale similar to those attained by large contract management companies. Members of these associations may benefit from volume purchasing, professional development programs, and peer-networking opportunities. The Society for Foodservice Management (SFM) is a professional association of individuals employed in or providing services to the on-site food and beverage industry. SFM

Exhibit 4 The Association for Healthcare Foodservice

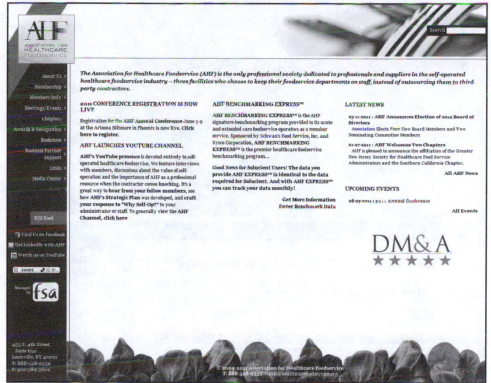

For more information about member services, access other areas of AHF's website at www.healthcarefoodservice.org.

provides support and education for the continuous improvement of on-site food and beverage professionals in this rapidly changing industry. The Association for Healthcare Foodservice (AHF) serves the interests of self-operated food and beverage facilities in the health care industry (see Exhibit 4). LeadingAge represents 5,500 mission-driven, not-for-profit nursing homes, continuing-care retirement communities, assisted living and senior housing facilities, and home and community-based service providers (see Exhibit 5). The website of the National Association of College & University Food Services (see Exhibit 6) describes how this nonprofit association addresses the needs of self-operated food and beverage departments in this segment of the on-site market.

Branded Food Options

In many segments of the on-site food and beverage market, both self-operated and contract-managed operations have linked with national chain restaurants and offer branded food options. By blending popular national brands and name-brand food products with their own menu offerings, on-site food and beverage operations can create more choices for their guests and capitalize on the consistent

Exhibit 5   LeadingAge

The LeadingAge website can be accessed at www.aahsa.org.

quality and service guests associate with branded foods. This can increase overall guest traffic in on-site food courts and other areas featuring branded outlets and may increase food revenues in nonbranded outlets as well.

Business and Industry Food and Beverage Operations

Business and industry is the largest segment of the on-site food and beverage market. The guest mix is primarily the workers, supervisors, middle managers, and top executives employed by the host organization and, secondarily, visitors to the organization who may include shareholders, customers, and distributors. The types of on-site food facilities for organizations within the business and industry segment generally include:

Exhibit 6 The National Association of College & University Food Services

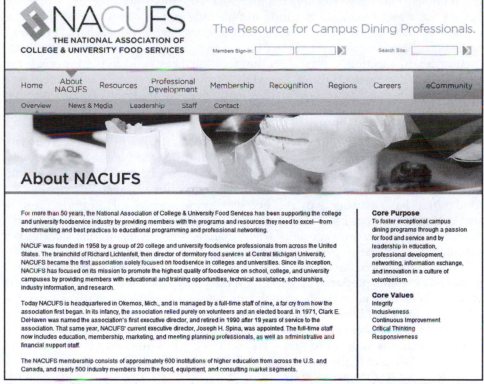

For more information about member services, access other areas of NACUFS's website at **www.nacufs.org.**

- Staff member dining areas
- Executive dining rooms
- Banquet facilities
- Vending services
- Mobile cart services
- Concession stores
- Concession vehicles

The number of food and beverage operations within the business and industry segment has declined in recent years as the economy has forced many businesses to shutter plants, particularly in traditional manufacturing areas such as states that produce automobiles and automobile parts. Many manufacturing plants that have remained open have been downsized (i.e., staff has been laid off), thus reducing the demand for the plants' food and beverage operations.

These operations have responded by adding day parts (e.g., breakfast) or adding more popular menu items to existing day parts to build business from remaining staff. For example, fair-trade, premium coffee has been added to break-fast menus to encourage workers to purchase their coffee once they arrive at work, not on the way to work. In addition to fair-trade coffee, cappuccinos, chai teas, espressos, and lattes are prepared in front of guests by a trained barista in some operations. Workers may also select fresh fruits, bagels, or pastries to complete their order. In addition to providing the traditional eggs and meats for breakfast, cooked-to-order omelet stations, breakfast burritos, and a sweet station (including crepes, French toast, pancakes, waffles, and specialty pastries) are also popular options. Healthier egg white or egg substitute omelets and turkey bacon appeal to health-conscious staff at breakfast.

The "cafeteria" label of days gone by has been dropped and replaced with "cafe," "eatery," and "bistro," as business and industry food and beverage operations strive to project a different image. Food courts have branded as well as non-branded food and beverage products available; nationally recognized branded food outlets have a distinctive draw because they are perceived as offering consistent quality. Decor has been modernized. Upgraded ambience may attract people from businesses nearby, especially when there is a relatively unique selection of products at competitive prices.

Another focus of business and industry food and beverage operations is promoting food items prepared to go. After a busy day, the last thing many workers want to do is think about what to make for dinner. It's easier to simply stop at the business's food and beverage outlet on the way out the door and select prepared food items to take home. The foods selected may range from reduced-carbohydrate menu items to pizza to salad. Workers in the building may be able to send their dinner choices to the outlet beforehand via e-mail or PDA so their orders are ready to go when they arrive at the outlet. If the outlet packages the food in a reusable bag, waste is reduced and at the same time workers are reminded of where they can place their next order for food to go.

Sustainability initiatives in business and industry food and beverage operations mirror those ecologically friendly efforts in commercial operations. Reducing waste, using local and organic ingredients, saving energy, and reducing the operation's carbon footprint are all sustainability goals that many food and beverage operations within the business and industry segment are pursuing.

Reducing Subsidies from Host Organizations

Factors in the overall business environment of host organizations significantly affect their on-site food and beverage operations. The most significant environmental factors are international expansion, increased automation, and consolidation through mergers and acquisitions. All three factors contribute to the downsizing of organizations and reduce the potential guest base for on-site food and beverage services. As organizations reduce their work forces, they are inclined to also review the amounts by which they subsidize the cost of providing on-site food services. In the past, while some host organizations expected their on-site food and beverage operations to at least break even, many organizations subsidized costs in an attempt to offer their staffs the lowest possible prices. Today, most host organizations want to minimize (or eliminate) these subsidies.

There are two fundamental ways by which a host organization can subsidize its on-site food and beverage operation. One is to subsidize the operation's overhead—the fixed costs of doing business. This entails covering all, or part, of the operation's administrative expenses and fixed costs such as energy, housekeeping, and maintenance. The other way is to subsidize the costs associated with daily operations. This entails picking up that portion of expenses that cannot be covered by revenues generated by the on-site food and beverage operation. Operational expenses include food, labor, serviceware, merchandising, insurance, and office supply expenses.

Helping a host organization reduce its overhead subsidy burden can be difficult for an on-site food and beverage operation. However, if a host organization allocates fixed costs on the basis of square footage, the on-site food and beverage operation can reduce its need for overhead subsidies by decreasing its space. On-site operations can reduce the square footage they need by capitalizing on new equipment and technology made available through partnering with chain restaurants or through contracting with management companies. Changing the service delivery systems can also impact overhead costs. For example, providing more take-out or "grab-and-go" meals and increasing mobile cart services could decrease the amount of space the operation needs for sit-down dining areas.

On-site food and beverage managers can also reduce the host organization's subsidy burden by generating more revenue. However, if meals are currently priced below costs, increasing participation levels at on-site food and beverage outlets will certainly increase total revenue but will also increase the total net loss for operations and, thereby, increase the subsidy needed from the host organization. Or, to put it another way, doing more business at a loss will only increase the magnitude of the loss. If participation rates stay constant, raising prices will increase revenue, decrease net operational losses, and reduce the operation's subsidy. However, if the majority of the guest mix is price-sensitive, raising prices could lower participation levels and perhaps even reduce the total amount of revenue. If so, increasing prices would, in effect, backfire and only serve to increase, rather than decrease, the subsidy needed from the host organization.

Price increases must be carefully considered in relation to guests' perceptions of value. In general, price increases are met with resistance from guests unless the perceived value is increased at the same time. One way to accomplish this is to raise prices while bundling items into combination packages or "value" meals. However, any strategy that involves increasing prices must be consistent with the host organization's objectives and overall strategies in providing on-site food and beverage service.

Some on-site food and beverage operations reduce host-organization subsidies by actively pursuing new sources of revenue. For example, one on-site food and beverage operation implemented a "Conferences After 5" program. After regular business hours, the operation's facilities and services were offered to local businesses, associations, and other outside organizations for meetings and catered events.

The need for subsidies might also be reduced through greater cost-control efforts. For example, it might be possible to lower food costs by lowering the quality of ingredients or by decreasing portion sizes. Again, guests' perceptions of value must be considered, because lowering quality without lowering prices may also lower participation rates; this would reduce overall revenue and end up costing the host organization more in subsidies. It might be possible to lower food costs by reducing the number of menu items offered. However, this is always a double-edged sword. Too little variety may decrease participation because guests become bored with the same menu items. However, too much variety may increase waste and cause food costs to rise. Generally, a combination of actions works best—for example, eliminating menu items that are high in cost, low in price, and low in popularity while, at the same time, adding menu items that are low in cost, reasonably priced, and at least as popular as the items taken off the menu. Depending on the guest mix, it might be possible to add more "upscale" menu items that can be priced higher but would still be perceived as a value to the target guests.

Reducing labor costs can be achieved by offering more self-service options and increasing vending services. In most cases, instead of completely eliminating a service, it is better to substitute a lower-cost alternative. For example, prepackaged food items might be substituted for cooked-to-order menu items. Or, centralized coffee and snack areas could be substituted for transport systems used to deliver similar food items throughout the organization.

Health Care Food and Beverage Operations

Health care organizations can be divided into several subsegments, including hospitals, psychiatric facilities, rehabilitation centers (sometimes referred to as "convalescent centers"), and eldercare facilities specializing in extended care and assisted living (often referred to as "nursing homes"). The guest mix for on-site food and beverage operations within these organizations varies. Guests include patients or residents, staff members (including administrators, technicians, maintenance and cleaning personnel, and therapists as well as doctors and nurses), visitors (including family members and friends of patients or residents), and members of the community (in cases where health care organizations cater events for local community groups).

The changing business environment of the health care industry is characterized by declining patient admissions and shorter patient stays, as well as by consolidations, acquisitions, and mergers of hospitals and other heath care organizations. These conditions have prompted changes in the management of health care food and beverage operations, affecting areas such as the selection of the type of menu (cyclical or restaurant style), food production systems (cook-chill, cook-freeze, or conventional), service delivery procedures (spoken menu concept, on-demand in-room dining, and chef visits), and cost-control systems.

When health care underwent dramatic changes in the late 1990s, due to cuts in Medicare and other factors, patients gained increased power to choose health care providers, especially when elective procedures were involved. This led administrators at hospitals and long-term-care organizations to view food and beverage service as a way to attract and retain patients.

Successful health care food and beverage organizations focus on five key areas. First is the menu; it should offer a variety of quality menu items. Next are recipes; there must be items on the menu whose recipes can be modified for patients and residents on restricted sodium or low-fat diets, yet still taste good. Third is image:

a health care food and beverage operation's image is positively affected when food is served on vibrantly colored trays, for example, rather than the bland pale green or gray trays of the past. Service is the fourth key area. Since patients or residents have greater power to choose, health care food and beverage operations must respond with better service if they hope to attract or retain patronage. In hospitals, one component of better service might be that the food and beverage service supervisor visits newly admitted patients to discuss the menu that the physician has ordered for them. The fifth and last area is communication. If the food and beverage service staff makes a point to communicate with patients or residents, they are more likely to be happy with the food that is served.

Going Healthy, Local, and "Green"

More food and beverage operations in the health care segment are adopting a "healthy food, healthy guests, healthy environment" philosophy. Antibiotic-free milk, fresh fruits and vegetables, whole grains and other less-processed foods, and antibiotic- and hormone-free meat products are being placed on menus with greater frequency. To add flavor, more herbs and spices are being used in preparation (often in liquid form to avoid the possibility of a choking hazard) rather than salt, which is an obvious plus for those on sodium-restricted diets.

In an attempt to reduce the use of canned and frozen foods, some health care food and beverage operations have implemented a "Farm to Fork" program in which locally grown and raised food ingredients are the products of choice. These efforts also help achieve sustainability goals. These food ingredients are both healthy for guests and supportive of the local community.

Some health care operations have become LEED (Leadership in Energy and Environmental Design) certified. These operations tie their focus on personal wellness to the wellness of the planet. Utilizing "green" power from wind turbines, hydropower, and geothermal power sources reduces carbon dioxide emissions into the air. Natural lighting from large windows and skylights adds to energy savings. Occupancy sensors in rooms shut off lights when no one is present. The use of outdoor air for ventilating systems, and ENERGY STAR™–rated equipment in kitchens help health care food and beverage operations "go green" as well. Other ecologically sound practices include using "green" chemicals for cleaning and sanitizing, using biodegradable containers for foods prepared to go, and selling spent fryer oil for conversion into biodiesel fuel.

Reinventing the Cafeteria

In the past, the only type of food and beverage center open to health care patients, staff members, and visitors was a cafeteria that was functional and efficient, but cold and uninviting in its design and decor. Typically, guests walked along a terrazzo floor, selected food items from a straight-line, stainless-steel serving counter, took their trays to metal-framed tables with plastic laminate tops, sat in tubular metal chairs with vinyl backs and seats, and "enjoyed" their meals surrounded by bland, sparsely decorated tile walls.

Today, health care cafeterias have undergone a name change and a face-lift. "Dining center," "dining area," and even "restaurant" are replacing the term "cafeteria," as the traditional cafeteria gives way to food and beverage operations offering made-from-scratch menu choices and more fresh foods. These operations are now designed and decorated to appeal to the operation's guest mix, reflect the image or theme of the health care organization or local community, and allow for the flexibility and mobility needed to coordinate changing menu items and featured cuisines. The reinvented health care cafeteria has become an open dining area with multiple food stations that increase choices for guests. Stations may include entrée and vegetable stations; salad, dessert, and beverage bars; and soup, delicatessen, grill, and pasta stations. Some health care organizations set food stations at angles in their dining areas to promote visual appeal as well as help merchandise food in retail display cases. Mobile carts are also used in dining and other areas. These carts may feature popcorn, specialty coffees, cookies, or other snacks.

Some of these new-style cafeterias sell pre-packaged salads, sandwiches, and other prepared-to-go foods to visitors and staff. Colorful posters and print ads located strategically throughout high-traffic areas of the health care facility can market these services. Some health care food and beverage facilities are installing kiosks in high-traffic areas (the lobby, for example, or near a waiting room) that offer beverages and a limited number of prepackaged food choices during hours when the cafeteria is closed.

Mobile, interchangeable food station equipment can help health care food and beverage operations easily accommodate changes in menus. Some health care organizations devote one or two food stations to new menu items or different international cuisines every week. Menus are also changing to offer guests lighter, healthier menu items. In general, menu changes follow trends found in the commercial sector of the food and beverage industry.

Tray Service—Hospitality Style

The traditional form of food and beverage service for patients in health care organizations is termed **tray service**. With tray service, a printed menu is sent to each patient the day before service. Patients circle the items they want to order for the following day. The marked menus are delivered to the kitchen. The next day, individual trays of food are assembled along tray lines in the kitchen area. The process is similar to that used by restaurants, hotels, and clubs for large banquets. Once assembled, the trays are grouped by floors or units, placed in carts, and transported to delivery points. Staff from the dietary department or from the nursing area deliver the trays to individual patients in their rooms.

While the traditional tray service system is a well-organized work process, it is a difficult system to integrate with other processes involving patients and often fails to meet patients' needs. For example, while food production areas enjoy the luxury of a 24-hour time delay from order to delivery of patient meals, the dynamics of daily patient care, such as early discharges, room transfers, diet changes, and medical tests, can disrupt the food delivery system, increase costs through greater waste, and create patient dissatisfaction with late meals or with meals that they received on time but did not order.

Spoken Menu Concept

To alleviate these and other food and beverage service problems, some health care organizations are implementing a spoken menu concept. This concept eliminates the traditional tray line and features a trained patient-care host to take food orders from patients, assemble the trays, deliver the trays to patients, pick up and clean the trays, complete calorie counts and fluid intake records, deliver supplements, and restock supplies on their assigned floors. With the spoken menu concept, the host asks patients for their next day's breakfast order as they serve their dinner meal; lunch and dinner orders are taken approximately two hours before the meal is delivered. The spoken menu concept often improves patient satisfaction, which may be due in part to the food order being taken closer to when the patient actually consumes the food, so that the meals more closely match the patient's actual food desires on that day (compared to the traditional system of choosing the menu 24-hours in advance).

On-Demand In-Room Dining

Some health care food and beverage organizations have changed to an on-demand, in-room dining delivery system for patient meals, allowing patients to order the food that they want whenever they want it. This gives patients more control over what they eat and when they eat it, making it more likely that the food ordered will be consumed. This increases patient satisfaction and reduces the amount of food that is thrown away. Patients may choose from regular or modified-diet menus that have been personalized for them, based on the dietary orders of their physicians. The menu is presented to each patient by a uniformed in-room dining associate, who also explains the diet and nutrition components of the menu and answers any questions the patient may have. The menu items typically are more attractive than traditional hospital fare and include such dishes as farm-raised salmon with honey mustard glaze, roasted vegetable quesadillas, grilled breast of chicken Rico, as well as made-to-order deli sandwiches, classic grill items, and omelets. To accompany the entrées, patients can choose from fresh fruits and vegetables, bakery products, and desserts. Menu items are prepared using a "Waldorf Suite"—a four-sided compact equipment island including a broiler, fryer, grill, pasta cooker, and set-up range, with refrigerated drawers for convenient food storage. The Waldorf Suite is designed for high-volume, rapid à la carte food production. Once a patient's food is prepared, a uniformed in-room dining associate delivers the tray to the patient.

Chef Visits

Some hospital on-site food and beverage operations find creative ways to involve the hospital chef in personalizing service to patients. For example, at one hospital, the chef visits a selected floor one evening each week, plates meals for patients in their rooms (family members who are visiting receive complimentary meals), and educates patients and visitors on culinary issues and cooking techniques related to nutrition and healthy food choices. The hospitality of the chef often improves patient and visitor satisfaction with the hospital's food and beverage service program.

College and University Food and Beverage Operations —

The design and decor of on-site food and beverage outlets in colleges and universities have also moved away from traditional cafeteria-style service to more

---

Trends in College and University Food and Beverage Service

Food and beverage operations on college and university campuses have changed in response to their guests' changing tastes and lifestyles. Many operations have added day parts (e.g., late night), particularly on weekends. A college or university food and beverage outlet that offers food and beverage service from 6 A.M. to 11 P.M. on weekdays may extend its hours until 2 A.M. on weekends, for example. Final exams week may also be a reason for extending an outlet's normal hours of operation.

College and university food and beverage operations are selling more coffees (particularly fair-trade and gourmet), grab-and-go sandwiches (particularly breakfast items), and gourmet salads. In food and beverage operations that feature food courts, guests can order comfort foods (e.g., turkey, mashed potatoes, and dressing), pizza, traditional burgers as well as those with unique toppings, fresh bakery products, and nonfried vegetables, all at one location.

Cooked-to-order menu items have strong appeal for today's students, since they are perceived as fresher. Some students believe that fresher ingredients mean that the product has more "food integrity"—that is, they do not contain harmful chemicals or pesticides. Colors are being used to emphasize different food preparation areas. The action of a culinary staff member preparing students' menu selections, just for them, fresh before their eyes, adds an entertainment component to the food and beverage experience.

Food and beverage outlet seating areas are being redesigned with a variety of seating options for meeting others or studying alone. Open spaces as well as intimate seating areas give guests choices. Natural lighting brightens the spaces and the moods of those who are sitting there studying during final exams week. Natural wood products enhance the feel of being ecologically friendly, since wood is a replaceable, reusable resource.

Colleges and universities that have agriculture programs are growing their own fruits and vegetables on farms or in green houses. For the food and beverage outlets at these schools, the phrase "local ingredients" takes on a whole new meaning. These homegrown products are not only prepared and served at campus residence halls, they may also be sold at fresh produce stands located on campus.

Today's guests of college and university food and beverage operations want choices. They do not want old-fashioned, out-of-date cafeteria service. They want food and beverages made for them, when they want them, anytime and anywhere.

Menu boards with digital displays appeal to today's generation of technophiles. Plasma screens with mouth-watering photographs of menu items and food items on display at cooking stations excite this generation; static displays, such as fixed menu boards, are boring to a generation that grew up multi-tasking. Students with ear buds in their ears, listening to music, will read a big-screen menu display while at the same time having a conversation with a friend, either in-person or via text messaging. Digital point-of-sale systems in college and university food and beverage operations are rushing to catch up with these multi-taskers.

modern service concepts adapted from commercial operations. The narrow, single-file, stainless-steel tray line has given way to kiosks, mobile carts, convenience stores, and open-area food courts with multiple food stations.

A college or university food court may simulate a mall, marketplace, or plaza and generally consists of "storefront" food outlets that may include delicatessen, bakery, grill, and gourmet coffee concepts as well as nationally branded outlets such as Panda Express, Burger King, and Subway. The addition of branded outlets in college and university food courts was made possible when national restaurant chains redesigned their traditional store units to make them smaller, reduce startup and operating costs, and take advantage of efficiencies brought about by new technology. Continuing advances have led some large universities to install several small food courts throughout their campuses. These operations are designed as separate kiosks along a counter, with service staff shifting as needed between kiosks; the entire system can often be served by a single cashier.

In college or university dining areas that feature a **scramble system**, students do not wait for portions to be plated by staff members behind a serving line. Instead, they go directly to the food stations of their choice. These stations might include display cooking stations offering international food items; self-serve pasta stations; pizza, grill, and wok stations; and traditional salad bars, beverage stations, and dessert stations. Flexible designs and mobile food stations that can be reconfigured as menu offerings change maximize choice and convenience for students.

The design and decor of college and university dining areas have changed from the traditional rows of tables set in military style to a variety of seating options, with the dining area's decor matching the featured cuisines. For example, one university sets tables with red-and-white-checkered tablecloths and candles in empty wine bottles to give the dining area an Italian motif; this change in decor matched menu changes that included adding anchovies, olives, and grated cheeses to the salad bar and Italian dessert items to the dessert station. Some colleges and universities have implemented a sports-grill dining concept, with high bar-style tables and stools arranged near large-screen television sets mounted on the walls.

Flexible Meal Plans

Increasing the participation of college students in meal plans is the challenge at most universities. In the past, board plans offered by many colleges and universities were designed to fit the needs of their on-site food and beverage operations rather than the needs of students. Students were assigned to specific campus dining halls, and meal transfers to other food and beverage outlets on campus were discouraged by inconvenient, bureaucratic procedures. Also, all students housed in residence halls generally paid the same board fee for the same number of breakfasts, lunches, and dinners—regardless of how many meals they wanted or actually consumed. This "one-plan-fits-all" approach has given way to flexible à la carte dining, made-to-order dining, and other meal plans that address the needs of students whose lifestyles and academic responsibilities may conflict with rigidly scheduled meal periods. Michigan State University is one of many universities that is using flexibility, variety, and marketing to attract students to take advantage of its meal plans (see Exhibit 7).

Exhibit 7   Student Meals at Michigan State University

Michigan State University's website (www.eatatstate.com) offers detailed information about campus food services for students.

In response to the demanding class and study schedules of students, many colleges and universities have implemented express breakfast bars, "grab-and-go" meals, and sack lunches and dinners at their residence halls. At some institutions, students phone a day in advance to order a prepared take-out meal; at others, students simply pack their own meals at designated self-service lines at food outlets. Still other institutions provide a take-out option at every meal period for students. Most students are pressed for time and often prefer meals and snacks that they can eat on the move. They are less willing to stand and wait in a serving line, and many don't want to eat in traditional dining halls; they prefer instead to take their food back to their rooms or eat it elsewhere. The convenience of take-out is important to today's busy students who want quick food options.

Serving Policies

Most college and university meal plans have "all-you-care-to-eat" policies for food served at dining halls. Lunches and dinners usually include a selection of three to four entrées, with access to dessert bars, salad bars, and fresh fruit baskets. When service is cafeteria-style, students can enter the serving line as often as they like. When using a dining hall meal credit at a snack bar or branded food court,

Meal Plans Today

Meal plans at colleges and universities have undergone huge changes in recent decades. To cite just one example, consider the following meal plan options at Michigan State University:

Residential Meal Plans

- Platinum
    - Unlimited meals at any Dining Hall
    - Combo-x-change once per day, M–F
    - Spartan Cash
    - Eight guest meal passes per semester
- Gold
    - Unlimited meals at any Dining Hall
    - Combo-x-change once per day, M–F
    - Spartan Cash
    - Four guest meal passes per semester
- Silver
    - Unlimited meals at any Dining Hall
    - Combo-x-change once per day, M–F
    - Spartan Cash can be added, but is not included with the Silver plan

Commuter Meal Plans

- Commuter 70
    - Access to 70 meals at any Dining Hall
    - Multiple accesses at any meal period
    - Unused meals roll over to the next semester
    - Access expires at the end of summer semester
    - Combo-x-change at any Culinary Services retail location
    - Flex Option at any Culinary Services retail location
- Commuter 10
    - Access to 10 meals at any Dining Hall
    - Multiple accesses at any meal period
    - Unused meals roll over to the next semester
    - Access expires at the end of summer semester
    - Combo-x-change at any Culinary Services retail location
    - Flex Option at any Culinary Services retail location

Faculty/Staff Meal Plans

- Any number of meals greater than 25
- Access to meals at any Dining Hall
- Sold in blocks of 10 (25, 35, 45, etc., all the way up to 105)
- Multiple accesses at any meal period
- Unused meals roll over to the next semester
- Access expires at the end of summer semester

(continued)

(continued)

- Combo-x-change at any Culinary Services retail location
- Flex Option at any Culinary Services retail location

There are 14 cafes, 20 "Sparty's" convenience stores, and a number of other dining options on the MSU campus. Captain Pea Pod's is a vegan/vegetarian outlet serving healthy vegetarian food options in one of the centrally located residence halls. The MSU Dairy Store serves campus-made ice creams (there is also a Dairy Store outlet in one of the residence halls). Organic food served in another residence hall is grown on MSU's Organic Farm, where food products are raised free from growth hormones, herbicides, insecticides, and pesticides. This outlet also features an organic peanut butter grinder.

Publisher is another resident hall cafe that specializes in hometown dinner and bar food favorites, such as freshly grilled sandwiches, hoagies, and wings. Riverwalk Market, a cafe in the graduate residence hall on campus, features over six different food stations with freshly made sandwiches, hot-out-of-the-oven pizza, a daily main course, grab-and-go salads and sandwiches, a salad and soup bar, and desserts.

The Gallery is advertised as an "exhibition of six artistic cook-for-show kitchens in a relaxed atmosphere." It includes Ciao! (featuring pizza and sub sandwiches); Latitudes (ethnic international menu choices); New Traditions (traditional comfort foods with a modern twist); Grill (burgers and chicken sandwiches); Berg (specialty salads), and Bliss (featuring cakes, ice creams, pies, and other desserts).

Union Square is a food and beverage outlet located in the MSU Union which serves pizza and calzones at Union Pizzeria, Mexican cuisine at Serrano's, and deli sandwiches, specialty coffees and teas, and MSU Dairy Store ice cream.

As you can see, students at Michigan State University have several meal plans and a wide variety of innovative food and beverage outlets to choose from, all on one university campus. Many colleges and universities across the country have similar programs, all designed to entice students, faculty, and others to patronize on-campus food and beverage services.

---

students are generally limited to a specific dollar value for the meal items they select. At many colleges and universities, serving policies are explained on their housing or food services Internet sites.

Menu Planning

The differences in menu planning between on-site college and university food and beverage operations and freestanding commercial restaurants emerge from the different needs and expectations of their guests. A loyal, repeat guest may dine at a freestanding restaurant as many as four or five times over a 30-day period. At each visit, the guest expects the same basic menu offerings. Daily specials are welcome, but the basic menu is a strong part of the attraction the restaurant has for the repeat guest. In contrast, a student with a full meal plan might dine at the residence hall more than 60 times a month. The last thing the student wants is the same basic menu offering the same items over and over again. This is why many on-site food and beverage operations at colleges and universities use cycle menus.

A **cycle menu** changes every day for a certain number of days, then repeats the cycle. Cycle menus vary; many are designed for 6-, 5-, or 4-week periods (the trend is toward shorter menu cycles). The frequency of menu changes challenges on-site college and university food and beverage operations to develop a number of ways to communicate each day's menu to guests. Colleges and universities generally post menus near the entrances to campus dining halls, increasingly on big flat-screen TVs. Some food and beverage programs put their entire cycle menu on a web page through the school's Internet site. Others provide a "dial-a-menu" service, enabling students to learn about the day's menu offerings by dialing a telephone number and listening to a recorded message.

Web pages and e-mail through the college's or university's computer network are popular ways for directors of food and beverage operations to communicate directly with students. Directors can use these communication channels to explain to students the cost-based pricing system of meal plans, gather feedback to improve service, and monitor students' acceptance of newly introduced menu items. Twitter, Facebook, Linked-In, and other social media are additional ways to communicate.

Encouraging Healthy Food Choices

Most colleges and universities offer meatless options on their cycle menus; many offer vegetarian menu choices at every meal period. Vegetarian options are becoming popular in the college and university environment, where learning new things and sampling new experiences are embraced and encouraged.

Healthy food trends in colleges and universities extend beyond vegetarian menu choices. Reduced-calorie and reduced-fat menu options are often available at each meal. Many campus food and beverage operations promote healthy choices on their menus and educate students on the basics of nutrition. Food guide pyramids, such as the one shown in Exhibit 8, appear on the websites of many college and university food and beverage operations. Managers of the food and beverage program at Stanford University distribute booklets to students that feature explanations of the basic nutritional guidelines of the American Dietetic Association and the American Heart Association. The university also displays nutritional analyses on cards in front of items in dining-area food stations.

Sustainability Issues

Many students who are interested in healthier menu options are also interested in sustainability issues, and there is a greater focus today on being ecologically friendly at many college and university food and beverage operations. More sustainable menu items in food and beverage operations are just the beginning. Working with food and beverage manufacturers and distributors to implement more humane treatment of animals is important to a growing number of college and university students. Purchasing only fish and seafood that are not endangered is another sustainability practice. Many students today expect that biodegradable serving containers will be used by campus food and beverage outlets, that "green" cleaning and maintenance chemicals will be purchased, and that leftover usable food will be donated to local homeless shelters.

Purchasing clean, nonpolluting power is another sustainability issue for college and university food and beverage operations. Rather than burning coal and

Exhibit 8   Educating Students on Nutrition Basics

University Residences and Dining Services
OFFICE OF STUDENT LIFE

Home
Nutrition
Dining Plans
Menus & Hours
Buckeye Bundles
F.A.Q.s
Employment
Donations and Advertising
Photo Galleries
University Catering
Contact

Nutrition Education

The "freshman 15" has become synonymous with college life, but armed with the right information, you can eat healthily easier than you think. For those that have special dietary requirements, food services has worked to make it as easy for you as possible to meet those needs.

Nutrition Counseling & Education

Free nutrition counseling and education is offered to OSU college students in the Student Wellness Center (RPAC). [More Information].

The New Food Guide Pyramid: My Pyramid Plan

The new food guide pyramid is designed to give you a better idea of how to eat healthfully. The food groups are the same as the old pyramid:

- **Grains**: This group includes wheat, rice, cornmeal, oats and cereal grain products like bread, pasta, tortillas, and oatmeal. Grains provide B vitamins, minerals and fiber.

- **Vegetables**: This group includes any vegetable, from broccoli to corn to potatoes to squash, in addition to 100% vegetable juices. Vegetables may be frozen, canned, dried or fresh, cooked or raw. Vegetables provide many vitamins, minerals and fiber.

- **Fruits**: This group includes frozen, dried, canned or fresh, cooked or raw fruits as well as 100% fruit juices. Fruits provide lots of vitamins and fiber.

- **Milk**: This group includes calcium-rich milk and most milk-based products, like cheese and yogurt. Products like cream cheese, sour cream and butter are NOT part of the milk group. Selections from this group should be low-fat or fat-free. Be aware of added sugars as in ice cream.

- **Meat and Beans**: This group includes beef, pork, poultry, fish, eggs, nuts, seeds, dried beans or peas and related products, like tofu. Choose lean or low-fat meats, and eat beans and nuts frequently. This group provides protein, iron, zinc and B vitamins.

- **Oils**: Oils like olive oil, vegetable oil or canola oil are fats from plant sources, and they are liquid at room temperature. Avoid hydrogenated oils, or trans fats, which are solid at room temperature. Fats, which are from animal sources, are solid at room temperature.

Unlike the old pyramid, each food group is represented now by a band that runs from the bottom of the pyramid to the top; this is because even within each food group, some choices are healthier than others. Whole grains such as wheat bread and brown rice should make up the base of the grain group, for example, while refined, white bread should be at the top. The width of each band gives you an idea of how much of one group you should consume each day in proportion to another. Aim for a variety of foods within each group and between groups, and aim for plenty of colorful fruits and vegetables. Keep in mind that exactly how much you need to eat depends on your age, sex, and activity level. Finally, the steps going up the side of the pyramid should remind you that daily physical activity is an essential part of a healthy lifestyle.

For more information on the My Pyramid Plan, visit www.mypyramid.gov.

Ohio State University's website (www.diningservices.osu.edu/nutrition) uses the food pyramid to educate students on the benefits of a well-balanced diet and encourages them to make healthy choices.

other fossil fuels, wind and geothermal power is preferred whenever possible, as these power sources minimize greenhouse gases and help reduce an operation's carbon footprint.

Summer Promotions

Today many college and university on-site food and beverage operations are actively promoting the availability of their services and facilities to non-student individuals and groups, particularly during the summer months when fewer students are on campus. One market that is targeted are organizations that want to book summer meetings or work groups on campus. Services that are promoted to these organizations include great food, Wi-Fi access, and all of the meeting rooms that are empty and available during this nonpeak usage time. Michigan State University's Culinary Services department, for example, advertises all-you-care-to-eat dining, à la carte dining, international and made-to-order food options, menus overseen by executive chefs, and various convenient dining locations on its website at www.eatatstate.com. In an effort to encourage more summer patronage from individuals as well, many colleges and universities offer discounted meal plans to faculty and staff during the summer; a meal-plan discount may be offered if the individual purchases 25 or more meals, for example.

Smart Card Technology

Technology such as the **smart card** enable colleges and universities to better manage the flexibility of their multiple meal plans. The computer chip embedded within a smart card can store large amounts of data. This enables colleges and universities to exercise control over a wide range of activities and transactions, such as accessing buildings, tracking meal plan credits, and processing cashless purchases. Smart card technology not only improves services but also offers a new level of safety and convenience for students and the entire campus community.

Smart cards at some universities also function as **debit cards**. Debit cards differ from credit cards in that the cardholder must establish value by depositing money in a personal account managed by a debit card center. Students deposit funds into a declining balance account and use the card to make food purchases at any of the university's food and beverage outlets. A certain amount each day can be transferred from the debit card balance to the card's vending stripe. The vending stripe is used to pay for the use of on-campus vending machines, laundry machines, photocopy machines, and other point-of-sale services. The cash value of the vending stripe is limited to a maximum of $50 because if the card is lost, stolen, or damaged, the cash value is lost and is not refundable. Given the card's convenience and incredible number of uses, a maximum risk factor of $50 seems reasonable in exchange for the safety and security of cashless purchases.

While many commercial food and beverage operations have been cautious and slow in accepting smart card technology, colleges and universities have generally embraced it and are pioneering its possibilities. Smart card systems at some colleges and universities eliminate the need for students to set up a debit account through the school and enable them to use automated teller machines (ATMs) to transfer funds from checking accounts at their own banks to the embedded computer chip on their university identification cards. These "smart" identification cards can be used in lieu of cash or checks to make purchases at on-campus and some off-campus retailers, as well as at campus vending machines, coin-operated laundries, and food and beverage outlets.

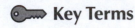 **Key Terms**

contract management company—An independent food and beverage company contracted to manage on-site food and beverage services (and possibly other services) within a host organization.

cycle menu—A menu that changes every day for a certain number of days, then repeats the cycle.

debit card—Plastic and similar in size to a credit card, a debit card requires the cardholder to deposit money at a debit card center or bank in advance of purchases; as purchases are made, the balance on the debit card falls.

host organization—A business or other organization that operates, or hires a contract management company to operate, an on-site food and beverage facility for use by the organization's staff members, managers, visitors, and others.

on-site food and beverage operations—Food and beverage facilities that operate within larger host organizations whose primary businesses are not that of providing food and beverage services.

scramble system—An open food and beverage area with multiple food stations that presents an alternative to the single-file serving line of traditional cafeteria service. Also called a scramble servery system or scatter system.

self-operated food and beverage services—On-site food and beverage operations whose managers and staff members are employed by the host organization.

smart card—Plastic and similar in size to a credit card, a smart card contains a computer chip capable of storing and transferring large amounts of data. College and university smart cards are used to control a wide range of activities and transactions, from accessing buildings to processing cashless purchases.

tray service—The traditional form of patient food and beverage service in health care organizations. Typically, a printed menu is sent to each patient the day before service; patients indicate the items they want, and the menus are returned to the kitchen. The next day, staff members assemble orders on trays, group the trays by floor or unit, and deliver them to patients.

 Review Questions

1. What are the major market segments of the on-site food and beverage industry?

2. How do self-operated on-site food and beverage facilities differ from on-site operations run by contract management companies?

3. How can on-site food and beverage operations in the business and industry segment help their host organizations reduce the subsidies they have to pay to support the food and beverage operations?

4. How are health care on-site food and beverage operations becoming more like commercial food and beverage operations?

5. How are some health care organizations changing the food and beverage service they provide to patients?

6. What are some examples of flexible meal plans that colleges and universities are providing to students?

7. How are colleges and universities using smart cards and debit cards?

 ## Case Study

Out with the Old, In with the New

Sylvia Castillo is the new food service director at the Sunnyside Nursing Home, a 120-bed facility where the average age of the occupants is 77. She is both a registered dietitian (R.D.) and a certified dietitian (C.D.). The American Dietetic Association provides the R.D. credentials for which one studies, passes a test, and stays current, earning points on a continuing basis. The state provides the certified designation.

Sylvia works for ADASPEC, a contract food service management firm with which the nursing home has contracted to provide food service to the facility's 120 occupants and 70 employees. The nursing home administrator, George Asti, felt that it was advantageous to hire a professional firm to provide the food service, since that is its expertise. The alternative, to operate food service using nursing home employees, known as "self-op," would likely be more expensive for the home, as it would not have the purchasing power of a large firm available to it, nor would it have a large pool of employees and others with specialized expertise like ADASPEC does. Sunnyside is charged for all food, labor, and related costs, plus a 2-percent management fee (on total costs) by ADASPEC. This is known as a fee-based contract.

Sylvia knows that Sunnyside operates a cycle menu on a four-week revolving basis. The residents have indicated, both verbally and through surveys, that they feel the food service is mediocre at best. They do not think there is enough variety, and the food is bland and unappealing visually.

Sylvia decides that her first task is to revise the luncheon menu, since lunch at a nursing home is the focal meal of the day for residents that age, more so than dinner. As a well-experienced food service professional, she knows she has to develop menus for a 28-day period (four weeks), have variety with two entrées per meal, consider the balance of the four food groups, which are: (A) meat, poultry, and fish, (B) fruits and vegetables, (C) starches, bread, grains, etc., and (D) dairy products such as milk, cheese, custards, etc. Plate presentations need color balance as well, and, of course, cost is a factor so the food budget doesn't break the bank.

Discussion Question

1. Assume you are in Sylvia's position. Develop a lunch menu for a seven-day period taking the aforementioned considerations into account.

This case was taken from William P. Fisher and Robert A. Ashley, *Case Studies in Commercial Food Service Operations* (Lansing, Mich.: American Hotel & Lodging Educational Institute, 2003).

References

Anonymous. "Insights You Should Know About the Ever-Greening Collegiate Environment...But Didn't Know to Ask!" PR Newswire. August 21, 2007.

———. "Iowa Gets 'Smart'." Foodservice Director. May 15, 2008. 21(5): 15.

———. "Locally Inspired." Foodservice Director. April 15, 2008. 21(4): 36.

———. "Report Outlines Leading Trend in Health Care Sector: Hospitals Nationwide Purchasing Local, Sustainable Food." PR Newswire. May 29, 2008.

———. "School Districts to Offer Menus with Food Made in Mich." Lansing State Journal. May 16, 2010: 9B.

Arthur, Gary. "Healthy Means 'Fresh'." Foodservice Director. August 15, 2009. 21(8): 56.

Boss, Donna L. "NACUFS' 50th Marks the Start of a New Journey." Nation's Restaurant News. July 28, 2008. 42(29): 12.

Brown, Ashley. "Love at First Bite: A Guide to the Best Places to Eat on Campus." Ingmagazine. March 2010: 5–6. twitter.com/ingmagazine

Duecy, Erica. "Grab-and-Go Items, Premium Coffee Big Trends on Campus." Nation's Restaurant News. November 28, 2005. 39(48): 18.

Elan, Elissa. "CDS's Oberstadt: Going Green Not One-Size-Fits-All Fix." Nation's Restaurant News. January 21, 2008. 42(3): 12.

———. "Nutrition, Brand Competition, Energy Woes Top NACUFS Agenda." Nation's Restaurant News. August 8, 2005. 39(32): 28.

Halaschek-Wiener, Franz. "Looking for 'Perks'." Foodservice Director. December 15, 2007. 20(12): 30.

Holaday, Susan. "A Model for Excellence." Foodservice Director. June 15, 2007. 20(6): 64.

———. "Breaking Down Breakfast." Foodservice Director. January 15, 2009. 22(1): 36.

———. "The New Color of Design." Foodservice Director. July 15, 2007. 20(7): 52.

Kidwell, Sheryl. "The Slow Switchover." Foodservice Director. October 15, 2008. 21(10): 28.

King, Paul. "2009 Menu Development Survey." Foodservice Director. March 15, 2009. 22(3): 26.

———. "Spartan Success." Foodservice Director. May 15, 2007. 20(5): 56.

Matthies, Mike. "Going Digital." Foodservice Director. September 15, 2008. 21(9): 54.

"Nutrition on the Menu." Chef Magazine. January 2009. 53(1): 20–21.

Pino, Carl. "Sustainability on the Menu." E: the Environmental Magazine. March/April 2008. 19(2): 30.

Ramsey, Lindsey. "Going for Gold." Foodservice Director. January 15, 2008. 21(1): 4.

———. "The New Cost of Doing Business." Foodservice Director. June 15, 2008. 21(6): 28.

Schilling, Becky. "Plowing Ahead." Foodservice Director. September 15, 2008. 21(9): 30.

Solnik, Claude. "Today's Corporate Dining Rooms Offer Healthier Choices and Employee-Friendly Surroundings." Long Island Business News. November 17, 2006: 1.

Walkup, Carolyn. "College Foodservice Learning to Live Green." Nation's Restaurant News. June 30, 2008. 42(26): 49.

Weisberg, Karen. "In Pursuit of Perfect Purees: One Operator's Quest." Foodservice Director. May 15, 2007. 20(5): 78.

———. "Resource Responsibility." Foodservice Director. September 15, 2007. 20(9): 60.

———. "Sustainable Success: The Power of One." Foodservice Director. January 15, 2007. 20(1): 46.

Internet Sites

For more information, visit the following Internet sites. Remember that Internet addresses can change without notice. If the site is no longer there, you can use a search engine to look for additional sites.

American Correctional Association
www.aca.org

ARAMARK
www.aramark.com

Association of Correctional Food Service Affiliates
www.acfsa.org

Association for Healthcare Foodservice
www.healthcarefoodservice.org

American Dietetic Association
www.eatright.org

Bon Appétit Management Company
www.bamco.com

California Polytechnic State University
www.calpolydining.com

The Campus Kitchens Project
www.campuskitchens.org

Compass Group
www.compass-group.com

Connecticut College Sprout!
http://sprout.conncoll.edu

Cornell Hospitality Quarterly
www.hotelschool.cornell.edu/research/chr/pubs/quarterly

FoodServiceDirector
www.fsdmag.com

Greening Princeton
www.princeton.edu/greening

LeadingAge
www.aahsa.org

Michigan State University
www.eatatstate.com

National Association of College &
  University Food Services
www.nacufs.org

Purdue University
www.housing.purdue.edu

School Nutrition Association
www.schoolnutrition.org

Society for Foodservice Management
www.sfm-online.org

Sodexo
www.sodexo.com

Stanford University
www.stanford.edu/dept/rde

Sustainable Endowments Institute
www.endowmentinstitute.org

University of Delaware
www.campusdish.com/en-US/CSE/
Delaware

The University of Houston
www.campusdish.com/en-US/CSSW/
UnivofHouston

University of Notre Dame
http://food.nd.edu

Yale Sustainable Food Project
www.yale.edu/sustainablefood

Appendix

Model Job Descriptions for Selected Positions in On-Site Food and Beverage Operations

The job descriptions presented in this section are for illustrative purposes only and should not be construed as recommendations or standards. While these job descriptions are typical, readers should keep in mind that each food and beverage operation has its own procedures and ways of dividing up job responsibilities.

JOB DESCRIPTION

POSITION TITLE: COUNTER PERSON

REPORTS TO: **Counter Supervisor**

POSITION SUMMARY: Performs a variety of duties relating to cafeteria-style service including greeting and serving customers, cold food preparation, stocking counters and steam table, and maintaining sanitation standards. Responsible customer service is a major component of this position.

DUTIES AND RESPONSIBILITIES:

1. Stocks counters, display refrigerators, salad bar, and steam table neatly, accurately, and timely as per menu.

2. Checks to insure that all display foods are merchandised attractively as per standards.

3. Displays food under appropriate hot or cold conditions as per standards.

4. Completes cold food preparation assignment neatly, accurately, and timely.

5. Handles cold food items appropriately during preparation.

6. Maintains appropriate portion control and merchandising standards when preparing cold food items.

7. Maintains proper food handling, safety and sanitation standards while preparing food, serving food, and clean-up.

8. Keeps display equipment clean and free of debris during meal service, as assigned.

9. Cleans tables and chairs, as assigned, by the start of each meal period. Arranges same as per diagram. Always checks for salt, pepper, and napkins, and stocks accordingly.

10. Cleans up spills during meal service immediately.

11. Cleans equipment, as assigned, thoroughly and timely.

12. Keeps floor in work or service area clean and free of debris.

13. Cleans work station thoroughly before leaving area for other assignment.

14. Greets customers courteously.

15. Handles customers swiftly. Does not allow for back-ups or snags in cafeteria line.

16. Consistently exhibits the ability to keep up with peak cafeteria hours and does so calmly, accurately, and efficiently.

17. Serves appropriate portion sizes as per standards.

18. Exhibits a cheerful and helpful manner when dealing with customers.

19. Demonstrates a complete understanding of daily menu items and explains same to customers accurately.

20. Serves food neatly and attractively as per standards.

21. Informs cook in a timely manner when food quantities are low.

(continued)

COUNTER PERSON (*continued*)

22. Maintains professional appearance at all times, clean and well-groomed as per standards.

23. Demonstrates complete understanding of department policies and procedures.

24. Exhibits outstanding attendance and punctuality and takes corrective action to prevent recurring absences.

25. Displays a positive and enthusiastic approach to all assignments.

26. Develops a positive working relationship with department and organization staff and avoids conflict.

27. Relays relevant comments received from customers directly to supervisor.

28. Views, as required, safety and risk management films and reviews fire safety and disaster plans.

29. Completes shift work, as assigned, timely and thoroughly in accordance with department standards.

PREREQUISITES:

Education: High school diploma or equivalent.

Experience: Demonstrated ability to understand and implement written and verbal instructions.

Physical: Position requires bending, standing, and walking the entire work day. Must be able to lift full pans, not to exceed 25 pounds. Light cleaning duties such as wiping tables and small equipment, sweeping and refilling stock. Must be able to speak clearly and listen attentively to guests and other staff members.

JOB DESCRIPTION

POSITION TITLE: **COUNTER SERVER**

REPORTS TO: **Shift Manager**

POSITION SUMMARY: Responsible for providing quick and efficient service to customers. Greets customers, takes their food and beverage orders, rings orders into register, and prepares and serves hot and cold drinks. Assemble food and beverage orders, checks them for completeness and accuracy and packages orders for on-premise or take-out. Collects payment from guest and makes change. Maintains cleanliness of counters and floors at all times.

DUTIES AND RESPONSIBILITIES:

1. Checks supplies in counter area and restocks items to ensure a sufficient supply throughout the shift.

2. Wipes off front counter with cleaning solution and a clean cloth. Keeps counter and floor clean at all times.

3. Greets customers and takes their orders. May give orders to cook or punch keys of register which records the order and computes the amount of the bill.

4. Serves drinks from dispensing machines or makes and serves hot drinks from water heat or coffee maker. Puts lid on drinks and places on tray with liner or in take-out container.

5. Picks up food items from serving bar or storage area. Places items on tray or in take-out containers. Checks orders to ensure that guest is receiving a complete and correct order.

6. Informs kitchen staff of shortages or special requests.

7. Collects payment from guest and makes change.

PREREQUISITES:

Education: Some high school. Must be able to perform simple mathematical calculations. Must be able to speak, read, write, and understand the primary language(s) used by guests who typically visit the work location.

Experience: Previous foodservice experience not required.

Physical: Must be able to stand and quickly walk for periods of up to four (4) hours in length and have the ability to bend and lift up to 10 pounds frequently. Must be able to speak clearly and listen attentively to guests and other staff members.

JOB DESCRIPTION

POSITION TITLE: COUNTER SUPERVISOR

REPORTS TO: Manager

POSITION SUMMARY: The Counter Supervisor directly supervises the daily operation of a specified unit and insures that daily schedules of activity and established quality standards are maintained. This includes the coordination of the individual and collective efforts of assigned staff.

DUTIES AND RESPONSIBILITIES:

1. Demonstrates complete understanding of departmental requirements and interprets their intent accurately to staff members.

2. Monitors daily performance of staff and ensures compliance with established timetables.

3. Monitors quality of products and services produced by staff and insures compliance with established standards.

4. Monitors sanitation and food-handling practices of assigned unit and insures staff compliance with established standards.

5. Routinely inspects areas of assigned responsibility and reports all substandard safety, security, or equipment conditions to Manager as observed by Manager.

6. Consistently monitors standards and makes recommendations for change as observed by Manager.

7. Supervises staff in a consistently fair and firm manner. Maintains steady productivity through close observation. Provides direction when necessary.

8. Schedules staff for assigned unit within daily F.T.E. allocation and projected workload.

9. Adjusts daily schedule and shifts personnel to complete essential duties when the need arises.

10. Coordinates work of staff to promote efficiency of operations

11. Consistently recommends actions necessary for staff discipline, terminations, promotions, etc.

12. Trains staff, as assigned, and assists with orientation of new staff members in a timely and efficient manner.

13. Schedules staff member time off so as not to interfere with heavy workload periods.

14. Monitors staff member attendance and notices all absence patterns and brings to the attention of management all relevant findings.

15. Monitors customer traffic and makes appropriate adjustments to decrease waiting time.

16. Monitors customer buying trends and makes relevant recommendations for product additions and deletions.

17. Accurately inventories supplies daily and requisitions items needed to meet par levels.

COUNTER SUPERVISOR (*continued*)

18. Ensures that supplies are utilized properly and cost-effectively as per standards.

19. Reports changes in menus or items substitutions to Managers.

20. Insures that all food and supplies are stored and/or maintained under proper conditions as per standards.

21. Monitors food and supply quality and makes relevant recommendations for product utilization.

22. Inspects all unit storage facilities each day so that proper temperatures and conditions are maintained, food is covered, labeled, and dated.

23. Completes counter supervisor reports in an accurate and timely manner.

24. Completes staff member appraisals in a timely fashion.

25. Keeps immediate supervisor informed of all relevant information including any diversions from normal activity, any substandard condition, personnel matters, etc.

26. Meets routinely with assigned staff to relay relevant information and encourage suggestions for service and/or quality improvements.

27. Works effectively and efficiently with other department supervisors and consistently demonstrates the ability to solve problems at this level.

28. Analyzes relevant data to make informed decisions compatible with department philosophy.

29. Treats staff with courtesy, respect, and empathy and displays good listening skills.

30. Displays team-building skills and always handles all assignments with a positive and enthusiastic attitude.

31. Maintains professional appearance as per standards.

PREREQUISITES:

Education: High school diploma or equivalent.

Experience: A minimum of two years as a counter server or equivalent position.

Physical: Position requires walking and giving direction most of the working day. May be required to push heavy food carts. May be required to lift trays of food or food items weighing up to 30 pounds.

JOB DESCRIPTION

POSITION TITLE: DIETITIAN

REPORTS TO: **Administrator/Director of Dietary Department**

POSITION SUMMARY: Provides consultation, guidance, direction, and support to Dietary Department Head in planning in the areas of clinical nutrition and food-service management. Provides information to promote quality food service and resident/patient nutritional care.

DUTIES AND RESPONSIBILITIES:

1. Participates in nutritional assessments, resident care conferences, discharge planning, and diet consultation.

2. Assists in determining policies for therapeutic nutrition and implementing nutritional care.

3. Assists Director in developing dietary policies and procedures.

4. May assist Director with budget development.

5. Assists Director in promoting work efficiency.

6. May assist in planning, remodeling, or new kitchen development.

7. May assist in new equipment selection and purchase.

8. Assists Director in promoting cost control in the department.

9. Assists Director in developing needed forms, schedules, checklists, and quality assurance forms to meet department objectives.

10. Assists Director in menu development and writing therapeutic diets.

11. Assists Director in development of standardized recipes and food preparation procedures to obtain quality food production.

12. Assists Director in developing a quality assurance program.

13. Evaluates audit findings and makes recommendations for change as appropriate.

14. Ensures that the department adheres to current regulations.

PREREQUISITES:

Education: College graduate in foods and nutrition or related field. Must be able to speak, read, write, and understand the primary language(s) of the work location. Must be sufficiently ambulatory and dexterous to move directly between and among the various areas of the kitchen and storage facilities, and to visit with patients, clients throughout the facility. Must be a registered dietitian.

Experience: Must have sound knowledge of the operations of a dietary department. Must understand LTC/hospital regulations. Minimum three years experience in LTC/hospital setting.

Physical: Some lifting of food cases and other forms of packaging may be required on occasion.

JOB DESCRIPTION

POSITION TITLE: DIRECTOR OF DIETARY DEPARTMENT

REPORTS TO: Administrator

POSITION SUMMARY: Provides overall management of the Dietary Department to ensure quality food and nutritional services to clients.

DUTIES AND RESPONSIBILITIES:

1. Responsible for overseeing purchasing, production, and service of food in a timely manner.

2. Responsible for departmental policy formulation and adherence and for procedure development.

3. Purchases supplies and equipment.

4. Directs the receipt, storage, and distribution of food products.

5. Responsible for establishing and maintaining departmental budget.

6. Maintains records to meet the needs of the department.

7. Hires, orients, trains, evaluates, disciplines, and terminates dietary department employees.

8. Develops and maintains work schedules.

9. Participates in department head meetings and other facility meetings as required.

10. Maintains security in the department.

11. Ensures that department is in compliance with all applicable federal and state regulations.

12. Coordinates dietary services with all other departments.

13. Maintains appropriate records of dietary staff members.

14. Orders food and supplies for the department.

15. Maintains inventory.

16. Monitors food preparation to ensure quality.

17. Maintains standardized recipe file and ensures guidelines are followed.

18. Develops menus with the assistance of the dietitian(s).

19. Ensures that food tray assembly is accurate.

20. Monitors entire therapeutic nutrition system to ensure optimum nutrition is obtained for all clients.

21. May interview new patient admissions. Charts in the medical record.

22. Attends client care conferences.

23. Processes diet orders to ensure the physician's directions are being carried through.

24. Periodically audits diet orders for accuracy.

(continued)

DIRECTOR OF DIETARY DEPARTMENT *(continued)*

25. May monitor food intake of residents. Addresses problems with dietitian and/or nursing services.

26. Monitors sanitation/safety standards in the department.

27. Complies with facility policies.

28. Conducts in-service training classes.

29. Conducts periodic dietary staff meetings.

30. Works to meet the goals of the facility with enthusiasm and a spirit of cooperation.

PREREQUISITES:

Education: Completion of a dietary manager training program required. Must be able to speak, read, write, and understand the primary language(s) of the work location. CDM preferred.

Experience: Must have good understanding of dietary management, quality food production, and therapeutic nutrition. Must possess leadership attributes coupled with administrative skills as demonstrated in prior positions.

Physical: Must be in good physical and mental health due to the multiple demands associated with the position.

JOB DESCRIPTION

POSITION TITLE: **DIRECTOR, DINING SERVICES**

REPORTS TO: **Executive Director, Campus Hospitality Services**

POSITION SUMMARY: Directs the foodservice operations and related activities that include multiple fine dining locations, the campus club, a snack bar, and catering.

DUTIES AND RESPONSIBILITIES:

1. Manages and directs the departmental staff consisting of both student and part-time workers.

2. Establishes policies and objective for Dining Services. Informs and discusses with managers and staff any changes in policy.

3. Responsible for staff and labor relations including the training and development of all staff members.

4. Collaborates with the Business Manager in determining the correct pricing of the daily bill of fare and board rates for meal contracts.

5. Plans and administers the Dining Service budgets.

6. Oversees the facilities maintenance and new construction programs.

7. Approves all expenditures for equipment.

8. Reviews all monthly, quarterly, and annual operating statements for each Dining Service unit with the Business Manager.

9. Formulates, administers, and oversees the planning of all capital projects.

10. Develops and implements all marketing programs.

11. Acts as a liaison with all student organizations.

12. Meets with student customers on a daily basis.

13. Meets with the union president every other week.

14. Acts as a hearing officer of all second-level union grievances.

15. Considers recommendations of the Labor/Management and Health/Safety committees.

16. Participates directly in union negotiations.

17. Schedules management staff to ensure proper coverage during downtimes and at catering functions.

18. Directs the proper implementation of in-house catering in all dining service units.

19. Responsible for the final pricing of all catering functions.

20. Formulates and implements any policy that affects the student worker program via the student General Manager and professional Unit Manager.

21. Ensures compliance with environmental laws including recycling, garbage disposal, and source reduction.

(continued)

DIRECTOR, DINING SERVICES (*continued*)

22. Conducts weekly management meetings.

23. Attends seminars and actively participates in professional organizations.

PREREQUISITES:

Education: Bachelor's degree from a hotel and restaurant school or a degree in business administration desired. Must be able to speak, read, write, and understand the primary language(s) of the work location.

Experience: Five years' experience in a large, multi-unit diversified university dining service operation, embracing budget/financial planning, production, marketing, purchasing, catering, and staff supervision responsibilities. A working knowledge of computer systems, construction projects, and collective bargaining agreements is required.

Physical: Must be able to maintain a rigorous 50- to 70-hour workweek. Some travel involved. On location, must be able to traverse a large campus area pursuant to daily and weekly supervisory responsibilities.

JOB DESCRIPTION

POSITION TITLE: FOODSERVICE DIRECTOR (HEALTH CARE)

REPORTS TO: Administrator/CEO

POSITION SUMMARY: Directs the delivery of professional food services which will be a material factor in producing cost-effective, positive financial and customer satisfaction results and a positive public image.

DUTIES AND RESPONSIBILITIES:

1. In conjunction with supervisory staff, develops systems and procedures for each departmental operation.

2. Investigates new methodology in health care and commercial foodservice delivery.

3. Maintains productivity data.

4. Makes regular reports on operations to organizational superior with recommendations for improvements as appropriate.

5. Jointly with superior and with input from staff, develops annual budgets for several cost centers, including coffee shop, cafeteria, patient services, and vending.

6. Analyzes and monitors cost and revenue budgets on an ongoing basis.

7. Makes necessary operational adjustments throughout the year to assure conformance with policy, procedures, and practices.

8. Keeps assistant and supervisors informed about budget performance. Solicits suggestions.

9. Investigates and recommends methodological and labor improvements to contain/reduce costs and increase income.

10. Interviews vendors, reviews bids, authorizes and monitors numerous supply and services contracts.

11. Helps determine specifications for and amounts of supplies and equipment needed for operations. Approves requisitions.

12. Appropriately utilizes expertise of others in the hospital such as Human Resources, Business Office.

13. Maintains records as required by hospital and outside agencies.

14. As requested, participates in planning for improvements in systems, services, physical facilities, new programs, cost containment, increasing revenue, etc.

15. Develops short- and long-range plans for the department, utilizes various resources such as internal research, hospital, and outside area.

16. Prepares written goals and objectives for entire department. Translates these into action plans for self and subordinate managers.

17. Prepares statistical forecasts for food and labor costs, catering sales and scheduling, etc.

FOODSERVICE DIRECTOR (HEALTH CARE) *(continued)*

18. On an ongoing basis, evaluates departmental and subordinate performance against established standards, goals, and objectives.

19. Develops and/or uses a variety of measurements to determine performance effectiveness, from statistics to input from the department and the company.

20. Directs the work of the entire department, through intermediate supervisors.

21. Interviews, selects, counsels, appraises performance, disciplines, and recommends salary and other personnel actions.

22. Prepares and oversees maintenance of confidential personnel records.

23. Seeks assistance to improve staffing/productivity, morale, and other aspects of staff member relations as appropriate from others in the company.

24. Assures that job descriptions and performance standards for each subordinate position are always current, complete, and properly utilized.

25. Supervises departmental education activities, including initial orientation and skills training for staff, students, and volunteers.

26. Assures that regular departmental meetings for entire staff are held to communicate plans, programs, and policies; to teach; to resolve problems; and to seek suggestions for improvements.

27. With individual subordinate supervisors, identifies development needs and counsels on personal development plans.

28. Makes recommendations to and works with company educators in design/support of programs.

29. Except as limited by policy, serves as spokesperson on departmental matters to community groups, vendors, government and health care agencies, and the press.

30. Represents the department in handling important inquiries or complaints from the public or refers these to others such as department assistants.

31. Develops brochures and other written materials about the department for public use.

32. Directs, plans, and coordinates food services for parties, banquets, socials, seminar meals, fundraisers, etc.

33. Coordinates services with those offered by other departments.

34. Participates in interdisciplinary task forces, in department head meetings, and similar joint activities.

35. Confers with other department heads regarding technical and administrative problems of nutrition services.

36. Deals with serious complaints from other departments. Clarifies issues, negotiates agreements.

37. Provides technical guidance and administrative direction over menu planning and the preparation and service of all food.

FOODSERVICE DIRECTOR (HEALTH CARE) *(continued)*

38. In health care situations: Reviews regular diet manuals as to costs and suitability. Standardizes recipes for menu requirements. Reviews therapeutic menus to ascertain conformance to prescription.

39. Makes frequent inspections of all work, storage, serving, and administrative areas to determine that regulations and directions governing handling and storing of supplies and equipment, methods of sanitation, maintenance of records, compilation of reports, and adherence standards are followed.

40. Reviews records and reports regarding costs of raw food; computation of daily food costs; inventory of equipment, food, and supplies; types of storage facilities available; patient and cafeteria menus; cafeteria sales reports and pricing; and various staff member time and cost records.

41. Oversees the selling, planning, pricing, and coordinating of all catering.

42. Visits customers and discusses and solves problems.

PREREQUISITES:

Education: Bachelor's degree in foodservice management, food & nutrition, business management, or related degree desired.

Experience: A minimum of 5 years in the hospitality industry in increasingly responsible foodservice supervisory positions.

Physical: Subject to wet floors, temperature extremes, and excessive noise. Position frequently involves long hours and widely diverse duties. Must be able to bend, stoop, and perform extensive walking. Must be able to move quickly to the different areas of the facility as demands require.

Index